The Qur'ān

The Qur'ān

TRANSLATED WITH A NEW INTRODUCTION

A. J. Droge

SHEFFIELD UK   BRISTOL CT

Published by Equinox Publishing Ltd.

UK: Office 415, The Workstation, 15 Paternoster Row, Sheffield, South Yorkshire S1 2BX

USA: ISD, 70 Enterprise Drive, Bristol, CT 06010

www.equinoxpub.com

This translation previously published in *The Qur'ān: A New Annotated Translation*, A. J. Droge, Equinox 2013.

© Arthur J. Droge 2022

All rights reserved. No part of this publication may be reproduced or transmitted in any form or by any means, electronic or mechanical, including photocopying, recording or any information storage or retrieval system, without prior permission in writing from the publishers.

British Library Cataloguing-in-Publication Data

A catalogue record for this book is available from the British Library.

ISBN-13 978 1 80050 095 2 (hardback)
         978 1 80050 096 9 (paperback)
         978 1 80050 097 6 (ePDF)
         978 1 80050 117 1 (ePub)

Library of Congress Cataloging-in-Publication Data

Names: Droge, Arthur J., 1953- translator.
Title: The Qur'an : translated with a new introduction / A. J. Droge.
Other titles: Qur'an. English. 2022.
Description: Bristol : Equinox Publishing Ltd, 2022. | Includes bibliographical references and index. | Summary: "Originally published in 2013 in an edition with annotations, commentary and other scholarly apparatus, Droge's widely praised translation is presented here as a stand-alone text, with a new introduction, ideal for students and general readers alike"-- Provided by publisher.
Identifiers: LCCN 2021042093 (print) | LCCN 2021042094 (ebook) | ISBN 9781800500952 (hardback) | ISBN 9781800500969 (paperback) | ISBN 9781800500976 (pdf) | ISBN 9781800501171 (epub)
Classification: LCC BP109 .D76 2022 (print) | LCC BP109 (ebook) | DDC 297.1/22521--dc23
LC record available at https://lccn.loc.gov/2021042093
LC ebook record available at https://lccn.loc.gov/2021042094

Typeset by Scribe Inc.

For the fearless Philip Davies
IN MEMORIAM

Contents

Preface	xi
Introduction: Is the Qur'ān in English Still the Qur'ān? Of Translators, Traitors, and Traders	xiii
Guide to Further Reading	xliii
Abbreviations	xlix
Timeline	li
The World of Islam c. 750 CE	liii
Synopsis: The Qur'ān at a Glance	lv

The Qur'ān

1	The Opening	1
2	The Cow	2
3	House of 'Imrān	24
4	Women	37
5	The Table	51
6	Livestock	62
7	The Heights	73
8	The Spoils	86
9	Repentance	91
10	Jonah	101
11	Hūd	108
12	Joseph	115
13	The Thunder	122
14	Abraham	126
15	Al-Ḥijr	130
16	The Bee	133
17	The Journey	140

Contents

18	The Cave	146
19	Mary	153
20	Ṭā' Hā'	157
21	The Prophets	163
22	The Pilgrimage	168
23	The Believers	173
24	The Light	177
25	The Deliverance	182
26	The Poets	186
27	The Ant	191
28	The Story	196
29	The Spider	201
30	The Romans	205
31	Luqmān	208
32	The Prostration	211
33	The Factions	213
34	Sheba	218
35	Creator	222
36	Yā' Sīn	225
37	The Ones Who Line Up	228
38	Ṣād	232
39	The Companies	235
40	Forgiver	240
41	Made Distinct	245
42	Consultation	248
43	Decoration	252
44	The Smoke	256
45	The Kneeling	258
46	The Sand Dunes	260
47	Muḥammad	263
48	The Victory	266
49	The Private Rooms	269
50	Qāf	271

Contents

51	The Scatterers	273
52	The Mountain	275
53	The Star	277
54	The Moon	279
55	The Merciful	281
56	The Falling	284
57	Iron	286
58	The Disputer	289
59	The Gathering	291
60	The Examined Woman	293
61	The Lines	295
62	The Assembly	296
63	The Hypocrites	297
64	Mutual Defrauding	298
65	Divorce	300
66	The Forbidding	302
67	The Kingdom	304
68	The Pen	306
69	The Payment Due	308
70	The Stairways	310
71	Noah	311
72	The Jinn	312
73	The Enwrapped One	314
74	The Cloaked One	315
75	The Resurrection	317
76	The Human	318
77	The Ones Sent Forth	320
78	The News	322
79	The Snatchers	323
80	He Frowned	324
81	The Shrouding	325
82	The Rending	326
83	The Defrauders	327

84	The Splitting	328
85	The Constellations	329
86	The Night Visitor	330
87	The Most High	331
88	The Covering	332
89	The Dawn	333
90	The Land	334
91	The Sun	335
92	The Night	336
93	The Morning Light	337
94	The Expanding	338
95	The Fig	339
96	The Clot	340
97	The Decree	341
98	The Clear Sign	342
99	The Earthquake	343
100	The Runners	344
101	The Striking	345
102	Rivalry	346
103	The Afternoon	347
104	The Slanderer	348
105	The Elephant	349
106	Quraysh	350
107	Assistance	351
108	Abundance	352
109	The Disbelievers	353
110	Help	354
111	The Fiber	355
112	Devotion	356
113	The Daybreak	357
114	Humans	358

Index to the Qur'ān   359

Preface

It was not long after the publication of *The Qur'ān: A New Annotated Translation* (2013) that several colleagues and friends began approaching me about the possibility of bringing out a translation-only edition. Initially, I balked at the suggestion, not just because I thought the extensive annotations were a major part of what made that edition distinctive, but even more, I confess, out of sheer exhaustion from the long and involved process of bringing it to print. What I really needed was a good lie-down. Slowly, however, I began to come around to their proposal. On many pages of the 2013 edition the annotations, even in a smaller typeface, are far more substantial than the primary text, and in some cases come close to swamping it entirely. The more I thought about it, the more the idea of a translation-only version began to make sense to me, not as a replacement for the 2013 edition, but as an alternative for readers who just want the text, the whole text, and nothing but the text. This is what you now hold in your hand, accompanied by a new introduction in which I reflect on the nature of translation in general and of the Qur'ān in particular. Save for the correction of a few typos and some minor adjustments necessitated by the removal of the annotations, the translation remains unchanged from the first edition (reprinted with corrections in 2017).

Among the many challenges of translating the Qur'ān are its unpredictable complexity, evocative associativeness, and polysemy. For these reasons, as well as more demanding theological ones, many translations cut, compress, paraphrase, and invent freely. I have taken a different approach. My translation aims not at elegance but strives for as literal a rendering of the Arabic as English will allow. It also endeavors to maintain consistency throughout in the translation of words and phrases, and even to mimic word order wherever possible. The result is a kind of Arabicized (or Qur'ānicized) English which tries to capture something of the power and pervasive strangeness of the original. Some may find the translation overly literal, even a bit awkward in places, but my hope is that more will gain access to the Qur'ān's distinctive idiom in a rendition that remains as close as possible to the way it is expressed in Arabic, with a minimum of smoothing and polishing. To that end, readers should be on alert for words and phrases not in the original Arabic, but which have been added on occasion for the sake of clarity. These, however, are always enclosed within parentheses. In this way readers will be able to distinguish the bones from the plaster of paris. Readers should feel free to skip the introductory essay, if they wish, and proceed directly

Preface

to the translation. They will find a comprehensive Index at the back, as well as an updated Guide to Further Reading, Timeline, Map, and Synopsis of each sūra following the introduction.

Once again I want to thank my publisher Janet Joyce for her encouragement, advice, and wise counsel. I should also like to thank Bradley Cox and Alvaro Estrada at Scribe Inc., who did such a masterful job of transforming the manuscript into a real book. Finally, I am happy to acknowledge my gratitude to the following friends and colleagues for their expertise, uncommon generosity, and good will at various times over the past seven years: Alaa Abu-Hijleh, Lindsay Atnip, James Beverley, Mark Durie, Elizabeth Key Fowden, Ayman Ibrahim, Umair Ali Khan, Bruce Lawrence, Allison Ray, Gabriel Said Reynolds, the late Andrew Rippin, and Shawkat Toorawa.

A.J.D.

Toronto

March 2, 2021

Introduction: Is the Qur'ān in English Still the Qur'ān?

OF TRANSLATORS, TRAITORS, AND TRADERS

In the following essay I offer some general reflections on the nature of translation (what is has been, what it can be, and what I think it should be), as well as on translation practice (free vs. literal, rhyme vs. reason, domestication vs. estrangement), before addressing the particular problems involved in translating the Qur'ān.[1]

1. Translators/Traitors

The old Italian pun, *traduttori, traditori*, is by now a hackneyed slogan and cliché, but I confess it still rings in my ears like a mischievous echo.[2] From the secure vantage point of the specialist, who needs no translation, anyone who would dare turn a literary masterpiece into another language – and call the two the same – is at best to be pitied and at worst decried. Add to this a strong religious component and you have the sad plight of the would-be Qur'ān translator. Since the Qur'ān is held by many to be a rendering into Arabic of a heavenly Book – literally, the 'Mother of the Book' (*umm al-kitāb*) – its message is inseparable from its linguistic medium. That is to say, since it is the translation that is revealed, rather than the divine archetype, the translation itself may not be retranslated

---

1. Earlier versions of this essay were presented at the inaugural meeting of the International Qur'anic Studies Association in November 2013 and at the second Cambridge Qur'ān Seminar in May 2015. I am grateful to both audiences for their comments and questions, which I have tried to take into account in this newly revised and expanded version. A special word of thanks is due to my Cambridge hosts, Yasmin Faghihi, Elizabeth Key Fowden, James Montgomery, and Shady Hekmat Nasser, for their kind invitation, splendid hospitality, and lively conversation. I am particularly indebted to Shawkat Toorawa, my fellow participant on both occasions, for his encouragement, collegiality, and wit.
2. As far as I can tell no one knows who first coined the pun. It appears in the following form, '*Traduttori, traditori.*,' in the poet and satirist Giuseppe Giusti's *Raccolta di proverbi toscani* (Firenze: F. Le Monnier, 1853) 179. Mark Davie speculates that this may have been an isolated occurrence without any literary antecedent. Nor is it clear how the pun escaped from Italy and became a free-floating, multilingual cliché. See further Davie's Oxford University Press blog (https://blog.oup.com/2012/09/traduttore-traditore-translator-traitor-translation/).

Introduction

without it ceasing to be the Qur'ān. Or at least so many have claimed. This does not necessarily imply that the Qur'ān cannot be translated, only that the result will be both imperfect and impotent – in short, not 'The Qur'ān' *sensu stricto*. Put differently, just as a magical incantation will not 'work' in translation, neither will Qur'ānic cantillation.

One does not have to look very far in the history of religions to find parallels to the phenomenon of Qur'ānic 'untranslatability.' After experimenting with Greek in the Hellenistic period, the later Judaism of the Rabbis came to the view that the Torah is only really the Torah in Hebrew, the language spoken by God and his angels.[3] In more recent times, Joseph Smith's translation of the Golden Plates revealed to him by the angel Moroni is an even closer analogue. Like the Qur'ān, the Book of Mormon cannot be modernized or retranslated in English without technically ceasing to be the Book of Mormon.[4] Even the late fourth-century Latin Bible – the Vulgate – itself a translation from Hebrew and Greek originals, strongly resisted the efforts to translate it into the vernacular languages of Europe, until the Reformation and the invention of printing changed everything.[5] The authorities may police the borders between texts as forcefully as between people, but in both cases their efforts are doomed to failure: like the human beings who produce them, books are inherently migratory.

It is important to stress at the outset that claims to untranslatability are always *secondary* to the texts about which the claim is made. In the case of the Qur'ān, later interpreters would marshal its dozen or so statements that it is an 'Arabic Qur'ān' (*qur'ān 'arabī*), and that its language is 'clear Arabic' (*'arabī mubīn*), to support the

---

3. Notwithstanding the fact that parts of the Jewish Bible are actually written in Aramaic, not Hebrew (Genesis 31.47, Jeremiah 10.11, Daniel 2.4b–7.28, Ezra 4.8–6.18, 7.12–26). But these passages amount to a mere 250 verses out of a total of more than 23,000. Medieval Jewish tradition accused the seventy Jewish scholars who allegedly translated the Hebrew scriptures into Greek – a translation that came to be known as the Septuagint – of plunging the world into darkness for three days; see Abraham Wasserstein and David J. Wasserstein, *The Legend of the Septuagint: From Classical Antiquity to Today* (Cambridge: Cambridge University Press, 2006) 51–83; Moshe Simon-Shoshan, 'The Tasks of the Translators: The Rabbis, the Septuagint, and the Cultural Politics of Translation,' *Prooftexts* 27 (2007) 1–39.

4. On this, see https://www.churchofjesuschrist.org/study/ensign/1993/04/news-of-the-church/modern-language-editions-of-the-book-of-mormon-discouraged?lang=eng. In translating the 'reformed Egyptian' of the plates, Joseph Smith was literally talking through his hat with the aid of a 'seer stone,' on which sentences appeared in English which he then dictated to his scribe, Oliver Cowdery. Smith published the translation as *The Book of Mormon* in 1830. Although the LDS Church discourages any updating or modernizing of the Book of Mormon in English, it has financed its translation and publication in over a hundred different languages.

5. A good example of how, in the course of events, a translation can sometimes usurp the place of its parent text and become a 'new original.' The King James translation of the Bible (1611) enjoys a similar status among many fundamentalist branches of Christianity.

Introduction

view that the Qur'ān can only be called *al-Qur'ān* without qualification in Arabic.[6] As the famous Andalusian polymath, Ibn Ḥazm (d. 456 AH/1064 CE), succinctly put it: 'Non-Arabic is not Arabic; therefore it is not Qur'ān.'[7] Hence the many circumlocutions in titles of English translations, such as *The Koran Interpreted* (Arberry), *The Meaning of the Glorious Koran* (Pickthall), *An Interpretation of the Qur'an* (Fakhry), and so on.[8] These attempts to steer clear of ever using the word 'translation' in relation to the Qur'ān is a good indicator of just how powerful is the doctrine of its untranslatability. Even so, we may still wonder whether the doctrine itself is Qur'ānic. Indeed, we may even wonder whether it is entirely in accord with Islamic tradition, for the date of the very first Qur'ān translation allegedly goes back to the lifetime of Muḥammad. According to one tradition, a companion of the Prophet, Salmān al-Fārisī, asked him for permission to translate the Qur'ān into Fārsī for the Persians, and, after he had showed him his translation of the opening sūra, *Sūrat al-Fātiḥa*, 'he [Muḥammad] permitted it.' Later, when Salmān had finished his translation, he wrote – *without qualification* – 'This is the Qur'ān which was sent down to Muḥammad.'[9] So much for the assertion of Ibn Ḥazm and others that a translation has no claim to the title *al-Qur'ān*.

2. Un/Translatable

Allow me to set these issues aside for the moment in order to place the problem of translation in a still wider frame, namely, the vexing problem of translatability itself: that is, the question of whether the meaning of *any* text – not just the Qur'ān – can be 'carried across' (Latin *translatio*) into another language, or whether the transfer of meaning is inherently impossible – and therefore quixotic, if not traitorous – because human experience itself is incommunicable across languages. This is sometimes called the 'Sapir-Whorf Hypothesis' (or 'Whorfianism' for short), after the two linguists who made it famous, but it is more generally referred to as the 'Hypothesis of Linguistic Relativity' or 'Linguistic Determinism.' It holds that since individual languages structure the data

---

6. 'Arabic Qur'ān': Q12.2; 20.113; 39.28; 41.3, 44; 42.7; 43.3; 'clear Arabic': Q16.103; 26.195; cf. Q13.37; 46.12.

7. Ibn Ḥazm was infamous for not mincing words. I owe this reference to Michael Cook, *The Koran: A Very Short Introduction* (Oxford/New York: Oxford University Press, 2000) 94, who adds: 'Yet every cloud has a silver lining: if a translation is not Koran, there need be no restrictions on touching it.'

8. Cf. the title of Abdur Raheem Kidwai's negative assessment of 21st-century translations of the Qur'ān: *God's Words, Man's Interpretations* (New Delhi: Viva Books, 2018). 'There is not a single translation,' Kidwai declares on page one, 'which may be recommended with confidence that it would enhance the readers' understanding of the meaning and the message of the Quran.'

9. For references, see Mohammad Jaffar Yahaghi, 'An Introduction to Early Persian Qur'anic Translations,' *Journal of Qur'anic Studies* 4 (2002) 105–109, esp. 105, 108 nn. 4 and 5. Whether or not this tradition is historically reliable is irrelevant; it would have important implications for later attempts to translate the Qur'ān into Persian.

Introduction

acquired through experience in their own particular ways, each linguistic community has its own construction of the world, which differs from that of every other linguistic community. Applied in its strongest form, the hypothesis would imply the impossibility of effective communication between the members of different linguistic communities, especially those coming from different language families.[10] Now, you will have to forgive my condensation of the matter, but I do not want simply to sidestep the challenge of linguistic relativism. So let me briefly tell you where I stand, and why. When the chips are down, my wager is on the notion that language itself *entails* translatability.[11]

Consider, for example, the phenomenon anthropologists and historians call 'silent trade' or 'silent barter,' a method by which traders who cannot speak each other's language can nevertheless exchange goods without talking. Herodotus provides our first account of the practice, but it is a recurring trans-cultural narrative. In his tale of the Carthaginians and their dealings with 'the people who live in a part of Libya beyond the Pillars of Herakles,' Herodotus relates the following:

> On reaching this country, the [Carthaginians] unload their goods, arrange them in orderly fashion along the beach, and then, returning to their boats, light a smoking fire. Seeing the smoke, the local inhabitants come down to the beach, place on the ground a certain quantity of gold in exchange for the goods, and go off again to a distance. The Carthaginians then come ashore and take a look at the gold. If they think it represents a fair price for their goods, they collect it and go away. If, on the other hand, it seems too little, they go back aboard and wait, and the local inhabitants come and add to the gold until they are satisfied. There is perfect honesty on both sides: the Carthaginians never touch the gold until it equals in value what they have offered for sale, and the local inhabitants never touch the goods until the gold has been taken away.[12]

Of interest to me here is the nexus of commerce and language: neither the existence of two different linguistic communities nor the absence of a translator renders communication impossible or keeps two peoples from trading, albeit silently, relying solely on each other's good will. This is what I mean when I say that language entails translatability, even, paradoxically, in a case where no words

---

10. See further Raquel de Pedro, 'The Translatability of Texts: A Historical Overview,' *Meta: Journal des Traducteurs / Meta: Translators' Journal* 44 (1999) 546–559, esp. 547–548.

11. Another way of putting this would be that the existence of linguistic universals ensures translatability; on this and related issues, see further John H. McWhorter, *The Language Hoax: Why the World Looks the Same in Any Language* (Oxford/New York: Oxford University Press, 2014).

12. Herodotus 4.196. I am indebted to the analysis of silent trade in Maurizio Bettini, *Vertere: Un'antropologia della traduzione nella cultura antica* (Torino: Einaudi, 2012) 144–175. According to Bettini, the emphasis on the honesty of the parties in silent trade points implicitly to an inherent characteristic of the absent translator: namely, his or her capacity to inspire or repel trust.

Introduction

are spoken. For the notion that someone speaks an untranslatable language is as incomprehensible as that a particular object is 'untradable.'[13]

Or allow me to put the matter this way: Just as some goods are more easily traded than other goods, so some texts are more easily translated than other texts. To be sure, there can be significant barriers to translation, as there are to trading, not the least being a lack of honesty, but while they are important to an understanding of why translation, as well as trading, can often be contentious, they do not strike me as theoretically puzzling in the way in which the Hypothesis of Linguistic Relativity would have it, at least in its strongest form. I prefer to think, then, in terms of the following spectrum: from 'relative untranslatability' at one extreme (e.g., glossolalia, *voces magicae*, nonsense rhymes, and so on), to 'optimum translatability' (e.g., yesterday's news).[14] Now, where might we locate the Qur'ān on such a spectrum?

Choose any language you wish – let's pick a tough one: Standard Chinese (Mandarin)[15] – and then consider the challenge of translating the following line from James Joyce's famously opaque novel, *Finnegans Wake*: 'Parysis, *tu sais*, crucycrooks, belongs to him who parises himself,' in comparison to a headline in one of yesterday's tabloids: 'Toronto woman, 56, dies after pit bull attack.' Translating the Qur'ān into English seems a good deal less daunting in comparison to translating Joyce into Chinese, and yet the latter has, in fact, been done, and to great popular acclaim. Dai Congrong's translation of *Finnegans Wake* was a best seller in China in 2013.[16] It seems clear, then, that while some texts may be more difficult to translate than others, the theory of untranslatability is relative. It is built entirely on exceptions.[17]

If untranslatability is relative, so also is optimum translatability, which Albrecht Neubert has defined as 'the degree obtained when denotative translation equivalence is the essential qualitative reference frame' between the source text and the target language.[18] This would apply in the case of translating the 'pit-bull story' into almost any language – 'dog attacks, kills woman' – less so in the case

---

13. Take the Walter White challenge: 'Name one thing in this world that is not negotiable' (*Breaking Bad* S3:E6 https://getyarn.io/yarn-clip/40918ed9-ea5f-4b47-bad2-0e92128da4d2). To assert, for example, that a particular object is 'priceless' is of a piece with the claim that a particular text is 'untranslatable.' Both are rhetorical and strategic. They are attempts to set an object or text above or outside the realm of the merely human (in other words, to jack up its price!).
14. Loosely following the classification scheme of Albrecht Neubert, as summarized by de Pedro, 'The Translatability of Texts' 553.
15. Tough, that is, for an English-speaker like me.
16. *Fenningen de Shouling Ye* sold out its first run of 8,000 copies (http://www.theguardian.com/books/2013/feb/05/finnegans-wake-china-james-joyce-hit).
17. So Georges Mounin: '. . . la théorie de l'intraduisibilité est construite toute entière sur des exceptions' (cited by Wolfram Wilss, *The Science of Translation: Problems and Methods* [Tübingen: Gunter Narr Verlag, 1982] 41).
18. See de Pedro, 'The Translatability of Texts' 557 n. 11.

of rendering Joyce into Chinese or the Qur'ān into English. Yet, even if the Qur'ān does not provide a case of optimum translatability, it does strike me as closer to that end of the spectrum than might initially be supposed or doctrinally held. Closer, that is, to translating yesterday's news than to rendering Joyce's *Finnegans Wake*. The reason is that the Qur'ān is very often in conversation with the Bible – its primary 'intertext,' if you will – and as a result a situation approaching 'denotative translation equivalence' exists, thanks to the previous labors of many who have 'carried the Bible across' into English.

Just as we cannot read Virgil's *Aeneid* without wondering how much of it is Homer, or the New Testament without wondering how much of it is the 'Old,' so too we cannot read the Qur'ān without shortly confronting the question of how much of it is the Bible. Indeed, without some knowledge of the Bible any reading of the Qur'ān is disadvantaged, and the challenges of translating it – both in the narrow and broad senses – only increase. But this is not just the case with the Qur'ān. When it comes to the so-called monotheist scriptures in general, they are almost always understood better in relation to what came before them, rather than to what came after; in short, to their prequels rather than their sequels.[19] As I see it, we cannot escape enquiry into the nature of the Qur'ān's 'intertextuality' (Kristeva) or 'creative misprision' (Bloom) or 'creation of its own precursor' (as Borges would put it), when at its inception lies the transposed meaning of another, antecedent work.[20] *In principle*, then, the Qur'ān presents the English translator with no more, and certainly no less, difficulty than the Bible. I underscore 'in principle,' because we do not as yet have a good English translation of the Bible – by that I mean a good *academic* translation – but that is a problem for another day.[21]

Now, I have endless patience when some of my best and dearest students inform me that: 'It is an admitted fact that the Qur'ān cannot be translated,' or that: 'There are no words in English that convey all the shades of meaning of *subḥāna* [one of their favorite examples] without spoiling the divinity of the message.' I have less patience with the special pleading of many religious savants who declare the Qur'ān's Arabic 'perfect' and 'untranslatable,' when it seems to me that translation lies at the very heart of the Qur'ān's own project. I will let that irony pass without comment for the moment, but I plan to come back to it.

---

19. Of course, this is not to diminish or denigrate what came after. More on this below.
20. Notice, for example, how even the Christian terms 'New' and 'Old' (Testament) transpose the Jewish Torah into a new articulation of meaning. This is how I conceive of the Qur'ān's extensive conversation with the Bible producing its own new articulation of meaning. The process is best thought of as creative, open ended, and above all scribal, rather than static, set for all time, and prophetic.
21. James D. Tabor has made a good beginning in this regard with *The Book of Genesis: A New Translation from the Transparent English Bible* (Charlotte: Genesis 2000 Press, 2020).

Introduction

3. Gained in Translation

First, let us consider an altogether different possibility: Can a translation ever equal or surpass its source? At the premiere of his now famous movie, *Apocalypse Now*, at Cannes in 1979, Francis Ford Coppola infamously boasted (through his French translator): 'My film isn't *about* Vietnam, my film *is* Vietnam.' Yet how could a film about something actually be more original than the thing itself? The Roman statesman Cicero (106–43 BCE) might well have conceded such a possibility. His ruminations on translation pervade many of his works, especially the oratorical and philosophical ones, and, in fact, it was the Romans themselves who were the first to reflect theoretically on the nature of translation. Curiously, at first sight, they conceived of Latin translations of originally Greek texts as intended for audiences who were bilingual. For his part, Cicero emphasized the need of having the right kind of person to carry out the translation. The orator, in his view, was the only reliable translator because he was someone who would not translate literally (*verbum pro verbo*), but would strive to reproduce the power of the words (*vis verborum*) and, in doing so, allow his own personality and judgment (*iudicium*) to surface – something which a mere interpreter (*interpres*) would be incapable of achieving.[22]

Cicero took what we would call considerable liberties in his translations, but this probably says more about us than it does about him. Our modern Western notion of translation as a literal (or 'faithful') rendering was quite alien to Roman literary culture in general, and Cicero in particular, who, like every true imperialist, endeavoured to appropriate and control the products of other cultures.[23] Cicero likened a word-for-word translation to counting out coins to the reader, when they should be paid by weight in precious metal. Notice the appeal here to an economy of exchange, but in an elite fashion: qualitative equivalence is what matters, not quantitative. In fact, from Cicero's perspective, the translating process should ideally end up replacing the Greek original, even for readers who already knew Greek. Just as, I submit, Coppola's *Apocalypse Now* has become for many viewers more real than reel.[24]

---

22. See esp. Cicero, *De officiis* 1.6; *De optimo genere oratorum* 14–18; and Siobhán McElduff, *Roman Theories of Translation: Surpassing the Source* (New York/London: Routledge, 2013). For the actual role of interpreters in Mediterranean antiquity, see Rachel Mairs, 'Translator, Traditor: The Interpreter as Traitor in Classical Tradition,' *Greece & Rome* 58 (2011) 64–81.

23. As Nietzsche remarked about the Romans, '[A]t that time one conquered by translating – not merely by leaving out the historical, but also by adding allusions to the present and, above all, crossing out the name of the poet and replacing it with one's own – not with any sense of theft but with the very best conscience of the *imperium Romanum*' (Friedrich Nietzsche, *The Gay Science*, ed. Bernard Williams, tr. Josefine Nauckhoff [Cambridge/New York: Cambridge University Press, 2001] 83). Today we would call this 'cultural appropriation' (a big no-no).

24. The second-century CE Latin writer, Aulus Gellius (*Noctes Atticae* 11.4), was the first not to condemn the practice of word-for-word translation, and to gesture towards

Introduction

Can a translation ever truly equal or surpass the original? And if so, should it, as Cicero suggests? These questions call to mind an episode towards the end of *Don Quixote* (1605/15), a work which itself purports to be a translation from the Arabic history of the shadowy Cide Hamete Benengeli,[25] when the Knight of the Sorrowful Face pays a visit to a print shop in Barcelona. (This is, by the way, the first instance of a fictional character entering such an establishment, and what do you think Quixote finds? A copy of *Don Quixote*!) Inside the shop Quixote sees as all manner of literary activity going on – 'printing in one place, correcting in another, typesetting here, revising there' – until he comes upon a gentleman who, he is told, 'has just translated a Tuscan book into our Castilian language.' Claiming to know a little Tuscan himself, Quixote quizzes the translator to test his mettle, and then holds forth:

> [T]ranslating from one language to another, unless it is from Greek and Latin, the queens of all languages, is like looking at Flemish tapestries from the wrong side, for although the figures are visible, they are covered by threads that obscure them, and cannot be seen with the smoothness and color of the right side. And translating from easy languages doesn't show any more ingenuity or eloquence than transcribing or copying from one piece of paper to another. And I don't mean to infer from this that the practice of translating is not deserving of praise, because there are other worse and less useful things that a man can do. From this reckoning I exempt two famous translators: one is Dr. Cristóbal de Figueroa, for his *Pastor Fido*, and the other is Don Juan de Jáurigui, for his *Aminta*, where they happily bring into question which is the translation and which the original.[26]

Lest we forget, these amusing musings on translation are delivered by a *loco* – Don Quixote is a madman – yet perhaps not so crazy that a Cicero would not have agreed with him. We, on the other hand, readily admit to what is *lost* in translation, but are we willing to entertain the possibility that reading a translation can be a substitute for reading the original? Is the Qur'ān in English still 'the

---

   modern ideas about translation practice. For the post-Ciceronian landscape of translation theory, see McElduff, *Roman Theories of Translation* 157-185. Bettini's broader thesis (*Vertere* 189-251) is that the notion of literal translation originates in Judeo-Christian literary culture, in which for the first time God is seen as 'speaking through writing.'

25. A 'pseudotranslation,' needless to say. On this phenomenon, see Brigitte Rath, 'Pseudotranslation,' ACLA State of the Discipline Report, 1 April 2014 (available at http://stateofthediscipline.acla.org/entry/pseudotranslation). On the meaning and significance of the name 'Cide Hamete Benengeli,' see the fascinating piece of detective work by Devin J. Stewart, 'Cide Hamete Benengeli, Narrator of *Don Quijote*,' *Medieval Encounters* 3 (1997) 111-127.

26. Miguel de Cervantes, *Don Quixote: A New Translation by Edith Grossman* (New York: Ecco, 2003) 873-874 (2.62), slightly altered. Cristóbal Suárez de Figueroa's translation of Giovanni Battista Guarini's *Il pastor Fido* (Venice 1590) was published in Naples in 1602; Juan de Jáurigui's translation of Torquato Tasso's *L'Aminta* (Parma 1573) was published in Rome in 1607.

Introduction

Qur'ān' – without qualification? Allow me take these questions a step farther and ask: Can a translation ever *surpass* the original on which it is based?

Some critics have said that Charles Baudelaire's translations of Edgar Allan Poe's poetry are superior to the original, and, whether their judgment is true or not, Poe does owe his literary stature to fans mostly outside the Anglophone world.[27] Let me take just one example, so that you can be the judge. Here are lines 7–12 of Poe's famous poem *The Raven* (1845), followed by Baudelaire's prose translation:

> Ah, distinctly I remember, it was in the bleak December;
> And each separate dying ember wrought its ghost upon the floor.
> Eagerly I wished the morrow; – vainly I had sought to borrow
> From my books surcease of sorrow – sorrow for the lost Lenore –
> For the rare and radiant maiden whom the angels name Lenore –
> Nameless *here* for evermore.[28]

The internal rhymes of 'remember,' 'December,' 'ember,' and 'morrow,' 'borrow,' 'sorrow' (repeated), along with the end rhymes of 'floor,' 'Lenore' (repeated), and 'evermore' clang, bang, and rattle in a way that sounds almost like a parody. Or at least so some critics have argued. Not even Byron's *Don Juan* is so heavily plodding, they say.

Now here is Baudelaire's prose rendering of the same lines in his *Le Corbeau* (1853):

> Ah! distinctement je me souviens que c'était dans le glacial décembre, et chaque tison brodait à son tour le plancher du reflet de son agonie. Ardemment je désirais le matin; en vain m'étais-je efforcé de tirer de mes livres un sursis à ma tristesse, ma tristesse pour ma Lénore perdue, pour la précieuse et rayonnante fille que les anges nomment Lénore – et qu'ici on ne nommera jamais plus.[29]

In contrast to Poe's original, here we find an overall fluidity and syllabic assonance that, even though it does not rhyme (perhaps *because* it does not rhyme), is still poetic and powerful. Or again, at least so some critics have argued. Baudelaire's translation appears true to the general sense of Poe's words, and the peculiarities of Poe can still be felt, but many of Baudelaire's turns of phrase are, these same critics contend, more beautiful than Poe's originals. December isn't just 'bleak,' it is 'icy' or 'frigid' (*glacial*). In contrast to Poe's 'each dying ember

---

27. Such luminaries as Henry James, T.S. Eliot, Aldous Huxley, and Harold Bloom have dismissed Poe's work as puerile, vulgar, and commonplace; Ralph Waldo Emerson referred to Poe as 'the jingle man,' and told a friend he could 'see nothing in *The Raven*.' For these references and more, see Harold Fromm, 'Genius or Fudge? The Clouded Alembics of Magister Poe,' *The Hudson Review* 45 (1992) 301–309; and the revisionist appraisal by Jerome McGann, *The Poet Edgar Allan Poe: Alien Angel* (Cambridge: Harvard University Press, 2014).
28. Available at https://www.poetryfoundation.org/poems/48860/the-raven.
29. Available at http://www.leboucher.com/pdf/poe/corbeau.pdf, along with the 1875 translation of *The Raven* by Stéphane Mallarmé.

Introduction

wrought its ghost upon the floor,' Baudelaire's 'loose' translation is far more descriptive and arresting: 'each ember in turn *was embroidering* the floor with the reflection of its agony.' Notice, too, that no retro-translation of this line would bring you very close to Poe's original. Finally, consider this counterfactual: What if Poe were a verse translation of Baudelaire? Would we reckon *The Raven* a translation of *Le Corbeau*? No, I rather think we would call it a sendup or parody of it.

Now as it happens, I think that Baudelaire has expressed better and more beautifully what Poe wanted to say, but that and $2.95 will get you a venti at Starbucks here in Toronto. My concern is *not* to convince you on this point. I offer it only as an example that, potentially at least, a translation can not only equal but surpass the original on which it is based, fully aware that in the final analysis it may be entirely subjective. But this in turn raises another, and to my translator's mind, more pressing question: By surpassing him, has Baudelaire translated Poe or traduced him? Put differently, is *Le Corbeau* an imitation or adaptation of *The Raven*, but not a translation of it?

Let us take another example, this time directly relevant to our topic. Here is *Sūrat al-Ikhlāṣ* (Q112.1–4) in Arabic transliteration, followed by what some readers might consider a clumsy word-for-word rendering.

1. *qul huwa 'llāhu 'aḥad*
    Say! 'He (is) God one'[30]
2. *allāhu 'l-ṣamad*
    God the Eternal[31]
3. *lam yalid wa-lam yūlad*
    He does not beget and was not begotten
4. *wa-lam yakun lahu kufuwan 'aḥad.*
    and (there) is not for him an equal one.'[32]

All four lines end in rhyme, but the variation in the number of syllables in each verse fails to produce anything that we would call poetic meter, at least not in a quantitative sense. Rather, the Qur'ān often resembles what is called 'accent poetry,' in which the feet are established by word accents and not by regular alterations of long and short syllables. Rap music is an analogue, as are nursery

---

30. The reading and construal of v. 1 vary considerably. Some early authorities (e.g., Ibn Masʿūd and Ubayy) are said to have lacked 'Say!' (*qul*). According to 'the reading of the Prophet,' both 'Say!' and the following 'He' (*huwa*) were omitted. Al Aʿmash read *al-wāḥid* ('the only one,' 'the unique') in place of *aḥad* ('one'), perhaps to avoid the unusual use of it here (for a somewhat similar construction, see Q6.19; 13.16; 39.4).
31. The meaning of *al-ṣamad* is uncertain. The word only occurs here in the entire Qur'ān. Other translations are 'self-sufficient,' 'eternally sought by all,' 'immanently indispensable' etc. It may be a cognate of *ṣamda* ('rock'); cf. the descriptions of God as 'rock' in the Bible (e.g., Psalm 18.2).
32. The word *kufuwan* ('equal,' 'peer,' 'one of equal standing') is another *hapax*.

Introduction

rhymes, Anglo-Saxon poetry, and so on.[33] There are also other features that give *al-Ikhlāṣ* a poetic feel. Notice, for example, the long sequence of 'l' sounds, beginning with the opening *qul* ('say'), which echo through the repeated name of God, and then into verses three and four. Notice also the contrasting pattern of affirmation (vv. 1–2) and negation (vv. 3–4). Finally, the repetition of *'aḥad* ('one') as the rhyme word in the last verse has the solemn effect of closure.

Now, here is Shawkat Toorawa's 'rhyming prose' translation of *Sūrat al-Ikhlāṣ*, which he renders 'Purity of Faith':[34]

1. Affirm: He is God, Matchless
2. God, Ceaseless,
3. Unbegetting, Birthless,
4. Without a single partner, Peerless.

You will see immediately that Toorawa has replaced the rather banal 'Say' (*qul*) with the much more potent 'Affirm,' thereby conveying to the reader that what we have here may be a creedal confession, perhaps intended for general liturgical repetition, much like its obvious intertext at Deuteronomy 6.4: *Shəma' Yisrā'ēl: YHWH elohēnū YHWH 'eḥād* ('Hear, O Israel: the Lord our God, the Lord is one'), the Arabic *'aḥad* recalling Hebrew *'eḥād*.[35] All four lines in Toorawa's translation end in rhyme, as they do in Arabic, but Toorawa renders the third verse (*lam yalid wa-lam yūlad*) with a mere two words ('Unbegetting, Birthless'), thus transforming a phrase into two epithets, and thereby producing a neat symmetry with the preceding epithets, 'Matchless' and 'Ceaseless.' (Notice that, as with Baudelaire's translation of Poe, one would be hard pressed to retro-translate Toorawa's third verse and arrive at the original Arabic.) The result is that, without forcing the lines into meter, Toorawa's translation nevertheless produces a kind of poetic cadence, or hip-hop-like pattern of affirmation: 'God, Matchless, God, Ceaseless, Unbegetting, Birthless.' This, in turn, makes the fourth and final line, somewhat plodding in Arabic (*wa-lam yakun lahu kufuwan aḥad*), all the more effective and powerful as it rolls out in English, right down to the alliterative final two words: 'Without a single partner, Peerless.' Notice here that Toorawa's choice to render the second and final *'aḥad* as 'Peerless,' rather than 'Matchless,' avoids the possible redundancy of the original. My only, slight criticism concerns this final line. I think a better rendering – *à la* Toorawa – would have been: 'He has no partner, Peerless.'

---

33. On this, see Devin J. Stewart, '*Saj'* in the Qur'ān: Prosody and Structure,' *Journal of Arabic Literature* 21 (1990) 101–139; idem, 'Divine Epithets and the Dibacchius: Clausulae and Qur'anic Rhythm,' *Journal of Qur'anic Studies* 15 (2013) 22–64.

34. Shawkat M. Toorawa, '"The Inimitable Rose," being Qur'anic *saj'* from *Sūrat al-Ḍuḥā* to *Sūrat al-Nās* (Q. 93–114) in English Rhyming Prose,' *Journal of Qur'anic Studies* 8 (2006) 143–155, quotation from 153.

35. Or, more likely: 'Hear O Israel: YHWH is our God, YHWH alone.' On this and other intertexts in Q112, see Angelika Neuwirth, 'Two Faces of the Qur'ān: Qur'ān and Muṣḥaf,' *Oral Tradition* 25 (2010) 141–156, esp. 150–153.

Introduction

The alliteration is maintained, but the 'He' picks up the very strange 'He' of the first verse and brings the syllable count of the first and last lines into alignment.

But this is quibbling. In my judgment, Toorawa's rendering is sheer brilliance. It is so good, in fact, that it slightly frightens my Arabophone students, who would otherwise dismiss the possibility that the Qur'ān could be translated into English and still be the Qur'ān. Yet, might one go even further, and argue that Toorawa's translation has surpassed the original, as some have said of Baudelaire's translation of Poe? It not only expresses better what *Sūrat al-Ikhlāṣ* wants to say, but it does so more beautifully. There, I've said it.[36] And I wager that Cicero, too, would have approved. Toorawa does not translate *verbum pro verbo*, or repay his reader by counting out coins; his version of *Sūrat al-Ikhlāṣ* relates the *vis verborum*, and in doing so repays his reader in precious metal, not a handful of coins. Notwithstanding this, we are once again faced with a more pertinent and pressing question: We must ask, as we did in the case of Baudelaire's translation of Poe, whether Toorawa has translated or traduced the Qur'ān by rendering it in the way that he has. Put differently, has Toorawa translated *Sūrat al-Ikhlāṣ* or rewritten it – however surpassing we may judge the literary merits of his rewriting to be?

Again, whether you agree with me about Baudelaire or Toorawa is not really the issue here. I merely wish to convince you that it is possible, *ex hypothesi*, for a translation to surpass its original. Yet there is much more at stake than just this. Once more, the crucial question is: By surpassing the original, has a translator traduced his source text? And the answer, I submit, is an unequivocal *yes*. But before I lay out the reasons why, let us linger a moment longer over a related issue. Even if a translation cannot (or must not) surpass the original, without also traducing it, this does not necessarily mean that a translation must inevitably result in loss. It seems to me that a translation might still surpass its original in terms of *utility*, which would constitute a considerable gain.

Take Shakespeare, for example. I simply do not get him in English, and neither do most of my Anglophone students. But they think they know at least this much: that when Juliet cries, 'O Romeo, Romeo, wherefore art thou Romeo,'[37] she is longing for her beloved, and wondering, Where oh where can he be? – Until, that is, they discover that this is not what Juliet is asking at all. When I show my students the same line in French translation, it is as if the scales have fallen from their eyes: 'ô Roméo, Roméo! Pourquoi es-tu Roméo?' Once they were blind, but now they see. The translation of the English word 'wherefore' by the French 'pourquoi' reveals that the former is just an old-fashioned way of asking 'why' rather than 'where.' What Juliet is lamenting, of course, is: 'O Romeo, why are you a Montague?' – alluding to the feud between her Capulet family and Romeo's

---

36. Again, with the same caveat stated above about my claim that Baudelaire expressed better and more beautifully what Poe wanted to say.
37. *Romeo & Juliet* II.ii.33.

Introduction

clan. Their love is impossible because of their family names, and so she asks him to change his allegiance, or else she will change hers.

Notice what has been lost in translation: the poetic meter of the line. The original English is (to my ear) clearly superior aesthetically to the literal French translation. Yet do not overlook what has been gained by reading Shakespeare *in French*: an understanding of the English original! On that score, at least, the translation is 'better' – or perhaps one should say, 'more useful' – than the original, not to mention underscoring the necessity of annotations for a reader removed in time and space from the original. There is no paradox or irony implied in saying that Shakespeare needs to be translated into English, any more than in saying that the Qur'ān needs to be translated into Arabic.

4. Domestication or Estrangement? Visiting Mr. Nabokov

In 1923, Walter Benjamin published his German translation of Baudelaire's *Tableaux Parisiens* (1857), the introduction to which contained Benjamin's famous essay, 'The Task of the Translator,' where he sketched out a general theory of the translatability of texts. There is a lot of theological mumbo jumbo in the piece, but I have taken away from it two important insights. For Benjamin, 'the question of whether a work is translatable has a dual meaning. Either: Will an adequate translator ever be found among the totality of its readers? Or, *more pertinently*: Does its nature lend itself to translation and [. . .] call for it?'[38] In the case of the Qur'ān, I think the answer to the latter question is a resounding yes. Quite apart from the traditional claim that the Qur'ān is itself a translation of a heavenly archetype, the Qur'ān's self-consciousness *as a text*, its acute awareness of its own 'Arabic tongue,' and its conversation with texts in other languages are all inextricably linked, and imply that the Qur'ān's original historical context, wherever and whenever it may have been, was a zone of multilingualism and translation. We do not have to wait for the ninth-century translation projects of the 'Bad Boys' of Baghdad or the 'Mad Monks' of Mār Sābā,[39] the Qur'ān is already striking testimony to the existence of a flourishing translation culture, involving the exchange of both ideas and texts, in its own time and place. Otherwise, what would be the point of the Qur'ān declaring itself to be an '*Arabic* Qur'ān'?[40] In short, we are dealing with a text whose very 'nature,' in the words of Benjamin,

---

38. Walter Benjamin, 'The Task of the Translator,' in idem, *Illuminations*, tr. Harry Zohn (New York: Schocken Books, 1968) 69–82, quotation from 70 (emphasis added).
39. On this burgeoning literary activity, see Shawkat M. Toorawa, *Ibn Abī Ṭāhir Ṭayfūr and Arabic Writerly Culture: A ninth-century bookman in Baghdad* (London/New York: RoutledgeCurzon, 2005) 102–122; and Tamar Pataridze, 'Christian Literature in Arabic in the Early Islamic Period,' *Le Muséon* 132 (2019) 199–222.
40. The specification 'Arabic Qur'ān' seems to imply the existence of 'other Qur'āns,' as it were, in other languages, as well as being an answer to some objection, perhaps that Hebrew was considered to be the *lingua sacra*; see Q12.2; 13.37; 16.103; 20.113; 39.28; 41.3; 42.7; 46.12.

Introduction

'lends itself to translation.' I quote him once more: '[B]y virtue of its translatability the original is closely connected with the translation; in fact, this connection is all the closer since it is no longer of importance to the original. We may call this connection a natural one, or, more specifically, *a vital connection*.'[41]

Benjamin's essay also put me onto the German poet and philosopher Rudolf Pannwitz (1881–1969), who thought that 'the basic error of the translator is that he preserves the state in which his own language happens to be instead of allowing his language to be powerfully affected by the [source text].'[42] 'Our translations,' Pannwitz wrote, 'even the best ones, proceed from the wrong premise. They want to turn Hindi, Greek, English into German instead of turning German into Hindi, Greek, English.'[43] Such a 'foreignizing strategy' is now associated with the work of Lawrence Venuti,[44] but it was first formulated by Friedrich Schleiermacher in his famous lecture 'On the Different Ways of Translating' (1813),[45] where he contrasted the method of 'bringing the foreign author to the reader' with that of 'taking the reader to the foreign author.' Schleiermacher demanded that translations from different languages into German should read and sound different. That is, the reader should be able to guess the Spanish behind a translation from Spanish, and the Greek behind a translation from Greek. Put simply, *estrangement* is always preferable to *domestication*. Whether it is the Qur'ān or the Bible, Homer or Herodotus, Cervantes or Dostoyevsky, a good, academic, 'thick translation'[46] ought to be similarly foreignizing and literal to the point of transparency, as well as strive to maintain consistency in the rendering of words and phrases, and even to mimic word order wherever possible. If, in the case of the Qur'ān or the Quixote, the result is a kind of 'Arabicized' or 'Castilianized' English, so much the better. A text's raw power and pervasive strangeness ought never to be subjected to smoothing and polishing.

Vladimir Nabokov took a radical stand on this issue in the course of working on his controversial translation of Pushkin's *Yevgeniy Onegin*, when he wrote,

---

41. Benjamin, 'The Task of the Translator' 71 (emphasis added).
42. Ibid. 81.
43. Ibid. 80.
44. See esp. Lawrence Venuti, *The Scandals of Translation: Towards an Ethics of Difference* (London/New York: Routledge, 1998).
45. Available in an English translation by Susan Bernofsky in Lawrence Venuti (ed.), *The Translation Studies Reader* (London/New York: Routledge, 2000) 43-63; see further Verena Lindemann, 'Friedrich Schleiermacher's Lecture "On the Different Methods of Translating" and the Notion of Authorship in Translation Studies,' in Teresa Seruya and José Miranda Justo (eds.), *Rereading Schleiermacher: Translation, Cognition and Culture* (Berlin/Heidelberg: Springer, 2015) 115-122.
46. I borrow the term from Kwame Anthony Appiah, 'Thick Translation,' *Callaloo* 16 (1993) 808-819, cited from Venuti (ed.), *The Translation Studies Reader* 417-429. Appiah defines it as 'a translation that aims to be of use in literary teaching; and . . . seeks with its annotations and its accompanying glosses to locate the text in a rich cultural and linguistic context' (ibid. 427).

Introduction

'The person who desires to turn a literary masterpiece into another language, has only one duty to perform, and this is to reproduce with absolute exactitude the whole text, and nothing but the text. The term "literal translation" is tautological, since anything but that is not truly a translation but an imitation, an adaptation or a parody.'[47] Nabokov called his translation of *Onegin* 'a pony' (i.e., a word-for-word translation). 'The clumsiest literal translation,' he insisted, 'is a thousand times more useful than the prettiest paraphrasing.'[48]

In the course of translating Pushkin, Nabokov said he had 'learned some facts and come to certain conclusions.' First, the facts:

> I take literalism to mean 'absolute accuracy.' If such accuracy sometimes results in the strange allegoric scene suggested by the phrase 'the letter has killed the spirit,' only one reason can be imagined: there must have been something wrong either with the original letter or with the original spirit, and this is not really a translator's concern.[49]

> 'Rhyme' rhymes with 'crime,' when Homer or *Hamlet* are rhymed [and, I would add, the Qur'ān as well]. The term 'free translation' smacks of knavery and tyranny. It is when the translator sets out to render the 'spirit' – not the textual sense – that he begins to traduce his author.[50]

> The problem, then, is a choice between rhyme and reason: can a translation while rendering with absolute fidelity the whole text, and nothing but the text, keep the form of the original, its rhythm and its rhyme? To the artist whom practice within the limits of one language, his own, has convinced that matter and manner are one, it comes as a shock to discover that a work of art can present itself to the would-be translator as split into form and content, and that the question of rendering one but not the other may arise at all. Actually what happens is still a monist's delight: shorn of its primary verbal existence, the original text will not be able to soar and to sing; but it can be very nicely dissected and mounted, and scientifically studied in all its organic details.[51]

So far the facts. Here are two conclusions Nabokov arrived at:

> 1. It is impossible to translate *Onegin* in rhyme. 2. It is possible to describe in a series of footnotes the modulations and rhymes of the text, as well as all its associations and other special features.[52]

These conclusions can be generalized. I want translations with copious footnotes, footnotes reaching up like skyscrapers to the top of this or that page so as to leave

---

47. Vladimir Nabokov, 'Problems of Translation: *Onegin* in English,' *Partisan Review* 22 (1955) 496–512, cited from Venuti (ed.), *The Translation Studies Reader* 71–83, quotations from 77.
48. Ibid.
49. Ibid. 81.
50. Ibid. 71.
51. Ibid. 77.
52. Ibid. 83.

Introduction

only the gleam of one textual line between commentary and eternity. I want such footnotes and the absolutely literal sense, with no emasculation and no padding – I want such sense and such notes for all the poetry in other tongues that still languishes in 'poetical' versions, begrimed and beslimed by rhyme.[53]

I have taken the liberty of quoting Nabokov at length not only because his ruminations on the translator's task have been formative in my own approach to translating the Qur'ān (however much I may have fallen short of them), but also because I think Nabokov's high bar ought to be the measure of any translation of a literary masterpiece that aspires to be an academic, 'thick translation.' Yet even so, in the case of the Qur'ān, a translator's problems are still not at an end.

5. Revelation, Ink (or, Why is God so Bookish?)

While there are many obstacles to overcome in translating the Qur'ān, these are not limited solely to the challenges the text itself presents.[54] The exegetical and biographical traditions about the Qur'ān and its Prophet can sometimes pose as great, if not greater, obstacles. Let me offer just one example, but first allow me to explain what I mean.

The Byzantine philosopher Proclus (412–485 CE), called 'the Successor,' was long considered to be the great systematizer of the Platonic 'revelation.' As a result, his works were taken to be the gateway to Plato when Christians, Jews, and Muslims in Late Antiquity sought to anchor their theologies in Greek philosophy. Far more than Plotinus (or anyone else for that matter), Proclus' voluminous writings *represented* Platonism for almost all scholars, theologians, and philosophers from the sixth century on, more or less until Friedrich Schleiermacher liberated Plato from the Platonic tradition in the early nineteenth century. The result of that liberation laid the groundwork not only for a new understanding of Plato, but also a better (i.e., more historically nuanced) understanding of the achievement of Proclus and the Platonic tradition. In my view, both the Qur'ān and the tradition about the Qur'ān are in need of a similar liberation, or in the immortal words of Gwyneth Paltrow, a 'conscious uncoupling.'[55]

---

53. Ibid.
54. Not the least of which is the absence of a critical edition. The Arabic text on which almost all English translations are based is known as the 'Egyptian standard' or 'Cairo edition,' first published in 1342 AH/1924 CE by a committee of Muslim scholars working under the auspices of the Egyptian government. Over time this edition has achieved a kind of *de facto* canonical status, but it is not, and never aspired to be, a critical edition.
55. As John Burton has cautioned, 'So long as we continue to approach the Qur'ān by means of the literature of Islam we must inevitably travel in a circle' (see his review of William Montgomery Watt, *Companion to the Qur'ān* [London: Allen & Unwin, 1967], in *Bulletin of the School of Oriental and African Studies* 32 [1969] 387–389, quotation from 388); cf. Walid A. Saleh: '[O]ur only task ... is to investigate the text [of the Qur'ān] on its own terms. [...] The moment we turn away from the tradition [about the Qur'ān] ... the picture becomes clear' (in idem, 'A Piecemeal Qur'ān: *Furqān* and

Introduction

One of the stories the Qur'ān tells about itself – the dominant one, it turns out – has to do with the 'sending down' or 'descent' of the Qur'ān as a 'book from heaven.' For the most part, the story is told in verbs derived from the triliteral root *n-z-l*, especially *nazzala* (form II) and *anzala* (form IV), both of which mean 'to send or bring down,' and occur some 250 times in the Qur'ān in a variety of contexts.[56] Indeed, the nominal of form II, *tanzīl* ('a sending down'), can even be employed as a shorthand designation for the Qur'ān itself, as in the following verses: 'Surely it is a sending down [*tanzīl*] indeed from the Lord of all peoples [. . .], so that you may be one of the warners, in a clear Arabic language' (Q26.192–195).[57]

The verb *nazzala* occurs famously at Q2.97, where the angel Gabriel is credited with having 'sent' or 'brought down' the Qur'ān on the Prophet's heart,[58] but

---

Its Meaning in Classical Islam and Modern Qur'ānic Studies,' *Jerusalem Studies in Arabic and Islam* 42 [2015] 31–71, quotations from 65, 69). The singular word 'tradition' is, of course, a misleading term, since it rarely speaks with a single voice, or reflects a unanimous point of view. By 'tradition' I mean centuries long, complex scholarly conversations, fraught with contradictions and unresolved tensions (and certainly no less interesting and important for that).

56. The distinction between these two verb forms is generally understood as factitive (II) and causative (IV), but in actual practice 'many verbs that produce Form II and Form IV show little or no appreciable difference in meaning' (Wheeler M. Thackston, *An Introduction to Koranic and Classical Arabic* [Bethesda: IBEX Publishers, 2000 (1994)] 197). As we shall see, this is the case with *nazzala* and *anzala*, which are used more or less synonymously and interchangeably in the Qur'ān. That is, the alternation in their use is to be attributed to stylistic impulse rather than to semantic choice. *Contra* Frederik Leemhuis, *The D and H Stems in Koranic Arabic* (Leiden: Brill, 1977) 20–36. Leemhuis' attempt to further differentiate the two forms in terms of the duration of an action is unpersuasive, and even he has to admit that the distinction 'is not applicable very often' and 'is not a basic opposition of factitive and causative' (28). Moreover, in instances of contextual ambiguity, Leemhuis too readily turns to Islamic tradition for clarification, which suggests that he presumes the traditional account of the Qur'ān's piecemeal revelation (e.g., see his appeal to al-Ṭabarī for confirmation of his construal of Q97.1, ibid. 27 and n. 25).

57. See also Q20.2-4 ('the Qur'ān . . . a sending down from One who created the earth and the high heavens'); 41.2-3 ('A sending down from the Merciful, the Compassionate. A Book – its verses made distinct – an Arabic Qur'ān for a people who know'), 42 ('[It is] a sending down from One wise, praiseworthy'); 56.77-80 ('Surely it is an honorable Qur'ān indeed, in a hidden Book. . . . [It is] a sending down from the Lord of all peoples'); 69.43 ('[It is] a sending down from the Lord of all peoples').

58. 'Say: "Whoever is an enemy to Gabriel – surely he has brought it down [*nazzalahu*] on your heart by the permission God, confirming what was before it, and as a guidance and good news to the believers."' Elsewhere this is attributed to the 'trustworthy spirit' (Q26.193; cf. 16.102). Although Gabriel is only mentioned by name three times in the Qur'ān, his depiction as the agent of God's revelation will not come as a surprise to readers attuned to biblical tradition, for this is the role he plays in both Jewish and Christian scriptures as well. Among many examples, see Daniel 8.15–26; 9.20–27; Luke 1.10–20, 26–37. In the verse immediately following (Q2.98), Gabriel is paired with Michael, as he is, for example, at 1 Enoch 9.1; 10.9–12; 40.9–10; 54.6;

Introduction

typically it is God himself who 'has sent down' the Qur'ān, just as he is the agent of revelation in general. On one occasion this is expressed in the first-person singular, when God speaks to the 'Sons of Israel' about the Qur'ān and its relationship to their own Book, the Torah of Moses:

> Believe in what I have sent down [*anzaltu*], confirming what is with you [i.e., the Torah], and do not be the first to disbelieve in it. (Q2.41)

But more often the verbs *nazzala* and *anzala* are found either in the third-person singular or the first-person plural. Here are a few key examples (and notice how the two verbs are used interchangeably):

> He [God] has sent down [*nazzala*] on you [sing.] the Book with the truth,[59] confirming what was before it, and He sent down [*anzala*] the Torah and the Gospel before (this) as guidance for the people. (Q3.3-4)

> Surely We sent it down [*anzalnāhu*] on a blessed night. (Q44.3)

> Surely We sent it down [*anzalnāhu*] on the Night of the Decree. (Q97.1)

In all four passages the perfect tense of the verb ('sent down' or 'have/has sent down') implies that the revelation of the Qur'ān was an act that occurred 'all at once' – indeed, on a *single* night – despite traditional claims that the Qur'ān was revealed to the Prophet at intervals over a period of some twenty years, right up until his death in 11 AH/632 CE. Further complicating the picture, Q2.185 refers to 'the month of Ramaḍān in which the Qur'ān was sent down [*unzila*].' Most later interpreters, notably the influential Persian scholar al-Ṭabarī (d. 310 AH/923 CE), tried to harmonize these passages by identifying the 'blessed night' (*laylatin mubārakatin*) of Q44.3 and the 'Night of the Decree' (*laylat al-qadr*) of Q97.1 as a single night, which they also claimed was one of the last ten nights in the 'month of Ramaḍān.' In doing so they took the perfect tense of the verb in these verses to refer to the descent of the Qur'ān *in its entirety* from the highest to the lowest of the seven heavens, whence it was revealed *piecemeal* to the Prophet by the angel Gabriel as occasion required.[60] There are, however, a host of other passages, like the examples cited above, that indicate the Qur'ān was revealed to the Prophet *all at once*. Here is a brief sampling of the evidence, spanning the so-called Meccan (610-622 CE) and Medinan (1-11 AH/622-632 CE) periods:

> Surely We have sent down [*anzalnā*] to you the Book. (Q4.105)

> God has sent down [*anzala*] on you the Book. (Q4.113)

71.8-9, 13; cf. Daniel 10.13, 21; 12.1; Jude 1.9; and Revelation 12.7-9. Unnamed angels play similar revelatory roles in the biblical books of Ezekiel and Zechariah.

59. Or 'in truth,' 'truly.'
60. On this extraordinarily clever exegetical strategy, with special attention to al-Ṭabarī, see Saleh, 'A Piecemeal Qur'ān' 53-57; cf. John Wansbrough, *Quranic Studies: Sources and Methods of Scriptural Interpretation*, Foreword, Translations, and Expanded Notes by Andrew Rippin (Amherst: Prometheus Books, 2004 [1977]) 37-38.

Introduction

Believe in God and His messenger, and the Book He has sent down [*nazzala*] on His messenger, and the Book that He sent down [*anzala*] before (this). (Q4.136)

This is a Book: We have sent it down [*anzalnāhu*], blessed, confirming what was before it. (Q6.92)

He [it is] who has sent down [*anzala*] to you [plur.] the Book.... Those to whom We have given [*ātaynāhumu*] the Book know that it has been sent down [*munazzalun*] from your Lord. (Q6.114)

A Book has been sent down [*unzila*] to you. (Q7.2)

Surely We have sent it down [*anzalnāhu*] as an Arabic Qur'ān, so that you [plur.] may understand. (Q12.2)

A Book – We have sent it down [*anzalnāhu*] to you. (Q14.1)

We have sent down [*nazzalnā*] on you the Book as an explanation for everything, and as a guidance and mercy, and as good news for those who submit. (Q16.89)

Praise [be] to God, who has sent down [*anzala*] on his servant the Book. (Q18.1)

A blessed Book – We have sent it down [*anzalnā*] to you, so that those with understanding may contemplate its verses and take heed. (Q38.29)

Surely We have sent down [*anzalnā*] to you the Book with the truth. (Q39.2)

These examples could easily be multiplied,[61] but they are sufficiently numerous to render problematic the traditional notion of a decades-long, piecemeal revelation of the Qur'ān. On the contrary, the clear implication of these passages is that the revelation of the Qur'ān in its entirety – that is, as a book – is a *fait*

---

61. See further Q2.136 ('Say [plur.]: "We believe in God, and what has been sent down [*unzila*] to us, and what has been sent down [*unzila*] to Abraham ... Moses and Jesus"'); 3.7 ('He [it is] who has sent down [*anzala*] on you the Book ...'), 84 ('Say [sing.]: "We believe in God, and what has been sent down [*unzila*] on us, and what has been sent down [*unzila*] on Abraham ..., and what was given [*ūtila*] to Moses, and Jesus, and the prophets from their Lord"'); 4.47 ('You who have been given the Book! Believe in what We have sent down [*nazzalnā*], confirming what is with you'); 5.48 ('We have sent down [*anzalnā*] to you the Book'); 6.155 ('This is a Book – We have sent it down [*anzalnāhu*], blessed'); 15.9 ('Surely we have sent down [*nazzalnā*] the Reminder'); 16.44 ('We have sent down [*anzalnā*] to you the Reminder'); 17.105 ('With the truth We have sent it down [*anzalnāhu*], and with the truth it has come down [*nazala*]'); 21.50 ('This is a blessed Reminder. We have sent it down [*anzalnāhu*]'); 29.47 ('We have sent down [*anzalnā*] the Book to you'), 51 ('Is it not sufficient for them that We have sent down [*anzalnā*] on you the Book to be recited to them?'); 39.41 ('Surely We have sent down [*anzalnā*] on you the Book ... with the truth'); 42.17 ('[It is] God who has sent down [*anzala*] the Book with the truth'); 46.30 ('Surely we [the Jinn] have heard a Book [which] has been sent down [*unzila*] after Moses, confirming what was before it, guiding to the truth and to a straight road'); 59.21 ('If We had sent down [*anzalnā*] this Qur'ān on a mountain, you would indeed have seen it humbled'); cf. Q2.23, 89, 176; 7.196; 8.41; 16.64; 25.1; 28.86; 29.46; 46.12; 57.25.

Introduction

accompli. But there is more. At least one other passage appears to render this idea emphatic. Here is Q76.23 in Arabic, followed by a simple, and at first glance obscure, word-for-word English translation:

innā naḥnu <u>nazzalnā</u> 'alayka 'l-qur'āna <u>tanzīlan</u>

Surely We – <u>We have sent down</u> on you the Qur'ān <u>a sending down</u>.

The problem is to figure out the particular sense of the verbal noun, 'a sending down' (*tanzīl*), which is used here as a cognate accusative to render emphatic the action of the main verb, 'We have sent down' (*nazzalnā*).[62] In this instance, the traditional understanding of *tanzīl* is that it means 'gradually' or 'in stages,' consistent with the view that the Qur'ān was revealed to the Prophet piece by piece over a period of two decades. And, not surprisingly, this is how many, though by no means all, translators render *tanzīl* at Q76.23. Here are a few representative examples drawn from widely used English translations, with the crucial word or words placed in italics:

It is We Who have sent down the Qur'ān to thee *by stages*.[63]

We have revealed the Qur'an to you *gradually*.[64]

VERILY, [O believer,] it is We who have bestowed from on high this Qur'an upon thee, *step by step* – truly a bestowal from on high.[65]

We have made known to you the Koran *by gradual revelation*.[66]

We Ourself have sent down this Qur'an to you [Prophet] *in gradual revelation*.[67]

All five translators construe the cognate accusative *tanzīl* ('a sending down') as emphasizing the duration of the action, rather than the moment of its effectuation, consistent with the traditional view of the Qur'ān's piecemeal composition. By contrast, Arthur J. Arberry preferred a simple, word-for-word rendering:

Surely We have sent down the Koran on thee, *a sending down*.[68]

But what, the reader may well ask, could 'sent down a sending down' possibly mean? It appears that here Arberry is taking *tanzīl* ('a sending down') in apposition with 'the Koran,' though he leaves this for the reader to discern, not by introducing an 'as' before 'a sending down,' only a comma. In so doing Arberry

---

62. The cognate accusative is one of the most common uses of the verbal noun in Qur'ānic Arabic, as well as in other Semitic languages.
63. Abdullah Yusuf Ali, *The Holy Qur'an* (Lahore: Shaikh Muḥammad Ashraf, 1934).
64. Ahmed Ali, *Al-Qur'ān: A Contemporary Translation* (Princeton: Princeton University Press, 1988).
65. Muhammad Asad, *The Message of the Qur'an* (Gibraltar: Dar Al-Andalus, 1980).
66. N.J. Dawood, *The Koran* (London: Penguin Books, 1999).
67. M.A.S. Abdel Haleem, *The Qur'an* (Oxford: Oxford University Press, 2004).
68. Arthur J. Arberry, *The Koran Interpreted*, 2 vols. (London: Allen & Unwin, 1955) 2.316.

Introduction

has chosen to ignore the fact that *tanzīl* is a cognate accusative, and instead taken it as just another name for the Qur'ān.[69] The five previous renderings are preferable precisely because they do not leave the reader in the lurch, trying to divine the meaning of Arberry's obscure rendering. Yet one may still ask whether they have translated the verse correctly, especially in light of the passages cited previously, or whether, in this case, they have been unduly swayed by the gravitational pull of later tradition.

In contrast to those translators who render *tanzīl* ('a sending down') as 'gradually' or 'in stages,' I contend that the cognate accusative is better construed as emphasizing the effectual, rather than the durative, action of the main verb *nazzalnā* (i.e., 'We *have* sent down'). In other words, the Qur'ān's revelation has taken place 'once and for all' – not over the course of twenty years or from the highest to the lowest heaven, for which there is no evidence in the Qur'ān, but to the Prophet himself (notice the 'on you' [*'alayka*]). Hence I have translated Q76.23: 'Surely We – We have sent down on you the Qur'ān *once and for all*.'[70] Such a rendering has a number of advantages. It is entirely in accord with the many passages previously cited, which described the revelation of the Qur'ān as a *fait accompli* – indeed, as occurring on a single night – as well as a host of other passages which refer to the Qur'ān as a book already in existence during the lifetime of the Prophet, even though Islamic tradition holds that it was not until the first caliph, Abū Bakr, that Zayd ibn Thābit and other scribes first the compiled the Qur'ān in book form.[71]

---

69. Cf. Marmaduke Pickthall, *The Meaning of the Glorious Koran* (London: Knopf, 1930): 'Lo! We, even We, have revealed unto thee the Qur'ān, *a revelation;*' and Seyyed Hossein Nasr *et al.* (eds.), *The Study Qur'ān: A New Translation and Commentary* (New York: HarperCollins, 2017): 'Truly We have sent down the Qur'ān upon thee *as a revelation,*' to which is appended the following annotation: 'This verse is understood as an indication of the *gradual manner* in which God revealed the Qur'ān, that is, *in periodic installments rather than all at once*' (emphasis added).

70. Cf. Richard Bell, *The Qur'ān: Translated, with a Critical Re-arrangement of the Surahs*, 2 vols. (Edinburgh: T. & T. Clark, 1937-1939): 'Verily it is We who have sent down to thee the Qur'ān *actually;*' and Alan Jones, *The Qur'ān*, (Exeter: Short Run Press, 2007): 'Truly We *have* sent down to you the Recitation' (emphasis added).

71. Notice, in particular, the frequent occurrence in the Qur'ān of such demonstrative expressions as: 'That is the Book' (Q2.2), 'This is a Book' (Q6.92, 155; 46.12), 'this Qur'ān' (Q6.19; 10.37; 12.3; 17.9, 41, 8, 89; 18.54; 25.30; 27.76; 30.58; 34.31; 39.27; 41.26; 43.31; 59.21), 'This is a Reminder' (Q21.24, 49; 38.49; 73.19; 76.29), and so on. Taken together the textual evidence points to the existence of an actual book in written form. *Contra* Saleh ('A Piecemeal Qur'ān 40–65), who argues that the Qur'ān's defense of its revelatory status is built upon the idea of it being a 'book-in-becoming.' My contention is that the Qur'ān's defense is instead built upon the fact of its existence as a 'book-in-actuality,' as, for example, Q6.155–156 clearly asserts: 'This is a Book – We have sent it down [*anzalnāhu*], blessed. [. . .] *Otherwise* you would say, "The Book has only been sent down [*unzila*] on two contingents [of people] before us."' The assertion here of the Qur'ān's existence, alongside the Torah and Gospel, is unmistakable, and constitutes the clearest refutation of the Prophet's opponents who demanded to be shown a 'heavenly book' (Q4.153; 17.93). Not that it would

Introduction

In order to gain a broader Qur'ānic perspective on how best to understand *tanzīl* ('a sending down') at Q76.23, we should consider a similar construction in an entirely different context where the stakes are not nearly so high. At Q25.25-26 the nominal form is again used as a cognate accusative to emphasize the action of the main verb, which this time occurs in the passive voice of form II and refers to the angels, who will be 'sent down' on the Last Day:

> On the Day when the sky is split open, (along) with the clouds, and the angels are sent down *once and for all*, the true kingdom that Day (will belong) to the Merciful, and it will be a hard Day for the disbelievers.

Here the expression 'sent down once and for all' – literally, 'sent down a sending down' (*nuzzila tanzīlan*) – clearly does not refer to a gradual or piecemeal process, but to an event that will occur on a *single* day, the Day of Judgment. It is, in fact, an emphatic response to the Prophet's skeptics, who had earlier questioned him as to why no angel 'had been sent down' (*unzila*) to be a 'warner' with him (Q25.7, repeated at v. 21). The answer is that the angels will be sent down – *once and for all* – on the Last Day.[72]

We find the same cognate accusative construction used again in another key passage about the Qur'ān's revelation (Q17.105-106):

> With the truth[73] We have sent it down [*anzalnāhu*], and with the truth it has come down [*nazala*]. We have sent you only as a bringer of good news and a warner. (It is) a Qur'ān – We have divided it, so that you may recite it to the people at intervals, and We have sent it down once and for all [*nazzalnāhu tanzīlan*].[74]

The tenor of the entire passage, not just the final statement, suggests an action that is complete. The declaration 'We have sent it down once and for all' (literally, 'sent it down a sending down') is yet another emphatic response to the

---

have mattered. The Qur'ān is also quite clear that it was their own disbelief that had placed them beyond the pale for persistently 'calling God's verses a lie and turning away' (Q6.157; cf. 6.21; 7.37; 10.15-17; 37.170; 61.6-7).

72. See the treatment of this passage in Leemhuis, *The D and H Stems in Koranic Arabic* 26: 'In XXV 25 the action is *momentary*: not the duration of the sending down is taken into consideration, but the moment of its effectuation.' Yet, Leemhuis then goes on to claim that 'XXV 21 on the other hand should be understood as: Why has it been *continuously* so that the angels were not being sent down' (26, emphasis added). But such a distinction is strained. My contention is that there is no semantic difference in these two verses between the passives of form II (*nuzzila*) and form IV (*unzila*).

73. Or 'In truth,' 'Truly.'

74. Notice how the sense of *anzalnāhu* (form IV) and *nazzalnāhu* (form II) is indistinguishable here, as well as how *nazala* (form I) is practically equivalent in meaning. Once again, their alternation is to be explained as a matter of style, not semantics. For reasons that can only be explained as deference to the traditional view, Arberry (*The Koran Interpreted* 1.314) translates the cognate accusative at Q17.106 as 'We have sent it down *successively*,' whereas at Q76.23, as we saw, he translated the very same construction as: 'We have sent down the Koran on you, *a sending down*.'

Introduction

Prophet's skeptics, who only a few lines earlier had challenged him to 'bring down' (*tunazzila*) a book from heaven (Q17.93). The statement that 'We have divided it' (*faraqnāhu*) does not appear to be a reference to a gradual or serial mode of revelation; it is more likely a reference to some division or versification of the text of the Qur'ān for the purpose of the Prophet's reading it aloud to the people 'at intervals.'[75]

More than a few passages attest to the idea that the Qur'ān was 'sent down' in the same way as the 'Torah' and 'Gospel' – that is, 'all at once' – as Q3.3-4 takes for granted: 'He has sent down on you the Book with the truth, confirming what was before it, and He sent down the Torah and the Gospel before (this).'[76] What would be so surprising about the fact that each of the three 'Books' had been revealed similarly, especially given the references in the Qur'ān to the idea of three 'parallel' Scriptures?[77] The traditional view of a gradual revelation of the Qur'ān is beginning to look like secondary claim *about the text*, rather than something firmly established *in the text*.

Now, lest there be any misunderstanding, I am not arguing that there is no textual evidence for the idea of a piecemeal Qur'ān, only that it is not nearly as widespread as is often presumed. Perhaps the strongest support for a serial mode of Qur'ānic revelation occurs at Q25.32:

> Those who disbelieve say, 'If only the Qur'ān were sent down [*nuzzila*] on him all of one piece.' (It has been sent down) in this way, so that We may make firm your heart by means of it. And We have arranged it very carefully.

The lament of the disbelievers here is almost unanimously understood as an objection to the Qur'ān's gradual mode of revelation. Nevertheless, one must always be cautious about putting too much weight on anything the Prophet's opponents say, simply because they are almost always wrong. Moreover, the precise

---

75. Or perhaps 'slowly' ('*alā mukthin* occurs only here). Cf. Saleh ('A Piecemeal Qur'ān' 39–43), who tries to build his case for a piecemeal revelation of the Qur'ān on the term *furqān*, apparently unaware that this term is also used as a designation for the Torah of Moses (Q2.53; 21.48). Likewise, Saleh (ibid. 43–50) sees another indication of the piecemeal manner of the Qur'ān's revelation in the root *f-ṣ-l* (e.g., *tafṣīl* at Q10.37; 12.111), and yet once again the same term is also applied to the Torah (e.g., Q6.154; 7.145). Since there is no reference in the Qur'ān to the piecemeal revelation of the Torah, it seems more likely that *tafṣīl* refers to some division or versification of the texts of both the Qur'ān and the Torah, for the purposes of their reading or recitation, rather than to their piecemeal revelation. As Saleh correctly notes, the root *f-ṣ-l* is also used to refer to the 'enumeration' of God's 'signs' (*āyāt*) in the natural world. But this is perfectly parallel, I submit, to the 'enumeration' of God's 'verses' (*āyāt*) in the textual world, rather than to a piecemeal revelation (cf. Q10.5; 13.2 and Q11.1; 41.3).
76. Cf. Q29.47. For the idea that Moses was given the Torah all at once, see Q2.53, 87; 5.44; 17.2, 4; for Jesus and the Gospel, see Q3.48; 5.46; 19.30; 57.27.
77. Articulated most explicitly at Q9.111, but see also Q2.136; 3.84; 5.48; 6.92; 29.46–47; 46.12.

Introduction

meaning of the phrase 'all of one piece' (*jumlatan wāḥidatan*) is not entirely clear on first reading. Are the opponents expressing their skepticism about the Qur'ān's *gradual revelation* to the Prophet, or are they challenging the Prophet's *piecemeal recitation* of a 'heavenly book' he claimed to possess? Only a few verses earlier these same opponents had dismissed what they had heard so far from the Prophet, and suspected that he was compiling a book in secret with the help of others:

> This is nothing but a lie! He has forged it, and other people have helped him with it. (. . .) Old tales! He has written it down, and it is dictated to him morning and evening (Q25.4-5).[78]

Here the disbelievers pointedly express their doubts, not about the physical existence of a book, only about its divine authorization. The Prophet's book, they allege, is merely a forgery. The verse immediately following is intended to put their skepticism to rest by stating definitively that it is God who 'has sent it down [*anzalahu*]' (Q25.6). The Qur'ān is no forgery, indeed, it is no ordinary book: its authorization is a divine *fait accompli*. When read in this context, the disbelievers' later challenge at Q25.32 may imply something quite different than is usually supposed. They are not objecting to the Qur'ān's serial mode of revelation, but to the Prophet's gradual or piecemeal recitation of it. Instead, they want to be shown the actual book he claimed had been 'sent down' to him from heaven.[79]

The second half of Q25.32 presents another difficulty, for the meaning of the adverb *kadhālika* ('thus' or 'in this way') depends on what is supplied parenthetically at the beginning of the sentence: '(It has [not?] been sent down) in this

---

78. Notice, by the way, the presumption of the Prophet's literacy, though tradition mostly holds that he could not read or write. Even allowing for its dismissive tone, it looks like the opponents are referring to something akin to a scribal school. (If one objects that the opponents are completely wrong about this, then one might similarly object that they are just as wrong when they asked why the Qur'ān was not sent down in one piece.) The association of revelation with 'pen and ink' (Q18.109; 31.27; 68.1b) deserves more attention than I can give to it here, but I would argue that it holds an important clue to the Qur'ān's scribal origins and its composition as a text. Who but scribes would insist that God is so bookish – indeed, a scribe himself – 'who teaches by the pen, teaches the human what he does not know' (Q96.4-5; cf. 80.11-16)?

79. This is what some of the unbelieving Jews are also said to have demanded of the Prophet at Q4.153: 'The People of the Book ask you to bring down on them a Book from the sky.' In other words, they challenged the Prophet to show them an actual 'heavenly book,' presumably like the physical 'tablets' that Moses had brought down from Sinai (cf. Q17.93). Of course, it was not only the disbelievers who issued challenges of this sort. On occasion the Prophet could give as good as he got. At Q28.49 he dared them to 'Bring a Book from God that is a better guide than these two' – referring to both the Torah *and* the Qur'ān – before adding sarcastically, 'I shall follow it, if you are truthful.' Such a challenge would make no sense if the Qur'ān did not actually exist *as a book*.

way, so that We may make firm your heart by means of it.' The adverb, too, is traditionally understood to confirm a gradual revelation of the Qur'ān, but quite a lot depends on the hypothetical parenthesis. An alternative such as '(We allow them to speak) in this way...' would shift completely the traditional understanding of the second half of the verse. The final sentence, 'We have arranged it very carefully,' presents still more problems. It is yet another instance of a cognate accusative – literally, 'We have arranged it an arranging' (*rattalnāhu tartīlan*) – and is usually taken to refer either to the manner of the recitation of the Qur'ān, or to its piecemeal revelation.[80] Yet there may be a third alternative, which I have tried to capture in my translation: namely, a divine declaration that the Qur'ān has been well composed.[81] Since, however, the expression *rattalnāhu tartīlan* only occurs here, its precise meaning is difficult to tease out on the basis of the text of the Qur'ān alone.[82]

6. Text and Tradition

Once again, let me be clear: I am not at pains to insist that there is no reference to a serial mode of revelation in the Qur'ān, only that many of the passages traditionally marshaled in support of such a view are more (or differently) complicated than Islamic tradition allows.[83] And my point is certainly not to denigrate that tradition as unreliable, but rather to distinguish between text and tradition in order to set the concerns of each in sharper relief. Thereby we can better appreciate the work of tradition, as it skillfully seeks to create space for its own theological interests, just as we are better able to discern a

---

80. As Saleh notes ('A Piecemeal Qur'ān' 51), the term *tartīl* later 'became a technical term for a style of Qur'ān recitation,' and this elocutionary meaning has influenced a number of translators (e.g., Arberry: 'We have chanted it very distinctly' and Nasr et al.: 'We have recited it unto thee in a measured pace'). Others, however, take the expression to refer, not to the recitation of the Qur'ān, but to its piecemeal revelation (e.g., Abdel Haleem: 'We gave it to you in gradual revelation' and Dawood: 'We have imparted it to you by gradual revelation;' cf. Saleh ['A Piecemeal Qur'ān' 41, 60]: 'we sent it down in pieces;' 'we have sent it in sections').

81. So also Pickthall: 'We have arranged it in right order.'

82. But cf. similar words addressed to the Prophet at Q73.4: *rattili ... tartīlan*, which I have chosen to translate similarly: 'arrange the Qur'ān very carefully.' In my view neither passage refers to the cantillation of the Qur'ān, or to its piecemeal revelation, but refers instead to the Qur'ān's arrangement and composition as an actual book.

83. See Q5.101 ('... when the Qur'ān is being sent down'); 20.114 ('Do not be in a hurry with the Qur'ān, before its inspiration is completed to you'); and 75.16–19 ('Do not move your tongue with it to hurry it. Surely on Us [depends] its collection and its recitation. When We recite it, follow its recitation'). I would only point out that such passages are far less numerous than those that attest to the Qur'ān existing as a book, above all the scores of passages employing the root *n-z-l*. At a minimum, both sets of passages should be allowed to stand in tension rather than be forcibly subordinated one to another with the goal of harmonizing them.

different set of concerns at stake in the Qur'ān itself.[84] Where tradition would differentiate the Qur'ān from its predecessors according to its serial mode of revelation, the Qur'ān registers its coherence with previous scriptures in having been revealed, like them, all at once. Even so, the text is mixed, and it appears that there is some inconsistency in the Qur'ān about whether it was delivered all at once or in stages. This may be yet another indication that the Qur'ān is more likely an archive of originally independent materials – with its share of contradictions and unresolved tensions – than a single book as is usually supposed.[85] Generally speaking, however, such a conclusion is not a possibility for a traditional scholar of the Qur'ān, any more than for a traditional scholar of the Bible. For it is always the task of tradition to strive for a clear and consistent vision, however much it always exceeds its grasp. By the sharpest possible contrast, the task of the translator is always provisional, and it is sometimes his job to complicate, not to clarify, much less smooth over and polish.

Some later interpreters would claim that it was the Qur'ān's serial mode of revelation that distinguished it from the revelation of the Torah to Moses.[86] And here we should consider for a moment the potential advantages – *for an exegete* – of a claim that the Qur'ān had been revealed over the course of some twenty years, rather than having been sent down all at once. For one thing it would set the Qur'ān apart from all other scriptures as unique in this regard, to say nothing of its Prophet. If Moses had been on the mountain with God for forty days and forty nights, the Prophet was the regular recipient of divine revelation for two decades. More importantly, the idea of a serial mode of revelation would offer an exegete a way to negotiate inconsistencies and contradictions in the text by being able to arrange them according to a scenario of an unfolding revelation at different times and places. The 'occasional' nature of revelation would also allow the exegete the possibility of prioritizing or ranking some passages over others – indeed of asserting that some allegedly 'earlier' passages had been abrogated or replaced by 'later' ones. Finally, if the Qur'ān had been delivered piecemeal, as occasion required, the exegete could then remove individual passages from their Qur'ānic contexts and recontextualize them within stories about the 'occasions of revelation' (*asbāb al-nuzūl*). And these new contexts would in turn furnish the exegete with new opportunities to play with the meaning of the text, with a view towards its ongoing relevance.[87]

---

84. This is what makes Saleh's 'A Piecemeal Qur'ān' so impressive methodologically, as well as exemplary for future work, even if I find myself in disagreement with him at several points.
85. If it is the case that the contents of the Qur'ān come from different times and places, this would explain why there are competing views about the mode of its revelation, and why it will continue to frustrate any attempt at harmonization on this score.
86. On this, see Wansbrough, *Quranic Studies* 37–38; and Saleh, 'A Piecemeal Qur'ān' 39–40.
87. On this, see esp. Andrew Rippin, 'The Function of *asbāb al-nuzūl* in Qur'ānic Exegesis,' *Bulletin of the School of Oriental and African Studies* 51 (1988) 1–20.

Introduction

Such interpretive strategies were not unique to Muslim exegetes but can also be found in the repertoires – 'the toolkits,' as it were – of Jewish and Christian interpreters of the Bible, for there were similarly conflicting views within Judaism and Christianity about the revelation of the Torah. Though some thought the Torah had been given to Moses directly by God – indeed, that God himself had written it with his own hand – others held that it was not God but an intermediary angel (or angels) who had delivered it to Moses. Some went so far as to claim that 'rebel angels' had sent down the Torah as part of a cosmic plot to enslave humanity. There were even some interpreters who, like their Muslim counterparts on the Qur'ān, claimed that the Torah had been transmitted in serial fashion – that is, 'scroll by scroll' – while others claimed that it had been revealed 'all at once.'[88]

To try to translate the Qur'ān and *only* the Qur'ān (i.e., apart from the tradition about it) is no small challenge – not the least because it flies in the face of both religious *and* academic orthodoxies – but it seems to me a challenge well worth taking up, because to conflate scripture and tradition does a disservice to both, just as was the case when Proclus was taken to be the gateway to Plato.

7. Translators/Traders

Just as we were told when we learned our maths that it was important to 'show our work,' so it is also incumbent on the translator to show his or hers, at least in a translation that aims to be of use in teaching. It is precisely at moments like this that the translator is obligated to point out difficulties, as well as to explain why certain choices have been made. Just as important, the translator ought to provide his or her reader with as many cross references as possible, to allow the reader the possibility of seeing individual passages in a wider textual and intertextual frame, as well the possibility of making up his or her own mind about the meaning of individual passages. This is what Appiah means by an academic or 'thick translation,' one that seeks through its annotations to situate the text by describing all its associations and other special features. Just as full disclosure is a prerequisite in every commercial transaction, so it should be in every translation. And it seems to me that such an academic translation is eminently worth doing.

If a translation should never paraphrase, neither should it ever sanitize. In an earlier essay on 'The Art of Translation' (1941) Nabokov wrote that of the '[t]hree grades of evil . . . in the queer world of verbal transmigration, [. . . t]he third, and worst, degree of turpitude is reached when a masterpiece is planished and patted into such a shape, vilely beautified in such a fashion as to conform to the notions and prejudices of a given public. This is a crime, to be punished by the stocks as plagiarists were in the shoebuckle days.'[89]

---

88. For example, see Babylonian Talmud, *Gittin* 60a.
89. Vladimir Nabokov, 'The Art of Translation,' *The New Republic* 105 (August 4, 1941) 160–162, quotation from 160. Of the first two errors, Nabokov wrote, 'The first, and lesser one, comprises obvious errors due to ignorance or misguided knowledge.

Introduction

I have tried to heed Nabokov's warning not only in translating the Qur'ān but also in teaching about it (after all, the two projects are really one). I refuse to 'planish and pat' *any* writ – holy or not – into shape or to sanitize and fetishize it. The simple peasant girl Aldonza Lorenzo is just fine the way she is. I do not need, nor do I want, to pretend that she is the princess Dulcinea del Toboso. But most of all, I do not want to be the errant knight, Don Quixote, who makes the fatal mistake of believing his beloved romances. After his strange, beautiful dream in the Cave of Montesinos, and after Sancho lies about what he saw while pretending to ride the magical horse Clavileño through the skies, Don Quixote whispers to his squire: 'Sancho, just as you want people to believe what you have seen in the sky, I want you to believe what I saw in the cave of Montesinos. And that is all I have to say.'[90] Individually, these are two of the funniest stories in the entire the novel, but when they are brought into conjunction in this way they become one of its saddest moments. 'I will believe in your fantasy if you believe in mine,' Quixote seems to be saying. I for one do not want to collude with others in believing Quixotic scriptures, though I recognize that that may make me a traitor in the eyes of some.

Translation, like trading, is a constant affair of the 'in between,' and as such there will always and inevitably be discrepancy. This means that no translation can ever be final or completely close the gap, and thus that the adequacy of every translation can and should be debated. Yet, however daunting the enterprise of translation may sometimes be, I am all in on the notion that 'language *entails* translatability,' as well as on its correlate, that 'there is no such thing as "religious language" in need of a special grammar, semantics or code book.'[91] To gamble otherwise – to reject the possibility of translation – is to adopt a model of incommensurability and unintelligibility, a model that condemns us to live in the world of Borges' Pierre Menard, in which a story must always be identically told, where a word can only be translated by itself.[92] Such a model denies the work of culture and the study of culture. For it is the inherent

---

> This is mere human frailty and thus excusable. The next step to Hell is taken by the translator who intentionally skips words or passages that he does not bother to understand or that might seem obscure or obscene to vaguely imagined readers; he accepts the blank look that his dictionary gives him without any qualms; or subjects scholarship to primness: he is as ready to know less than the author as he is to think he knows better.'

90. Cervantes, *Don Quixote* 727 (2.41 end).
91. Hans H. Penner, 'Interpretation,' in Willi Braun and Russell T. McCutcheon (eds.), *Guide to the Study of Religion* (London/New York: Cassell, 2000) 57-71, quotations from 69 (emphasis in original) and 70.
92. Jorge Luis Borges, 'Pierre Menard, Author of the *Quixote*,' in idem, *Labyrinths: Selected Stories & Other Writings*, ed. D.A. Yates and J.E. Irby (New York: New Directions Books, 1964) 36-44, esp. 43. I owe this reference to Jonathan Z. Smith, 'A Twice-told Tale: The History of the History of Religions' History,' *Numen* 48 (2001) 131-146, esp. its peroration.

Introduction

problem of translation – that 'this' is never quite 'that,' and that acts of interpretation are required – that animates the human sciences and, indeed, marks us as human(e) beings.[93] To play just a little with Alfred Korzybski's famous aphorism, that 'a map is not the territory': a translation is not the text – but translations are all we possess.[94]

---

93. On this problem, see Jonathan Z. Smith, 'Differential Equations: On Constructing the Other,' in idem, *Relating Religion: Essays in the History of Religions* (Chicago/London: University of Chicago Press, 2004) 230–250. Elsewhere Smith has argued that 'explanation is, at heart, an act of translation, of redescription' ('The Topography of the Sacred,' in *Relating Religion* 101–116, quotation from 105–106).
94. Alfred Korzybski, 'A Non-Aristotelian System and its Necessity for Rigour in Physics and Mathematics,' in idem, *Science and Sanity: An Introduction to Non-Aristotelian Systems and General Semantics* (Lancaster: The International Non-Aristotelian Publishing Co./Science Press Printing Co., 1933) 758; with a nod to Jonathan Z. Smith, *Map is Not Territory: Studies in the History of Religions* (Leiden: Brill, 1978) 309: 'Map is not territory – but maps are all we possess.'

Guide to Further Reading

The following selective bibliography focuses exclusively on the Qur'ān, rather than including works about Muḥammad and the origins and early history of Islam. It has been compiled to reflect a spectrum of critical viewpoints and approaches, ranging from 'traditionalist' to 'revisionist.' Aside from a few notable exceptions, it is limited to recent works in English, and to books rather than articles in journals, encyclopedias, and essay collections (though references to the latter are included). Additional bibliography will be found in the footnotes and bibliographies of the works listed here, as well as in the new exhaustive bibliography compiled by Morterza Karimi-Nia (listed under 'General reference works' below). Readers may also wish to consult the following journals for new publications on a wide variety of texts and topics relevant to Qur'ānic studies, as well as for reviews of recently published books in the field: *Arabica, Al-Bayān: Journal of Qur'ān and Ḥadīth Studies, Bulletin of the School of Oriental and African Studies, Comparative Islamic Studies, International Journal of Middle East Studies, Jerusalem Studies in Arabic and Islam, Journal of the American Oriental Society, Journal of Near Eastern Studies, Journal of Qur'anic Studies, Journal of Semitic Studies, Journal of the International Qur'anic Studies Association, Revue of Qur'anic Research, Studia Islamica,* and *The Muslim World.* Finally, the *Index Islamicus* is a database that indexes literature on Islam, the Middle East, and the Muslim world.

(On) English translations of the Qur'ān

Abdel Haleem, M.A.S. *The Qur'an*. Oxford: Oxford University Press, 2004.

Ali, A. *Al-Qur'ān: A Contemporary Translation*. Princeton: Princeton University Press, 1988.

Arberry, A.J. *The Koran Interpreted*. 2 vols. London: Allen & Unwin, 1955.

Asad, M. *The Message of the Qur'ān*. Gibraltar: Al-Andalus, 1984.

Bell, R. *The Qur'ān: Translated, with a Critical Re-arrangement of the Surahs*. 2 vols. Edinburgh: T. & T. Clark, 1937–1939.

Droge, A.J. *The Qur'ān: A New Annotated Translation*. Sheffield: Equinox, 2013.

Elmarsafy, Z. *The Enlightenment Qur'an: The Politics of Translation and the Construction of Islam*. Oxford: Oneworld, 2009.

Fakhry, M. *An Interpretation of the Qur'an: English Translation of the Meanings*. New York: New York University Press, 2002.

Jones, A. *The Qur'ān*. Exeter: Short Run Press, 2007.

Khalidi, T. *The Qur'an: A New Translation*. London: Penguin, 2008.

Lawrence, B.B. *The Koran in English: A Biography*. Princeton: Princeton University Press, 2017.

Qarai, A.Q. *The Qur'an: With a Phrase-by-Phrase English Translation*. 2nd ed. Elmhurst: Tahrike Tarsile Qur'an, 2011.

Mohammed, K. 'Assessing English Translations of the Qur'an.' *The Middle East Quarterly* 12 (2005) 58–71.

Nasr, S.H. et al. *The Study Qur'an: A New Translation and Commentary*. San Francisco: HarperOne, 2015.

Pickthall, M. *The Meaning of the Glorious Koran*. London: Knopf, 1930.

Yusuf Ali, A. *The Holy Qur'an: Text, Translation and Commentary*. Lahore: Shaikh Muḥammad Ashraf, 1934.

General reference works

Karimi-Nia, M. *Bibliography of Qur'anic Studies in European Languages*. Qum: Center for Translation of the Holy Quran, 2013.

Kassis, H.E. *A Concordance of the Qur'an*. Berkeley: University of California Press, 1983.

Leaman, O. (ed.) *The Qur'an: An Encyclopedia*. London: Routledge, 2006.

McAuliffe, J.D. (ed.) *The Encyclopaedia of the Qur'ān*. 5 vols. Leiden: Brill, 2001–2006.

Mir, M. *Dictionary of Qur'ānic Terms and Concepts*. New York: Garland, 1987.

Paret, R. *Der Koran: Kommentar und Konkordanz*. Stuttgart: Kohlhammer, 1971.

Peters, F.E. *A Reader on Classical Islam*. Princeton: Princeton University Press, 1994.

Watt, W.M. *Companion to the Qur'ān*. Oxford: Oneworld, 1994 [1967].

Introductions to the Qur'ān

Abdel Haleem, M.A.S. *Understanding the Qur'an: Themes and Style*. London: Tauris, 2000.

Cook, M. *The Koran: A Very Short Introduction*. Oxford: Oxford University Press, 2000.

Ernst, C.F. *How to Read the Qur'an: A New Guide, with Select Translations*. Chapel Hill: University of North Carolina Press, 2011.

Esack, F. *The Qur'an: A User's Guide*. Oxford: Oneworld, 2005.

Gade, A.M. *The Qur'ān: An Introduction*. Oxford: Oneworld, 2010.

Ibrahim, A.S. *A Concise Guide to the Quran: Answering Thirty Critical Questions*. Grand Rapids: Baker Academic, 2020.

Lawrence, B. *The Qur'an: A Biography*. New York: Atlantic Monthly Press, 2006.

Mattson, I. *The Story of the Qur'an: Its History and Place in Muslim Life*. Oxford: Blackwell, 2008.

McAuliffe, J.D. (ed.) *The Cambridge Companion to the Qur'ān*. Cambridge: Cambridge University Press, 2006.

McAuliffe, J.D. (ed.) *The Qur'ān*. Norton Critical Editions. London: W.W. Norton & Co., 2017.

Rahman, F. *Major Themes of the Qur'ān*. 2nd ed. Chicago: University of Chicago Press, 2009 [1980].

Rippin, A. (ed.) *The Blackwell Companion to the Qur'ān*. Oxford: Blackwell, 2006.

Reynolds, G.S. *The Qur'an and the Bible: Text and Commentary*. New Haven/London: Yale University Press, 2018.

Robinson, N. *Discovering the Qur'an: A Contemporary Approach to a Veiled Text*, 2nd ed. Washington, DC: Georgetown University Press, 2003.

Sells, M. *Approaching the Qur'án: The Early Revelations*. Ashland: White Cloud Press, 1999.

Sinai, N. *The Qur'an: A Historical-Critical Introduction* (Edinburgh: Edinburgh University Press, 2017).

Watt, W.M. and R. Bell. *Bell's Introduction to the Qur'ān*. Edinburgh: Edinburgh University Press, 1970.

Welch, A.T. art. 'al-Ḳur'ān.' *Encyclopaedia of Islam*. 2nd ed. 12 vols. Leiden: Brill, 1954–2004. 5.400–429 [orig. 1981].

Special studies

As-Said, L. *The Recited Koran: A History of the First Recorded Version*. Ed. and tr. B. Weiss, M.A. Rauf, and M. Berger. Princeton: Darwin Press, 1975.

Ayoub, M. *The Qur'an and Its Interpreters*. 2 vols. Albany: SUNY Press, 1984–1992.

Boullata, I.J. (ed.) *Literary Structures of Religious Meaning in the Qur'ān*. Richmond: Curzon, 2000.

Burton, J. 'Those are the High-flying Cranes.' *Journal of Semitic Studies* 15 (1970) 246–265.

Burton, J. *The Collection of the Qur'ān*. Cambridge: Cambridge University Press, 1977.

El-Awa, S.M.S. *Textual Relations in the Qur'ān: Relevance, Coherence and Structure*. London: Routledge, 2005.

El-Badawi, E. and P. Sanders (eds.) *Communities of the Qur'an: Dialogue, Debate, and Diversity in the 21st Century*. London: Oneworld Academic, 2019.

Gätje, H. *The Qur'ān and its Exegesis: Selected Texts with Classical and Modern Muslim Interpretations*. Ed. and tr. A.T. Welch. Oxford: Oneworld, 1996 [1971].

Gwyne, R.W. *Logic, Rhetoric, and Legal Reasoning in the Qur'ān: God's Arguments*. London: RoutledgeCurzon, 2004.

Hawting, G.R. and A.-K. Shareef. (eds.) *Approaches to the Qur'an*. London: Routledge, 1993.

Guide to Further Reading

Hidayatullah, A.A. *Feminist Edges of the Qur'an*. Oxford: Oxford University Press, 2014.

Izutsu, T. *God and Man in the Koran: Semantics of the Koranic Weltanschauung*. Tokyo: The Keio Institute of Cultural and Linguistic Studies, 1964.

Izutsu, T. *Ethico-Religious Concepts in the Qur'ān*. Montreal: McGill University Press, 2002 [1966].

Jeffrey, A. *The Foreign Vocabulary of the Qur'ān*. Baroda: Oriental Institute, 1938.

Jeffrey, A. *The Qur'ān as Scripture*. New York: Russell F. Moore, 1952.

Jomier, J. *The Great Themes of the Qur'an*. London: SCM Press, 1997.

Klar, M. (ed.) *Structural Dividers in the Qur'an*. London: Routledge, 2020.

Madigan, D.A. *The Qur'ān's Self-Image: Writing and Authority in Islam's Scripture*. Princeton: Princeton University Press, 2001.

Mir, M. *Coherence in the Qur'ān*. Indianapolis: American Trust Publications, 1986.

Neuwirth, A. *Studien zur Komposition der mekkanischen Suren*. 2., erweiterte Auflage. Berlin: Walter de Gruyter, 2007.

Neuwirth, A. *The Qur'an and Late Antiquity: A Shared Heritage*. Tr. S. Wilder. New York: Oxford University Press, 2019.

Neuwirth, A. et al. (eds.) *The Qur'ān in Context: Historical and Literary Investigations into the Qur'anic Milieu*. Leiden: Brill, 2010.

O'Shaughnessy, T.J. *Eschatological Themes in the Qur'ān*. Manila: Loyola School of Theology, 1986.

Reeves, J.C. (ed.) *Bible and Qur'ān: Essays in Scriptural Intertextuality*. Atlanta: Society of Biblical Literature, 2003.

Reynolds, G.S. *The Qur'ān and Its Biblical Subtext*. London: Routledge, 2010.

Reynolds, G.S. *Allah: God in the Qur'an*. New Haven/London: Yale University Press, 2020.

Reynolds, G.S. (ed.) *The Qur'ān in Its Historical Context*. London: Routledge, 2008.

Reynolds, G.S. (ed.) *New Perspectives on the Qur'ān: The Qur'ān in Its Historical Context 2*. London: Routledge, 2011.

Rippin, A. *The Qur'an and its Interpretive Tradition*. Aldershot: Variorum/Ashgate, 2001.

Rippin, A. (ed.) *The Qur'an: Formative Interpretation*. Aldershot: Ashgate, 1999.

Rippin, A. (ed.) *The Qurán: Style and Contents*. Aldershot: Ashgate, 2001.

Rubin, U. *Between Bible and Qur'ān: The Children of Israel and the Islamic Self-Image*. Princeton: Darwin Press, 1999.

Saleh, W. 'In Search of a Comprehensible Qur'ān: A Survey of Some Recent Scholarly Works.' *Bulletin of the Royal Institute for Inter-Faith Studies* 5 (2003) 143–162.

Sirry, M. *Scriptural Polemics: The Qur'ān and Other Religions*. Oxford: Oxford University Press, 2014.

Smith, J.Z. 'Religion and Bible.' *Journal of Biblical Literature* 128 (2009) 5–27.

Stowasser, B.F. *Women in the Qur'an, Traditions, and Interpretation.* New York: Oxford University Press, 1994.

Tlili, S. *Animals in the Qur'an.* Cambridge: Cambridge University Press, 2012.

Tottoli, R. *Biblical Prophets in the Qur'ān and Muslim Literature.* Richmond: Curzon, 2002.

Wadud, A. *Qur'an and Woman: Rereading the Sacred Text from a Woman's Perspective.* Oxford: Oxford University Press, 1999.

Wansbrough, J. *Quranic Studies: Sources and Methods of Scriptural Interpretation.* Foreword, Translations, and Expanded Notes by Andrew Rippin. Amherst: Prometheus Books, 2004 [1977].

Wheeler, B. *Prophets in the Quran: An Introduction to the Quran and Muslim Exegesis.* London: Continuum, 2002.

Wheeler, B. *Moses in the Quran and Islamic Exegesis.* London: RoutledgeCurzon, 2002.

Widengren, G. *Muḥammad, the Apostle of God, and his Ascension.* Uppsala: A.B. Lundequistska Bokhandeln, 1955.

Wild, S. (ed.) *The Qur'an as Text.* Leiden: Brill, 1996.

Wild, S. (ed.) *Self-Referentiality in the Qur'ān.* Wiesbaden: Harrassowitz, 2006.

ABBREVIATIONS

AH	indicates dates according to the Islamic calendar (from Latin *anno Hegirae*, or 'in the year of the Hijra'), also called the 'Hijrī calendar' (*al-taqwīm al-hijrī*). Year 1 AH = 622 CE.
BCE	indicates dates before the Common Era, equivalent to BC ('before Christ') in the Christian Gregorian calendar.
c.	circa.
CE	indicates dates according to the Common Era, equivalent to AD (from Latin *anno Domini*, or 'in the year of the Lord') of the Christian Gregorian calendar.
cf.	compare.
d.	died.
e.g.	for example.
fem.	feminine.
i.e.	that is.
lacuna	a missing section of a text. In this edition a lacuna in the text is marked by [...].
lit.	literally.
masc.	masculine.
n.	note.
nn.	notes.
par.	parallel.
plur.	plural.
Q	Qur'ān; references to the Qur'ān are cited as follows: Q sūra # . verse # (versification is according to the Cairo edition).
sing.	singular.
v.	verse.
vv.	verses.

Timeline

The following dates are all CE ('Common Era'). Many dates are approximate, and some open to doubt.

527–565	reign of Byzantine emperor Justinian
530–579	reign of Sassanid Persian emperor Khusro I
537	dedication of the church of Hagia Sophia
540	Khusro I takes Antioch
540–561	period of Persian/Byzantine warfare
c. 570–632	dates for Muḥammad
572–591	period of Persian/Byzantine warfare
582–602	reign of Byzantine emperor Maurice
591–628	reign of Sassanid Persian emperor Khusro II
c. 600	compilation of the Babylonian Talmud
602–629	period of Persian/Byzantine warfare
610–641	reign of Byzantine emperor Heraclius
610	Muḥammad's first 'vision'
613	Persians take Antioch
614	Persians take Jerusalem
619	Persians take Alexandria
622	Muḥammad's flight from Mecca to Medina, beginning of the Muslim era (16 July)
627	final campaign of Heraclius in Persia
629	Muslims take Mecca
632–661	rule of Muḥammad's successors ('caliphs'), Abū Bakr (632–634), 'Umar (634–644), 'Uthmān (644–656), and 'Alī (656–661)
635	Muslims take Damascus

Timeline

636	Muslim victory over the Byzantines at the battle of Yarmuk (end of Byzantine control of Syria), Muslim victory over the Persians at the battle of al-Qādisiyya (Sassanid empire declines),
637	Muslims take Antioch
638	Muslims take Jerusalem
642	Muslims take Alexandria
644–656	caliphate of 'Uthmān, during which the text of the Qur'ān was definitively fixed, according to Muslim tradition
661–750	Umayyad caliphate, rules from Damascus
677	Muslim siege of Constantinople
691	completion of Dome of the Rock
692–724	Al-Hajjaj, Ummayad governor of Iraq
695	first Muslim coins minted
698	Muslims take Carthage
699	Arabic replaces Greek in administration
711	Muslims invade Spain
715	completion of Great Mosque of Damascus
717	defeat of Muslims at Constantinople
732	Franks defeat Muslims at the battle of Tours/Poitiers
750	revolt of the Abbasids, beginning of the Abbasid caliphate
750–1258	Abbasid caliphate, rules from Baghdad
c. 755–1031	independent Umayyad dynasty in Spain

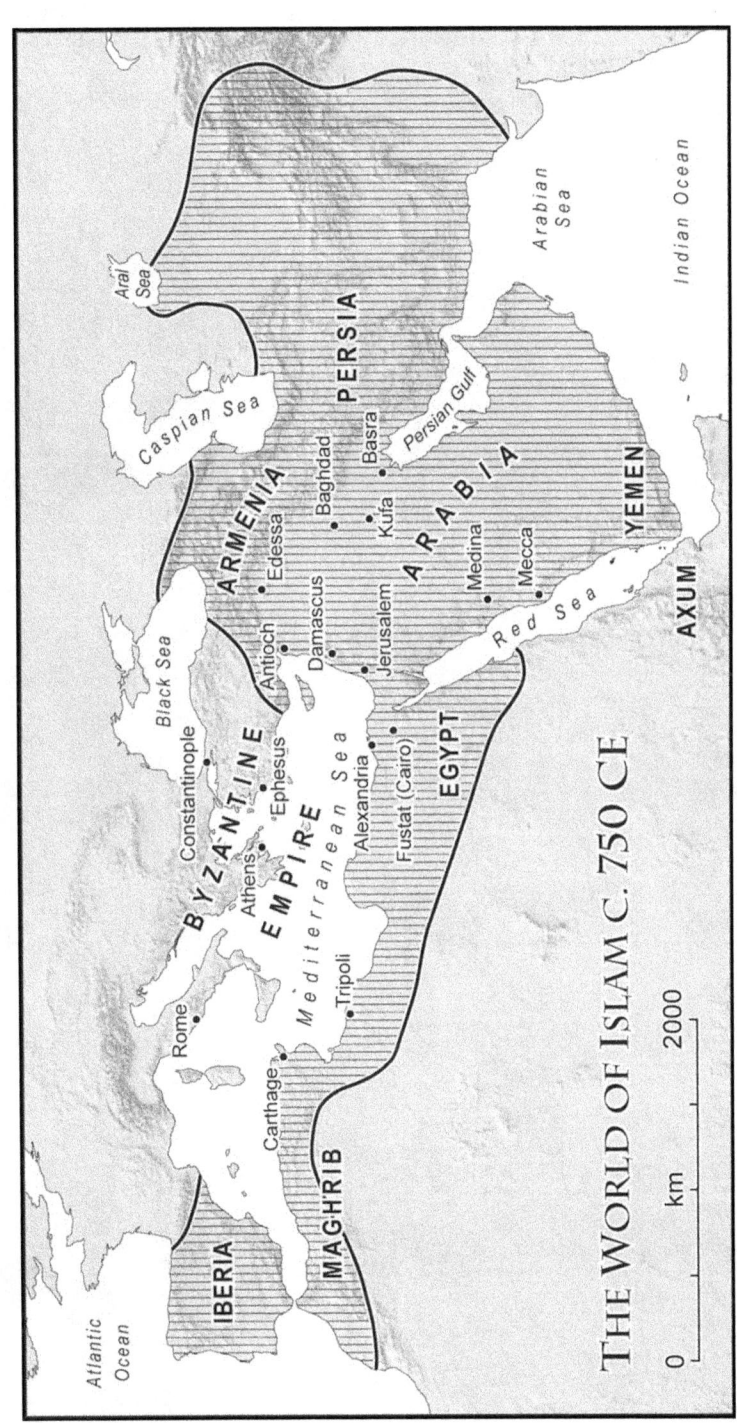

The Muslim world c. 750 CE

Synopsis: The Qur'ān at a Glance

1 The Opening
As its title suggests, this short prayer serves as the introduction to the Qur'ān, though it has also had several other names (e.g., 'The Praise'). It is sometimes referred to as the 'mother' or 'essence of the Qur'ān' (*umm al-Qur'ān*), and is an important part of worship, both public and private. Whether it was originally part of the Qur'ān is uncertain. The early codex (*muṣḥaf*) of Ibn Mas'ūd (d. 32 AH/652/3 CE) is said to have omitted it.

2 The Cow
By far the longest sūra, Q2 defies easy summary. It includes accounts of Adam's fall, Moses and Pharaoh, Israel's disobedience, and the religion of Abraham and his building of God's 'House,' toward which prayer is now directed. Instruction on a wide variety of topics occupies most of the second half of the sūra (on food, retaliation, wills, fasting, fighting, pilgrimage, marriage, divorce, usury, almsgiving, and prayer). Its title comes from the story of 'the cow' which the Israelites were commanded to sacrifice (Q2.67–71).

3 House of 'Imrān
This sūra opens with a pronouncement about the divine origin of the Qur'ān, including its relationship to the previous scriptures of Jews and Christians. After this come stories of Zachariah, Mary, Jesus and his disciples, and Abraham as a Muslim. Criticism of Jewish disbelief, exhortation to the believers, and encouragement in the aftermath of defeat occupy most of the remainder of the sūra. Its title derives from the reference to the 'house of 'Imrān' at Q3.33.

4 Women
This sūra takes its name from the many instructions regarding women, but it also offers guidance on a variety of other topics, including the treatment of orphans, marriage, property, inheritance, and fighting. The Prophet is put forward as God's representative and the supreme arbiter of all disputes. There are also polemical passages against the 'hypocrites' and 'People of the Book,' as well as a dispute about the crucifixion of Jesus.

5 The Table

This sūra offers instruction on a variety of topics (e.g., prayer, pilgrimage, and food), and prescribes punishment for certain offenses (e.g., murder and theft). Several passages condemn various 'pagan' practices, but many more are critical of Jewish disobedience and Christian doctrine, and believers are warned against entering into alliance with the 'People of the Book.' Q5 receives its title from the miraculous 'table' of food sent down to Jesus and his disciples (Q5.111–115).

6 Livestock

This sūra emphasizes the creative power of the one God, especially as manifested in the 'signs' of an ordered natural world. On that basis it attacks the folly of idolatry, charging that other so-called gods are really 'jinn.' The story of Abraham's rejection of idols is repeated, and a parallel is drawn between the 'religion' of Abraham and the Prophet, as well as between the 'Books' given to Moses and the Prophet. Its title is a reference to the practice of dedicating 'livestock' to other gods besides God (Q6.136–139).

7 The Heights

Following an introductory reference to 'the Book' and a warning about judgment, Q7 falls into three main parts: the story of Iblīs and Adam's fall (Q7.10–25), a series of stories about the destruction of disobedient peoples of the past (Q7.59–102), and the story of Moses, Pharaoh, and the Sons of Israel (Q7.103–174). The sūra receives its title from the enigmatic reference to 'the heights' at Q7.46.

8 The Spoils

Most of this sūra concerns the victory of Muslim forces over their opponents, including directives about the distribution of 'spoils' (Q8.1, 41).

9 Repentance

This sūra deals with various matters connected with fighting for the cause of God. It opens with a renunciation of all treaty obligations with the 'idolaters' (Q9.1–28). This is followed by a short exhortation to fight against the 'People of the Book' (Q9.29–35). Then comes a sustained diatribe against the 'hypocrites' and others for their refusal to fight alongside the Prophet (Q9.38–106). It concludes by emphasizing again the duty to fight for the cause (Q9.119–129). Q9 is the only sūra in the Cairo edition that is not introduced by the *basmala* (though the codex of Ibn Mas'ūd is said to have included it). The title comes from the reference to 'repentance' at Q9.104, but it is also known as 'The Renunciation' (*al-Barā'a*) from its first word.

10 Jonah

This sūra opens with a declaration of God's creative power, followed by a condemnation of idolatry. The certainty of judgment and the authenticity of the

Qur'ān are also stressed. A final section contains stories about Noah and Moses (Q10.71–103). It receives its title from the reference to 'Jonah's people' at Q10.98.

11 Hūd
This sūra is made up almost entirely of stories about the following messengers: Noah, Hūd, Ṣāliḥ, Abraham, Lot, Shuʿayb, and Moses.

12 Joseph
This sūra is devoted almost entirely to the story of Joseph, beloved son of Jacob. While there are many parallels between the Qur'ānic version and the account in Genesis 37–50, there are also some striking differences. In contrast to his biblical counterpart, Jacob is a prophet who is not tricked into thinking Joseph was killed. The Qur'ānic Jacob is also clairvoyant, even though he cannot physically see, and in the end miraculously receives his sight when Joseph's shirt is laid over his face.

13 The Thunder
This sūra is an assemblage of short passages touching on a variety of topics, including God's power and providence, rewards and punishments, and encouragement to the Prophet. It takes its name from 'the thunder' that praises God at Q13.13.

14 Abraham
This sūra, like the previous one, is an assemblage of short passages touching on a variety of topics, including a brief recounting of the stories of Moses and other messengers, human ingratitude for God's blessings, and the prayer of Abraham, from which it receives its title.

15 Al-Ḥijr
This sūra contains accounts of the rebellion of Iblīs (Q15.26–48) and the angels' visits to Abraham and Lot (Q15.49–77). Two short stories of punishment follow: the people of 'the Grove' and the inhabitants of 'al-Ḥijr' (Q15.78–84). Q15 concludes with a series of admonitions to the Prophet.

16 The Bee
This sūra treats a variety of topics and themes. In general it extols God's creative power and condemns the foolishness of idolatry. It takes its title from the reference to the bees (Q16.68–69), which are 'inspired' by God and only one of many signs of his providence. A later section (Q16.98–105) sheds important light on the recitation and revelation of the Qur'ān.

17 The Journey
This sūra opens with the famous and tantalizingly brief report of a 'night journey.' A variety of topics then follow, including a series of commandments resembling

the Decalogue in form and content (Q17.22–39a), as well as passages dealing with the nature and purpose of the Qur'ān. The Prophet's role as the 'messenger' is emphasized, and disbelievers are chastised for their objection that he is merely a 'human being' who does not perform any miracles. Q17 is also known as the 'Sons of Israel' from the references to the Banū Isrā'īl at its beginning and end.

18 The Cave
This sūra is distinctive for being composed almost entirely of stories. The three main ones are: the 'Men of the Cave' (Q18.9–26), Moses and the servant (18.60–82), and Dhū-l-Qarnayn, a figure usually identified with Alexander the Great (18.83–98).

19 Mary
This sūra begins with a series of stories about earlier prophets. The longest of these is the story of Mary and Jesus (Q19.16–36), from which Q19 receives its title. The remainder of the sūra explains the role of angels, responds to objections about the resurrection, and pronounces judgment on disbelievers.

20 Ṭā' Hā'
This sūra is devoted almost entirely to the story of Moses (Q20.9–101). It features accounts of his early life, call to be a messenger, struggles with Pharaoh, exodus from Egypt, and finally the episode of 'the calf.' Q20 concludes with sections on the Last Day and the covenant with Adam. It receives its title from the two letters with which it begins.

21 The Prophets
This sūra begins with a warning of approaching judgment, and condemns idolatry in the face of God's power and providence. Its second half is comprised of a series of stories about earlier 'prophets' (Q21.48–91), from which Q21 receives its title. Many of these prophets have counterparts among biblical figures.

22 The Pilgrimage
This sūra takes its title from the reference to the Ḥajj, the pilgrimage originally established by Abraham (Q22.26–38). In addition to dealing with matters connected with the pilgrimage, it condemns those who deny believers access to the 'Sacred Mosque,' and concludes with an address to the believers, urging them to remain steadfast to the religion of Abraham.

23 The Believers
This sūra opens with an enumeration of the virtues of believers. It then extols the signs of God's power and providence, relates accounts of previous messengers, and emphasizes the certainty of resurrection and judgment.

24 The Light

This sūra takes its title from the reference to God as 'the light of the heavens and the earth' (Q24.35). It is comprised for the most part of regulations governing the household, including appropriate dress, conduct, and sexual behavior.

25 The Deliverance

This sūra begins by responding to the disbelievers' rejection of the Prophet and his message, and then warns them by way of examples of earlier generations who were punished for similar disbelief. The second half of the sūra is mainly devoted to the signs of God's power and providence discernible in the natural world. It concludes with a description of the characteristic qualities of God's servants.

26 The Poets

This sūra is made up almost entirely of stories about the following messengers: Moses, Abraham, Noah, Hūd, Ṣāliḥ, Lot, and Shuʿayb, all linked together by a recurring refrain (Q26.8–9). It receives its title from the dismissive reference to 'the poets' at Q26.224–225.

27 The Ant

This sūra opens with a reference to the Qur'ān as 'guidance and good news' and closes with a description of the Day of Judgment. It recounts the stories of previous messengers, including one about Solomon and the Queen of Sheba. The theme of God's power and uniqueness is also emphasized. It receives its title from 'the ant' that speaks in the story of Solomon (Q27.18).

28 The Story

This sūra is devoted almost entirely to the story of Moses, featuring accounts of his childhood and early life, his call to be a messenger, and finally his struggles with Pharaoh (with a later addendum on the story of Qārūn/Korah). It concludes with three scenes of judgment and a final word of encouragement to the Prophet. Q28 receives its title from 'the story' Moses recounts at Q28.25.

29 The Spider

This sūra begins by exhorting believers to remain steadfast in the face of opposition, and then recounts the stories of seven previous messengers. It also describes the nature of 'the Book' revealed to the Prophet and its relationship to the previous scriptures of the 'People of the Book.' It takes its title from the parable of 'the spider' at Q29.41.

30 The Romans

This sūra opens with a reference to a military defeat of the Byzantine empire, which is followed by a prophecy of their ultimate victory over the Sassanid

Persians. It then extols the signs of God's power in the natural world as evidence of his benevolence and ability to raise the dead.

31 Luqmān

This sūra takes its title from the story of Luqmān, a sage who presents his son with a succinct version of his wisdom (Q31.12–19). Among its many diverse themes, Q31 extols the signs of God's power and providence, and warns disbelievers of the certainty of judgment.

32 The Prostration

This sūra opens with a pronouncement about the truth of the Qur'ān. It then extols God's power as creator and defends the resurrection against the objection of disbelievers, whose fate is contrasted with the ultimate vindication of believers. Q32 takes its title from the 'prostration' of believers in worship (Q32.15).

33 The Factions

This sūra deals mainly with the Prophet's marriage to a woman formerly married to his adopted son, as well as with other matters concerning his wives. It receives its title from the description of an attack against the believers of the city of Yathrib by 'factions' of their enemies (Q33.9–27).

34 Sheba

The main subject of this sūra is the certainty of judgment and resurrection. It receives its title from the story of the people of Sheba (Q34.15–21).

35 Creator

The first part of this sūra is in the form of an address to the people, setting forth the claims of God (Q35.1–17). It then shifts to address the Prophet, consoling him with the reminder of previous messengers who also faced rejection (Q35.18–26). It concludes with the different fates awaiting believers and disbelievers. Q35 takes its title from the reference to God as 'creator' in the opening verse, but is also called 'the angels' (*al-Malā'ika*) from another word in the first verse.

36 Yā' Sīn

This sūra begins with an affirmation of the Prophet's mission. It then relates a parable about a 'disbelieving city,' enumerates the signs of God's power and providence, and describes the different fates awaiting believers and disbelievers. Q36 receives its title from the two letters with which it begins.

37 The Ones Who Line Up

This sūra opens with an emphatic declaration of the unity and creative power of God. Next come sections on the resurrection and the different fates awaiting believers and disbelievers, followed by stories of previous messengers from Noah to Jonah. Its title refers to the angels standing in assembly around the divine throne (Q37.1, 165).

38 Ṣād

The first part of this sūra describes the defiance of the Prophet's contemporaries. Next come stories of David, Solomon, Job, and several others. It then describes the different fates awaiting believers and disbelievers, before concluding with the story of Iblīs. Q38 takes its title from the letter with which it begins.

39 The Companies

This sūra opens with pronouncements about divine origin of the Qur'ān and the unity and creative power of God. The remainder of sūra contrasts the different fates awaiting believers and disbelievers, before concluding with a vivid description of Judgment Day. Q39 receives its title from the reference to the righteous and wicked entering the Garden and Gehenna in 'companies' (Q39.71, 73).

40 Forgiver

This is the first of a group of seven sūras (Q40–46) known as the 'Ḥawāmīm,' from the two letters (Ḥā' Mīm) with which they all begin. It consists mainly of the story of Moses, with a number of features that distinguish it from other versions of his story in the Qur'ān. Q40 takes its name from one of the divine epithets in its opening verses, but it is also known as al-Mu'min, from 'the believer' in the house of Pharaoh who tried to dissuade his people from opposing Moses (Q40.28–45).

41 Made Distinct

This sūra extols God as creator and pronounces judgment on those who refuse to recognize the signs of his power and providence. Its title comes from a word used to describe the Qur'ān (Q41.3, 44), though it is also known as 'The Prostration' (the same title as Q32).

42 Consultation

This sūra opens by extolling the power and majesty of God and stresses the purpose of the Qur'ān as a warning. Next comes a declaration of the unity of religion in the face of religious differences. The contrasting fates of believers and disbelievers occupy much of the remainder of the sūra. The conclusion is noteworthy for the light it sheds on different modes of revelation. Q42 receives its title from the reference to the believers' 'consultation' among themselves at Q42.38.

43 Decoration

This sūra condemns the folly of idolatry, especially the idea that God has 'daughters,' and warns of the dangers of persistent disbelief. It goes on to recount the stories of Moses and Jesus, and concludes with a vivid scene of judgment. Q43 receives its title from the 'decoration' referred to at Q43.35.

44 The Smoke

This sūra opens with a declaration of the 'sending down' of the Qur'ān during a single night, followed by a warning that punishment is coming. It recounts the story of Pharaoh and the Sons of Israel, defends the idea of resurrection, and concludes with a description of the rewards and punishments awaiting the righteous and wicked. Q44 takes its title from the reference to the appearance of a heavenly 'smoke' which will be a sign of the Last Day (Q44.10).

45 The Kneeling

This sūra opens with a declaration of the 'sending down' of the Qur'ān and an enumeration of the signs of God's power and providence in nature. The Prophet is then urged to follow God's path independently of the 'Sons of Israel.' Q45 concludes with a judgment scene, at which each community will be found 'kneeling' (Q45.28).

46 The Sand Dunes

This is the last of a group of seven sūras known as the 'Ḥawāmīm,' from the two letters (Ḥā' Mīm) with which they all begin. It opens with a declaration of the 'sending down' of the Qur'ān, and then condemns the folly of idolatry in the face of God's power and providence. The Prophet is set forth as a typical messenger whose 'Book' confirms the 'Book of Moses.' Next comes the story of the punishment of the people of 'Ād, followed by one about a band of jinn who came to believe after listening to the Prophet recite from the Qur'ān. A conclusion stresses the certainty of resurrection and judgment. The title of Q46 refers to 'the sand dunes' where the 'Ād were destroyed (Q46.21).

47 Muḥammad

Much of this sūra is concerned with matters of war. It receives its title from one of the rare mentions of Muḥammad's name at Q47.2.

48 The Victory

This sūra opens with the promise of victory and offers encouragement to the Prophet and those who have sworn allegiance to him. It takes its title from the 'victory' mentioned in the opening verse.

49 The Private Rooms

This sūra deals with the conduct of the Prophet's followers in their interactions with him and each other. It concludes with a criticism of the bedouin Arabs. Q49 takes its name from a word that is said to refer to the private living quarters of the Prophet's wives (Q49.4).

50 Qāf

This sūra begins by defending the resurrection through an appeal to the signs of God's power and providence in nature. It stresses the certainty of death and judgment, and concludes with some words of advice for the Prophet. Q50 takes its title from the letter with which it begins.

51 The Scatterers

This sūra opens with a series of vivid affirmations of the certainty and imminence of the Day of Judgment. Next comes the story of Abraham and his guests, followed by briefer reports of the punishment of Pharaoh and the peoples of 'Ād, Thamūd, and Noah. A final section extols God's power and providence. Q51 takes its name from a word in the opening verse.

52 The Mountain

This sūra opens with a series of affirmations of the certainty and imminence of the Day of Judgment. This is followed by a description of the delights awaiting the righteous in Paradise. The latter half of the sūra is an unrelenting diatribe against the disbelievers. Q52 receives its title from the reference to Mount Sinai in the opening verse.

53 The Star

This sūra opens with reports of two 'visions.' These are followed by a section rejecting the idea that angels are the 'daughters of God.' It concludes with a summary of the contents of 'the scrolls of Moses and Abraham.' Q53 takes its title from 'the star' mentioned in the opening verse.

54 The Moon

This sūra is made up almost entirely of stories about earlier generations who were destroyed for their disobedience, all linked together by a recurring refrain which ends with the question, 'Is there anyone who takes heed?' Fittingly, both the beginning and the end warn that judgment is near. Q54 receives its title from the opening reference to the moon being split open, a sign that the end is at hand.

55 The Merciful

The first half of this sūra recounts God's blessings; the second half describes the punishments of the wicked and rewards of the righteous. One of its distinctive features is that it addresses both humans and jinn in the form of a refrain that is repeated some thirty-one times ('Which of the blessings of your Lord will you two call a lie?'). Q55 takes its title from the opening reference to God as 'the Merciful.'

56 The Falling

This sūra opens with a vivid description of the Last Day, when people will be divided into three classes – 'the foremost' and 'the companions on the right and left' – whose rewards and punishments are then described. The second half of the sūra extols God's power and providence, and praises the Qur'ān. Q56 receives its title from the 'falling' of Judgment referred to in the opening verse.

57 Iron

This sūra opens by extolling the glory of God, and then appeals for belief in and support of the Prophet and his cause. It describes the different fates awaiting the 'hypocrites' and believers, and concludes with a reference to the previous messengers Abraham, Noah, and Jesus. Q57 receives its title from the mention of 'iron,' which God has sent down along with 'the Book' and 'the scale' (Q57.25).

58 The Disputer

This sūra takes its title from a woman who 'disputed' her husband's attempt to end their marriage by means of a pre-Islamic formula. The case concludes by stipulating the penalty for anyone who continues to use such a formula in the future. The rest of the sūra is a warning that those who conspire against the Prophet, or otherwise oppose him, will suffer defeat both in this world and the next.

59 The Gathering

Most of this sūra concerns the expulsion of the disbelievers among the 'People of the Book' from their homes and the division of spoils. It concludes with an exhortation to fear God, whose surpassing glory is revealed in his many different epithets. Q59 receives its title from 'the gathering' of the disbelievers for exile (Q59.2).

60 The Examined Woman

This sūra warns believers about secret alliances with the enemy. It also gives instructions on how to treat women who leave their husbands to join the believers, as well as what to do about the wives of believers who run off.

61 The Lines

This sūra consists of several short passages. Notable among them is a section on Israel's opposition to Moses, Jesus, and finally the Prophet, whose coming (under the name of 'Aḥmad') Jesus is said to have predicted. Q61 takes its title from the reference to troops drawn up in battle 'lines' (Q61.4).

Synopsis: The Qur'ān at a Glance

62 The Assembly

This sūra consists of several short passages. The Prophet is identified as a 'native' messenger, Jewish exceptionalism is criticized, and prayer is established on Friday, the 'day of assembly,' from which Q62 receives its title.

63 The Hypocrites

This sūra is comprised of two passages, one describing 'the hypocrites' (whence its title), and the other admonishing the believers.

64 Mutual Defrauding

This sūra extols the glory, power, and knowledge of God, and then describes the different fates awaiting believers and disbelievers. It concludes by encouraging believers to remain steadfast and contribute to the cause. Q64 receives its title from a word whose exact meaning and significance are uncertain (Q64.9).

65 Divorce

As its title indicates, this sūra is mostly comprised of regulations concerning divorce (similar to those found at Q2.226–232). It also alludes briefly to the punishment of previous cities and mentions the future reward of believers, before concluding with a striking reference to the creation of the 'seven heavens.'

66 The Forbidding

The first half of this sūra deals with an incident between the Prophet and his wives, though the exact circumstances remain obscure. It concludes by giving famous examples from the past of both believing and disbelieving women. The title comes from God's chastisement of the Prophet for forbidding himself what God has permitted (Q66.1).

67 The Kingdom

This sūra consists mostly of short passages, many of which revolve around the theme of the knowledge and power of God, in whose hand is 'the kingdom.' It concludes with a series of declarations reinforcing this theme.

68 The Pen

This sūra opens with a denial that the Prophet is 'possessed,' before turning to denounce one of his opponents directly. Next comes a parable warning against arrogant self-satisfaction, followed by a section on eschatological rewards and punishments, and a concluding exhortation to the Prophet. Q68 receives its title from the opening verse in which God swears 'by the pen,' perhaps referring to the idea of God's written revelation or the Book of Destiny by which everything is ordained.

69 The Payment Due

This sūra begins with a reference to several previous peoples who dismissed the threat of impending punishment and were destroyed. It then describes the terror of the Last Day and Judgment, and concludes with God affirming the truth of the Qur'ān. Its title comes from its first word.

70 The Stairways

This sūra begins by responding to a question about the coming punishment. A description of those who will enter the Garden follows. It then concludes by assuring the Prophet that his opponents are doomed. Q70 takes its title from the reference to the 'stairways' or 'ladders' to heaven on which the angels descend and ascend (Q70.3).

71 Noah

As its title indicates, this sūra is devoted to Noah, including details not found in other iterations of his story in the Qur'ān.

72 The Jinn

This sūra begins with a report of a band of jinn who heard the Prophet reciting the Qur'ān. Their affirmation of belief makes up the first half of the sūra; the latter half contains a series of pronouncements by the Prophet.

73 The Enwrapped One

This sūra opens with the Prophet being urged to spend the night attending to the Qur'ān. This is followed by a warning to the people and an appeal for belief. It concludes with a modification of what was imposed at the beginning of the sūra. Q73 receives its title from the opening address to the Prophet as 'the one wrapped up in his robe.'

74 The Cloaked One

This sūra is a collection of diverse passages. It opens with a command to the Prophet to 'arise and warn.' This is followed by sections dealing with an opponent, the number of angels guarding Hell, and the fate of those who disregard the message. Q74 takes its title from the opening address to the Prophet as 'the one wrapped up in his cloak.'

75 The Resurrection

This sūra is a collection of short passages, most of which revolve around the Last Day and God's power to raise the dead. Noteworthy among them is a section dealing with the Prophet's method of reciting the Qur'ān. Its title comes from the oath with which it begins.

Synopsis: The Qur'ān at a Glance

76 The Human

This sūra opens with a reference to the generation of humans, describes the rewards of the righteous, and closes with an exhortation to the Prophet to remain steadfast. It also goes under the name 'Time' (Ar. *al-Dahr*).

77 The Ones Sent Forth

This sūra, unified by the theme of impending judgment, opens with a series of vivid affirmations of the certainty of the Last Day, and then, just as vividly, describes the signs that will accompany it. The remainder of the sūra is a series of eschatological 'woes' directed against those who deny God's judgment. Q77 takes its name from a word in the opening verse, probably referring to the winds of an approaching storm as a metaphor for the imminent arrival of the Last Day.

78 The News

This sūra, which begins with 'the news' of impending judgment, extols the power and providence of God, and describes the events of the Last Day, including the different fates awaiting the righteous and wicked.

79 The Snatchers

This sūra opens with a series of affirmations that lead into a dramatic representation of sinners at the resurrection. This is followed by an abridged version of the story of Moses, as well as passages on God's providential power, and the different fates awaiting the righteous and wicked. Q79 receives its title from the opening verse.

80 He Frowned

This sūra begins by admonishing the Prophet to persevere in the face of apparent failure. Next come sections on the authority of the written message and human ingratitude for God's providential care. It concludes with a vivid scene of the Last Day. The title comes from its first word.

81 The Shrouding

This sūra consists of two passages: the first is a description of events of the Last Day; the other relates a vision on the part of the Prophet. Its title comes from 'the shrouding' of the sun (Q81.1), one of the cosmic signs that the Last Day is at hand.

82 The Rending

This sūra falls into three related parts: the events of the Last Day, the certainty of Judgment, and an explanation of Judgment Day. Its title comes from 'the rending' of the sky, one of the cosmic signs that the Last Day is at hand.

83 The Defrauders

As its title suggests, this sūra opens with a denunciation of those who cheat others by giving 'short measure.' Their punishment is then contrasted with the fate of the righteous.

84 The Splitting

This sūra opens with a description of events of the Last Day that will culminate in the resurrection and judgment. It concludes with a warning to those who reject the Qur'ān. Its title comes from 'the splitting' of the sky, one of the cosmic signs that the Last Day is at hand.

85 The Constellations

This sūra promises punishment for the wicked and rewards for the righteous.

86 The Night Visitor

This sūra stresses God's power to raise the dead and the accountability of each individual before him. In conclusion the Prophet is told to leave the disbelievers alone temporarily. Its title comes from a word in the opening verse.

87 The Most High

This sūra promises the Prophet God's support in reciting the Qur'ān, and commends those who accept its message. It concludes by emphasizing the superiority of the future life over the present one. Its title is one of God's many epithets.

88 The Covering

This sūra contrasts the fates of the righteous and the wicked on the Day of Judgment. It concludes with an exhortation to the Prophet to continue in his role as a 'warner.'

89 The Dawn

Following a mysterious oath, this sūra describes the punishment of earlier generations and concludes with an anticipation of the final judgment.

90 The Land

This sūra criticizes those who take the easy path and neglect the steep ascent to virtue. Only the latter path leads to the promised rewards, wheras the former ends in certain punishment.

91 The Sun

This sūra consists of two passages. The first is a series of contrasting oaths that culminate in the contrast between true success and failure. The second recounts the story of the people of Thamūd, who were destroyed for their evildoing.

92 The Night
This sūra, like the previous one, begins with a series of oaths that culminate in a contrast between the two ways in life, and concludes with the different fates awaiting the righteous and wicked.

93 The Morning Light
This sūra offers the Prophet reassurance and encouragement. It is noteworthy for the light it may shed on his former life.

94 The Expanding
This sūra, like the previous one (with which it may be connected), offers the Prophet reassurance by recounting God's past favor. Its title derives from a word in the opening verse.

95 The Fig
This sūra is concerned to alleviate any doubt or hesitancy the Prophet may have had about proclaiming the coming Judgment.

96 The Clot
This sūra, regarded by some as the first revelation, opens with an exhortation to the Prophet to 'recite' in the name of God the creator. The second part is a warning to one of the Prophet's opponents. Q96 takes its name from a word in the second verse. It is also known as 'Recite' (*Iqra'*) from its opening command.

97 The Decree
This short sūra describes the night on which the Qur'ān was sent down.

98 The Clear Sign
This sūra explains the cause of religious divisions, and then describes the different fates awaiting the righteous and wicked.

99 The Earthquake
This short sūra describes 'the earthquake' that will occur on the Day of Resurrection, when the dead will come forth from the grave for judgment.

100 The Runners
This sūra decries people's ingratitude to God and their lust for wealth.

Synopsis: The Qur'ān at a Glance

101 The Striking
This sūra vividly describes an event of the Last Day called 'the striking.'

102 Rivalry
This sūra condemns competition for wealth and status.

103 The Afternoon
This sūra is a short declaration of the impoverished state of human existence.

104 The Slanderer
This sūra attacks wealthy critics of the Prophet and his followers.

105 The Elephant
This sūra recounts how God thwarted the plot of the 'companions of the elephant.'

106 Quraysh
This sūra is an appeal to the Quraysh to worship God in gratitude for his benefits. It is sometimes joined to 'The Elephant' (Q105) to produce a single sūra.

107 Assistance
This sūra links neglect of the poor to denial of the Judgment, before turning to condemn false piety. Its title comes from the last word in the final verse.

108 Abundance
This sūra offers the Prophet encouragement after insult.

109 The Disbelievers
This sūra declares the Prophet's complete break with the disbelievers.

110 Help
This sūra foresees the coming of triumph of the Prophet's movement.

111 The Fiber
This sūra is a denouncement of an opponent and his wife. It is also named 'Lahab' (al-Lahab) and 'Perished' (Tabbat).

112 Devotion
This sūra emphasizes the oneness and uniqueness of God. For that reason it is also known as 'The Unity' (al-Tawḥīd).

113 The Daybreak

The final two sūras of the Qur'ān are known as the 'sūras of taking refuge.' The first is an apotropaic prayer to ward off magic.

114 Humans

This sūra is an apotropaic prayer to ward off evil suggestions.

The Qur'ān

1 ❊ The Opening

1 In the Name of God, the Merciful, the Compassionate.

2 Praise (be) to God, Lord of all peoples, **3** the Merciful, the Compassionate, **4** Master of the Day of Judgment. **5** You we serve and You we seek for help. **6** Guide us to the straight path: **7** the path of those whom You have blessed, not (the path) of those on whom (Your) anger falls, nor of those who go astray.

2 ❈ THE COW

In the Name of God, the Merciful, the Compassionate

1 Alif Lām Mīm.
2 That is the Book – (there is) no doubt about it – a guidance for the ones who guard (themselves), 3 who believe in the unseen, and observe the prayer, and contribute from what We have provided them, 4 and who believe in what has been sent down to you, and what was sent down before you, and they are certain of the Hereafter. 5 Those (stand) on guidance from their Lord, and those – they are the ones who prosper. 6 Surely those who disbelieve – (it is) the same for them whether you warn them or do not warn them. They will not believe. 7 God has set a seal on their hearts and on their hearing, and on their sight (there is) a covering. For them (there is) a great punishment.

8 (There are) some who say, 'We believe in God and in the Last Day,' but they are not believers. 9 They try to deceive God and the believers, but they only deceive themselves, though they do not realize (it). 10 In their hearts is a sickness, so God has increased their sickness, and for them (there is) a painful punishment because they have lied. 11 When it is said to them, 'Do not foment corruption on the earth,' they say, 'We are setting (things) right.' 12 Is it not a fact that they – they are the ones who foment corruption, though they do not realize (it)? 13 When it is said to them, 'Believe as the people believe,' they say, 'Shall we believe as the fools believe?' Is it not a fact that they – they are the fools, but they do not know (it)? 14 When they meet those who believe, they say, 'We believe,' but when they go privately to their satans, they say, 'Surely we are with you. We were only mocking.' 15 God will mock them, and increase them in their insolent transgression, wandering blindly. 16 Those are the ones who have purchased error with the (price of) guidance. Their transaction has not profited (them), and they have not been (rightly) guided. 17 Their parable is like the parable of the one who kindled a fire. When it lit up what was around him, God took away their light, and left them in darkness – they do not see. 18 Without hearing or speech or sight – so they do not return. 19 Or (it is) like a cloudburst from the sky, with darkness and thunder and lightning. They put their fingers in their ears because of the thunderbolts, afraid of death – God surrounds the disbelievers. 20 The lightning almost takes away their sight. Whenever it flashes for them, they walk in it, but when it becomes dark over them, they stand (still). If God (so) pleased, He could indeed take away their hearing and their sight. Surely God is powerful over everything.

The Cow

21 People! Serve your Lord, who created you and those who were before you, so that you may guard (yourselves). **22** (He it is) who made the earth as a couch for you, and the sky a dome, and sent down water from the sky, by means of which He produced fruits as a provision for you. So do not set up rivals to God, when you know (better). **23** If you are in doubt about what We have sent down to Our servant, then bring a sūra like it, and call your witnesses, other than God, if you are truthful. **24** If you do not (do this), and you will not (do it), then guard (yourselves) against the Fire – its fuel is people and stones – which is prepared for the disbelievers.

25 Give good news to those who believe and do righteous deeds, that for them (there are) Gardens through which rivers flow. Whenever they are provided with fruit from there as provision, they will say, 'This is what we were provided with before,' (for) they will be given similar things (to eat). There they will also have pure spouses, and there they will remain.

26 Surely God is not ashamed to strike a parable even of a gnat or anything above it. As for those who believe, they know that it is the truth from their Lord, but as for those who disbelieve, they will say, 'What does God intend by this parable?' He leads many astray by it and guides many by it, but He does not lead any astray by it except the wicked, **27** who break the covenant of God, after its ratification, and sever what God has commanded to be joined, and foment corruption on the earth. Those – they are the losers. **28** How can you disbelieve in God, when you were (once) dead and He gave you life? Then He causes you to die, then He gives you life (again), (and) then to Him you are returned? **29** He (it is) who created for you what is on the earth – all (of it). Then He mounted (upward) to the sky and fashioned them (as) seven heavens. He has knowledge of everything.

30 (Remember) when your Lord said to the angels, 'Surely I am placing on the earth a ruler.' They said, 'Will You place on it someone who will foment corruption on it, and shed blood, while we glorify (You) with Your praise and call You holy?' He said, 'Surely I know what you do not know.' **31** And He taught Adam the names – all of them. Then He presented them to the angels, and said, 'Inform Me of the names of these, if you are truthful.' **32** They said, 'Glory to You! We have no knowledge except for what You have taught us. Surely You – You are the Knowing, the Wise.' **33** He said, 'Adam! Inform them of their names.' And when he had informed them of their names, He said, 'Did I not say to you, "Surely I know the unseen (things) of the heavens and the earth"? I know what you reveal and what you have concealed.'

34 (Remember) when We said to the angels, 'Prostrate yourselves before Adam,' and they prostrated themselves, except Iblīs. He refused and became arrogant, and was one of the disbelievers. **35** And We said, 'Adam! Inhabit the Garden, you and your wife, and eat freely of it wherever you please, but do not go near this tree, or you will both be among the evildoers.' **36** Then Satan caused them both to slip from there, and to go out from where they were. And We said, 'Go down, some of you an enemy to others! The earth is a dwelling place for you, and enjoyment (of life) for a time.' **37** Then Adam received certain words from his Lord, and He turned to him (in forgiveness). Surely He – He is the One who turns (in forgiveness), the Compassionate. **38** We said, 'Go down from it – all (of you)! If any guidance comes to you from Me, whoever follows My guidance – (there will be) no fear on them, nor will they sorrow. **39** But those who disbelieve and call Our signs a lie – those are the companions of the Fire. There they will remain.'

40 Sons of Israel! Remember My blessing which I bestowed on you. Fulfill My covenant (and) I shall fulfill your covenant, and Me – fear Me (alone). **41** Believe in what I have sent down, confirming what is with you, and do not be the first to disbelieve in it. Do not sell My signs for a small price, and guard (yourselves) against Me. **42** Do not mix the truth with falsehood, and do not conceal the truth when you know (better). **43** Observe the prayer and give the alms, and bow with the ones who bow. **44** Do you command the people to piety and forget yourselves, though you recite the Book? Will you not understand? **45** Seek help in patience and the prayer. Surely it is hard indeed, except for the humble, **46** who think that they will meet their Lord, and that they will return to Him. **47** Sons of Israel! Remember My blessing which I bestowed on you, and that I have favored you over all peoples. **48** Guard (yourselves) against a Day when no one will intercede for another at all, and no intercession will be accepted from him, and no compensation taken from him, nor will they be helped.

49 (Remember) when We rescued you from the house of Pharaoh. They were inflicting on you the evil punishment, slaughtering your sons and sparing your women. In that was a great test from your Lord. **50** And when We parted the sea for you, We rescued you, and We drowned the house of Pharaoh while you were looking on.

51 (Remember) when We appointed for Moses forty nights. Then you took the calf after he (was gone), and you were evildoers. **52** Then We pardoned you after that, so that you might be thankful. **53** And (remember) when We gave Moses the Book and the Deliverance, so that you might be (rightly) guided. **54** And when Moses said to his people, 'My people! Surely you have done yourselves evil by taking the calf. So turn to your Creator (in repentance), and kill one another. That will be better for you in the sight of your Creator.' Then He turned to you (in forgiveness). Surely He – He is the One who turns (in forgiveness), the Compassionate.

55 (Remember) when you said, 'Moses! We shall not believe you until we see God openly,' and the thunderbolt took you while you were looking on. **56** Then We raised you up after your death, so that you might be thankful. **57** And We overshadowed you (with) the cloud, and We sent down on you the manna and the quails: 'Eat from the good things which We have provided you.' They did not do Us evil, but they did themselves evil.

58 (Remember) when We said, 'Enter this town and eat freely of it wherever you please, and enter the gate in prostration and say: "Ḥiṭṭa."'[1] We shall forgive you

---

1. Ḥiṭṭa: meaning uncertain.

The Cow

your sins and increase the doers of good.' **59** But those who did evil exchanged a word other than that which had been spoken to them. So We sent down on those who did evil wrath from the sky, because they were acting wickedly.

60 (Remember) when Moses asked for water for his people, and We said, 'Strike the rock with your staff,' and (there) gushed forth from it twelve springs. All the people already knew their drinking place: 'Eat and drink from the provision of God, and do not act wickedly on the earth, fomenting corruption.'

61 (Remember) when you said, 'Moses! We cannot endure just one kind of food. Call on your Lord for us, that He may bring forth for us some of what the earth grows: its green herbs, its cucumbers, its corn, its lentils, and its onions.' He said, 'Would you exchange what is worse for what is better? Go (back) down to Egypt! Surely you will have what you ask for.' Humiliation and poverty were stamped upon them, and they incurred the anger of God. That was because they had disbelieved in the signs of God, and killed the prophets without any right. That was because they disobeyed and went on transgressing. **62** Surely those who believe, and those who are Jews, and the Christians, and the Sabians[2] – whoever believes in God and the Last Day, and does righteousness – they have their reward with their Lord. (There will be) no fear on them, nor will they sorrow.

63 (Remember) when We took a covenant with you, and raised the mountain above you: 'Hold fast what We have given you, and remember what is in it, so that you may guard (yourselves).' **64** Then you turned away after that, and if (it were) not (for the) favor of God on you, and His mercy, you would indeed have been among the losers. **65** Certainly you know those of you who transgressed in (the matter of) the sabbath, and (that) We said to them, 'Become apes, skulking away!' **66** We made it a punishment for their own time and what followed, and an admonition for the ones who guard (themselves).

67 (Remember) when Moses said to his people, 'Surely God commands you to slaughter a cow.' They said, 'Do you take us in mockery?' He said, 'I take refuge with God from being one of the ignorant.' **68** They said, 'Call on your Lord for us, so that He may make clear to us what it (should be).' He said, 'Surely He says, "Surely it is to be a cow, not old and not young, (but) an age between that." Do what you are commanded!' **69** They said, 'Call on your Lord for us, so that He may make clear to us what color it (should be).' He said, 'Surely He says, "Surely it is to be a yellow cow, its color bright, delighting to the onlookers."' **70** They said, 'Call on your Lord for us, so that He may make clear to us what (kind) it (should be). Surely cows are all alike to us. And surely (then), if God pleases, we shall indeed be (rightly) guided.' **71** He said, 'Surely He says, "Surely it is to be a cow, not broken in to plough the earth or to water the field, (but one that is) sound, without any blemish on it."' They said, 'Now you have brought the truth.' So they slaughtered it, though they nearly did not.

---

2. *Sabians*: it is not clear who the Ṣābi'ūn are.

The Cow

72 (Remember) when you[3] killed a man, and you argued about it, but God brought forth what you were concealing. **73** So We said, 'Strike him with part of it.' In this way God brings the dead to life, and shows you His signs so that you may understand. **74** Then your hearts became hardened after that, and they (became) like stones or even harder. Surely (there are) some stones indeed from which rivers gush forth, and surely (there are) some indeed which have been split open, so that water comes out of them, and surely (there are) some indeed which fall down from fear of God. God is not oblivious of what you do.

75 Are you[4] eager that they should believe you, even though a group of them has already heard the word of God, (and) then altered it after they had understood it – and they know (they have done this)? **76** When they meet those who believe, they say, 'We believe,' but when some of them meet with others, they say, 'Do you report to them what God has disclosed to you, so that they may dispute with you by means of it in the presence of your Lord? Will you not understand?' **77** Do they not know that God knows what they keep secret and what they speak aloud? **78** Some of them are common people – they do not know the Book, only wishful thinking, and they only conjecture. **79** So woe to those who write the Book with their (own) hands, (and) then say, 'This is from God,' in order to sell it for a small price. Woe to them for what their hands have written, and woe to them for what they earn. **80** And they say, 'The Fire will only touch us for a number of days.' Say: 'Have you taken a covenant with God? God will not break His covenant. Or do you say about God what you do not know? **81** Yes indeed! Whoever commits evil and is encompassed by his sin – those are the companions of the Fire. There they will remain. **82** But those who believe and do righteous deeds – those are the companions of the Garden. There they will remain.'

83 (Remember) when We took a covenant with the Sons of Israel: 'Do not serve (anyone) but God, and (do) good to parents and family, and the orphans, and the poor, and speak well to the people, and observe the prayer and give the alms.' Then you turned away in aversion, except for a few of you. **84** And when We took a covenant with you: 'Do not shed your (own) blood, and do not expel your (own) people) from your homes,' then you agreed (to it) and bore witness. **85** Then you became those who were killing yourselves, and expelling some of you from their homes, supporting each other against them in sin and enmity. And if they come to you as captives, you ransom (them), though their expulsion was forbidden to you. Do you believe in part of the Book and disbelieve in part? What is the payment for the one among you who does that, except disgrace in this present life, and on the Day of Resurrection they will be returned to the harshest punishment? God is not oblivious of what you do. **86** Those are the ones who have purchased this present life with (the price of) the Hereafter. The punishment will not be lightened for them, nor will they be helped.

---

3. *you*: plur.
4. *you*: plur.

The Cow

87 Certainly We gave Moses the Book, and followed up after him with the messengers, and We gave Jesus, son of Mary, the clear signs, and supported him with the holy spirit. (But) whenever a messenger brought you what you yourselves did not desire, did you become arrogant, and some you called liars and some you killed? **88** And they say, 'Our hearts are covered.' No! God has cursed them for their disbelief, and so little will they believe. **89** When (there) came to them a Book from God, confirming what was with them – though before (this) they had asked for victory against those who disbelieved – when what they recognized came to them, they disbelieved in it. So the curse of God is on the disbelievers. **90** Evil is what they have sold themselves for: they disbelieve in what God has sent down, (because of) envy that God should send down some of His favor on whomever He pleases of His servants. So they have incurred anger upon anger, and for the disbelievers (there is) a humiliating punishment.

91 When it is said to them, 'Believe in what God has sent down,' they say, 'We believe in what has been sent down on us,' but they disbelieve in anything after that, when it is the truth confirming what is with them. Say: 'Why did you kill the prophets of God before, if you were believers?' **92** Certainly Moses brought you the clear signs, (but) then you took the calf after he (was gone), and you were evildoers. **93** And when We took a covenant with you, and raised the mountain above you: 'Hold fast what We have given you, and hear,' they said, 'We hear and disobey.' And they were made to drink the calf in their hearts because of their disbelief. Say: 'Evil is what your belief commands you, if you are believers.'

94 Say: 'If the Home of the Hereafter with God is yours alone, to the exclusion of the people, and not for (the rest of) the people, wish for death, if you are truthful.' **95** But they will never wish for it because of what their (own) hands have sent forward. God knows the evildoers. **96** Indeed you will find them the most desirous of people for life – even more so than the idolaters. One of them wishes to live for a thousand years, but (even) such a long life will not spare him from the punishment. God sees what they do.

97 Say: 'Whoever is an enemy to Gabriel – surely he has brought it down on your heart by the permission of God, confirming what was before it, and as a guidance and good news to the believers. **98** Whoever is an enemy to God, and His angels, and His messengers, and Gabriel and Michael – surely God is an enemy to the disbelievers.' **99** Certainly We have sent down to you[5] clear signs, and no one disbelieves them except the wicked. **100** Whenever they have made a covenant, did a group of them toss it away? No! Most of them do not believe. **101** When a messenger came to them from God, confirming what was with them, a group of those who were given the Book tossed the Book of God behind their backs, as if they did not know (about it). **102** And they followed what the satans used to recite over the kingdom of Solomon. Solomon did not disbelieve, but the satans disbelieved. They taught the people magic, and what had been sent down to

---

5. *you*: sing.

the two angels (in) Babylon, Hārūt and Mārūt.[6] Neither of them taught anyone, unless they both (first) said, 'We are only a temptation, so do not disbelieve.' And they learned from both of them how to separate a husband from his wife. Yet they did not harm anyone in this way, except by the permission of God. What they learned (only) harmed them and did not benefit them. Certainly they knew that whoever buys it has no share in the Hereafter. Evil indeed is what they have sold themselves for, if (only) they knew. **103** If they had believed and guarded (themselves), a reward from God (would) indeed (have been) better, if (only) they knew.

104 You who believe! Do not say, 'Observe us,' but say, 'Regard us,' and hear. For the disbelievers (there is) a painful punishment. **105** Those who disbelieve among the People of the Book, and the idolaters, do not like (it) that anything good should be sent down on you[7] from your Lord. But God chooses whomever He pleases for His mercy, and God is full of great favor. **106** Whatever verse We cancel or cause to be forgotten, We bring a better (one) than it, or (one) similar to it. Do you[8] not know that God is powerful over everything? **107** Do you not know that God – to Him (belongs) the kingdom of the heavens and the earth, and you have no ally and no helper other than God. **108** Or do you wish to question your messenger, as Moses was questioned before? Whoever exchanges belief for disbelief has indeed gone astray from the right way. **109** Many of the People of the Book would like (it) if you turned back into disbelievers, after your believing, (because of) jealousy on their part, after the truth has become clear to them. So pardon and excuse (them), until God brings His command. Surely God is powerful over everything. **110** Observe the prayer and give the alms. Whatever good you send forward for yourselves, you will find it with God. Surely God sees what you do.

111 They say, 'No one will enter the Garden unless they are Jews or Christians.' That is their wishful thinking. Say: 'Bring your proof, if you are truthful.' **112** Yes indeed! Whoever submits his face to God, and he is a doer of good, has his reward with his Lord. (There will be) no fear on them, nor will they sorrow. **113** The Jews say, 'The Christians have no ground to stand on;' and the Christians say, 'The Jews have no ground to stand on,' though they (both) recite the Book. In this way those who have no knowledge say something similar to their saying. God will judge between them on the Day of Resurrection concerning their differences.

114 And who is more evil than the one who prevents the mosques of God from having His name remembered in them, and strives for their destruction? Those – it was not for them to enter them except in fear. For them (there is) disgrace in this world, and a great punishment for them in the Hereafter. **115** The East and the West (belong) to God, so wherever you turn, there is the face of God. Surely God is embracing, knowing.

---

6. *Hārūt and Mārūt*: reference obscure.
7. *you*: plur.
8. *you*: sing.

The Cow

116 They say, 'God has taken a son.' Glory to Him! No! Whatever is in the heavens and the earth (belongs) to Him. All are obedient before Him **117** – Originator of the heavens and the earth. When He decrees something, He simply says to it, 'Be!' and it is.

118 Those who have no knowledge say, 'If only God would speak to us or a sign come to us.' In this way those who were before them said something similar to their saying. Their hearts are alike. We have already made the signs clear to a people (who) are certain (in their belief). **119** Surely We have sent you with the truth, as a bringer of good news and a warner. You will not be questioned about the companions of the Furnace.

120 Neither the Jews nor the Christians will ever be pleased with you until you follow their creed. Say: 'Surely the guidance of God – it is the (true) guidance.' If indeed you follow their (vain) desires, after the knowledge which has come to you, you will have no ally and no helper against God. **121** Those to whom We have given the Book recite it as it should be recited. Those (people) believe in it. But whoever disbelieves in it – those (people) – they are the losers.

122 Sons of Israel! Remember My blessing which I bestowed on you, and that I have favored you over all peoples. **123** Guard (yourselves) against a Day when no one will intercede for another at all, and no compensation will be accepted from him, and no intercession will benefit him, nor will they be helped.

124 (Remember) when his Lord tested Abraham with (certain) words, and he fulfilled them. He said, 'Surely I am going to make you a leader for the people.' He said, 'And of my descendants?' He said, 'My covenant does not extend to the evildoers.' **125** And when We made the House a place of meeting and security for the people, and (said), 'Take the standing place of Abraham as a place of prayer,' and We made a covenant with Abraham and Ishmael: 'Both of you purify My House for the ones who go around (it), and the ones who are devoted to it, and the ones who bow, (and) the ones who prostrate themselves.' **126** And when Abraham said, 'My Lord, make this land secure, and provide its people with fruits – whoever of them who believes in God and the Last Day,' He said, 'And whoever disbelieves – I shall give him enjoyment (of life) for a little (while), (and) then I shall force him to the punishment of the Fire – and it is an evil destination!' **127** And when Abraham raised up the foundations of the House, and Ishmael (with him): 'Our Lord, accept (this) from us. Surely You – You are the Hearing, the Knowing. **128** Our Lord, make us both submitted to You, and (make) from our descendants a community submitted to You. And show us our rituals, and turn to us (in forgiveness). Surely You – You are the One who turns (in forgiveness), the Compassionate. **129** Our Lord, raise up among them a messenger from among them, to recite Your signs to them, and to teach them the Book and the wisdom, and to purify them. Surely You – You are the Mighty, the Wise.'

130 Who prefers (another creed) to the creed of Abraham except the one who makes a fool of himself? Certainly We have chosen him in this world, and surely in the Hereafter he will indeed be among the righteous. **131** When his Lord said to him, 'Submit!,' he said, 'I have submitted to the Lord of all peoples.' **132** And Abraham charged his sons with this, and Jacob (did too): 'My sons! Surely God has chosen the (true) religion for you, so do not die without submitting.' **133** Or were you witnesses when death approached Jacob, when he said to his sons, 'What will you serve after me?' They said, 'We will serve your God, and the God of your fathers, Abraham, and Ishmael, and Isaac: one God – to Him we submit.' **134** That community has passed away. To it what it has earned, and to you what you have earned. You will not be questioned about what they have done.

135 They say, 'Be Jews or Christians, (and then) you will be (rightly) guided.' Say: 'No! The creed of Abraham the Ḥanīf.[9] He was not one of the idolaters.' **136** Say:[10] 'We believe in God, and what has been sent down to us, and what has been sent down to Abraham, and Ishmael, and Isaac, and Jacob, and the tribes, and what was given to Moses and Jesus, and what was given to the prophets from their Lord. We make no distinction between any of them, and to Him we submit.' **137** If they believe in something like what you believe in, they have been (rightly) guided, but if they turn away, they are only in defiance. God will be sufficient for you[11] against them. He is the Hearing, the Knowing.

138 The dye(ing) of God, and who is better than God at dye(ing)? We serve Him. **139** Say: 'Do you dispute with us about God, when He is our Lord and your Lord? To us our deeds and to you your deeds. We are devoted to Him. **140** Or do you say, "Abraham, and Ishmael, and Isaac, and Jacob, and the tribes were Jews or Christians"?' Say: 'Do you know better, or God? Who is more evil than the one who conceals a testimony which he has from God? God is not oblivious of what you do.' **141** That community has passed away. To it what it has earned, and to you what you have earned. You will not be questioned about what they have done.

142 The fools among the people will say, 'What has turned them from the direction (of prayer) which they were (facing) toward?' Say: 'The East and the West (belong) to God. He guides whomever He pleases to a straight path.' **143** In this way We have made you a community (in the) middle, so that you may be witnesses over the people, and that the messenger may be a witness over you. And We established the direction (of prayer) which you[12] were (facing) toward only so that We might know the one who would follow the messenger from the one who would turn back on his heels. Surely it was hard indeed, except for those whom God guided. But God was not one to let your[13] belief go to waste. Surely God is indeed kind (and) compassionate with the people.

---

9. *Ḥanīf*: meaning uncertain.
10. *Say*: plur. imperative.
11. *you*: sing.
12. *you*: sing.
13. *your*: plur.

The Cow

144 We do see you[14] turning your face about in the sky, and We shall indeed turn you in a direction which you will be pleased with. Turn your face in the direction of the Sacred Mosque, and wherever you are, turn your faces in its direction. Surely those who have been given the Book know indeed that it is the truth from their Lord. God is not oblivious of what they do. **145** Yet even if you bring every sign to those who have been given the Book, they will not follow your direction. You are not a follower of their direction, nor are they followers of each other's direction. If indeed you follow their (vain) desires, after the knowledge which has come to you, surely then you will indeed be among the evildoers. **146** Those to whom We have given the Book recognize it, as they recognize their (own) sons, yet surely a group of them indeed conceals the truth – and they know (it). **147** The truth is from your Lord, so do not be one of the doubters. **148** Each has a direction to which he turns. So race (toward doing) good deeds. Wherever you may be, God will bring you all together. Surely God is powerful over everything.

149 From wherever you go forth, turn your face toward the Sacred Mosque. Surely it is the truth indeed from your Lord. God is not oblivious of what you do. **150** From wherever you go forth, turn your face toward the Sacred Mosque. And wherever you are, turn your faces toward it, so that the people will not have any argument against you – except for the evildoers among them; do not fear them, but fear Me – and so that I may complete My blessing on you, and that you may be (rightly) guided, **151** even as We have sent among you a messenger from among you. He recites to you Our signs, and purifies you, and teaches you the Book and the wisdom, and teaches you what you did not know. **152** So remember Me (and) I shall remember you. Be thankful to Me and do not be ungrateful to Me.

153 You who believe! Seek help in patience and prayer. Surely God is with the patient. **154** Do not say of anyone who is killed in the way of God, '(They are) dead.' No! (They are) alive, but you do not realize (it). **155** We shall indeed test you with some (experience) of fear and hunger, and loss of wealth and lives and fruits. But give good news[15] to the patient, **156** who say, when a smiting smites them, 'Surely we (belong) to God, and surely to Him we return.' **157** Those – on them (there are) blessings from their Lord, and mercy. Those – they are the (rightly) guided ones.

158 Surely al-Ṣafā and al-Marwa are among the symbols[16] of God. Whoever performs pilgrimage to the House or performs visitation – (there is) no blame on him if he goes around both of them. And whoever does good voluntarily – surely God is thankful, knowing.

159 Surely those who conceal what We have sent down of the clear signs and the guidance, after We have made it clear to the people in the Book, those – God will

---

14. *you*: sing.
15. *give good news*: sing. imperative.
16. *symbols*: meaning uncertain (Ar. *shaʿāʾir*).

curse them, and the cursers will curse them, **160** except for those who turn (in repentance), and set (things) right, and make (it) clear. Those – I shall turn to them (in forgiveness). I am the One who turns (in forgiveness), the Compassionate. **161** Surely those who disbelieve, and die while they are disbelievers, those – on them is the curse of God, and the angels, and the people all together. **162** There (they will) remain – the punishment will not be lightened for them, nor will they be spared.

163 Your God is one God – (there is) no god but Him, the Merciful, the Compassionate. **164** Surely in the creation of the heavens and the earth, and the alternation of the night and the day, and the ship which runs on the sea with what benefits the people, and the water which God sends down from the sky, and by means of it gives the earth life after its death, and He scatters on it all (kinds of) creatures, and (in the) changing of the winds, and the clouds controlled between the sky and the earth – (all these are) signs indeed for a people who understand. **165** But (there are) some of the people who set up rivals to God. They love them with a love like (that given to) God. Yet those who believe are stronger in love for God. If (only) those who do evil could see (the Day), when they will see the punishment, that the power (belongs) to God altogether, and that God is harsh in punishment. **166** When those who were followed disown those who followed them, and they see the punishment, and the ties with them are cut, **167** and those who followed say, 'If (only) we had (another) turn, so that we might disown them as they have disowned us.' In this way God will show them their deeds as regrets for them. They will never escape from the Fire.

168 People! Eat from what is permitted (and) good on the earth, and do not follow the footsteps of Satan. Surely he is clear enemy to you. **169** He only commands you to evil and immorality, and to say about God what you do not know. **170** When it is said to them, 'Follow what God has sent down,' they say, 'No! We shall follow what we found our fathers doing' – even though their fathers did not understand anything and were not (rightly) guided? **171** The parable of those who disbelieve is like the parable of the one who calls out to what hears nothing but a shout and a cry. Without hearing or speech or sight – they do not understand.

172 You who believe! Eat from the good things which We have provided you, and be thankful to God, if it is Him you serve. **173** He has only forbidden to you: the dead (animal), and the blood, and swine's flesh, and what has been dedicated to (a god) other than God. But whoever is forced (by necessity), not desiring or (deliberately) transgressing – no sin (rests) on him. Surely God is forgiving, compassionate.

174 Surely those who conceal what God has sent down of the Book, and sell it for a small price, those – they will not eat (anything) but the Fire in their bellies. God will not speak to them on the Day of Resurrection, nor will He purify them. For them (there is) a painful punishment. **175** Those are the ones who have purchased error with the (price of) guidance, and punishment with the (price of) forgiveness. How determined they are to (reach) the Fire! **176** That is because God has sent down the Book with the truth. Surely those who differ about the Book are indeed in extreme defiance.

177 Piety is not turning your faces toward the East and the West, but (true) piety (belongs to) the one who believes in God and the Last Day, and the angels, and the Book, and the prophets, and (who) gives his wealth, despite his love for it, to family, and the orphans, and the poor, and the traveler, and the beggars, and for the (freeing of) slaves, and (who) observes the prayer and gives the alms, and those who fulfill their covenant when they have made it, and those who are patient under violence and hardship, and in times of peril. Those are the ones who are truthful, and those – they are the ones who guard (themselves).

178 You who believe! The (law of) retaliation is prescribed for you in (the case of) those who have been killed: the free man for the free man, the slave for the slave, and the female for the female. But whoever is granted any pardon for it by his brother, it should be (done) rightfully, and payment should be rendered with kindness. That is a concession from your Lord, and a mercy. Whoever transgresses after that – for him (there is) a painful punishment. **179** In the (law of) retaliation (there is) life for you – those (of you) with understanding! – so that you may guard (yourselves).

180 It is prescribed for you, when death approaches one of you, if he leaves behind any goods, (to make) bequests for parents and family rightfully. (It is) an obligation on the ones who guard (themselves). **181** And whoever changes it after hearing (it) – the sin (rests) only on those who change it. Surely God is hearing, knowing. **182** But whoever suspects any injustice or sin from the one making the bequest, and resolves (the matter) between them – no sin (rests) on him. Surely God is forgiving, compassionate.

183 You who believe! Fasting is prescribed for you, as it was prescribed for those who were before you, so that you may guard (yourselves). **184** (Fast for) a number of days. Whoever of you is sick or on a journey, (let him fast) a certain number of other days. And for those who can afford it, (there is) a ransom: feeding a poor person. Whoever does good voluntarily – it is better for him. But to fast is better for you, if (only) you knew.

185 The month of Ramaḍān, in which the Qur'ān was sent down as a guidance for the people, and as clear signs of the guidance and the deliverance: so whoever of you is present during the month, let him fast in it, but whoever of you is sick or on a journey, (let him fast) a certain number of other days. God wishes to make it easy for you, and does not wish any hardship for you. And (He wishes) that you should fulfill the number (of days), and that you should magnify God for having guided you, and that you should be thankful. **186** When My servants ask you about Me, surely I am near. I respond to the call of the caller when he calls on Me. So let them respond to Me, and believe in Me, so that they may be led aright.

The Cow

187 It is permitted to you on the night of the fast to have sexual relations with your wives. They are a covering for you, and you are a covering for them. God knows that you have been betraying yourselves (in this regard), and has turned to you (in forgiveness) and pardoned you. So now have relations with them, and seek what God has prescribed for you. And eat and drink, until a white thread may be discerned from a black thread at the dawn. Then keep the fast completely until night, and do not have relations with them while you are devoted to the mosques. Those are the limits (set by) God, so do not go near them. In this way God makes clear His signs to the people, so that they may guard (themselves).

188 Do not consume your wealth among yourselves by means of falsehood, nor offer it to the judges, so that you may consume some of the property of the people sinfully, when you know (better).

189 They ask you about the new moons. Say: 'They are appointed times for the people, and for the pilgrimage.'

It is not piety to come to (your) houses from their backs, but (true) piety (belongs to) the one who guards (himself). Come to (your) houses by their doors, and guard (yourselves) against God, so that you may prosper.

190 Fight in the way of God against those who fight against you, but do not commit aggression. Surely God does not love the aggressors. **191** And kill them wherever you come upon them, and expel them from where they expelled you. Persecution is worse than killing. But do not fight them near the Sacred Mosque until they fight you there. If they fight you, kill them – such is the payment for the disbelievers. **192** But if they stop (fighting) – surely God is forgiving, compassionate. **193** Fight them until (there) is no persecution and the religion is God's. But if they stop, (let there be) no aggression, except against the evildoers. **194** The sacred month for the sacred month; sacred things are (subject to the law of) retaliation. Whoever commits aggression against you, commit aggression against him in the same manner (as) he committed aggression against you. Guard (yourselves) against God, and know that God is with the ones who guard (themselves).

195 Contribute in the way of God. Do not cast (yourselves) to destruction with your own hands, but do good. Surely God loves the doers of good.

196 Complete the pilgrimage and the visitation for God. But if you are prevented, (make) whatever offering is easy to obtain. Do not shave your heads until the offering has reached its lawful place. Whoever of you is sick or has an injury to his head, (there is) a ransom of fasting or a freewill offering or a sacrifice. When you are secure, whoever makes use of (the time from) the visitation until the pilgrimage, (let him make) whatever offering is easy to obtain. Whoever cannot find (an offering), (let him perform) a fast of three days during the pilgrimage, and seven (days) when you return. That is ten (days) in all. That is for the one whose family is not present at the Sacred Mosque. Guard (yourselves) against God, and know that God is harsh in retribution.

The Cow

197 The pilgrimage (falls in certain) specified months. Whoever undertakes the pilgrimage in them – (there should be) no sexual relations or wickedness or quarreling during the pilgrimage. Whatever good you do, God knows it. And take provision (for the journey), but surely the best provision is the guarding (of oneself). So guard (yourselves) against Me, those (of you) with understanding!

198 There is no blame on you in seeking favor from your Lord. When you press on from 'Arafāt, remember God at the Sacred Monument, and remember Him as He has guided you, though before you were indeed among those who had gone astray. **199** Then press on from where the people press on, and ask forgiveness from God. Surely God is forgiving, compassionate. **200** When you have performed your rituals, remember God, as you remember your fathers, or (even with) greater remembrance. (There are) some of the people who say, 'Our Lord, give us (good) in this world.' For them (there will be) no share in the Hereafter. **201** But (there are others) of them who say, 'Our Lord, give us good in this world and good in the Hereafter, and guard us against the punishment of the Fire.' **202** Those – for them (there will be) a portion of what they have earned, and God is quick at the reckoning.

203 Remember God during a (certain) number of days. Whoever hurries (through it) in two days – no sin (rests) on him, and whoever delays – no sin (rests) on him, (at least) for the one who guards (himself). Guard (yourselves) against God, and know that you will be gathered to Him.

204 Among the people (there is) one who impresses you[17] (with) his speech in this present life, and who calls God to witness about what is in his heart, though he is the most contentious of opponents. **205** And when he turns away, he strives to foment corruption on the earth, and to destroy the crops and livestock. God does not love the (fomenting of) corruption. **206** When it is said to him, 'Guard (yourself) against God,' false pride carries him away to more sin. Gehenna will be enough for him – it is an evil bed indeed! **207** But among the people (there is) one who sells himself,[18] seeking the approval of God. God is kind with (His) servants.

208 You who believe! Enter into unity all together, and do not follow the footsteps of Satan. Surely he is a clear enemy to you. **209** But if you slip, after the clear signs have come to you, know that God is mighty, wise.

210 Do they expect (anything) but God to come to them in the shadow of the clouds with the angels? The affair has been decided, and to God (all) affairs return. **211** Ask the Sons of Israel how many of the clear signs We gave them. Whoever changes the blessing of God after it has come to him – surely God is harsh in retribution. **212** This present life is made to appear enticing to those who disbelieve, and they ridicule those who believe. But the ones who guard (themselves) will be

---

17. *you*: sing.
18. *sells himself*: into slavery (here used metaphorically of 'service' to God).

The Cow

above them on the Day of Resurrection. God provides for whomever He pleases without reckoning.

213 The people were (once) one community. Then God raised up the prophets as bringers of good news and warners, and with them He sent down the Book with the truth to judge among the people concerning their differences. Only those who had been given it differed concerning it, after the clear signs had come to them, (because of) envy among themselves. And God guided those who believed to the truth concerning which they differed, by His permission. God guides whomever He pleases to a straight path.

214 Or did you think that you would enter the Garden before you had experienced what those who passed away before you experienced? Violence and hardship touched them, and they were (so) shaken that the messenger, and those who believed with him, said, 'When will the help of God come?' Is it not a fact that the help of God is near?

215 They ask you (about) what they should contribute. Say: 'Whatever good you have contributed is for parents and family, and the orphans, and the poor, and the traveler. Whatever good you do, surely God knows about it.'

216 Fighting is prescribed for you, though it is hateful to you. You may happen to hate a thing though it is good for you, and you may happen to love a thing though it is bad for you. God knows and you do not know. **217** They ask you about the sacred month – (about) fighting during it. Say: 'Fighting during it is a serious (matter), but keeping (people) from the way of God – and disbelief in Him – and the Sacred Mosque, and expelling its people from it, (are even) more serious in the sight of God. Persecution is more serious than killing.' They will not stop fighting you until they turn you back from your religion, if they can. Whoever of you turns away from his religion and dies while he is a disbeliever, those – their deeds have come to nothing in this world and the Hereafter. Those are the companions of the Fire. There they will remain. **218** Surely those who believe, and those who have emigrated and struggled in the way of God, those – they hope for the mercy of God. God is forgiving, compassionate.

219 They ask you about wine and games of chance. Say: 'In both of them (there is) great sin, but (also some) benefits for the people, yet their sin is greater than their benefit.'

They ask you about what they should contribute. Say: 'The excess.' In this way God makes clear to you the signs, so that you may reflect **220** in this world and the Hereafter.

They ask you about the orphans. Say: 'Setting right (their affairs) for them is good. And if you become partners with them, (they are) your brothers. God knows the one who foments corruption from the one who sets (things) right. If God (so) pleased, He could indeed cause you to suffer. Surely God is mighty, wise.'

The Cow

221 Do not marry idolatrous women until they believe. A believing slave girl is better than a (free) idolatrous woman, even if she pleases you. And do not marry idolatrous men until they believe. A believing slave is better than a (free) idolatrous man, even if he pleases you. Those (people) – they call (you) to the Fire, but God calls (you) to the Garden and forgiveness, by His permission. He makes clear His signs to the people, so that they may take heed.

222 They ask you about menstruation. Say: 'It is harmful.[19] Withdraw from women in menstruation, and do not go near them until they are clean. When they have cleansed themselves, come to them as God has commanded you.' Surely God loves hose who turn (in repentance), and He loves those who purify themselves. **223** Your women are (like) a field for you, so come to your field when you wish, and send forward (something) for yourselves. Guard (yourselves) against God, and know that you will meet Him. And give good news to the believers.

224 Do not, on account of your oaths, make God an obstacle to doing good, and guarding (yourselves), and setting (things) right among the people. Surely God is hearing, knowing. **225** God will not take you to task for a slip in your oaths, but He will take you to task for what your hearts have earned. God is forgiving, forbearing.

226 For those who renounce their wives, (there is) a waiting period of four months. If they return – surely God is forgiving, compassionate. **227** But if they are determined to divorce – surely God is hearing, knowing. **228** (Let) the divorced women wait by themselves for three periods. It is not permitted to them to conceal what God has created in their wombs, if they believe in God and the Last Day. Their husbands have a better right to take them back in that (period), if they wish to set (things) right. Women rightfully have the same privilege (as is exercised) over them, but men have a rank above them. God is mighty, wise.

229 Divorce (may take place) twice, (with the option of) retaining (them) rightfully, or sending (them) away with kindness. It is not permitted to you to take (back) anything of what you have given them, unless the two of them fear that they cannot maintain the limits (set by) God. But if you fear that they cannot maintain the limits (set by) God, (there is) no blame on either of them in what she ransoms (herself) with. Those are the limits (set by) God, so do not transgress it. Whoever transgresses the limits (set by) God, those – they are the evildoers. **230** If he divorces her, she is not permitted to him (to marry) after that, until she marries another husband. And then if he divorces her, (there is) no blame on (either of) them to return to each other, if they think that they can maintain the limits (set by) God. Those are the limits (set by) God. He makes it clear to a people who know.

231 When you divorce women, and they have reached (the end of) their term, either retain them rightfully, or send them away rightfully. Do not retain them

---

19. *harmful*: i.e. ritually defiling.

The Cow

harmfully, so that you transgress. Whoever does that has done himself evil. Do not take the signs of God in mockery, but remember the blessing of God on you, and what he has sent down to you of the Book and the wisdom. He admonishes you by means of it. Guard (yourselves) against God, and know that God has knowledge of everything. **232** When you divorce women, and they have reached (the end of) their term, do not prevent them from marrying their (new) husbands, when they make an agreement together rightfully. That is what anyone who believes in God and the Last Day is admonished. That is purer for you, and cleaner. God knows and you do not know.

233 Mothers shall nurse their children for two full years, for those who wish to complete the nursing (period). (It is an obligation) on the father for him (to supply) their provision and their clothing rightfully. No one is to be burdened beyond their capacity. A mother is not to suffer on account of her child, nor a father on account of his child. The (father's) heir has a similar (obligation) to that. If the two of them wish, by mutual consent and consultation, to wean (the child earlier), (there is) no blame on (either of) them. And if you wish to seek nursing for your children, (there is) no blame on you, provided you pay what you have rightfully promised. Guard (yourselves) against God, and know that God sees what you do.

234 Those of you who are taken, and leave behind wives – (let the widows) wait by themselves for fourteen months. When they have reached (the end) of their waiting period, (there is) no blame on you for what they may rightfully do with themselves. God is aware of what you do. **235** (There is) no blame on you concerning the proposals you offer to women, or (the proposals) you conceal within yourselves. God knows that you will be thinking about them. But do not make a proposal to them in secret, unless you speak rightful words. And do not tie the knot of marriage until the prescribed (term) has reached its end. Know that God knows what is within you. So beware of Him, and know that God is forgiving, forbearing.

236 (There is) no blame on you if you divorce women whom you have not touched, nor promised any bridal gift to them. Yet provide for them rightfully – the wealthy according to his means, and the poor according to his means – (it is) an obligation on the doers of good. **237** If you divorce them before you have touched them, but you have already promised them a bridal gift, (give them) half of what you have promised, unless they relinquish (it), or he relinquishes (it) in whose hand is the knot of marriage. To relinquish (it) is nearer to the guarding (of oneself), and do not forget generosity among you. Surely God sees what you do.

238 Watch over[20] the prayers, and the middle prayer. And stand before God obedient. **239** If you fear (danger), (pray) on foot or (while) riding. But when you are secure, remember God, since He has taught you what you did not know.

---

20. *Watch over*: plur. imperative.

240 Those of you who (are about to be) taken, and (are going to) leave behind wives, (let them make) a bequest for their wives: provision for the year without evicting (them from their homes). But if they do leave, (there is) no blame on you for what they may rightfully do with themselves. God is mighty, wise. **241** For divorced women (there is) a rightful provision – (it is) an obligation on the ones who guard (themselves). **242** In this way God makes clear to you His signs, so that you may understand.

243 Have you[21] not considered those who went forth from their homes – and they were thousands – afraid of death? And God said to them, 'Die!' (But) then He brought them to life. Surely God is indeed full of favor to the people, but most of the people are not thankful (for it). **244** So fight in the way of God, and know that God is hearing, knowing. **245** Who is the one who will lend to God a good loan, and He will double it for him many times? God withdraws and extends (His provision), and to Him you will be returned.

246 Have you[22] not considered the assembly of the Sons of Israel after (the time of) Moses? They said to a prophet of theirs, 'Raise up a king for us, (and) we shall fight in the way of God.' He said, 'Is it possible that, if fighting is prescribed for you, you will not fight?' They said, 'Why should we not fight in the way of God, when we have been expelled from our homes and our children?' Yet when fighting was prescribed for them, they (all) turned away, except for a few of them. God has knowledge of the evildoers.

247 And their prophet said to them, 'Surely God has raised up for you Saul as king.' They said, 'How can he possess the kingship over us, when we are more deserving of the kingship than him, and he has not been given abundant wealth?' He said, 'Surely God has chosen him (to be) over you, and has increased him abundantly in knowledge and stature. God gives His kingdom to whomever He pleases. God is embracing, knowing.'

248 And their prophet said to them, 'Surely the sign of his kingship is that the ark will come to you. In it is a Sakīna from your Lord, and a remnant of what the house of Moses and the house of Aaron left behind. The angels (will) carry it. Surely in that is a sign indeed for you, if you are believers.'

249 When Saul set out with his forces, he said, 'Surely God is going to test you by means of a river. Whoever drinks from it is not on my side, but whoever does not taste it is surely on my side, except for whoever scoops (it) up with his hand.' But they (all) drank from it, except for a few. So when he crossed it, he and those who believed with him, they said, 'We have no strength today against Goliath and his forces.' But those who thought that they would meet God said, 'How many a small cohort has overcome a large cohort by the permission of God? God is with the patient.' **250** So when they went forth to (battle) Goliath and his forces said,

---

21. *you*: sing.
22. *you*: sing.

The Cow

'Our Lord, pour out on us patience, and make firm our feet, and help us against the people who are disbelievers.' **251** And they routed them by the permission of God, and David killed Goliath, and God gave him the kingdom and the wisdom, and taught him about whatever He pleased. If God had not repelled some of the people by means of others, the earth would indeed have been corrupted. But God is full of favor to all peoples.

252 Those are the signs of God. We recite them to you in truth. Surely you are indeed one of the envoys. **253** Those are the messengers – We have favored some of them over others. (There were) some of them to whom God spoke, and some of them He raised in rank. And We gave Jesus, son of Mary, the clear signs, and supported him with the holy spirit. If God had (so) pleased, those who (came) after them would not have fought each other, after the clear signs had come to them. But they differed, and (there were) some of them who believed and some of them who disbelieved. If God had (so) pleased, they would not have fought each other. But God does whatever He wills.

254 You who believe! Contribute from what We have provided you, before a Day comes when (there will be) no bargaining, and no friendship, and no intercession. The disbelievers – they are the evildoers.

255 God – (there is) no god but Him, the Living, the Everlasting. Slumber does not overtake Him, nor sleep. To Him (belongs) whatever is in the heavens and whatever is on the earth. Who is the one who will intercede with Him, except by His permission? He knows whatever is before them and whatever is behind them, but they cannot encompass any of His knowledge, except whatever He pleases. His throne comprehends the heavens and the earth. Watching over both of them does not weary him. He is the Most High, the Almighty.

256 (There is) no compulsion in religion. The right (course) has become clearly distinguished from error. Whoever disbelieves in al-Ṭāghūt,[23] and believes in God, has grasped the firmest handle, (which) does not break. God is hearing, knowing. **257** God is the ally of those who believe. He brings them out of the darkness into the light. But those who disbelieve – their allies are al-Ṭāghūt, who bring them out of the light into the darkness. Those are the companions of the Fire. There they will remain.

258 Have you[24] not considered the one who disputed (with) Abraham concerning his Lord, because God had given him the kingdom? When Abraham said, 'My Lord is the One who gives life and causes death,' he said, 'I give life and cause death.' Abraham said, 'Surely God brings the sun from the East, so you bring it from the West.' And then the one who disbelieved was confounded. God does not guide the people who are evildoers.

---

23. *al-Ṭāghūt*: meaning uncertain; perhaps 'other gods' or 'idols' (cf. Q16.36; 39.17), but elsewhere another name for Satan (Q4.60, 76).

24. *you*: sing.

The Cow

259 Or (have you not considered) the example of the one who passed by a town that had collapsed in ruins? He said, 'How will God give this (town) life after its death?' So God caused him to die for a hundred years, (and) then raised him up. He said, 'How long have you remained (dead)?' He said, 'I have remained (dead) for a day or part of a day.' He said, 'No! You have remained (dead) for a hundred years. Look at your food and drink, it has not spoiled, and look at your donkey – and (this happened) so that We might make you a sign to the people – and look at the bones, how We raise them up, (and) then clothe them with flesh.' So when it became clear to him, he said, 'I know that God is powerful over everything.'

260 (Remember) when Abraham said, 'My Lord, show me how You give the dead life.' He said, 'Have you not believed?' He said, 'Yes indeed! But (show me) to satisfy my heart.' He said, 'Take four birds, and take them close to you, then place a piece of them on each hill, (and) then call them. They will come rushing to you. Know that God is mighty, wise.'

261 The parable of those who contribute their wealth in the way of God is like the parable of a grain of corn that grows seven ears: in each ear (there are) a hundred grains. (So) God doubles for whomever He pleases. God is embracing, knowing. **262** Those who contribute their wealth in the way of God, (and) then do not follow up what they have contributed (with) insult and injury, for them – their reward is with their Lord. (There will be) no fear on them, nor will they sorrow. **263** Rightful words and forgiveness are better than a freewill offering followed by injury. God is wealthy, forbearing.

264 You who believe! Do not invalidate your freewill offerings by insult and injury, like the one who contributes his wealth in order to be seen by the people, but who does not believe in God and the Last Day. His parable is like the parable of a smooth rock with dirt on top of it. A heavy rain smites it (and) leaves it bare. They have no power over anything they have earned. God does not guide the people who are disbelievers. **265** But the parable of those who contribute their wealth, seeking the approval of God and confirmation for themselves, is like the parable of a garden on a hill. A heavy rain smites it, and it yields its produce twofold. And if a heavy rain does not smite it, a shower (does). God sees what you do.

266 Would any of you like to have a garden of date palms and grapes, (with) rivers flowing through it, and in it (there is) every (kind of) fruit for him? (Then) old age smites him, and he has (only) weak children. Then a whirlwind, with a fire in it, smites it. Then it was burned. In this way God makes clear to you the signs, so that you will reflect.

267 You who believe! Contribute from the good things you have earned, and from what We have produced for you from the earth. And do not designate for contributions bad things, when you would never take them (yourselves), except with disdain. Know that God is wealthy, praiseworthy.

268 Satan promises you poverty, and commands you to immorality, but God promises you forgiveness from Him, and favor. God is embracing, knowing.

269 He gives wisdom to whomever He pleases, and whoever is given wisdom has been given much good. Yet no one takes heed except those with understanding.

270 Whatever contribution you make, and whatever vow you vow, surely God knows it. But the evildoers have no helper.

271 If you make freewill offerings publicly, that is excellent, but if you hide it and give it to the poor, that is better for you, and will absolve you of some of your evil deeds. God is aware of what you do.

272 Their guidance is not (dependent) on you,[25] but God guides whomever He pleases. Whatever good you contribute is for yourselves, even though you contribute (as a result of) seeking the face of God. And whatever good you contribute will be repaid to you in full, and you will not be done evil. **273** (Freewill offerings are) for the poor who are constrained in the way of God, and are unable to strike forth on the earth. The ignorant suppose them to be rich because of (their) self-restraint, but you know them by their mark – they do not constantly beg from people. Whatever good you contribute, surely God knows it. **274** Those who contribute their wealth in the night and in the day, in secret and in open, for them – their reward is with their Lord. (There will be) no fear on them, nor will they sorrow.

275 Those who devour usury will not stand, except as one stands whom Satan has overthrown by (his) touch. That is because they have said, 'Trade is just like usury,' though God has permitted trade and forbidden usury. Whoever receives an admonition from his Lord, and stops (practicing usury), will have whatever is past, and his case is in the hands of God, but whoever returns (to usury) – those are the companions of the Fire. There they will remain. **276** God destroys usury but causes freewill offerings to bear interest. God does not love any ungrateful one (or) sinner. **277** Surely those who believe and do righteous deeds, and observe the prayer and give the alms, for them – their reward is with their Lord. (There will be) no fear on them, nor will they sorrow.

278 You who believe! Guard (yourselves) against God, and give up the usury that is (still) outstanding, if you are believers. **279** If you do not, be on notice of war from God and His messenger. But if you turn (in repentance), you will have your principal. You will not have committed evil or been done evil. **280** If he[26] should be in hardship, (let there be) a postponement until (there is) some relief (of his situation). But that you remit (it as) a freewill offering is better for you, if (only) you knew. **281** Guard (yourselves) against a Day on which you will be returned to God. Then everyone will be paid in full what they have earned – and they will not be done evil.

282 You who believe! When you contract a debt with one another for a fixed term, write it down. Let a scribe write it down fairly between you, and let the scribe not

---

25. *you*: sing.

26. *he*: the debtor, who is obligated to return the principal.

refuse to write it down, seeing that God has taught him. So let him write, and let the one who owes the debt dictate, and let him guard (himself) against God his Lord, and not diminish anything from it. If the one who owes the debt is weak of mind or body, or unable to dictate himself, let his ally dictate fairly. And call in two of your men as witnesses, or, if there are not two men, then one man and two women, from those present whom you approve of as witnesses, so that if one of the two women goes astray, the other will remind her. And let the witnesses not refuse when they are called on. Do not disdain to write it down, (however) small or large, with its due date. That is more upright in the sight of God, more reliable for witnessing (it), and (makes it) more likely that you will not be in doubt (afterwards) – unless it is an actual transaction you exchange among yourselves, and then there is no blame on you if you do not write it down. But take witnesses when you do business with each other. Only let the scribe or the witness not injure either party, or, if you do, that is wickedness on your part. So guard (yourselves) against God. God teaches you, and God has knowledge of everything.

283 And if you are on a journey, and do not find a scribe, (let) a security be taken. But if one of you trusts another, let him who is trusted pay back what is entrusted, and let him guard (himself) against God his Lord. Do not conceal the testimony. Whoever conceals it, surely he is sinful – (that is) his heart. God knows what you do.

284 To God (belongs) whatever is in the heavens and whatever is on the earth. Whether you reveal what is within you or hide it, God will call you to account for it. He forgives whomever He pleases and He punishes whomever He pleases. God is powerful over everything.

285 The messenger believes in what has been sent down to him from his Lord, and (so do) the believers. Each one believes in God, and His angels, and His Books, and His messengers. We make no distinction between any of His messengers. And they say, 'We hear and obey. (Grant us) Your forgiveness, our Lord. To You is the (final) destination.'

286 God does not burden any person beyond his capacity. What they have earned is either to their credit or against their account.

'Our Lord, do not take us to task if we forget or make a mistake. Our Lord, do not lay on us a burden such as You laid on those before us. Our Lord, do not burden us beyond what we have the strength (to bear). Pardon us, and forgive us, and have compassion on us. You are our Protector. Help us against the people who are disbelievers.'

3 ✵ House of 'Imrān

In the Name of God, the Merciful, the Compassionate

1 Alif Lām Mīm.

2 God – (there is) no god but Him, the Living, the Everlasting. 3 He has sent down on you[1] the Book with the truth, confirming what was before it, and He sent down the Torah and the Gospel 4 before (this) as guidance for the people, and (now) He has sent down the deliverance. Surely those who disbelieve in the signs of God – for them (there is) a harsh punishment. God is mighty, a taker of vengeance.

5 Surely God – nothing is hidden from Him on the earth or in the sky. 6 He (it is) who fashions you in the wombs as He pleases. (There is) no god but Him, the Mighty, the Wise.

7 He (it is) who has sent down on you the Book, of which some verses are clearly composed – they are the mother of the Book – but others are ambiguous. As for those in whose hearts (there is) a turning aside, they follow the ambiguous part of it, seeking (to cause) trouble and seeking its interpretation. No one knows its interpretation except God. And (as for) the ones firmly grounded in knowledge, they say, 'We believe in it. All (of it) is from our Lord.' Yet no one takes heed except those with understanding. 8 'Our Lord, do not cause our hearts to turn aside after You have guided us, and grant us mercy from Yourself. Surely You – You are the Giver. 9 Our Lord, surely You will gather the people for a Day – (there is) no doubt about it. Surely God will not break the appointment.'

10 Surely those who disbelieve – neither their wealth nor their children will be of any use against God. And those – they will be fuel for the Fire, 11 like the case of the house of Pharaoh, and those who were before them, who called Our signs a lie. God seized them because of their sins, and God is harsh in retribution. 12 Say to those who disbelieve: 'You will be conquered and gathered into Gehenna – it is an evil bed!' 13 There was a sign for you in the two cohorts which met: one cohort fighting in the way of God, and another disbelieving. They saw them twice as many (as themselves) with (their own) eyesight. God supports with His help whomever He pleases. Surely in that is a lesson indeed for those have sight.

14 Enticing to the people is love of desires: women and sons, qinṭārs upon qinṭārs of gold and silver (coins), and the finest horses, cattle, and fields. That is the provision of this present life. But God – with Him is the best place of return.

---

1. *you*: sing.

House of 'Imrān

15 Say: 'Shall I inform you of (something) better than that? For the ones who guard (themselves), (there are) Gardens with their Lord, through which rivers flow, there to remain, and (there are) pure spouses and approval from God.' God sees (His) servants **16** who say, 'Our Lord, surely we believe. Forgive us our sins and guard us against the punishment of the Fire.' **17** (They are) the patient, the truthful, the obedient, those who contribute, the askers of forgiveness in the mornings.

18 God has borne witness that (there is) no god but Him – and (so have) the angels, and the people of knowledge, (who) uphold justice. (There is) no god but Him, the Mighty, the Wise. **19** Surely the religion with God is Islam. Those who were given the Book did not differ until after the knowledge had come to them, (because of) envy among themselves. Whoever disbelieves in the signs of God – surely God is quick at the reckoning. **20** If they dispute with you, say: 'I have submitted to God, and (so have) those who follow me.' And say to those who have been given the Book, and to the common people: 'Have you submitted?' If they submit, they have been (rightly) guided, but if they turn away – only (dependent) on you is the delivery (of the message). God sees (His) servants.

21 Surely those who disbelieve in the signs of God, and kill the prophets without any right, and kill those of the people who command justice – give them news of a painful punishment. **22** Those are the ones whose deeds come to nothing in this world and the Hereafter. They will have no helpers.

23 Have you[2] not considered those who were given a portion of the Book? They were called to the Book of God in order that it might judge between them. Then a group of them turned away in aversion. **24** That is because they said, 'The Fire will only touch us for a number of days.' What they forged has deceived them in their religion. **25** How (will it be) when We gather them for a Day – (there is) no doubt about it – and everyone will be paid in full what he has earned, and they will not be done evil? **26** Say: 'God! Master of the kingdom, You give the kingdom to whomever You please and You take away the kingdom from whomever You please. You exalt whomever You please and You humble whomever You please. In Your hand is the good. Surely You are powerful over everything. **27** You cause the night to pass into the day, and cause the day to pass into the night. You bring forth the living from the dead, and bring forth the dead from the living. You provide for whomever You please without reckoning.'

28 Let not the believers take the disbelievers as allies, rather than the believers – whoever does that, he has nothing from God – unless you guard (yourselves) against them as a precaution. God warns you to beware of Him. To God is the (final) destination. **29** Say: 'Whether you hide what is in your hearts or reveal it, God knows it. He knows whatever is in the heavens and whatever is on the earth. God is powerful over everything.' **30** On the Day when everyone will find

---

2. *you*: sing.

House of 'Imrān

the good he has done brought forward, and (also) the evil he has done, he will wish that there were a great distance between himself and it. God warns you to beware of Him. God is kind with (His) servants. **31** Say: 'If you love God, follow me. God will love you and will forgive you your sins. God is forgiving, compassionate.' **32** Say: 'Obey God and the messenger!' If they turn away – surely God does not love the disbelievers.

33 Surely God has chosen Adam and Noah, and the house of Abraham and the house of 'Imrān[3] over all peoples, **34** some of them descendents of others. God is hearing, knowing.

35 (Remember) when the wife of 'Imrān said, 'My Lord, surely I vow to You what is in my belly, (to be) dedicated (to Your service). Accept (it) from me. Surely You – You are the Hearing, the Knowing.' **36** And when she had delivered her, she said, 'My Lord, surely I have delivered her, a female' – God knew very well what she had delivered, (since) the male is not like the female – 'and I have named her Mary, and I seek refuge for her with You, and for her descendants, from the accursed Satan.' **37** So her Lord accepted her fully and caused her to grow up well, and Zachariah took charge of her. Whenever Zachariah entered upon her (in) the place of prayer, he found a provision (of food) with her. He said, 'Mary! Where does this (food) come to you from?' She said, 'It is from God. Surely God provides for whomever He pleases without reckoning.' **38** There Zachariah called on his Lord. He said, 'My Lord, grant me a good descendant from Yourself. Surely You are the Hearer of the call.' **39** And the angels called him while he was standing, praying in the place of prayer: 'God gives you good news of John, confirming a word from God. (He will be) a man of honor, and an ascetic, and a prophet from among the righteous.' **40** He said, 'My Lord, how shall I have a boy, when old age has already come upon me and my wife cannot conceive?' He said, 'So (it will be)! God does whatever He pleases.' **41** He said, 'My Lord, make a sign for me.' He said, 'Your sign is that you will not speak to the people for three days, except by gestures. Remember your Lord often, and glorify (Him) in the evening and the morning.'

42 And (remember) when the angels said, 'Mary! Surely God has chosen you and purified you, and He has chosen you over all other women. **43** Mary! Be obedient to your Lord, and prostrate yourself and bow with the ones who bow.' **44** – That is one of the stories of the unseen. We inspired you[4] (with) it. You were not with them when they cast their pens (as lots to see) which of them would take charge of Mary. Nor were you with them when they were disputing. – **45** When the angels said, 'Mary! Surely God gives you good news of a word from Him: his name is the Messiah, Jesus, son of Mary, eminent in this world and the Hereafter, and one of those brought near. **46** He will speak to the people (while he is still) in the cradle and in adulthood, and (he will be) one of the righteous.' **47** She said,

---

3. *'Imrān*: father of Mary.
4. *you*: sing.

House of 'Imrān

'My Lord, how shall I have a child, when no man has touched me?' He said, 'So (it will be)! God creates whatever He pleases. When He decrees something, He simply says to it, "Be!" and it is.'

48 And He will teach him the Book and the wisdom, and the Torah and the Gospel. **49** And (He will make him) a messenger to the Sons of Israel. 'Surely I have brought you a sign from your Lord: I shall create for you the form of a bird from clay. Then I will breathe into it and it will become a bird by the permission of God. And I shall heal the blind and the leper, and give the dead life by the permission of God. And I shall inform you of what you may eat, and what you may store up in your houses. Surely in that is a sign indeed for you, if you are believers. **50** And (I come) confirming what was before me of the Torah, and to make permitted to you some things which were forbidden to you (before). I have brought you a sign from your Lord, so guard (yourselves) against God, and obey me. **51** Surely God is my Lord and your Lord, so serve Him! This is a straight path.'

52 When Jesus perceived disbelief from them, he said, 'Who will be my helpers to God?' The disciples said, 'We will be the helpers of God. We believe in God. Bear witness that we submit. **53** Our Lord, we believe in what You have sent down, and we follow the messenger. So write us down among the witnesses.'

54 They schemed, but God schemed (too), and God is the best of schemers. **55** (Remember) when God said, 'Jesus! Surely I am going to take you and raise you to Myself, and purify you from those who disbelieve. And I am going to place those who follow you above those who disbelieve until the Day of Resurrection. Then to Me is your return, and I shall judge between you concerning your differences. **56** As for those who disbelieve, I shall punish them (with) a harsh punishment in this world and the Hereafter. They will have no helpers.' **57** As for those who believe and do righteous deeds, He will pay them their rewards in full. God does not love the evildoers. **58** That – We recite it to you[5] from the signs and the wise Reminder.

59 Surely the likeness of Jesus is, with God, as the likeness of Adam. He created him from dust, (and) then He said to him, 'Be!' and he was. **60** The truth (is) from your Lord, so do not be one of the doubters. **61** Whoever disputes with you about him, after what has come to you of the knowledge, say: 'Come, let us call our sons and your sons, our wives and your wives, ourselves and yourselves. Then let us pray earnestly and place the curse of God upon the liars.' **62** Surely this – it indeed is the true account. (There is) nothing of (the nature of) a god but God. Surely God – He indeed is the Mighty, the Wise. **63** If they turn away – surely God knows the fomenters of corruption.

64 Say: 'People of the Book! Come to a word (which is) common between us and you: "We do not serve (anyone) but God, and do not associate (anything) with

---

5. *you*: sing.

Him, and do not take each other as Lords instead of God.'" If they turn away, say:[6] 'Bear witness that we are Muslims.'

65 People of the Book! Why do you dispute about Abraham, when the Torah and the Gospel were not sent down until after him. Will you not understand? **66** There you are! Those who have disputed about what you know. Why do you dispute about what you do not know? God knows, but you do not know. **67** Abraham was not a Jew, nor a Christian, but he was a Ḥanīf,[7] a Muslim. He was not one of the idolaters. **68** Surely the people nearest to Abraham are those indeed who followed him, and this prophet, and those who believe. God is the ally of the believers.

69 A contingent of the People of the Book would like to lead you astray, but they only lead themselves astray, though they do not realize (it). **70** People of the Book! Why do you disbelieve in the signs of God, when you are witnesses (to them)? **71** People of the Book! Why do you mix the truth with falsehood, and conceal the truth, when you know (better)? **72** A contingent of the People of the Book has said, 'Believe in what has been sent down on those who believe at the beginning of the day, and disbelieve at the end of it, perhaps (then) they may return.' **73** And: 'Do not believe (anyone) except the one who follows your religion.' Say: 'Surely the (true) guidance is the guidance of God – that anyone should be given what you have been given, or (that) they should dispute with you before your Lord!' Say: 'Surely favor is in the hand of God. He gives it to whomever He pleases. God is embracing, knowing. **74** He chooses whomever He pleases for His mercy, and God is full of great favor.'

75 Among the People of the Book (there is) one who, if you[8] entrust him with a qinṭār,[9] will pay it back to you, but among them (there is) one who, if you entrust him with a dīnār, will not pay it back to you unless you stand over him. That is because they say, 'There is no way (of obligation) on us concerning the common people.' They speak lies against God, and they know (it). **76** Yes indeed! Whoever fulfills his covenant and guards (himself) – surely God loves the ones who guard (themselves). **77** Surely those who sell the covenant of God and their oaths for a small price will have no share in the Hereafter. God will not speak to them or look at them on the Day of Resurrection, nor will He purify them. For them (there is) a painful punishment.

78 Surely (there is) indeed a group of them who twist their tongues with the Book, so that you will think it is from the Book, when it is not from the Book. And they say, 'It is from God,' when it is not from God. They speak lies against God, and they know (it). **79** It is not (possible) for a human being that God should give him

---

6. *say*: plur. imperative.
7. *Ḥanīf*: meaning uncertain.
8. *you*: sing.
9. *qinṭār*: a large sum of money.

House of 'Imrān

the Book, and the judgment, and the prophetic office, (and) then he should say to the people, 'Be my servants instead of God's.' Rather (he would say), 'Be rabbis by what you have been teaching of the Book and by what you have been studying (of it).' **80** He would not command you to take the angels and the prophets as Lords. Would he command you to disbelief after you have submitted?

81 (Remember) when God took a covenant with the prophets: 'Whatever indeed I have given you of the Book and wisdom, when a messenger comes to you confirming what is with you, you are to believe in him and you are to help him.' He said, 'Do you agree and accept My burden on that (condition)?' They said, 'We agree.' He said, 'Bear witness, and I shall be with you among the witnesses.' **82** Whoever turns away after that, those – they are the wicked.

83 Do they desire a religion other than God's, when whoever is in the heavens and the earth has submitted to Him, willingly or unwillingly, and to Him they will be returned? **84** Say: 'We believe in God, and what has been sent down on us, and what has been sent down on Abraham, and Ishmael, and Isaac, and Jacob, and the tribes, and what was given to Moses, and Jesus, and the prophets from their Lord. We make no distinction between any of them, and to Him we submit.' **85** Whoever desires a religion other than Islam, it will not be accepted from him, and in the Hereafter he will be one of the losers.

86 How will God guide a people who have disbelieved after having believed, and (after) they have borne witness that the messenger is true, and the clear signs have come to them? God does not guide the people who are evildoers. **87** Those – their payment is that on them (rests) the curse of God, and the angels, and the people all together. **88** There (they will) remain – the punishment will not be lightened for them, nor will they be spared **89** – except for those who turn (in repentance) after that and set (things) right. Surely God is forgiving, compassionate. **90** Surely those who disbelieve after their believing, (and) then increase in disbelief – their repentance will not be accepted. And those – they are the ones who go astray. **91** Surely those who disbelieve, and die while they are disbelievers – not all the world's gold would be accepted from (any) one of them, even if he (tried to) ransom (himself) with it. Those – for them (there is) a painful punishment. They will have no helpers.

92 You will not attain piety until you contribute from what you love, and whatever you contribute, surely God knows it.

93 All food was permitted to the Sons of Israel, except for what Israel forbade himself before the Torah was sent down. Say: 'Bring the Torah and read it, if you are truthful.' **94** Whoever forges lies against God after that, those – they are the evildoers. **95** Say: 'God has spoken the truth, so follow the creed of Abraham the Ḥanīf. He was not one of the idolaters.'

96 Surely the first House laid down for the people was indeed that at Becca, a blessed (House) and a guidance for all peoples. **97** In it are clear signs: the standing place of Abraham. Whoever enters it is secure. Pilgrimage to the House is (an obligation) on the people to God – (for) anyone who is able (to make) a way to it. Whoever disbelieves – surely God is wealthy beyond all peoples.

98 Say: 'People of the Book! Why do you disbelieve in the signs of God, when God is a witness of what you do?' **99** Say: 'People of the Book! Why do you keep those who believe from the way of God, desiring (to make) it crooked, when you are witnesses? God is not oblivious of what you do.'

100 You who believe! If you obey a group of those who have been given the Book, they will turn you back (into) disbelievers after having believed. **101** Yet how can you disbelieve, when the signs of God are recited to you, and His messenger is among you? Whoever holds fast to God has been guided to a straight path.

102 You who believe! Guard (yourselves) against God – guarding (yourselves) against Him is an obligation – and (see to it that) you do not die unless you have submitted. **103** And hold fast to the rope of God – all (of you) – and do not become divided. Remember the blessing of God on you: when you were enemies and He united your hearts, so that by His blessing you became brothers. You were on the brink of a pit of the Fire, and He saved you from it. In this way God makes clear to you His signs, so that you may be (rightly) guided.

104 Let there be (one) community of you, calling (people) to good, and commanding right and forbidding wrong. Those – they are the ones who prosper. **105** Do not be like those who became divided and differed, after the clear signs had come to them. Those – for them (there is) a great punishment, **106** on the Day when (some) faces will become white and (other) faces will become black. As for those whose faces are blackened: 'Did you disbelieve after having believed? Taste the punishment for what you were disbelieving!' **107** As for those whose faces are whitened, (they will be) in the mercy of God. There they will remain. **108** Those are the signs of God. We recite them to you[10] in truth. God does not intend evil to any peoples. **109** To God (belongs) whatever is in the heavens and whatever is on the earth. To God all affairs are returned.

110 You are the best community (ever) brought forth for humankind, commanding right and forbidding wrong, and believing in God. If the People of the Book had believed, it would indeed have been better for them. Some of them are believers, but most of them are wicked. **111** They will not cause you any harm, except for a (little) hurt. And if they fight you, they will turn their backs to you, (and) then they will not be helped. **112** Humiliation will be stamped upon them wherever they are found, unless (they grasp) a rope from God and a rope from the people. They have incurred the anger of God, and poverty will be stamped upon them. That is because they have disbelieved in the signs of God and killed the prophets without any right. That is because they have disobeyed and transgressed.

113 (Yet) they are not (all) alike. Among the People of the Book (there is) a community (which is) upstanding. They recite the signs of God during the hours of

---

10. *you*: sing.

House of 'Imrān

the night and prostrate themselves. **114** They believe in God and the Last Day, and command right and forbid wrong, and are quick in the (doing of) good deeds. Those are among the righteous. **115** Whatever good they do, they will not be denied (the reward of) it. God knows the ones who guard (themselves). **116** Surely those who disbelieve – neither their wealth nor their children will be of any use against God – those are the companions of the Fire. There they will remain. **117** The parable of what they contribute in this present life is like the parable of a freezing wind, which smites the field of a people who have done themselves evil, and destroys it. God did not do them evil, but they did themselves evil.

118 You who believe! Do not take outsiders as intimate friends. They will not fail to cause you ruin. They desire what you are distressed at. (Their) hatred is already apparent from their mouths, but what their hearts hide is (even) greater. We have already made clear to you the signs, if you are understanding. **119** There you are! You are those who love them, but they do not love you. You believe in the Book – all of it. And when they meet you they say, 'We believe,' but when they are alone, they bite their fingers at you out of rage. Say: 'Die in your rage! Surely God knows what is in the hearts.' **120** If some good touches you, it distresses them, but if some evil smites you, they gloat over it. Yet if you are patient and guard (yourselves), their plot will not harm you at all. Surely God encompasses what they do.

121 (Remember) when you[11] went out early from your family to post the believers (in their) positions for the battle – God is hearing, knowing – **122** when two contingents of you were inclined to lose courage, though God was their ally – in God let the believers put their trust. **123** Certainly God helped you[12] at Badr, when you were an utterly insignificant (force). So guard (yourselves) against God, that you may be thankful.

124 (Remember) when you said to the believers, 'Is it not sufficient for you that your Lord increases you with three thousand angels (specially) sent down? **125** Yes indeed! If you are patient and guard (yourselves), and they come against you suddenly, your Lord will increase you with five thousand angels (specially) designated.' **126** God only intended that as good news for you, and to satisfy your hearts by means of it. Help (comes) only from God, the Mighty, the Wise, **127** so that He might cut off a part of those who disbelieve, or disgrace them, so that they would turn back disappointed. **128** You[13] have nothing to do with the matter, whether He turns to them (in forgiveness) or punishes them. Surely they are evildoers. **129** To God (belongs) whatever is in the heavens and whatever is on the earth. He forgives whomever He pleases and He punishes whomever He pleases. God is forgiving, compassionate.

---

11. *you*: sing.
12. *you*: plur.
13. You: sing.

House of 'Imrān

130 You who believe! Do not devour usury, (making it) double and redouble, but guard (yourselves) against God, so that you may prosper. **131** And guard (yourselves) against the Fire which is prepared for the disbelievers.

132 Obey God and the messenger, so that you may receive compassion. **133** And be quick to (obtain) forgiveness from your Lord, and a Garden – its width (is like) the heavens and the earth – prepared for the ones who guard (themselves), **134** who contribute (alms) in prosperity and adversity, and who choke back their anger and pardon the people. God loves the doers of good, **135** and those who, when they commit immorality or do themselves evil, remember God and ask forgiveness for their sins – and who forgives sins but God? – and do not persist in (doing) what they did, when they know (better). **136** Those – their payment is forgiveness from their Lord, and Gardens through which rivers flow, there to remain. Excellent is the reward of the doers!

137 Customary practices have passed away before you. Travel the earth and see how the end was for the ones who called (it) a lie. **138** This is an explanation for the people, and a guidance and admonition for the ones who guard (themselves).

139 Do not grow weak and do not sorrow, when you are the prevailing (force), if you are believers. **140** If a wound has touched you, a similar wound has already touched the enemy. We cause days like this to alternate among the people, so that God may know those who believe, and that He may take martyrs from you – God does not love the evildoers – **141** and so that God may purge those who believe, and destroy the disbelievers. **142** Or did you think that you would enter the Garden, when God did not yet know those of you who would struggle, and know the (ones who would be) patient? **143** Certainly you were desiring death before you met it. Now you have seen it, and you are staring (at it).

144 Muḥammad is only a messenger. Messengers have already passed away before him. If he dies or is killed, will you turn back on your heels? Whoever turns back on his heels will not harm God at all. God will repay the thankful. **145** It is not (given) to anyone to die, except by the permission of God – (it is) determined (in) writing. Whoever desires the reward of this world, We shall give him (a share) of it, and whoever desires the reward of the Hereafter, We shall give him (a share) of it. We shall repay the thankful.

146 How many a prophet has fought, (and along) with him (fought) many thousands? Yet they did not weaken at what smote them in the way of God. They were not weak nor did they humiliate themselves. God loves the patient. **147** All that they said was, 'Our Lord, forgive us our sins and our wantonness in our affair, and make firm our feet, and give us victory over the people who are disbelievers.' **148** So God gave them the reward of this world and the good reward of the Hereafter. God loves the doers of good.

149 You who believe! If you obey those who disbelieve, they will turn you back on your heels, and you will return as losers. **150** No! God is your Protector. He is the best of helpers. **151** We shall cast dread into the hearts of those who disbelieve,

House of 'Imrān

because they have associated with God what He has not sent down any authority for. Their refuge is the Fire. Evil is the dwelling place of the evildoers!

152 Certainly God fulfilled His promise to you when you were killing them by His permission, until you lost courage and argued about the matter, and disobeyed after He had shown you what you love. (There are) some of you who desire this world, and some of you who desire the Hereafter. Then He turned you away from them, so that He might test you. Certainly He has pardoned you. God is full of favor to the believers.

153 (Remember) when you were going up, and not turning aside for anyone, and the messenger was calling to you from behind: He repaid you (with) distress upon distress, so that you might not sorrow over what eluded you or what smote you. God is aware of what you do. **154** Then, after the distress, He sent down on you security: a slumber covering a contingent of you, but (another) contingent (of you) was obsessed about themselves, thinking about God (something) other than the truth – thought(s) of the (time of) ignorance. They were saying, 'Do we have any part at all in the affair?' Say: 'Surely the affair – all of it – (belongs) to God.' They hide within themselves what they do not reveal to you. They were saying, 'If we had any part in the affair, we would not have been killed here.' Say: '(Even) if you had been in your houses, those for whom death was written would (still) indeed have gone forth to the places where they lie (dead).' (That happened) in order that God might test what was in your hearts, and that He might purge what was in your hearts. God knows what is in the hearts. **155** Surely those of you who turned back on the day the two forces met – (it was) only Satan (who) caused them to slip because of something they had earned. Certainly God has pardoned them. Surely God is forgiving, forbearing.

156 You who believe! Do not be like those who disbelieve, and say of their brothers when they strike forth on the earth or are on a raid, 'If they had been with us, they would not have died or been killed' – so that God may make that a (cause of) regret in their hearts. (It is) God (who) gives life and causes death. God sees what you do. **157** If indeed you are killed in the way of God, or die – forgiveness from God, and mercy, are indeed better than what they accumulate. **158** If indeed you die or are killed, you will indeed be gathered to God. **159** (It was) by a mercy from God (that) you have been soft on them. If you had been harsh (and) stern of heart, they would indeed have deserted from your ranks. So pardon them, and ask forgiveness for them, and consult with them about the affair. When you have made up your mind, put your trust in God. Surely God loves the ones who put their trust (in Him). **160** If God helps you, (there is) no one to overcome you, but if He forsakes you, who (is there) who (will) help you after Him? In God let the believers put their trust.

161 It is not for a prophet to defraud. Whoever defrauds will bring what he has defrauded on the Day of Resurrection. Then everyone will be paid in full what they have earned – and they will not be done evil. **162** Is the one who follows after the approval of God like the one who incurs the anger of God? His refuge

House of 'Imrān

will be Gehenna – and it is an evil destination! **163** They (have different) ranks with God, and God sees what they do. **164** Certainly God bestowed favor on the believers when He raised up among them a messenger from among them, to recite His signs to them, and to purify them, and to teach them the Book and the wisdom, though before (this) they were indeed clearly astray. **165** Why, when a smiting smote you – you had already smitten twice (as many in comparison to) it – did you say, 'How is this?' Say: 'You yourselves are to blame. Surely God is powerful over everything.'

166 What smote you on the day when the two forces met (happened) by the permission of God, so that He might know the (true) believers, **167** and that He might know those who played the hypocrite. It was said to them, 'Come, fight in the way of God, or defend!' But they said, 'If we knew (how) to fight, we would indeed follow you.' They were nearer to disbelief that day than to belief. They were saying with their mouths what was not in their hearts. But God knows what they were concealing – **168** those who said of their brothers, when they (themselves) sat (at home), 'If they had obeyed us, they would not have been killed.' Say: 'Avert death from yourselves, if you are truthful.'

169 Do not think of those who have been killed in the way of God as dead. No! (They are) alive with their Lord (and) provided for, **170** gloating over what God has given them of his favor, and welcoming the good news about those who have not (yet) joined them of those who stayed behind – that (there will be) no fear on them, nor will they sorrow. **171** They welcome the good news of blessing from God, and favor, and that God does not let the reward of the believers go to waste. **172** Those who responded (to the call of) God and the messenger after the wound had smitten them – for those of them who have done good and guarded (themselves), (there is) a great reward. **173** (They are) those to whom the people said, 'Surely the enemy has gathered against you, so fear them!' But it increased them in belief, and they said, 'God is enough for us. Excellent is the Guardian.' **174** So they turned back by the blessing and favor of God, without any evil touching them. They followed after the approval of God, and God is full of great favor. **175** That is only Satan (who) frightens his allies. Do not fear them, but fear Me, if you are believers.

176 Do not let those who are quick to disbelieve cause you sorrow. Surely they will not harm God at all. God does not wish to assign to them any share in the Hereafter. For them (there is) a great punishment. **177** Surely those who have purchased disbelief with the (price of) belief will not harm God at all. For them (there is) a painful punishment. **178** And let not those who disbelieve think that We spare them for their own good. We only spare them so that they will increase in sin! For them (there is) a humiliating punishment. **179** God is not one to leave the believers in (the situation) you are in until He separates the bad from the good. Nor is God one to inform you of the unseen, but God chooses from His messengers whomever He pleases. So believe in God and His messengers. If you believe and guard (yourselves), for you (there is) a great reward. **180** And let not those who

House of 'Imrān

are stingy with what God has given them of His favor think that it is good for them. No! It is bad for them. What they are stingy with will be hung about their necks on the Day of Resurrection. To God (belongs) the inheritance of the heavens and the earth. God is aware of what you do.

181 Certainly God has heard the words of those who said, 'Surely God is poor and we are rich.' We shall write down what they have said, along with their killing the prophets without any right, and We shall say, 'Taste the punishment of the burning (Fire)! **182** That is for what your (own) hands have sent forward, and (know) that God is not an evildoer to (His) servants.'

183 Those (are the same people) who said, 'Surely God has made us promise not to believe in any messenger until he brings a sacrifice which fire devours.' Say: 'Messengers have come to you before me with the clear signs, and with that which you spoke of. So why did you kill them, if you are truthful?' **184** If they call you a liar, (know that) messengers have been called liars before you, who brought the clear signs, and the scriptures, and the illuminating Book.

185 Every person will taste death, and you will only be paid your rewards in full on the Day of Resurrection. Whoever is removed from the Fire and admitted to the Garden has triumphed. This present life is nothing but a deceptive enjoyment. **186** You will indeed be tested concerning your wealth and your lives, and you will indeed hear from those who were given the Book before you, and from those who are idolaters, much hurt. But if you are patient and guard (yourselves) – surely that is one of the determining factors in (all) affairs.

187 (Remember) when God took a covenant with those who had been given the Book: 'You shall indeed make it clear to the people, and shall not conceal it.' But they tossed it behind their backs, and sold it for a small price. Evil is what they purchased! **188** Do not think (that) those who gloat over what they have brought, and like to be praised for what they have not done – do not think that they are in (a place of) safety from the punishment. For them (there is) a painful punishment. **189** To God (belongs) the kingdom of the heavens and the earth. God is powerful over everything.

190 Surely in the creation of the heavens and the earth, and (in) the alternation of the night and the day, (there are) signs indeed for those with understanding, **191** who remember God, whether standing or sitting or (lying) on their sides, and reflect on the creation of the heavens and the earth: 'Our Lord, You have not created this in vain. Glory to You! Guard us against the punishment of the Fire. **192** Our Lord, surely You – whomever You cause to enter the Fire, You have disgraced him. The evildoers will have no helpers. **193** Our Lord, surely we have heard a caller calling (us) to belief (saying): "Believe in your Lord!" So we have believed. Our Lord, forgive us our sins, and absolve us of our evil deeds, and take us with the pious. **194** Our Lord, give us what You have promised us on (the assurance of) Your messengers, and do not disgrace us on the Day of Resurrection. Surely You will not break the appointment.' **195** And their Lord responded to them: 'Surely I do not let a deed of anyone of you go to waste – whether male or female – you are all alike. Those who have emigrated, and were expelled from their homes, and suffered harm in My way, and have fought and been killed – I shall indeed absolve them of their evil deeds, and I shall indeed cause them to enter Gardens through which rivers flow. A reward from God! God – with Him is the best reward.'

196 Do not let the disbelievers' comings and goings in the lands deceive you. **197** A little enjoyment (of life), then their refuge is Gehenna – it is an evil resting place! **198** But the ones who guard (themselves) against their Lord – for them (there are) Gardens through which rivers flow, there to remain. A reception from God! And what is with God is better for the pious.

199 Surely (there are) some of the People of the Book who indeed believe in God, and what has been sent down to you, and what has been sent down to them, humbling themselves before God. They do not sell the signs of God for a small price. Those – for them their reward is with their Lord. Surely God is quick at the reckoning.

200 You who believe! Be patient and strive in patience, and be steadfast, and guard (yourselves) against God, so that you may prosper.

4 ❈ Women

In the Name of God, the Merciful, the Compassionate

1 People! Guard (yourselves) against your Lord, who created you from one person, and from him created his wife, and scattered from the two of them many men and women. And guard (yourselves) against God, whom you ask each other questions about, and (guard yourselves against) the wombs.¹ Surely God is watching over you.

2 Give the orphans their property, and do not exchange the bad for the good, and do not consume their property along with your own. Surely it is a great crime. 3 If you fear that you will not act fairly toward the orphan girls, marry what seems good to you of the women: two, or three, or four. But if you fear that you will not be fair, (marry only) one, or what your right (hands) own.² That (will make it) more likely that you will not be biased.³ 4 Give the women their dowries as a gift. If they remit to you any part of it on their own, consume it with satisfaction (and) pleasure. 5 Do not give the foolish your property which God has assigned to you to maintain, but provide for them by means of it and clothe them, and speak to them rightful words. 6 Test the orphan girls until they reach (the age of) marriage. If you perceive right judgment in them, hand over their property to them. Do not consume it wantonly or hastily before they are grown up. Whoever is wealthy should refrain (from using it), and whoever is poor should use (it) rightfully. And when you do hand over their property to them, take witnesses over them. God is sufficient as a reckoner.

7 To the men (belongs) a portion of what parents and family leave, and to the women (belongs) a portion of what parents and family leave, (whether there is) a little of it or a lot, an obligatory portion. 8 When the family, the orphans, and the poor are present at the distribution (of the estate), provide for them from it, and speak to them rightful words. 9 Let those fear who, if they left behind them weak descendants, would fear for them. Let them guard (themselves) against God, and speak a direct word. 10 Surely those who consume the property of the orphans in an evil manner, they only consume fire in their bellies, and they will burn in a blazing (Fire).

---

1. *the wombs*: meaning obscure.
2. *what your right (hands) own*: i.e. female slaves.
3. *biased*: meaning uncertain.

Women

11 God charges you concerning your children: to the male, a share equal to two females. But if they be (only) women, more than two, then to them two-thirds of what he leaves. But if there be (only) one, then to her a half. And to his parents, to each of them, a sixth of what he leaves, if he has children. But if he has no children, and his heirs are his parents, then to his mother a third. And if he has brothers, then to his mother the sixth, after any bequest he may have made or any debt (has been paid). Whether your fathers or your sons are of most benefit to you,[4] you do not know. (This is) an obligation from God. Surely God is knowing, wise.

12 And to you a half of what your wives leave, if they have no children. But if they have children, then to you the fourth of what they leave, after any bequest they may have made or any debt (has been paid). And to them the fourth of what you leave, if you have no children. But if you have children, then to them the eighth of what you leave, after any bequest you may have made or any debt (has been paid). If a man or a woman has no direct heir, but has a brother or a sister, then to each of them the sixth. But if they are more (numerous) than that, then they share in the third, after any bequest he may have made or any debt (has been paid), without prejudice (to anyone). (This is) a directive from God. God is knowing, forbearing.

13 Those are the limits (set by) God. Whoever obeys God and His messenger – He will cause him to enter Gardens through which rivers flow, there to remain. That is the great triumph! **14** But whoever disobeys God and His messenger, and transgresses His limits – He will cause him to enter the Fire, there to remain. For him (there is) a humiliating punishment.

15 (As for) those of your women who commit immorality, call witnesses against them, four of you. If they bear witness (to the truth of the allegation), confine them in their houses until death takes them, or God makes a way for (dealing with) them. **16** And (if) two of you commit it, harm both of them. But if they turn (in repentance) and set (things) right, let them be. Surely God turns (in forgiveness), compassionate. **17** But God only turns (in forgiveness) to those who do evil in ignorance, (and) then turn (in repentance) soon after. Then God will turn to them (in forgiveness). God is knowing, wise. **18** But (His) turning (in forgiveness) is not for those who continue to do evil deeds, and only when death approaches say, 'Surely I turn (in repentance) now.' Nor (does He turn in forgiveness) to those who die while they are still disbelievers. Those – for them We have prepared a painful punishment.

19 You who believe! It is not permitted to you to inherit women against their will. And do not prevent them, so that you may take part of what you have given them, unless they commit clear immorality. Associate with them rightfully. If you dislike them, it may be that you dislike something in which God has placed

---

4. *of most benefit to you*: or 'most entitled to benefit from you.'

much good. **20** And if you wish to exchange a wife for (another) wife, and you have given one of them a qinṭār,[5] take (back) none of it. Would you take it (back by) slander and clear sin? **21** How can you take it (back), seeing that one of you has gone into the other, and they have taken a firm pledge from you?

22 Do not marry women whom your fathers have married, unless it is a thing of the past. Surely it is an immorality, an abhorrent thing, and an evil way. **23** Forbidden to you are: your mothers, your daughters, your sisters, your paternal aunts, your maternal aunts, (your) brothers' daughters, (your) sisters' daughters, the mothers who have nursed you, (those who are) your sisters by nursing, your wives' mothers, and your stepdaughters who are in your care, (born) of wives you have gone into – but if you have not gone into them, (there is) no blame on you – and wives of your sons, those of your own loins, and that you should have two sisters at the same time, unless it is a thing of the past. Surely God is forgiving, compassionate. **24** And (also forbidden to you are) married women, except what your right (hands) own. (This is) a written decree of God for you. (All women) beyond that are permitted to you to seek (to obtain) by means of your wealth, taking (them) in marriage, not in immorality. So (because of) what you enjoy from them in this way, give them their marriage gifts as an obligation. (There is) no blame on you in anything you may give them by mutual agreement beyond this obligation. Surely God is knowing, wise.

25 Whoever among you cannot wait to marry believing, free women, (let them take) believing young women from what your right (hands) own. God knows your belief, (for) you are all alike. Marry them with the permission of their families, and give them their rightful marriage gifts, (as) married women, not (as) women who commit immorality or take secret lovers. But if they commit immorality after they are married, they will be liable to half the punishment (inflicted) on free women. That (provision) is for those of you who fear sin. Yet to be patient (would be) better for you. God is forgiving, compassionate. **26** God wishes to make (things) clear to you, and to guide you in the customary ways of those who were before you, and to turn toward you (in forgiveness). God is knowing, wise. **27** God wishes to turn toward you (in forgiveness), but those who follow (their) lusts wish you to swerve far away. **28** God wishes to lighten (your burdens) for you, (for) the human was created weak.

29 You who believe! Do not consume your property among yourselves by means of falsehood, but (let there) be a transaction among you by mutual agreement. And do not kill one another. Surely God is compassionate with you. **30** Whoever does that in enmity and evil – We shall burn him in a Fire. That is easy for God. **31** If you avoid the gross (sins) of what you are forbidden (to commit), We shall absolve you of your (other) evil deeds, and We shall cause you to enter (through) an entrance of honor.

---

5. *qinṭār*: i.e. a large sum of money as a marriage gift.

32 Do not long for what God has bestowed in favor on some of you over others. To the men (belongs) a portion of what they have earned, and to the women (belongs) a portion of what they have earned. Ask God for some of His favor. Surely God has knowledge of everything. **33** To everyone We have appointed heirs of what parents and family leave; and those with whom your right (hands) have made contract, give them their portion. Surely God is a witness over everything.

34 Men are supervisors of women because God has favored some of them over others, and because they have contributed from their wealth. Righteous women are obedient, watching over (affairs) in the absence (of their husbands)[6] because God has watched over (them). (As for) those women whom you fear may be rebellious: admonish them, avoid them in bed, and (finally) strike them. If they obey you, do not seek (any further) way against them. Surely God is most high, great. **35** If you fear a breach between the two,[7] raise up an arbiter from his family and an arbiter from her family. If they both wish to set (things) right, God will effect a reconciliation between the two. Surely God is knowing, aware.

36 Serve God, and do not associate anything with Him, and (do) good to parents and to family, and the orphans, and the poor, and the neighbor who is related and the neighbor who is a stranger, and the companion at your side, and the traveler, and what your right (hands) own.

Surely God does not love anyone who is arrogant (and) boastful, **37** (nor) those who are stingy, and (who) command the people to be stingy, and conceal what God has given them of his favor. We have prepared for the disbelievers a humiliating punishment. **38** (Nor does God love) those who contribute their wealth to show off (before) the people, and who do not believe in God and the Last Day. Whoever has Satan for his comrade – he is an evil comrade! **39** What (harm would it do) them if they believed in God and the Last Day, and contributed from what God has provided them? But God knows about them. **40** Surely God does not do (even) a speck's weight of evil. If it is a good (deed), He doubles it, and gives from Himself a great reward. **41** How (will it be) when We bring from each community a witness, and bring you as a witness against them (all)? **42** On that Day those who have disbelieved and disobeyed the messenger will wish that the earth were leveled with them. But they will not (be able to) conceal (any) account from God.

43 You who believe! Do not go near the prayer when you are drunk, until you know what you are saying, or (when you are) defiled, unless (you are) travelers (on the) way, until you wash yourselves. If you are sick or on a journey, or if one of you has come from the toilet, or if you have touched women, and you do not find any water, take clean soil and wipe your faces and your hands. Surely God is pardoning, forgiving.

---

6. *watching over (affairs) in the absence (of their husbands)*: meaning obscure (lit. 'watching over the unseen').
7. *the two*: husband and wife.

Women

44 Have you[8] not considered those have been given a portion of the Book? They purchase error and wish that you[9] would go astray from the way. **45** God knows about your enemies. God is sufficient as an ally, and God is sufficient as a helper. **46** Some of those who are Jews alter words from their positions, and they say, 'We hear and disobey,' and 'Hear, and do not hear,' and 'Observe us,' twisting with their tongues and vilifying the religion. If they had said, 'We hear and obey,' and 'Hear,' and 'Regard us,' it would indeed have been better for them, and more just. But God has cursed them for their disbelief, and so they do not believe, except for a few.

47 You who have been given the Book! Believe in what We have sent down, confirming what is with you, before We obliterate faces, and turn them on their backs, or curse them as We cursed the men of the sabbath,[10] and God's command is done. **48** Surely God does not forgive (anything) being associated with Him, but He forgives what is other than that for whomever He pleases. Whoever associates (anything) with God has forged a great sin. **49** Do you not see those who claim purity for themselves? No! (It is) God (who) purifies whomever He pleases – and they will not be done evil in the slightest. **50** See how they forge lies against God. That suffices as a clear sin.

51 Do you not see those who have been given a portion of the Book? They believe in al-Jibt and al-Ṭāghūt,[11] and they say to those who disbelieve, 'These are better guided (as to the) way than those who believe'? **52** Those are the ones whom God has cursed, and whomever God has cursed – for him you will not find any helper. **53** Or do they have a portion of the kingdom? If that were so, they do not give the people the slightest thing. **54** Or are they jealous of the people for what God has given them of His favor? Yet We gave the house of Abraham the Book and the wisdom, and We gave them a great kingdom. **55** (There are) some of them who believe in it, and some of them who keep (people) from it. Gehenna is sufficient as a blazing (Fire). **56** Surely those who disbelieve in Our signs – We shall burn them in a Fire. Whenever their skins are completely burned, We shall exchange their skins for others, so that they may (continue to) feel the punishment. Surely God is mighty, wise. **57** But those who believe and do righteous deeds – We shall cause them to enter Gardens through which rivers flow, there to remain forever. There they will have pure spouses, and We shall cause them to enter sheltering shade.

58 Surely God commands you to pay back deposits to their (rightful) owners, and when you judge between the people, to judge with justice. Surely God gives you admonition which is excellent. Surely God is hearing, seeing.

---

8. *you*: sing.
9. *you*: plur.
10. *men of the sabbath*: see Q7.163–167.
11. *al-Jibt and al-Ṭāghūt*: reference uncertain; probably other names for Satan (see Q4.60, 76 below).

59 You who believe! Obey God, and obey the messenger and those (who have) the command among you. If you argue about anything, refer it to God and the messenger, if you believe in God and the Last Day. That is better and fairer in interpretation.

60 Have you[12] not considered those who claim that they believe in what has been sent down to you, and what was sent down before you? They wish to go (with their disputes) to al-Ṭāghūt for judgment. Yet they have been commanded to disbelieve in him. Satan wishes to lead them very far astray. **61** When it is said to them, 'Come to what God has sent down, and to the messenger,' you see the hypocrites keeping (people) from you. **62** How (will it be) when a smiting smites them for what their (own) hands have sent forward? Then they will come to you swearing, 'By God! We wanted nothing but good and reconciliation.' **63** Those are the ones who – God knows what is in their hearts. So turn away from them, and admonish them, and speak to them effective words about themselves.

64 We have not sent any messenger, except that he should be obeyed, by the permission of God. If, when they did themselves evil, they had come to you and asked forgiveness from God, and the messenger had asked forgiveness for them, they would indeed have found God turning (in forgiveness), compassionate. **65** But no! By your Lord! They will not believe until they make you judge concerning their disputes. Then they would have no difficulty with what you decided, and would submit (in full) submission. **66** If We had prescribed for them: 'Kill one another' or 'Go forth from your homes,' they would not have done it, except for a few of them. Yet if they had done what they were admonished (to do), it would indeed have been better for them, and a firmer foundation (for them). **67** And then We would indeed have given them a great reward from Us, **68** and indeed guided them to a straight path. **69** Whoever obeys God and the messenger are with those whom God has blessed: the prophets, and the truthful, and the martyrs, and the righteous. Those are good companions! **70** That is the favor of God. God is sufficient as a knower.

71 You who believe! Take your precautions. Go forth in detachments or go forth all together. **72** Surely among you (there is) the one indeed who lags behind, and if a smiting smites you, he says, 'God has blessed me because I was not a martyr with them.' **73** But if indeed some favor from God smites you, he will indeed say – as if there had not been any friendship between you and him – 'Would that I had been with them and attained a great triumph!' **74** So let those who sell this present life for (the price of) the Hereafter fight in the way of God. Whoever fights in the way of God – whether he is killed or conquers – We shall give him a great reward. **75** What is with you (that) you do not fight in the way of God, and (on behalf of) the weak among the men, women, and children, who say, 'Our Lord, bring us out of this town of the evildoers, and appoint for us an ally from Yourself, and appoint for us a helper from Yourself'? **76** Those who believe fight in the

---

12. *you*: sing.

way of God, and those who disbelieve fight in the way of al-Ṭāghūt. So fight the allies of Satan! Surely the plot of Satan is weak.

77 Have you[13] not considered those to whom it was said, 'Restrain your hands, and observe the prayer and give the alms'? Then, when fighting is prescribed for them, suddenly (there is) a group of them who fear the people as (much as) they fear God, or even more. And they say, 'Our Lord, why have you prescribed fighting for us? Why not spare us for a time near (at hand)?' Say: 'The enjoyment of this world is a small thing, but the Hereafter is better for the one who guards (himself). You will not be done evil in the slightest.' 78 Wherever you are, death will overtake you, even though you are in well-built towers. And if some good smites them, they say, 'This is from God,' but if some evil smites them, they say, 'This is from you.'[14] Say: 'Everything is from God.' What is (the matter) with these people? They hardly understand any report.

79 Whatever good smites you[15] is from God, and whatever evil smites you is from yourself. We have sent you as a messenger to the people. God is sufficient as a witness. 80 Whoever obeys the messenger has obeyed God, but whoever turns away – We have not sent you as a watcher over them. 81 They say, '(We pledge) obedience (to you).' But when they go forth from your presence, a contingent of them plans by night (to do) other than what you say. God is writing down what they plan. So turn away from them and put your trust in God. God is sufficient as a guardian.

82 Do they not contemplate the Qur'ān? If it were from any other than God, they would indeed have found in it much contradiction.

83 When any matter comes to them concerning security or fear, they divulge it. But if they were to refer it to the messenger and to those (who have) the command among them, those who investigate (such things) would indeed have known (about) it. If (it were) not (for the) favor of God on you,[16] and His mercy, you would indeed have followed Satan, except for a few (of you).

84 Fight in the way of God! You are only responsible for yourself, but urge on the believers. It may be that God will restrain the violence of those who disbelieve. God is harsher in violence, and harsher in punishing.

85 Whoever intercedes with a good intercession will have a portion of it for himself, but whoever intercedes with an evil intercession will have a portion of it for himself. God is powerful over everything.

86 When you receive a greeting, reply with a better greeting, or return it. Surely God is a reckoner of everything.

---

13. *you*: sing.
14. *you*: sing.
15. *you*: sing.
16. *you*: plur.

Women

87 God – (there is) no god but Him. He will indeed gather you to the Day of Resurrection – (there is) no doubt about it. Who is more truthful than God in report?

88 What is (the matter) with you? (Are there) two cohorts (of you) concerning the hypocrites, when God has overthrown them for what they have earned? Do you wish to guide the one whom God has led astray? Whomever God has led astray – you[17] will not find a way for him. **89** They want you[18] to disbelieve as they have disbelieved, and then you would be alike. Do not take any allies from them, until they emigrate in the way of God. If they turn back, seize them and kill them wherever you find them. Do not take any ally or helper from them, **90** except those who join a people with whom you have a treaty, or who come to you with their hearts restrained from fighting you or fighting their own people. If God had (so) pleased, He would indeed have given them power over you, and they would indeed have fought you. If they withdraw from you, and do not fight you but offer you peace, God has not made a way for you against them. **91** You will find others wishing that they were safe from you, and safe from their (own) people. Whenever they are returned to temptation, they are overwhelmed by it. If they do not withdraw from you alone, and offer you peace, and restrain their hands, seize them and kill them wherever you come upon them. Those (people) – We give you clear authority against them.

92 It is not for a believer to kill a believer, except by mistake. Whoever kills a believer by mistake, (the penalty is) the setting free of a believing slave, and compensation (is to be) paid to his family, unless they remit (it as) a freewill offering. If he[19] is from a people (who are) an enemy to you, and he is a believer, (the penalty is) the setting free of a believing slave. If he is from a people with whom you have a treaty, compensation (is to be) paid to his family and the setting free of a believing slave. Whoever does not find (the means to do that), (the penalty is) a fast for two months consecutively – a repentance (prescribed) by God. God is knowing, wise. **93** Whoever kills a believer intentionally, his payment is Gehenna – there to remain. God will be angry with him, and curse him, and prepare a great punishment for him.

94 You who believe! When you strike forth in the way of God, be discerning, and do not say to the one who offers you peace, 'You are not a believer,' seeking (the fleeting) goods of this present life. For (there are) many spoils with God. You (too) were like that before, but God bestowed favor on you. So be discerning. Surely God is aware of what you do.

95 Those of the believers who sit (at home) – other than the injured – are not equal with the ones who struggle in the way of God with their wealth and their lives. God favors in rank the ones who struggle with their wealth and their lives

---

17. *you*: sing.
18. *you*: plur.
19. *he*: i.e. the victim.

Women

over the ones who sit (at home). To each God has promised the good (reward), but God favors (with) a great reward the ones who struggle over the ones who sit (at home): **96** (higher) ranks from Him, and forgiveness and mercy. Surely God is forgiving, compassionate.

97 Surely those who – (when) the angels take them (while they are doing) themselves evil – they[20] will say, 'What (condition) were you in?' They[21] will say, 'We were weak on the earth.' They[22] will say, 'Was God's earth not wide (enough), so that you might have emigrated in it?' And those – their refuge is Gehenna – and it is an evil destination! – **98** except for the (truly) weak among the men, women, and children, (who) were not able (to devise) a plan and were not guided to a way (of escape). **99** Those – God may pardon them, (for) God is pardoning, forgiving. **100** Whoever emigrates in the way of God will find on the earth many places of refuge and abundance (of provisions). And whoever goes forth from his house, emigrating to God and His messenger, (and) then death overtakes him – his reward falls on God (to pay). Surely God is forgiving, compassionate.

101 When you strike forth on the earth, there is no blame on you to shorten the prayer, if you fear that those who disbelieve may attack you. Surely the disbelievers are your clear enemies. **102** When you are among them, and establish the prayer for them, let a contingent of them stand with you, and let them take their weapons. When they have prostrated themselves, let them be behind you, and let another contingent (which has) not prayed come (forward) and pray with you. Let them take their precautions and their weapons. Those who disbelieve want you to be oblivious of your weapons and your baggage. Then they would launch an attack on you (all at) once. (There is) no blame on you if you lay down your weapons because of the harmful effect of rain on you or (because) you are sick. But take your precautions. Surely God has prepared for the disbelievers a humiliating punishment. **103** When you[23] have finished the prayer, remember God, whether standing or sitting or (lying) on your sides. Then, when you are secure, observe the prayer. Surely the prayer is a written decree for the believers at appointed times. **104** But do not grow weak in seeking out the enemy. If you are suffering, surely they (too) are suffering as you are suffering, while what you hope for from God they do not hope for. God is knowing, wise.

105 Surely We have sent down to you the Book with the truth, so that you may judge between the people by what God has shown you. Do not be an advocate on behalf of the treacherous. **106** Ask forgiveness from God. Surely God is forgiving, compassionate. **107** Do not dispute on behalf of those who betray themselves. Surely God does not love anyone who is a traitor (or) sinner. **108** They hide themselves from the people, but they do not hide themselves from God. For

---

20. *they*: the angels.
21. *They*: those the angels take away.
22. *They*: the angels.
23. *you*: plur.

He is with them when they plan by night (with) the words He finds displeasing. God encompasses what they do. **109** There you are! Those who have disputed on their behalf in this present life, but who will dispute with God on their behalf on the Day of Resurrection? Or who will be a guardian over them? **110** Whoever does evil or does himself evil, (and) then asks forgiveness from God, he will find God is forgiving, compassionate. **111** Whoever earns sin, only earns it against himself. God is knowing, wise. **112** Whoever earns a mistake or sin, (and) then hurls it against an innocent person, will bear (the burden of) slander and clear sin. **113** If (it were) not (for the) favor of God on you, and His mercy, a contingent of them was indeed determined to lead you astray. But they only lead themselves astray; they will not harm you at all. God has sent down on you the Book and the wisdom, and He has taught you what you did not know. The favor of God on you is great. **114** (There is) no good in much of their secret talk, except for the one who commands voluntary giving, or what is right, or setting (things) right among the people. Whoever does that, seeking the approval of God – We shall give him a great reward. **115** But whoever breaks with the messenger after the guidance has become clear to him, and follows a way other (than that) of the believers – We shall turn him (over) to what he has turned to, and burn him in Gehenna – and it is an evil destination!

116 Surely God does not forgive (anything) being associated with Him, but He forgives what is other than that for whomever He pleases. Whoever associates (anything) with God has gone very far astray. **117** They only call on females instead of Him. They only call on a rebellious Satan. **118** God cursed him, and he said, 'I shall indeed take an obligatory portion of Your servants, **119** and I shall indeed lead them astray and fill them with longings, and I shall indeed command them and they will cut off the ears of the cattle. I shall indeed command them and they will alter the creation of God.' Whoever takes Satan as an ally, instead of God, has lost utterly (and) clearly. **120** He makes promises to them and fills them with longings. Yet Satan does not promise them (anything) but deception. **121** Those – their refuge is Gehenna, and they will not find any place of escape from it. **122** But those who have believed and done righteous deeds, We shall cause them to enter Gardens through which rivers flow, there to remain forever – the promise of God in truth! Who is more truthful than God in speaking?

123 (This) is not[24] (in accord) with your[25] wishful thinking, nor (in accord with the) wishful thinking of the People of the Book. Whoever does evil will be repaid with it, and he will not find for himself any ally or helper other than God. **124** But whoever does righteous deeds – whether male or female – and he is a believer, those will enter the Garden – and they will not be done evil in the slightest.

---

24. *(This) is not...*: the meaning of this sentence is obscure.

25. *your*: sing.

125 Who is better in religion than one who submits his face to God, and is a doer of good, and follows the creed of Abraham the Ḥanīf?[26] God took Abraham as a friend. 126 To God (belongs) whatever is in the heavens and whatever is on the earth. God encompasses everything.

127 They ask you for a pronouncement about women. Say: 'God makes a pronouncement to you about them, and what is recited to you in the Book (gives instruction) about female orphans to whom you do not give what is prescribed for them, though you wish to marry them, and (about) the weak among the children, and that you secure justice for the orphans. Whatever good you do, surely God knows about it.'

128 If a woman fears rebelliousness from her husband, or desertion, (there is) no blame on the two of them if they set (things) right between themselves. Setting (things) right is better, but people are prone to greed. If you do good and guard (yourselves) – surely God is aware of what you do.

129 You will not be able to act fairly among the women,[27] even though you are eager (to do so). But do not turn completely away (from one of them) so that you leave her, as it were, in suspense. If you set (things) right and guard (yourselves) – surely God is forgiving, compassionate. 130 But if the two of them separate, God will enrich each (of them) from His abundance. God is embracing, wise.

131 To God (belongs) whatever is in the heavens and whatever is on the earth. Certainly We have charged those who were given the Book before you, and you (as well), 'Guard (yourselves) against God!' But if you disbelieve – surely to God (belongs) whatever is in the heavens and whatever is on the earth. God is wealthy, praiseworthy.

132 To God (belongs) whatever is in the heavens and whatever is on the earth. God is sufficient as a guardian. 133 If He (so) pleases, He will do away with you, people, and bring others (in your place). God is powerful over that.

134 Whoever desires the reward of this world – with God is the reward of this world and the Hereafter. God is hearing, seeing.

135 You who believe! Be supervisors in justice, witnesses for God, even if it is against yourselves or your parents and family. Whether he be rich or poor, God (stands) closer to both of them. Do not follow (your vain) desire or you will (not) act fairly. If you turn aside or turn away – surely God is aware of what you do.

136 You who believe! Believe in God and His messenger, and the Book He has sent down on His messenger, and the Book which He sent down before (this). Whoever disbelieves in God and His angels, and His Books and His messengers, and the Last Day, has gone very far astray. 137 Surely those who have believed, then

---

26. *Ḥanīf*: meaning uncertain.
27. *the women*: i.e. their wives.

disbelieved, then believed (again), then disbelieved (again), (and) then increased in disbelief – God will not forgive them or guide them (to the) way.

138 Give the hypocrites the news that for them (there is) a painful punishment **139** – those who take the disbelievers as allies instead of the believers. Do they seek honor with them? Surely honor (belongs) to God altogether. **140** He has already sent down on you[28] in the Book: 'When you hear the signs of God being disbelieved and mocked, do not sit with them until they banter about some other topic. Otherwise you will surely be like them.' Surely God is going to gather the hypocrites and the disbelievers into Gehenna – all (of them). **141** (The hypocrites are) those who wait (to see what happens) with you.[29] If a victory comes to you from God, they say, 'Were we not with you?' But if a portion (of good fortune) falls to the disbelievers, they say, 'Did we not prevail over you, and protect you from the believers?' God will judge between you on the Day of Resurrection. God will not make a way for the disbelievers over the believers.

142 The hypocrites (try to) deceive God, but He deceives them. When they stand up for the prayer, they stand up in a lazy fashion, showing off (before) the people, but they do not remember God, except a little, **143** wavering between (this and) that, (belonging) neither to these nor to those. Whomever God leads astray – you[30] will not find a way for him.

144 You who believe! Do not take disbelievers as allies instead of the believers. Do you wish to give God clear authority against you?

145 Surely the hypocrites will be in the lowest level of the Fire, and you will not find for them any helper, **146** except those who turn (in repentance), and set (things) right, and hold fast to God, and devote their religion to God. Those are with the believers, and God will give the believers a great reward. **147** Why would God punish you, if you are thankful and believe? God is thankful, knowing.

148 God does not love the public utterance of evil words, except (by one) who has suffered evil. God is hearing, knowing. **149** If you do good openly or you hide it, or you pardon an evil – surely God is pardoning, powerful.

150 Surely those who disbelieve in God and His messengers, and wish to make a distinction between God and His messengers, and say, 'We believe in part, but disbelieve in part,' and wish to take a way between (this and) that, **151** those – they in truth are the disbelievers. And We have prepared for the disbelievers a humiliating punishment. **152** But those who believe in God and His messengers, and make no distinction between any of them, those – He will give them their rewards. God is forgiving, compassionate.

153 The People of the Book ask you to bring down on them a Book from the sky. They had already asked Moses for (something) greater than that, for they said,

---

28. *you*: plur.
29. *you*: plur.
30. *you*: sing.

Women

'Show us God openly!' So the thunderbolt took them for their evildoing. Then they took the calf, after the clear signs had come to them. But We pardoned them for that, and We gave Moses clear authority. **154** And We raised the mountain above them, with their covenant, and We said to them, 'Enter the gate in prostration.' And We said to them, 'Do not transgress the sabbath.' And We made a firm covenant with them. **155** So for their breaking their covenant, and their disbelief in the signs of God, and their killing the prophets without any right, and their saying, 'Our hearts are covered' – No! God set a seal on them for their disbelief, so they do not believe, except for a few – **156** and for their disbelief, and their saying against Mary a great slander, **157** and for their saying, 'Surely we killed the Messiah, Jesus, son of Mary, the messenger of God' – yet they did not kill him, nor did they crucify him, but it (only) seemed like (that) to them. Surely those who differ about him[31] are indeed in doubt about him.[32] They have no knowledge about him,[33] only the following of conjecture. Certainly they did not kill him. **158** No! God raised him up to Himself. God is mighty, wise. **159** Yet (there is) not one of the People of the Book except that he will indeed believe in it before his death, and on the Day of Resurrection he will be a witness against them.

160 So for the evildoing of those who are Jews, We have made (certain) good things forbidden to them which were permitted to them (before), and (also) for their keeping many (people) from the way of God. **161** And (for) their taking usury, when they were forbidden (to take) it, and (for) their consuming the wealth of the people by means of falsehood, We have prepared for the disbelievers among them a painful punishment. **162** But the ones who are firm in knowledge among them – and the believers – believe in what has been sent down to you, and what has been sent down before you. And the ones who observe the prayer, and who give the alms, and who believe in God and the Last Day, those – We shall give them a great reward.

163 Surely We have inspired you as We inspired Noah and the prophets after him, and as We inspired Abraham, and Ishmael, and Isaac, and Jacob, and the tribes, and Jesus, and Job, and Jonah, and Aaron, and Solomon, and We gave David (the) Psalms, **164** and messengers We have already recounted to you before, and messengers We have not recounted to you – but God spoke to Moses directly – **165** (and) messengers bringing good news and warning, so that the people might have no argument against God after (the coming of) the messengers. God is mighty, wise.

166 But God bears witness to what He has sent down to you – He sent it down with His knowledge – and the angels (also) bear witness. Yet God is sufficient as a witness. **167** Surely those who disbelieve and keep (people) from the way of God – they have gone very far astray. **168** Surely those who disbelieve and do evil – God

---

31. *him*: or 'it.'
32. *him*: or 'it.'
33. *him*: or 'it.'

Women

will not forgive them, nor will He guide them (to any) road, **169** except the road to Gehenna, there to remain forever. That is easy for God. **170** People! The messenger has brought you the truth from your Lord, so believe! (It will be) better for you. But if you disbelieve – surely to God (belongs) whatever is in the heavens and the earth. God is knowing, wise.

171 People of the Book! Do not go beyond the limits in your religion, and do not say about God (anything) but the truth. The Messiah, Jesus, son of Mary, was only a messenger of God, and His word, which He cast into Mary, and a spirit from Him. So believe in God and His messengers, but do not say, 'Three.' Stop! (It will be) better for you. God is only one God. Glory to Him! (Far be it) that He should have a son! To Him (belongs) whatever is in the heavens and whatever is on the earth. God is sufficient as a guardian. **172** The Messiah does not disdain to be a servant of God, nor will the angels, the ones brought near. Whoever disdains His service and becomes arrogant – He will gather them to Himself – all (of them). **173** As for those who believe and do righteous deeds, He will pay them their rewards in full and increase them from His favor. But as for those who have become disdainful and arrogant, He will punish them with a painful punishment. They will not find for themselves any ally or helper other than God.

174 People! A proof has come to you from your Lord: We have sent down to you a clear light. **175** As for those who believe in God and hold fast to Him, He will cause them to enter into mercy from Himself, and favor, and He will guide them to Himself (on) a straight path.

176 They ask you for a pronouncement. Say: 'God makes a pronouncement to you about the person who leaves no direct heirs. If a man perishes without children, but has a sister, then to her a half of what he leaves, and he is her heir if she has no children. If there are two (sisters), then to them two-thirds of what he leaves. If there are brothers and sisters, then to the male a share equal to two females. God makes (this) clear to you, so that you do not go astray. God has knowledge of everything.

Sūra 4

5 ✸ The Table

In the Name of God, the Merciful, the Compassionate

1 You who believe! Fulfill (your) pledges.

Permitted to you (to eat) is (any) animal of the livestock,[1] except for what is recited to you. The hunting (of wild game) is not permitted when you are (in a state of) sanctity. Surely God decrees whatever He wills.

2 You who believe! Do not profane the symbols[2] of God, nor the sacred month, nor the offering, nor the ornaments, nor (those) going to the Sacred House seeking favor from their Lord and approval. But when you are free (from your state of sanctity), hunt (wild game). Do not let hatred of the people who kept you from (going to) the Sacred Mosque provoke you to commit aggression. Help one another to piety and the guarding (of yourselves), and do not help each other to sin and enmity. Guard (yourselves) against God. Surely God is harsh in retribution.

3 Forbidden to you (to eat) are: the dead (animal), and the blood, and swine's flesh, and what has been dedicated to (a god) other than God, and the strangled (to death), and the beaten (to death), and the fallen (to death), and the gored (to death), and what a wild animal has devoured – except what you have slaughtered – and what has been sacrificed on stones. And (it is forbidden) that you should divide by divination arrows – that is wickedness for you.

Today those who disbelieve have no hope of (ever destroying) your religion. So do not fear them, but fear Me. Today I have perfected your religion for you, and I have completed My blessing on you, and I have approved Islam for you as a religion.

But if anyone is forced by hunger, without intending to sin – surely God is forgiving, compassionate.

4 They ask you what is permitted to them (to eat). Say: 'The good things are permitted to you, and what you have taught some of (your) hunting animals (to catch), training (them), (and) teaching them some of what God has taught you. So eat from what they catch for you, and mention the name of God over it, and guard (yourselves) against God. Surely God is quick at the reckoning.' **5** Today the good things are permitted to you, and the food of those who have been given the Book is permitted to you, and your food is permitted to them.

---

1. *livestock*: lit. 'cattle.'
2. *symbols*: meaning uncertain (Ar. *sha'ā'ir*).

The Table

(Permitted to you are) the chaste women among the believers, and the chaste women among those who have been given the Book before you, once you have given them their marriage gifts, taking (them) in marriage, not in immorality, nor taking (them) as secret lovers. Whoever disbelieves in the faith, his deed has come to nothing, and in the Hereafter he will be one of the losers.

6 You who believe! When you stand up for the prayer, wash your faces and your hands up to the elbows, and wipe your heads and your feet up to the ankles. If you are defiled, purify yourselves. If you are sick or on a journey, or if one of you has come from the toilet, or if you have touched women, and you do not find any water, take clean earth and wipe your faces and your hands with it. God does not wish to place any difficulty on you, but He wishes to purify you and to complete His blessing on you, so that you may be thankful.

7 Remember the blessing of God on you, and His covenant with which He bound you, when you said, 'We hear and obey.' Guard (yourselves) against God. Surely God knows what is in the hearts.

8 You who believe! Be supervisors for God, witnesses in justice, and do not let hatred of a people provoke you to act unfairly. Act fairly! It is nearer to guarding (yourselves). Guard (yourselves) against God. Surely God is aware of what you do. **9** God has promised those who believe and do righteous deeds (that there is) forgiveness for them and a great reward. **10** But those who disbelieve and call Our signs a lie – those are the companions of the Furnace.

11 You who believe! Remember the blessing of God on you. When a people were determined to stretch out their hands against you, He restrained their hands from you. Guard (yourselves) against God, and in God let the believers put their trust.

12 Certainly God took a covenant with the Sons of Israel, and We raised up among them twelve chieftains, and God said, 'Surely I am with you. If indeed you observe the prayer and give the alms, and believe in My messengers and support them, and lend to God a good loan, I shall indeed absolve you of your evil deeds, and cause you to enter Gardens through which rivers flow. But whoever of you disbelieves after that has gone astray from the right way.'

13 For their breaking their covenant, We cursed them and made their hearts hard. They alter words from their positions, and have forgotten part of what they were reminded of. You will continue to see treachery from them, except for a few of them. Yet pardon them and excuse (them). Surely God loves the doers of good.

14 And with those who say, 'Surely we are Christians,' We took a covenant, but they have forgotten part of what they were reminded of. So We stirred up enmity and hatred among them, until the Day of Resurrection, and (then) God will inform them about what they have done.

15 People of the Book! Our messenger has come to you, making clear to you much of what you have been hiding of the Book, and overlooking much. Now a light

The Table

and a clear Book from God has come to you. **16** By means of it God guides those who follow after His approval (in the) ways of peace, and He brings them out of the darkness to the light, by His permission, and guides them to a straight path.

17 Certainly they disbelieve who say, 'Surely God – He is the Messiah, son of Mary.' Say: 'Who could do anything against God if He wished to destroy the Messiah, son of Mary, and his mother, and whoever is on the earth – all (of them) together? To God (belongs) the kingdom of the heavens and the earth, and whatever is between them. He creates whatever He pleases. God is powerful over everything.'

18 The Jews and the Christians say, 'We are the sons of God, and His beloved.' Say: 'Then why does He punish you for your sins? No! You are human beings, (part) of what He created. He forgives whomever He pleases and He punishes whomever He pleases. To God (belongs) the kingdom of the heavens and the earth, and whatever is between them. To Him is the (final) destination.'

19 People of the Book! Our messenger has come to you, making (things) clear to you after an interval between the messengers, in case you should say, 'No bringer of good news has come to us, nor any warner.' Now a bringer of good news and a warner has come to you. God is powerful over everything.

20 (Remember) when Moses said to his people, 'My people! Remember the blessing of God on you, when He made prophets among you, and made you kings, and gave you what He had not given to any among all peoples. **21** My people! Enter the Holy Land which God has prescribed for you, and do not turn your backs, or you will turn out (to be) losers.' **22** They said, 'Moses! Surely (there is) an oppressive people in it, and we shall not (be able to) enter it until they depart from it. If they depart from it, we shall enter (it).' **23** Two men among those who feared (God), whom God had blessed, said, 'Enter (through) the gate against them. When you have entered it, you will be victorious. Put your trust in God, if you are believers.' **24** They said, 'Moses! Surely we shall never enter it as long as they remain in it. So you and your Lord go, and both of you fight. Surely we shall be sitting here.' **25** He said, 'My Lord, surely I have no control over (anyone) but myself and my brother. Make a separation between us and this wicked people.' **26** He[3] said, 'Surely it is forbidden to them for forty years, while they wander on the earth. So do not grieve over this wicked people.'

27 Recite to them the story of Adam's two sons in truth: when they both offered a sacrifice, and it was accepted from one of them, but was not accepted from the other. (One) said, 'I shall indeed kill you.' (The other) said, 'God only accepts (offerings) from the ones who guard (themselves). **28** If indeed you stretch out your hand against me, to kill me, (still) I shall not stretch out my hand against you, to kill you. Surely I fear God, Lord of all peoples. **29** Surely I wish that you would incur my sin and your sin, so that you may be one of the companions of the Fire. That is the reward of the evildoers.' **30** Then his (own) self compelled

---

3. *He*: God.

The Table

him to the killing of his brother. So he killed him and became one of the losers. **31** Then God raised up a raven, scratching in the earth, to show him how to hide the shame of his brother. He said, 'Woe is me! Am I unable to be like this raven, and hide the shame of my brother?' And then he became one of the regretful.

32 From that time We prescribed for the Sons of Israel that whoever kills a person, except (in retaliation) for another, or (for) fomenting corruption on the earth, (it is) as if he had killed all the people. And whoever gives (a person) life, (it is) as if he had given all the people life. Certainly Our messengers have brought them the clear signs, yet even after that many of them act wantonly on the earth.

33 The penalty (for) those who wage war (against) God and His messenger, and who strive in fomenting corruption on the earth, is that they be killed or crucified, or their hands and feet on opposite sides be cut off, or they be banished from the earth. That is a disgrace for them in this world, and in the Hereafter (there will be) a great punishment for them, **34** except those who turn (in repentance) before you have them in your power. Know that God is forgiving, compassionate.

35 You who believe! Guard (yourselves) against God, and seek access to Him, and struggle in His way, so that you may prosper. **36** Surely those who disbelieve, even if they had whatever is on the earth – all (of it) and as much again – to ransom (themselves) with it from punishment on the Day of Resurrection, it would not be accepted from them. For them (there is) a painful punishment. **37** They will wish to get out of the Fire, but they will not get out of it. For them (there is) a lasting punishment.

38 (As for) the male thief and the female thief: cut off their hands as a penalty for what they have done – a punishment from God. God is mighty, wise. **39** Whoever turns (in repentance) after his evildoing and sets (things) right – surely God will turn to him (in forgiveness). Surely God is forgiving, compassionate. **40** Do you not know that God – to Him (belongs) the kingdom of the heavens and the earth – He punishes whomever He pleases and He forgives whomever He pleases. God is powerful over everything.

41 Messenger! Do not let those who are quick to disbelief cause you sorrow. (They are) among those who say with their mouths, 'We believe,' but their hearts do not believe. Among those who are Jews (there are) those who listen to lies, (and who) listen to (other) people who have not come to you. They alter words from their positions, (and) say, 'If you are given it, take it, but if you are not given it, beware.' If God wishes to test anyone, you will not have any (help) for him against God. Those are the ones whose hearts God does not wish to purify. For them (there is) disgrace in this world, and in the Hereafter (there will be) a great punishment for them. **42** (They are) listeners to lies (and) consumers of what is forbidden. If they come to you, judge between them or turn away from them. If you turn away from them, they will not harm you at all. But if you judge, judge between them in justice. Surely God loves the ones who act fairly. **43** Yet how will they make you (their) judge, when they have the Torah, containing the judgment of God, (and) then turn away after that? Those (people) are not with the believers.

44 Surely We sent down the Torah, containing guidance and light. By means of it the prophets who had submitted rendered judgment for those who were Jews, and (so did) the rabbis and the teachers, with what they were entrusted of the Book of God, and they were witnesses to it. So do not fear the people, but fear Me, and do not sell My signs for a small price. Whoever does not judge by what God has sent down, those – they are the disbelievers. **45** We prescribed for them in it: 'The life for the life, and the eye for the eye, and the nose for the nose, and the ear for the ear, and the tooth for the tooth, and (for) the wounds retaliation.' But whoever remits it as a freewill offering, it will be an atonement for him. Whoever does not judge by what God has sent down, those – they are the evildoers.

46 And in their footsteps We followed up with Jesus, son of Mary, confirming what was with him of the Torah, and We gave him the Gospel, containing guidance and light, and confirming what was with him of the Torah, and as guidance and admonition to the ones who guard (themselves). **47** So let the People of the Gospel judge by what God has sent down in it. Whoever does not judge by what God has sent down, those – they are the wicked.

48 And We have sent down to you the Book with the truth, confirming what was with him of the Book, and as a preserver of it. So judge between them by what God has sent down, and do not follow their (vain) desires (away) from what has come to you of the truth. For each of you We have made a pathway and an open road. If God had (so) pleased, He would indeed have made you one community, but (He did not do so) in order to test you by what He has given you. So race (toward doing) good deeds. To God is your return – all (of you) – and then He will inform you about your differences. **49** (So) judge between them by what God has sent down, and do not follow their (vain) desires, and beware of them in case they tempt you (to turn away) from any part of what God has sent down to you. If they turn away, know that God intends to smite them for some of their sins. Surely many of the people are wicked indeed. **50** Is it the judgment of the (time of) ignorance they seek? Yet who is better in judgment than God, for a people who are certain (in their belief)?

51 You who believe! Do not take the Jews and the Christians as allies. They are allies of each other. Whoever of you takes them as allies is already one of them. Surely God does not guide the people who are evildoers. **52** Yet you[4] see those in whose hearts is a sickness – they are quick (to turn) to them, (and) they say, 'We fear that disaster may smite us.' But it may be that God will bring the victory, or some command from Himself, and they will be full of regret for what they kept secret within themselves. **53** But those who believe will say, 'Are these those who

---

4. *you*: sing.

The Table

swore by God the most solemn of their oaths: (that) surely they were indeed with you? Their deeds have come to nothing, and they are the losers.'

54 You who believe! Whoever of you turns back from his religion, God will bring (another) people whom He loves, and who love Him, (who are) humble toward the believers, mighty toward the disbelievers, (who) struggle in the way of God, and do not fear the blame of anyone. That is the favor of God. He gives it to whomever He pleases. God is embracing, knowing. 55 Your only ally is God, and His messenger, and the believers who observe the prayer and give the alms, and who bow. 56 Whoever takes God as an ally, and His messenger, and those who believe – surely the faction of God, they are the victors.

57 You who believe! Do not take those who take your religion in mockery and jest as allies, (either) from those who were given the Book before you, or (from) the disbelievers. Guard (yourselves) against God, if you are believers. 58 When you make the call to prayer, they take it in mockery and jest. That is because they are a people who do not understand. 59 Say: 'People of the Book! Do you take vengeance on us (for any other reason) than that we believe in God and what has been sent down to us, and what was sent down before (this), and because most of you are wicked?' 60 Say: 'Shall I inform you of (something) worse than that? Retribution with God! Whomever God has cursed, and whomever He is angry with – some of whom He made apes, and pigs, and slaves of al-Ṭāghūt[5] – those are in a worse situation and farther astray from the right way.'

61 When they come to you,[6] they say, 'We believe,' but they have already entered in disbelief and will depart in it. God knows what they are concealing. 62 You see many of them being quick to sin and enmity, and consuming what is forbidden. Evil indeed is what they have done! 63 Why do the rabbis and the teachers not forbid them from their saying what is a sin and (from) their consuming what is forbidden? Evil indeed is what they have done!

64 The Jews say, 'The hand of God is chained.' (May) their hands (be) chained, and (may) they (be) cursed for what they say! No! Both His hands are outstretched: He gives as He pleases. What has been sent down to you from your Lord will indeed increase many of them in insolent transgression and disbelief. We have cast enmity and hatred among them until the Day of Resurrection. Whenever they light the fire of war, God extinguishes it. But they strive (at) fomenting corruption on the earth, and God does not love the fomenters of corruption. 65 Had the People of the Book believed and guarded (themselves), We would indeed have absolved them of their evil deeds, and caused them to enter Gardens of Bliss. 66 Had they observed the Torah and the Gospel, and what was sent down to them from their Lord, they would indeed have eaten from (what was) above them and

---

5. *slaves of al-Ṭāghūt*: or 'worshippers of other gods,' or perhaps 'of Satan.'
6. *you*: plur.

The Table

from (what was) beneath their feet. Some of them are a moderate community, but most of them – evil is what they do.

67 Messenger! Deliver what has been sent down to you from your Lord. If you do not, you have not delivered His message. God will protect you from the people. Surely God does not guide the people who are disbelievers. **68** Say: 'People of the Book! You are (standing) on nothing until you observe the Torah and the Gospel, and what has been sent down to you from your Lord.' But what has been sent down to you from your Lord will indeed increase many of them in insolent transgression and disbelief. So do not grieve over the people who are disbelievers. **69** Surely those who believe, and those who are Jews, and the Sabians,[7] and the Christians – whoever believes in God and the Last Day, and does righteousness – (there will be) no fear on them, nor will they sorrow.

70 Certainly We took a covenant with the Sons of Israel, and We sent messengers to them. Whenever a messenger brought them what they themselves did not desire, some they called liars and some they killed. **71** They thought that there would be no trouble (for them), so they became blind and deaf. Then God turned to them (in forgiveness), (and) then many of them became blind and deaf (again). Yet God sees what they do.

72 Certainly they have disbelieved who say, 'Surely God – He is the Messiah, son of Mary,' when the Messiah said, 'Sons of Israel! Serve God, my Lord and your Lord. Surely he who associates (anything) with God, God has forbidden him (from) the Garden, and his refuge is the Fire. The evildoers have no helpers.' **73** Certainly they have disbelieved who say, 'Surely God is the third of three,' when (there is) no god but one God. If they do not stop what they are saying, a painful punishment will indeed strike those of them who disbelieve. **74** Will they not turn to God (in repentance) and ask forgiveness from Him? God is forgiving, compassionate. **75** The Messiah, son of Mary, was only a messenger. Messengers have passed away before him. His mother was a truthful woman. They both ate food. See how We make clear the signs to them, then see how deluded they are. **76** Say: 'Do you serve what has no power to (cause) you harm or benefit, instead of God (alone)? God – He is the Hearing, the Knowing.' **77** Say: 'People of the Book! Do not go beyond the limits in your religion, (saying anything) other than the truth, and do not follow (the vain) desires of a people who went astray before (you). They have led many astray, and they have gone astray from the right way.'

78 Those of the Sons of Israel who disbelieved were cursed by the tongue of David and Jesus, son of Mary – that was because they disobeyed and were transgressing. **79** They did not forbid each other any evildoing. Evil indeed is what they have done! **80** You see many of them taking those who disbelieve as allies. Evil indeed is what they have sent forward for themselves! That (is why) God became angry with them, and in the punishment they will remain. **81** If they had believed in

---

7. *Sabians*: it is not clear who the Ṣābi'ūn are.

The Table

God and the prophet, and what has been sent down to him, they would not have taken them as friends. But many of them are wicked.

82 Certainly you will find that the most violent of people in enmity to the believers are the Jews and the idolaters. Certainly you will find that the closest of them in affection to the believers are those who say, 'We are Christians.' That is because (there are) priests and monks among them, and because they are not arrogant. **83** When they hear what has been sent down to the messenger, you see their eyes overflowing with tears because of what they recognize of the truth. They say, 'Our Lord, we believe, so write us down among those who bear witness. **84** Why should we not believe in God and (in) what has come to us of the truth, when we are eager for our Lord to cause us to enter with the people who are righteous?' **85** So God has rewarded them for what they said (with) Gardens through which rivers flow, there to remain. That is the reward for the doers of good. **86** But those who disbelieve and call Our signs a lie, those are the companions of the Furnace.

87 You who believe! Do not forbid the good things which God has permitted to you, and do not transgress. Surely God does not love the transgressors. **88** Eat from what God has provided you as permitted (and) good, and guard (yourselves) against God – the One in whom you are believers.

89 God will not take you to task for a slip in your oaths, but He will take you to task for what you have pledged by oath. Atonement for it is the feeding of ten poor persons with the average (amount of food) which you feed your households, or clothing them, or the setting free of a slave. Whoever does not find (the means to do that), (the penalty is) a fast for three days. That is the atonement for your oaths when you have sworn (them, and broken them). But guard your oaths! In this way God makes clear to you His signs, so that you may be thankful.

90 You who believe! Wine, games of chance, stones, and divination arrows are an abomination, part of the work of Satan. So avoid it in order that you may prosper. **91** Satan only wishes to cause enmity and hatred among you with wine and games of chance, and to keep you from the remembrance of God and from the prayer. Will you refrain? **92** Obey God, and obey the messenger, and beware! If you do turn away, know that only (dependent) on Our messenger is the clear delivery (of the message).

93 (There is) no blame on those who believe and do righteous deeds for what they may have eaten, so long as they guard (themselves) and believe and do righteous deeds, (and) then (again) guard (themselves) and believe, (and) then (again) guard (themselves) and do good. God loves the doers of good.

94 You who believe! God will indeed test you with some of the wild game which your hands and spears obtain, so that God may know who fears Him in the unseen. Whoever transgresses after that, for him (there is) a painful punishment.

95 You who believe! Do not kill wild game when you are (in a state of) sanctity. Whoever of you kills it intentionally, (there is) a penalty equivalent (to) what he

The Table

has killed from the livestock – as two just men among you will determine it – as an offering to reach the Ka'ba. Or (there is) a penalty of the feeding of poor persons, or the equivalent of that in fasting, so that he may taste the consequence of his action. God pardons whatever is past, but whoever returns (to repeat his offense) – God will take vengeance on him. God is mighty, a taker of vengeance.

96 Permitted to you is the wild game of the sea and its food, as a provision for you and for the travelers. But forbidden to you is the wild game on the shore, as long as you are (in a state of) sanctity. Guard (yourselves) against God, the One to whom you will be gathered.

97 God has made the Ka'ba – the Sacred House – an establishment for the people, and (also) the sacred month, the offering, and the ornaments. That is so that you may know that God knows whatever is in the heavens and whatever is on the earth, and that God has knowledge of everything. **98** Know that God is harsh in retribution, and that God is forgiving, compassionate. **99** Nothing (depends) on the messenger except the delivery (of the message). God knows what you[8] reveal and what you conceal.

100 Say: 'The bad and the good are not equal, even though the abundance of bad may cause you to wonder.' Guard (yourselves) against God – those (of you) with understanding! – so that you may prosper.

101 You who believe! Do not ask about anything which, if it were disclosed to you, would distress you. But if you do ask about it, when the Qur'ān is being sent down, it will be disclosed to you. God pardons it, (for) God is forgiving, forbearing. **102** A people before you asked about it, (and) then became disbelievers in it. **103** God has not appointed any baḥīra or sā'iba or waṣīla or ḥāmi,[9] but those who disbelieve forge lies against God. Most of them do not understand. **104** When it is said to them, 'Come to what God has sent down, and to the messenger,' they say, 'What we found our fathers doing is (good) enough for us.' Even if their fathers had no knowledge and were not (rightly) guided? **105** You who believe! Look to yourselves. No one who goes astray can harm you, if you are (rightly) guided. To God is your return – all (of you) – and then He will inform you about what you have done.

106 You who believe! When death approaches one of you, the testimony among you at the time (of making) bequests will be (that of) two just men of you, or two others of (a people) other than you, if you strike forth on the earth and the smiting of death smites you. Detain them both after the prayer, and let them both swear by God, if you have your doubts (about them): 'We will not sell it[10] for a price, even if he happens to be a family member, and we will not conceal

---

8. *you*: plur.
9. *baḥīra or sā'iba or waṣīla or ḥāmi*: perhaps a reference to different kinds of animals dedicated to other gods (cf. Q6.136–139).
10. *it*: their testimony.

The Table

the testimony of God. Surely then we would indeed be among the sinners.' **107** If it is discovered that they both (were guilty of) sin,[11] let two others take their place, from those who have a rightful claim against the two former (false witnesses), and let them both swear by God: 'Certainly our testimony is truer than the testimony of the other two, and we have not transgressed. Surely then we would indeed be among the evildoers.' **108** That will make it more likely that they will give testimony directly, or (else) they will be afraid that (their) oaths will be turned back after they have sworn them. Guard (yourselves) against God and hear! God does not guide the people who are wicked.

109 On the Day when God gathers the messengers, He will say, 'What response were you given?' They will say, 'We have no knowledge. Surely You – You are the Knower of the unseen.'

110 (Remember) when God said, 'Jesus, son of Mary! Remember My blessing on you and on your mother, when I supported you with the holy spirit, (and) you spoke to the people (while you were still) in the cradle, and in adulthood. And when I taught you the Book and the wisdom, and the Torah and the Gospel. And when you created the form of a bird from clay by My permission, and you breathed into it, and it became a bird by My permission, and you healed the blind and the leper by My permission. And when you brought forth the dead by My permission, and when I restrained the Sons of Israel from (violence against) you. When you brought them the clear signs, those among them who had disbelieved said, "This is nothing but clear magic."'

111 (Remember) when I inspired the disciples: 'Believe in Me and in My messenger.' They said, 'We believe. Bear witness that we submit.' **112** And when the disciples said, 'Jesus, son of Mary! Is your Lord able to send down on us a table from the sky?,' he said, 'Guard (yourselves) against God, if you are believers.' **113** They said, 'We wish to eat from it and satisfy our hearts, so that we may know with certainty that you have spoken truthfully to us, and that we may be among the witnesses to it.' **114** Jesus, son of Mary, said, 'God! Our Lord, send down on us a table from the sky, to be a festival for us – for the first of us and last of us – and a sign from You. Provide for us, (for) You are the best of providers.' **115** God said, 'Surely I am going to send it down on you. Whoever of you disbelieves after that – surely I shall punish him (with) a punishment (as) I have not punished anyone among all peoples.'

116 (Remember) when God said, 'Jesus, son of Mary! Did you say to the people, "Take me and my mother as two gods instead of God (alone)"?' He said, 'Glory to You! It is not for me to say what I have no right (to say). If I had said it, You would have known it. You know what is within me, but I do not know what is within You. Surely You – You are the Knower of the unseen. **117** I only said to them what You commanded me: "Serve God, my Lord and your Lord!" And

---

11. *sin*: of giving false testimony.

The Table

I was a witness over them as long as I was among them. But when You took me, You became the Watcher over them. You are a Witness over everything. **118** If You punish them – surely they are Your servants. If You forgive them – surely You are the Mighty, the Wise.' **119** God said, 'This is the Day when their truthfulness will benefit the truthful. For them (there are) Gardens through which rivers flow, there to remain forever. God is pleased with them, and they are pleased with Him. That is the great triumph!' **120** To God (belongs) the kingdom of the heavens and the earth, and whatever is in them. He is powerful over everything.

6 ❖ Livestock

In the Name of God, the Merciful, the Compassionate

1 Praise (be) to God, who created the heavens and the earth, and made the darkness and the light! Then (despite that) those who disbelieve equate (others) with their Lord. **2** He (it is) who created you from clay, then decreed a time – and a time appointed by Him – then (despite that) you are in doubt. **3** He is God in the heavens and on the earth. He knows your secret and your public utterance, and He knows what you earn. **4** Yet not a sign comes to them from the signs of their Lord without their turning away from it. **5** They called the truth a lie when it came to them, but the story of what they were mocking will come to them.

6 Do they not see how many a generation We have destroyed before them? We established them on the earth in a way in which We have not established you, and We sent the sky (down) on them in abundance (of rain), and made rivers to flow beneath them, and then We destroyed them because of their sins, and produced another generation after them. **7** Even if We had sent down on you[1] a Book (written) on papyrus, and they touched it with their hands, those who disbelieve would indeed have said, 'This is nothing but clear magic.' **8** They say, 'If only an angel were sent down on him.' Even if We had sent down an angel, the matter would indeed have been decided, (and) then they would not be spared. **9** Even if We had made him an angel, We would indeed have made him a man, and have confused for them what they are confusing. **10** Certainly messengers have been mocked before you, but those of them who ridiculed (were) overwhelmed (by) what they were mocking. **11** Say: 'Travel the earth and see how the end was for those who called (it) a lie.'

12 Say: 'To whom (belongs) whatever is in the heavens and the earth?' Say: 'To God. He has prescribed mercy for Himself. He will indeed gather you to the Day of Resurrection – (there is) no doubt about it. Those who have lost their (own) selves, they do not believe. **13** To Him (belongs) whatever dwells in the night and the day. He is the Hearing, the Knowing.'

14 Say: 'Shall I take any other ally than God, Creator of the heavens and the earth, when He feeds (others) and is not fed?' Say: 'Surely I have been commanded to be the first of those who have submitted,' and: 'Do not be one of the idolaters!' **15** Say: 'Surely I fear, if I disobey my Lord, the punishment of a great Day.' **16** Whoever

---

1. *you*: sing.

Livestock

is turned from it on that Day – He has had compassion on him. That is the clear triumph! **17** If God touches you[2] with any harm, (there is) no one to remove it but Him, and if He touches you with any good – He is powerful over everything. **18** He is the Supreme One above His servants. He is the Wise, the Aware.

19 Say: 'What thing (is) greater as a witness?' Say: 'God is witness between me and you, and I have been inspired (with) this Qur'ān so that I may warn you by means of it, and whomever it reaches. Do you indeed bear witness that (there are) other gods with God?' Say: 'I do not bear witness.' Say: 'He is only one God. Surely I am free of what you associate.' **20** Those to whom We have given the Book recognize it, as they recognize their own sons. Those who have lost their (own) selves, they do not believe. **21** Who is more evil than the one who forges a lie against God, or calls His signs a lie? Surely the evildoers will not prosper. **22** On the Day when We shall gather them – all (of them) – We shall say to those who associated, 'Where are your associates whom you used to claim (as gods)?' **23** Then their only excuse will be to claim, 'By God, our Lord! We have not been idolaters.' **24** See how they lie against themselves, and (how) what they forged has abandoned them!

25 (There are) some of them who listen to you, but We have made coverings over their hearts, so that they do not understand it, and a heaviness in their ears. If they see any sign, they do not believe in it, so that when they come to dispute with you, those who disbelieve say, 'This is nothing but old tales.' **26** They keep (others) from it, and keep (themselves) from it, but they only destroy themselves, though they do not realize (it). **27** If (only) you could see when they are made to stand before the Fire: they will say, 'Would that we (could) be returned, and had not called the signs of our Lord a lie, but were among the believers.' **28** No! What they were hiding before has (now) become apparent to them. Even if they were returned, they would indeed return to what they were forbidden. Surely they are liars indeed!

29 They say, 'There is nothing but our present life. We are not going to be raised up.' **30** If (only) you could see when they are made to stand before their Lord: He will say, 'Is this not the truth?' They will say, 'Yes indeed! By our Lord!' He will say, 'Taste the punishment for what you were disbelieving.' **31** Lost (are) those who call the meeting with God a lie – until, when the Hour comes upon them unexpectedly, they say, 'Alas for us, because of what we neglected concerning it!' They bear their burdens on their backs. Is it not a fact that evil is what they bear? **32** This present life is nothing but jest and diversion. Yet the Home of the Hereafter is indeed better for the ones who guard (themselves). Will you not understand?

33 We know that what they say causes you[3] sorrow. Yet surely they do not call you a liar, but the evildoers are denying the signs of God. **34** Certainly messengers

---

2. *you*: sing.
3. *you*: sing.

Livestock

have been called liars before you, yet they patiently endured being called liars, and suffered harm, until Our help came to them. No one can change the words of God. Certainly some of the story has (already) come to you about the envoys (before you). **35** But if their aversion is hard on you, (even) if you were able to seek out an opening in the earth, or a ladder into the sky, to bring them a sign [. . .].[4] If God had (so) pleased, He would indeed have gathered them to the guidance. Do not be one of the ignorant. **36** Only those who hear respond, but the dead – God will raise them up. Then to Him they will be returned.

37 They (also) say, 'If only a sign were sent down on him from his Lord.' Say: 'Surely God is able to send down a sign,' but most of them do not know (it). **38** (There is) no creature on the earth, nor (any) bird flying with both its wings, but (they are) communities like you. We have not neglected anything in the Book. Then to their Lord they will be gathered. **39** Those who call Our signs a lie are deaf and speechless in the darkness. Whomever God pleases, He leads astray, and whomever He pleases, He places him on a straight path. **40** Say: 'Do you see yourselves? If the punishment of God comes upon you, or the Hour comes upon you, will you call on (any god) other than God, if you are truthful?' **41** No! You will call on Him, and He will remove what you call on Him for, if He pleases, and you will forget what you associate.

42 Certainly We have sent to communities before you, and We seized them with violence and hardship, so that they might humble themselves. **43** If only they had humbled themselves when Our violence came upon them! But their hearts were hard, and Satan made what they were doing appear enticing to them. **44** So when they forgot what they were reminded of, We opened on them the gates of everything, until they gloated over what they were given, when (once again) We seized them unexpectedly, and suddenly they were in despair. **45** So the last remnant of the people who did evil was cut off. Praise (be) to God, Lord of all peoples!

46 Say: 'Do you see? If God takes away your hearing and your sight, and sets a seal on your hearts, who is a god other than God to bring it (back) to you?' See how We vary the signs? Then they (still) turn away. **47** Say: 'Do you see yourselves? If the punishment of God comes upon you, unexpectedly or openly, will any be destroyed but the people who are evildoers?' **48** We send the envoys only as bringers of good news and warners. Whoever believes and sets (things) right – (there will be) no fear on them, nor will they sorrow. **49** But those who call Our signs a lie – the punishment will touch them because they were acting wickedly.

50 Say: 'I do not say to you, "The storehouses of God are with me." I do not know the unseen, nor do I say to you, "I am an angel." I only follow what I am inspired (with).' Say: 'Are the blind and the sighted equal? Will you not reflect?'

---

4. [. . .]: there may be a lacuna here, but the meaning is that even if the Prophet could miraculously descend into the earth or ascend into heaven, the disbelievers would still not be convinced.

Livestock

51 Warn by means of it those who fear that they will be gathered to their Lord – they have no ally and no intercessor other than Him – so that they may guard (themselves). **52** And do not drive away those who call on their Lord in the morning and the evening, desiring His face. Nothing of their account (falls) on you, and nothing of your account (falls) on them, (that) you should drive them away and so become one of the evildoers. **53** In this way We have tested some of them by means of others, so that they will say, 'Are these (the ones) on whom God has bestowed favor among us?' Is it not God (who) knows the thankful? **54** When those who believe in Our signs come to you, say: 'Peace (be) upon you! Your Lord has prescribed mercy for Himself. Whoever of you does evil in ignorance, (and) then turns (in repentance) after that and sets (things) right – surely He is forgiving, compassionate.' **55** In this way We make the signs distinct, and (We do this) so that the way of the sinners may become clear.

56 Say: 'Surely I am forbidden to serve those whom you call on instead of God.' Say: 'I do not follow your (vain) desires, (for) then I would indeed have gone astray, and not be one of the (rightly) guided.' **57** Say: 'I (stand) on a clear sign from my Lord, but you have called it a lie. What you seek to hurry is not in my power. Judgment (belongs) only to God. He recounts the truth, and He is the best of judges.' **58** Say: 'If what you seek to hurry were in my power, the matter would indeed have been decided between you and me. God knows about the evildoers.'

59 With Him are the keys of the unseen. No one knows them but Him. He knows whatever is on the shore and the sea. Not a leaf falls but He knows of it. (There is) not a grain in the darkness of the earth, and nothing ripe or withered, but (it is recorded) in a clear Book. **60** He (it is) who takes you in the night, and He knows what you have earned in the day. Then He raises you up in it, so that an appointed time may be completed. Then to Him is your return, (and) then He will inform you about what you have done. **61** He is the Supreme One over His servants. He sends watchers over you, until, when death comes to one of you, Our messengers take him – and they do not neglect (their duty). **62** Then they are returned to God, their true Protector. Is it not a fact that judgment (belongs) to Him? He is the quickest of reckoners.

63 Say: 'Who rescues you from the dangers of the shore and the sea? You call on Him in humility and in secret: "If indeed He rescues us from this, we shall indeed be among the thankful."' **64** Say: 'God rescues you from it, and from every distress, (but) then you associate.'[5] **65** Say: 'He is the One able to raise up punishment against you, from above you or from beneath your feet, or to confuse you (into different) parties, and make some of you taste violence from others.' See how We vary the signs, so that they may understand. **66** But your people have called it a lie, when it is the truth. Say: 'I am not a guardian over you. **67** Every prophecy will come true. Soon you will know!'

---

5. *associate*: other gods with God.

Livestock

68 When you see those who banter about Our signs, turn away from them until they banter about some other topic. If Satan makes you forget (this), do not sit, after (you give) the Reminder, with the people who are evildoers. **69** Nothing of their account (falls) on the ones who guard (themselves), but (it is) a reminder, so that they (too) may guard (themselves). **70** Leave those who take their religion as jest and diversion. This present life has deceived them. Remind (them) by means of it, in case a person be given up to destruction for what he has earned. He has no ally and no intercessor other than God. Even if he were to offer any equal compensation, it would not be accepted from him. Those are the ones who are given up to destruction for what they have earned. For them (there will be) a drink of boiling (water) and a painful punishment, because they were disbelieving.

71 Say: 'Shall we call on what does not benefit us or harm us, instead of God (alone), and turn back on our heels after God has guided us? – Like the one whom the satans have lured on the earth, (and he is) confused, though he has companions who call him to the guidance (saying): "Come to us"?' Say: 'Surely the guidance of God – it is the (true) guidance, and we have been commanded to submit to the Lord of all peoples, **72** and (to say), "Observe the prayer and guard (yourselves) against Him, (for) He is the One to whom you will be gathered."' **73** He (it is) who created the heavens and the earth in truth. On the day when He says 'Be!' it is. His word is the truth, and the kingdom (will belong) to Him on the Day when there will be a blast on the trumpet. (He is) the Knower of the unseen and the seen. He is the Wise, the Aware.

74 (Remember) when Abraham said to his father Āzar: 'Do you take idols as gods? Surely I see you and your people are clearly astray.' **75** In this way We were showing Abraham the kingdom of the heavens and the earth, and (this took place) so that he might be one of those who are certain. **76** When night descended on him, he saw a star. He said, 'This is my Lord.' But when it set, he said, 'I do not love what vanishes.' **77** When he saw the moon rising, he said, 'This is my Lord.' But when it set, he said, 'Surely if my Lord does not guide me, I shall indeed be one of the people who go astray.' **78** When he saw the sun rising, he said, 'This is my Lord – this is greater!' But when it set, he said, 'My people! Surely I am free of what you associate. **79** Surely I have turned my face to Him who created the heavens and the earth – a Ḥanīf.[6] I am not one of the idolaters.' **80** But his people disputed with him. He said, 'Do you dispute with me about God, when He has indeed guided me? I do not fear what you associate with Him, unless (it be) that my Lord wills something (against me). My Lord comprehends everything in knowledge. Will you not take heed? **81** How should I fear what you have associated, when you are not afraid to associate with God what He has not sent down on you any authority for?' Which of the two groups has (more) right to security, if you know? **82** Those who have believed, and have not confused their belief with evildoing, those – for them (there is) the (true) security, and they are (rightly)

---

6. *Ḥanīf*: meaning uncertain.

guided. **83** That (was) Our argument. We gave it to Abraham against his people. We raise in rank whomever We please. Surely your Lord is wise, knowing.

84 And We granted him Isaac and Jacob – each one We guided, and Noah We guided before (them) – and of his descendants (were) David, and Solomon, and Job, and Joseph, and Moses, and Aaron – in this way We repay the doers of good – **85** and Zachariah, and John, and Jesus, and Elijah – each one was of the righteous – **86** and Ishmael, and Elisha, and Jonah, and Lot – each one We favored over all peoples **87** – and some of their fathers, and their descendants, and their brothers. We chose them and guided them to a straight path. **88** That is the guidance of God. He guides by means of it whomever He pleases of His servants. If they had associated, what they did would indeed have come to nothing for them. **89** Those are the ones to whom We gave the Book, and the judgment, and the prophetic office. If these (people) disbelieve in it, We have already entrusted it to a people who do not disbelieve in it. **90** Those are the ones whom God has guided. Follow their guidance. Say: 'I do not ask you for any reward for it. It is nothing but a reminder to all peoples.'

91 They have not measured God (with) due measure, when they said, 'God has not sent down anything on a human being.' Say: 'Who sent down the Book which Moses brought as a light and a guidance for the people? You make it (into) sheets of papyrus – you reveal (some of) it, but you hide much (of it). And you were taught what you did not know – neither you nor your fathers.' Say: 'God,' and leave them in their banter (while) they jest.

92 This is a Book: We have sent it down, blessed, confirming what was before it. And (We sent it down) so that you may warn the Mother of Towns and those around it. Those who believe in the Hereafter believe in it, and they keep guard over their prayers. **93** Who is more evil than the one who forges a lie against God, or says, 'I am inspired,' when he is not inspired at all, or the one who says, 'I will send down the equivalent of what God has sent down'?

If (only) you could see when the evildoers are in the throes of death, and the angels are stretching out their hands (saying): 'Out with yourselves! Today you are repaid (with) the punishment of humiliation, because you spoke about God (something) other than the truth, and (because) you behaved arrogantly toward His signs.' **94** 'Certainly you have come to Us individually, as We created you the first time, and you have left what We bestowed on you behind your backs. Nor do We see with you your intercessors, whom you claimed to be associates (with God) on your behalf. Certainly (the bond) between you has been cut, and what you used to claim (as gods) has abandoned you.'

95 Surely God is the splitter of the grain and the date seed. He brings forth the living from the dead, and brings forth the dead from the living. That is God. How are you (so) deluded? **96** (He is) the splitter of the dawn, and has made the night for rest, and the sun and moon for reckoning. That is the decree of the Mighty, the Knowing. **97** He (it is) who has made the stars for you, so that you might be

Livestock

guided by them in the darkness of the shore and the sea. We have made the signs distinct for a people who know. **98** And He (it is) who produced you from one person, and (gave you) a dwelling place and a place of deposit. We have made the signs distinct for a people who understand. **99** He (it is) who has sent down water from the sky, and We have brought forth by means of it vegetation of every (kind), and brought forth green (leaves). We bring forth from it thick-clustered grain, and from the date palm, from its sheath, (We bring forth) bunches of dates near (at hand), and gardens of grapes, and olives, and pomegranates, alike and different. Look at its fruit, when it bears fruit, and its ripening. Surely in that are signs indeed for a people who believe.

100 They make the jinn associates with God, when He created them, and they assign to Him sons and daughters without any knowledge. Glory to Him! He is exalted above what they allege. **101** Originator of the heavens and the earth – how can He have a son when He has no consort, (and) when He created everything and has knowledge of everything? **102** That is God, your Lord. (There is) no god but Him, Creator of everything. So serve Him! He is guardian over everything. **103** Sight does not reach Him, but He reaches sight. He is the Astute, the Aware.

104 Now evidence has come to you from your Lord: whoever sees – it is to his advantage, and whoever is blind – it is to his disadvantage. I am not a watcher over you. **105** In this way We vary the signs, so that they will say, 'You have studied,' and that We may make it clear to a people who know. **106** Follow what you are inspired (with) from your Lord – (there is) no god but Him – and turn away from the idolaters. **107** If God had (so) pleased, they would not have been idolaters. We have not made you a watcher over them, nor are you a guardian over them. **108** Do not revile those (gods) on whom they call instead of God, or they will revile God in enmity without any knowledge. In this way We make their deed(s) appear enticing to every community. Then to their Lord is their return, and He will inform them about what they have done.

109 They have sworn by God the most solemn of their oaths: if indeed a sign comes to them, they will indeed believe in it. Say: 'The signs (are) only with God.' What will make you realize that, when it does come, they will not believe? **110** We shall turn their hearts and their sight away (from the sign), just as (We did when) they did not believe in it the first time, and We shall leave them in their insolent transgression, wandering blindly. **111** Even if We had sent down the angels to them, and the dead had spoken to them, and (even if) We had gathered together everything against them head on, they would (still) not believe, unless God (so) pleased. But most of them are ignorant.

112 In this way We have assigned to every prophet an enemy – satans of the humans and jinn – some of them inspiring others (with) decorative speech as a deception. If your Lord had (so) pleased, they would not have done it. So leave them and what they forge. **113** And (it is) so that the hearts of those who do not believe in the Hereafter may incline to it, and that they may be delighted by it, and that they may acquire what they are acquiring. **114** Shall I seek (anyone) other than God as a judge? He (it is) who has sent down to you[7] the Book, set forth distinctly. Those to whom We have (already) given the Book know that it is sent down from your Lord with the truth. Do not be one of the doubters.

115 Perfect is the word of your Lord in truth and justice. No one can change His words. He is the Hearing, the Knowing. **116** If you[8] obey the majority of those on the earth, they will lead you astray from the way of God. They only follow conjecture and they only guess. **117** Surely your Lord – He knows who goes astray from His way and He knows the ones who are (rightly) guided.

118 Eat from that over which the name of God has been mentioned, if you are believers in His signs. **119** What is (the matter) with you that you do not eat from that over which the name of God has been mentioned, when He has already made distinct for you what He has forbidden you (to eat), unless you are forced to (eat) it? Surely many are indeed led astray by their (vain) desires without realizing (it). Surely your Lord – He knows about the transgressors. **120** Forsake (both) obvious and hidden sin. Surely those who earn sin will be repaid for what they have earned. **121** Do not eat that over which the name of God has not been mentioned. Surely it is wickedness indeed! Surely the satans inspire their allies, so that they may dispute with you. If you obey them, surely you will be idolaters indeed! **122** Is the one who was dead, and We gave him life (again), and made for him a light to walk by among the people, like the one who is to be compared to (a person) in the darkness from which he never emerges? In this way what they have done was made to appear enticing to the disbelievers.

123 In this way We have placed in every town great ones among its sinners, so that they may scheme there. Yet they do not scheme against (anyone) but themselves, though they do not realize (it). **124** When a sign comes to them, they say, 'We will not believe until we are given (something) similar to what was given to the messengers of God.' God knows where He places His message. Disgrace in God's sight will smite those who have sinned, and (also) a harsh punishment, for what they were scheming. **125** Whomever God intends to guide, He expands his heart to Islam, and whomever He intends to lead astray, He makes his heart narrow (and) constricted, as if he were climbing up into the sky. In this way God places the abomination on those who do not believe. **126** This is the path of your Lord – straight. We have made the signs distinct for a people who take heed. **127** For them (there is) the Home of peace with their Lord. He is their ally for what they have done.

128 On the Day when He will gather them all together: 'Assembly of the jinn! You have acquired many of humankind.' And their allies among humankind will say,

---

7. *you*: plur.
8. *you*: sing.

Livestock

'Our Lord, some of us have profited by others, but (now) we have reached our time which You appointed for us.' He will say, 'The Fire is your dwelling place, there to remain' – except for whomever God pleases. Surely your Lord is wise, knowing. **129** In this way We make some of the evildoers allies of others for what they have earned.

130 'Assembly of jinn and humans! Did messengers not come to you from among you, recounting to you My signs and warning you of the meeting of this Day of yours?' They will say, 'We bear witness against ourselves.' This present life deceived them, and they bear witness against themselves that they were disbelievers. **131** That (is because) your Lord was not one to destroy the towns in an evil manner, while their people were oblivious. **132** And for each (there are) ranks according to what they have done, and your Lord is not oblivious of what they do. **133** Your Lord is the wealthy One, the One full of mercy. If He (so) pleases, He will do away with you, and appoint as a successor after you whomever He pleases, just as He produced you from the descendants of another people. **134** Surely what you are promised will indeed come, and you cannot escape (it). **135** Say: 'My people! Do as you are able. Surely I am going to do (what I can). Soon you will know to whom the final Home (belongs). Surely he – the evildoers will not prosper.'

136 They assign to God a portion of the crops and the livestock which He created, and they say, 'This is for God' – so they claim – 'and this is for our associates.'⁹ But what is for their associates does not reach God, and what is for God reaches their associates. Evil is what they judge! **137** In this way their associates made the killing of their children appear enticing to many of the idolaters, in order that they might bring them to ruin and confuse their religion for them. If God had (so) pleased, they would not have done it. So leave them and what they forge. **138** They say, 'These livestock and crops are forbidden. No one may eat them, except for whomever we please' – so they claim – 'and livestock whose backs have been forbidden, and livestock over which the name of God is not to be mentioned' – forging (lies) against Him. He will repay them for what they have forged. **139** They say, 'What is in the bellies of these livestock is exclusively for our males and forbidden to our wives. But if it is (born) dead, they will (all) be partakers in it.' He will repay them for their attributing (these things to Him). Surely He is wise, knowing. **140** Lost (are) those who kill their children in foolishness, without any knowledge, and forbid what God has provided them, forging (lies) against God. They have gone astray and are not (rightly) guided.

141 He (it is) who produces gardens, trellised and untrellised, and date palms and crops of diverse produce, and olives and pomegranates, alike and different. Eat from its fruits when it bears fruit, and give its due (portion) on the day of its harvest. But do not act wantonly. Surely He does not love the wanton. **142** And of the livestock (there are some for) burden and (some for) slaughter. Eat from

---

9. *our associates*: other gods.

what God has provided you, and do not follow the footsteps of Satan. Surely he is clear enemy to you.

143 Eight pairs: two of the sheep, and two of the goats. Say: 'Has He forbidden the two males or the two females? Or what the wombs of the two females contain? Inform me with knowledge, if you are truthful.' **144** And two of the camels, and two of the cows. Say: 'Has He forbidden the two males or the two females? Or what the wombs of the two females contain? Or were you witnesses when God charged you with this (command)? Who is more evil than the one who forges a lie against God, in order to lead the people astray without (their) realizing (it)? Surely God does not guide the people who are evildoers.'

145 Say: 'I do not find in what I have been inspired (with anything) forbidden to one who eats of it, unless it is (already) dead, or blood (which is) shed, or swine's flesh – surely it is an abomination – or – something wicked – it has been dedicated to (a god) other than God.' But whoever is forced (by necessity), not desiring or (deliberately) transgressing – surely your Lord is forgiving, compassionate.

146 To those who are Jews We have forbidden every (animal) with claws, and of the cows and the sheep and goats We have forbidden to them their fat, except what their backs carry, or their entrails, or what is mixed with the bone. We repaid them that for their envy.[10] Surely We are truthful indeed. **147** If they call you a liar, say: 'Your Lord is full of abundant mercy, but His violence will not be turned back from the people who are sinners.'

148 The idolaters will say, 'If God had (so) pleased, we would not have been idolaters, nor our fathers, nor would we have forbidden anything.' In this way the people before them called (it) a lie, until they tasted Our violence. Say: 'Do you have any knowledge? Bring it forth for us! You only follow conjecture and you only guess.' **149** Say: 'To God (belongs) the conclusive argument. If He had (so) pleased, He would indeed have guided you all.' **150** Say: 'Produce your witnesses who (will) bear witness that God has forbidden this.' If they do bear witness, do not bear witness with them. Do not follow the desires of those who call Our signs a lie, and who do not believe in the Hereafter, and (who) equate (others) with their Lord.

151 Say: 'Come! I will recite what your Lord has forbidden to you: Do not associate anything with Him, and (do) good to parents, and do not kill your children because of poverty – We shall provide for you and them – and do not go near (any) immoral deeds, neither what is obvious of them nor what is hidden, and do not kill the person whom God has forbidden (to be killed), except by right. That is what He has charged you with, so that you may understand. **152** Do not go near the property of the orphan, except to improve it, until he reaches his maturity. Fill up the measure and the scale in justice. We do not burden anyone beyond

---

10. *their envy*: i.e. jealousy that God has now chosen others to receive his revelation (see Q2.90).

Livestock

their capacity. When you speak, be fair, even if he is a family member. Fulfill the covenant of God. That is what He has charged you with, so that you may take heed. **153** And (know) that this is My straight path. So follow it, and do not follow the ways (of others), or it will diverge with you from His way. That is what He has charged you with, so that you may guard (yourselves).'

154 Then We gave Moses the Book, complete for the one who does good, and a distinct setting forth of everything, and a guidance and mercy, so that they might believe in the meeting with their Lord. **155** And this is a Book: We have sent it down, blessed. Follow it and guard (yourselves), so that you may receive compassion. **156** Otherwise you would say, 'The Book has only been sent down on two contingents (of people) before us, and we were indeed oblivious of their studies.' **157** Or you would say, 'If (only) the Book had been sent down to us, we would indeed have been better guided than them.' Yet a clear sign has come to you from your Lord, and a guidance and mercy. Who is more evil than the one who calls the signs of God a lie, and turns away from them? We shall repay those who turn away from Our signs (with) an evil punishment for their turning away. **158** Do they expect (anything) but the angels to come to them, or your Lord to come, or one of the signs of your Lord to come? On the Day when one of the signs of your Lord comes, belief will not benefit anyone who did not believe before, or (who did not) earn some good through his belief. Say: '(Just) wait! Surely We (too) are waiting.'

159 Surely those who have divided up their religion and become (different) parties – you are no part of them. Their affair (belongs) only to God, and He will inform them about what they have done. **160** Whoever brings a good deed will have ten equal to it, but whoever brings an evil deed will only be paid the equal of it – and they will not be done evil. **161** Say: 'Surely my Lord has guided me to a straight path, a right religion, the creed of Abraham the Ḥanīf. He was not one of the idolaters.'

162 Say: 'Surely my prayer and my sacrifice, and my living and my dying, are for God, Lord of all peoples. **163** He has no associate. With that I have been commanded, and I am the first of those who submit.'

164 Say: 'Shall I seek a Lord other than God, when He is the Lord of everything? No one earns (anything) except against himself, and no one bearing a burden bears the burden of another. Then to your Lord is your return, (and) then He will inform you about your differences.' **165** He (it is) who has made you rulers on the earth, and raised some of you above others in rank, so that He might test you by what He has given you. Surely your Lord is quick in retribution, yet surely He is indeed forgiving, compassionate.

7 ✹ The Heights

In the Name of God, the Merciful, the Compassionate

1 Alif Lām Mīm Ṣād.

2 A Book sent down to you – so let there be no heaviness in your heart because of it – in order that you may warn by means of it, and as a reminder to the believers. **3** Follow[1] what has been sent down to you from your Lord, and do not follow any allies other than Him. Little do you take heed!

4 How many a town have We destroyed! Our violence came upon it at night, or (while) they were relaxing at midday. **5** Their only cry, when Our violence came upon them, was that they said, 'Surely We were evildoers!' **6** We shall indeed question those to whom (a messenger) was sent, and We shall indeed question the envoys. **7** We shall indeed recount to them with knowledge, (for) We were not absent. **8** The weighing on that Day (will be) the true (weighing). Whoever's scales are heavy, those – they are the ones who prosper, **9** but whoever's scales are light, those are the ones who have lost their (own) selves, because of the evil they have done to Our signs.

10 Certainly We have established you on the earth, and provided for you a means of living on it – little thanks you show! **11** Certainly We created you, (and) then fashioned you. Then We said to the angels, 'Prostrate yourselves before Adam,' and they prostrated themselves, except Iblīs. He was not one of those who prostrated themselves. **12** He[2] said, 'What kept you from prostrating yourself when I commanded you?' He[3] said, 'I am better than him.[4] You created me from fire, but You created him from clay.' **13** He said, 'Go down from here! It is not for you to be arrogant here. Get out! Surely you are one of the disgraced.' **14** He said, 'Spare me until the Day when they are raised up.' **15** He said, 'Surely you are one of the spared.' **16** He said, 'Because you have made me err, I shall indeed sit (in wait) for them (on) Your straight path. **17** Then I shall indeed come upon them, from before them and from behind them, and from their right and from their left, and You will not find most of them thankful.' **18** He said, 'Get out of here, detested

---

1. *Follow*: plur. imperative.
2. *He*: God.
3. *He*: Iblīs.
4. *him*: Adam.

The Heights

(and) rejected! Whoever of them follows you – I shall indeed fill Gehenna with you all!'

19 'Adam! Inhabit the Garden, you and your wife, and eat freely of it wherever you please, but do not go near this tree, or you will both be among the evildoers.' **20** Then Satan whispered to them both, to reveal to them both what was hidden from them of their shameful parts. He said, 'Your Lord has only forbidden you both from this tree to keep you both from becoming two angels, or from becoming two of the immortals.' **21** And he swore to them both, 'Surely I am indeed one of your trusty advisers.' **22** So he caused them both to fall by means of deception. And when they both had tasted the tree, their shameful parts became apparent to them, and they both began fastening on themselves some leaves of the Garden. But their Lord called to them both, 'Did I not forbid you both from that tree, and say to you both, "Surely Satan is a clear enemy to you"?' **23** They both said, 'Our Lord, we have done ourselves evil. If You do not forgive us, and have compassion on us, we shall indeed be among the losers.' **24** He said, 'Go down, some of you an enemy to others! The earth is a dwelling place for you, and enjoyment (of life) for a time.' **25** He said, 'On it you will live and on it you will die, and from it you will be brought forth.'

26 Sons of Adam! We sent down on you clothing – it covers your shameful parts – and feathers. Yet the clothing of guarding (yourselves) – that is better. That is one of the signs of God, so that they may take heed.

27 Sons of Adam! Do not let Satan tempt you, as he drove your parents out of the Garden, stripping both of them of their clothing in order to show both of them their shameful parts. Surely he sees you – he and his ilk – from where you do not see them. Surely We have made the satans allies of those who do not believe.

28 When they commit immorality, they say, 'We found our fathers doing it, and God has commanded us (to do) it.' Say: 'Surely God does not command immorality. Do you say about God what you do not know?' **29** Say: 'My Lord has commanded justice. Set your faces in every mosque, and call on Him, devoting (your) religion to Him. As He brought you about, (so) will you return. **30** (One) group He has guided, and (another) group – their going astray was deserved. Surely they have taken the satans as allies instead of God, and they think that they are (rightly) guided.'

31 Sons of Adam! Take your adornment in every mosque, and eat and drink, but do not act wantonly. Surely He does not love the wanton. **32** Say: 'Who has forbidden the adornment of God which He has brought forth for His servants, and the good things of (His) provision?' Say: 'It is exclusively for those who have believed in this present life on the Day of Resurrection.' In this way We make the signs distinct for a people who know.

33 Say: 'My Lord has only forbidden immoral deeds – (both) what is obvious of them and what is hidden – and all sin and envy – without any right – and that you associate with God what He has not sent down any authority for, and that you

The Heights

say about God what you do not know.' **34** For every community (there is) a time. When their time comes, they will not delay (it) by an hour, nor will they advance (it by an hour).

35 Sons of Adam! If messengers from among you should come to you, recounting to you My signs, whoever guards (himself) and sets (things) right – (there will be) no fear on them, nor will they sorrow. **36** But those who call Our signs a lie, and become arrogant about it – those are the companions of the Fire. There they will remain. **37** Who is more evil than the one who forges a lie against God, or calls His signs a lie? Those – their portion of the Book will reach them, until, when Our messengers come to them, to take them, they say, 'Where is what you used to call on (as gods) instead of God?' They will say, 'They have abandoned us,' and they will bear witness against themselves that they were disbelievers.

38 He will say, 'Enter into the Fire, among the communities of jinn and humans who have passed away before you.' Whenever a (new) community enters, it curses its sister (community), until, when they have all followed each other into it, the last of them will say to the first of them, 'Our Lord, these led us astray, so give them a double punishment of the Fire.' He will say, 'To each a double, but you do not know.' **39** And the first of them will say to the last of them, 'You have no advantage over us, so taste the punishment for what you have earned.'

40 Surely those who call Our signs a lie, and are arrogant about it – the gates of the sky will not be opened for them, nor will they enter the Garden, until the camel passes through the eye of the needle. In this way We repay the sinners. **41** They have a bed in Gehenna, and coverings above them. In this way We repay the evildoers. **42** But those who believe and do righteous deeds – We do not burden anyone beyond their capacity – those are the companions of the Garden. There they will remain. **43** We shall strip away whatever rancor is in their hearts. Beneath them rivers will flow, and they will say, 'Praise (be) to God, who has guided us to this! We would not have been guided if God had not guided us. Certainly the messengers of our Lord have brought the truth.' And they will be called out to: 'That is the Garden! You have inherited it for what you have done.' **44** The companions of the Garden will call out to the companions of the Fire: 'We have found what our Lord promised us (to be) true. So have you found what your Lord promised (to be) true?' They will say, 'Yes!' And then a caller will call out among them: 'The curse of God is on the evildoers, **45** who keep (people) from the way of God and desire (to make) it crooked, and they are disbelievers in the Hereafter.'

46 Between both (groups) of them (there is) a partition, and on the heights[5] (there are) men who recognize each (of them) by their marks, and they call out to the companions of the Garden: 'Peace (be) upon you! They have not entered it, as much as they were eager (to do so).' **47** And when their sight is turned toward the companions of the Fire, they say, 'Our Lord, do not place us among the people

---

5. *heights*: the meaning of Ar. *a'rāf* is uncertain.

The Heights

who are evildoers.' **48** The men of the heights will call out to men whom they recognize by their marks, (and) say, 'Your hoarding is of no use to you, nor what you were arrogant (about). **49** Are these[6] the ones whom you swore God would not reach with (His) mercy? Enter the Garden! (There will be) no fear on you, nor will you sorrow.'

50 And the companions of the Fire will call out to the companions of the Garden: 'Pour some water on us, or some of what God has provided you!' They will say, 'Surely God has forbidden both to the disbelievers, **51** who have taken their religion as diversion and jest. This present life has deceived them.' So today We forget them as they forgot the meeting of this Day of theirs, and because they have denied Our signs.

52 Certainly We have brought them a Book – We have made it distinct on (the basis of) knowledge – as a guidance and mercy for a people who believe. **53** Do they expect anything but its interpretation?[7] On the Day when its interpretation comes, those who forgot it before will say, 'The messengers of our Lord have brought the truth. Have we any intercessors to intercede for us? Or (may) we return so that we might do other than what we have done?' They have lost their (own) selves, and what they forged has abandoned them.

54 Surely your Lord is God, who created the heavens and the earth in six days. Then He mounted the throne. The night covers the day, which it pursues urgently, and the sun, and the moon, and the stars are subjected, (all) by His command. Is it not (a fact) that to Him (belong) the creation and the command? Blessed (be) God, Lord of all peoples!

55 Call on your Lord in humility and in secret. Surely He does not love the transgressors. **56** Do not foment corruption on the earth after it has been set right, and call on Him in fear and in eagerness. Surely the mercy of God is near to the doers of good. **57** He (it is) who sends the winds as good news before His mercy, until, when it brings a cloud heavy (with rain), We drive it to some barren land, and send down water by means of it, and bring forth by means of it every (kind of) fruit. In this way We bring forth the dead, so that you may take heed. **58** (As for) the good land, its vegetation comes forth by the permission of its Lord, but (as for) the bad, (its vegetation) comes forth only poorly. In this way We vary the signs for a people who are thankful.

59 Certainly We sent Noah to his people, and he said, 'My people! Serve God! You have no god other than Him. Surely I fear for you the punishment of a great Day.' **60** The assembly of his people said, 'Surely we see you are indeed clearly astray.' **61** He said, 'My people! There is nothing astray in me, but I am a messenger from the Lord of all peoples. **62** I deliver to you the messages of my Lord and I offer advice to you. I know from God what you do not know. **63** Are you amazed that a

---

6. *these*: the group in heaven.
7. *interpretation*: i.e. the fulfillment of its promises and threats.

reminder has come to you from your Lord by means of a (mere) man from among you, so that he may warn you, and that you may guard (yourselves), and that you may receive compassion?' 64 But they called him a liar, so We rescued him and those with him in the ship, and We drowned those who called Our signs a lie. Surely they were a blind people.

65 And to ʿĀd (We sent) their brother Hūd. He said, 'My people! Serve God! You have no god other than Him. Will you not guard (yourselves)?' 66 The assembly of those who disbelieved among his people said, 'Surely we see you are indeed in foolishness, and surely we think you are indeed one of the liars.' 67 He said, 'My people! There is no foolishness in me, but I am a messenger from the Lord of all peoples. 68 I deliver to you the messages of my Lord and I am a trustworthy adviser for you. 69 Are you amazed that a reminder has come to you from your Lord by means of a (mere) man from among you, so that he may warn you? (Remember) when He made you successors after the people of Noah, and increased you in size abundantly. Remember the blessings of God, so that you may prosper.' 70 They said, 'Have you come to us (with the message) that we should serve God alone, and forsake what our fathers have served? Bring us what you promise us, if you are one of the truthful.' 71 He said, 'Abomination and anger from your Lord have fallen upon you. Will you dispute with me about names which you have named, you and your fathers? God has not sent down any authority for it. (Just) wait! Surely I shall be one of those waiting with you.' 72 So We rescued him and those with him by a mercy from Us, and We cut off the last remnant of those who called Our signs a lie and were not believers.

73 And to Thamūd (We sent) their brother Ṣāliḥ. He said, 'My people! Serve God! You have no god other than Him. A clear sign has come to you from your Lord: this is the she-camel of God, a sign for you. Let her graze on God's earth, and do not touch her with evil, or a painful punishment will seize you. 74 Remember when He made you rulers after ʿĀd and settled you on the earth: you took palaces from its plains, and carved houses out of the mountains. Remember the blessings of God, and do not act wickedly on the earth, fomenting corruption.' 75 The assembly of those who were arrogant among his people said to those who were weak, to those of them who believed, 'Do you (really) know that Ṣāliḥ is an envoy from his Lord?' They said, 'Surely We are believers in what he has been sent with.' 76 Those who were arrogant said, 'Surely we are disbelievers in what you have believed.' 77 So they wounded the she-camel, and disdained the command of their Lord, and said, 'Ṣāliḥ! Bring us what you promise us, if you are one of the envoys.' 78 And then the earthquake seized them, and morning found them leveled in their home(s). 79 So he turned away from them, and said, 'My people! Certainly I have delivered to you the message of my Lord and I offered advice to you, but you do not like advisers.'

80 And Lot, when he said to his people, 'Do you commit (such) immorality (as) no one among all peoples has committed before you? 81 Surely you approach

The Heights

men with lust instead of women. Yes! You are a wanton people.' **82** But the only response of his people was that they said, 'Expel them from your town, (for) surely they are men who keep themselves clean.' **83** So We rescued him and his family, except his wife – she was one of those who stayed behind. **84** And We rained down on them a rain. See how the end was for the sinners!

85 And to Midian (We sent) their brother Shu'ayb. He said, 'My people! Serve God! You have no god other than Him. A clear sign has come to you from your Lord. Fill up the measure and the scale, and do not shortchange the people of their wealth, and do not foment corruption on the earth after it has been set right. That is better for you, if you are believers. **86** And do not sit in every path making threats, and keeping from the way of God those who believe in Him, and desiring (to make) it crooked. Remember when you were few (in number) and He multiplied you. And see how the end was for the fomenters of corruption! **87** If (there is) a contingent of you who believe in that with which I have been sent, and a contingent who do not believe, be patient until God judges between us, (for) He is the best of judges.' **88** The assembly of those who were arrogant among his people said, 'We shall indeed expel you, Shu'ayb, and those who believe with you, from our town, or else you will indeed return to our creed.' He said, 'Even if we are unwilling? **89** We would have forged a lie against God, if we returned to your creed after God rescued us from it. It is not for us to return to it, unless God our Lord (so) pleases. Our Lord comprehends everything in knowledge. In God we have put our trust. Our Lord, disclose the truth between us and our people, (for) You are the best of disclosers.' **90** The assembly of those who disbelieved among his people said, 'If indeed you follow Shu'ayb, surely then you will be losers indeed.' **91** And then the earthquake seized them, and morning found them leveled in their home(s). **92** Those who called Shu'ayb a liar – (it was) as if they had not lived in prosperity there. Those who called Shu'ayb a liar – they were the losers. **93** So he turned away from them, and said, 'My people! Certainly I have delivered to you the messages of my Lord and I offered advice to you. How shall I grieve over a disbelieving people?'

94 We have not sent any prophet to a town, except that We seized its people with violence and hardship, so that they might humble themselves. **95** Then We exchanged good for evil, until they forgot (about it), and said, 'Hardship and prosperity have touched our fathers.' So We seized them unexpectedly, when they did not realize (it). **96** Yet if the people of the towns had believed and guarded (themselves), We would indeed have opened on them blessings from the sky and the earth. But they called (it) a lie, so We seized them for what they had earned.

97 Do the people of the towns feel secure that Our violence will not come upon them at night, while they are sleeping? **98** Or do the people of the towns feel secure that Our violence will not come upon them in the daylight, while they jest? **99** Do they feel secure against the scheme of God? No one feels secure against the scheme of God except the people who are losers. **100** Or is it not a guide for those

The Heights

who inherit the earth after its (former) people that, if We (so) please, We could smite them because of their sins, and We could set a seal on their hearts so that they do not hear?

101 Those were the towns – We recount to you[8] some of their stories. Certainly their messengers brought them the clear signs, but they were not (able) to believe what they had called a lie before. In this way God sets a seal on the hearts of the disbelievers. **102** We did not find any covenant with most of them, but We found most of them wicked.

103 Then, after them, We raised up Moses with Our signs to Pharaoh and his assembly, but they did evil to them. See how the end was for the fomenters of corruption! **104** Moses said, 'Pharaoh! Surely I am a messenger from the Lord of all peoples. **105** (There is) an obligation on (me) that I do not say about God (anything) but the truth. I have brought you a clear sign from your Lord, so send forth the Sons of Israel with me.' **106** He said, 'If you have come with a sign, bring it, if you are one of the truthful.' **107** So he cast (down) his staff, and suddenly it became a real snake. **108** And he drew forth his hand, and suddenly it became white to the onlookers. **109** The assembly of the people of Pharaoh said, 'Surely this man is a skilled magician indeed. **110** He wants to expel you from your land. So what do you command?' **111** They said, 'Put him and his brother off (for a while), and send searchers into the cities **112** to bring you every skilled magician.'

113 And the magicians came to Pharaoh, (and) said, 'Surely for us (there will be) a reward indeed, if we are the victors.' **114** He said, 'Yes, and surely you will indeed be among the ones brought near.' **115** They said, 'Moses! Are you going to cast (first), or are we to be the ones who cast?' **116** He said, 'Cast!' So when they cast, they bewitched the eyes of the people, and terrified them, and produced a great (feat of) magic. **117** And We inspired Moses: 'Cast (down) your staff!,' and suddenly it swallowed up what they were falsely contriving. **118** So the truth came to pass, and what they were doing was invalidated. **119** They were overcome there, and turned back disgraced. **120** And the magicians were cast (down) in prostration. **121** They said, 'We believe in the Lord of all peoples, **122** the Lord of Moses and Aaron.' **123** Pharaoh said, 'You have believed in Him before I gave you permission. Surely this is indeed a scheme which you have schemed in the city to expel its people from it. But soon you will know! **124** I shall indeed cut off your hands and your feet on opposite sides, (and) then I shall indeed crucify you – all (of you)!' **125** They said, 'Surely we are going to return to our Lord. **126** You are not taking vengeance on us (for any other reason) than that we believed in the signs of our Lord when they came to us. Our Lord, pour out on us patience, and take us as ones who have submitted.'

127 The assembly of the people of Pharaoh said, 'Will you leave Moses and his people to foment corruption on the earth and to forsake you and your gods?'

---

8. *you*: sing.

The Heights

He said, 'We shall kill their sons and keep their women alive. Surely we shall be supreme over them!' **128** Moses said to his people, 'Seek help from God and be patient. Surely the earth (belongs) to God. He causes whomever He pleases of His servants to inherit it. The outcome (belongs) to the ones who guard (themselves).' **129** They said, 'We have suffered harm before you came to us and after you came to us.' He said, 'It may be that your Lord will destroy your enemy and make you rulers on the earth, and then see how you will act.'

130 Certainly We seized the house of Pharaoh with years (of famine), and scarcity of fruits, so that they might take heed. **131** But when good came to them, they said, 'This (belongs) to us,' but if evil smote them, they attributed it to the evil omen of Moses and those who were with him. Is it not a fact that their evil omen was with God? But most of them did not know (it). **132** And they said, 'Whatever kind of sign you[9] bring us, to bewitch us by means of it, we are not going to believe in you.' **133** So We sent on them the flood, and the locusts, and the lice, and the frogs, and the blood, as distinct signs. But they became arrogant and were a sinful people. **134** When the wrath fell upon them, they said, 'Moses! Call on your Lord for us by whatever covenant He has made with you. If indeed you remove this wrath from us, we shall indeed believe in you, and send forth the Sons of Israel with you.' **135** But when We removed the wrath from them, until a time they reached (later), suddenly they broke (their promise). **136** So We took vengeance on them and drowned them in the sea, because they called Our signs a lie and were oblivious of them. **137** And We caused the people who were weak to inherit the land We had blessed – the east (parts) and the west (parts) of it – and the best word of your Lord was fulfilled for the Sons of Israel, because they were patient. And We destroyed what Pharaoh and his people had been making and what they had been building.

138 We crossed the sea with the Sons of Israel, and they came upon a people devoted to their idols. They said, 'Moses! Make for us a god like the gods they have.' He said, 'Surely you are an ignorant people. **139** Surely these – what they (are engaged) in (will be) destroyed, and what they are doing is worthless.' **140** He said, 'Shall I seek a god for you other than God, when He has favored you over all peoples?'

141 (Remember) when We rescued you from the house of Pharaoh. They were inflicting on you the evil punishment, killing your sons and sparing your women. In that was a great test from your Lord. **142** And We appointed for Moses (a period of) thirty night(s), and We completed them with ten (more), so the meeting with his Lord was completed in forty night(s). And Moses said to his brother Aaron, 'Be ruler in my place among my people, and set (things) right, and do not follow the way of the fomenters of corruption.' **143** And when Moses came to Our meeting, and his Lord spoke to him, he said, 'My Lord, show me (Yourself), so that I may look at You.' He said, 'You will not see Me, but look at the mountain. If

---

9. *you*: Moses.

it remains in its place, you will see Me.' But when his Lord revealed His splendor to the mountain, He shattered it, and Moses fell down thunderstruck. And when he recovered, he said, 'Glory to You! I turn to You (in repentance), and I am the first of the believers.' **144** He said, 'Moses! I have chosen you over the people for My messages and for My word. So take what I have given you, and be one of the thankful.'

145 And We wrote for him on the Tablets an admonition of everything, and a distinct setting forth of everything: 'So hold it fast, and command your people to take the best of it. I shall show you the home of the wicked. **146** I shall turn away from My signs those who are arrogant on the earth without any right. Even if they see every sign, they will not believe in it. And if they see the right way, they will not take it as a way, but if they see the way of error, they will take it as a way. That (is) because they called Our signs a lie and were oblivious of them. **147** Those who have called Our signs a lie, and (also) the meeting of the Hereafter – their deeds come to nothing. Will they be repaid (for anything) except for what they have done?'

148 And the people of Moses, after he (was gone), made a calf out of their ornaments – a (mere) image of it (having) a mooing sound. Did they not see that it could not speak to them or guide them to a way? (Yet) they made it and became evildoers. **149** But when they stumbled and saw that they had gone astray, they said, 'If indeed our Lord does not have compassion on us, and does not forgive us, we shall indeed be among the losers.' **150** When Moses returned to his people, in anger (and) grief, he said, 'Evil is what you have done as my successors, after I (left you). Have you sought to hurry the command of your Lord?' And he cast (down) the Tablets, and seized his brother's head, dragging him toward himself. He said,[10] 'Son of my mother! Surely the people thought me weak, and nearly killed me. So do not let (my) enemies gloat over me, and do not place me among the people who are evildoers.' **151** He said, 'My Lord, forgive me and my brother, and cause us to enter into Your mercy, (for) You are the most compassionate of the compassionate.' **152** Surely those who made the calf – anger from their Lord will reach them, and humiliation in this present life. In this way We repay the forgers (of lies). **153** But those who do evil deeds, (and) then turn (in repentance) after that, and believe – surely after that your Lord is indeed forgiving, compassionate.

154 When the anger of Moses abated, he took (up) the Tablets, and in their inscription (there was) a guidance and mercy for those who fear their Lord. **155** And Moses chose his people – seventy men – for Our meeting. So when the earthquake seized them, he said, 'My Lord, if You had pleased, You could have destroyed them before, and me (as well). Will You destroy us for what the foolish among us have done? It is only Your test by which You lead astray whomever You please and guide whomever You please. You are our ally, so forgive us and have

---

10. *He said*: Aaron addresses Moses, then Moses prays.

The Heights

compassion on us, (for) You are the best of forgivers. **156** And prescribe for us good in this world and in the Hereafter. Surely we have turned to You.' He said, 'My punishment – I smite with it whomever I please, but My mercy comprehends everything. I shall prescribe it for the ones who guard (themselves), and give the alms, and those who – they believe in Our signs – **157** those who follow the messenger, the prophet of the common people, whom they find written in their Torah and Gospel. He will command them what is right and forbid them what is wrong, and he will permit them good things and forbid them bad things, and he will deliver them of their burden and the chains that were on them. Those who believe in him, and support him and help him, and follow the light which has been sent down with him, those – they are the ones who will prosper.'

158 Say: 'People! Surely I am the messenger of God to you – all (of you) – (the messenger of) the One to whom (belongs) the kingdom of the heavens and the earth. (There is) no god but Him. He gives life and causes death. So believe in God and His messenger, the prophet of the common people, who believes in God and His words, (and) follow him, so that you may be (rightly) guided.'

159 Among the people of Moses (there was) a community which guided by the truth, and by means of it acted fairly. **160** We divided them (into) twelve tribes as communities, and We inspired Moses, when his people asked him for water: 'Strike the rock with your staff,' and (there) gushed forth from it twelve springs – each tribe knew its drinking place – and We overshadowed them (with) the cloud, and We sent down on them the manna and the quails: 'Eat from the good things which We have provided you.' They did not do Us evil, but they did themselves evil.

161 (Remember) when it was said to them, 'Inhabit this town and eat of it wherever you please, and say: "Ḥiṭṭa,"[11] and enter the gate in prostration. We shall forgive you your sins and increase the doers of good.' **162** But those of them who did evil exchanged a word other than that which had been spoken to them. So We sent down on them wrath from the sky, because of the evil they were doing.

163 Ask them about the town which was near the sea, when they transgressed in (the matter of) the sabbath, when their fish came to them on the day of their sabbath, (swimming) right to the shore. But on the day when they did not observe the sabbath, they did not come to them. In this way We were testing them because they were acting wickedly. **164** (Remember) when a (certain) community of them said, 'Why do you admonish a people whom God is going to destroy or punish (with) a harsh punishment?' They said, '(As) an excuse to your Lord, and so that they might guard (themselves).' **165** So when they forgot what they were reminded of, We rescued those who had been forbidding evil, and We seized the evildoers with a violent punishment because they were acting wickedly. **166** So when they disdained what they had been forbidden from, We said to them, 'Become apes, skulking away!'

---

11. Ḥiṭṭa: meaning uncertain.

The Heights

167 (Remember) when your Lord proclaimed (that) He would indeed raise up against them – until the Day of Resurrection – those who would inflict them (with) evil punishment. Surely your Lord is indeed quick in retribution, yet surely He is indeed forgiving, compassionate.

168 We divided them (into) communities on the earth, some of them righteous and some of them other than that, and We tested them with good things and bad, so that they might return. **169** And after them came successors (who) inherited the Book, taking (the fleeting) goods of this lower (world) and saying, 'It will be forgiven us.' And if there comes to them goods like that (again), they will take them. Has the covenant of the Book not been taken upon them, (namely) that they should not say about God (anything) but the truth? And have they (not) studied what is in it? The Home of the Hereafter is better for the ones who guard (themselves). Will you not understand? **170** Those who hold fast the Book and observe the prayer – surely We do not let the reward of those who set (things) right go to waste.

171 (Remember) when We shook the mountain above them, as if it were a canopy, and they thought it was going to fall on them: 'Hold fast what We have given you, and remember what is in it, so that you may guard (yourselves).'

172 (Remember) when your Lord took from the sons of Adam – from their loins – their descendants, and made them bear witness about themselves: 'Am I not your Lord?' They said, 'Yes indeed! We bear witness.' (We did that) so that you would not say on the Day of Resurrection, 'Surely we were oblivious of this,' **173** or say, 'Our fathers were idolaters before (us), and we are descendants after them. Will You destroy us for what the perpetrators of falsehood did?' **174** In this way We make the signs distinct, so that they will return.

175 Recite to them the story of the one to whom We gave Our signs, but he passed them by, and Satan followed him, and he became one of those who are in error. **176** If We had (so) pleased, We would indeed have raised him by it, but he clung to the earth and followed his (vain) desire. So his parable is like the parable of the dog: If you attack it, it lolls its tongue out, or if you leave it alone, it (still) lolls its tongue out. That is the parable of the people who called Our signs a lie. So recount the account, that they may reflect.

177 Evil is the parable of the people who called Our signs a lie, but (who only) did themselves evil. **178** Whoever God guides is the (rightly) guided one, and whoever He leads astray, those – they are the losers. **179** Certainly We have created for Gehenna many of the jinn and humans: they have hearts, but they do not understand with them; they have eyes, but they do not see with them; they have ears, but they do not hear with them. Those (people) are like cattle – No! They are (even) farther astray! Those – they are the oblivious.

180 To God (belong) the best names. So call on Him with them, and leave those who pervert His names. They will be repaid for what they have done.

181 Among those whom We have created is a community which guides by the truth and by means of it acts fairly. **182** But those who call Our signs a lie – We shall

The Heights

lead them on step by step without their realizing it, **183** and I shall spare them – surely My plan is strong. **184** Do they not reflect? Their companion is not possessed. He is only a clear warner. **185** Do they not look into the kingdom of the heavens and the earth, and whatever things God has created, and that it may be that their time has already drawn near? So in what (kind of) proclamation will they believe after this? **186** Whoever God leads astray has no guide. He leaves them in their insolent transgression, wandering blindly.

187 They ask you about the Hour: 'When is its arrival?' Say: 'Knowledge of it is only with my Lord. No (one) will reveal it at its (appointed) time but He. It is heavy in the heavens and the earth, (but) it will only come upon you unexpectedly.' They ask you as if you are well informed about it. Say: 'Knowledge of it is only with God, but most of the people do not know (it).' **188** Say: 'I have no power to (cause) myself benefit or harm, except for whatever God pleases. If I had knowledge of the unseen, I would indeed have acquired much good, and evil would not have touched me. I am only a warner and bringer of good news to a people who believe.'

189 He (it is) who created you from one person, and made from him his spouse, so that he might dwell with her. And when he covered her, she bore a light burden and passed on with it (unnoticed). But when she became heavy, they both called on God their Lord, 'If indeed You give us a righteous (son), we shall indeed be among the thankful.' **190** But when He gave them a righteous (son), they set up associates for Him in (return for) what He had given them. Yet God is exalted above what they associate. **191** Do they associate (with Him) what does not create anything, since they are (themselves) created? **192** They cannot (give) them any help, nor can they (even) help themselves. **193** If you[12] call them to the guidance, they will not follow you. (It is) the same for you whether you call them or you remain silent.

194 Surely those you call on instead of God are servants like you. So call on them and let them respond to you, if you are truthful. **195** Do they have feet with which they walk, or do they have hands with which they grasp, or do they have eyes with which they see, or do they have ears with which they hear? Say: 'Call on your associates, (and) then plot against me and do not spare me! **196** Surely my ally is God, who has sent down the Book. He takes the righteous as allies. **197** Those you call on instead of Him cannot help you, nor can they (even) help themselves.' **198** If you[13] call them to the guidance, they do not hear. You see them looking at you, but they do not see.

199 Take the excess, and command what is right, and turn away from the ignorant. **200** If any provocation from Satan provokes you, take refuge with God. Surely He is hearing, knowing. **201** Surely the ones who guard (themselves), when a circler

---

12. *you*: plur.
13. *you*: plur.

from Satan touches them, remember,[14] and suddenly they see (clearly). **202** But their brothers increase them in error, (and) then they do not stop.

203 When you do not bring them a sign, they say, 'If only you would choose (to do) it.' Say: 'I only follow what I am inspired (with) from my Lord. This is evidence from your Lord, and a guidance and mercy for a people who believe.' **204** When the Qur'ān is recited, listen to it and remain silent, so that you may receive compassion.

205 Remember your Lord within yourself, in humility and in fear, and without loud words, in the mornings and the evenings. Do not be one of the oblivious. **206** Surely those who are with your Lord are not too proud to serve Him. They glorify Him and prostrate themselves before Him.

---

14. *remember*: i.e. call God to mind.

8 ✵ The Spoils

In the Name of God, the Merciful, the Compassionate

1 They ask you about the spoils. Say: 'The spoils (belong) to God and the messenger. So guard (yourselves) against God, and set right what is between you. Obey God and His messenger, if you are believers.'

2 Only those are believers who, when God is mentioned, their hearts become afraid, and when His signs are recited to them, it increases them in belief. They put their trust in their Lord. 3 Those who observe the prayer, and contribute from what We have provided them, 4 those – they are the true believers. For them (there are) ranks (of honor) with their Lord, and forgiveness and generous provision.

5 – As your Lord brought you[1] forth from your house with the truth, when a group of the believers were indeed unwilling, 6 disputing with you about the truth after it had become clear, as if they were being driven to death with their eyes wide open.

7 (Remember) when God was promising you[2] that one of the two contingents would be yours, and you were wanting the unarmed one to be yours, but God wished to verify the truth by His words, and to cut off the last remnant of the disbelievers, 8 so that He might verify the truth and falsify the false, even though the sinners disliked (it). 9 (Remember) when you were calling on your Lord for help, and He responded to you: 'I am going to increase you with a thousand angels following behind.' 10 God did it only as good news, and that your hearts might be satisfied by it. Help (comes) only from God. Surely God is mighty, wise.

11 (Remember) when He covered you with slumber as a security from Him, and sent down on you water from the sky, so that He might purify you by means of it, and take away from you the abomination of Satan,[3] and that he might strengthen your hearts, and make firm (your) feet by means of it. 12 When your[4] Lord inspired the angels: 'I am with you,[5] so make firm those who believe. I shall cast dread into the hearts of those who disbelieve. So strike above (their) necks,

---

1. *you*: sing.
2. *you*: plur.
3. *abomination of Satan*: reading 'abomination' (Ar. *rijs*) instead of 'wrath' (*rijz*); probably referring to 'idolatry' (cf. Q22.30).
4. *your*: sing.
5. *you*: plur.

The Spoils

and strike (off) all their fingers!' **13** That was because they broke with God and His messenger, and whoever breaks with God and His messenger – surely God is harsh in retribution. **14** 'That is for you! So taste it! And (know) that the punishment of the Fire is for the disbelievers.'

15 You who believe! When you encounter those who disbelieve advancing (for battle), do not turn (your) backs to them. **16** Whoever turns his back to them on that day – unless turning aside to fight or to join (another) cohort – he has incurred the anger of God. His refuge will be Gehenna – and it is an evil destination!

17 You[6] did not kill them, but God killed them, and you[7] did not throw when you threw, but God threw, and (He did that) in order to test the believers (with) a good test from Himself. Surely God is hearing, knowing. **18** That is for you![8] (Know) that God weakens the plot of the disbelievers. **19** If you ask for a victory, the victory has already come to you. And if you stop, it will be better for you. But if you return, We shall return (too), and your cohort will be of no use to you, even if it should be numerous. (Know) that God is with the believers.

20 You who believe! Obey God and His messenger, and do not turn away from him when you hear (him). **21** Do not be like those who say, 'We hear,' when they do not hear. **22** Surely the worst of creatures in the sight of God are the deaf (and) the speechless – those that do not understand. **23** If God had known any good in them, He would indeed have made them hear. But (even) if He had made them hear, they would indeed have turned away in aversion.

24 You who believe! Respond to God and to the messenger, when he calls you to what gives you life. Know that God stands between a person and his (own) heart, and that to Him you will be gathered. **25** Guard (yourselves) against trouble, which will indeed smite not just the evildoers among you, and know that God is harsh in retribution.

26 Remember when you were few (and) weak on the earth, (and) you feared that the people might snatch you away, and He gave you refuge, and supported you with His help, and provided you with good things, so that you might be thankful. **27** You who believe! Do not betray God and the messenger, and do not betray your pledges when you know (better). **28** Know that your wealth and your children are a test, and that God – with Him (there is) a great reward. **29** You who believe! If you guard (yourselves) against God, He will grant deliverance for you, and absolve you of your evil deeds, and forgive you. God is full of great favor.

30 (Remember) when those who disbelieved were scheming against you,[9] to confine you, or kill you, or expel you. They were scheming but God was scheming (too), and God is the best of schemers. **31** When Our signs are recited to them, they

---

6. *You*: plur.
7. *you*: sing.
8. *you*: plur.
9. *you*: sing.

The Spoils

say, 'We have already heard (this). If we wished, we could indeed say (something) like this. This is nothing but old tales.' **32** And (remember) when they said, 'God! If this is the truth from You, rain down on us stones from the sky or bring us a painful punishment.' **33** But God was not one to punish them while you were among them, and God was not one to punish them while they were asking for forgiveness. **34** But what (excuse) have they (now) that God should not punish them, when they are keeping (people) from (going to) the Sacred Mosque, and they are not its (true) allies? Its only allies are the ones who guard (themselves), but most of them do not know (it). **35** Their prayer at the House is nothing but whistling and clapping of hands. So taste the punishment for what you disbelieve!

36 Surely those who disbelieve spend their wealth to keep (people) from the way of God – and they will (continue to) spend it. Then it will be a (cause of) regret for them, (and) then they will be overcome. Those who disbelieve will be gathered into Gehenna, **37** so that God may separate the bad from the good, and place the bad one on top of the other, and so pile them all up, and place them in Gehenna. Those – they are the losers. **38** Say to those who disbelieve (that) if they stop, whatever is already past will be forgiven them, but if they return, the customary way of those of old has already passed away. **39** Fight them[10] until (there) is no persecution, and the religion – all of it – (belongs) to God. If they stop – surely God sees what they do. **40** If they turn away, know that God is your Protector. Excellent is the Protector, and excellent is the Helper!

41 Know that whatever spoils you take, a fifth of it (belongs) to God and to the messenger, and to family, and the orphans, and the poor, and the traveler, if you believe in God and what We sent down on Our servant on the Day of Deliverance, the day the two forces met. God is powerful over everything.

42 (Remember) when you were on the nearer side, and they on the farther side, and the caravan was below you. (Even) if you had set a time (to fight), you would indeed have failed to keep the appointment. But (the battle took place) so that God might decide the affair – it was done! – (and it took place) so that those who perished might perish on (the basis of) a clear sign, and that those who lived might live on (the basis of) a clear sign. Surely God is indeed hearing, knowing.

43 (Remember) when God showed them to you[11] in your dream as (only) a few, and if had He shown them as many, you[12] would indeed have lost courage, and indeed argued about the matter. But God kept (you) safe. Surely He knows what is in the hearts. **44** (Remember) when He showed them to you[13] – when you met – as few in your eyes, and He made you (appear as) few in their eyes. (This took place) so that God might decide the affair – it was done! To God all affairs are returned.

---

10. *Fight them*: plur. imperative.
11. *you*: sing.
12. *you*: plur.
13. *you*: plur.

The Spoils

45 You who believe! When you encounter a (hostile) cohort, stand firm, and remember God often, so that you may prosper. **46** Obey God and His messenger, and do not argue, so that you lose courage and your strength fails. And be patient. Surely God is with the patient. **47** Do not be like those who went forth from their homes boastfully, and to show off to the people, and to keep (them) from the way of God. God encompasses what they do.

48 (Remember) when Satan made their deeds appear enticing to them, and said, '(There is) no one among the people to defeat you today. Surely I am your neighbor.' But when the two cohorts saw each other, he turned on his heels, and said, 'Surely I am free of you, (for) surely I see what you do not see. Surely I fear God, (for) God is harsh in retribution.'

49 (Remember) when the hypocrites and those in whose hearts is a sickness were saying: 'Their religion has deceived these (people).' But whoever puts his trust in God – surely God is mighty, wise. **50** If (only) you[14] could see when the angels take those who have disbelieved, striking their faces and their backs, and (saying): 'Taste the punishment of the burning (Fire)! **51** That is for what your (own) hands have sent forward, and (know) that God is not an evildoer to (His) servants.' **52** (It will be) like the case of the house of Pharaoh, and those who were before them: they disbelieved in the signs of God, so God seized them for their sins. Surely God is strong, harsh in retribution. **53** That is because God is not one to change the blessing with which He has blessed a people, until they change what is within themselves. (Know) that God is hearing, knowing. **54** Like the case of the house of Pharaoh, and those who were before them: they called the signs of their Lord a lie, so We destroyed them for their sins, and We drowned the house of Pharaoh. All were evildoers.

55 Surely the worst of creatures in the sight of God are those who disbelieve – and they will not believe – **56** those of them with whom you[15] have made a treaty, (and) then they break their treaty every time, and they do not guard (themselves). **57** If you come upon them in war, scatter with them those who are behind them, so that they may take heed. **58** If you fear treachery from a people, toss (the treaty) back at them likewise. Surely God does not love the treacherous. **59** Do not let those who disbelieve think they have gotten away. Surely they will not escape. **60** Prepare for them whatever force and cavalry you[16] can, to terrify by this means the enemy of God and your enemy, and others besides them. You do not know them, but God knows them. Whatever you contribute in the way of God will be repaid to you in full, and you will not be done evil. **61** If they incline toward peace, you[17] incline toward it (as well). Put (your) trust in God. Surely He is the Hearing, the Knowing. **62** But if they intend to deceive you – surely God is

---

14. *you*: sing.
15. *you*: sing.
16. *you*: plur.
17. *you*: sing.

The Spoils

enough for you. He (it is) who supported you with His help and with the believers, **63** and He has brought their hearts together. If you had spent what is on the earth – all (of it) – you could not have brought their hearts together. But God has brought their hearts together. Surely He is mighty, wise.

64 Prophet! God is enough for you, and whoever follows you of the believers. **65** Prophet! Urge on the believers to the fighting. If (there) are twenty of you (who are) patient, they will overcome two hundred, and if (there) are a hundred of you, they will overcome a thousand of those who disbelieve, because they are a people without understanding. **66** Now God has lightened (the task) for you,[18] and He knows that (there is) weakness in you. If (there) are a hundred of you (who are) patient, they will overcome two hundred, and if (there) are a thousand of you, they will overcome two thousand by the permission of God. God is with the patient.

67 It is not for a prophet to have captives, until he has subdued (the enemy) on the earth. You[19] desire (the fleeting) goods of this world, but God desires the Hereafter. God is mighty, wise. **68** Were it not for a preceding Book from God, a great punishment would indeed have touched you for what you took. **69** So eat from what you have taken as spoils as permitted (and) good, and guard (yourselves) against God. Surely God is forgiving, compassionate.

70 Prophet! Say to the captives in your hands: 'If God knows of any good in your hearts, He will give you (something) better than what has been taken from you, and He will forgive you. Surely God is forgiving, compassionate.' **71** But if they intend to betray you, they have already betrayed God before (that). So He has given (you) power over them. God is knowing, wise.

72 Surely those who have believed and emigrated, and struggled with their wealth and their lives in the way of God, and those who have given refuge and help, those – they are allies of each other. But those who have believed and not emigrated – their protection is not (an obligation) on you[20] at all, until they emigrate. Yet if they seek your help in the (matter of) religion, (their) help is (an obligation) on you, unless (it be) against a people with whom you have a treaty. God sees what you do.

73 Those who disbelieve are allies of each other. Unless you do this (too), (there) will be trouble on the earth and great corruption. **74** But those who have believed, and emigrated, and struggled in the way of God, and those who have given refuge and help, those – they are the true believers. For them (there is) forgiveness and generous provision. **75** But those who have believed after that, and emigrated, and struggled (along) with you, they (too) belong to you. Yet those related by blood are closer to one another in the Book of God. Surely God has knowledge of everything.

---

18. *you*: plur.
19. *You*: plur.
20. *you*: plur.

9 ✣ Repentance

1 A renunciation from God and His messenger to those of the idolaters with whom you have made a treaty: **2** 'Move about (freely) on the earth for four months, and know that you cannot escape God, and that God will disgrace the disbelievers.'

3 And a proclamation from God and His messenger to the people on the day of the great pilgrimage: 'God renounces the idolaters, and (so does) His messenger. If you turn (in repentance), it will be better for you, but if you turn away, know that you cannot escape God.'

Give those who disbelieve news of a painful punishment, **4** except those of the idolaters with whom you have made a treaty, (and who) since then have not failed you in anything and have not supported anyone against you. Fulfill their treaty with them until their term. Surely God loves the ones who guard (themselves).

5 Then, when the sacred months have passed, kill[1] the idolaters wherever you find them, and seize them, and besiege them, and sit (in wait) for them at every place of ambush. If they turn (in repentance), and observe the prayer and give the alms, let them go their way. Surely God is forgiving, compassionate. **6** If one of the idolaters seeks your protection, grant him protection until he hears the word of God. Then convey him to his place of safety – that is because they are a people who have no knowledge.

7 How can the idolaters have a treaty with God and with His messenger, except those with whom you have made a treaty at the Sacred Mosque? So long as they go straight with you, go straight with them. Surely God loves the ones who guard (themselves). **8** How (can there be a treaty with them)? If they were to prevail over you, they would not respect any bond or agreement with you. They please you with their mouths, but their hearts refuse (you). Most of them are wicked. **9** They have sold the signs of God for a small price, and kept (people) from His way. Surely evil is what they have done. **10** They do not respect any bond or agreement with a believer. Those – they are the transgressors. **11** If they turn (in repentance), and observe the prayer and give the alms, (they are) your brothers in the religion. We make the signs distinct for a people who know. **12** But if they break their oaths, after their treaty, and vilify your religion, fight the leaders of disbelief – surely they have no (binding) oaths – so that they stop (fighting).

---

1. *kill*: plur. imperative.

Repentance

13 Will you[2] not fight (against) a people who have broken their oaths, and are determined to expel the messenger, and started (to attack) you the first time? Are you afraid of them? God – (it is more) right that you should fear Him, if you are believers. **14** Fight them! God will punish them by your hands, and disgrace them, and help you against them, and heal the hearts of a people who believe, **15** and take away (all) rage from their hearts. God turns (in forgiveness) to whomever He pleases. God is knowing, wise.

16 Or did you think that you would be left (in peace), when God did not (yet) know those of you who have struggled, and have not taken any ally other than God and His messenger and the believers? God is aware of what you do. **17** It is not for the idolaters to inhabit the mosques of God, (while) bearing witness against themselves of disbelief. Those – their deeds have come to nothing, and in the Fire they will remain. **18** Only he will inhabit the mosques of God who believes in God and the Last Day, and observes the prayer and gives the alms, and does not fear (anyone) but God. It may be that those – they will be among the (rightly) guided ones.

19 Do you make the giving of water to the pilgrims and the inhabiting of the Sacred Mosque like the one who believes in God and the Last Day and struggles in the way of God? They are not equal with God, and God does not guide the people who are evildoers. **20** Those who have believed, and emigrated, and struggled in the way of God with their wealth and their lives are higher in rank with God. Those – they are the triumphant. **21** Their Lord gives them good news of mercy from Himself, and approval, and (there are) Gardens for them in which (there is) lasting bliss, **22** there to remain forever. Surely God – with Him is a great reward.

23 You who believe! Do not take your fathers and your brothers as allies, if they prefer disbelief over belief. Whoever among you takes them as allies, those – they are the evildoers. **24** Say: 'If your fathers, and your sons, and your brothers, and your wives, and your clan, and wealth you have acquired, and (business) transaction(s) you fear (may) fall off, and dwellings you take pleasure in are dearer to you than God and His messenger, and struggling in His way, then wait until God brings His command. God does not guide the people who are wicked.'

25 Certainly God has helped you on many (battle)fields, and on the day of Ḥunayn, when your multitude impressed you but was of no use to you at all, and the earth was too narrow for you, despite its breadth, and you turned back, retreating. **26** Then God sent down His Sakīna on His messenger and on the believers, and He sent down forces you did not see, and punished those who disbelieved – that was the payment of the disbelievers. **27** Then, after that, God turns (in forgiveness) to whomever He pleases. God is forgiving, compassionate.

28 You who believe! Only the idolaters are impure, so let them not go near the Sacred Mosque after this, their (final) year. If you fear poverty, God will enrich you from His favor, if He pleases. Surely God is knowing, wise.

---

2. *you*: plur. (throughout this section).

Repentance

29 Fight those who do not believe in God or the Last Day, and do not forbid what God and His messenger have forbidden, and do not practice the religion of truth – from among those who have been given the Book – until they pay tribute out of hand, and they are disgraced.

30 The Jews say, 'Ezra is the son of God,' and the Christians say, 'The Messiah is the son of God.' That is their saying with their mouths. They imitate the saying of those who disbelieved before (them). (May) God fight them. How are they (so) deluded? **31** They have taken their teachers and their monks as Lords instead of God, and (also) the Messiah, son of Mary, when they were only commanded to serve one God. (There is) no god but Him. Glory to Him above what they associate! **32** They want to extinguish the light of God with their mouths, but God refuses (to do anything) except perfect His light, even though the disbelievers dislike (it). **33** He (it is) who has sent His messenger with the guidance and the religion of truth, so that He may cause it to prevail over religion – all of it – even though the idolaters dislike (it).

34 You who believe! Surely many of the teachers and the monks consume the wealth of the people by means of falsehood, and keep (people) from the way of God. Those who hoard the gold and the silver, and do not spend it in the way of God – give them news of a painful punishment. **35** On the Day when it will be heated in the Fire of Gehenna, and their foreheads and their sides and their backs will be branded with it: 'This is what you hoarded for yourselves, so taste what you have hoarded!'

36 Surely the number of months with God is twelve, (written) in the Book of God on the day when He created the heavens and the earth. Of them, four are sacred. That is the right religion. Do not do yourselves evil during them, but fight (against) the idolaters all together, as they fight you all together, and know that God is with the ones who guard (themselves). **37** The postponement is an increase of disbelief by which those who disbelieve go astray. They make it profane (one) year, and make it sacred (another) year, to adjust the number (of months) God has made sacred, and to profane what God has made sacred. The evil of their deeds is made to appear enticing to them, but God does not guide the people who are disbelievers.

38 You who believe! What is (the matter) with you? When it is said to you, 'Go forth in the way of God,' you slump to the earth. Are you pleased with this present life, rather than the Hereafter? Yet what enjoyment (there is) of this present life is only a little (thing) in (comparison to) the Hereafter. **39** If you do not go forth, He will punish you (with) a painful punishment, and exchange a people other than you. You will not harm Him at all, (for) God is powerful over everything. **40** If you do not help him, God has already helped him, when those who disbelieved expelled him, the second of two: when the two were in the cave,[3]

---

3. *when the two were in the cave*: said to refer to the Prophet's flight from Mecca, when he and Abū Bakr took shelter in a cave near Mecca until their pursuers abandoned the chase.

Repentance

(and) when he said to his companion, 'Do not sorrow, (for) surely God is with us.' Then God sent down His Sakīna on him, and supported him with forces which you did not see, and made the word of those who disbelieved the lowest, while the word of God is the highest. God is mighty, wise.

41 Go forth, light and heavy, and struggle in the way of God with your wealth and your lives. That is better for you, if (only) you knew. **42** If it were (some fleeting) gain near (at hand), and an easy journey, they would indeed have followed you,[4] but the distance is (too) far for them. (Still) they will swear by God, 'If we had been able, we would indeed have gone out with you.' (In this way) they destroy themselves. But God knows: 'Surely they are liars indeed!'

43 God pardon you![5] Why did you give them permission, before (it was) clear to you (who were) those who spoke the truth, and (before) you knew (who were) the liars? **44** Those who believe in God and the Last Day do not ask your permission, so that they may struggle with their wealth and their lives. God knows the ones who guard (themselves). **45** Only those who do not believe in God and the Last Day ask your permission, and their hearts are filled with doubt, and they waver in their doubt. **46** If they had intended to go forth, they would indeed have made some preparation for it. But God disliked their going forth, so He held them back, and it was said (to them), 'Sit (at home) with the ones who sit.' **47** If they had gone forth with you,[6] they would have added to you nothing but ruin, and would indeed have run around in your midst, seeking to stir up trouble among you – and some of you would have listened to them. But God knows the evildoers. **48** Certainly they sought to stir up trouble before (this), and upset matters for you,[7] until the truth came and the command of God prevailed, even though they were unwilling. **49** (There is) one of them who says, 'Give me permission, and do not tempt me.' Is it not (a fact) that they have (already) fallen into temptation? Surely Gehenna will indeed encompass the disbelievers.

50 If some good smites you,[8] it distresses them, but if some smiting smites you, they say, 'We took hold of our affair before (this),' and they turn away, gloating. **51** Say: 'Nothing smites us except what God has prescribed for us. He is our Protector, and in God let the believers put (their) trust.' **52** Say: 'Do you wait for anything in our case except for one of the two good (rewards)? But we are waiting in your case for God to smite you with punishment from Him or at our hands. (Just) wait! Surely we shall be waiting with you.'

53 Say: 'Contribute willingly or unwillingly, it will not be accepted from you. Surely you are a wicked people.' **54** Nothing prevents their contributions being

---

4. *you*: sing.
5. *you*: sing.
6. *you*: plur.
7. *you*: sing.
8. *you*: sing.

accepted from them, except that they have not believed in God and in His messenger, and they do not come to the prayer, except in a lazy fashion, and they do not contribute, except unwillingly.

55 Do not let their wealth and their children impress you. God only intends to punish them by means of it in this present life, and (that) they themselves should pass away while they are disbelievers. **56** They swear by God that they indeed belong to you, but they do not belong to you. They are a people who are afraid. **57** If they could find a shelter, or caves, or a place to hide, they would indeed resort to it and rush off.

58 (There is) one of them who finds fault with you concerning freewill offerings. Yet if they are given (a share) of it, they are pleased, but if they are not given (a share) of it, they are angry. **59** If (only) they had been pleased with what God gave them, and His messenger, and had said, 'God is enough for us. God will give us (more) of His favor, and (so will) His messenger. Surely we turn in hope to God.' **60** Freewill offerings are only for the poor and the needy, and the ones who collect it, and the ones whose hearts are united, and for the (freeing of) slaves, and the (relief of) debtors, and for the way of God, and the traveler. (That is) an obligation from God. God is knowing, wise.

61 (There are) some of them who hurt the prophet, and say, 'He is all ears!' Say: 'Good ears for you! He believes in God and believes in the believers, and (he is) a mercy for those of you who believe. But those who hurt the messenger of God – for them (there is) a painful punishment.' **62** They swear to you by God in order to please you, but God and His messenger – (it is more) right that they should please Him, if they are believers. **63** Do they not know that the one who opposes God and His messenger – surely for him (there is) the Fire of Gehenna, there to remain? That is the great humiliation!

64 The hypocrites are afraid that a sūra will be sent down against them, informing them of what is in their hearts. Say: 'Go on mocking! Surely God will bring forth what you are afraid of.' **65** If indeed you ask them, they will indeed say, 'We were only bantering and jesting.' Say: 'Were you mocking God, and His signs, and His messenger? **66** Do not make excuses! You have disbelieved after your believing. If We pardon (one) contingent of you, We will punish (another) contingent because they have been sinners.' **67** The hypocrite men and the hypocrite women are all alike. They command wrong and forbid right, and they withdraw their hands. They have forgotten God, so He has forgotten them. Surely the hypocrites – they are the wicked. **68** God has promised the hypocrite men and the hypocrite women, and the disbelievers, the Fire of Gehenna, there to remain. It will be enough for them. God has cursed them, and for them (there is) a lasting punishment. **69** Like those before you: they were stronger than you in power and (had) more wealth and children, and they took enjoyment in their share. You have taken enjoyment in your share, as those before you took enjoyment in their share. You have bantered as they bantered. Those – their deeds

Repentance

have come to nothing in this world and the Hereafter. And those – they are the losers. **70** Has no story come to them of those who were before them: the people of Noah, and ʿĀd, and Thamūd, and the people of Abraham, and the companions of Midian, and the overturned (cities)? Their messengers brought them the clear signs. God was not one to do them evil, but they did themselves evil.

71 The believing men and the believing women are allies of each other. They command right and forbid wrong, they observe the prayer and give the alms, and they obey God and His messenger. Those – God will have compassion on them. God is mighty, wise. **72** God has promised the believing men and the believing women Gardens through which rivers flow, there to remain, and good dwellings in Gardens of Eden – but the approval of God is greater. That is the great triumph!

73 Prophet! Struggle against the disbelievers and the hypocrites, and be stern with them. Their refuge is Gehenna – and it is an evil destination! **74** They swear by God that they did not say (it), but certainly they have said the word of disbelief, and have disbelieved after their submission. They determined (to do) what they did not attain, and they took vengeance for no other reason than that God and His messenger had enriched them from His favor. If they turn (in repentance) it will be better for them, but if they turn away, God will punish them (with) a painful punishment in this world and the Hereafter. They have no ally and no helper on the earth.

75 (There is) one of them who has made a covenant with God: 'If He gives us some of His favor, we shall indeed make contributions and indeed be among the righteous.' **76** But when He gave them some of His favor, they were stingy with it and turned away in aversion. **77** So He placed hypocrisy in their hearts until the Day when they meet Him, because they broke (with) God (concerning) what they promised Him, and because they have lied. **78** Do they not know that God knows their secret and their secret talk, and that God is the Knower of the unseen? **79** Those who find fault with those of the believers who contribute voluntarily, and those who ridicule those (believers) who do not find (anything to offer) but their effort – God has ridiculed them, and for them (there is) a painful punishment. **80** Ask forgiveness for them or do not ask forgiveness for them. (Even) if you ask forgiveness for them seventy times, God will not forgive them. That is because they have disbelieved in God and His messenger. God does not guide the wicked.

81 The ones who stayed behind gloated over their sitting (at home) behind the messenger of God, and disliked (it) that they should (have to) struggle with their wealth and their lives in the way of God. They said, 'Do not go forth in the heat.' Say: 'The Fire of Gehenna is hotter!' If (only) they understood! **82** So let them laugh a little (now) and weep a lot in payment for what they have earned. **83** If God brings you back to some contingent of them, and they ask your permission to go forth, say: 'You will never go forth with me, nor will you ever fight any enemy with me. Surely you were pleased with sitting (at home) the first time, so sit with the ones who stay behind.'

Repentance

84 Never pray over anyone of them who has died, nor stand over his grave. Surely they disbelieved in God and His messenger, and died while they were wicked. **85** Do not let their wealth and their children impress you. God only intends to punish them by means of it in this world, and (that) they themselves should pass away while they are disbelievers.

86 When a sūra is sent down (stating): 'Believe in God, and struggle alongside His messenger,' the wealthy among them ask your permission, and say, 'Let us be with the ones who sit (at home).' **87** They are pleased to be with the ones who stay behind, and a seal is set on their hearts, and so they do not understand. **88** But the messenger and those who believe with him have struggled with their wealth and their lives. And those – for them (there are) the good things, and those – they are the ones who prosper. **89** God has prepared for them Gardens through which rivers flow, there to remain. That is the great triumph!

90 The excuse-makers among the Arabs came to get permission for themselves, and those who lied to God and His messenger sat (at home). A painful punishment will smite those of them who disbelieve. **91** There is no blame on the weak or on the sick or on those who find nothing to contribute, if they are true to God and His messenger. (There is) no way against the doers of good – God is forgiving, compassionate – **92** nor against those (to) whom, when they came to you for you to give them mounts, you said, 'I cannot find a mount for you.' They turned away, and their eyes were full of the tears of sorrow, because they did not find anything to contribute. **93** The way is only open against those who ask your permission when they are rich. They are pleased to be with the ones who stay behind. God has set a seal on their hearts, but they do not know (it).

94 They will make excuses to you[9] when you return to them. Say: 'Do not make excuses, (for) we do not believe you. God has already informed us of the reports about you. God will see your deed, and (so will) His messenger. Then you will be returned to the Knower of the unseen and the seen, and He will inform you about what you have done.' **95** They will swear to you[10] by God, when you turn back to them, that you may turn away from them. Turn away from them, (for) surely they are an abomination. Their refuge is Gehenna – a payment for what they have earned. **96** They will swear to you[11] in order that you may be pleased with them. Yet (even) if you are pleased with them, surely God will not be pleased with the people who are wicked.

97 The Arabs are (even) stronger in disbelief and hypocrisy, and more likely not to know the limits of what God has sent down on His messenger. God is knowing, wise. **98** Among the Arabs (there is) one who regards what he contributes as a fine, and waits for the wheels (of fortune to turn) against you. The wheel of evil

---

9. *you*: plur.
10. *you*: plur.
11. *you*: plur.

Repentance

(will turn) against them! God is hearing, knowing. **99** Among the Arabs (there is) one who believes in God and the Last Day, and takes what he contributes as a (means of) drawing near to God, and (likewise) the prayers of the messenger. Is it not a fact that it is a (means of) drawing near for them? God will cause them to enter into His mercy. God is forgiving, compassionate.

100 The foremost – the first of the emigrants and the helpers, and those who have followed them in doing good – God is pleased with them and they are pleased with Him. He has prepared for them Gardens through which rivers flow, there to remain forever. That is the great triumph!

101 Some of the Arabs who (dwell) around you are hypocrites, and some of the people of the city (also). They have become obstinate in (their) hypocrisy. You[12] do not know them, (but) We know them, (and) We shall punish them twice. Then they will be returned to a great punishment. **102** Others have acknowledged their sins. They have mixed a righteous deed and another (that is) evil. It may be that God will turn (in forgiveness) to them. Surely God is forgiving, compassionate. **103** Take from their wealth a contribution, to cleanse them and purify them by means of it, and pray over them. Surely your prayers are a rest for them. God is hearing, knowing. **104** Do they not know that God – He accepts repentance from His servants and takes (their) contributions, and that God – He is the One who turns (in forgiveness), the Compassionate? **105** Say: 'Work! God will see your deed, and (so will) His messenger and the believers, and you will be returned to the Knower of the unseen and the seen, and He will inform you about what you have done.' **106** (There are) others (who will be) deferred to the command of God, (to see) whether He will punish them or turn (in forgiveness) to them. God is knowing, wise.

107 Those who have taken a mosque (to cause) harm and disbelief and division among the believers, and (to provide) a place of ambush for those who fought against God and His messenger before – they will indeed swear, 'We wanted nothing but good!' But God bears witness: 'Surely they are liars indeed!' **108** Never stand in it! A mosque founded from the first day on the (obligation of) guarding (oneself) is indeed (more) worthy for you to stand in. In it (there are) are men who love to purify themselves, and God loves the ones who purify themselves. **109** So is someone who founded his building on (the obligation of) guarding (oneself) against God, and (on His) approval, better, or someone who founded his building on the brink of a crumbling precipice, (which) then collapsed with him into the Fire of Gehenna? God does not guide the people who are evildoers. **110** Their building which they have built will continue (to be a cause of) doubt in their hearts, unless their hearts are cut (to pieces). God is knowing, wise.

111 Surely God has purchased from the believers their lives and their wealth with (the price of) the Garden (in store) for them. They fight in the way of God, and they kill and are killed. (That is) a promise binding on Him in the Torah, and

---

12. *You*: sing.

the Gospel, and the Qur'ān. Who fulfills his covenant better than God? So welcome the good news of the bargain you have made with Him. That is the great triumph! **112** The ones who turn (in repentance), the ones who serve, the ones who praise, the ones who wander, the ones who bow, the ones who prostrate themselves, the ones who command right, and the ones who forbid wrong, (and) the ones who keep the limits of God – give good news to the believers.

113 It is not for the prophet and those who believe to ask forgiveness for the idolaters, even though they may be family, after it has become clear to them that they are the companions of the Furnace. **114** Abraham's asking forgiveness for his father was only because of a solemn promise he had made to him. But when it became clear to him that he was an enemy to God, he disowned him. Surely Abraham was indeed kind (and) forbearing. **115** God is not one to lead a people astray after He has guided them, until He makes clear to them what they should guard (themselves) against. Surely God has knowledge of everything. **116** Surely God – to Him (belongs) the kingdom of the heavens and the earth. He gives life and causes death. You have no ally and no helper other than God.

117 Certainly God has turned (in forgiveness) to the prophet, and (to) the emigrants and the helpers who followed him in the hour of hardship, after the hearts of a group of them had nearly turned aside. Then He turned to them (in forgiveness). Surely He was kind (and) compassionate with them. **118** And to the three who stayed behind, when the earth became narrow for them despite its breadth, and they themselves were constrained, and they thought that (there was) no shelter from God except (going) to Him, then He turned to them (in forgiveness), so that they might (also) turn (in repentance). Surely God – He is the One who turns (in forgiveness), the Compassionate.

119 You who believe! Guard (yourselves) against God, and be with the truthful. **120** It is not for the people of the city, and those of the Arabs who (dwell) around them, to lag behind the messenger of God, nor should they prefer their lives to his. That is because no thirst and no weariness and no emptiness smites them in the way of God, nor do they make any attack (that) enrages the disbelievers, nor do they take any gain from an enemy, except that a righteous deed is thereby written down for them. Surely God does not let the reward of the doers of good go to waste. **121** Nor do they make any contribution, small or great, nor cross any wādī, except that it is written down for them, so that God may repay them (for the) best of what they have done.

122 It is not for the believers to go forth all together. Why not have a contingent of every group of them go forth, so that they may gain understanding in religion, and that they may warn their people when they return to them, so that they (in turn) may beware?

123 You who believe! Fight those of the disbelievers who are close to you, and let them find sternness in you, and know that God is with the ones who guard (themselves).

124 Whenever a sūra is sent down, some of them say, 'Which of you has this increased in belief?' As for those who believe, it increases them in belief, and they welcome the good news. **125** But as for those in whose hearts is a sickness, it increases them in abomination (added) to their abomination, and they die while they are disbelievers. **126** Do they not see that they are tested every year once or twice? Yet still they do not turn (in repentance), nor do they take heed.

127 Whenever a sūra is sent down, some of them look at others: 'Does anyone see you?' Then they turn away. God has turned away their hearts, because they are a people who do not understand.

128 Certainly a messenger has come to you from among you. What you suffer is a mighty (weight) on him, (for he has) concern over you, (and he is) kind (and) compassionate with the believers.

129 If they turn away, say: 'God is enough for me. (There is) no god but Him. In Him have I put my trust. He is the Lord of the great throne.'

10 ✻ JONAH

In the Name of God, the Merciful, the Compassionate

1 Alif Lām Rā'. Those are the signs of the wise Book.

2 Is it amazing to the people that We have inspired a man from among them: 'Warn the people, and give good news to those who believe, that for them (there is) a sure footing with their Lord'? (But) the disbelievers say, 'Surely this (man) is a clear magician indeed.'

3 Surely your Lord is God, who created the heavens and the earth in six days. Then He mounted the throne. He directs the (whole) affair. (There is) no intercessor without His permission. That is God, your Lord, so serve Him! Will you not take heed? 4 To Him is your return – all (of you) – the promise of God in truth! Surely He brought about the creation, (and) then He restores it, so that He may repay those who believe and do righteous deeds in justice. But those who disbelieve – for them (there is) a drink of boiling (water) and a painful punishment, because they were disbelieving.

5 He (it is) who made the sun an illumination, and the moon a light, and determined it by stations, so that you might know the number of the years and the reckoning (of time). God created that only in truth. He makes the signs distinct for a people who know. 6 Surely in the alternation of the night and the day, and (in) what God has created in the heavens and the earth, (there are) signs indeed for a people who guard (themselves).

7 Surely those who do not expect to meet Us, and are satisfied with this present life and feel secure in it, and those who are oblivious of Our signs, 8 those – their refuge is the Fire for what they have earned. 9 Surely those who believe and do righteous deeds – their Lord guides them for their belief. Beneath them rivers flow in Gardens of Bliss. 10 Their call there is: 'Glory to You, God!,' and their greeting there is: 'Peace!,' and the last (part) of their call is: 'Praise (be) to God, Lord of all peoples!'

11 If God were to hurry the evil for the people, (as) their seeking to hurry the good, their time would indeed have been completed for them. But We leave those who do not expect the meeting with Us in their insolent transgression, wandering blindly.

12 When hardship touches a person, he calls on Us, (whether lying) on his side or sitting or standing. But when We have removed his hardship from him, he

Jonah

continues on, as if he had not called on Us about the hardship (that) had touched him. In this way what the wanton do is made to appear enticing to them.

13 Certainly We destroyed the generations before you when they did evil, when their messengers brought them the clear signs and they would not believe. In this way We repay the people who are sinners. **14** Then, after them, We made you rulers on the earth, so that We might see how you would do.

15 When Our signs are recited to them as clear signs, those who do not expect the meeting with Us say, 'Bring a different Qur'ān than this one, or change it.' Say: 'It is not for me to change it of my own accord. I only follow what I am inspired (with). Surely I fear, if I disobey my Lord, the punishment of a great Day.' **16** Say: 'If God had (so) pleased, I would not have recited it to you, nor would He have made it known to you. I had already spent a lifetime among you before it (came to me). Will you not understand?' **17** Who is more evil than the one who forges a lie against God, or calls His signs a lie? Surely the sinners will not prosper.

18 They serve what neither harms them nor benefits them, instead of God (alone), and they say, 'These are our intercessors with God.' Say: 'Will you inform God about what He does not know either in the heavens or on the earth? Glory to Him! He is exalted above what they associate.' **19** The people were (once) one community, then they differed. Were it not for a preceding word from your Lord, it would indeed have been decided between them concerning their differences. **20** They say, 'If only a sign were sent down on him from his Lord.' Say: 'The unseen (belongs) only to God. (Just) wait! Surely I shall be one of those waiting with you.' **21** When We give the people a taste of mercy, after hardship has touched them, suddenly they (devise) some scheme against Our signs. Say: 'God is quicker (at devising) a scheme. Surely Our messengers are writing down what you are scheming.'

22 He (it is) who enables you to travel on the shore and the sea, until, when you are on the ship, and they sail with them by means of a fair wind, and they gloat over it, a violent wind comes upon it and the waves come at them from every side, and they think they are encompassed by them. (Then) they call on God, devoting (their) religion to Him: 'If indeed you rescue us from this, we shall indeed be among the thankful.' **23** Yet when He has rescued them, suddenly they become greedy on the earth without any right. People! Your envy is only against yourselves – (the fleeting) enjoyment of this present life. Then to Us is your return, and We shall inform you about what you have done.

24 A parable of this present life: (It is) is like water which We send down from the sky, and (there) mingles with it the vegetation of the earth from which the people and livestock eat, until, when the earth takes on its decoration and is adorned, and its people think that they have power over it, Our command comes on it by night or by day, and We cut it down, as if it had not flourished the day before. In this way We make the signs distinct for a people who reflect.

Jonah

25 God calls to the Home of peace, and guides whomever He pleases to a straight path. 26 For those who have done good, (there is) the good (reward) and more (besides). Neither dust nor humiliation will cover their faces. Those are the companions of the Garden. There they will remain. 27 But those who have done evil deeds – (the) payment for an evil deed is (an evil) like it – humiliation will cover them. They will have no protector from God. (It will be) as if their faces were covered (with) pieces of the darkness of night. Those are the companions of the Fire. There they will remain.

28 On the Day when We shall gather them all together, then We shall say to those who associated: '(Take) your place, you and your associates!' Then We shall separate them, and their associates will say, 'You were not serving us. 29 God is sufficient as a witness between us and you that we were indeed oblivious of your service.' 30 There every person will stand trial (for) what he has done, and they will be returned to God, their true Protector, and (then) what they forged will abandon them.

31 Say: 'Who provides for you from the sky and the earth? Or who has power over hearing and sight? Who brings forth the living from the dead, and brings forth the dead from the living, and who directs the (whole) affair?' Then they will say, 'God.' So say: 'Will you not guard (yourselves)?' 32 That is God, your true Lord. And what (is there) after the truth except straying (from it)? How (is it that) you are turned away? 33 In this way the word of your Lord has proved true against those who acted wickedly: 'They will not believe.' 34 Say: '(Is there) any of your associates who (can) bring about the creation, (and) then restore it?' Say: 'God – He brings about the creation, (and) then He restores it. How are you (so) deluded?' 35 Say: '(Is there) any of your associates who (can) guide to the truth?' Say: 'God – He guides to the truth. Is He who guides to the truth more worthy to be followed, or he who does not guide unless he is guided? What is (the matter) with you? How do you judge?' 36 Most of them only follow conjecture, (and) surely conjecture is of no use at all against the truth. Surely God is aware of what they do.

37 This Qur'ān is not the kind (of Book) that could have been forged apart from God. (It is) a confirmation of what was before it, and a distinct setting forth of the Book – (there is) no doubt about it – from the Lord of all peoples. 38 Or do they say, 'He has forged it'? Say: 'Then bring a sūra like it, and call on anyone you can, other than God, if you are truthful.' 39 No! They have called a lie what they cannot encompass in (their) knowledge of it, and when the interpretation of it has not (yet) come to them. Those who were before them called (it) a lie (too), and see how the end was for the evildoers!

40 (There is) one of them who believes in it, and (there is) one of them who does not believe in it, but your Lord knows the ones who foment corruption. 41 If they call you a liar, say: 'To me my deed, and to you your deed. You are free of what I do, and I am free of what you do.' 42 (There is) one of them who listens to you, but can

Jonah

you make the deaf hear, when they do not understand? **43** (There is) one of them who looks to you, but can you guide the blind, when they do not see? **44** Surely God does not do the people any evil at all, but the people do themselves evil.

45 On the Day when He gathers them, (it will seem) as if they had remained (in the grave) only for an hour of the day, (and) they will recognize each other. Lost (are) those who called the meeting with God a lie, and were not (rightly) guided. **46** Whether We show you some of that which We promise them, or take you, to Us is their return. Then God is a witness over what they do. **47** For every community (there is) a messenger. When their messenger comes, it will be decided between them in justice – and they will not be done evil.

48 They say, 'When (will) this promise (come to pass), if you[1] are truthful?' **49** Say: 'I do not have power to (cause) myself harm or benefit – except whatever God pleases. For every community (there is) a time. When their time comes, they will not delay (it) by an hour, nor will they advance (it by an hour).' **50** Say: 'Do you see? If His punishment comes to you by night or by day, what (part) of it would the sinners seek to hurry? **51** When it falls, will you believe in it? Now? When you had been seeking to hurry it?' **52** Then it will be said to those who have done evil: 'Taste the punishment of eternity! Are you being repaid (for anything) except for what you have earned?'

53 They ask you to inform them: 'Is it true?' Say: 'Yes, by my Lord! Surely it is true indeed! You will not escape (it).' **54** If each person who has done evil had all that is on the earth, he would indeed (try to) ransom (himself) with it. They will be full of secret regret when they see the punishment. It will be decided between them in justice – and they will not be done evil. **55** Is it not a fact that to God (belongs) whatever is in the heavens and the earth? Is it not a fact that the promise of God is true? But most of them do not know (it). **56** He gives life and causes death, and to Him you will be returned.

57 People! An admonition has come to you from your Lord, and a healing for what is in the hearts, and a guidance and mercy for the believers. **58** Say: 'In the favor of God and in His mercy – let them gloat over that, (for) it is better than what they accumulate.' **59** Say: 'Have you seen what God has sent down for you from (His) provision, yet you have made some of it forbidden and (some) permitted?' Say: 'Has God given permission to you, or do you forge (lies) against God?' **60** What will they think who forge lies against God on the Day of Resurrection? Surely God is indeed full of favor to the people, but most of them are not thankful (for it).

61 You[2] are not (engaged) in any matter, nor do you recite any recitation of it, nor do you[3] do any deed, except (that) We are witnesses over you when you are

---

1. *you*: plur.
2. *You*: sing.
3. *you*: plur.

Jonah

busy with it. Not (even) the weight of a speck on the earth or in the sky escapes from your Lord, nor (is there anything) smaller than that or greater, except (that it is recorded) in a clear Book. **62** Is it not a fact that the allies of God – (there will be) no fear on them, nor will they sorrow? **63** Those who believe and guard (themselves) – **64** for them (there is) good news in this present life and in the Hereafter. No one can change the words of God. That is the great triumph! **65** Do not let their speech cause you[4] sorrow. Surely honor (belongs) to God altogether. He is the Hearing, the Knowing.

66 Is it not a fact that to God (belongs) whoever is in the heavens and whoever is on the earth? They follow – those who call on associates other than God – they only follow conjecture and they only guess. **67** He (it is) who made the night for you to rest in and the day to see. Surely in that are signs indeed for a people who hear.

68 They say, 'God has taken a son.' Glory to Him! He is the wealthy One. To Him (belongs) whatever is in the heavens and whatever is on the earth. You have no authority for this (claim). Do you say about God what you do not know? **69** Say: 'Surely those who forge lies against God will not prosper.' **70** A (little) enjoyment in this world, then to Us is their return. Then We (shall) make them taste the harsh punishment for what they have disbelieved.

71 Recite to them the story of Noah: when he said to his people, 'My people! If my stay (here) and my reminding (you) by the signs of God are hard on you, yet in God have I put my trust. So put together your plan, (you) and your associates. Then do not let your plan (be a cause of) distress for you. Then decide about me and do not spare me. **72** If you turn away, (know that) I have not asked you for any reward. My reward (depends) only on God, and I have been commanded to be one of those who submit.' **73** But they called him a liar, so We rescued him and those who were with him in the ship, and We made them successors, and We drowned those who called Our signs a lie. See how the end was for the ones who were warned!

74 Then, after him, We raised up messengers for their people, and they brought them the clear signs. But they would not believe in what they had called a lie before. In this way We set a seal on the hearts of the transgressors.

75 Then, after them, We raised up Moses and Aaron for Pharaoh and his assembly with Our signs, but they became arrogant and were a sinful people. **76** When the truth came to them from Us, they said, 'Surely this is clear magic indeed.' **77** Moses said, 'Do you say (this) about the truth, when it has come to you? Is this magic? Yet magicians do not prosper.' **78** They said, 'Have you come to us in order to turn us away from what we found our fathers doing, and (in order that) you two (might) have greatness on the earth? We do not believe in you two.' **79** And Pharaoh said, 'Bring me every skilled magician.' **80** When the magicians came, Moses said to them, 'Cast (down) what you are going to cast.' **81** Then,

---

4. *you*: sing.

Jonah

when they had cast, Moses said, 'What you have brought is magic. Surely God will invalidate it. Surely God does not set right any deed of the fomenters of corruption. **82** God verifies the truth by His words, even though the sinners dislike (it).' **83** So no one believed in Moses, except for the descendants of his people, out of fear that Pharaoh and their assembly would persecute them. Surely Pharaoh was indeed haughty on the earth. Surely he was indeed one of the wanton.

84 Moses said, 'My people! If you believe in God, put your trust in Him, if you have submitted.' **85** They said, 'In God we have put our trust. Our Lord, do not make us an (object of) persecution for the people who are evildoers, **86** but rescue us by Your mercy from the people who are disbelievers.' **87** And We inspired Moses and his brother: 'Establish houses for your people in Egypt, and make your houses a direction (of prayer), and observe the prayer, and give good news to the believers.' **88** Moses said, 'Our Lord, surely You have given Pharaoh and his assembly splendor and wealth in this present life, Our Lord, so that they might lead (people) astray from Your way. Our Lord, obliterate their wealth and harden their hearts, so that they do not believe until they see the painful punishment.' **89** He said, 'The request of both of you has been answered. So both of you go straight, and do not follow the way of those who do not know.'

90 And We crossed the sea with the Sons of Israel, and Pharaoh and his forces followed them (out of) envy and enmity, until, when the drowning overtook him, he said, 'I believe that (there is) no god but the One in whom the Sons of Israel believe. I am one of those who submit.' **91** 'Now? When you had disobeyed before and were one of the fomenters of corruption? **92** Today We rescue you with your body, so that you may be a sign for those who succeed you. Yet surely many of the people are indeed oblivious of Our signs.' **93** Certainly We settled the Sons of Israel in a sure settlement and provided them with good things. They did not (begin to) differ until (after) the knowledge had come to them. Surely your Lord will decide between them on the Day of Resurrection concerning their differences.

94 If you are in doubt about what We have sent down to you, ask those who have been reciting the Book before you. The truth has come to you from your Lord, so do not be one of the doubters. **95** And do not be one of those who call the signs of God a lie, or you will be one of the losers. **96** Surely those against whom the word of your Lord has proved true will not believe, **97** even though every sign comes to them, until they see the painful punishment. **98** Why was there no town which believed, and its belief benefited it, except the people of Jonah? When they believed, We removed from them the punishment of disgrace in this present life and gave them enjoyment (of life) for a time. **99** If your Lord had (so) pleased, whoever was on the earth would indeed have believed – all of them together. Will you compel the people until they become believers? **100** It is not for any person to believe, except by the permission of God. He places abomination on those who do not understand.

Jonah

101 Say: 'See what is in the heavens and the earth!' But signs and warnings are of no use to a people who do not believe. **102** Do they expect (anything) but the same as the days of those who passed away before them? Say: '(Just) wait! Surely I shall be one of those waiting with you.' **103** Then We rescue Our messengers and those who believe. In this way – (it is) an obligation on Us – We shall rescue the believers.

104 Say: 'People! If you are in doubt about my religion, (know that) I do not serve those whom you serve instead of God, but I serve God, the One who takes you. I have been commanded to be one of the believers' **105** And: 'Set your face to the religion (as) a Ḥanīf,[5] and do not be one of the idolaters. **106** Do not call on what can neither benefit nor harm you, instead of God (alone). If you do, surely then you will be one of the evildoers. **107** If God touches you with any harm, (there is) no one to remove it but Him, and if He intends for you any good, (there is) no one to turn back His favor. He smites with it whomever He pleases of His servants. He is the Forgiving, the Compassionate.'

108 Say: 'People! The truth has come to you from your Lord. Whoever is (rightly) guided, is guided only for himself, and whoever goes astray, goes astray only against himself. I am not a guardian over you.'

109 Follow what you are inspired (with), and be patient until God judges, (for) He is the best of judges.

---

5. *Ḥanīf*: meaning uncertain.

11 ✺ Hūd

In the Name of God, the Merciful, the Compassionate

1 Alif Lām Rā'.

A Book – its verses have been clearly composed (and) then made distinct – (sent down) from One (who is) wise, aware.

2 'Do not serve (anyone) but God! Surely I am a warner and bringer of good news to you from Him.' **3** And: 'Ask forgiveness from your Lord, then turn to Him (in repentance). He will give you good enjoyment (of life) for an appointed time, and give His favor to everyone (deserving) of favor. If you turn away – surely I fear for you the punishment of a great Day. **4** To God is your return. He is powerful over everything.'

5 Is it not a fact that they cover their hearts to hide from Him? Is it not (a fact) that (even) when they cover themselves with their clothing, He knows what they keep secret and what they speak aloud? Surely He knows what is in the hearts. **6** (There is) not a creature on the earth but its provision (depends) on God. He knows its dwelling place and its storage place. Everything is (recorded) in a clear Book. **7** He (it is) who created the heavens and the earth in six days – and His throne was upon the water – that He might test you (to see) which of you is best in deed.

If indeed you say, 'Surely you will be raised up after death,' those who disbelieve will indeed say, 'This is nothing but clear magic.' **8** If indeed We postpone the punishment from them until a set period (of time), they will indeed say, 'What is holding it back?' Is it not (a fact) that on the Day when it comes to them, it will not be diverted from them, and what they were mocking will overwhelm them? **9** If indeed We give a person a taste of mercy from Us, (and) then We withdraw it from him, surely he is indeed despairing (and) ungrateful. **10** But if indeed We give him a taste of blessing, after hardship has touched him, he will indeed say, 'The evils have gone from me.' Surely he is indeed gloating (and) boastful **11** – except those who are patient and do righteous deeds. Those – for them (there is) forgiveness and a great reward.

12 Perhaps you are leaving out part of what you are inspired (with), and your heart is weighed down by it, because they say, 'If only a treasure were sent down on him or an angel came with him?' You are only a warner. God is guardian over everything. **13** Or do they say, 'He has forged it'? Say: 'Then bring ten sūras forged like it, and call on whomever you can, other than God, if you are truthful.' **14** If they do not respond to you, know that it has been sent down with the knowledge

Hūd

of God, and that (there is) no god but Him. So (will) you submit? **15** Whoever desires this present life and its (passing) splendor – We shall pay them in full for their deeds in it, and they will not be shortchanged in it. **16** Those are the ones who – for them there is nothing in the Hereafter but the Fire. What they have done will come to nothing there. What they have done will be in vain.

17 Is the one who (stands) on a clear sign from his Lord, and recites it as a witness from Him, and before it was the Book of Moses as a model and mercy [...]?[1] Those believe in it, but whoever disbelieves in it from the factions – the Fire is his appointed place. So do not be in doubt about it. Surely it is the truth from your Lord, but most of the people do not believe.

18 Who is more evil than the one who forges a lie against God? Those will be presented before their Lord, and the witnesses will say, 'These are those who lied against their Lord.' Is it not (a fact) that the curse of God is on the evildoers, **19** who keep (people) from the way of God and desire (to make) it crooked, and they are disbelievers in the Hereafter? **20** Those – they cannot escape (Him) on the earth, and they have no allies other than God. The punishment will be doubled for them. They could not hear and did not see. **21** Those are the ones who have lost their (own) selves, and what they forged has abandoned them. **22** (There is) no doubt that they will be the worst losers in the Hereafter. **23** Surely those who believe, and do righteous deeds, and humble themselves to their Lord – those are the companions of the Garden. There they will remain. **24** The parable of the two groups is like the blind and the deaf, and the sighted and the hearing. Are they equal in comparison? Will you not take heed?

25 Certainly We sent Noah to his people: 'I am a clear warner for you. **26** Do not serve (anyone) but God! Surely I fear for you the punishment of a painful Day.' **27** The assembly of those who disbelieved of his people said, 'We do not see you as (anything) but a human being like us, and we do not see following you (any) but the worst (and) most gullible of us. We do not see in you any superiority over us. No! We think you are liars.' **28** He said, 'My people! Do you see? If I (stand) on a clear sign from my Lord, and He has given me mercy from Himself, but it has been obscured for you, shall we compel you (to accept) it when you are unwilling? **29** My people! I do not ask you for any money for it. My reward (depends) only on God. I am not going to drive away those who believe. Surely they are going to meet their Lord, but I see that you are an ignorant people. **30** My people! Who would help me against God if I drove them away? Will you not take heed? **31** I do not say to you, "I possess the storehouses of God," nor do I know the unseen. And I do not say, "I am an angel," nor do I say to those your eyes look down on, "God will not give them any good." God knows what is in them. Surely then I would indeed be one of the evildoers.' **32** They said, 'Noah!

---

1. [...]: something appears to be missing here; perhaps originally a contrast was drawn between the Prophet's authority (namely, the Qur'ān and, before it, the Torah) and that of his (Jewish?) opponents (cf. Q46.12).

Hūd

You have disputed with us, and disputed (too) much with us. Bring us what you promise us, if you are one of the truthful.' **33** He said, 'Only God will bring it to you, if He (so) pleases, and you will not escape. **34** My advice will not benefit you – (even) if I wish to advise you – if God wishes to make you err. He is your Lord, and to Him you will be returned.'

35 Or do they say, 'He has forged it'? Say: 'If I have forged it, my sin is on me, but I am free of the sins you commit.'

36 And Noah was inspired: 'None of your people will believe, except for the one who has (already) believed, so do not be distressed by what they have done. **37** Build the ship under Our eyes and Our inspiration, and do not address Me concerning those who have done evil. Surely they are going to be drowned.' **38** And he was building the ship, and whenever the assembly of his people passed by him, they ridiculed him. He said, 'If you ridicule us, surely we shall ridicule you as you ridicule. **39** Soon you will know (on) whom punishment will come, disgracing him, and on whom a lasting punishment will descend.' **40** – Until, when Our command came and the oven boiled, We said, 'Load into it two of every kind, a pair, and your family – except for the one against whom the word has (already) gone forth – and whoever has believed.' But only a few had believed with him. **41** And he said, 'Sail in it! In the name of God (is) its running and its anchoring. Surely my Lord is indeed forgiving, compassionate.' **42** It ran with them in (the midst of) waves like mountains, and Noah called out to his son, since he was in a place apart, 'My son! Sail with us and do not be with the disbelievers!' **43** He said, 'I shall take refuge on a mountain (that) will protect me from the water.' He[2] said, '(There is) no protector today from the command of God, except for the one on whom He has compassion.' And the waves came between them, and he was among the drowned.

44 And it was said: 'Earth! Swallow your water! And sky! Stop!' And the waters subsided, and the command was accomplished, and it came to rest on al-Jūdī. And it was said: 'Away with the people who were evildoers!' **45** And Noah called out to his Lord, and said, 'My Lord, surely my son is one of my family, and surely Your promise is the truth, and You are the most just of judges.' **46** He said, 'Noah! Surely he is not one of your family. Surely it is an unrighteous deed. So do not ask Me about what you have no knowledge of. Surely I admonish you not to be one of the ignorant.' **47** He said, 'My Lord, surely I take refuge with You for asking You about what I have no knowledge of, and unless You forgive me and have compassion on me, I shall be one of the losers.' **48** It was said, 'Noah! Go down with peace from Us, and blessings on you and on the communities of those who are with you. But (to other) communities We shall give enjoyment (of life), (and) then a painful punishment from Us will touch them.' **49** That is one of the stories of the unseen. We inspired you (with) it. You did not know it, (neither) you nor your people, before (this). So be patient. Surely the outcome (belongs) to the ones who guard (themselves).

---

2. *He*: Noah.

Hūd

50 And to 'Ād (We sent) their brother Hūd. He said, 'My people! Serve God! You have no god other than Him. You are nothing but forgers (of lies). **51** My people! I do not ask you for any reward for it. My reward (depends) only on the One who created me. Will you not understand?' **52** And: 'My people! Ask forgiveness from your Lord, then turn to Him (in repentance). He will send the sky (down) on you in abundance (of rain), and increase you in strength upon your strength. Do not turn away as sinners.' **53** They said, 'Hūd! You have not brought us any clear sign, and we are not going to abandon our gods on your saying, (for) we do not believe in you. **54** We (can) only say (that) one of our gods has seized you with evil.' He said, 'Surely I call God to witness, and you bear witness (too), that I am free of what you associate, **55** other than Him. So plot against me, all of you, (and) then do not spare me. **56** Surely I have put my trust in God, my Lord and your Lord. (There is) no creature He does not seize by its hair. Surely my Lord is on a straight path. **57** If you turn away, I have delivered to you what I was sent to you with, and my Lord will make another people succeed you, and you will not harm Him at all. Surely my Lord is a watcher over everything.' **58** And when Our command came, We rescued Hūd, and those who believed with him, by a mercy from Us, and We rescued them from a stern punishment. **59** That was 'Ād: they denied the signs of their Lord, and disobeyed His messengers, and followed the command of every stubborn tyrant. **60** And they were followed in this world (by) a curse, and on the Day of Resurrection: 'Is it not a fact that 'Ād disbelieved their Lord? Is it not, "Away with 'Ād, the people of Hūd"?'

61 And to Thamūd (We sent) their brother Ṣāliḥ. He said, 'My people! Serve God! You have no god other than Him. He produced you from the earth and settled you in it. So ask forgiveness from Him, (and) then turn to Him (in repentance). Surely my Lord is near (and) responsive.' **62** They said, 'Ṣāliḥ! You were among us as someone in whom hope was placed before. Do you forbid us to serve what our fathers have served? Surely we are in grave doubt indeed about what you call us to.' **63** He said, 'My people! Do you see? If I (stand) on a clear sign from my Lord, and He has given me mercy from Himself, who would help me against God if I disobeyed Him? You would only increase my loss. **64** My people! This is the she-camel of God, a sign for you. Let her graze on God's earth, and do not touch her with evil, or a punishment near (at hand) will seize you.' **65** But they wounded her, and he said, 'Enjoy (yourselves) in your home(s) for three days – that is a promise not to be denied.' **66** And when Our command came, We rescued Ṣāliḥ, and those who believed with him, by a mercy from Us, and from the disgrace of that day. Surely your Lord – He is the Strong, the Mighty. **67** And the cry seized those who did evil, and morning found them leveled in their homes. **68** (It was) as if they had not lived in prosperity there. 'Is it not a fact that Thamūd disbelieved their Lord? Is it not, "Away with Thamūd"?'

69 Certainly Our messengers brought Abraham the good news. They said, 'Peace!' He said, 'Peace!,' and did not delay in bringing a roasted calf. **70** When he saw their hands not reaching for it, he became suspicious of them and began to feel

Hūd

fear of them. They said, 'Do not fear! Surely we have been sent to the people of Lot.' **71** His wife was standing (there), and she laughed. And so We gave her the good news of Isaac, and after Isaac, Jacob. **72** She said, 'Woe is me! Shall I give birth when I am an old woman and my husband here is an old man? Surely this is an amazing thing indeed!' **73** They said, 'Are you surprised by the command of God? The mercy of God and His blessings (be) upon you, People of the House! Surely He is indeed praiseworthy, glorious.' **74** When the fright had left Abraham and the good news had come to him, he was disputing with Us concerning the people of Lot. **75** Surely Abraham was indeed tolerant, kind, (and) turning (in repentance). **76** 'Abraham! Turn away from this! Surely it has come – the command of your Lord. Surely they – a punishment is coming upon them which cannot be turned back.'

77 And when Our messengers came to Lot, he became distressed about them, and felt powerless (to protect) them, and he said, 'This is a hard day.' **78** His people came to him, rushing to him, (for) they had been in the habit of doing evil deeds before (this). He said, 'My people! These are my daughters, they are purer for you. So guard (yourselves) against God, and do not disgrace me concerning my guests. Is (there) no one among you of right mind?' **79** They said, 'Certainly you know that we have no right to your daughters, and surely you know indeed what we want.' **80** He said, 'If only I had the strength for you, or could take refuge in a strong supporter!' **81** They said, 'Lot! Surely we are messengers of your Lord. They will not reach you. So journey with your family in a part of the night, and let none of you turn around, except your wife, (for) surely what is about to smite them is going to smite her. Surely their appointment is the morning. Is the morning not near?' **82** So when Our command came, We turned it upside down, and rained on it stones of baked clay, one after another, **83** marked in the presence of your Lord. It is not far from the evildoers.

84 And to Midian (We sent) their brother Shu'ayb. He said, 'My people! Serve God! You have no god other than Him. Do not diminish the measure or the scale. Surely I see you in prosperity, but surely I fear for you the punishment of an overwhelming day. **85** My people! Fill up the measure and the scale in justice, and do not shortchange the people of their wealth, and do not act wickedly on the earth, fomenting corruption. **86** A remnant of God is better for you, if you are believers. I am not a watcher over you.' **87** They said, 'Shu'ayb! Does your prayer command you that we should abandon what our fathers have served, or that (we should abandon) doing what we please with our wealth? Surely you – you indeed are the tolerant (and) right-minded one.' **88** He said, 'My people! Have you considered? If I (stand) on a clear sign from my Lord, and He has provided me with good provision from Himself [. . .].³ I do not wish to go behind your backs to (do) what I forbid you from. I only wish to set (things) right, as much as I am able, but

---

3. *[. . .]*: there is a lacuna here, which can be restored on the basis of the parallel at Q11.63 above ('who would help me against God if I disobeyed Him?').

Hūd

my success is only with God. In Him I have put my trust, and to Him I turn (in repentance). **89** My people! Do not let my defiance (of you) provoke you to sin, or something will smite you similar to what smote the people of Noah, or the people of Hūd, or the people of Ṣāliḥ. And the people of Lot are not far from you. **90** Ask forgiveness from your Lord, (and) then turn to Him (in repentance). Surely my Lord is compassionate, loving.'

91 They said, 'Shu'ayb! We do not understand much of what you say. Surely we indeed see you as weak among us. But (for) your gang (of followers) we would indeed have stoned you, (for) you are not mighty against us.' **92** He said, 'My people! Is my gang (of followers) mightier against you than God? Have you taken Him (as something to cast) behind you? Surely my Lord encompasses what you do. **93** My people! Do as you are able. Surely I am going to do (what I can). Soon you will know the one (on) whom punishment will come, disgracing him, and the one who is a liar. (Just) watch! Surely I am watching with you.' **94** And when Our command came, We rescued Shu'ayb, and those who believed with him, by a mercy from Us. And the cry seized those who did evil, and morning found them leveled in their homes. **95** (It was) as if they had not lived there. 'Is it not away with Midian, (just) as Thamūd was done away with?'

96 Certainly We sent Moses with Our signs and clear authority **97** to Pharaoh and his assembly, but they followed the command of Pharaoh, when the command of Pharaoh was not right-minded. **98** He will precede his people on the Day of Resurrection, and lead them to the Fire. Evil is the place (to which they are) led! **99** They were followed in this (world by) a curse, and on the Day of Resurrection – evil is the gift (they will be) given!

100 That is from the stories of the towns (which) We recount to you. Some of them are (still) standing and some (are already) cut down. **101** Yet We did not do them evil, but they did themselves evil. Their gods, on whom they called instead of God, were of no use to them at all, when the command of your Lord came, and they only added to their ruin. **102** Such was the seizing of your Lord, when He seized the towns while they were doing evil. Surely His seizing was painful (and) harsh. **103** Surely in that is a sign indeed for whoever fears the punishment of the Hereafter. That is a Day to which the people will be gathered, and that is a Day (that will be) witnessed. **104** We postpone it only for a set time. **105** (When that) Day comes, no one will speak, except by His permission. Some of them will be miserable, and some happy. **106** As for those who are miserable, (they will be) in the Fire, where (there will be) a moaning and panting for them, **107** remaining there as long as the heavens and the earth endure, except as your Lord pleases. Surely your Lord accomplishes whatever He pleases. **108** But as for those who are happy, (they will be) in the Garden, there to remain as long as the heavens and the earth endure, except as your Lord pleases – an unceasing gift. **109** Do not be in doubt about what these (people) serve: they only serve as their fathers served before (them). Surely We shall indeed pay them their portion in full, undiminished.

Hūd

110 Certainly We gave Moses the Book, and then differences arose about it. Were it not for a preceding word from your Lord, it would indeed have been decided between them. Surely they are in grave doubt indeed about it. **111** Surely each (of them) – your Lord will indeed pay them in full for their deeds. Surely He is aware of what they do.

112 So go straight, as you have been commanded, (you) and those who have turned (in repentance) with you. Do not transgress insolently,[4] (for) surely He sees what you do. **113** Do not incline[5] toward those who do evil, or the Fire will touch you – you have no allies other than God – (and) then you will not be helped. **114** And observe the prayer[6] at the two ends of the day and at the approach of the night. Surely good (deeds) take away evil (ones). That is a reminder to the mindful. **115** And be patient. Surely God does not let the reward of the doers of good go to waste.

116 If only there had been a remnant of men, among the generations before you, to forbid the (fomenting of) corruption on the earth – aside from a few of those whom We rescued among them. But those who did evil pursued what luxury they were given to delight in, and became sinners. **117** Yet your Lord was not one to destroy the towns in an evil manner, while its people were setting (things) right. **118** If your Lord had (so) pleased, He would indeed have made the people one community, but they will continue to differ, **119** except for the one on whom your Lord has compassion, and for that (purpose) He created them. But the word of your Lord is fulfilled: 'I shall indeed fill Gehenna with jinn and humans – all (of them)!'

120 Everything We recount to you[7] from the stories of the messengers (is) what We make firm your heart with, and by this means the truth has come to you, and an admonition, and a reminder to the believers. **121** Say to those who do not believe: 'Do as you are able. Surely we are going to do (what we can).' **122** And: '(Just) wait! Surely we (too) are waiting.'

123 To God (belongs) the unseen in the heavens and the earth, and to Him the affair – all of it – will be returned. So serve Him and put your trust in Him! Your[8] Lord is not oblivious of what you[9] do.

---

4. *Do not transgress...*: plur. imperative.
5. *Do not incline*: plur. imperative.
6. *observe the prayer*: sing. imperative.
7. *you*: sing.
8. *Your*: sing.
9. *you*: plur.

12 ✤ Joseph

In the Name of God, the Merciful, the Compassionate

1 Alif Lām Rā'. Those are the signs of the clear Book. **2** Surely We have sent it down as an Arabic Qur'ān, so that you[1] may understand.

3 We shall recount to you[2] the best of accounts in what We have inspired you (with of) this Qur'ān, though before it you were indeed one of the oblivious.

4 (Remember) when Joseph said to his father, 'My father! Surely I saw eleven stars, and the sun and the moon. I saw them prostrating themselves before me.' **5** He said, 'My son! Do not recount your vision to your brothers or they will hatch a plot against you. Surely Satan is a clear enemy to humans. **6** In this way your Lord will choose you, and teach you about the interpretation of dreams, and complete His blessing on you and on the house of Jacob, as He completed it before on your fathers, Abraham and Isaac. Surely your Lord is knowing, wise.'

7 Certainly in (the story of) Joseph and his brothers (there) are signs for the ones who ask.

8 (Remember) when they said, 'Joseph and his brother are indeed dearer to our father than we, (even) though we are a (large) group. Surely our father is indeed clearly astray. **9** Kill Joseph, or cast him (into some other) land, so that your father's favor will be exclusively for you, and after that you will be a righteous people.' **10** A speaker among them said, 'Do not kill Joseph, but cast him to the bottom of the well, (and) some caravan will pick him up – if you are going to do (anything).'

11 They said, 'Our father! Why do you not trust us with Joseph? Surely we shall indeed look after him. **12** Send him out with us tomorrow to enjoy (himself) and jest. Surely we shall indeed watch over him.' **13** He said, 'Surely I – it sorrows me indeed that you should take him away – I fear that the wolf may eat him while you are oblivious of him.' **14** They said, 'If indeed the wolf eats him, when we are (so large) a group, surely then we (would be) losers indeed.'

15 When they had taken him away, and agreed to put him in the bottom of the well, We inspired him: 'You will indeed inform them about this affair (of theirs), though they will not realize (who you are).' **16** And they came to their father in the evening, weeping. **17** They said, 'Our father! Surely we went off racing (one

---

1. *you*: plur.
2. *you*: sing.

Joseph

another), and we left Joseph (behind) with our things, and the wolf ate him. But you will not believe us, even though we are truthful.' **18** And they brought his shirt with fake blood on it. He said, 'No! You have only contrived a story for yourselves. Patience is becoming (for me), and God is the One to be sought for help against what you allege.'

19 A caravan came, and they sent their water-drawer, and he let down his bucket. He said, 'Good news! This is a young boy (here).' And they hid him as merchandise, but God knew what they were doing. **20** And they sold him for a small price, a number of dirhams, (for) they had no interest in him. **21** The one who bought him, (being) from Egypt, said to his wife, 'Make his dwelling place honorable. It may be that he will benefit us, or we may adopt him as a son.' In this way We established Joseph in the land, and (this took place) in order that We might teach him about the interpretation of dreams. God is in control of His affair, but most of the people do not know (it). **22** When he reached his maturity, We gave him judgment and knowledge. In this way We repay the doers of good.

23 She, in whose house he was, tried to seduce him, and she closed the doors, and said, 'Come here, you!' He said, 'God's refuge! Surely he is my lord,[3] and he has given me a good dwelling place. Surely the evildoers do not prosper.' **24** Certainly she was obsessed with him, and he would have been obsessed with her, if (it had) not (been) that he saw a proof of his Lord. (It happened) in this way in order that We might turn evil and immorality away from him. Surely he was one of Our devoted servants. **25** They both raced to the door, and she tore his shirt from behind. They both met her husband at the door. She said, 'What penalty (is there) for (someone) who intended (to do) evil to your family, except that he should be imprisoned or (suffer) a painful punishment?' **26** He said, 'She tried to seduce me!' (Just then) a witness of her household bore witness: 'If his shirt is torn from the front, she has been truthful, and he is one of the liars. **27** But if his shirt is torn from behind, she has lied, and he is one of the truthful.' **28** So when he saw his shirt torn from behind, he said, 'Surely it is a plot of you women! Surely your plot is grave. **29** Joseph, turn away from this. And you (woman), ask forgiveness for your sin. Surely you are one of the sinners!'

30 Some women in the city said, 'The wife of that mighty one has been trying to seduce her young man. He has affected her deeply (with) love. Surely we see (that) she is indeed clearly astray.' **31** When she heard their cunning (gossip), she sent for them, and prepared a banquet for them, and gave each one of them a knife. Then she said (to Joseph), 'Come forth to (wait on) them.' When they saw him, they admired him, and cut their hands, and said, 'God preserve (us)! This is no (mere) mortal. This is nothing but a splendid angel!' **32** She said, 'That is the one you blamed me about. I certainly did try to seduce him, but he defended himself, and (now) if he does not do what I command him, he will indeed be imprisoned, and become one of the disgraced.' **33** He said, 'My Lord, prison is

---

3. *my lord*: Joseph's Egyptian master.

preferable to me than what they invite me to. But unless You turn their plot away from me, I shall give in to them, and I shall become one of the ignorant.' **34** Then his Lord responded to him, and turned their plot away from him. Surely He – He is the Hearing, the Knowing.

35 Then it became apparent to them,[4] after they had seen the signs,[5] (that) they should imprison him for a time. **36** And two young men entered the prison with him. One of them said, 'Surely I saw myself (in a dream) pressing wine,' and the other said, 'Surely I saw myself (in a dream) carrying bread on my head, from which the birds were eating. Inform us about its interpretation. Surely we see you are one of the doers of good.' **37** He said, 'Before any food comes to either of you for provision, I shall inform each of you about its interpretation before it comes to you. That is part of what my Lord has taught me. Surely I have forsaken the creed of a people (who) do not believe in God and (who) are disbelievers in the Hereafter, **38** and I have followed the creed of my fathers, Abraham, and Isaac, and Jacob. (It) was not for us to associate anything with God. That is part of the favor of God to us and to the people, but most of the people are not thankful (for it). **39** My two companions of the prison! Are various Lords better, or God, the One, the Supreme? **40** Instead of Him, you only serve names which you have named, you and your fathers. God has not sent down any authority for it. Judgment (belongs) only to God. He has commanded you not to serve (anyone) but Him. That is the right religion, but most of the people do not know (it). **41** My two companions of the prison! As for one of you, he will give his lord wine to drink, and as for the other, he will be crucified, and birds will eat from his head. The matter about which you two asked for a pronouncement has been decided.' **42** He said to the one of them he thought would be released, 'Mention me in the presence of your lord.' But Satan made him forget to mention (him) to his lord. So he remained in the prison for several years.

43 The king said, 'Surely I saw (in a dream) seven fat cows, (and) seven lean ones are eating them, and seven green ears (of corn) and others dry. Assembly! Make a pronouncement to me about my vision, if you can interpret visions.' **44** They said, 'A jumble of dreams. We know nothing of the interpretation of dreams.' **45** But the one who had been released (from prison) said – (for) he remembered after a period (of time) – 'I shall inform you about its interpretation. So send me.' **46** 'Joseph, you truthful man! Make a pronouncement to us about the seven fat cows (and) seven lean ones eating them, and the seven green ears (of corn) and others dry, in order that I may return to the people, so that they will know.' **47** He said, 'You will sow for seven years as usual, but what you harvest leave in its ear, except a little from which you may eat. **48** Then, after that, will come seven hard (years), (which will) devour what you stored up for them, (all) except a little of

---

4. *them*: the men of the city.
5. *the signs*: that Joseph posed a threat to their women.

Joseph

what you preserved. **49** Then, after that, will come a year in which the people will have rain, and in which they will press.'

50 The king said, 'Bring him to me!' But when the messenger came to him, he[6] said, 'Return to your lord and ask him, "What (about the) case of the women who cut their hands?" Surely my Lord knew of their plot.' **51** He[7] said, 'What is this business of yours, when you tried to seduce Joseph?' They said, 'God preserve (us)! We know no evil against him.' The wife of the mighty one said, 'Now the truth has come to light. I tried to seduce him, but surely he is indeed one of the truthful.' **52** 'That (is) so that he[8] may know that I[9] did not betray him in secret, and that God does not guide the plot of the treacherous. **53** Yet I do not pronounce myself innocent, (for) surely the self is indeed an instigator of evil, except as my Lord has compassion. Surely my Lord is forgiving, compassionate.'

54 The king said, 'Bring him to me! I want him for myself.' So when he spoke to him, he said, 'Surely this day you are secure with us (and) trustworthy.' **55** He said, 'Set me over the storehouses of the land. Surely I am a skilled overseer.' **56** In this way We established Joseph in the land. He settled in it wherever he pleased. We smite whomever We please with Our mercy, and We do not let the reward of the doers of good go to waste. **57** But the reward of the Hereafter is indeed better for those who believe and guard (themselves).

58 The brothers of Joseph came, and they entered upon him. He recognized them, but they did not know him. **59** When he had supplied them with their supplies, he said, 'Bring me a brother of yours from your father. Do you not see that I fill up the measure, and that I am the best of hosts? **60** But if you do not bring him to me, (there will be) no measure for you with me, and you will not come near me.' **61** They said, 'We shall solicit his father for him. Surely we shall indeed do (so).' **62** He said to his young men, 'Put their merchandise[10] (back) in their packs, so that they will recognize it when they turn back to their family, (and) so that they will return (here).'

63 When they returned to their father, they said, 'Our father! The measure was refused us,[11] so send our brother[12] (back) with us, (and) we shall get the measure. Surely we shall indeed watch over him.' **64** He said, 'Shall I trust you with him as I trusted you with his brother before? God is the best Watcher, and He (is) the most compassionate of the compassionate.' **65** When they opened their belongings, they found their merchandise returned to them. They said, 'Our father,

---

6. *he*: Joseph.
7. *He*: the king.
8. *he*: the woman's husband (this and the following verse are spoken by Joseph).
9. *I*: Joseph.
10. *merchandise*: what the brothers had brought with them to barter for corn.
11. *was refused us*: i.e. future supplies of corn were denied.
12. *our brother*: Benjamin, according to Genesis 42.36.

Joseph

what (more) do we desire? This is our merchandise returned to us. We shall supply (food for) our family, and watch over our brother, and get an extra measure of a camel(-load). That is an easy measure.' **66** He said, 'I shall not send him with you until you give me a promise from God that you will indeed bring him (back) to me, unless you are surrounded.' When they had given him their pledge, he said, 'God is guardian over what we say.' **67** And he said, 'My sons! Do not enter by one gate, but enter by different gates. I am of no use to you at all against God. Judgment (belongs) only to God. In Him have I put my trust, and in Him let the trusting put their trust.'

68 When they had entered in the way their father commanded them – it was of no use to them at all against God, but (it was only) a need in Jacob himself which he satisfied. Surely he was indeed full of knowledge because of what We had taught him, but most of the people do not know (it). **69** And when they entered upon Joseph, he took his brother to himself and said, 'Surely I am your brother, so do not be distressed at what they have done.'

70 When he had supplied them with their supplies, he put the drinking cup in the pack of his brother. Then a crier cried out, 'Caravan! Surely you are thieves indeed!' **71** They said as they approached them, 'What is it you are missing?' **72** They said, 'We are missing the king's cup. To the one who brings it a camel-load (will be given). I guarantee it.' **73** They said, 'By God! Certainly you know (that) we did not come to foment corruption on the earth. We are not thieves.' **74** They said, 'What will the penalty for it be, if you are liars?' **75** They said, 'The penalty for it (will be): the one in whose pack it is found, he (will be) liable for it. In this way we repay the evildoers.' **76** So he[13] began with their packs before (searching) his brother's pack, (and) then he brought it out of his brother's pack. In this way We plotted for (the sake of) Joseph. He was not one to take his brother, in (accord with) the religion of the king, unless God had (so) pleased. We raise in rank whomever We please, and above everyone who has knowledge is the One who knows.

77 They said, 'If he steals, a brother of his has stolen before.' But Joseph kept it secret within himself and did not reveal it to them. He said, 'You are (in) a bad situation. God knows what you are alleging.' **78** They said, 'Great one! Surely he has a father (who is) very old, so take one of us (in) his place. Surely we see (that) you are one of the doers of good.' **79** He said, 'God's refuge! That we should take (anyone) except (the one) in whose possession we found our things! Surely then we (would be) evildoers indeed.' **80** So when they had given up hope of (moving) him, they withdrew in private conversation. The eldest of them said, 'Do you not know that your father has already taken you under a promise from God? And (that) before that you neglected (to keep your promise) concerning Joseph? I shall not leave the land until my father gives me permission or (until) God judges for me.[14] He is the best of judges. **81** Return to your father and say, "Our father!

---

13. *he*: Joseph.
14. *judges for me*: or 'decides in my favor.'

Joseph

Surely your son has stolen. We bear witness only about what we know. We were not observers of the unseen. **82** Ask (the people of) the town where we were, and (those in) the caravan in which we have come. Surely we are truthful indeed.'"

83 He[15] said, 'No! You have only contrived a story for yourselves. Patience is becoming (for me). It may be that God will bring them all to me. Surely He – He is the Knowing, the Wise.' **84** He turned away from them and said, 'My sorrow for Joseph!' And his eyes became white from the grief, and he choked back his sadness. **85** They said, 'By God! You will never stop mentioning Joseph until you are frail or are on the verge of death.' **86** He said, 'I only complain (of) my anguish and my grief to God, (for) I know from God what you do not know. **87** My sons! Go and search out news of Joseph and his brother, and do not despair of the comfort of God. Surely everyone has hope of the comfort of God, except for the people who are disbelievers.'

88 When they entered upon him,[16] they said, 'Great one! Hardship[17] has touched us and our house, and we have brought merchandise of little value. Fill up the measure for us and be charitable to us. Surely God rewards the charitable.' **89** He said, 'Do you know what you did with Joseph and his brother, when you were ignorant?' **90** They said, 'Are you indeed Joseph?' He said, 'I am Joseph, and this is my brother. God has bestowed favor on us. Surely the one who guards (himself) and is patient – surely God does not let the reward of the doers of good go to waste.' **91** They said, 'By God! Certainly God has preferred you over us, and we have been sinners indeed.' **92** He said, '(There is) no reproach on you today. God will forgive you, (for) He is the most compassionate of the compassionate. **93** Go with this shirt of mine and cast it on my father's face. He will regain (his) sight. And (then) bring me your family all together.'

94 When the caravan set forth, their father said, 'Surely I do indeed perceive the scent of Joseph, though you may think me senile.' **95** They said, 'By God! Surely you are indeed in your (same) old error.' **96** So when the bringer of good news came (to him), he cast it on his face and (his) sight returned. He said, 'Did I not say to you, "Surely I know from God what you do not know"?' **97** They said, 'Our father! Ask forgiveness for us for our sins. Surely we have been sinners.' **98** He said, 'I shall ask my Lord for forgiveness for you. Surely He – He is the Forgiving, the Compassionate.'

99 When they entered upon Joseph, he took his parents to himself and said, 'Enter Egypt, if God pleases, secure.' **100** He raised his parents on the throne, and they (all) fell down before him in prostration. And he said, 'My father! This is the interpretation of my vision from before. My Lord has made it (come) true. He has been good to me, when He brought me out of the prison, and when He brought

---

15. *He*: Jacob.
16. *him*: Joseph.
17. *Hardship*: i.e. famine.

Joseph

you out of the desert, after Satan had caused strife between me and my brothers. Surely my Lord is astute to whatever He pleases. Surely He – He is the Knowing, the Wise. **101** My Lord, you have given me some of the kingdom, and taught me some of the interpretation of dreams. Creator of the heavens and the earth, You are my ally in this world and the Hereafter. Take me as one who has submitted, and join me with the righteous.'

102 That is one of the stories of the unseen. We inspired you (with) it. You were not with them when they agreed on their plan and were scheming. **103** Most of the people are not going to believe, even if you are eager (for that). **104** You do not ask them for any reward for it. It is nothing but a reminder to all peoples. **105** How many a sign in the heavens and the earth do they pass by! Yet they turn away from it. **106** Most of them do not believe in God, unless they associate. **107** Do they feel secure that a covering of God's punishment will not come upon them, or that the Hour will not come upon them unexpectedly, when they do not realize (it)? **108** Say: 'This is my way. I call (you) to God on (the basis of) evidence – I and whoever follows me. Glory to God! I am not one of the idolaters.'

109 We have not sent (anyone) before you except men whom We inspired from the people of the towns. Have they not traveled on the earth and seen how the end was for those who were before them? The Home of the Hereafter is indeed better for those who guard (themselves). Do you not understand? **110** – Until, when the messengers had given up hope, and thought that they had been called liars, Our help came to them, and those whom We pleased were rescued. But Our violence was not turned back from the people who were sinners. **111** Certainly in their accounts (there is) a lesson for those with understanding.

It is not a forged proclamation, but a confirmation of what was before it, and a distinct setting forth of everything, and a guidance and mercy for a people who believe.

13 ❋ The Thunder

In the Name of God, the Merciful, the Compassionate

1 Alif Lām Mīm Rā'. Those are the signs of the Book. What has been sent down to you from your Lord is the truth, but most of the people do not believe.

2 (It is) God who raised up the heavens without pillars that you (can) see. Then He mounted the throne, and subjected the sun and the moon, each one running (its course) for an appointed time. He directs the (whole) affair. He makes the signs distinct, so that you[1] may be certain of the meeting with your Lord. **3** He (it is) who stretched out the earth, and placed on it firm mountains and rivers. And of all the fruits He has placed on it two in pairs. He covers the day with the night. Surely in that are signs indeed for a people who reflect. **4** On the earth (there are) parts neighboring (each other), and gardens of grapes, and (fields of) crops, and palm trees, (growing in) bunches and singly, (all) watered with one water. Yet We favor some of it over others in fruit. Surely in that are signs indeed for a people who understand.

5 If you[2] are amazed, their saying is amazing: 'When we have turned to dust, shall we indeed (return) in a new creation?' Those are the ones who have disbelieved in their Lord, and those – the chains will be on their necks – those are the companions of the Fire. There they will remain. **6** They seek to hurry you with the evil before the good, though the examples (of punishment) have already happened before them. Surely your Lord is indeed full of forgiveness for the people, despite their evildoing, yet surely your Lord is (also) indeed harsh in retribution.

7 Those who disbelieve say, 'If only a sign were sent down on him from his Lord.' You are only a warner, and for every people (there is) a guide.

8 God knows what every female bears, and (in) what (way) the womb shrinks and (in) what (way) it swells. Everything with Him has (its) measure. **9** (He is) the Knower of the unseen and the seen, (He is) the Great, the Exalted. **10** (It is) the same (for) any of you who keeps (his) saying secret or makes it public, and (for) anyone who hides in the night or goes about in the day. **11** For him (there is) a following, before him and behind him, who watch over him by the command of God. Surely God does not change what is in a people, until they change what is in themselves. And when God

---

1. *you*: plur.
2. *you*: sing.

wishes evil for a people, (there is) no turning (it) back for them. They have no ally other than Him.

12 He (it is) who shows you the lightning – in fear and desire – and He produces the clouds heavy (with rain). **13** The thunder glorifies (Him) with His praise, and the angels (too) out of awe of Him. He sends the thunderbolts, and smites with it whomever He pleases. Yet they dispute about God, when He is mighty in power. **14** The true call (is) to Him, and those whom they call on instead of Him do not respond to them at all. (They are) only like someone stretching out his hands toward water, so that it may reach his mouth, but it does not reach it. The call of the disbelievers only goes astray. **15** Whatever is in the heavens and the earth prostrates before God, willingly and unwillingly, and (so do) their shadows in the morning and the evenings.

16 Say: 'Who is Lord of the heavens and the earth?' Say: 'God.' Say: 'Have you taken allies other than Him? They do not have power to (cause) themselves benefit or harm.' Say: 'Are the blind and the sighted equal, or are the darkness and the light equal? Or have they set up associates for God who have created a creation like His, so that the creation is (all) alike to them?' Say: 'God is the Creator of everything. He is the One, the Supreme.'

17 He sends down water from the sky, and the wādīs flow, (each) in its measure, and the torrent carries a rising (layer of) froth (on top), like the froth that arises from what they heat in the fire, seeking some ornament or utensil. In this way God strikes (a parable of) the true and the false. As for the froth, it becomes worthless, but as for what benefits the people, it remains on the earth. In this way God strikes parables.

18 For those who respond to their Lord (there is) the good (reward), but those who do not respond to Him – (even) if they had what is on the earth – all (of it) – and as much again, they would indeed (try to) ransom (themselves) with it. Those – for them (there is) the evil reckoning. Their refuge is Gehenna – it is an evil bed!

19 Is the one who knows that what has been sent down to you from your Lord is the truth, like the one who is blind? Only those with understanding take heed: **20** those who fulfill the covenant of God and do not break the compact, **21** and who join together what God has commanded to be joined with it, and fear their Lord, and are afraid of the evil reckoning, **22** and who are patient in seeking the face of their Lord, and observe the prayer, and contribute from what We have provided them, in secret and in open, and avert evil by means of the good. Those – for them (there is) the outcome of the Home: **23** Gardens of Eden which they (will) enter, and (also) those who were righteous among their fathers, and their wives, and their descendants. The angels (will) come in to them from every gate: **24** 'Peace (be) upon you because you were patient! Excellent is the outcome of the Home!'

25 But those who break the covenant of God, after its ratification, and sever what God has commanded to be joined, and foment corruption on the earth, those

– for them (there is) the curse, and for them (there is) the evil Home. **26** God extends (His) provision to whomever He pleases, and restricts (it). They gloat over this present life, but this present life is nothing but a (fleeting) enjoyment in (comparison to) the Hereafter.

27 Those who disbelieve say, 'If only a sign were sent down on him from his Lord.' Say: 'Surely God leads astray whomever He pleases and guides to Himself whoever turns (to Him).' **28** Those who believe and whose hearts are secure in the remembrance of God – surely hearts are secure in the remembrance of God – **29** those who believe and do righteous deeds – for them (there is) happiness and a good (place of) return.

30 In this way We have sent you among a community – before it (other) communities have already passed away – in order that you might recite to them what We have inspired you (with). Yet they disbelieve in the Merciful. Say: 'He is my Lord – (there is) no god but Him. In Him I have put my trust, and to Him is my turning (in repentance).' **31** If (only there were) a Qur'ān by which the mountains were moved, or by which the earth were split open, or by which the dead were spoken to. No! The affair (belongs) to God altogether. Have those who believe no hope that, if God (so) pleased, He would indeed guide all the people? (As for) those who disbelieve, a striking will continue to smite them for what they have done, or it will descend near their home(s), until the promise of God comes. Surely God will not break the appointment. **32** Certainly messengers have been mocked before you, but I spared those who disbelieved. Then I seized them – and how was my retribution?

33 Is He who stands over every person for what he has earned [. . .]?[3] They have set up associates for God. Say: 'Name them! Or will you inform Him about what He does not know on the earth, or about what is said openly?' No! Their scheming is made to appear enticing to those who disbelieve, and they are kept from the way. Whoever God leads astray has no guide. **34** For them (there is) punishment in this present life, yet the punishment of the Hereafter is indeed harder. They have no defender against God.

35 A parable of the Garden which is promised to the ones who guard (themselves): through it rivers flow, its fruit is unending, and (also) its shade. That is the outcome for the ones who guard (themselves), but the outcome for the disbelievers is the Fire.

36 Those to whom We have given the Book rejoice in what has been sent down to you, though some among the factions reject part of it. Say: 'I am only commanded to serve God, and not to associate (anything) with Him. To Him do I call (you), and to Him is my return.'

37 In this way We have sent it down as an Arabic judgment. If indeed you follow their (vain) desires, after what has come to you of the knowledge, you will have

---

3. *[. . .]*: there appears to be a lacuna here.

The Thunder

no ally and no defender against God. **38** Certainly We sent messengers before you, and gave them wives and descendants, but it was not for any messenger to bring a sign, except by the permission of God. For every (period of) time (there is) a written decree. **39** God blots out whatever he pleases, and He confirms (whatever He pleases). With Him is the mother of the Book.

40 Whether We let you see part of what We promise them, or We take you, only (dependent) on you is the delivery (of the message). (Dependent) on Us is the reckoning. **41** Do they not see that We come to the land, pushing back its borders? God judges, (and there is) no revision of His judgment. He is quick at the reckoning.

42 Those who were before them schemed, but the scheme (belongs) to God altogether. He knows what every person earns, and soon the disbelievers will know to whom the outcome of the Home (belongs). **43** Those who disbelieve say, 'You are not an envoy.' Say: 'God is sufficient as a witness between me and you, and (so is) whoever has knowledge of the Book.'

14 ❖ Abraham

In the Name of God, the Merciful, the Compassionate

1 Alif Lām Rā'.

A Book – We have sent it down to you, so that you may bring the people out of the darkness to the light, by the permission of their Lord, to the path of the Mighty, the Praiseworthy. 2 God who – to Him (belongs) whatever is in the heavens and whatever is on the earth. Woe to the disbelievers because of a harsh punishment! 3 Those who love this present life more than the Hereafter, and keep (people) from the way of God, and desire (to make) it crooked – those are far astray!

4 We have not sent any messenger except in the language of his people, so that he might make (things) clear to them. Then God leads astray whomever He pleases and guides whomever He pleases. He is the Mighty, the Wise.

5 Certainly We sent Moses with Our signs: 'Bring your people out of the darkness to the light, and remind them of the days of God.' Surely in that are signs indeed for every patient (and) thankful one.

6 (Remember) when Moses said to his people, 'Remember the blessing of God on you, when He rescued you from the house of Pharaoh. They were inflicting on you the evil punishment, and slaughtering your sons and sparing your women. In that was a great test from your Lord.' 7 And (remember) when your Lord proclaimed, 'If indeed you are thankful, I shall indeed give you more, but if indeed you are ungrateful, surely My punishment is harsh indeed.' 8 And Moses said, '(Even) if you disbelieve, you and whoever is on the earth all together – surely God is indeed wealthy, praiseworthy.'

9 Has no story come to you[1] of those who were before you: the people of Noah, 'Ād, Thamūd, and those who (came) after them? No one knows them but God. Their messengers brought them the clear signs, but they put their hands in their mouths, and said, 'Surely We disbelieve in what you are sent with, and surely we are in grave doubt indeed about what you call us to.' 10 Their messengers said, '(Is there any) doubt about God, Creator of the heavens and the earth? He calls you so that He may forgive you of your sins and spare you for an appointed time.' They said, 'You are nothing but human beings like us. You want to keep us from what our fathers have served. Bring us some clear authority (for this).' 11 Their messengers said to them, 'We are nothing but human beings like you, but God

---

1. *you*: plur.

Abraham

bestows favor on whomever He pleases of His servants. It is not for us to bring you any authority, except by the permission of God. In God let the believers put their trust. **12** Why should we not put our trust in God, when He has guided us to our ways. Indeed we shall patiently endure whatever harm you do us. In God let the trusting put their trust.' **13** Those who had disbelieved said to their messengers, 'We shall indeed expel you from our land, or (else) you will return to our creed.' Then their Lord inspired them: 'We shall indeed destroy the evildoers **14** and cause you to inhabit the land after them. That is for whoever fears My position and fears My promise.'

15 They asked for victory, and every stubborn tyrant despaired. **16** Behind him is Gehenna, and he is given a drink of filthy water. **17** He gulps it but can hardly swallow it. Death comes upon him from every side, yet he does not die, and behind him is a stern punishment.

18 A parable of those who disbelieve in their Lord: their deeds are like ashes, on which the wind blows strongly on a stormy day. They have no power over anything of what they have earned. That is straying far.

19 Do you not see that God created the heavens and the earth in truth? If He (so) pleases, He will do away with you and bring a new creation. **20** That is no great matter for God.

21 They will come forth to God all together, and the weak will say to those who were arrogant, 'Surely we were your followers, so are you going relieve us (now) of any of the punishment of God?' They will say, 'If God had guided us, we would indeed have guided you. (It is) the same for us whether we become distressed or are patient. (There is) no place of escape for us.' **22** And Satan will say, when the matter is decided, 'Surely God promised you a true promise, and I (too) promised you, (but) then I broke (my promise) to you. I had no authority over you, except that I called you and you responded to me. So do not blame me, but blame yourselves. I am not going to help you, nor are you going to help me. Surely I disbelieved in your associating me (with God) before.' Surely the evildoers – for them (there is) a painful punishment. **23** But those who believe and do righteous deeds – they are made to enter Gardens through which rivers flow, there to remain by the permission of their Lord. Their greeting there is: 'Peace!'

24 Do you not see how God has struck a parable? A good word is like a good tree. Its root is firm and its branch (reaches) to the sky, **25** giving its fruit every season by the permission of its Lord. God strikes parables for the people so that they may take heed. **26** But the parable of a bad word is like a bad tree, uprooted from the earth, without any support for it. **27** God makes firm those who believe by the firm word in this present life and in the Hereafter. But God leads astray the evildoers. God does whatever He pleases.

28 Do you not see those who have exchanged the blessing of God for disbelief, and caused their people to descend to the home of ruin – **29** Gehenna – where they will burn? It is an evil dwelling place! **30** They have set up rivals to God in

Abraham

order to lead (people) astray from His way. Say: 'Enjoy (yourselves)! Surely your destination is to the Fire!'

31 Say to My servants who believe (that) they should observe the prayer, and contribute from what We have provided them, in secret and in open, before a Day comes when (there will be) no bargaining and no friendship.

32 (It is) God who created the heavens and the earth, and sent down water from the sky, and brought forth fruits by means of it as a provision for you. And He subjected the ship to you, to run on the sea by His command, and subjected the rivers to you. **33** And He subjected the sun and the moon to you, both being constant (in their courses), and subjected the night and the day to you. **34** He has given you some of all that you have asked Him for. If you (try to) number God's blessing, you will not (be able to) count it. Surely the human is indeed an evildoer (and) ungrateful!

35 (Remember) when Abraham said, 'My Lord, make this land secure, and keep me and my sons away from serving the idols. **36** My Lord, surely they have led many of the people astray. Whoever follows me, surely he belongs to me, and whoever disobeys me – surely You are forgiving, compassionate. **37** Our Lord, I have settled some of my descendants in a wādī without any cultivation, near your Sacred House, Our Lord, in order that they may observe the prayer. So cause the hearts of some of the people to yearn toward them, and provide them with fruits, so that they may be thankful. **38** Our Lord, You know what we hide and what we speak aloud. Nothing is hidden from God (either) on the earth or in the sky. **39** Praise (be) to God, who has granted me Ishmael and Isaac in (my) old age. Surely my Lord is indeed the Hearer of the call. **40** My Lord, make me observant of the prayer, and (also) some of my descendants, our Lord, and accept my call. **41** Our Lord, forgive me, and my parents, and the believers, on the Day when the reckoning takes place.'

42 Do not think (that) God is oblivious of what the evildoers do. He is only sparing them for a Day when (their) eyes will stare, **43** (as they go) rushing with their heads raised up, unable to turn back their gaze, and their hearts empty. **44** Warn the people (of) a Day when the punishment will come to them, and those who have done evil will say, 'Our Lord, spare us for a time near (at hand)! We shall respond to Your call and follow the messengers.' 'Did you not swear before that (there would be) no end for you? **45** You dwell in the (same) dwelling places as those who did themselves evil, and it became clear to you how We dealt with them, and (how) We struck parables for you. **46** They schemed their scheme, but their scheme was known to God, even though their scheme was (such as) to remove the mountains by it.'

47 Do not think (that) God is going to break His promise to His messengers. Surely God is mighty, a taker of vengeance. **48** On the Day when the earth will be changed (into something) other (than) the earth, and the heavens (as well), and they will go forth to God, the One, the Supreme, **49** and you will see the sinners

Abraham

on that Day bound together in chains, **50** their clothing (made) of pitch, and the Fire will cover their faces, **51** so that God may repay everyone for what he has earned. Surely God is quick at the reckoning.

52 This is a delivery for the people, and (it is delivered) so that they may be warned by means of it, and that they may know that He is one God, and that those with understanding may take heed.

15 ✼ Al-Ḥijr

In the Name of God, the Merciful, the Compassionate

1 Alif Lām Rā'. Those are the signs of the Book and a clear Qur'ān.

2 Perhaps those who disbelieve (will) wish, if they had submitted [. . .].[1] 3 Leave them (to) eat and enjoy (themselves), and (let their) hope divert them. Soon they will know! 4 We have not destroyed any town without its having a known decree. 5 No community precedes its time, nor do they delay (it).

6 They have said: 'You on whom the Reminder has been sent down! Surely you are possessed indeed! 7 Why do you not bring the angels to us, if you are one of the truthful?' 8 We only send down the angels with the truth, and then they will not be spared. 9 Surely We have sent down the Reminder, and surely We are indeed its Watchers. 10 Certainly We sent (messengers) before you among the parties of old, 11 yet not one messenger came to them whom they did not mock. 12 In this way We put it into the hearts of the sinners – 13 they do not believe in it, though the customary way of those of old has already passed away. 14 (Even) if We opened on them a gate of the sky, and they were going up through it continually, 15 they would (still) indeed say, 'Our sight is bewildered! No! We are a bewitched people!'

16 Certainly We have made constellations in the sky, and made it appear enticing for the onlookers, 17 and protected it from every accursed satan 18 – except any who (may) steal in to overhear, then a clear flame pursues him. 19 And the earth – We stretched it out, and cast on it firm mountains, and caused everything (that is) weighed to sprout in it. 20 We have made for you a means of living on it, and (for those creatures) for which you are not providers. 21 The storehouses of everything are only with Us, and We send it down only in a known measure. 22 We send the fertilizing winds, and We send down water from the sky and give it to you to drink. You are not the storekeepers of it. 23 Surely We – We indeed give life and cause death, and We are the inheritors. 24 Certainly We know the ones who press forward among you, and certainly We know the ones who lag behind. 25 Surely your Lord – He will gather them. Surely He is wise, knowing.

26 Certainly We created the human from dry clay, from molded mud, 27 and the (ancestor of the) jinn, We created him before (that) from scorching fire.

28 (Remember) when your Lord said to the angels: 'Surely I am going to create a human being from dry clay, from molded mud. 29 When I have fashioned him,

---

1. [. . .]: there appears to be a lacuna here.

Al-Ḥijr

and breathed some of My spirit into him, fall down before him in prostration.' **30** So the angels prostrated themselves – all of them together **31** – except Iblīs. He refused to be with the ones who prostrated themselves. **32** He said, 'Iblīs! What is (the matter) with you that you are not with the ones who prostrated themselves?' **33** He said, 'I am not (one) to prostrate myself before a human being whom you have created from dry clay, from molded mud.' **34** He said, 'Get out of here! Surely you are accursed! **35** Surely the curse (is going to remain) on you until the Day of Judgment.' **36** He said, 'My Lord, spare me until the Day when they are raised up.' **37** He said, 'Surely you are one of the spared **38** – until the Day of the known time.' **39** He said, 'My Lord, because You have made me err, I shall indeed make (things) appear enticing to them on the earth, and I shall indeed make them err – all (of them) **40** – except for Your devoted servants among them.' **41** He said, 'This is the straight path (incumbent) on Me. **42** Surely My servants – you will not have any authority over them, except for whoever follows you of the ones who are in error. **43** Surely Gehenna is indeed their appointed place – all (of them). **44** It has seven gates: to each gate a part of them is assigned. **45** (But) surely the ones who guard (themselves) will be in (the midst of) gardens and springs: **46** "Enter it in peace, secure!" **47** We shall strip away whatever rancor is in their hearts. (As) brothers (they will recline) on couches, facing each other. **48** No weariness will touch them there, nor will they be expelled from it.'

49 Inform My servants that I am the Forgiving, the Compassionate, **50** and that My punishment is the painful punishment. **51** And inform them about the guests of Abraham: **52** when they entered upon him, and said, 'Peace!,' he said, 'Surely we are afraid of you.' **53** They said, 'Do not be afraid. Surely we give you good news of a knowing boy.' **54** He said, 'Do you give me good news, even though old age has touched me? What good news do you give me?' **55** They said, 'We give you good news in truth, so do not be one of the despairing.' **56** He said, 'Who despairs of the mercy of his Lord, except for the ones who go astray?' **57** He said, 'What is your business, you envoys?' **58** They said, 'Surely we have been sent to a people who are sinners, **59** except for the house(hold) of Lot. Surely we shall indeed rescue them – all (of them) **60** – except his wife. We have determined that she indeed (will be) one of those who stay behind.'

61 When the envoys came to the house(hold) of Lot, **62** he said, 'Surely you are a people unknown (to me).' **63** They said, 'No! We have brought you what they were in doubt about. **64** We have brought you the truth. Surely we are truthful indeed. **65** So journey with your family in a part of the night, but you follow behind them. Let none of you turn around, but proceed where you are commanded.' **66** We decreed for him that command, that the last remnant of these (people) would be cut off in the morning. **67** The people of the city came welcoming the good news. **68** He said, 'Surely these are my guests, so do not shame me. **69** Guard (yourselves) against God, and do not disgrace me.' **70** They said, 'Did we not forbid you from all peoples?' **71** He said, 'These are my daughters, if you would do (it).' **72** By your life! Surely they were wandering blindly in their drunkenness. **73** So the cry seized

Al-Ḥijr

them at sunrise. **74** We turned (the city) upside down and rained on them stones of baked clay. **75** Surely in that are signs indeed for the discerning. **76** Surely it is indeed on a (path)way (which still) exists. **77** Surely in that is a sign indeed for the believers.

78 The people of the Grove were evildoers indeed, **79** so We took vengeance on them. Surely both of them are indeed in a clear record.

80 Certainly the people of al-Ḥijr called the envoys liars. **81** We gave them Our signs, but they turned away from it. **82** They carved secure houses out of the mountains, **83** but the cry seized them in the morning. **84** What they had earned was of no use to them.

85 We did not create the heavens and the earth, and whatever is between them, except in truth. Surely the Hour is coming indeed, so excuse (them) gracefully. **86** Surely your Lord – He is the Creator, the Knowing.

87 Certainly We have given you seven of the oft-repeated (stories), and the great Qur'ān.

88 Do not yearn after what We have given classes of them to enjoy, and do not sorrow over them, but lower your wing to the believers, **89** and say: 'Surely I am the clear warner.'

90 – As We have sent (it) down on the dividers, **91** those who have cut the Qur'ān (into) parts. **92** By your Lord! We shall indeed question them all **93** about what they have done.

94 Break forth with what you are commanded, and turn away from the idolaters. **95** Surely We are sufficient for you (against) the mockers, **96** who set up another god with God. Soon they will know! **97** Certainly We know that you – your heart is distressed by what they say. **98** Glorify your Lord with praise, and be one of those who prostrate themselves, **99** and serve your Lord, until the certainty comes to you.

16 ❁ The Bee

In the Name of God, the Merciful, the Compassionate

1 The command of God has come! Do not seek to hurry it. Glory to Him! He is exalted above what they associate.

2 He sends down the angels with the spirit of His command on whomever He pleases of His servants: 'Give warning that (there is) no god but Me, so guard (yourselves) against Me!'

3 He created the heavens and the earth in truth. He is exalted above what they associate. **4** He created the human from a drop, and suddenly he (becomes) a clear adversary. **5** And the cattle – He created them for you. (There is) warmth in them and (other) benefits, and from them you eat. **6** And (there is) beauty in them for you, when you bring them in and when you lead them out. **7** They carry your loads to a land you would (otherwise) not reach without exhausting yourselves. Surely your Lord is indeed kind, compassionate. **8** (He also created) horses and mules and donkeys for you to ride, and for display. And He creates what you do not know. **9** (It is incumbent) on God (to set the) direction of the way, yet (there is) deviation from it. If He had (so) pleased, He would indeed have guided you all.

10 He (it is) who sends down water from the sky. From it you have (something to) drink, and from it vegetation (grows) on which you pasture (livestock). **11** By means of it He causes the crops to grow for you, and (also) olives, and date palms, and grapes, and all (kinds of) fruit. Surely in that is a sign indeed for a people who reflect. **12** He subjected the night and the day for you, and the sun and the moon, and the stars (are) subjected by His command. Surely in that are signs indeed for a people who understand. **13** And whatever He has scattered for you on the earth (with) its various colors – surely in that is a sign indeed for a people who take heed. **14** He (it is) who subjected the sea, so that you may eat fresh fish from it, and bring out of it an ornament which you wear, and you see the ship cutting through it, and (it is) so that you may seek some of His favor, and that you may be thankful. **15** And He cast on the earth firm mountains, so that it does not sway with you (on it), and rivers and (path)ways, that you may guide yourselves, **16** and landmarks (too). And by the stars they guide (themselves). **17** Is the One who creates like the one who does not create? Will you not take heed? **18** If you (try to) number God's blessing, you will not (be able to) count it. Surely God is indeed forgiving, compassionate.

The Bee

19 God knows what you keep secret and what you speak aloud. 20 Those they call on instead of God do not create anything, since they are (themselves) created. 21 (They are) dead, not alive, and they do not realize when they will be raised up. 22 Your God is one God. Those who do not believe in the Hereafter – their hearts are defiant, and they are arrogant. 23 (There is) no doubt that God knows what they keep secret and what they speak aloud. Surely He does not love the arrogant.

24 When it is said to them, 'What has your Lord sent down?,' they say, 'Old tales!' 25 – that they may bear their own burdens fully on the Day of Resurrection, and (also) some of the burdens of those whom they led astray without (their) realizing (it). Evil is what they will bear! 26 Those who were before them schemed, but God came (against) their building from the foundations, and the roof fell down on them from above them, and the punishment came upon them from where they did not realize (it would). 27 Then on the Day of Resurrection He will disgrace them, and say, 'Where are My associates for whose sake you broke away?' Those who were given the knowledge will say, 'Surely today disgrace and evil are on the disbelievers, 28 those who – the angels take them (while they are doing) themselves evil.' They will offer peace: 'We were not doing anything evil.' 'Yes indeed (you were)! Surely God is aware of what you have done. 29 So enter the gates of Gehenna, there to remain. Evil indeed is the dwelling place of the arrogant!'

30 And it is said to those who guard (themselves), 'What has your Lord sent down?' They say, 'Good!' For those who do good in this world (there is) good, but the Home of the Hereafter is indeed better. Excellent indeed is the Home of the ones who guard (themselves) 31 – Gardens of Eden, which they will enter, through which rivers flow, where they will have whatever they please. In this way God repays the ones who guard (themselves), 32 those who – the angels take them (while they are doing) good. They will say, 'Peace (be) upon you! Enter the Garden for what you have done.'

33 Do they expect (anything) but the angels to come to them, or the command of your Lord to come? So did those who were before them. God did not do them evil, but they did themselves evil. 34 So the evils of what they had done smote them, and what they were mocking overwhelmed them.

35 The idolaters say, 'If God had (so) pleased, we would not have served anything other than Him, neither we nor our fathers, and we would not have forbidden anything other than Him.' So did those who were before them. (Does anything depend) on the messengers except the clear delivery (of the message)? 36 Certainly We have raised up in every community a messenger (saying): 'Serve God and avoid al-Ṭāghūt!'[1] (There were) some of them whom God guided, and some whose going astray was deserved. Travel the earth and see how the end was for

---

1. *al-Ṭāghūt*: meaning uncertain; perhaps 'other gods' or 'idols' (cf. Q2.256; 39.17), or another name for Satan (Q4.60, 76).

The Bee

the ones who called (it) a lie. **37** If you are eager for their guidance – surely God does not guide those whom He leads astray. They will have no helpers.

38 They have sworn by God the most solemn of their oaths: 'God will not raise up anyone who dies!' Yes indeed! (It is) a promise (binding) on Him in truth, but most of the people do not know (it). **39** (They will be raised) so that He may make clear their differences to them, and so that those who disbelieved may know that they were liars. **40** Our only word to a thing, when We intend it, is that We say to it, 'Be!' and it is.

41 Those who emigrate in (the way of) God, after they have been done evil – We shall indeed give them a good settlement in this world, but the reward of the Hereafter is indeed greater, if (only) they knew. **42** (They are) those who are patient and put their trust in their Lord.

43 We have not sent (anyone) before you except men whom We inspired – just ask the People of the Reminder, if you do not know (it) – **44** with the clear signs and the scriptures, and We have sent down to you the Reminder, so that you may make clear to the people what has been sent down to them, and that they will reflect.

45 Do those who have schemed evils feel secure that God will not cause the earth to swallow them, or that the punishment will not come upon them from where they do not realize? **46** Or that He will not seize them in their comings and goings, and they will not be able to escape? **47** Or that He will not seize them with a (sudden) fright? Surely your Lord is indeed kind, compassionate.

48 Do they not see anything of what God has created? (How) its shadows revolve from the right and the left, prostrating themselves before God, and they are humble? **49** Whatever is in the heavens and whatever is on the earth prostrates itself before God – every living creature and the angels (too) – and they are not arrogant. **50** They fear their Lord above them, and they do what they are commanded.

51 God has said: 'Do not take two gods. He is only one God. So Me – fear Me (alone)!' **52** To Him (belongs) whatever is in the heavens and the earth, and to Him (belongs) the religion forever. Will you guard (yourselves) against (anyone) other than God? **53** Whatever blessing you have is from God. Then when hardship touches you, (it is) to Him you cry out. **54** Then when He removes the hardship from you, suddenly a group of you associates with their Lord, **55** to show ingratitude for what We have given them. Enjoy (yourselves)! Soon you will know!

56 They assign to what they do not know a portion of what We have provided them. By God! Surely you will indeed be questioned about what you have forged. **57** And they assign daughters to God – glory to Him! – and to themselves (they assign) what they desire. **58** When one of them is given news of a female (child), his face turns dark and he chokes back his disappointment. **59** He hides himself from the people because of the evil of what he has been given news about. Should he keep it in humiliation or bury it in the dust? Is it not evil what they judge? **60** An evil parable (is fitting) for those who do not believe in the Hereafter, but (only) the highest parable (is fitting) for God. He is the Mighty, the Wise.

The Bee

61 If God were to take the people to task for their evildoing, He would not leave on it any living creature. But He is sparing them until an appointed time. When their time comes, they will not delay (it) by an hour, nor will they advance (it by an hour). **62** They assign to God what they (themselves) dislike, and their tongues allege the lie that the best is for them. (There is) no doubt that the Fire (is fitting) for them, and that they (will) be rushed (into it).

63 By God! Certainly We sent messengers to communities before you, but Satan made their deeds appear enticing to them. So he is their ally today, and for them (there is) a painful punishment. **64** We have not sent down on you the Book, except for you to make clear their differences to them, and (We have sent it down) as a guidance and mercy for a people who believe.

65 (It is) God (who) sends down water from the sky, and by means of it gives the earth life after its death. Surely in that is a sign indeed for a people who hear. **66** And surely in the cattle is a lesson indeed for you: We give you to drink from what is in their bellies – between excretions and blood – pure milk, pleasant tasting to the drinkers. **67** And from the fruits of the date palms and the grapes, from which you take an intoxicating drink and a good provision – surely in that is a sign indeed for a people who understand.

68 And your Lord inspired the bee: 'Make hives among the mountains, and among the trees, and among what they construct. **69** Then eat from all the fruits, and follow the ways of your Lord subserviently.' (There) comes forth from their bellies a drink of various colors, in which (there is) healing for the people. Surely in that is a sign indeed for a people who reflect.

70 (It is) God (who) creates you. Then He will take you. But among you (there is) one who is reduced to the worst (stage) of life, so that he knows nothing after (having had) knowledge. Surely God is knowing, powerful.

71 God has favored some of you over others in the (matter of) provision, but those who have been favored do not give over their provision to what their right (hands) own, so (that) they are (all) equal in that respect. Is it the blessing of God they deny? **72** God has given you wives from yourselves, and from your wives He has given you sons and grandsons, and He has provided you with good things. Do they believe in falsehood, and do they disbelieve in the blessing of God? **73** Do they serve, instead of God, what has no power to provide anything for them from the heavens or the earth, nor are they able (to do anything)? **74** Do not strike any parables for God. Surely God knows and you do not know.

75 God strikes a parable: a slave (who is) owned – he has no power over anything – and (another) whom We have provided with a good provision from Us, and he contributes from it in secret and in public. Are they equal? Praise (be) to God! No! But most of them do not know (it).

76 God strikes a parable: two men, one of them cannot speak – he has no power over anything, and he is a burden on his master – wherever he directs him, he

The Bee

does not bring (back anything) good. Is he equal to the one who commands justice and is himself on a straight path?

77 To God (belongs) the unseen of the heavens and the earth, and the affair of the Hour is only like a blink of the eye, or it is nearer. Surely God is powerful over everything.

78 (It is) God (who) brought you forth from the bellies of your mothers – you did not know a thing – and made for you hearing and sight and hearts, so that you may be thankful. **79** Do they not see the birds, subjected in the midst of the sky? No one holds them (up) but God. Surely in that are signs indeed for a people who believe.

80 God has made (a place of) rest for you from your houses, and made houses for you from the skins of the livestock, which you find light (to carry) on the day of your departure and on the day of your encampment. And from their wool and their fur and their hair (He has made for you) furnishings and enjoyment for a time.

81 God has made (places of) shade for you from what He has created, and made (places of) cover for you from the mountains, and made clothing for you to guard you from the heat, and clothing to guard you from your (own) violence. In this way He completes His blessing on you, so that you will submit. **82** If they turn away – only (dependent) on you is the clear delivery (of the message). **83** They recognize the blessing of God, (and) then they reject it. Most of them are ungrateful.

84 On the Day when We raise up a witness from every community, then no permission (to speak) will be given to those who have disbelieved, nor will they be allowed to make amends. **85** When those who have done evil see the punishment, it will not be lightened for them, nor will they be spared.

86 When those who were idolaters see their associates, they will say, 'Our Lord, these are our associates, on whom we used to call instead of You.' But they will cast (back) at them the word: 'Surely you are liars indeed!' **87** And they will offer peace to God on that Day, and (then) what they have forged will abandon them.

88 Those who disbelieve and keep (people) from the way of God – We shall increase them in punishment upon punishment because they were fomenting corruption.

89 On the Day when We raise up in every community a witness against them from among them, and bring you as a witness against these (people) [. . .].[2] We have sent down on you the Book as an explanation for everything, and as a guidance and mercy, and as good news for those who submit.

90 Surely God commands justice and good, and giving to family, and He forbids immorality, and wrong, and envy. He admonishes you so that you may take heed.

---

2. [. . .]: there appears to be a lacuna here.

The Bee

91 Fulfill the covenant of God, when you have made a covenant, and do not break (your) oaths after their confirmation, when you have made God a guarantor over you. Surely God is aware of what you do.

92 Do not be like the one who unraveled her yarn, after (it was) firmly spun, (into) broken strands, (by) taking your oaths as a (means of) deception between you, because (one) community is more numerous than (another) community. God is only testing you by means of it. He will indeed make clear to you your differences on the Day of Resurrection. **93** If God had (so) pleased, He would indeed have made you one community, but He leads astray whomever He pleases and guides whomever He pleases. You will indeed be questioned about what you have done.

94 Do not take your oaths as a (means of) deception between you, so that a foot should slip after its standing firm, and you taste evil for having kept (people) from the way of God, and (there be) for you a great punishment. **95** Do not sell the covenant of God for a small price. Surely what is with God is better for you, if (only) you knew. **96** What is with you fails, but what is with God lasts, and We shall indeed pay those who are patient their reward for the best of what they have done. **97** Whoever does righteousness – whether male or female – and he is a believer – We shall indeed give him a good life, and We shall indeed pay them their reward for the best of what they have done.

98 When you recite the Qur'ān, take refuge with God from the accursed Satan. **99** Surely he has no authority over those who believe and put their trust in their Lord. **100** His authority is only over those who take him as an ally, and those who associate (other gods) with Him.

101 When We exchange a verse in place of (another) verse – and God knows what He sends down – they say, 'You are only a forger!' No! Most of them do not know (anything).

102 Say: 'The holy spirit has brought it down from your Lord in truth, to make firm those who believe, and as a guidance and good news for those who submit.' **103** Certainly We know that they say, 'Only a human being teaches him.' The language of the one to whom they perversely allude is foreign, but this language is clear Arabic. **104** Surely those who do not believe in the signs of God – God will not guide them, and for them (there is) a painful punishment. **105** Only they forge lies who do not believe in the signs of God. Those – they are the liars!

106 Whoever disbelieves in God after having believed – except for someone who is compelled, yet his heart is (still) secure in belief – and whoever expands his heart in disbelief – on them is anger from God, and for them (there is) a great punishment. **107** That is because they loved this present life over the Hereafter, and because God does not guide the disbelievers. **108** Those – God has set a seal on their hearts and their hearing and their sight. And those – they are the oblivious. **109** (There is) no doubt that in the Hereafter they (will be) the losers.

110 Then surely your Lord – to those who emigrated after having been persecuted, (and) then struggled and were patient – surely your Lord after that is

The Bee

indeed forgiving, compassionate, **111** on the Day when each person will come disputing on his own behalf, and each person will be paid in full for what he has done – and they will not be done evil.

112 God strikes a parable: a town was secure (and) at rest, its provision coming to it in abundance from every place, but it was ungrateful for the blessings of God. So God caused it to wear the clothing of hunger and fear for what they had been doing. **113** Certainly a messenger had come to them from among them, but they called him a liar. So the punishment seized them while they were doing evil.

114 Eat from what God has provided you as permitted (and) good, and be thankful for the blessing of God, if it is Him you serve. **115** He has only forbidden you: the dead (animal), and the blood, and swine's flesh, and what has been dedicated to (a god) other than God.' But whoever is forced (by necessity), not desiring or (deliberately) transgressing – surely God is forgiving, compassionate. **116** (As) for what your tongues (may) allege, do not speak the (following) lie: 'This is permitted but that is forbidden,' so that you forge lies against God. Surely those who forge lies against God – they will not prosper. **117** A little enjoyment (of life), and (then) for them (there is) a painful punishment.

118 To those who are Jews, We have forbidden what We recounted to you before. We did not do them evil, but they did themselves evil. **119** Then surely your Lord – to those who have done evil in ignorance, (and) then repented and set (things) right – surely your Lord after that is indeed forgiving, compassionate.

120 Surely Abraham was a community obedient before God – a Ḥanīf[3] – yet he was not one of the idolaters. **121** (He was) thankful for His blessings. He chose him and guided him to a straight path. **122** We gave him good in this world, and surely in the Hereafter he will indeed be among the righteous. **123** Then We inspired you: 'Follow the creed of Abraham the Ḥanīf. He was not one of the idolaters.'

124 The sabbath was only made for those who differed concerning it. Surely on the Day of Resurrection your Lord will judge between them concerning their differences.

125 Call to the way of your Lord with wisdom and good admonition, and dispute with them by means of what is better. Surely your Lord – He knows who goes astray from His way, and He knows the ones who are (rightly) guided.

126 If you[4] take retribution, take it in the same way as retribution was taken against you. But if indeed you are patient – it is indeed better for the ones who are patient. **127** And you[5] be patient (too). Yet your patience (comes) only with (the help of) God. Do not sorrow over them, and do not be in distress because of what they are scheming. **128** Surely God is with those who guard (themselves), and those who do good.

---

3. *Ḥanīf*: meaning uncertain.
4. *you*: plur.
5. *you*: sing.

17 ✢ The Journey

In the Name of God, the Merciful, the Compassionate

1 Glory to the One who sent His servant on a journey by night from the Sacred Mosque to the Distant Mosque, whose surroundings We have blessed, so that We might show him some of Our signs. Surely He – He is the Hearing, the Seeing.

2 We gave Moses the Book, and made it a guidance for the Sons of Israel: 'Do not take any guardian other than Me!' **3** (They were) descendants of those whom We carried with Noah. Surely he was a thankful servant. **4** And We decreed for the Sons of Israel in the Book: 'You will indeed foment corruption on the earth twice, and you will indeed rise to a great height.' **5** When the first promise came (to pass), We raised up against you servants of Ours, men of harsh violence, and they invaded (your) homes, and it was a promise fulfilled. **6** Then We returned to you (another) chance against them, and increased you with wealth and sons, and made you more numerous. **7** 'If you do good, you do good for yourselves, but if you do evil, (it is likewise) for yourselves.' When the second promise came (to pass), (We raised up against you servants of Ours) to cause you distress, and to enter the Temple as they entered it the first time, and to destroy completely what they had conquered. **8** It may be that your Lord will have compassion on you. But if you return, We shall return, and We have made Gehenna a prison for the disbelievers.

9 Surely this Qur'ān guides to that which is more upright, and gives good news to the believers who do righteous deeds, that for them (there is) a great reward, **10** and that those who do not believe in the Hereafter – We have prepared for them a painful punishment. **11** But the human calls for evil (as if) calling for good, (for) the human is (always) hasty.

12 We have made the night and the day as two signs: We have blotted out the sign of the night and made the sign of the day to (let you) see, so that you may seek some favor from your Lord, and that you may know the number of the years and the reckoning (of time). Everything – We have made it distinct.

13 And every human – We have fastened his fate to him on his neck, and We shall bring forth a book for him on the Day of Resurrection, which he will find unrolled. **14** 'Read your book! You are sufficient today as a reckoner against yourself.'

15 Whoever is (rightly) guided, is guided only for himself, and whoever goes astray, goes astray only against himself. No one bearing a burden bears the burden of another. We never punish until We have raised up a messenger.

The Journey

16 When We wish to destroy a town, We (first) command its affluent ones, and they act wickedly in it, so that the word against it is proved true, and We destroy it completely. **17** How many generations have We destroyed after Noah! Your Lord is sufficient (as One who) is aware of (and) sees the sins of His servants.

18 Whoever desires this hasty (world) – We hasten to (give) him in it whatever We please to whomever We wish. Then We have made Gehenna for him, (where) he will burn, condemned (and) rejected. **19** But whoever desires the Hereafter and strives with effort for it, and he is a believer, those – their striving will be thanked. **20** Each one We increase – these and those – with some gift of your Lord. The gift of your Lord is not limited. **21** See how We have favored some of them over others. Yet the Hereafter is indeed greater in ranks (of honor) and greater in favor.

22 Do not set up another god with God, or you will sit down condemned (and) forsaken.

23 Your Lord has decreed that you do not serve any but Him, and (that you do) good to your parents, whether one or both of them reaches old age with you. Do not say to them, 'Uff,' and do not repulse them, **24** but speak to them an honorable word. And conduct yourself humbly toward them out of mercy, and say: 'My Lord, have compassion on both of them, as they brought me up (when I was) small.' **25** Your Lord knows what is in you. If you are righteous, surely He is forgiving to those who regularly turn (to Him in repentance).

26 Give the family member his due, and the poor and the traveler, but do not squander (your wealth) wastefully. **27** Surely the squanderers are brothers of the satans, and Satan is ungrateful to his Lord. **28** But if you turn away from them, seeking a mercy from your Lord that you expect, speak to them a gentle word. **29** Do not keep your hand chained to your neck, nor extend it all the way, or you will sit down blamed (and) impoverished. **30** Surely your Lord extends (His) provision to whomever He pleases, and restricts (it). Surely He is aware of His servants (and) sees (them).

31 Do not kill your children for fear of poverty. We will provide for them and for you. Surely their killing is a great sin.

32 Do not go near adultery. Surely it is an immoral act and evil as a way.

33 Do not kill the person whom God has forbidden (to be killed), except by right. Whoever is killed in an evil manner – We have given authority to his ally, but he should not be excessive in the killing, (for) surely he has been helped.

34 Do not go near the property of the orphan, except to improve it, until he reaches his maturity.

Fulfill the covenant. Surely you are responsible for a covenant.

35 Fill up the measure when you measure, and weigh with the straight balance. That is better and fairer in interpretation.

36 Do not pursue what you have no knowledge of. Surely the hearing and the sight and the heart – all those you are responsible for.

The Journey

37 Do not walk on the earth in jubilation. Surely you will not plumb the depths of the earth, nor reach the mountains in height. **38** All that – the evil of it – is hateful in the sight of your Lord. **39** That is some of the wisdom your Lord has inspired you (with).

Do not set up another god with God, or you will be cast into Gehenna, blamed (and) rejected. **40** Has your Lord distinguished you with sons and taken (for Himself) females from the angels? Surely you speak a dreadful word indeed! **41** Certainly We have varied (the signs) in this Qur'ān, so that they may take heed, but it only increases them in aversion (to it). **42** Say: 'If there were (other) gods with Him, as they say, they would indeed have sought a way to the Holder of the throne.' **43** Glory to Him! He is exalted a great height above what they say. **44** The seven heavens and the earth, and whatever is in them, glorify Him, and (there is) nothing that does not glorify (Him) with His praise, but you[1] do not understand their glorifying. Surely He is forbearing, forgiving.

45 When you recite the Qur'ān, We place between you and those who do not believe in the Hereafter an obscuring veil. **46** And We make coverings over their hearts, so that they do not understand it, and a heaviness in their ears. When you mention your Lord alone in the Qur'ān, they turn their backs in aversion (to it). **47** We know what they listen to when they listen to you, and when they (are in) secret talk, when the evildoers say, 'You are only following a man (who is) bewitched.' **48** See how they strike parables for you! But they have gone astray and cannot (find) a way.

49 They say, 'When we have become bones and fragments, shall we indeed be raised up as a new creation?' **50** Say: 'Become stones or iron, **51** or something greater still in your estimation!' And then they will say, 'Who will restore us?' Say: '(He) who created you the first time.' And then they will shake their heads at you, and say, 'When will it be?' Say: 'It may be that it is near **52** – the Day when He will call you, and you will respond with His praise, and you will think that you remained (in the grave) only for a little (while).'

53 Say to My servants (that) they should say that which is best. Surely Satan provokes discord among them. Surely Satan is a clear enemy to humankind. **54** Your Lord knows about you.[2] If He pleases, He will have compassion on you, or if He pleases, He will punish you. We have not sent you[3] as a guardian over them. **55** Your Lord knows whatever is in the heavens and the earth. Certainly We have favored some of the prophets over others, and We gave David (the) Psalms.

56 Say: 'Call on those whom you have claimed (as gods) instead of Him. They have no power (to) remove hardship from you, nor (to) change (it).' **57** Those whom they call on seek access to their Lord, whichever of them (may be) nearest, and

---

1. *you*: plur.
2. *you*: plur.
3. *you*: sing.

The Journey

they hope for His mercy and fear His punishment. Surely the punishment of your Lord is something to beware of.

58 (There is) no town that We are not going to destroy before the Day of Resurrection, or are not going to punish (with a) harsh punishment. That is written in the Book.

59 Nothing prevented Us from sending the signs, except that those of old called them a lie. We gave Thamūd the she-camel as a visible (sign), but they did her evil. We send the signs only to frighten.

60 (Remember) when We said to you, 'Surely your Lord encompasses the people,' and We made the vision which We showed you only a test for the people, and (also) the cursed tree in the Qur'ān. We frighten them, but it only increases them in great(er) insolent transgression.

61 (Remember) when We said to the angels, 'Prostrate yourselves before Adam,' and they prostrated themselves, except Iblīs. He said, 'Shall I prostrate myself before one whom You have created (from) clay?' **62** He said, 'Do You see this (creature) whom You have honored above me? If indeed You spare me until the Day of Resurrection, I shall indeed root out his descendants, except for a few.' **63** He said, 'Go, and any of them who follows you! Surely Gehenna will be your payment – an ample payment! **64** Scare any of them you can with your voice, and assemble against them with your cavalry and your infantry, and associate with them in (their) wealth and children, and make promises to them.' Yet Satan does not promise them (anything) but deception. **65** 'Surely My servants – you will have no authority over them.' Your Lord is sufficient as a guardian.

66 Your Lord (it is) who drives the ship on the sea for you, so that you may seek some of His favor. Surely He is compassionate with you. **67** When hardship touches you on the sea, (all those) whom you call on abandon (you), except Him, but when He has delivered you (safely) to the shore, you turn away. The human is ungrateful. **68** Do you feel secure that He will not cause the shore to swallow you, or send a sandstorm against you? Then you will find no guardian for yourselves. **69** Or do you feel secure that He will not send you back into it a second time, and send a hurricane against you, and drown you because you were ungrateful? Then you will find no attendant (to help) you with it against Us.

70 Certainly We have honored the sons of Adam, and carried them on the shore and the sea, and provided them with good things, and favored them greatly over many of those whom We have created.

71 On the Day when We shall call all people with their record, whoever is given his book in his right (hand) – those will read their book, and they will not be done evil in the slightest. **72** Whoever is blind in this (world will be) blind in the Hereafter, and farther astray (from the) way.

73 Surely they almost tempted you away from what We inspired you (with), so that you might forge against Us (something) other than it, and then they would indeed have taken you as a friend. **74** And had We not made you (stand) firm, you would almost have been disposed toward them a little. **75** Then We would have made you taste the double of life and the double of death, (and) then you would have found no helper for yourself against Us. **76** They almost scared you from the land, so that they might expel you from it, but then they would not have remained (there) after you, except for a little (while). **77** (That was Our) customary way (concerning) those of Our messengers whom We sent before you, and you will find no change in Our customary way.

78 Observe the prayer at the setting of the sun until the darkness of the night, and (deliver) a recitation at the dawn – surely a recitation at the dawn is witnessed. **79** And a part of the night – keep watch in it as a gift for you. It may be that your Lord will raise you up to a praised position. **80** And say: 'My Lord, cause me to enter a truthful entrance, and cause me to exit a truthful exit, and grant me authority from Yourself (to) help (me).' **81** And say: 'The truth has come and falsehood has passed away. Surely falsehood is (bound) to pass away.'

82 What We send down of the Qur'ān is a healing and mercy for the believers, but it only increases the evildoers in loss. **83** When We bless a person, he turns away and distances himself, but when evil touches him, he is in despair. **84** Say: 'Each does according to his own disposition, but your Lord knows who is best guided (as to the) way.'

85 They ask you about the spirit. Say: 'The spirit (comes) from the command of my Lord. You have only been given a little knowledge (of it).'

86 If We (so) pleased, We could indeed take away what We have inspired you (with). Then you would find no guardian for yourself against Us concerning it, **87** except as a mercy from your Lord. Surely His favor toward you is great.

88 Say: 'If indeed humans and jinn joined together to produce something like this Qur'ān, they would not produce anything like it, even if they were supporters of each other.' **89** Certainly We have varied (the signs) for the people in this Qur'ān by means of every (kind of) parable, yet most of the people refuse (everything) but disbelief.

90 They say, 'We shall not believe you until you cause a spring to gush forth for us from the earth, **91** or (until) you have a garden of date palms and grapes, and cause rivers to gush forth abundantly in the midst of it, **92** or (until) you make the sky fall on us in fragments, as you have claimed, or (until) you bring God and the angels before (us), **93** or (until) you have a decorative house, or (until) you ascend into the sky. And we shall not believe in your ascent until you bring down on us a book, so that we may read it.' Say: 'Glory to my Lord! Am I anything but a human being, a messenger?'

94 What prevented the people from believing when the guidance came to them, except that they said, 'Has God sent a human being as a messenger?' **95** Say: 'If there were angels walking contentedly on the earth, We would indeed have sent down on them an angel from the sky as a messenger.' **96** Say: 'God is sufficient

The Journey

as a witness between me and you. Surely He is aware of His servants (and) sees (them).' **97** Whoever God guides is the (rightly) guided one, and whoever He leads astray – you will not find for them any allies other than Him. We shall gather them on the Day of Resurrection on their faces – without sight or speech or hearing. Their refuge is Gehenna – whenever it dies down We increase (for) them a blazing (Fire). **98** That is their payment because they disbelieved in Our signs, and said, 'When we have become bones and fragments, shall we indeed be raised up as a new creation?' **99** Do they not see that God, who created the heavens and the earth, is able to create their equivalent? He has appointed a time for them – (there is) no doubt about it – yet the evildoers refuse (everything) but disbelief.

100 Say: '(Even) if you possessed the storehouses of my Lord's mercy, you would (still) hold back (out of) a fear (of) spending (it). Humans are stingy.'

101 Certainly We gave Moses nine clear signs – (just) ask the Sons of Israel. (Remember) when he came to them, and Pharaoh said to him, 'Moses! Surely I think you are bewitched indeed.' **102** He said, 'Certainly you know that no one has sent down these (signs) as clear proofs except the Lord of the heavens and the earth. Pharaoh! Surely I think you are doomed indeed.' **103** He wanted to scare them from the land, but We drowned him and those who were with him – all (of them). **104** After that We said to the Sons of Israel, 'Inhabit the land, and when the promise of the Hereafter comes, We shall bring you (all together) as a mob.'

105 With the truth We have sent it down, and with the truth it has come down, and We have sent you only as a bringer of good news and a warner. **106** (It is) a Qur'ān – We have divided it, so that you may recite it to the people at intervals, and We have sent it down once and for all. **107** Say: 'Believe in it, or do not believe. Surely those who were given the knowledge before it – when it is recited to them, they fall down on their chins in prostration, **108** and say, "Glory to our Lord! Surely our Lord's promise has been fulfilled indeed." **109** They fall down on their chins weeping, and it increases them in humility.'

110 Say: 'Call on God or call on the Merciful – whichever you call on, to Him (belong) the best names.' And do not be loud in your prayer, nor silent in it, but seek a way between that.

111 Say: 'Praise (be) to God, who has not taken a son, and has no associate in the kingdom, nor has He any (need of) an ally (to protect Him) from disgrace.' Magnify Him (with all) magnificence.

18 ❖ The Cave

In the Name of God, the Merciful, the Compassionate

1 Praise (be) to God, who has sent down on His servant the Book! He has not made in it any crookedness. 2 (He has made it) right: to warn of harsh violence from Himself, and to give good news to the believers who do righteous deeds, that for them (there is) a good reward 3 in which they will remain forever, 4 and to warn those who have said, 'God has taken a son.' 5 They have no knowledge about it, nor (did) their fathers. Monstrous is the word (that) comes out of their mouths! They say nothing but a lie. 6 Perhaps you are going to destroy yourself by following after them, if they do not believe in this proclamation. 7 Surely We have made what is on the earth a splendor for it, so that We may test them (to see) which of them is best in deed. 8 And surely We shall make what is on it barren soil.

9 Or did you[1] think that the companions of the cave and al-Raqīm[2] were an amazing thing among Our signs? 10 (Remember) when the young men took refuge in the cave, and said, 'Our Lord, grant us mercy from Yourself, and furnish the right (course) for us in our situation.' 11 So We sealed up their ears in the cave for a number of years, 12 and then We raised them up (again), so that We might know which of the two factions would better count (the length of) time (they had) remained (there).

13 We shall recount to you their story in truth: Surely they were young men who believed in their Lord, and We increased them in guidance. 14 We strengthened their hearts, when they stood up and said, 'Our Lord is the Lord of the heavens and the earth. We do not call on any god other than Him. Certainly we would then have spoken an outrageous thing. 15 These people of ours have taken gods other than Him. If only they would bring some clear authority concerning them! Who is more evil than the one who forges a lie against God? 16 When you have withdrawn from them, and what they serve instead of God, take refuge in the cave. Your Lord will display some of His mercy to you, and will furnish some relief for you in your situation.'

17 And you (would) see the sun when it rose, inclining from their cave toward the right, and when it set, passing them by on the left, while they were in the open part of it. That was one of the signs of God. Whoever God guides is the (rightly)

---

1. *you*: sing.
2. *al-Raqīm*: reference obscure.

The Cave

guided one, and whoever He leads astray – you will not find for him an ally guiding (him). **18** And you (would) think them awake, even though they were asleep, and We were turning them (now) to the right and (now) to the left, while their dog (lay) stretched out (with) its front paws at the door (of the cave). If you (had) observed them, you would indeed have turned away from them in flight, and indeed been filled (with) dread because of them.

19 So We raised them up (again) that they might ask questions among themselves. A speaker among them said, 'How long have you remained (here)?' Some said, 'We have (only) remained (here) a day, or part of a day.' Others said, 'Your Lord knows how long you have remained (here). So send one of you with this paper (money)[3] of yours to the city, and let him see which (part) of it (has the) purest food, and let him bring you a supply of it. But let him be astute, and let no one realize (who) you (are). **20** Surely they – if they become aware of you – they will stone you, or make you return to their creed, and then you will never prosper.' **21** So We caused (the people of the city) to stumble upon them, in order that they might know that the promise of God is true, and that the Hour – (there is) no doubt about it. When they[4] argued among themselves about their situation, they said, 'Build over them a building. Their Lord knows about them.' Those who prevailed over their situation said, 'We shall indeed take (to building) a place of worship over them.'

22 Some say, '(There were) three, the fourth of them was their dog.' But others say, '(There were) five, the sixth of them was their dog' – guessing about what is unknown. Still others say, '(There were) seven, the eighth of them was their dog.' Say: 'My Lord knows about their number. No one knows (about) them except a few.' So do not dispute about them, except (on) an obvious point, and do not ask for a pronouncement about them from any of them. **23** And do not say of anything, 'Surely I am going to do that tomorrow,' **24** except (with the proviso): 'If God pleases.' And remember your Lord, when you forget, and say, 'It may be that my Lord will guide me to something nearer the right (way) than this.'

25 They remained in their cave for three hundred years and (some) add nine (more). **26** Say: 'God knows about how long they remained (there). To Him (belongs) the unseen of the heavens and the earth. How well He sees and hears! They have no ally other than Him, and He does not associate anyone in His judgment.'

27 Recite what you have been inspired (with) of the Book of your Lord. No one can change His words, and you will find no refuge other than Him. **28** Be patient within yourself with those who call on their Lord in the morning and the evening, desiring His face, and do not let your eyes turn away from them, desiring the (passing) splendor of this present life. Do not obey (anyone) whose heart We

---

3. *paper (money)*: Ar. *wariq* (lit. 'leaf' or 'sheet') seems to imply paper money, though most commentators interpret it as 'silver coins.'
4. *they*: the people of the city.

The Cave

have made oblivious of Our remembrance, and (who only) follows his desire and whose concern is (only) excess.

29 Say: 'The truth is from your Lord. Whoever pleases, let him believe, and whoever pleases, let him disbelieve.' Surely We have prepared a Fire for the evildoers – its walls will encompass them. If they call for help, they will be helped with water like molten metal (which) will scald their faces. Evil is the drink and evil the resting place! **30** Surely those who believe and do righteous deeds – surely We do not allow the reward of anyone who does a good deed to go to waste. **31** Those – for them (there are) Gardens of Eden through which rivers flow. There they will be adorned with bracelets of gold, and they will wear green clothes of silk and brocade, reclining there on couches. Excellent is the reward, and good the resting place!

32 Strike for them a parable of two men: We made for one of them two gardens of grapes, and surrounded both with date palms, and placed between them (a field of) crops. **33** Each of the two gardens produced its fruit and did not fail in any way. And We caused a river to gush forth between them. **34** So he had fruit. And he said to his companion, while he was talking with him, 'I am greater than you in wealth, and mightier in family.' **35** And he entered his garden, doing himself evil, (for) he said, 'I do not think that this will ever perish, **36** nor do I think the Hour is coming. If indeed I am returned to my Lord, I shall indeed find a better (place of) return than this.' **37** His companion said to him, while he was talking with him, 'Do you disbelieve in Him who created you from dust, then from a drop, (and) then fashioned you as a man? **38** But as for us, He is God, my Lord, and I do not associate anyone with my Lord. **39** Why did you not say, when you entered your garden, "What God pleases," (for there is) no power except in God? If you see me as inferior to you in wealth and children, **40** it may be that my Lord will give me (something) better than your garden, and send on it a reckoning from the sky, so that it becomes slippery soil, **41** or its water sinks (into the earth), so that you will not be able to find it.' **42** And (all) his fruit was overwhelmed, and in the morning he began wringing his hands over what he had spent on it, (for) it had collapsed on its trellises, and he said, 'I wish I had not associated anyone with my Lord!' **43** But there was no cohort to help him, other than God, and he was helpless. **44** In such a case protection (belongs only) to God, the True One. He is best in reward, and best in final outcome.

45 Strike for them a parable of this present life: (It is) like water which We send down from the sky, and the vegetation of the earth mingles with it, and it becomes stubble which the winds scatter. God is powerful over everything. **46** Wealth and sons are the (passing) splendor of this present life, but the things that endure – righteous deeds – are better in reward with your Lord, and better in hope.

47 On the Day when We shall cause the mountains to move, and you see the earth coming forth, and We gather them so that We do not leave any of them behind, **48** and they are presented before your Lord in lines: 'Certainly you have come to Us as We created you the first time. Yet you claimed that We had not set an

The Cave

appointment for you!' **49** And the Book will be laid down, and you will see the sinners apprehensive because of what is in it, and they will say, 'Woe to us! What (kind of) Book is this? It omits nothing small or great, but it has counted it?' And they will find what they have done presented (to them), and your Lord will not do anyone evil.

50 (Remember) when We said to the angels: 'Prostrate yourselves before Adam,' and they prostrated themselves, except Iblīs. He was one of the jinn, and acted wickedly (against) the command of his Lord. Do you take him and his descendants as allies instead of Me, when they are your enemy? Evil is the exchange for the evildoers! **51** I did not make them witnesses of the creation of the heavens and the earth, nor of the creation of themselves. I am not one to take those who lead (others) astray (for) support.

52 On the Day when He will say, 'Call those who you claimed were My associates,' they will call them, but they will not respond to them – (for) We have set between them a place of destruction.[5] **53** The sinners will see the Fire and think that they are about to fall into it, but they will find no escape from it.

54 Certainly We have varied (the signs) for the people in this Qur'ān by means of every (kind of) parable, yet the people remain contentious for the most part. **55** Nothing prevented the people from believing, when the guidance came to them, and from asking forgiveness from their Lord, except that the customary way of those of old should come upon them, or the punishment come upon them head on. **56** We send the envoys only as bringers of good news and warners, but those who disbelieve dispute by means of falsehood in order to refute the truth with it. They have taken My signs and what they were warned about in mockery. **57** Who is more evil than the one who, having been reminded by the signs of his Lord, turns away from them, and forgets what his hands have sent forward? Surely We have made coverings over their hearts, so that they do not understand it, and a heaviness in their ears. Even if you call them to the guidance, they will never be guided. **58** Yet your Lord is the Forgiving, the One full of mercy. If He were to take them to task for what they have earned, He would indeed hurry the punishment for them. Yet for them (there is) an appointment from which they will find no escape. **59** Those towns – We destroyed them when they did evil, and We set an appointment for their destruction.

60 (Remember) when Moses said to his young man, 'I shall not give up until I reach the junction of the two seas, or (else) I shall go on for a long time.' **61** When they reached the junction of them, they forgot their fish, (for) it had taken its way into the sea, swimming off. **62** So when they had passed beyond (that place), he said to his young man, 'Bring us our morning meal. We have indeed become weary from this journey of ours.' **63** He[6] said, 'Did you see when we took refuge

---

5. *place of destruction*: meaning obscure.
6. *He*: the young man.

The Cave

at the rock?[7] Surely I forgot the fish – none other than Satan made me forget to remember it – and it took its way into the sea – an amazing thing!' **64** He[8] said, 'That is what we were seeking!'[9] So they returned, retracing their footsteps. **65** And they found a servant,[10] one of Our servants to whom We had given mercy from Us, and whom We had taught knowledge from Us. **66** Moses said to him, 'Shall I follow you on (the condition) that you teach me some of what you have been taught (of) right (knowledge)?' **67** He said, 'Surely you will not be able (to have) patience with me. **68** How could you have patience for what you cannot encompass in (your) awareness of it?' **69** He said, 'You will find me, if God pleases, patient, and I shall not disobey you in any command.' **70** He said, 'If you follow (me), do not ask me about anything, until I mention it to you.'

71 So they both[11] set out (and continued on) until, when they sailed in the ship, he[12] made a hole in it. He[13] said, 'Have you made a hole in it in order to drown its passengers? You have indeed done a dreadful thing!' **72** He said, 'Did I not say, "Surely you will not be able (to have) patience with me?"' **73** He said, 'Do not take me to task for what I forgot, and do not burden me (with) hardship in my affair.' **74** So they both set out (and continued on) until, when they met a young boy, he killed him. He said, 'Have you killed an innocent person, other than (in retaliation) for a person? Certainly you have done a terrible thing!' **75** He said, 'Did I not say to you, "Surely you will not be able (to have) patience with me?"' **76** He said, 'If I ask you about anything after this, do not keep me as a companion. You have had enough excuses from me.' **77** So they both set out (and continued on) until, when they came to the people of a town, they asked its people for food, but they refused to offer them hospitality. They both found in it a wall on the verge of collapse, and he[14] set it up. He[15] said, 'If you had wished, you could indeed have taken a reward for that.' **78** He said, 'This is the parting between me and you. (Now) I shall inform you about the interpretation of what you were not able (to have) patience with. **79** As for the ship, it belonged to poor people working on the sea, and I wanted to damage it, (because) behind them (there) was a king seizing

---

7. *the rock*: reference obscure.
8. *He*: Moses.
9. *That is what we were seeking*: Moses now realizes that the water in which the fish came to life was the 'spring of immortality,' for which he had been searching all along.
10. *a servant*: this mysterious figure remains unnamed, though a majority of commentators call him al-Khaḍr (or al-Khiḍr), 'the green man,' but other possibilities have been suggested (e.g. the prophet Elijah, or Utnapishtim in the *Epic of Gilgamesh*).
11. *they both*: Moses and the mysterious servant.
12. *he*: the mysterious servant.
13. *He*: Moses.
14. *he*: the servant.
15. *He*: Moses.

The Cave

every ship by force. **80** As for the young boy, his parents were believers, and we feared that he would burden them both (with) insolent transgression and disbelief. **81** We wanted their Lord to give to them both in exchange (one) better than him in purity, and closer (to them) in affection. **82** As for the wall, it belonged to two orphan boys in the city, and underneath it was a treasure belonging to them both, (for) their father had been a righteous man. Your Lord wanted them both to reach their maturity, and bring forth their treasure as a mercy from your Lord. I did not do it on my (own) command. That is the interpretation (of) what you were not able (to have) patience with.'

83 They ask you about Dhū-l-Qarnayn.[16] Say: 'I shall recite to you a remembrance of him. **84** Surely We established him on the earth and gave him a way of access to everything. **85** He followed (one such) way of access **86** until, when he reached the setting of the sun, he found it setting in a muddy spring, and he found next to it a people. We said, "Dhū-l-Qarnayn! Either punish (them) or do them (some) good." **87** He said, "As for the one who does evil, we shall punish him. Then he will be returned to his Lord, and He will punish him (with) a terrible punishment. **88** But as for the one who believes, and does righteousness, for him (there is) the good payment, and we shall speak to him something easy from our command."

89 Then he followed (another) way of access **90** until, when he reached the rising (place) of the sun, he found it rising on a people for whom We had not provided any shelter from it. **91** So (it was), but We had already encompassed what his situation was in (our) awareness. **92** Then he followed (another) way of access **93** until, when he arrived (at the place) between the two barriers, he found on this side of them a people hardly able to understand (his) speech. **94** They said, "Dhū-l-Qarnayn! Surely Gog and Magog are fomenting corruption on the earth. Shall we pay tribute to you on (the condition) that you construct a barrier between us and them?" **95** He said, "What my Lord has established me with is better. Help me with a force, (and) I shall construct a rampart between you and them. **96** Bring me blocks of iron!" – Until, when he had made level (the gap) between the two cliffs, he said, "Blow!" – Until, when he had made it a fire, he said, "Bring me (blocks of brass)! I will pour molten brass over it." **97** So they[17] were not able to surmount it, nor were they able (to make) a hole in it. **98** He said, "This is a mercy from my Lord. But when the promise of my Lord comes, He will shatter it. The promise of my Lord is true.'"

99 We shall leave some of them on that Day crashing into each other, and there will be a blast on the trumpet, and We shall gather them all together. **100** We shall present Gehenna on that Day to the disbelievers, **101** whose eyes were covered from My remembrance and (who) were not capable (of) hearing. **102** Do

---

16. *Dhū-l-Qarnayn*: lit. 'He of the two horns;' usually identified with Alexander the Great (d. 323 BCE), whose widely circulating image on coins depicted him in the guise of the two-horned god Zeus-Ammon.

17. *they*: Gog and Magog.

The Cave

those who disbelieve think that they can take My servants as allies instead of Me? Surely We have prepared Gehenna as a reception for the disbelievers.

103 Say: 'Shall We inform you about the worst losers in (regard to their) deeds? **104** (They are) those whose striving goes astray in this present life, even though they think that they are doing good in (regard to their) work. **105** Those – (they are) those who disbelieve in the signs of their Lord and in the meeting with Him. So their deeds have come to nothing. We shall not assign any weight to them on the Day of Resurrection. **106** That is their payment – Gehenna – because they disbelieved and took My signs and My messengers in mockery. **107** (But) surely those who believe and do righteous deeds – for them (there will be) Gardens of Paradise as a reception, **108** there to remain. They will not desire any removal from there.'

109 Say: 'If the sea were ink for the words of my Lord, the sea would indeed give out before the words of my Lord would give out, even if We brought (another sea) like it as an extension.'

110 Say: 'I am only a human being like you. I have received inspiration that your God is one God. So whoever expects the meeting with his Lord, let him do righteous deeds and not associate anyone in the service of his Lord.'

19 ✤ Mary

In the Name of God, the Merciful, the Compassionate

1 Kāf Hā' Yā' 'Ayn Ṣād.

2 A remembrance of the mercy of your Lord (to) His servant Zachariah: 3 When he called on his Lord in secret, 4 he said, 'My Lord, surely I – (my) bones have become weak within me, and (my) head is aflame (with) white (hair), but I have not been disappointed in calling on You (before), my Lord. 5 Surely I fear (who) the heirs (will be) after me, (for) my wife cannot conceive. So grant me from Yourself an heir, 6 (who) will inherit from me and inherit from the house of Jacob, and make him, my Lord, pleasing.' 7 'Zachariah! Surely We give you good news of a boy. His name (will be) John. We have not given (this) name to anyone before.' 8 He said, 'My Lord, how shall I have a boy, when my wife cannot conceive and I have already reached extreme old age?' 9 He said, 'So (it will be)! Your Lord has said, "It is easy for Me, seeing that I created you before, when you were nothing."' 10 He said, 'My Lord, give me a sign.' He said, 'Your sign is that you will not speak to the people for three days exactly.' 11 So he came out to his people from the place of prayer and inspired them: 'Glorify (Him) morning and evening.'

12 'John! Hold fast the Book!' And We gave him the judgment as a child, 13 and grace from Us, and purity. He was one who guarded (himself), 14 and was dutiful to his parents. He was not a tyrant (or) disobedient. 15 Peace (be) upon him, the day he was born, and the day he dies, and the day he is raised up alive.

16 And remember in the Book Mary: When she withdrew from her family to an eastern place, 17 and took a veil apart from them, We sent to her Our spirit, and it took for her the form of a human being exactly. 18 She said, 'Surely I take refuge with the Merciful from you, if you are one who guards (yourself).' 19 He said, 'I am only a messenger of your Lord (sent) to grant you a boy (who is) pure.' 20 She said, 'How can I have a boy, when no human being has touched me, nor am I a prostitute?' 21 He said, 'So (it will be)! Your Lord has said: "It is easy for Me. And (it is) to make him a sign to the people and a mercy from Us. It is a thing decreed."'

22 So she conceived him, and withdrew with him to a place far away. 23 The pains of childbirth drove her to the trunk of the date palm. She said, 'I wish I had died before (this) and was completely forgotten!' 24 And then he[1] called out to her from

---

1. *he*: the infant Jesus.

Mary

beneath her, 'Do not sorrow! Your Lord has made a stream beneath you. 25 Shake the trunk of the date palm toward you, and it will drop on you fresh ripe (dates). 26 Eat and drink and be comforted. If you see any human being, say: "Surely I have vowed a fast to the Merciful, and so I shall not speak to any human today."'

27 Then she brought him to her people, carrying him. They said, 'Mary! Certainly you have brought something strange. 28 Sister of Aaron! Your father was not a bad man, nor was your mother a prostitute.' 29 But she referred (them) to him. They said, 'How shall we speak to one who is in the cradle, a (mere) child?' 30 He said, 'Surely I am a servant of God. He has given me the Book and made me a prophet. 31 He has made me blessed wherever I am, and He has charged me with the prayer and the alms as long as I live, 32 and (to be) respectful to my mother. He has not made me a tyrant (or) miserable. 33 Peace (be) upon me, the day I was born, and the day I die, and the day I am raised up alive.'

34 That was Jesus, son of Mary – a statement of the truth about which they are in doubt. 35 It is not for God to take any son. Glory to Him! When He decrees something, He simply says to it, 'Be!' and it is. 36 'Surely God is my Lord and your Lord, so serve Him! This is a straight path.'

37 But the factions differed among themselves. So woe to those who disbelieve on account of (their) witnessing a great Day! 38 How well they will hear on it! How well they will see on the Day when they come to Us! But the evildoers today are clearly astray. 39 Warn them of the Day of Regret, when the matter will be decided while they are (still) oblivious and disbelieving. 40 Surely We shall inherit the earth, and whoever is on it, and to Us they will be returned.

41 And remember in the Book Abraham: Surely he was a man of truth, a prophet. 42 When he said to his father, 'My father! Why do you serve what does not hear and does not see, and is of no use to you at all? 43 My father! Surely some knowledge has come to me that has not come to you. So follow me, and I shall guide you to an even path. 44 My father! Do not serve Satan! Surely Satan is disobedient to the Merciful. 45 My father! I fear that punishment from the Merciful will touch you, and you become an ally of Satan.' 46 He said, 'Do you forsake my gods, Abraham? If indeed you do not stop, I shall indeed stone you. So leave me for a long time!' 47 He said, 'Peace (be) upon you! I shall ask forgiveness for you from my Lord. Surely He has been gracious to me. 48 I shall withdraw from you and what you call on instead of God, and I shall call on my Lord. It may be that I shall not be disappointed in calling on my Lord.' 49 So when he had withdrawn from them and what they were serving instead of God, We granted him Isaac and Jacob, and each one We made a prophet. 50 We granted them some of Our mercy, and We assigned to them a true (and) high reputation.

51 And remember in the Book Moses: Surely he was devoted, and he was a messenger, a prophet. 52 We called him from the right side of the mountain, and We brought him near in conversation. 53 And We granted him some of Our mercy: his brother Aaron, a prophet.

Mary

54 And remember in the Book Ishmael: Surely he was true to the promise, and he was a messenger, a prophet. **55** He commanded his people with the prayer and the alms, and he was pleasing before his Lord.

56 And remember in the Book Idrīs:[2] Surely he was a man of truth, a prophet. **57** We raised him up to a high place.

58 Those were the ones whom God has blessed among the prophets from the descendants of Adam, and from those We carried with Noah, and from the descendants of Abraham and Israel, and from those whom We have guided and chosen. When the signs of the Merciful were recited to them, they fell down in prostration and weeping. **59** But after them came successors (who) neglected the prayer and followed (their own) desires. Soon they will meet error **60** – except for the one who turns (in repentance), and believes, and does righteousness. Those will enter the Garden, and they will not be done evil at all **61** – Gardens of Eden, which the Merciful has promised to His servants in the unseen. Surely He – His promise will come to pass. **62** There they will not hear any frivolous talk, only 'Peace!' And there they will have their provision morning and evening. **63** That is the Garden which We give as an inheritance to those of Our servants who guard (themselves).

64 'We[3] only come down by the command of your Lord. To Him (belongs) whatever is before us and whatever is behind us, and whatever is between that. Your Lord is not forgetful **65** – Lord of the heavens and the earth, and whatever is between them. So serve Him and be patient in His service! Do you know (another) name for Him?'

66 The human says, 'When I am dead, shall I indeed be brought forth alive?' **67** Does the human not remember that We created him before, when he was nothing? **68** By your Lord! We shall indeed gather them together, and (also) the satans. Then We shall indeed bring them around Gehenna (on) bended knees. **69** Then We shall indeed draw out from each party those of them (who are) most (in) rebellion against the Merciful. **70** Then indeed We shall know those who most deserve burning with it. **71** (There is) not one of you (who is) not coming to it – (that) is for your Lord an inevitability decreed. **72** Then We shall rescue the ones who guarded (themselves), and leave the evildoers in it (on) bended knees.

73 When Our signs are recited to them as clear signs, those who disbelieve say to those who believe, 'Which of the two groups is better in status and better as a cohort?' **74** But how many a generation We have destroyed before them! They were better in wealth and outward appearance. **75** Say: 'Whoever is astray, let the Merciful prolong his life until, when they see what they are promised – either the punishment or the Hour – they will know who is worse in position and weaker in forces.' **76** But God will increase in guidance those who are guided. And the things that endure – righteous deeds – are better with your Lord, and better in return.

---

2. *Idrīs*: probably Ezra (derived from 'Esdras,' the Greek form of the name).
3. *We*: the angels.

Mary

77 Have you seen the one who disbelieves in Our signs, and says, 'I shall indeed be given wealth and children'? **78** Has he looked into the unseen, or has he taken a covenant with the Merciful? **79** By no means! We shall write down what he says, and We shall increase the punishment for him. **80** We shall inherit from him what he says, and he will come to Us alone.

81 They have taken gods other than God, so that they might be a (source of) honor for them. **82** By no means! They will deny their service, and they will be opposed to them. **83** Do you not see that We have sent the satans against the disbelievers to incite them. **84** So do not be in a hurry with them. We are only counting for them a (certain) number (of years). **85** On the Day when We shall gather to the Merciful the ones who guarded (themselves) like a delegation, **86** and drive the sinners into Gehenna like a herd, **87** they will have no power of intercession, except for the one who has taken a covenant with the Merciful.

88 They say, 'The Merciful has taken a son.' **89** Certainly you have put forth something abhorrent! **90** The heavens are nearly torn apart because of it, and the earth split open, and the mountains collapse in pieces **91** – that they should attribute to the Merciful a son, **92** when it is not fitting for the Merciful to take a son.

93 (There is) no one in the heavens and the earth who comes to the Merciful except as a servant. **94** Certainly He has counted them and numbered them exactly. **95** Each one of them will come to Him on the Day of Resurrection alone. **96** Surely those who believe and do righteous deeds – to them the Merciful will show (His) love.

97 Surely We have made it easy in your language, so that you may give good news by means of it to the ones who guard (themselves), and warn by means of it a contentious people. **98** But how many a generation We have destroyed before them! Do you see a single one of them, or hear (even) a whisper of them?

20 ☸ Ṭā' Hā'

In the Name of God, the Merciful, the Compassionate

1 Ṭā' Hā'.
2 We have not sent down the Qur'ān on you for you to be miserable, 3 but as a reminder to the one who fears 4 – as a sending down from the One who created the earth and the high heavens. 5 The Merciful is mounted upon the throne. 6 To Him (belongs) whatever is in the heavens and whatever is on the earth, and whatever is between them, and whatever is beneath the ground. 7 If you speak the word publicly, surely He knows the secret and (what is even) more hidden. 8 God – (there is) no god but Him. To Him (belong) the best names.

9 Has the story of Moses come to you? 10 When he saw a fire, he said to his family, 'Stay (here). Surely I perceive a fire. Perhaps I shall bring you a flaming torch from it, or I shall find at the fire guidance.' 11 But when he came to it, he was called: 'Moses! 12 Surely I am your Lord, so take off your shoes. Surely you are in the holy wādī of Ṭuwā. 13 I have chosen you, so listen to what is inspired. 14 Surely I am God – (there is) no god but Me. So serve Me, and observe the prayer for My remembrance! 15 Surely the Hour is coming – I almost hide it, so that every person may be repaid for what he strives after. 16 So do not let anyone who does not believe in it, and who (only) follows his (own) desire, keep you from it, or you will be brought to ruin.'

17 'What is that in your right (hand), Moses?' 18 He said, 'It is my staff. I lean on it, and I bring down leaves with it to (feed) my sheep, and I have other uses for it.' 19 He said, 'Cast it (down), Moses!' 20 So he cast it, and suddenly it became a slithering snake. 21 He said, 'Take hold of it, and do not fear. We shall restore it to its former state. 22 Now draw your hand to your side. It will come out white, unharmed – another sign. 23 (We have done this) to show you one of Our greatest signs.'

24 'Go to Pharaoh! Surely he has transgressed insolently.' 25 He said, 'My Lord, expand my heart for me, 26 and make my task easy for me. 27 Untie the knot from my tongue, 28 so that they may understand my words. 29 And appoint an assistant for me from my family: 30 Aaron, my brother. 31 Strengthen me through him, 32 and associate him in my task, 33 so that we may glorify You often, 34 and remember You often. 35 Surely you see us.' 36 He said, 'You are granted your request, Moses.'

37 'Certainly We bestowed favor on you another time, 38 when We inspired your mother (with) what was inspired: 39 "Cast him into the ark, and cast it into the

sea, and let the sea throw it up on the shore, and an enemy to Me and an enemy to him will take him." But I cast love on you from Me, and (I did this) so that you might be brought up under My eye. **40** When your sister went out, she said, "Shall I direct you to (someone) who will take charge of him?" And We returned you to your mother, so that she might be comforted and not sorrow. And (then) you killed a man, and We rescued you from that distress, and We tested you thoroughly. So you remained for (some) years with the people of Midian, (and) then you came (here), according to a decree, Moses.'

41 'I have brought you up for Myself. **42** Go, you and your brother, with My signs, and do not be lax in My remembrance. **43** Go, both of you, to Pharaoh. Surely he has transgressed insolently. **44** But speak to him a soft word. Perhaps he may take heed or fear.' **45** They said, 'Our Lord, surely we are afraid that he may act rashly against us, or that he may transgress insolently.' **46** He said, 'Do not be afraid! Surely I am with both of you. I hear and I see. **47** So go to him, both of you, and say: "We are two messengers of your Lord, so send forth the Sons of Israel with us, and do not punish them. We have brought you a sign from your Lord. Peace (be) upon anyone who follows the guidance! **48** Surely we have been inspired that the punishment (will fall) on anyone who calls (it) a lie and turns away."'

49 He[1] said, 'And who is your Lord, Moses?' **50** He said, 'Our Lord is the One who gave everything its creation, (and) then guided (it).' **51** He said, 'What (about the) case of the former generations?' **52** He said, 'The knowledge of it is with my Lord in a Book. My Lord does not go astray, nor does He forget. **53** (It is He) who made the earth as a cradle for you, and put (path)ways in it for you, and sent down water from the sky. And by means of it We brought forth pairs of various (kinds of) vegetation. **54** Eat (of it) and pasture your livestock (on it). Surely in that are signs indeed for those with reason. **55** We created you from it, and into it We shall return you, and from it We shall bring you forth another time.'

56 Certainly We showed him Our signs, all of them, but he called (them) a lie and refused. **57** He said, 'Have you come to bring us forth from our land by your magic, Moses? **58** We shall indeed bring you magic like it. So set an appointment between us and you – We shall not break it, nor will you – at a fair place.' **59** He said, 'Your appointment is on the Day of Splendor. Let the people be gathered at morning light.'

60 So Pharaoh turned away, and put together his plot. Then he came (again). **61** Moses said to them, 'Woe to you! Do not forge a lie against God, or He will destroy you with a punishment. Whoever forges (a lie) has failed.' **62** So they disputed their situation among themselves, but they kept their talk secret. **63** They said, 'Surely these two magicians want to expel you from your land by their magic, and to do away with your exemplary way (of life). **64** So put together your plot, (and) then line up. He who has the upper hand today will indeed prosper.'

---

1. *He*: Pharaoh, in Pharaoh's court.

Ṭā' Hā'

65 They said, 'Moses! Are you going to cast or shall we be first to cast?' **66** He said, 'No! You cast (first)!' And suddenly their ropes and their staffs seemed to him to be moving as a result of their magic. **67** So Moses felt fear within himself. **68** We said to him, 'Do not be afraid! Surely you will be the superior one. **69** Cast (down) what is in your right (hand), and it will swallow up what they have made. What they have done is only a magician's trick, and the magician does not prosper, (no matter) where he comes.'

70 And the magicians were cast (down) in prostration. They said, 'We believe in the Lord of Aaron and Moses.' **71** He[2] said, 'Have you believed in him before I gave you permission? Surely he indeed is your master, the (very) one who taught you magic? I shall indeed cut off your hands and your feet on opposite sides, and I shall indeed crucify you on the trunks of date palms, and you will indeed know which of us is harsher in punishment, and more lasting.' **72** They said, 'We shall not prefer you over the clear signs which have come to us, nor (over) Him who created us. So decree whatever you are going to decree. You can only decree for this present life. **73** Surely we have believed in our Lord, so that He may forgive us our sins and the magic you forced us to (practice). God is better and more lasting.'

74 Surely the one who comes to his Lord as a sinner, surely for him (there is) Gehenna, where he will neither die nor live. **75** But whoever comes to Him as a believer, (and) he has done righteous deeds, those – for them (there are) the highest ranks: **76** Gardens of Eden, through which rivers flow, there to remain. That is the payment for the one who purifies himself.

77 Certainly We inspired Moses: 'Journey with My servants, and strike for them a dry passage in the sea, without fear of being overtaken or being afraid.' **78** So Pharaoh followed them with his forces, but (there) covered them of the sea what covered them. **79** Pharaoh led his people astray and did not guide (them).

80 Sons of Israel! We have rescued you from your enemy, and made a covenant with you at the right side of the mountain, and sent down on you the manna and the quails: **81** 'Eat from the good things which We have provided you, but do not transgress insolently in that, or My anger will descend on you. Whoever My anger falls on has perished. **82** Yet surely I am indeed forgiving to whoever turns (in repentance) and believes, and does righteousness, (and) then is (rightly) guided.'

83 'What has made you hurry (ahead) of your people, Moses?' **84** He said, 'They are close on my footsteps, but I have hurried (ahead) to you, my Lord, in order that You might be pleased.' **85** He[3] said, 'Surely We have tempted your people after you (left them), and al-Sāmirī[4] has led them astray.' **86** So Moses returned to his people, angry (and) sorrowful. He said, 'My people! Did your Lord not promise

---

2. *He*: Pharaoh.
3. *He*: God.
4. *al-Sāmirī*: perhaps 'the Samaritan,' but the meaning is uncertain.

Ṭā' Hā'

you a good promise? Did (the time of) the covenant last too long for you, or did you wish that the anger of your Lord would descend on you, and so you broke (your) appointment with me?' **87** They said, 'We did not break (our) appointment with you by our (own) will, but we were loaded with burdens of the ornaments of the people, and we cast them (down), and so did al-Sāmirī.' **88** Then he brought forth for them a calf, a (mere) image of it (having) a mooing sound, and they said, 'This is your god, and the god of Moses, though he has forgotten.' **89** Did they not see that it did not return a word to them, and had no power to (cause) them harm or benefit? **90** Certainly Aaron had said to them before, 'My people! You are only being tempted by it. Surely your Lord is the Merciful, so follow me and obey my command!' **91** They said, 'We shall continue (to be) devoted to it until Moses returns to us.'

92 He[5] said, 'Aaron! What prevented you, when you saw them going astray, **93** from following me? Did you disobey my command?' **94** He said, 'Son of my mother! Do not seize (me) by my beard or by my head! Surely I was afraid that you would say, "You have caused a division among the Sons of Israel, and you have not respected my word."' **95** He[6] said, 'What was this business of yours, al-Sāmirī?' **96** He said, 'I saw what they did not see, and I took a handful (of dust) from the footprint of the messenger, and I tossed it. In this way my mind contrived (it) for me.' **97** He[7] said, 'Go! Surely it is yours in this life to say, "Do not touch (me)!" And surely for you (there is) an appointment – you will not break it. Look at your god which you remained devoted to! We shall indeed burn it (and) then scatter it as dust in the sea. **98** Your only god is God – (there is) no god but Him – who comprehends everything in knowledge.'

99 In this way We recount to you some of the stories of what has already gone before, and We have given you a reminder from Us. **100** Whoever turns away from it, surely he will bear a burden on the Day of Resurrection. **101** [. . .][8] there to remain, and evil (will be the) load for them on the Day of Resurrection.

102 On the Day when there is a blast on the trumpet – and We shall gather the sinners on that Day blue – **103** they will murmur among themselves: 'You have remained (in the grave) only for ten (days).' **104** We know what they will say, when the best of them in way (of life) will say, 'You have remained only for a day.'

105 They ask you about the mountains. Say: 'My Lord will scatter them as dust, **106** and He will leave it a barren plain **107** in which you will not see any crookedness or curve.'

108 On that Day they will follow the Caller, in whom (there is) no crookedness, and voices will be hushed before the Merciful, so that you will hear nothing

---

5. *He*: Moses.
6. *He*: Moses.
7. *He*: Moses.
8. *[. . .]*: there appears to be a lacuna here.

Ṭā' Hā'

but a faint murmur. **109** On that Day intercession will not be of any benefit, except for the one to whom the Merciful gives permission, and whose word He approves. **110** He knows what is before them and what is behind them, but they do not encompass Him in knowledge. **111** Faces will be humbled before the Living, the Everlasting. Whoever carries (a load of) evildoing will have failed, **112** but whoever does any righteous deeds – and he is a believer – he will not fear (any) evil or dispossession.

113 In this way We have sent it down as an Arabic Qur'ān, and We have varied some of the promise(s) in it, so that they may guard (themselves), or so that it may arouse in them a reminder. **114** Exalted is God, the true King! Do not be in a hurry with the Qur'ān, before its inspiration is completed to you, but say: 'My Lord, increase me in knowledge.'

115 Certainly We made a covenant with Adam before, but he forgot, and We found in him no determination. **116** (Remember) when We said to the angels, 'Prostrate yourselves before Adam,' and they prostrated themselves, except Iblīs. He refused. **117** And We said, 'Adam! Surely this is an enemy to you and to your wife. Do not let him expel you both from the Garden, and you become miserable. **118** Surely it is yours not to hunger there or go naked, **119** nor to thirst there or be exposed to the sun.' **120** But Satan whispered to him. He said, 'Adam! Shall I direct you to the Tree of Immortality, and (to) a kingdom that does not decay?' **121** So they both ate from it, and their shameful parts became apparent to them, and they both began fastening on themselves some leaves of the Garden, and Adam disobeyed his Lord and erred. **122** Then his Lord chose him, and turned to him (in forgiveness), and guided (him). **123** He said, 'Go down from it, both of you together, some of you an enemy to others. If any guidance comes to you from Me, whoever follows My guidance will not go astray, nor become miserable. **124** But whoever turns away from My reminder, surely for him (there will be) a life of deprivation, and We shall gather him blind on the Day of Resurrection.' **125** He will say, 'My Lord, why have you gathered me blind, when I had sight before?' **126** He will say, 'So (it is). Our signs came to you, but you forgot them, so today you are forgotten.' **127** In this way We repay anyone who acts wantonly and does not believe in the signs of his Lord. Yet the punishment of the Hereafter is indeed harsher and more lasting.

128 Is it not a guide for them how many generations We destroyed before them, (seeing that) they walk in (the midst of) their dwelling places? Surely in that are signs indeed for those with reason. **129** Were it not for a preceding word from your Lord, it would indeed be close at hand – but (there is) a time appointed (for punishment). **130** So be patient with what they say, and glorify your Lord with praise before the rising of the sun, and before its setting, and during the hours of the night, and glorify (Him) at the ends of the day, so that you may find satisfaction. **131** Do not yearn after what We have given classes of them to enjoy – the flower of this present life – that We may test them by means of it. The provision of your Lord is better and more lasting. **132** Command your family (to observe) the prayer, and be patient in it. We do not ask you for provision. We provide for you, and the outcome (is) for the guarding (of yourself).

133 They say, 'If only he would bring us a sign from his Lord.' Has there not come to them a clear sign (of) what was in the former pages? **134** If We had destroyed them with a punishment before him, they would indeed have said, 'Our Lord, if only you had sent us a messenger, so that we might have followed your signs before we were humiliated and disgraced?' **135** Say: 'Each one is waiting, so you wait (too), and then you will know who are the followers of the even path, and who is (rightly) guided.'

21 ❈ THE PROPHETS

In the Name of God, the Merciful, the Compassionate

1 Their reckoning has drawn near to the people, while they are turning away oblivious. 2 No new reminder comes to them from their Lord, without their listening to it while they jest, 3 their hearts diverted. Those who do evil keep their talk secret: 'Is this (anything) but a human being like you? Will you surrender to magic when you see (it)?' 4 Say:[1] 'My Lord knows the words (spoken) in the sky and the earth. He is the Hearing, the Knowing.' 5 'No!' they say, '(It is) a jumble of dreams! No! He has forged it! No! He is a poet! Let him bring us a sign, as the ones of old were sent (with signs).' 6 Not one town which We destroyed before them believed. Will they believe?

7 We have not sent (anyone) before you except men whom We inspired – just ask the People of the Reminder, if you do not know (it) – 8 nor did We give them a body not eating food, nor were they immortal. 9 But We were true to them in the promise, so We rescued them and whomever We pleased, and We destroyed the wanton. 10 Certainly We have sent down to you[2] a Book in which (there is) your reminder. Will you not understand?

11 How many a town (which) was doing evil have We smashed, and produced another people after it! 12 And when they sensed Our violence, suddenly they began fleeing from it. 13 'Do not flee, but return to what luxury you were given to delight in, and (to) your dwellings, so that you may be questioned.' 14 They said, 'Woe to us! Surely we have been evildoers.' 15 This cry of theirs did not stop until We cut them down (and) snuffed (them) out.

16 We did not create the sky and the earth, and whatever is between them, in jest. 17 If We wanted to choose a diversion, We would indeed have chosen it from Ourselves, if We were going to do (anything). 18 No! We hurl the truth against falsehood, and it breaks its head, and suddenly it passes away. Woe to you for what you allege!

19 To Him (belongs) whoever is in the heavens and the earth, and those who are in His presence are not (too) proud for His service, nor do they grow weary (of it). 20 They glorify (Him) night and day – they do not cease.

---

1. *Say*: following the alternative reading 'Say' (Ar. *qul*) instead of 'He said' (*qāla*), which seems unlikely here (and at Q21.112 below).
2. *you*: plur.

The Prophets

21 Or have they taken gods from the earth? Do they raise (the dead)? **22** If there were any gods in the two of them[3] other than God, the two would indeed go to ruin. So glory to God, Lord of the throne, above what they allege! **23** He will not be questioned about what He does, but they will be questioned. **24** Or have they taken gods other than Him? Say: 'Bring your proof! This is a Reminder (for) those who are with me, and a Reminder (for) those who were before me.' But most of them do not know the truth, so they turn away. **25** We have not sent any messenger before you except that We inspired him: '(There is) no god but Me, so serve Me!'

26 They say, 'The Merciful has taken a son.' Glory to Him! No! (They are) honored servants. **27** They do not precede Him in speech, but they act on His command. **28** He knows what is before them and what is behind them, and they do not intercede, except for the one whom He approves, and they are apprehensive because of fear of Him. **29** Whoever of them says, 'Surely I am a god instead of Him,' We repay that one with Gehenna. In this way We repay the evildoers.

30 Do those who disbelieve not see that the heavens and the earth were (once) a solid mass, and We split the two of them apart, and We made every living thing from water? Will they not believe? **31** We have placed on the earth firm mountains, so that it does not sway with them (on it), and placed in it passes (to serve) as (path)ways, so that they might be guided. **32** And We have made the sky as a guarded roof. Yet they (still) turn away from its signs. **33** He (it is) who created the night and the day, and the sun and the moon, each floating in (its own) orbit.

34 We have not granted immortality to any human being before you. If you die, will they live forever? **35** Every person will taste death. We try you[4] with evil and good as a test, and to Us you will be returned. **36** When those who disbelieve see you,[5] they take you only in mockery: 'Is this the one who makes mention of your gods?' Yet they (become) disbelievers at any mention of the Merciful. **37** The human was created out of haste. I shall show you[6] My signs, so do not ask Me to hasten (them). **38** But they say, 'When (will) this promise (come to pass), if you[7] are truthful?' **39** If (only) those who disbelieved knew the time when they will not be able to hold off the Fire from their faces and from their backs, nor will they be helped! **40** No! It will come upon them unexpectedly, and confound them, and they will not be able to turn it back, nor will they be spared. **41** Certainly messengers have been mocked before you, but those of them who ridiculed (were) overwhelmed (by) what they were mocking.

---

3. *the two of them*: the dual refers to 'the heavens and the earth.'
4. *you*: plur.
5. *you*: sing.
6. *you*: plur.
7. *you*: plur.

The Prophets

42 Say: 'Who will guard you in the night and the day from the Merciful?' No! They (still) turn away from (any) reminder of their Lord. **43** Or do they have gods other than Us to protect them? They are not able to help themselves, nor will they have any companions (to shield them) from Us. **44** No! We gave these (people) and their fathers enjoyment (of life), until life had lasted a long time for them. Do they not see that We come to the land, pushing back its borders? Are they the victors? **45** Say: 'I warn you only (in accord) with the inspiration.' But the deaf do not hear the call when they are warned. **46** If indeed a whiff of the punishment of your Lord should touch them, they would indeed say, 'Woe to us! Surely we – we have been evildoers.' **47** We shall lay down the scales of justice for the Day of Resurrection, and no one will be done any evil. (Even) if there is (only) the weight of a mustard seed, We shall produce it, and We are sufficient as reckoners.

48 Certainly We gave Moses and Aaron the Deliverance, and a light, and a reminder to the ones who guard (themselves), **49** who fear their Lord in the unseen, and they are apprehensive of the Hour. **50** And this is a blessed Reminder. We have sent it down. Will you reject it?

51 Certainly We gave Abraham his right (path) before (them), (for) We knew him. **52** (Remember) when he said to his father and his people: 'What are these images which you are devoted to?' **53** They said, 'We found our fathers serving them.' **54** He said, 'Certainly you and your fathers were clearly astray.' **55** They said, 'Have you brought us the truth, or are you one of those who jest?' **56** He said, 'No! Your Lord – Lord of the heavens and the earth – is the One who created them, and I am one of the witnesses to this. **57** By God! I shall indeed plot (to destroy) your idols after you have turned away, withdrawing.' **58** So he broke them into pieces, (all) except a big one they had, so that they would return to it. **59** They said, 'Who has done this with our gods? Surely he is indeed one of the evildoers.' **60** They said, 'We heard a young man mentioning them – he is called Abraham.' **61** They said, 'Bring him before the eyes of the people, so that they may bear witness.' **62** They said, 'Have you done this with our gods, Abraham?' **63** He said, 'No! This big one of them did it. Just ask them, if they are able to speak.' **64** And they turned to each other, and said, 'Surely you – you are the evildoers.' **65** Then they became utterly confused: 'Certainly you know (that) these do not speak.' **66** He said, 'Do you serve what does not benefit you at all, or harm you, instead of God (alone)? **67** Uff to you and to what you serve instead of God! Will you not understand?' **68** They said, 'Burn him, and help your gods, if you are going to do (anything).' **69** We said, 'Fire! Be coolness and peace for Abraham!' **70** They intended a plot against him, but We made them the worst losers, **71** and We rescued him, and Lot, (and brought them) to the land which We have blessed for all peoples.

72 And We granted him Isaac, and Jacob as a gift, and each (of them) We made righteous. **73** And We made them leaders (who) guide (others) by Our command, and We inspired them (with) the doing of good deeds, and the observance of the prayer and the giving of the alms, and they served Us.

The Prophets

74 And Lot – We gave him judgment and knowledge, and we rescued him from the town which was doing bad things. Surely they were an evil people (and) wicked. 75 And We caused him to enter Our mercy. Surely He was one of the righteous.

76 And Noah – when he called out before (that), and We responded to him, and rescued him and his family from great distress. 77 We helped him against the people who called Our signs a lie. Surely they were an evil people, so We drowned them – all (of them)!

78 And David and Solomon – when they rendered judgment concerning the field, when the people's sheep had grazed in it – We were witnesses to their judgment. 79 And We caused Solomon to understand it, and to each We gave judgment and knowledge. And (along) with David We subjected the mountains and the birds to glorify (Us) – We were the doers (of it). 80 And We taught him the making of clothing to protect you from your (own) violence. Are you thankful? 81 And to Solomon (We subjected) the wind, blowing strongly at his command to the land which We have blessed – We have knowledge of everything. 82 And among the satans, (there were) those who dived for him and did other work besides – We were watching over them.

83 And Job – when he called on his Lord, 'Surely hardship has touched me, and You are the most compassionate of the compassionate.' 84 We responded to him, and removed what hardship was upon him, and We gave him his family, and as much again, as a mercy from Us, and a reminder to the ones who serve.

85 And Ishmael, and Idrīs,[8] and Dhū-l-Kifl[9] – each one was among the patient. 86 And We caused them to enter Our mercy. Surely they were among the righteous.

87 And Dhū-l-Nūn[10] – when he went away angry, and thought that We had no power over him, but he called out in the darkness: '(There is) no god but You. Glory to You! Surely I – I have been one of the evildoers.' 88 We responded to him and rescued him from (his) distress. In this way We rescue the believers.

89 And Zachariah – when he called out to his Lord: 'My Lord, do not leave me alone, when You are the best of inheritors.' 90 We responded to him, and granted him John, and set his wife right for him. Surely they were quick in the (doing of) good deeds, and they used to call on Us in hope and fear, and humble (themselves) before Us.

91 And she[11] who guarded her private part – We breathed into her some of Our spirit, and made her and her son a sign to all peoples: 92 'Surely this community of yours is one community, and I am your Lord. So serve Me!' 93 But they cut up their affair among them. (Yet) all (of them) will return to Us. 94 Whoever does

---

8. *Idrīs*: probably Ezra (derived from 'Esdras,' the Greek form of the name).
9. *Dhū-l-Kifl*: some commentators suggest the prophet Ezekiel, others Elijah.
10. *Dhū-l-Nun*: probably Jonah (lit. 'he of the fish').
11. *She*: Mary.

The Prophets

any righteous deeds – and he is a believer – (there will be) no ingratitude for his striving. Surely We are writing (them) down for him.

95 (There is) a ban on any town which We have destroyed: they shall not return **96** until, when Gog and Magog are opened, and they come swooping down from every height, **97** and the true promise draws near, and suddenly (there) it (is)! The eyes of those who disbelieved (will be) staring (and they will say): 'Woe to us! We were oblivious of this. No! We were evildoers.' **98** 'Surely you, and what you were serving instead of God, are stones for Gehenna – you will go down to it.' **99** If these had been gods, they would not have gone down to it, but everyone (of them) will remain in it. **100** In it (there is) a moaning for them, and in it they do not hear (anything else).

101 Surely those for whom the best (reward) has gone forth from Us – those will be (kept) far from it. **102** They will not hear (even) a slight sound of it, and they will remain in what they themselves desired. **103** The great terror will not cause them sorrow, and the angels will meet them: 'This is your Day which you were promised.'

104 On the Day when We shall roll up the sky like the rolling up of a scroll for the writings: as We brought about the first creation, (so) We shall restore it – (it is) a promise (binding) on Us. Surely We shall do (it)! **105** Certainly We have written in the Psalms, after the Reminder: 'The earth – My righteous servants will inherit it.' **106** Surely in this (there is) a delivery indeed for a people who serve.

107 We have sent you only as a mercy to all peoples. **108** Say: 'I am only inspired that your God is one God. Are you going to submit?' **109** If they turn away, say: 'I have proclaimed to all of you equally, but I do not know whether what you are promised is near or far. **110** Surely He knows what is spoken publicly and He knows what you conceal. **111** I do not know. Perhaps it is a test for you, and enjoyment (of life) for a time.' **112** Say:[12] 'My Lord, judge in truth! Our Lord is the Merciful – the One to be sought for help against what you allege.'

---

12. *Say*: following the alternative reading 'Say' (Ar. *qul*) instead of 'He said' (*qāla*), which seems unlikely here (and at Q21.4 above).

22 ❖ The Pilgrimage

In the Name of God, the Merciful, the Compassionate

1 People! Guard (yourselves) against your Lord! Surely the earthquake of the Hour is a great thing. **2** On the Day when you[1] see it, every nursing woman will forget what she has nursed, and every pregnant female will deliver her burden, and you[2] will see the people drunk when they are not drunk – but the punishment of God is harsh! **3** Yet among the people (there is) one who disputes about God without any knowledge, and follows every rebellious satan. **4** It is written about him: 'He who takes him as an ally – he will lead him astray and guide him to the punishment of the blazing (Fire).'

5 People! If you are in doubt about the raising up – surely We created you from dust, then from a drop, then from a clot, (and) then from a lump, formed and unformed, so that We may make (it) clear to you. We establish in the wombs what We please for an appointed time, then We bring you forth as a child, (and) then (We provide for you) so that you may reach your maturity. Among you (there is) one who is taken, and among you (there is) one who is reduced to the worst (stage) of life, so that he knows nothing after (having had) knowledge. And you see the earth withered, but when We send down water on it, it stirs and swells, and grows (plants) of every beautiful kind. **6** That is because God – He is the Truth, and because He gives the dead life, and because He is powerful over everything, **7** and because the Hour is coming – (there is) no doubt about it – and because God will raise up those who are in the graves.

8 Yet among the people (there is) one who disputes about God without any knowledge or guidance, or an illuminating Book, **9** (who) turns away in scorn to lead (people) astray from the way of God. For him (there is) disgrace in this world, and on the Day of Resurrection We shall make him taste the punishment of the burning (Fire): **10** 'That is for what your (own) hands have sent forward, and (know) that God is not an evildoer to (His) servants.' **11** Among the people (there is also) one who serves God sitting on the fence. If some good smites him, he is satisfied with it, but if some trouble smites him, he is overturned (by it). He loses this world and the Hereafter. That – it is the clearest loss! **12** Instead of God, he calls on what does not harm him, and what does not benefit him. That – it is

---

1. *you*: plur.
2. *you*: sing.

The Pilgrimage

straying the farthest! **13** He calls indeed on one whose harm is nearer than his benefit. Evil indeed is the protector, and evil indeed the friend!

14 Surely God will cause those who believe and do righteous deeds to enter Gardens through which rivers flow. Surely God does whatever He wills. **15** Whoever thinks that God will not help him in this world and the Hereafter, let him stretch a rope to the sky. Then let him cut (it), and see whether his scheme will take away what enrages (him). **16** In this way We have sent it down as signs – clear signs – and because God guides whomever He wills.

17 Surely those who believe, and those who are Jews, and the Sabians,[3] and the Christians, and the Magians, and the idolaters – surely God will distinguish between them on the Day of Resurrection. Surely God is a witness over everything. **18** Do you not see that God – whoever is in the heavens and whoever is on the earth prostrates before Him, and (so do) the sun, and the moon, and the stars, and the mountains, and the trees, and the animals, and many of the people? But (there are) many for whom the punishment is justified, and whomever God humiliates, (there is) no one to honor him. Surely God does whatever He pleases.

19 These two disputants dispute about their Lord. But those who disbelieve – clothes of fire have been cut for them, and boiling (water) will be poured (on them) from above their heads, **20** by which what is in their bellies and (their) skins will be melted. **21** And for them (there are) hooked rods of iron. **22** Whenever they want to come out of it, because of (their) agony, they will be sent back into it, and: 'Taste the punishment of the burning (Fire)!' **23** Surely God will cause those who believe and do righteous deeds to enter Gardens through which rivers flow. There they will be adorned with bracelets of gold and (with) pearls, and there their clothes (will be of) silk. **24** They have been guided to good speech, and they have been guided to the path of the Praiseworthy.

25 Surely those who disbelieve and keep (people) from the way of God and the Sacred Mosque, which We have made for the people equally – the resident there and the visitor – and whoever intends to pervert it in an evil manner – We shall make him taste a painful punishment.

26 (Remember) when We settled the place of the House for Abraham: 'Do not associate anything with Me, but purify My House for the ones who go around (it), and the ones who stand, and the ones who bow, (and) the ones who prostrate themselves. **27** And proclaim the pilgrimage among the people. Let them come to you on foot and on every lean animal. They will come from every remote mountain pass, **28** so that they may witness things of benefit to them, and mention the name of God, on (certain) specified days, over whatever animal of the livestock He has provided them: "Eat from them, and feed the wretched poor." **29** Then let them bring an end to their ritual state, and fulfill their vows, and go around the ancient House.'

---

3. *Sabians*: it is not clear who the Ṣābi'ūn are.

The Pilgrimage

30 That (is the rule). Whoever respects the sacred things of God – it will be better for him with his Lord. Permitted to you (to eat) are the livestock, except for what is recited to you. Avoid the abomination of the idols, and avoid the speaking of falsehood, **31** (being) Ḥanīfs[4] before God, not associating (anything) with Him. Whoever associates (anything) with God – (it is) as if he has fallen from the sky, and the birds snatched him away, or (as if) the wind has swept him away to some far off place.

32 That (is the rule). Whoever respects the symbols of God – surely that (comes) from the guarding of (your) hearts. **33** (There are) benefits for you in this up to an appointed time. Then their lawful place is to the ancient House.

34 For every community We have appointed a ritual: that they should mention the name of God over whatever animal of the livestock He has provided them. Your God is one God, so submit to Him. And give good news to the humble, **35** those who, when God is mentioned, their hearts become afraid, and the ones who are patient with whatever smites them, and the ones who observe the prayer, and contribute from what We have provided them. **36** The (sacrificial) animals – We have appointed them for you among the symbols of God: there is good for you in them. So mention the name of God over them, (as they stand) in lines. Then when their sides fall (to the ground), eat from them, and feed the needy and the beggar. In this way We have subjected them to you, so that you may be thankful. **37** Its flesh will not reach God, nor its blood, but the guarding (of yourselves) will reach Him from you. In this way He has subjected them to you, so that you may magnify God because He has guided you. Give good news to the doers of good. **38** Surely God will repel (evil) from those who believe. Surely God does not love any traitor (or) ungrateful one.

39 Permission is given to those who fight because they have been done evil – and surely God is indeed able to help them – **40** those who have been expelled from their homes without any right, only because they said, 'Our Lord is God.' But if God had not repelled some of the people by the means of others, many monasteries, and churches, and synagogues, and mosques, in which the name of God is mentioned often, would indeed have been destroyed. God will indeed help the one who helps Him – surely God is indeed strong, mighty – **41** those who, if We establish them on the earth, observe the prayer and give the alms, and command right and forbid wrong. To God (belongs) the outcome of all affairs.

42 If they call you a liar, the people of Noah called (him) a liar before you, and (so did) 'Ād, and Thamūd, **43** and the people of Abraham, and the people of Lot, **44** and the companions of Midian, and Moses was called a liar (too). I spared the disbelievers, then I seized them, and how was My loathing (of them)! **45** How many a town have We destroyed while it was doing evil, so it is (now) collapsed on its supports! (How many) an abandoned well and well-built palace! **46** Have

---

4. Ḥanīfs: meaning uncertain.

The Pilgrimage

they not traveled on the earth? Do they have hearts to understand with or ears to hear with? Surely it is not the sight (which) is blind, but the hearts within the chests (which) are blind. **47** They seek to hurry you with the punishment. God will not break His promise. Surely a day with your Lord is like a thousand years of what you count. **48** How many a town have I spared while it was doing evil! Then I seized it. To Me is the (final) destination. **49** Say: 'People! I am only a clear warner for you.' **50** Those who believe and do righteous deeds – for them (there is) forgiveness and generous provision. **51** But those who strive against Our signs to obstruct (them) – those are the companions of the Furnace.

52 We have not sent any messenger or any prophet before you, except that, when he began to wish, Satan cast (something) into his wishful thinking. But God cancels what Satan casts, (and) then God clearly composes His verses – surely God is knowing, wise – **53** so that He may make what Satan casts a test for those in whose hearts is a sickness, and whose hearts are hardened – and surely the evildoers are indeed in extreme defiance – **54** and so that those who have been given the knowledge may know that it is the truth from your Lord, and may believe in it, and so that their hearts may be humble before Him. Surely God is indeed guiding those who believe to a straight path.

55 Those who disbelieve will continue (to be) in doubt about it, until the Hour comes upon them unexpectedly, or the punishment of a barren Day comes upon them. **56** The kingdom on that Day (will belong) to God. He will judge between them. Those who believe and do righteous deeds (will be) in Gardens of Bliss, **57** but those who disbelieve and call Our signs a lie – for them (there will be) a humiliating punishment.

58 Those who have emigrated in the way of God, (and) then were killed or died, God will indeed provide them (with) a good provision. Surely God – He indeed is the best of providers. **59** He will indeed cause them to enter by an entrance with which they will be pleased. Surely God is indeed knowing, forbearing. **60** That (will be so). And whoever takes retribution with the same retribution he suffered, (and) then is sought out – God will indeed help him. Surely God is indeed pardoning, forgiving.

61 That is because God causes the night to pass into the day, and causes the day to pass into the night, and because God is hearing, seeing. **62** That is because God – He is the Truth, and because what they call on instead of Him, that is the falsehood, and because God is the Most High, the Great. **63** Do you not see that God sends down water from the sky, (and) then the earth becomes green? God is astute, aware. **64** To Him (belongs) whatever is in the heavens and whatever is on the earth. Surely God – He indeed is the wealthy One, the Praiseworthy. **65** Do you not see that God has subjected to you whatever is on the earth, and the ship that runs on the sea by His command, and (that) He holds up the sky so that it does not fall upon the earth, except by His permission? Surely God is indeed kind (and) compassionate with the people. **66** He (it is) who gave you life, then

The Pilgrimage

He causes you to die, (and) then He will give you life (again). Surely the human is ungrateful indeed.

67 For every community we have appointed a ritual which they practice. So let them not argue with you about the matter, but call (them) to your Lord. Surely you are indeed on a straight guidance. **68** If they dispute with you, say: 'God knows what you do. **69** God will judge between you on the Day of Resurrection concerning your differences.' **70** Do you not know that God knows whatever is in the sky and the earth? Surely that is in a Book. Surely that is easy for God.

71 Instead of God, they serve what He has not sent down any authority for, and what they have no knowledge of. The evildoers will have no helper. **72** When Our signs are recited to them as clear signs, you recognize defiance in the faces of those who disbelieve – they all but attack those who recite Our signs to them. Say: 'Shall I inform you about (something) worse than that? The Fire! God has promised it to those who disbelieve – and it is an evil destination!'

73 People! A parable is struck, so listen to it. Surely those you call on instead of God will not create a fly, even if they joined together for it. And if a fly were to snatch anything away from them, they would not (be able to) rescue it from it. Weak is the seeker and the sought (alike)! **74** They have not measured God (with) the measure due Him. Surely God is indeed strong, mighty.

75 God chooses messengers from the angels and from the people. Surely God is hearing, seeing. **76** He knows what is before them and what is behind them. To God all affairs are returned.

77 You who believe! Bow and prostrate yourselves, and serve your Lord, and do good, so that you may prosper. **78** And struggle for God with the struggling due Him. He has chosen you, and has not placed any difficulty on you in the (matter of) religion: the creed of your father Abraham. He named you Muslims, (both) before and in this, so that the messenger might be a witness against you, and that you might be witnesses against humankind. So observe the prayer and give the alms, and hold fast to God. He is your Protector. Excellent is the Protector, and excellent is the Helper!

23 ❖ THE BELIEVERS

In the Name of God, the Merciful, the Compassionate

1 The believers have prospered **2** who are humble in their prayers, **3** and who turn away from frivolous talk, **4** and who give the alms, **5** and who guard their private parts, **6** except from their wives or what their right (hands) own[1] – surely then they are not (to be) blamed, **7** but whoever seeks beyond that, those – they are the transgressors – **8** and those who keep their pledges and their promise(s), **9** and who guard their prayers. **10** Those – they are the inheritors **11** who will inherit Paradise. There they will remain.

12 Certainly We created the human from an extract of clay. **13** Then We made him a drop in a secure dwelling place, **14** then We made a clot (from) the drop, then We made a lump (from) the clot, then We made bones (from) the lump, then We clothed the bones (with) flesh, (and) then We (re)produced him as another creature. So blessed (be) God, the best of creators! **15** Then, after that, you will indeed die, **16** (and) then surely on the Day of Resurrection you will be raised up.

17 Certainly We created above you seven orbits, and We were not oblivious of the creation. **18** We send down water from the sky in (due) measure, and cause it to settle in the earth – and surely We are able indeed to take it away. **19** By means of it We produce gardens of date palms and grapes for you, in which (there are) many fruits for you, and from which you eat, **20** and a tree (which) comes forth from Mount Sinai (which) bears oil and seasoning[2] for eaters. **21** Surely in the cattle[3] is a lesson indeed for you: We give you to drink from what is in their bellies, and in them (there are) many benefits for you, and from them you eat. **22** On them, and on the ship (as well), you are carried.

23 Certainly We sent Noah to his people, and he said, 'My people! Serve God! You have no god other than Him. Will you not guard (yourselves)?' **24** But the assembly of those who disbelieved among his people said, 'This is nothing but a human being like you. He wants to gain superiority over you. If God had (so) pleased, He would indeed have sent down angels. We have not heard of this among our fathers of old. **25** He is nothing but a man possessed. Wait on him for a time.' **26** He said, 'My Lord, help me, because they are calling me a liar.' **27** So

---

1. *what their right (hands) own*: i.e. their female slaves (cf. Q4.3, 24).
2. *seasoning*: meaning uncertain.
3. *cattle*: or 'livestock' in general.

The Believers

We inspired him: 'Build the ship under Our eyes and Our inspiration, and when Our command comes and the oven boils, put into it two of every kind, a pair, and your family – except for him against whom the word has (already) gone forth. Do not address Me concerning those who have done evil. Surely they are going to be drowned! **28** When you have boarded the ship – you and (those) who are with you – say: "Praise (be) to God, who has rescued us from the people who were evildoers!" **29** And say: "My Lord, bring me to land (at) a blessed landing place, (for) You are the best of those who bring to land."' **30** Surely in that are signs indeed. Surely We have been testing (people) indeed.

31 Then, after them, We produced another generation, **32** and We sent among them a messenger from among them: 'Serve God! You have no god other than Him. Will you not guard (yourselves)?' **33** But the assembly of his people, those who disbelieved and called the meeting of the Hereafter a lie, even though We had given them luxury in this present life, said, 'This is nothing but a human being like you. He eats from what you eat, and drinks from what you drink. **34** If indeed you obey a human being like you, surely then you will be the losers indeed. **35** Does he promise you that when you are dead, and become dust and bones, that you will be brought forth? **36** Away! Away with what you are promised! **37** There is nothing but our present life. We die, and we live, and we are not going to be raised up. **38** He is nothing but a man who has forged a lie against God. We are not believers in him.' **39** He said, 'My Lord, help me, because they are calling me a liar.' **40** He said, 'In a little (while) they will indeed be full of regret.' **41** Then the cry seized them in truth, and We turned them into ruins. Away with the people who are evildoers!

42 Then, after them, We produced other generations. **43** No community precedes its time, nor do they delay (it). **44** Then We sent Our messengers in succession: whenever its messenger came to a community, they called him a liar. So We caused some of them to follow others, and We turned them (into) stories. Away with a people who do not believe!

45 Then We sent Moses and his brother Aaron, with Our signs and clear authority, **46** to Pharaoh and his assembly, but they became arrogant and were a haughty people. **47** They said, 'Shall we believe in two human beings like us, when their people are serving us?' **48** So they called them both liars, and were among the destroyed.

49 Certainly We gave Moses the Book, so that they might be (rightly) guided. **50** And We made the son of Mary and his mother a sign, and We gave them both refuge on high ground, (where there was) a hollow (as) a dwelling place and a flowing spring: **51** 'Messengers! Eat from the good things, and do righteousness! Surely I am aware of what you do. **52** Surely this community of yours is one community, and I am your Lord. So guard (yourselves) against Me!' **53** But they cut their affair (in two) between them (over the) scriptures, each faction gloating over what was with them. **54** Leave them in their flood (of confusion) for a time.

The Believers

55 Do they think that in increasing them with wealth and children **56** We are quick to do them good? No! But they do not realize (it).

57 Surely those who – they are apprehensive on account of fear of their Lord, **58** and those who – they believe in the signs of their Lord, **59** and those who – they do not associate (anything) with their Lord, **60** and those who give what they give, while their hearts are afraid because they are going to return to their Lord – **61** (it is) those who are quick in the (doing of) good deeds, and they are foremost in them.

62 We do not burden anyone beyond his capacity, and with Us is a Book (which) speaks in truth – and they will not be done evil. **63** No! But their hearts are in a flood (of confusion) about this, and they have deeds other than that, which they (will continue to) do **64** – until, when We seize their affluent ones with the punishment, suddenly they cry out. **65** 'Do not cry out today! Surely you will receive no help from Us. **66** My signs were recited to you, but you turned on your heels, **67** being arrogant toward it, (and) forsaking (one who was) conversing by night.'

68 Have they not contemplated the word? Or did (there) come to them what did not come to their fathers of old? **69** Or did they not recognize their messenger, and so rejected him? **70** Or do they say, 'He is possessed'? No! He brought them the truth, but most of them were averse to the truth. **71** If the truth had followed their desires, the heavens and the earth and whatever is in them would indeed have been corrupted. No! We brought them their Reminder, but they turned away from their Reminder. **72** Or do you ask them for payment? Yet the payment of your Lord is better, and He is the best of providers. **73** Surely you indeed call them to a straight path, **74** and surely those who do not believe in the Hereafter are indeed deviating from the path. **75** Even if We had compassion on them, and removed whatever hardship they had, they would indeed persist in their insolent transgression, wandering blindly. **76** Certainly We have seized them with the punishment (already), but they did not submit themselves to their Lord, nor were they humble. **77** – Until, when We open a gate of harsh punishment on them, suddenly they are in despair about it.

78 He (it is) who has produced for you hearing and sight and hearts – little thanks you show! **79** He (it is) who has scattered you on the earth, and to Him you will be gathered. **80** He (it is) who gives life and causes death, and to Him (belongs) the alternation of the night and the day. Will you not understand? **81** No! They said just what those of old said. **82** They said, 'When we are dead, and turned to dust and bones, shall we indeed be raised up? **83** We have been promised this before – we and our fathers. This is nothing but old tales.'

84 Say: 'To whom (does) the earth and whatever is on it (belong), if you know?' **85** They will say, 'To God.' Say: 'Will you not take heed?' **86** Say: 'Who is Lord of the seven heavens, and Lord of the great throne?' **87** They will say, 'To God.' Say: 'Will you not guard (yourselves)?' **88** Say: 'Who is (it) in whose hand is the kingdom of everything, (who) protects and needs no protection, if you know?'

The Believers

89 They will say, 'To God.' Say: 'How are you (so) bewitched?' **90** No! We have brought them the truth. Surely they are liars indeed! **91** God has not taken a son, nor is there any (other) god with Him. Then each god would indeed have gone off with what he had created, and some of them would indeed have exalted (themselves) over others. Glory to God above what they allege! **92** (He is the) Knower of the unseen and the seen. He is exalted above what they associate.

93 Say: 'My Lord, if You show me what they are promised, **94** my Lord, do not place me among the people who are evildoers.' **95** Surely We are able indeed to show you what We promise them. **96** Repel the evil with that which is better. We know what they allege. **97** And say: 'My Lord, I take refuge with You from the incitements of the satans, **98** and I take refuge with You, my Lord, from their being present with me.'

99 – Until, when death comes to one of them, he says, 'My Lord, send me back, **100** so that I may do righteousness concerning what I left (undone).' By no means! Surely it is (only) a word which he says. Behind them is a barrier, until the Day when they will be raised up.

101 When there is a blast on the trumpet, (there will be) no (claims of) kinship among them on that Day, nor will they ask each other questions. **102** Whoever's scales are heavy, those – they are the ones who prosper, **103** but whoever's scales are light, those are the ones who have lost their (own) selves – remaining in Gehenna. **104** The Fire will scorch their faces, while they grimace in it. **105** 'Were My signs not recited to you, and did you not call them a lie?' **106** They will say, 'Our Lord, our miserableness overcame us, and we were a people in error. **107** Our Lord, bring us out of it! Then if we return (to evil), surely we shall be evildoers.' **108** He will say, 'Skulk away into it, and do not speak to Me! **109** Surely there was a group of My servants (who) said, "Our Lord, we believe, so forgive us, and have compassion on us, (for) You are the best of the compassionate." **110** But you took them (in) ridicule, until they made you forget My remembrance, and you were laughing at them. **111** Surely I have repaid them today for their patience. Surely they – they are the triumphant!' **112** He will say, 'How long did you remain in the earth, (by) number of years?' **113** They will say, 'We remained a day, or part of a day. Ask those who keep count.' **114** He will say, 'You remained only a little (while) – if only you knew! **115** Did you think that We created you in vain, and that you would not be returned to Us?'

116 Exalted is God, the true King! (There is) no god but Him, Lord of the honorable throne. **117** Whoever calls on another god with God – for which he has no proof – his reckoning is with his Lord. Surely he will not prosper, (nor will) the disbelievers. **118** Say: 'My Lord, forgive and have compassion, (for) You are the best of the compassionate.'

24 ❊ THE LIGHT

In the Name of God, the Merciful, the Compassionate

1 A sūra – We have sent it down and made it obligatory, and We have sent down in it clear signs, so that you[1] may take heed.

2 The adulterous woman and the adulterous man – flog each one of them a hundred lashes, and let no pity for the two of them affect you concerning the religion of God, if you believe in God and the Last Day. And let a group of the believers witness their punishment. **3** The adulterous man shall marry no one but an adulterous woman or an idolatrous woman, and the adulterous woman – no one shall marry her but an adulterous man or an idolatrous man. That is forbidden to the believers.

4 Those who hurl (accusations) against women of reputation, (and) then do not bring four witnesses, flog them eighty lashes, and do not accept their testimony ever (again). Those – they are the wicked, **5** except for those who turn (in repentance) after that and set (things) right. Surely God is forgiving, compassionate. **6** Those who hurl (accusations) against their wives, and have no witnesses except themselves, the testimony of such a person shall be to bear witness four times 'by God,' that he is indeed one of the truthful, **7** and the fifth time, that the curse of God (be) upon him if he is one of the liars. **8** And it shall avert the punishment from her that she bear witness four times 'by God,' that he is indeed one of the liars, **9** and the fifth time, that the anger of God (be) upon her if he is one of the truthful. **10** And if (it were) not (for the) favor of God on you, and His mercy, and that God turns (in forgiveness), wise [. . .].[2]

11 Surely those who brought the lie are a group of you. Do not think it a bad (thing) for you – No! It is good for you! Each one of them will bear what sin he has earned, and the one who took upon himself the greater part of it – for him (there will be) a great punishment. **12** Why, when you heard it, did the believing men and the believing women not think better of themselves, and say, 'This is a clear lie'? **13** Why did they not bring four witnesses concerning it? Since they did not bring the witnesses, they are liars in the sight of God. **14** If (it were) not (for the) favor of God on you, and His mercy, in this world and the Hereafter, a great punishment would have touched you for what you spread about. **15** When you

---

1. *you*: plur.
2. [. . .]: this sentence is incomplete, either inadvertently or for rhetorical effect ('anacoluthon'); cf. v. 20 below.

were receiving it with your tongues, and speaking with your mouths what you had no knowledge of, and thought it was a trivial (thing), when with God it was a mighty (thing) – **16** why, when you heard it, did you not say, 'It is not for us to speak about this. Glory to You! This is a great slander'? **17** God admonishes you from ever returning to such a thing (again), if you are believers. **18** God makes clear to you the signs. God is knowing, wise. **19** Surely those who love (allegations of) immorality to circulate among those who believe – for them (there is) a painful punishment in this world and the Hereafter. God knows, and you do not know. **20** If (it were) not (for the) favor of God on you, and His mercy, and that God is kind, compassionate [. . .].

21 You who believe! Do not follow the footsteps of Satan. Whoever follows the footsteps of Satan – surely he commands (what is) immoral and wrong. If (it were) not (for the) favor of God on you, and His mercy, not one of you would ever have been pure. God purifies whomever He pleases. God is hearing, knowing.

22 Let not those of you who possess favor and abundance swear against giving (support) to family, and the poor, and the ones who emigrate in the way of God, but let them pardon and excuse (them). Would you not like God to forgive you? God is forgiving, compassionate.

23 Surely those who hurl (accusations) against chaste women – the oblivious (but) believing women – are accursed in this world and the Hereafter. For them (there is) a great punishment. **24** On the Day when their tongues, and their hands, and their feet will bear witness against them about what they have done, **25** on that Day God will pay them their just due in full, and they will know that God – He is the clear Truth.

26 The bad women for the bad men, and the bad men for the bad women. And the good women for the good men, and the good men for the good women – those are (to be declared) innocent of what they say.[3] For them (there is) forgiveness and generous provision.

27 You who believe! Do not enter houses other than your (own) houses, until you ask permission and greet its inhabitants. That is better for you, so that you may take heed. **28** But if you do not find anyone inside, do not enter it until permission is given to you. If it is said to you, 'Go away,' go away. It is purer for you. God is aware of what you do. **29** There is no blame on you that you enter uninhabited houses, where (there is) enjoyment for you. God knows what you reveal and what you conceal.

30 Say to the believing men (that) they (should) lower their sight and guard their private parts. That is purer for them. Surely God is aware of what they do. **31** And say to the believing women (that) they (should) lower their sight and guard their private parts, and not show their charms, except for what (normally) appears of them. And let them draw their head coverings over their breasts, and not

---

3. *innocent of what they say*: i.e. innocent of whatever 'bad people' may say about them.

The Light

show their charms, except to their husbands, or their fathers, or their husbands' fathers, or their sons, or their husbands' sons, or their brothers, or their brothers' sons, or their sisters' sons, or their women, or what their right (hands) own, or such men as attend (them who) have no (sexual) desire, or children (who are) not (yet) aware of women's nakedness. And let them not stamp their feet to make known what they hide of their charms. Turn to God (in repentance) – all (of you) – believers, so that you may prosper.

32 Marry off the unmarried among you, and (also) the righteous among your male slaves and your female slaves. If they are poor, God will enrich them from His favor. God is embracing, knowing. **33** Let those who do not find (the means for) marriage abstain, until God enriches them from His favor. Those who seek the writ,[4] among what your right (hands) own, write (it) for them, if you know any good in them, and give them some of the wealth of God which He has given you. And do not force your young women into prostitution, if they wish (to live in) chastity, so that you may seek (the fleeting) goods of this present life. Whoever forces them – surely God is forgiving (and) compassionate (to them) after their being forced.

34 Certainly We have sent down to you[5] clear signs, and an example of those who passed away before you, and an admonition for those who guard (themselves).

35 God (is the) light of the heavens and the earth. A parable of His light (is) like a niche in which (there is) a lamp, the lamp in a glass, the glass as it were a brilliant star, lit from a blessed tree, an olive (tree) neither (of the) East nor (of the) West, whose oil would almost shine, even if no fire touched it – light upon light – God guides to His light whomever He pleases, and God strikes parables for the people, and God has knowledge of everything – **36** in houses (which) God permitted to be raised up, and in which His name was remembered. Glorifying Him there, in the mornings and the evenings, **37** were men (whom) neither (any business) transaction nor (any) bargaining would divert from the remembrance of God, or (from) observing the prayer and giving the alms. They feared a Day on which the hearts and the sight would be overturned, **38** so that God might repay them (for the) best of what they had done, and increase them from His favor. God provides for whomever He pleases without reckoning.

39 But those who disbelieve – their deeds are like a mirage in a desert which the thirsty man thinks (to be) water, until, when he comes to it, he finds it (to be) nothing, but he finds God beside him, and then He pays him his account in full. God is quick at the reckoning. **40** Or (he is) like the darkness in a deep sea – a wave covers him, above which is (another) wave, above which is a cloud – darkness upon darkness. When he puts out his hand, he can hardly see it. The one to whom God does not give light has no light (at all).

---

4. *the writ*: of manumission.
5. *you*: plur.

The Light

41 Do you not see that God – whatever is in the heavens and the earth glorifies Him, and (so do) the birds spreading (their wings in flight)? Each one knows its prayer and its glorifying, and God is aware of what they do. **42** To God (belongs) the kingdom of the heavens and the earth. To God is the (final) destination. **43** Do you not see that God drives the clouds, then gathers them, then makes them (into) a mass, and then you see the rain come forth from the midst of it? He sends down mountains (of them) from the sky, in which (there is) hail, and He smites whomever He pleases with it, and turns it away from whomever He pleases. The flash of His lightning almost takes away the sight. **44** God alternates the night and the day. Surely in that is a lesson indeed for those who have sight. **45** God has created every living creature from water. (There are) some of them who walk on their bellies, and some of them who walk on two feet, and some of them who walk on four. God creates whatever He pleases. Surely God is powerful over everything. **46** Certainly We have sent down clear signs. God guides whomever He pleases to a straight path.

47 They say, 'We believe in God and the messenger, and we obey.' Then, after that, a group of them turns away. Those are not with the believers. **48** When they are called to God and His messenger, so that he may judge between them, suddenly a group of them turns away. **49** But if (they think) the truth is on their side, they come to him readily. **50** (Is there) a sickness in their hearts, or do they doubt, or do they fear that God will be unjust to them, and His messenger (too)? No! Those – they are the evildoers. **51** The only saying of the believers, when they are called to God and His messenger, so that he may judge between them, is that they say, 'We hear and obey.' Those – they are the ones who prosper. **52** Whoever obeys God and His messenger, and fears God, and guards (himself) against Him, those – they are the triumphant. **53** They have sworn by God the most solemn of their oaths: if indeed you command them, they will indeed go forth. Say: 'Do not swear! Honorable obedience (is sufficient). Surely God is aware of what you do.' **54** Say: 'Obey God, and obey the messenger! If you turn away, (there is) only on him what is laid on him, and (only) on you what is laid on you. But if you obey him, you will be (rightly) guided. Nothing (depends) on the messenger except the clear delivery (of the message).'

55 God has promised those of you who believe and do righteous deeds that He will indeed make them rulers on the earth, (even) as He made those who were before them rulers, and (that) He will indeed establish their religion for them – that which He has approved for them – and (that) He will indeed give them security in exchange for their former fear: 'They will serve Me, not associating anything with Me. Whoever disbelieves after that, those – they are the wicked.' **56** Observe the prayer and give the alms, and obey the messenger, so that you may receive compassion. **57** Do not think (that) those who disbelieve are able to escape (God) on the earth. Their refuge is the Fire – and it is indeed an evil destination!

58 You who believe! Let those whom your right (hands) own, and those of you who have not reached the (age of) puberty, ask permission of you at three times

The Light

(of the day) – before the dawn prayer, and when you lay down your clothes at the noon hour, and after the evening prayer – the three (times) of nakedness for you. But beyond those (times) there is no blame on you or on them in going about among each other. In this way God makes clear to you the signs. God is knowing, wise. **59** When your children reach the (age of) puberty, let them ask permission (before entering), as those before them asked permission. In this way God makes clear to you His signs. God is knowing, wise. **60** And your women who are past childbearing and have no hope of marriage, there is no blame on them that they lay down their clothes, (as long as there is) no flaunting of (their) charms. But that they abstain is better for them. God is hearing, knowing.

61 There is no blame on the blind, and no blame on the disabled, and no blame on the sick, nor on yourselves, that you eat at your houses, or your fathers' houses, or your mothers' houses, or your brothers' houses, or your sisters' houses, or your paternal uncles' houses, or your paternal aunts' houses, or your maternal uncles' houses, or your maternal aunts' houses, or (at houses) of which you possess the keys, or (at the house) of your friend. There is no blame on you that you eat together or in separate groups. When you enter (these) houses, greet one another (with) a greeting from God, blessed (and) good. In this way God makes clear to you the signs, so that you may understand.

62 Only those are believers who believe in God and His messenger, and who, when they are with him on some common matter, do not go away until they ask his permission. Surely those who ask your permission – those are the ones who believe in God and His messenger. When they ask your permission for some affair of theirs, give permission to whomever you please of them, and ask forgiveness for them from God. Surely God is forgiving, compassionate.

63 Do not make the messenger's calling of you like the calling of some of you to others. God already knows those of you who slip away secretly. Let those who go against his command beware, or trouble will smite them, or a painful punishment will smite them.

64 Is it not a fact that to God (belongs) whatever is in the heavens and the earth? He already knows what you are up to, and on the Day when they will be returned to Him, He will inform them about what they have done. God has knowledge of everything.

25 ❈ The Deliverance

In the Name of God, the Merciful, the Compassionate

1 Blessed (be) the One who sent down the Deliverance on His servant, so that he may be a warner to all peoples **2** – the One who – to Him (belongs) the kingdom of the heavens and the earth. He has not taken a son, nor has He any associate in the kingdom. He created everything and decreed it exactly. **3** Yet they have taken gods other than Him. They do not create anything, since they are (themselves) created, and do not have power to (cause) themselves harm or benefit, and do not have power over death or life or raising up.

4 Those who disbelieve say, 'This is nothing but a lie! He has forged it, and other people have helped him with it.' So they have come to evil and falsehood. **5** And they say, 'Old tales! He has written it down, and it is dictated to him morning and evening.' **6** Say: 'He has sent it down – He who knows the secret in the heavens and the earth. Surely He is forgiving, compassionate.'

7 They say, 'What is wrong with this messenger? He eats food and walks about in the markets. If only an angel were sent down to him to be a warner with him, **8** or a treasure were cast (down) to him, or he had a garden from which to eat.' The evildoers say, 'You are only following a man (who is) bewitched.' **9** See how they strike parables for you! But they have gone astray and cannot (find) a way. **10** Blessed is He who, if He pleases, will give you (what is) better than that – Gardens through which rivers flow – and He will give you palaces.

11 No! They have called the Hour a lie – and We have prepared a blazing (Fire) for whoever calls the Hour a lie. **12** When it sees them from a place far off, they will hear its raging and moaning. **13** When they are cast into a narrow part of it, bound in chains, they will call out there (for) destruction. **14** 'Do not call out today (for) one destruction, but call out (for) many destruction(s)!' **15** Say: 'Is that better, or the Garden of Eternity which is promised to the ones who guard (themselves)? It is their payment and (final) destination.' **16** Remaining there, they will have whatever they please. It is a promise (binding) on your Lord, (something) to be asked for.

17 On the Day when He will gather them and what they serve instead of God, He will say, 'Did you lead astray these servants of Mine, or did they (themselves) go astray from the way?' **18** They will say, 'Glory to You! It was not fitting for us to take any allies other than You, but You gave them and their fathers enjoyment (of life), until they forgot the Reminder and became a ruined people.' **19** 'So they

The Deliverance

have called you a liar in what you say, and you are incapable of turning (it) aside or (finding any) help. Whoever among you does evil – We shall make him taste a great punishment.'

20 We have not sent any of the envoys before you, except that they indeed ate food and walked about in the markets. We have made some of you a test for others: 'Will you be patient?' Your Lord is seeing. **21** Those who do not expect to meet Us say, 'If only the angels were sent down on us, or we saw our Lord?' Certainly they have become arrogant within themselves, and behaved with great disdain.

22 On the Day when they see the angels, (there will be) no good news that Day for the sinners, and they will say, 'An absolute ban!' **23** We shall press forward to whatever deeds they have done, and make them scattered dust. **24** The companions of the Garden on that Day (will be in) a better dwelling place and a finer resting place. **25** On the Day when the sky is split open, (along) with the clouds, and the angels are sent down all at once, **26** the true kingdom that Day (will belong) to the Merciful, and it will be a hard Day for the disbelievers. **27** On the Day when the evildoer bites down on both his hands, he will say, 'Would that I had taken a way with the messenger! **28** Woe to me! Would that I had not taken So-and-so as a friend! **29** Certainly he led me astray from the Reminder, after it came to me. Satan is the betrayer of humankind.'

30 The messenger said, 'My Lord! Surely my people have taken this Qur'ān (as a thing to be) shunned.' **31** In this way We have assigned to every prophet an enemy from the sinners. Yet your Lord is sufficient as a guide and helper. **32** Those who disbelieve say, 'If only the Qur'ān were sent down on him all of one piece?' (It has been sent down) in this way, so that We may make firm your heart by means of it. And We have arranged it very carefully. **33** They do not bring you any parable, except (that) We have (already) brought you the truth, and (something) better in exposition. **34** Those who are going to be gathered to Gehenna on their faces – those will be worse in position and farther astray (from the) way.

35 Certainly We gave Moses the Book, and appointed his brother Aaron as an assistant with him. **36** We said, 'Both of you go to the people who have called Our signs a lie.' And We destroyed them completely. **37** And the people of Noah – when they called the messengers liars – We drowned them, and made them a sign for the people. We have prepared for the evildoers a painful punishment. **38** And 'Ād, and Thamūd, and the companions of al-Rass,[1] and many generations between that. **39** Each – We struck parables for it, and each We destroyed completely. **40** Certainly they have come upon the town which was rained on by an evil rain. Have they not seen it? No! They do not expect any raising up.

41 When they see you, they take you only in mockery: 'Is this the one whom God has raised up as a messenger? **42** He would indeed have led us astray from our gods, had we not been patient toward them.' Soon they will know, when they see

---

1. *companions of al-Rass*: reference obscure (they are mentioned only here and at Q50.12).

The Deliverance

the punishment, who is farther astray (from the) way. **43** Do you see the one who takes his own desire as his god? Will you be a guardian over him? **44** Or do you think that most of them hear or understand? They are just like cattle – No! They are (even) farther astray (from the) way!

45 Have you not regarded your Lord, how He has stretched out the shadow? If He had (so) pleased, He would indeed have made it stand still. Then We made the sun a guide for it, **46** (and) then We drew it to Us gradually. **47** He (it is) who has made the night as a covering for you, and made sleep as a rest, and He has made the day as a raising up. **48** He (it is) who has sent the winds as good news before His mercy, and We have sent down pure water from the sky, **49** so that We might give some barren land life by means of it, and give it as a drink to some of what We have created – livestock and many people. **50** Certainly We have varied it among them so that they might take heed, yet most of the people refuse (everything) but disbelief. **51** If We had (so) pleased, We would indeed have raised up a warner in every town. **52** So do not obey the disbelievers, but struggle mightily against them by means of it.

53 He (it is) who has let loose the two seas, this one sweet and fresh, and this (other) one salty (and) bitter, and placed between them a barrier, and an absolute ban. **54** He (it is) who created a human being from water, and made him related by blood and by marriage, (for) Your Lord is powerful. **55** Yet they serve what neither benefits them nor harms them, instead of God (alone). The disbeliever (always) allies himself against his Lord. **56** We have sent you only as a bringer of good news and a warner. **57** Say: 'I do not ask you for any reward for it, except for whoever pleases to take a way to his Lord.' **58** Put your trust in the Living One who does not die, and glorify (Him) with His praise. He is sufficient (as One who) is aware of the sins of His servants, **59** who created the heavens and the earth, and whatever is between them, in six days. Then He mounted the throne (as) the Merciful. Ask anyone (who is) aware about Him! **60** But when it is said to them, 'Prostrate yourselves before the Merciful,' they say, 'What is the Merciful? Shall we prostrate ourselves before what you command us?' And it (only) increases them in aversion (to Him). **61** Blessed is He who has made constellations in the sky, and has made a lamp in it, and an illuminating moon. **62** He (it is) who has made the night and the day a succession – for anyone who wishes to take heed or wishes to be thankful.

63 The servants of the Merciful are those who walk humbly on the earth, and when the ignorant address them, say: 'Peace!' **64** (They are) those who spend the night prostrating themselves and standing before their Lord, **65** and those who say, 'Our Lord, turn away from us the punishment of Gehenna. Surely its punishment is torment! **66** Surely it is an evil dwelling and resting place!' **67** And (they are) those who, when they contribute, are neither wanton nor stingy, but right between that, **68** and those who do not call on another god with God, and do not kill the person whom God has forbidden (to be killed), except by right, and do

The Deliverance

not commit adultery – whoever does that will meet (his) penalty. **69** The punishment will be doubled for him on the Day of Resurrection, and he will remain in it humiliated, **70** except for the one who turns (in repentance), and believes, and does a righteous deed – and those, God will change their evil deeds (into) good ones, (for) God is forgiving, compassionate. **71** Whoever turns (in repentance) and does righteousness, surely he turns to God in complete repentance. **72** (They are) those who do not bear false witness, and, when they pass by any frivolous talk, they pass by with dignity, **73** and those who, when they are reminded by the signs of their Lord, do not fall down over it, deaf and blind, **74** and those who say, 'Our Lord, grant us comfort (to our) eyes from our wives and descendants, and make us a model for the ones who guard (themselves).' **75** Those will be repaid with the exalted room because they were patient, and there they will meet a greeting and 'Peace!' **76** There they will dwell – it is good as a dwelling and resting place.

77 Say: 'My Lord would not care about you, if it were not for your prayer. But you have called (it) a lie, so it will be close at hand.'

26 ❖ The Poets

In the Name of God, the Merciful, the Compassionate
1 Ṭā' Sīn Mīm. 2 Those are the signs of the clear Book.

3 Perhaps you are going to destroy yourself because they do not believe. 4 If We (so) please, We shall send down on them a sign from the sky, and their necks will stay bowed before it. 5 But no new reminder comes to them from the Merciful without their turning away from it. 6 They have called (it) a lie, so the story of what they were mocking will come to them. 7 Do they not look at the earth – how many (things) of every excellent kind We have caused to grow in it? 8 Surely in that is a sign indeed, but most of them are not believers. 9 Surely your Lord – He indeed is the Mighty, the Compassionate.

10 (Remember) when your Lord called to Moses: 'Go to a people who are evildoers, 11 the people of Pharaoh. Will they not guard (themselves)?' 12 He said, 'My Lord, surely I fear that they will call me a liar, 13 and my heart will be distressed, and my tongue will not work. So send for Aaron. 14 They (also) have a crime against me, and I fear they will kill me.' 15 He said, 'By no means! Go, both of you, with Our signs. Surely We shall be with you, hearing (everything). 16 So come, both of you, to Pharaoh, and say: "Surely we are the messenger of the Lord of all peoples. 17 Send forth the Sons of Israel with us."'

18 He said, 'Did we not bring you up among us as a child, and did you not remain among us for some years of your life? 19 Yet you did the deed you did, and were one of the ungrateful.' 20 He said, 'I did it when I was one of those who had gone astray, 21 and I fled from you when I became afraid of you. But my Lord granted me judgment, and made me one of the envoys. 22 And is that a blessing you bestow on me, that you have enslaved the Sons of Israel?'

23 Pharaoh said, 'What is the Lord of all peoples?' 24 He said, 'The Lord of the heavens and the earth, and whatever is between them, if you (would) be certain.' He[1] said to those who were around him, 25 'Do you not hear?' 26 He[2] said, 'Your Lord and the Lord of your fathers of old.' 27 He said, 'Surely your messenger who has been sent to you is possessed indeed.' 28 He said, 'The Lord of the East and the West, and whatever is between them, if you (would) understand.' 29 He said, 'If indeed you take a god other than me, I shall indeed make you one of

---

1. *He*: Pharaoh.
2. *He*: Moses.

the imprisoned.' **30** He said, 'Even if I brought you something clear?' **31** He said, 'Bring it, if you are one of the truthful.' **32** So he cast (down) his staff, and suddenly it became a real snake, **33** and he drew forth his hand, and suddenly it became white to the onlookers. **34** He said to the assembly around him, 'Surely this is a skilled magician indeed. **35** He wants to expel you from your land by his magic. So what do you command?' **36** They said, 'Put him and his brother off (for a while), and raise up searchers in the cities **37** to bring you every skilled magician.' **38** So the magicians were gathered together for the meeting on a day made known. **39** And it was said to the people, 'Will you (too) gather together?' **40** 'Perhaps we will follow the magicians, if they are the victors.'

41 When the magicians came, they said to Pharaoh, '(Will there) surely (be) for us a reward indeed, if we are the victors?' **42** He said, 'Yes, and surely then you will indeed be among the ones brought near.' **43** Moses said to them, 'Cast (down) what you are going to cast.' **44** So they cast their ropes and their staffs, and said, 'By the honor of Pharaoh! Surely we shall be the victors indeed.' **45** And then Moses cast his staff, and suddenly it swallowed up what they were falsely contriving. **46** And the magicians were cast (down) in prostration. **47** They said, 'We believe in the Lord of all peoples, **48** the Lord of Moses and Aaron.' **49** He said, 'You have believed in him before I gave you permission. Surely he is indeed your master, the (very) one who taught you magic. But soon indeed you will know! I shall indeed cut off your hands and your feet on opposite sides, and I shall indeed crucify you – all (of you)!' **50** They said, 'No harm! Surely we are going to return to our Lord. **51** Surely we are eager that our Lord should forgive us our sins, because we are the first of the believers.'

52 And We inspired Moses: 'Journey with My servants. Surely you will be followed.' **53** So Pharaoh sent searchers into the cities: **54** 'Surely these (people) are indeed a small band, **55** and surely they are indeed enraging us, **56** but surely we are indeed all vigilant.' **57** So We brought them forth from gardens and springs, **58** and treasures and an honorable place. **59** So (it was), and We caused the Sons of Israel to inherit them. **60** So they followed them at sunrise, **61** and when the two forces saw each other, the companions of Moses said, 'Surely we are indeed overtaken!' **62** He said, 'By no means! Surely my Lord is with me. He will guide me.' **63** And so We inspired Moses: 'Strike the sea with your staff!' And it parted, and each part was like a great mountain. **64** We brought the others near to that place, **65** and We rescued Moses and those who were with him – all (of them). **66** Then We drowned the others. **67** Surely in that is a sign indeed, but most of them do not believe. **68** Surely your Lord – He indeed is the Mighty, the Compassionate.

69 Recite to them the story of Abraham: **70** When he said to his father and his people, 'What do you serve?' **71** They said, 'We serve idols, and continue (to be) devoted to them.' **72** He said, 'Do they hear you when you call, **73** or do they benefit you or harm (you)?' **74** They said, 'No! But we found our fathers doing so.' **75** He said, 'Do you see what you have been serving, **76** you and your fathers who

The Poets

preceded (you)? **77** Surely they are an enemy to me – except the Lord of all peoples, **78** who created me, and He guides me, **79** and who – He gives me food and gives me drink, **80** and when I am sick, He heals me. **81** He (it is) who causes me to die, (and) then gives me life, **82** and who – I am eager that He should forgive me my sin on the Day of Judgment. **83** My Lord, grant me judgment, and join me with the righteous, **84** and assign to me a good reputation among later (generations). **85** Make me one of the inheritors of the Garden of Bliss. **86** And forgive my father, (for) surely he is one of those who have gone astray. **87** Do not disgrace me on the Day when they are raised up, **88** the Day when neither wealth nor children will benefit (them), **89** except for the one who comes to God with a sound heart. **90** The Garden will be brought near for the ones who guard themselves, **91** and the Furnace will come forth for the ones who are in error. **92** And it will be said to them, "Where is what you were serving **93** instead of God? (Can) they defend you or defend themselves?" **94** And then they will be tossed into it – they and the ones who are in error – **95** and the forces of Iblīs – all (of them). **96** They will say, as they are disputing there, **97** "By God! We were indeed far astray, **98** when we made you³ equal with the Lord of all peoples. **99** (It was) only the sinners who led us astray. **100** (Now) we have no intercessors, **101** and no true friend. **102** If only we had (another) turn, and (could) be among the believers!'" **103** Surely in that is a sign indeed, but most of them do not believe. **104** Surely your Lord – He indeed is the Mighty, the Compassionate.

105 The people of Noah called the envoys liars: **106** When their brother Noah said to them, 'Will you not guard (yourselves)? **107** Surely I am a trustworthy messenger for you, **108** so guard (yourselves) against God and obey me. **109** I do not ask you for any reward for it. My reward (depends) only on the Lord of all peoples. **110** Guard (yourselves) against God and obey me.' **111** They said, 'Shall we believe you, when (only) the worst (people) follow you?' **112** He said, 'What do I know about what they have done? **113** Their reckoning is only with my Lord, if (only) you realized (it). **114** I am not going to drive away the believers. **115** I am only a clear warner.' **116** They said, 'If indeed you do not stop, Noah, you will indeed be one of the stoned.' **117** He said, 'My Lord, surely my people have called me a liar, **118** so disclose (the truth) decisively between me and them, and rescue me and those of the believers who are with me.' **119** So We rescued him, and those who were with him, in the loaded ship. **120** Then, after that, We drowned the rest. **121** Surely in that is a sign indeed, but most of them do not believe. **122** Surely your Lord – He indeed is the Mighty, the Compassionate.

123 'Ād called the envoys liars: **124** When their brother Hūd said to them, 'Will you not guard (yourselves)? **125** Surely I am a trustworthy messenger for you, **126** so guard (yourselves) against God and obey me. **127** I do not ask you for any reward for it. My reward (depends) only on the Lord of all peoples. **128** Do you build a sign on every high place in vain, **129** and take strongholds in the hope

---

3. *you*: their gods.

The Poets

that you may remain there? **130** And when you attack (someone), do you attack like tyrants? **131** Guard (yourselves) against God and obey me. **132** Guard (yourselves) against the One who has increased you with what you know. **133** He has increased you with livestock and sons, **134** and gardens and fountains. **135** Surely I fear for you the punishment of a great day.' **136** They said, '(It is) the same for us whether you admonish (us) or are not one of the admonishers. **137** This is nothing but the creation of those of old. **138** We are not going to be punished.' **139** So they called him a liar, and We destroyed them. Surely in that is a sign indeed, but most of them do not believe. **140** Surely your Lord – He indeed is the Mighty, the Compassionate.

141 Thamūd called the envoys liars: **142** When their brother Ṣāliḥ said to them, 'Will you not guard (yourselves)? **143** Surely I am a trustworthy messenger for you, **144** so guard (yourselves) against God and obey me. **145** I do not ask you for any reward for it. My reward (depends) only on the Lord of all peoples. **146** Will you be left secure in what is here, **147** in gardens and springs, **148** and (fields of) crops and date palms (with) its slender sheath? **149** Will you (continue to) carve houses out of the mountains with skill? **150** Guard (yourselves) against God and obey me. **151** Do not obey the command of the wanton, **152** those who foment corruption on the earth and do not set (things) right.' **153** They said, 'You are only one of the bewitched. **154** You are nothing but a human being like us. Bring (us) a sign, if you are one of the truthful.' **155** He said, 'This is a she-camel: to her a drink and to you a drink, on a day made known. **156** Do not touch her with evil, or the punishment of a great day will seize you.' **157** But they wounded her, and morning found them full of regret, **158** and the punishment seized them. Surely in that is a sign indeed, but most of them do not believe. **159** Surely your Lord – He indeed is the Mighty, the Compassionate.

160 The people of Lot called the envoys liars: **161** When their brother Lot said to them, 'Will you not guard (yourselves)? **162** Surely I am a trustworthy messenger for you, **163** so guard (yourselves) against God and obey me. **164** I do not ask you for any reward for it. My reward (depends) only on the Lord of all peoples. **165** Do you approach the males of all peoples, **166** and leave your wives whom your Lord created for you? Yes! You are a people who transgress!' **167** They said, 'If indeed you do not stop, Lot, you will indeed be one of the expelled.' **168** He said, 'Surely I am one of those who despise what you do. **169** My Lord, rescue me and my family from what they do.' **170** So We rescued him and his family – all of them – **171** except for an old woman among those who stayed behind. **172** Then We destroyed the others. **173** We rained down on them a rain, and evil was the rain on those who had been warned! **174** Surely in that is a sign indeed, but most of them do not believe. **175** Surely your Lord – He indeed is the Mighty, the Compassionate.

176 The people of the Grove called the envoys liars: **177** When Shu'ayb said to them, 'Will you not guard (yourselves)? **178** I am a trustworthy messenger for you, **179** so guard (yourselves) against God and obey me. **180** I do not ask you for any

The Poets

reward for it. My reward (depends) only on the Lord of all peoples. **181** Fill up the measure, and do not be cheaters, **182** and weigh with the even scale, **183** and do not shortchange the people of their wealth, and do not act wickedly on the earth, fomenting corruption. **184** Guard (yourselves) against the One who created you and the multitudes of old.' **185** They said, 'You are only one of the bewitched. **186** You are nothing but a human being like us. Surely we think (that) you are indeed one of the liars. **187** Make fragments of the sky fall on us, if you are one of the truthful.' **188** He said, 'My Lord knows what you are doing.' **189** But they called him a liar, and the punishment of the Day of Shadow seized them. Surely it was the punishment of a great day. **190** Surely in that is a sign indeed, but most of them do not believe. **191** Surely your Lord – He indeed is the Mighty, the Compassionate.

192 Surely it is indeed a sending down from the Lord of all peoples. **193** The trustworthy spirit has brought it down **194** on your heart, so that you may be one of the warners, **195** in a clear Arabic language. **196** Surely it is indeed in the scriptures of those of old. **197** Was it not a sign for them that it was known to the learned of the Sons of Israel? **198** If We had sent it down on one of the foreigners, **199** and he had recited it to them, they would not have believed in it. **200** In this way We put it into the hearts of the sinners. **201** They will not believe in it until they see the painful punishment, **202** and it will come upon them unexpectedly, when they do not realize (it), **203** and they will say, 'Are we going to be spared?' **204** Do they seek to hurry Our punishment? **205** Have you considered? If We give them enjoyment (of life) for (some) years, **206** (and) then what they were promised comes upon them, **207** what use will the enjoyment they were given be to them? **208** We have not destroyed any town without its having warners **209** as a reminder. We have not been evildoers.

210 The satans have not brought it down. **211** It is not fitting for them (to do), nor are they able (to). **212** Surely they are removed indeed from the hearing (of it). **213** Do not call on another god (along) with God, or you will be one of the punished. **214** Warn your clan, **215** and lower your wing to whoever follows you of the believers. **216** If they disobey you, say: 'I am free of what you do.' **217** Put your trust in the Mighty, the Compassionate, **218** who sees you when you stand, **219** and when you turn about among the ones who prostrate themselves. **220** Surely He – He is the Hearing, the Knowing.

221 Shall I inform you[4] on whom the satans come down? **222** They come down on every liar (and) sinner. **223** They listen attentively, but most of them are liars. **224** And the poets – the ones who are in error follow them. **225** Do you[5] not see that they wander in every wādī, **226** and that they say what they do not do? **227** – except for those who believe, and do righteous deeds, and remember God often, and defend themselves after they have suffered evil. Those who have done evil will come to know what a complete overturning they will suffer.

---

4. *you*: plur.
5. *you*: sing.

27 ✹ THE ANT

In the Name of God, the Merciful, the Compassionate

1 Ṭā' Sīn. Those are the signs of the Qur'ān and a clear Book, **2** a guidance and good news for the believers, **3** who observe the prayer and give the alms, and they are certain of the Hereafter. **4** Those who do not believe in the Hereafter – We have made their deeds appear enticing to them, and they wander blindly. **5** Those are the ones for whom (there is) an evil punishment, and in the Hereafter they will be the worst losers. **6** Surely you have indeed received the Qur'ān from One (who is) wise, knowing.

7 (Remember) when Moses said to his family: 'Surely I perceive a fire. I shall bring you some news of it, or I shall bring you a flame – a torch – so that you may warm yourselves.' **8** But when he came to it, he was called: 'Blessed is He who is in the fire, and whoever is around it. Glory to God, Lord of all peoples! **9** Moses! Surely I am God, the Mighty, the Wise.' **10** And: 'Cast (down) your staff!' When he saw it wiggling as if it were a snake, he turned around, retreating, and did not look back. 'Moses! Do not fear! Surely in My presence the envoys do not fear **11** – except for the one who has done evil, (and) then has exchanged good after evil – surely I am forgiving, compassionate. **12** Put your hand inside your cloak. It will come out white, unharmed – (these are two) among nine signs for Pharaoh and his people. Surely they are a wicked people.' **13** But when Our signs came to them visibly, they said, 'This is clear magic.' **14** They denied them, even though they were convinced of them in themselves, out of evil and haughtiness. See how the end was for the fomenters of corruption!

15 Certainly We gave David and Solomon knowledge, and they said, 'Praise (be) to God, who has favored us over many of His believing servants!' **16** Solomon inherited (it) from David, and said, 'People! We have been taught the speech of birds, and we have been given (some) of everything. Surely this – it indeed is clear favor.' **17** Gathered before Solomon were his forces – jinn, and men, and birds – and they were arranged (in rows) **18** – until, when they came upon the Wādī of the Ants, an ant said, 'Ants! Enter your dwellings, or Solomon and his forces will crush you without realizing (it).' **19** But he[1] smiled, laughing at its words, and said, 'My Lord, (so) dispose me that I may be thankful for your blessing with which You have blessed me and my parents, and that I may do

---

1. *he*: Solomon.

The Ant

righteousness (that) pleases You, and cause me to enter, by Your mercy, among your righteous servants.'

20 He reviewed the birds, and said, 'Why do I not see the hudhud? Or is it one of the absent? **21** I shall indeed punish it severely, or slaughter it, or it will bring me a clear authority.' **22** But it did not stay (away) for long, and said, 'I have encompassed what you have not encompassed, and I have brought you reliable news from (the people of) Sheba. **23** Surely I found a woman ruling over them, and she has been given (some) of everything, and she has a great throne. **24** I found her and her people prostrating themselves before the sun instead of God. Satan has made their deeds appear enticing to them, and he has kept them from the way, and they are not (rightly) guided. **25** (He did this) so that they would not prostrate themselves before God, who brings forth what is hidden in the heavens and the earth. He knows what you hide and what you speak aloud. **26** God – (there is) no god but Him, Lord of the great throne.' **27** He said, 'We shall see whether you have spoken the truth or are one of the liars. **28** Go with this letter of mine, and cast it (down) to them. Then turn away from them and see what they return.'

29 She[2] said, 'Assembly! Surely an honorable letter has been cast (down) to me. **30** Surely it is from Solomon, and surely it (reads): "In the Name of God, the Merciful, the Compassionate. **31** Do not exalt yourselves over me, but come to me in surrender."' **32** She said, 'Assembly! Make a pronouncement to me about my affair. I do not decide any affair until you bear me witness.' **33** They said, 'We are full of strength and full of harsh violence, but the affair (belongs) to you. See what you will command.' **34** She said, 'Surely kings, when they enter a town, corrupt it, and make the upper class of its people the lowest, and that is what they will do. **35** Surely I am going to send a gift to them, and see what the envoys bring back.'

36 When he[3] came to Solomon, he[4] said, 'Would you increase me with wealth, when what God has given me is better than what He has given you? No! (It is) you (who) gloat over your own gift. **37** Return to them! We shall indeed come upon them with forces which they have no power to face, and we shall indeed expel them from there in humiliation, and they will be disgraced.' **38** He said, 'Assembly! Which of you will bring me her throne before they come to me in surrender?' **39** A crafty one of the jinn said, 'I will bring it to you before you (can) rise from your place. Surely I have strength for it (and am) trustworthy.' **40** One who had knowledge of the Book said, 'I will bring it to you in the wink of an eye.' So when he[5] saw it set before him, he said, 'This is from the favor of my Lord to test me (to see) whether I am thankful or ungrateful. Whoever is thankful is thankful only for his own good, and whoever is ungrateful – surely my Lord is wealthy, generous.' **41** He said, 'Disguise her throne for her. We shall see whether she is (rightly)

---

2. *She*: the Queen of Sheba.
3. *he*: the Queen's envoy.
4. *he*: Solomon.
5. *he*: Solomon.

guided or is one of those who are not (rightly) guided.' **42** So when she came, it was said, 'Is your throne like this?' She said, 'It seems like it.' 'And we[6] had been given the knowledge before her, and were in surrender, **43** but what she served, instead of God, kept her back. Surely she was from a disbelieving people.' **44** It was said to her, 'Enter the palace.' When she saw it, she thought it was a pool (of water), and she uncovered her legs. He said, 'Surely it is a polished palace of crystal.' She said, 'My Lord, surely I have done myself evil. I surrender with Solomon to God, Lord of all peoples.'

45 Certainly We sent to Thamūd their brother Ṣāliḥ: 'Serve God!' And suddenly they were two groups disputing each other. **46** He said, 'My people! Why do you seek to hurry the evil before the good? Why do you not ask forgiveness from God, so that you may receive compassion?' **47** They said, 'We have an evil omen about you and those who are with you.' He said, 'Your evil omen is with God. But you are a people being tested!' **48** In the city (there) was a group of nine persons who were fomenting corruption on the earth, and not setting (things) right. **49** They said, 'Swear to each other by God, "We shall indeed attack him and his family by night." Then we shall indeed say to his ally, "We were not witnesses of the destruction of his family" and "Surely we are truthful indeed."' **50** They schemed a scheme, but We (too) schemed a scheme, though they did not realize (it). **51** See how the end of their scheme was: We destroyed them and their people – all (of them)! **52** Those are their houses, collapsed because of the evil they did. Surely in that is a sign indeed for a people who know. **53** And We rescued those who believed and guarded (themselves).

54 And Lot, when he said to his people: 'Do you commit immorality with your eyes open? **55** Do you indeed approach men with lust instead of women? But you are an ignorant people!' **56** The only response of his people was that they said, 'Expel the house(hold) of Lot from your town, (for) surely they are men who keep themselves clean.' **57** So We rescued him and his family, except for his wife. We decreed that she (would be) one of those who stayed behind. **58** And We rained down on them a rain. Evil was the rain on those who had been warned!

59 Say: 'Praise (be) to God, and peace (be) upon His servants whom He has chosen!' Is God better, or what they associate? **60** Or (is He not better) who created the heavens and the earth, and sent down water from the sky for you, and then by means of it We cause orchards to grow, full of beauty, whose trees you could never grow? (Is there any other) god with God? No! But they are a people who equate (others to Him). **61** Or (is He not better) who made the earth a dwelling place, and placed rivers in the midst of it, and made firm mountains for it, and placed a partition between the two seas? (Is there any other) god with God? No! But most of them do not know (it). **62** Or (is He not better) who responds to the distressed (person) when he calls on Him and removes the evil, and establishes

---

6. *And we . . .* : spoken by members of the Queen's entourage, who claim to have been 'in surrender' (i.e. 'Muslims') all along.

you as rulers on the earth? (Is there any other) god with God? Little do you take heed! **63** Or (is He not better) who guides you in the darkness of the shore and the sea, and who sends the winds as good news before His mercy? (Is there any other) god with God? God is exalted above what they associate! **64** Or (is He not better) who brings about the creation, (and) then restores it, and who provides for you from the sky and the earth? (Is there any other) god with God? Say: 'Bring your proof, if you are truthful.'

65 Say: 'No one in the heavens or the earth knows the unseen except God. They do not realize when they will be raised up. **66** No! Their knowledge is confused concerning the Hereafter. No! They are in doubt about it. No! They are blind to it.'

67 Those who disbelieve say, 'When we have become dust, and our fathers (too), shall we indeed be brought forth? **68** Certainly we have been promised this before, we and our fathers. This is nothing but old tales.' **69** Say: 'Travel the earth and see how the end was for the sinners.' **70** Do not sorrow over them, nor be in distress because of what they are scheming.

71 They say, 'When (will) this promise (come to pass), if you[7] are truthful?' **72** Say: 'It may be that part of what you seek to hurry is bearing down on you (now).' **73** Surely your Lord is indeed full of favor to the people, but most of them are not thankful (for it). **74** Surely your Lord indeed knows what their hearts conceal and what they speak aloud. **75** (There is) nothing hidden in the sky or the earth, except (that it is recorded) in a clear Book.

76 Surely this Qur'ān recounts to the Sons of Israel most of their differences, **77** and surely it is indeed a guidance and mercy to the believers. **78** Surely your Lord will decide between them by His judgment. He is the Mighty, the Knowing. **79** Put your trust in God, (for) surely you (stand) on the clear truth. **80** Surely you cannot make the dead to hear, nor can you make the deaf to hear the call, when they turn away, withdrawing. **81** Nor can you guide the blind out of their straying. You cannot make (anyone) hear, except the one who believes in Our signs, and so they submit.

82 When the word falls upon them, We shall bring forth for them a creature from the earth, (which) will speak to them: 'The people were not certain of Our signs.' **83** On the Day when We shall gather from every community a crowd of those who have called Our signs a lie, and they are arranged (in rows) **84** – until, when they come, He will say, 'Did you call My signs a lie, when you did not encompass them in knowledge, or what (it was) you were doing?' **85** And the word will fall upon them because of the evil they have done, and they will not speak.

86 Do they not see that We made the night for them to rest in, and the day to see? Surely in that are signs indeed for a people who believe. **87** On the Day when there is a blast on the trumpet, and whoever is in the heavens and whoever is on the earth will be terrified, except for whomever God pleases, and all will come to

---

7. *you*: plur.

The Ant

Him humbled, **88** and you[8] see the mountains, supposedly solid, yet passing by (as) the clouds pass by – (such is) the work of God who has perfected everything. Surely He is aware of what you do. **89** (On that Day) whoever brings a good (deed) will have a better one than it, and they will be secure from the terror of that Day. **90** But whoever brings an evil (deed), they will be cast down face first into the Fire: 'Are you repaid (for anything) except for what you have done?'

91 'I have only been commanded to serve the Lord of this land, who has made it sacred. To Him everything (belongs). And I have been commanded to be one of those who submit, **92** and to recite the Qur'ān. Whoever is (rightly) guided is guided only for himself, and whoever goes astray [. . .].'[9] Say: 'I am only one of the warners.' **93** And say: 'Praise (be) to God! He will show you His signs and you will recognize them. Your Lord is not oblivious of what you do.'

---

8. *you*: sing.

9. *[. . .]*: this sentence is incomplete, either inadvertently or for rhetorical effect ('anacoluthon').

28 ❈ The Story

In the Name of God, the Merciful, the Compassionate

1 Ṭā' Sīn Mīm. **2** Those are the signs of the clear Book.

3 We recite to you some of the story of Moses and Pharaoh in truth, for a people who believe: **4** Surely Pharaoh had exalted himself on the earth, and divided its people (into) parties, weakening one contingent of them (by) slaughtering their sons and sparing their women. Surely he was one of the fomenters of corruption. **5** But We wanted to bestow favor on those who were weak on the earth, and make them leaders, and make them the inheritors, **6** and to establish them on the earth, and show Pharaoh and Haman, and their forces, what they had to beware of from them.

7 We inspired Moses' mother: 'Nurse him, and when you fear for him, cast him into the sea, but do not fear and do not sorrow. Surely We are going to return him to you, and make him one of the envoys.' **8** And the house of Pharaoh picked him up, so that he might be an enemy to them and a (cause of) sorrow. Surely Pharaoh and Haman, and their forces, were sinners. **9** The wife of Pharaoh said, '(He is) a comfort to me and to you. Do not kill him! It may be that he will benefit us, or we may adopt him as a son.' But they did not realize (what they were doing). **10** The next day the heart of Moses' mother was empty. She would almost have betrayed him, if We had not strengthened her heart, so that she might be one of the believers. **11** She said to his sister, 'Follow him.' So she watched him on the sly, though they did not realize (it). **12** Before (this) We had forbidden any wet nurses for him, so she said, 'Shall I direct you to the people of a household who will take charge of him for you, and look after him?' **13** And We returned him to his mother, so that she might be comforted and not sorrow, and that she might know that the promise of God is true. But most of them do not know (it). **14** When he reached his maturity and established (himself), We gave him judgment and knowledge. In this way We reward the doers of good.

15 He entered the city at a time when its people were oblivious, and in it he found two men fighting: the one of his (own) party, and the other of his enemies. The one who was of his (own) party called him for help against the one who was of his enemies. So Moses struck him, and finished him off. He said, 'This is the work of Satan. Surely he is a clear enemy (who) leads (people) astray.' **16** He said, 'My Lord, surely I have done myself evil. Forgive me!' So God forgave him. Surely He – He is the Forgiving, the Compassionate. **17** He said, 'My Lord, because of the blessing with which You have blessed me, I shall not be a supporter of the sinners.'

The Story

18 The next day he was in the city, afraid (and) watchful, when suddenly the one who had sought his help the day before cried out to him for help (again). Moses said to him, 'Surely you are in error indeed!' **19** But when he was about to attack the one who was an enemy to them both, he said, 'Moses! Do you intend to kill me as you killed (that) person yesterday? You only want to be a tyrant on the earth, and you do not want to be one of those who set (things) right.' **20** And (just then) a man came running from the farthest part of the city. He said, 'Moses! Surely the assembly is taking counsel about you, to kill you. So get out! Surely I am one of your trusty advisers.' **21** So he went forth from it, afraid (and) watchful. He said, 'My Lord, rescue me from the people who are evildoers.'

22 When he turned his face toward Midian, he said, 'It may be that my Lord will guide me to the right way.' **23** And when he came to the water of Midian, he found by it a community of the people watering (their flocks), and besides them he found two women driving off their flocks. He said, 'What is the matter with you two?' They said, 'We may not water (our flocks) until the shepherds drive off (their flocks), and our father is very old.' **24** So he watered (their flocks) for them. Then he turned aside to the shade, and said, 'My Lord, surely I am in need of whatever good You may send down to me.' **25** Then one of the two women came to him, walking shyly. She said, 'My father calls you, so that he may pay you a reward for your watering (our flocks) for us.' When he had come to him and recounted the story to him, he said, 'Do not fear! You have escaped from the people who are evildoers.' **26** One of the two women said, 'My father! Hire him, (for) surely the best man whom you can hire is the strong (and) the trustworthy one.' **27** He said, 'Surely I wish to marry you to one of these two daughters of mine, on (the condition) that you hire yourself to me for eight years. But if you complete ten, that will be of your own accord, (for) I am not about to make it a hardship for you. You will find me, if God pleases, one of the righteous.' **28** He said, 'That is between me and you. No matter which of the two terms I fulfill, (let there be) no enmity against me. God is guardian over what we say.'

29 When Moses had fulfilled the term and traveled with his family, he perceived a fire on the side of the mountain. He said to his family, 'Stay (here). Surely I perceive a fire. Perhaps I shall bring you some news of it, or some wood from the fire, so that you may warm yourselves.' **30** But when he came to it, he was called out to from the right side of the wādī, in the blessed hollow, from the tree: 'Moses! Surely I am God, Lord of all peoples.' **31** And: 'Cast (down) your staff!' And when he saw it wiggling as if it were a snake, he turned around, retreating, and did not look back. 'Moses! Come forward and do not fear! Surely you are one of the secure. **32** Put your hand into your cloak. It will come out white, unharmed. Now draw your hand to your side from fear. Those are two proofs from your Lord for Pharaoh and his assembly. Surely they are a wicked people.' **33** He said, 'My Lord, surely I have killed one of them, and I fear that they will kill me. **34** My brother Aaron – he is more eloquent than me in speech. Send him with me as a support (who) will confirm me. Surely I fear that they will call me a liar.' **35** He said, 'We shall strengthen your arm by means of your brother, and give authority to both of you, so that they will be no match for you because of Our signs. You two, and whoever follows you, will be the victors.'

36 When Moses brought them Our clear signs, they said, 'This is nothing but a magic trick. We have not heard of this among our fathers of old.' **37** But Moses said, 'My Lord knows who brings the guidance from Him, and to whom the final Home (belongs). Surely the evildoers will not prosper.' **38** Pharaoh said, 'Assembly! I know of no other god for you than me. So light a fire for me, Haman, on the clay, and make a tower for me, so that I may look at the god of Moses. Surely I think he is indeed one of the liars.' **39** He and his forces became arrogant on the earth without any right, and thought that they would not be returned to Us. **40** So We seized him and his forces, and tossed them into the sea. See how the end was for the evildoers! **41** We made them leaders (who) call (others) to the Fire, and on the Day of Resurrection they will not be helped. **42** We pursued them in this world with a curse, and on the Day of Resurrection they will be among the scorned.

43 Certainly We gave Moses the Book, after We had destroyed the former generations, as evidence for the people, and a guidance and mercy, so that they might take heed. **44** You were not on the western side when We decreed the command to Moses, nor were you among the witnesses. **45** But We produced (other) generations, and life was prolonged for them. You were not dwelling among the people of Midian, reciting to them Our signs, when We were sending (messengers). **46** You were not on the side of the mountain when We called out (to Moses), but (you were sent) as a mercy from your Lord, so that you might warn a people to whom no warner had come before you, so that they might take heed. **47** If (it were) not that a smiting might smite them for what their hands have sent forward, and (that) they might say, 'Our Lord, why did You not send a messenger to us, so that we might have followed Your signs, and (so) been among the believers [...]?'[1] **48** Yet when the truth did come to them from Us, they said, 'If only he were given the same as what Moses was given.' Did they not disbelieve in what was given to Moses before? They said, 'Two magic (tricks) supporting each other,' and they said, 'Surely we are disbelievers in all (of it).' **49** Say: 'Bring a Book from God that is a better guide than these two[2] – I shall follow it, if you are truthful.' **50** If they do not respond to you, know that they are only following their (vain) desires. And who is farther astray than the one who follows his desire without guidance from God? Surely God does not guide the people who are evildoers. **51** Certainly We have caused the word to reach them, so that they may take heed.

52 Those to whom We gave the Book before it – they believe in it. **53** When it is recited to them, they say, 'We believe in it. Surely it is the truth from our Lord. Surely we were Muslims before it.' **54** Those – they will be given their reward twice over for what they have endured. They avert evil by means of the good, and

---

1. [...]: there appears to be a lacuna here.
2. *these two*: i.e. the Torah and Qur'ān.

The Story

contribute from what We have provided them. **55** When they hear any frivolous talk, they turn away from it, and say, 'To us our deeds and to you your deeds. Peace (be) upon you! We do not seek out the ignorant.'

56 Surely you will not guide whomever you like, but God guides whomever He pleases, and knows the ones who are (rightly) guided. **57** They say, 'If we follow the guidance with you, we shall be snatched from our land.' Have We not established a secure sanctuary for them, where fruits of every kind are brought as a provision from Us? But most of them do not know (it). **58** How many a town have We destroyed (which) boasted of its means of livelihood! Those are their dwelling places (which remain) uninhabited after them, except for a few. We became the inheritors! **59** Yet your Lord was not one to destroy the towns until He had raised up a messenger in their mother (city), reciting Our signs to them. We would not have destroyed the towns unless their people had been evildoers.

60 Whatever thing you have been given is (only) an enjoyment of this present life, and its (passing) splendor, but what is with God is better and more lasting. Will you not understand? **61** Is the one whom We have promised a good promise, and (who) receives it, like the one whom We have given the enjoyment of this present life, (and) then on the Day of Resurrection will be one of those brought forward (to the punishment)?

62 On the Day when He will call them, and say, 'Where are My associates whom you used to claim (as gods)?,' **63** those against whom the word has proved true will say, 'Our Lord, these are those whom we made err. We made them err as we had erred. We disown (them) before You. They were not serving us.' **64** And it will be said, 'Call your associates!' And they will call them, but they will not respond to them, and they will see the punishment. If only they had been guided!

65 On the Day when He will call them, and say, 'What response did you give the envoys?' **66** The news will be dark for them on that Day, nor will they ask each other questions. **67** But as for the one who turns (in repentance), and believes, and does righteousness, it may be that he will be one of those who prosper.

68 Your Lord creates whatever He pleases, and chooses (whomever He pleases) – the choice is not theirs. Glory to God! He is exalted above what they associate. **69** Your Lord knows what their hearts conceal and what they speak aloud. **70** He is God – (there is) no god but Him. To Him (be) praise, at the first and at the last! To Him (belongs) the judgment, and to Him you will be returned.

71 Say: 'Have you considered? If God makes the night continuous for you until the Day of Resurrection, what god other than God will bring you light? Will you not hear?' **72** Say: 'Have you considered? If God makes the day continuous for you until the Day of Resurrection, what god other than God will bring you night to rest in? Will you not see? **73** But out of His mercy He has made the night and the day for you, so that you may rest in it, and that you may seek some of His favor, and that you may be thankful.'

The Story

74 On the Day when He will call them, and say, 'Where are My associates whom you used to claim (as gods)?' **75** We shall draw out a witness from every community, and say, 'Bring your proof!' And then they will know that the truth (belongs) to God, and what they have forged will abandon them.

76 Surely Qārūn was one of the people of Moses, and acted oppressively toward them. We had given him treasures, the keys of which would indeed have been a burden for a group (of men) endowed with strength. (Remember) when his people said to him, 'Do not gloat! Surely God does not love those who gloat. **77** But seek the Home of the Hereafter by means of what God has given you, and do not forget your portion of this world. Do good, as God has done good to you, and do not seek to foment corruption on the earth. Surely God does not love the fomenters of corruption.' **78** He said, 'I have been given it only because of the knowledge (that is) in me.' Did he not know that God had destroyed those of the generations before him who were stronger than him and had accumulated more? The sinners will not be questioned about their sins. **79** So he went forth to his people in his splendor. Those who desired this present life said, 'Would that we had the same as what has been given to Qārūn! Surely he is indeed the possessor of great good luck.' **80** But those to whom knowledge had been given said, 'Woe to you! The reward of God is better for the one who believes and does righteousness. But no one will obtain it except the patient.' **81** So We caused the earth to swallow him and his home, and he had no cohort to help him, other than God, and he was not one of those who could help themselves. **82** In the morning those who had longed (to be in) his place the day before were saying, 'Woe (to Qārūn)! Surely God extends (His) provision to whomever He pleases of His servants, and restricts (it). If God had not bestowed favor on us, He would indeed have caused (the earth) to swallow us (too). Woe to him! The disbelievers will not prosper.'

83 That is the Home of the Hereafter: We assign it to those who do not desire haughtiness on the earth, nor corruption. The outcome (belongs) to the ones who guard (themselves). **84** Whoever brings a good (deed) will have a better one than it, and whoever brings an evil (deed) – those who have done evil deeds will only be repaid for what they have done.

85 Surely He who made the Qur'ān obligatory for you will indeed return you to (your) home. Say: 'My Lord knows who brings the guidance, and who is clearly astray.' **86** You did not expect that the Book would be cast (down) to you, except as a mercy from your Lord. So do not be a supporter of the disbelievers. **87** Let them not keep you from the signs of God, after they have been sent down to you, but call (people) to your Lord, and do not be one of the idolaters. **88** Do not call on another god (along) with God. (There is) no god but Him. Everything perishes except His face. To Him (belongs) the judgment, and to Him you will be returned.

29 ❊ THE SPIDER

In the Name of God, the Merciful, the Compassionate

1 Alif Lām Mīm.

2 Do the people think that they will be left (in such a position) that they (can) say, 'We believe,' but (that) they will not be tested? **3** Certainly We tested those who were before them, and God will indeed know those who are truthful, and He will indeed know the liars. **4** Or do those who do evil deeds think that they will escape Us? Evil is what they judge! **5** Whoever expects the meeting with God – surely the time of God is coming indeed! He is the Hearing, the Knowing. **6** Whoever struggles, struggles only for himself. Surely God is indeed wealthy beyond all peoples. **7** Those who believe and do righteous deeds – We shall indeed absolve them of their evil deeds, and indeed repay them (for the) best of what they have done.

8 We have charged each person (to do) good to his parents, but if they both struggle with you – to make you associate with Me what you have no knowledge of – do not obey them. To Me is your return, and I shall inform you about what you have done. **9** Those who believe and do righteous deeds – We shall indeed cause them to enter among the righteous.

10 Among the people (there is) one who says, 'We believe in God,' but when he is hurt in (the way of) God, he takes the persecution of the people as the punishment of God. But if indeed help comes to you from your Lord, they indeed say, 'Surely we were with you.' Does God not know what is in the hearts of all? **11** God indeed knows those who believe, and He indeed knows the hypocrites.

12 Those who disbelieve say to those who believe, 'Follow our way, and let us bear your sins.' Yet they cannot bear a single one of their own sins. Surely they are liars indeed! **13** But they will indeed bear their burdens, and (other) burdens with their burdens, and on the Day of Resurrection they will indeed be questioned about what they have forged.

14 Certainly We sent Noah to his people, and he stayed among them a thousand years, minus fifty years, and then the flood seized them while they were doing evil. **15** But We rescued him and (his) companions on the ship, and made it a miracle for all peoples.

16 And Abraham, when he said to his people: 'Serve God, and guard (yourselves) against Him. That is better for you, if (only) you knew. **17** Instead of God, you only serve idols, and you create a lie. Surely those whom you serve, instead of God,

The Spider

do not possess any provision for you. Seek (your) provision from God, and serve Him, and be thankful to Him – to Him you will be returned. **18** But if you call (it) a lie, (know that) communities called (it) a lie before you. Nothing (depends) on the messenger except the clear delivery (of the message).'

19 Do they not see how God brings about the creation, (and) then restores it? Surely that is easy for God. **20** Say: 'Travel the earth and see how He brought about the creation. Then God produces the latter growth. Surely God is powerful over everything. **21** He punishes whomever He pleases and has compassion on whomever He pleases – and to Him you will be returned. **22** You cannot escape (Him) either on the earth or in the sky, and you have no ally and no helper other than God.' **23** Those who disbelieve in the signs of God and the meeting with Him – those have no hope of My mercy, and those – for them (there is) a painful punishment.

24 But the only response of his people was that they said, 'Kill him, or burn him!' And then God rescued him from the fire. Surely in that are signs indeed for a people who believe. **25** And he said, 'Instead of God, you have only taken idols (in a bond of) friendship among you in this present life. Then on the Day of Resurrection some of you will deny others, and some will curse others, and your refuge will be the Fire, and you will have no helpers.' **26** Lot believed in him, and said, 'I am going to flee to my Lord. Surely He – He is the Mighty, the Wise.' **27** And We granted him Isaac and Jacob, and We placed among his descendant the prophetic office and the Book. We gave him his reward in this world, and in the Hereafter he will indeed be among the righteous.

28 And Lot, when he said to his people: 'Surely you commit (such) immorality (as) no one among all peoples has committed before you. **29** Do you indeed approach men, and cut off the way,[1] and commit wrong in your meeting?' But the only response of his people was that they said, 'Bring us the punishment of God, if you are one of the truthful.' **30** He said, 'My Lord, help me against the people who foment corruption.' **31** When Our messengers brought Abraham the good news, they said, 'Surely we are going to destroy the people of this town, (for) its people are evildoers.' **32** He said, 'Surely Lot is in it.' They said, 'We know who is in it. We shall indeed rescue him and his family, except his wife. She will be one of those who stay behind.' **33** When Our messengers came to Lot, he became distressed about them, and felt powerless (to protect) them, but they said, 'Do not fear and do not sorrow. Surely we are going to rescue you and your family, except your wife. She will be one of those who stay behind. **34** Surely We are going to send down wrath from the sky on the people of this town, because they have acted wickedly.' **35** Certainly We have left some of it as a clear sign for a people who understand.

36 And to Midian (We sent) their brother Shu'ayb. He said, 'My people! Serve God and expect the Last Day. Do not act wickedly on the earth, fomenting corruption.'

---

1. *cut off the way*: of producing children.

The Spider

37 But they called him a liar, so the earthquake seized them, and morning found them leveled in their home(s).

38 And 'Ād and Thamūd – it is clear to you from their dwellings. Satan made their deeds appear enticing to them, and kept them from the way, though they saw (it) clearly.

39 And Qārūn, and Pharaoh, and Haman – certainly Moses brought them the clear signs, but they became arrogant on the earth. Yet they did not outrun (Us). **40** We seized each one for his sin. We sent a sandstorm against one of them, and another of them was seized by the cry, and We caused the earth to swallow (yet) another of them, and We drowned (still) another of them. Yet God was not one to do them evil, but they did themselves evil.

41 The parable of those who take allies other than God is like the parable of the spider: it takes a house, but surely the house of the spider is indeed the most feeble of houses – if (only) they knew. **42** Surely God knows whatever they call on instead of Him. He is the Mighty, the Wise. **43** Those parables – We strike them for the people, but no one understands them except the ones who know. **44** God created the heavens and the earth in truth. Surely in that is a sign indeed for the believers.

45 Recite what you have been inspired (with) of the Book, and observe the prayer. Surely the prayer forbids immorality and wrong, yet the remembrance of God is indeed greater. God is aware of what you do. **46** Do not dispute with the People of the Book, except with what is better – except for those of them who do evil. And say: 'We believe in what has been sent down to us, and what has been sent down to you. Our God and your God is one, and to Him we submit.' **47** In this way We have sent down the Book to you. Those to whom We have given the Book believe in it, and among these (people) (there are) some who believe in it. No one denies Our signs but the disbelievers.

48 You were not accustomed to read from any book before it, or to write it with your right (hand), (for) then the perpetrators of falsehood would indeed have had (reason to) doubt (you). **49** No! It is clear signs in the hearts of those who have been given knowledge. No one denies Our signs but the evildoers.

50 They say, 'If only signs were sent down on him from his Lord.' Say: 'The signs are only with God. I am only a clear warner.' **51** Is it not sufficient for them that We have sent down on you the Book to be recited to them? Surely in that is a mercy indeed, and a reminder to a people who believe. **52** Say: 'God is sufficient as a witness between me and you.' He knows whatever is in the heavens and the earth. Those who believe in falsehood and disbelieve in God, those – they are the losers.

53 They seek to hurry you with the punishment. If it were not for an appointed time, the punishment would indeed have come upon them (already). Yet it will indeed come upon them unexpectedly, when they do not realize (it). **54** They seek to hurry you with the punishment. Surely Gehenna will indeed encompass

The Spider

the disbelievers. **55** On the Day when the punishment will cover them – from above them and from beneath their feet – (then) He will say, 'Taste what you have done!'

56 My servants who believe! Surely My earth is wide, so serve Me! **57** Every person will taste death, then to Us you will be returned. **58** Those who have believed and done righteous deeds – We shall indeed settle them in exalted rooms of the Garden, through which rivers flow, there to remain. Excellent is the reward of the doers, **59** who are patient and trust in their Lord.

60 How many a creature (there is which) does not carry its own provision, yet God provides for it and for you. He is the Hearing, the Knowing. **61** If indeed you ask them, 'Who created the heavens and the earth, and subjected the sun and the moon?,' they will indeed say, 'God.' How then are they (so) deluded? **62** God extends (His) provision to whomever He pleases of His servants, and restricts (it) from him (whom He pleases). God has knowledge of everything. **63** If indeed you ask them, 'Who sends down water from the sky, and by means of it gives the earth life after its death?,' they will indeed say, 'God.' Say: 'Praise (be) to God!' But most of them do not understand.

64 This present life is nothing but jest and diversion. Surely the Home of the Hereafter – it is life indeed, if (only) they knew. **65** When they sail in the ship, they call on God, devoting (their) religion to Him. But when He brings them safely to the shore, suddenly they associate (other gods with Him). **66** Let them be ungrateful for what We have given them, and enjoy (themselves). Soon they will know! **67** Do they not see that We established a secure sanctuary (for them), while all around them the people are plundered? Do they believe in falsehood, but disbelieve in the blessing of God?

68 Who is more evil than the one who forges a lie against God, or calls the truth a lie when it comes to him? Is there not in Gehenna a dwelling place for the disbelievers? **69** But those who struggle for Us, We shall indeed guide them in Our ways. Surely God is indeed with the doers of good.

30 ❊ The Romans

In the Name of God, the Merciful, the Compassionate

1 Alif Lām Mīm.

2 The Romans have been conquered 3 in the nearer (part) of the land, but after their conquering, they will conquer 4 in a few years. The affair (belongs) to God before and after, and on that day the believers will gloat 5 over the help of God. He helps whomever He pleases. He is the Mighty, the Compassionate.

6 The promise of God! God will not break His promise, but most of the people do not know (it). 7 They perceive (only) what is obvious in this present life, but they are oblivious of the Hereafter. 8 Do they not reflect within themselves? God did not create the heavens and the earth, and whatever is between them, except in truth and (for) an appointed time. Yet surely many of the people are indeed disbelievers in the meeting with their Lord. 9 Have they not traveled on the earth and seen how the end was for those who were before them? They were stronger than them in power, and they ploughed the earth and populated it more than they have populated it. Their messengers brought them the clear signs. God was not one to do them evil, but they did themselves evil. 10 Then the end of those who had done evil was evil, because they had called the signs of God a lie and mocked them.

11 God brings about the creation, then restores it, (and) then to Him you will be returned. 12 On the Day when the Hour strikes, the sinners will despair. 13 They will not have any intercessors among their associates, but they (will come to) disbelieve in their associates. 14 On the Day when the Hour strikes, on that Day they will be separated. 15 As for those who have believed and done righteous deeds, they will be made happy in a meadow. 16 But as for those who have disbelieved, and called Our signs a lie, and the meeting of the Hereafter, those will be brought forward to the punishment. 17 So glory to God, when you come to evening and when you come to morning. 18 Praise (be) to Him in the heavens and the earth – and at night and when you appear (in the day)! 19 He brings forth the living from the dead, and brings forth the dead from the living. He gives the earth life after its death, and in this way you (too) will be brought forth.

20 (One) of His signs is that He created you from dust, and now you are human beings spreading (far and wide). 21 (Another) of His signs is that He created spouses for you from yourselves, so that you may live with them, and He has established love and mercy between you. Surely in that are signs indeed for a

people who reflect. **22** (Another) of His signs is the creation of the heavens and the earth, and the variety of your languages and colors. Surely in that are signs indeed for those who know. **23** (Another) of His signs is your sleeping by night and day, and your seeking some of His favor. Surely in that are signs indeed for a people who hear. **24** (Another) of His signs (is that) He shows you lightning – in fear and desire – and He sends down water from the sky, and by means of it gives the earth life after its death. Surely in that are signs indeed for a people who understand. **25** (Another) of His signs is that the sky and the earth stand (fast) by His command. Then, when He calls you out of the earth once and for all, suddenly you will come forth. **26** To Him (belongs) whoever is in the heavens and the earth: all are obedient before Him. **27** He (it is) who brings about the creation, then restores it – it is easy for Him. (Only) the highest parable in the heavens and the earth (is fitting) for Him. He is the Mighty, the Wise.

28 He has struck a parable for you from yourselves: Among what your right (hands) own,[1] do you have associates in what We have provided you with, so that you are (all) equal in that respect – (you) fearing them as you fear each other? In this way We make the signs distinct for a people who understand.

29 No! Those who do evil follow their own (vain) desires without any knowledge. So who will guide those whom God has led astray? They have no helpers. **30** Set your face to the religion (as) a Ḥanīf[2] – the creation of God for which He created humankind. (There is) no change in the creation of God. That is the right religion, but most of the people do not know (it) – **31** turning to Him (in repentance). Guard (yourself) against Him, and observe the prayer, and do not be one of the idolaters, **32** one of those who have divided up their religion and become parties, each faction gloating over what was with them. **33** When hardship touches the people, they call on their Lord, turning to Him (in repentance). Then, when He gives them a taste of mercy from Himself, suddenly a group of them associates (other gods) with their Lord. **34** Let them be ungrateful for what We have given them: 'Enjoy (yourselves)! Soon you will know!' **35** Or have We sent down any authority on them (for this), and does it speak about what they associate with Him?

36 When We give the people a taste of mercy, they gloat over it, but if some evil smites them because of what their (own) hands have sent forward, suddenly they despair. **37** Do they not see that God extends (His) provision to whomever He pleases, and restricts (it)? Surely in that are signs indeed for a people who believe.

38 Give the family its due, and the poor, and the traveler – that is better for those who desire the face of God, and those – they are the ones who prosper. **39** Whatever you give in usury, in order that it may increase on the wealth of the people, does not increase with God, but what you give in alms, desiring the face of God – those are the ones who gain double.

---

1. *what your right (hands) own*: slaves.
2. *Ḥanīf*: meaning uncertain.

The Romans

40 (It is) God who created you, then provided for you, then causes you to die, (and) then gives you life. (Are there) any of your associates who (can) do any of that? Glory to Him! He is exalted above what they associate. **41** Corruption has appeared on the shore and the sea because of what the hands of the people have earned, so that He may give them a taste of what they have done, that they may return. **42** Say: 'Travel the earth and see how the end was for those who were before (you). Most of them were idolaters.'

43 Set your face to the right religion, before a Day comes from God which cannot be turned back. On that Day they will be divided: **44** whoever disbelieves – his disbelief (will be) on him, but whoever does righteousness – they are smoothing (the way) for themselves, **45** so that He may repay from His favor those who believe and do righteous deeds. Surely He does not love the disbelievers.

46 (One) of His signs is that He sends the winds as bringers of good news, so that He may give you a taste of His mercy, and that the ship may run by His command, and that you may seek some of His favor, and that you may be thankful. **47** Certainly We sent messengers to their people before you, and they brought them the clear signs. Then We took vengeance on those who sinned, but it was an obligation on Us (to) help the believers. **48** (It is) God who sends the winds, and it stirs up a cloud, and He spreads it in the sky as He pleases, and breaks it into fragments, and you see the rain coming forth from the midst of it. When He smites with it whomever He pleases of His servants, suddenly they welcome the good news, **49** though before (this), before it was sent down on them, they were in despair. **50** Observe the traces of the mercy of God, how He gives the earth life after its death. Surely that One will indeed give the dead life. He is powerful over everything. **51** If indeed We send a wind, and they see it growing yellow, they indeed remain disbelievers after that. **52** You cannot make the dead to hear, nor can you make the deaf to hear the call when they turn away, withdrawing. **53** You cannot guide the blind out of their straying, nor can you make (anyone) hear, except for those who believe in Our signs, and so they submit. **54** (It is) God who created you from weakness, then after weakness He made strength, (and) then after strength He made weakness and grey hair. He creates whatever He pleases. He is the Knowing, the Powerful.

55 On the Day when the Hour strikes, the sinners will swear they remained (in the grave) only for an hour – that is how deluded they were – **56** but those who have been given knowledge and belief will say (to them), 'You have remained in the Book of God until the Day of Raising Up, and this is the Day of Raising Up, but you did not know (it).' **57** On that Day their excuses will not benefit those who have done evil, nor will they be allowed to make amends.

58 Certainly We have struck for the people every (kind of) parable in this Qur'ān. But if indeed you bring them a sign, those who disbelieve will indeed say, 'You are nothing but perpetrators of falsehood.' **59** In this way God sets a seal on the hearts of those who do not know. **60** So be patient! Surely the promise of God is true. And (let) not those who are uncertain unsettle you.

31 ❊ Luqmān

In the Name of God, the Merciful, the Compassionate

1 Alif Lām Mīm. **2** Those are the signs of the wise Book, **3** a guidance and mercy for the doers of good, **4** who observe the prayer and give the alms, and they are certain of the Hereafter. **5** Those (depend) on guidance from their Lord, and those – they are the ones who prosper. **6** But among the people (there is) one who buys a diverting tale to lead (others) astray from the way of God without any knowledge, and to take it in mockery. Those – for them (there is) a humiliating punishment. **7** When Our signs are recited to him, he turns away arrogantly, as if he had not heard them, as if (there were) a heaviness in his ears. So give him news of a painful punishment! **8** Surely those who believe and do righteous deeds – for them (there are) Gardens of Bliss, **9** there to remain. The promise of God in truth! He is the Mighty, the Wise.

10 He created the heavens without any pillars you (can) see, and He cast on the earth firm mountains, so that it does not sway with you (on it), and He scattered on it all (kinds of) creatures. And We sent down water from the sky, and caused (things) of every excellent kind to grow in it. **11** This is the creation of God. Show me what those (whom you worship) instead of Him have created. No! The evildoers are clearly astray.

12 Certainly We gave Luqmān wisdom: 'Be thankful to God. Whoever is thankful is thankful only for himself, and whoever is ungrateful – surely God is wealthy, praiseworthy.'

13 (Remember) when Luqmān said to his son, when he was admonishing him: 'My son! Do not associate (anything) with God. Surely the association (of anything) with God is a great evil indeed.'

14 We have charged the human concerning his parents – his mother bore him in weakness upon weakness, and his weaning took two years – 'Be thankful to Me and to your parents. To Me is the (final) destination.' **15** But if they both struggle with you – to make you associate with Me what you have no knowledge of – do not obey them. Keep rightful company with them in this world, but follow the way of the one who turns to Me (in repentance). Then to Me is your return, and I shall inform you about what you have done.'

16 'My son! Surely it – if it should be (only) the weight of a mustard seed, and it should be in a rock, or in the heavens, or on the earth, God will bring it forth. Surely God is astute, aware. **17** My son! Observe the prayer, and command right

Luqmān

and forbid wrong. Bear patiently whatever smites you – surely that is one of the determining factors in (all) affairs. **18** Do not turn your cheek to the people, and do not walk on the earth in jubilation. Surely God does not love anyone who is arrogant (and) boastful. **19** Be modest in your walking, and lower your voice. Surely the most hateful of voices is the voice of donkeys.'

20 Do you[1] not see that God has subjected to you whatever is in the heavens and whatever is on the earth, and has lavished on you His blessings, both outwardly and inwardly? But among the people (there is) one who disputes about God without any knowledge or guidance or illuminating Book. **21** When it is said to them, 'Follow what God has sent down,' they say, 'No! We will follow what we found our fathers doing.' Even if Satan were calling them to the punishment of the blazing (Fire)? **22** Whoever submits his face to God, being a doer of good, has grasped the firmest handle. To God (belongs) the outcome of all affairs. **23** Whoever disbelieves – do not let his disbelief cause you[2] sorrow. To Us is their return, and We shall inform them about what they have done. Surely God knows what is in the hearts. **24** We give them enjoyment (of life) for a little (while), then We force them to a stern punishment. **25** If indeed you ask them, 'Who created the heavens and the earth?,' they will indeed say, 'God.' Say: 'Praise (be) to God!' But most of them do not know (it). **26** To God (belongs) whatever is in the heavens and the earth. Surely God – He is the wealthy One, the Praiseworthy.

27 Even if all the trees on the earth were pens, and the sea (were ink) – (and) extending it (were) seven seas after it – the words of God would (still) not give out. God is mighty, wise.

28 Your creation and your raising up are only as (that of) a single person. God is hearing, seeing.

29 Do you not see that God causes the night to pass into the day, and causes the day to pass into the night, and has subjected the sun and the moon, each one running (its course) for an appointed time, and that God is aware of what you do? **30** That is because God – He is the Truth, and what they call on instead of Him – that is the falsehood, and because God is the Most High, the Great. **31** Do you not see that the ship runs on the sea by the blessing of God, so that He may show you some of His signs? Surely in that are signs indeed for every patient (and) thankful one. **32** And when wave(s) cover them like shadows, they call on God, devoting (their) religion to Him. But when He has brought them safely to the shore, some of them become lax. No one denies Our signs except every traitor (and) ungrateful one.

33 People! Guard (yourselves) against your Lord, and fear a Day when no father will offer any compensation for his son, and no son will offer any compensation for his father. Surely the promise of God is true, so do not let this present

---

1. *you*: plur.
2. *you*: sing.

Luqmān

life deceive you, and do not let the Deceiver deceive you about God. **34** Surely God – with Him is the knowledge of the Hour. He sends down the rain, and He knows what is in the wombs, but no person knows what he will earn tomorrow, and no person knows in what (place on) earth he will die. Surely God is knowing, aware.

32 ❖ THE PROSTRATION

In the Name of God, the Merciful, the Compassionate

1 Alif Lām Mīm.

2 (The) sending down of the Book – (there is) no doubt about it – (is) from the Lord of all peoples. **3** Or do they say, 'He has forged it'? No! It is the truth from your Lord, so that you may warn a people to whom no warner has come before you, so that they may be (rightly) guided.

4 (It is) God who created the heavens and the earth, and whatever is between them, in six days. Then He mounted the throne. You have no ally and no intercessor other than Him. Will you not take heed? **5** He directs the (whole) affair from the sky to the earth; then it will go up to Him in a day, the measure of which is a thousand years of what you count. **6** That One is the Knower of the unseen and the seen, the Mighty, the Compassionate, **7** who made well everything He created. He brought about the creation of the human from clay, **8** then He made his progeny from an extract of despicable water, **9** then He fashioned him and breathed into him some of His spirit, and made for you hearing and sight and hearts. Little thanks you show!

10 They say, 'When we have gotten lost in the earth, shall we indeed (return) in a new creation?' But they are disbelievers in the meeting with their Lord. **11** Say: 'The angel of death, who is put in charge of you, will take you, (and) then you will be returned to your Lord.' **12** If (only) you (could) see when the sinners are hanging their heads before their Lord: 'Our Lord, (now) we have seen and heard, so let us return (and) we shall do righteousness. Surely (now) we are certain.' **13** 'If We had (so) pleased, We would indeed have given every person his guidance. But My word has proved true: "I shall indeed fill Gehenna with jinn and humans – all (of them)!" **14** So taste (the punishment) because you have forgotten the meeting of this Day of yours. Surely We have forgotten you! Taste the punishment of eternity for what you have done!'

15 Only those believe in Our signs who, when they are reminded of them, fall down in prostration and glorify their Lord with praise. They are not arrogant. **16** They forsake their beds (during the night) to call on their Lord in fear and eagerness, and they contribute from what We have provided them. **17** No one knows what comfort is hidden (away) for them in payment for what they have done. **18** So is the one who believes like the one who is wicked? They are not equal! **19** As for those who believe and do righteous deeds, for them (there are)

The Prostration

Gardens of the Refuge, as a reception for what they have done. **20** But as for those who act wickedly, their refuge is the Fire. Whenever they want to come out of it, they will be sent back into it, and it will be said to them: 'Taste the punishment of the Fire which you called a lie!' **21** And We shall indeed make them taste the nearer punishment, before the greater punishment, so that they may return. **22** Who is more evil than the one who is reminded of the signs of his Lord, (and) then turns away from them? Surely We are going to take vengeance on the sinners.

23 Certainly We gave Moses the Book – so do not be in doubt of meeting Him – and We made it a guidance for the Sons of Israel. **24** And We appointed from among them leaders (who) guide (others) by Our command, when they were patient and were certain of Our signs. **25** Surely your Lord – He will distinguish between them on the Day of Resurrection concerning their differences.

26 Is it not a guide for them how many generations We have destroyed before them, (seeing that) they walk in (the midst of) their dwelling places? Surely in that are signs indeed. Will they not hear? **27** Do they not see that We drive water to the barren earth, and bring forth crops by means of it, from which their livestock and they themselves eat? Will they not see? **28** They say, 'When will the victory take place, if you are truthful?' **29** Say: 'On the Day of Victory, their belief will not benefit those who disbelieve, nor will they be spared.' **30** So turn away from them, and wait. Surely they (too) are waiting.

33 ❖ THE FACTIONS

In the Name of God, the Merciful, the Compassionate

1 Prophet! Guard (yourself) against God, and do not obey the disbelievers and the hypocrites. Surely God is knowing, wise. 2 Follow what you are inspired (with) from your Lord. Surely God is aware of what you do. 3 Put your trust in God, (for) God is sufficient as a guardian.

4 God has not placed two hearts inside anyone. He has not made your wives whom you declare to be as your mothers' backs[1] your (real) mothers, nor has He made your adopted sons your (real) sons. That is what you say with your mouths, but God speaks the truth and guides (you) to the (right) way. 5 Call them by (the names of) their (real) fathers: that is more just in the sight of God. If you do not know their (real) fathers, (regard them) as your brothers in religion, and your clients. There is no blame on you in any mistakes you have made, but only in what your hearts have intended. God is forgiving, compassionate.

6 The prophet is closer to the believers than they are to themselves, and his wives are their mothers, but those related by blood are closer to one another in the Book of God than the believers and the emigrants – but you should do right by your allies. That is written in the Book.

7 (Remember) when We took a covenant with the prophets – and from you, and from Noah, and Abraham, and Moses, and Jesus, son of Mary – We took a firm covenant with them, 8 so that He might question the truthful about their truthfulness. He has prepared a painful punishment for the disbelievers.

9 You who believe! Remember the blessing of God on you, when the forces came upon you, and We sent against them a wind, and (also) forces which you did not see. God sees what you do. 10 When they came upon you from above you and from below you, and when (your) sight turned aside and (your) hearts reached (your) throats, and you were thinking about God (all kinds of) thoughts, 11 there and then the believers were tested and severely shaken. 12 And when the hypocrites, and those in whose hearts is a sickness, said, 'God and His messenger have promised us nothing but deception.' 13 And when a group of them said, 'People of Yathrib! (There is) no dwelling place for you (here), so return!' And (another) contingent of them was asking permission of the prophet, saying, 'Surely our

---

1. *declare to be as your mothers' backs*: meaning obscure; said to be a pre-Islamic formula for ending a marriage.

The Factions

houses are vulnerable' – yet they were not vulnerable, they only wished to flee. **14** If an entrance had been made against them from that side, (and) then they had been asked (to join in) the troublemaking, they would indeed have done it, and scarcely have hesitated with it. **15** Certainly they had made a covenant with God before (this), that they would not turn their backs, and a covenant with God is (something) to be responsible for. **16** Say: 'Flight will not benefit you. If you flee from death or killing, you will only enjoy (life) a little (while).' **17** Say: 'Who is the one who will protect you against God, if He intends evil for you, or intends mercy for you?' They will not find for themselves any ally or helper other than God.

18 God knows those of you who are a hindrance, and those who say to their brothers, 'Come to us,' but who seldom come out to the battle, **19** (in their) greed toward you.[2] When fear comes (upon them), you[3] see them looking at you, their eyes rolling around like one who faints at the point of death. But when fear departs, they sting you[4] with (their) sharp tongues (in their) greed for the good (that has come to you). Those – they have not believed. God has made their deeds worthless. That is easy for God. **20** They think (that) the factions have not gone away. If the factions come (again), they will wish that they were living in the desert among the Arabs, asking for news of you. Yet (even) if they were among you, they would seldom fight. **21** Certainly the messenger of God has been a good example for you – for the one who hopes in God and the Last Day, and remembers God often.

22 When the believers saw the factions, they said, 'This is what God and His messenger promised us, and God and His messenger were truthful.' It only increased them in belief and submission. **23** Among the believers are men who have been truthful to the covenant which they made with God: some of them have fulfilled their vow, and some of them are (still) waiting (to do so). They have not changed in the least, **24** so that God may repay the truthful for their truthfulness, and punish the hypocrites, if He (so) pleases, or turn to them (in forgiveness). Surely God is forgiving, compassionate. **25** God turned back those who disbelieved in their rage, and they did not attain any advantage. God was sufficient for the believers in the fighting. Surely God is strong, mighty. **26** He brought down from their fortifications those of the People of the Book who supported them, and cast dread into their hearts. You killed a group (of them), and took captive (another) group. **27** And He caused you to inherit their land, their homes, and their wealth, and a land you had not set foot on. God is powerful over everything.

28 Prophet! Say to your wives: 'If you desire this present life and its (passing) splendor, come! I shall make provision for you, and release you gracefully. **29** But if you desire God and His messenger, and the Home of the Hereafter – surely God has prepared a great reward for the doers of good among you.' **30** Wives of the

---

2. *you*: plur.
3. *you*: sing.
4. *you*: plur.

The Factions

prophet! Whoever among you commits clear immorality, for her the punishment will be doubled. That is easy for God. **31** But whoever among you is obedient to God and His messenger, and does righteousness – We shall give her her reward twice over. We have prepared a generous provision for her. **32** Wives of the prophet! You are not like any of the (other) women. If you guard (yourselves), do not be beguiling in (your) speech, or he in whose heart is a sickness will become lustful, but speak in a rightful fashion. **33** Stay in your houses, and do not flaunt (yourselves) with the flaunting of the former ignorance, but observe the prayer and give the alms, and obey God and His messenger. God only wishes to take away the abomination from you, People of the House, and to purify you completely. **34** Remember what is recited in your houses of the signs of God and the wisdom. Surely God is astute, aware.

35 Surely the submitting men and the submitting women, the believing men and the believing women, the obedient men and the obedient women, the truthful men and the truthful women, the patient men and the patient women, the humble men and the humble women, the charitable men and the charitable women, the fasting men and the fasting women, the men who guard their private parts and the women who guard (them), the men who remember God often and the women who remember (Him) – for them God has prepared forgiveness and a great reward.

36 It is not for a believing man or a believing woman, when God and His messenger have decided a matter, to have the choice in their matter. Whoever disobeys God and His messenger has very clearly gone astray.

37 (Remember) when you said to the one whom God had blessed, and whom you had blessed: 'Keep your wife to yourself, and guard (yourself) against God,' and you hid within yourself what God was going to reveal, and feared the people, when God had a better right that you feared Him. So when Zayd[5] had gotten what he needed from her, We married her to you, so that there should not be any blame on the believers concerning the wives of their adopted sons, when they have gotten what they needed from them. The command of God was (to be) fulfilled. **38** There is no blame on the prophet concerning what God has made obligatory for him. (That was) the customary way of God concerning those who passed away before – and the command of God is a determined decree – **39** who were delivering the messages of God, and fearing Him, and not fearing anyone but Him. God is sufficient as a reckoner.

40 Muḥammad is not the father of any of your men, but the messenger of God and the seal of the prophets. God has knowledge of everything.

41 You who believe! Remember God often, **42** and glorify Him morning and evening. **43** He (it is) who prays over you, and His angels (do too), to bring you out of the darkness to the light. He is compassionate with the believers. **44** On the Day

---

5. *Zayd*: the Prophet's adopted son, Zayd ibn-Ḥāritha.

The Factions

when they meet Him, their greeting will be: 'Peace!' He has prepared a generous reward for them.

45 Prophet! Surely We have sent you as a witness, and as a bringer of good news and a warner, **46** and as one calling to God, by His permission, and as an illuminating lamp. **47** Give good news to the believers that they have great favor from God. **48** Do not obey the disbelievers and the hypocrites. Ignore their hurt and put your trust in God. God is sufficient as a guardian.

49 You who believe! When you marry believing women (and) then divorce them before you touch them, you have no waiting period to count for them. So make provision for them, and release them gracefully.

50 Prophet! Surely We have made lawful for you your wives to whom you have granted their marriage gifts, and what your right (hand) owns from what God has given you, and the daughters of your paternal uncles and paternal aunts, your maternal uncles and maternal aunts, who have emigrated with you, and any believing woman, if she gives herself to the prophet, and if the prophet wishes to take her in marriage. (That is) exclusively for you, apart from the believers – We know what We have made obligatory for them concerning their wives and what their right (hands) own – so that there may be no blame on you. God is forgiving, compassionate. **51** You may put off whomever you please of them, and you may take to yourself whomever you please. And whomever you desire of those you have set aside, (there is) no blame on you (if you take her again). That is more appropriate, so that they may be comforted and not sorrow, and (that) they may be pleased with what you give them – all of them. God knows what is in your hearts. God is knowing, forbearing. **52** Beyond (that) women are not permitted to you, nor (is it permitted to you) to take (other) wives in exchange for them, even though their beauty pleases you, except for what your right (hand) owns. God is watching over everything.

53 You who believe! Do not enter the houses of the prophet to (attend) a meal without waiting (until it) is ready, unless permission is given to you. But when you are invited, enter, and when you have eaten, disperse, and do not linger for conversation. Surely that is hurtful to the prophet, and he is ashamed of you, but God is not ashamed of the truth. When you ask them for anything, ask them from behind a veil. That is purer for your hearts and their hearts. It is not for you to hurt the messenger of God, nor to marry his wives after him – ever. Surely that is a great (offense) in the sight of God. **54** Whether you reveal a thing or hide it, surely God has knowledge of everything.

55 (There is) no blame on them concerning their fathers, or their sons, or their brothers, or their brothers' sons, or their sisters' sons, or their women, or what their right (hands) own. But guard (yourselves) against God. Surely God is a witness over everything.

56 Surely God and His angels pray for the prophet. You who believe! You pray for him (too), and greet him (with a worthy) greeting. **57** Surely those who hurt God

The Factions

and His messenger – God has cursed them in this world and the Hereafter, and has prepared a humiliating punishment for them. **58** Those who hurt believing men and believing women – other than what they have earned – they will indeed bear (the burden of) slander and clear sin.

59 Prophet! Say to your wives, and your daughters, and the believing women, to draw some of their outer clothes over themselves. That is more appropriate for their being recognized, and not hurt. God is forgiving, compassionate.

60 If indeed the hypocrites do not stop – and those in whose hearts is a sickness, and those who cause commotion in the city – We shall indeed incite you against them, (and) then they will not be your neighbors there, except for a little (while). **61** (They will be) accursed! Wherever they are found, they will be seized and completely killed. **62** (That was) the customary way of God concerning those who have passed away before, and you will find no change in the customary way of God.

63 The people ask you about the Hour. Say: 'Knowledge of it is only with God. What will make you know? Perhaps the Hour is near.' **64** Surely God has cursed the disbelievers, and prepared for them a blazing (Fire), **65** there to remain forever. They will not find any ally or helper. **66** On the Day when their faces will be turned about in the Fire, they will say, 'Oh, would that we had obeyed God, and obeyed the messenger!' **67** And they will say, 'Our Lord, surely we obeyed our men of honor and our great men, and they led us astray from the way. **68** Our Lord, give them a double (share) of the punishment, and curse them with a great curse!'

69 You who believe! Do not be like those who hurt Moses, but God cleared him of what they said, and he was eminent in the sight of God. **70** You who believe! Guard (yourselves) against God, and speak a direct word. **71** He will set right your deeds for you, and forgive you your sins. Whoever obeys God and His messenger has attained a great triumph.

72 Surely We offered the trust to the heavens and the earth, and the mountains, but they refused to bear it, and were afraid of it, and (instead) the human bore it. Surely he has become an evildoer (and) ignorant. **73** (It is) so that God might punish the hypocrite men and the hypocrite women (alike), and the idolatrous men and the idolatrous women alike, and so that God might turn (in forgiveness) to the believing men and the believing women (alike). God is forgiving, compassionate.

34 ❖ Sheba

In the Name of God, the Merciful, the Compassionate

1 Praise (be) to God – to Him (belongs) whatever is in the heavens and whatever is on the earth – and to Him (be) praise in the Hereafter! He is the Wise, the Aware. 2 He knows what penetrates into the earth and what comes forth from it, and what comes down from the sky and what goes up into it. He is the Compassionate, the Forgiving.

3 Those who disbelieve say, 'The Hour will not come upon us.' Say: 'Yes indeed! By my Lord! It will indeed come to you! (He is the) Knower of the unseen. Not (even) the weight of a speck in the heavens and the earth escapes from Him, nor (is there anything) smaller than that or greater, except (that it is recorded) in a clear Book 4 – so that He may repay those who believe and do righteous deeds.' Those – for them (there is) forgiveness and generous provision. 5 But those who strive against Our signs to obstruct (them), those – for them (there is) a punishment of painful wrath. 6 But those who have been given the knowledge see (that) what has been sent down to you from your Lord is the truth, and (that) it guides to the path of the Mighty, the Praiseworthy.

7 Those who disbelieve say, 'Shall we direct you to a man who will inform you (that) when you have been completely torn to pieces, you will indeed (return) in a new creation? 8 Has he forged a lie against God, or is he possessed?' No! Those who do not believe in the Hereafter are in punishment and far astray. 9 Do they not look to what is before them and what is behind them of the sky and the earth? If We (so) please, We could cause the earth to swallow them, or make fragments of the sky fall on them. Surely in that is a sign indeed for every servant who turns (in repentance).

10 Certainly We gave David favor from Us: 'You mountains! Return (praises) with him, and you birds (too)!' And We made iron malleable for him: 11 'Make full (coats of armor), and measure (well) in the sewing (of them).' And: 'Do righteousness, (for) surely I see what you do.' 12 And to Solomon (We subjected) the wind, its morning was a month's (journey), and its evening was a month's (journey), and We made a spring of molten brass to flow for him. And among the jinn, (there were) those who worked for him by the permission of his Lord. Whoever of them turns aside from Our command – We shall make him taste the punishment of the blazing (Fire). 13 They made for him whatever he pleased: places of prayer, and statues, and basins like cisterns, and fixed cooking pots. 'House of David!

Work in thankfulness, (for) few of My servants are thankful!' **14** And when We decreed death for him, nothing indicated his death to them except a creature of the earth devouring his staff. When he fell down, it became clear to the jinn that, if they had known the unseen, they would not have remained in the humiliating punishment.[1]

15 Certainly for Sheba there was a sign in their dwelling place – two gardens, on the right and left: 'Eat from the provision of your Lord, and be thankful to Him. A good land and a forgiving Lord.' **16** But they turned away, so We sent on them the flood of 'Arim, and We replaced for them their two gardens (with) two gardens producing bitter fruit, and tamarisks, and a few lote trees. **17** We repaid them that because they disbelieved. We do not repay (anyone) but the ungrateful? **18** We set between them and the towns which We have blessed (other) towns (which are still) visible, and We measured out the traveling (distance) between them: 'Travel among them by night and day in security!' **19** But they said, 'Our Lord, lengthen (the distance) between our journeys.'[2] They did themselves evil, so We made them legendary, and We tore them completely to pieces. Surely in that are signs indeed for every patient (and) thankful one. **20** Certainly Iblīs confirmed his conjecture about them, and they followed him, except for a group of the believers. **21** But he had no authority over them, except that We might know the one who believed in the Hereafter from the one who was in doubt about it. Your Lord is a watcher over everything.

22 Say: 'Call on those whom you claim (as gods) instead of God! They do not possess (even) the weight of a speck in the heavens or on the earth. They have no partnership in (the creation of) either of them, nor has He any support from them.' **23** Intercession will be of no benefit with Him, except for the one to whom He gives permission – until, when terror is removed from their hearts, they say, 'What did your Lord say?,' and they say, 'The truth. He is the Most High, the Great.' **24** Say: 'Who provides for you from the heavens and the earth?' Say: 'God. Surely (either) we or you (stand) indeed on guidance, or (are) clearly astray.'

25 Say: 'You will not be questioned about what sins we have committed, nor shall we be questioned about what you do.'

26 Say: 'Our Lord will gather us together, (and) then disclose the truth between us, (for) He is the Discloser, the Knowing.'

27 Say: 'Show me those whom you have joined with Him as associates. By no means (can you do so)! No! He (alone) is God, the Mighty, the Wise.'

28 We have sent you only as a bringer of good news and a warner to the people all together. But most of the people do not know (it).

---

1. *if they had known the unseen . . .* : i.e. if the jinn had known that Solomon was dead, they would not have continued their demeaning labor.
2. *lengthen (the distance) between our journeys*: meaning obscure.

Sheba

29 They say, 'When (will) this promise (come to pass), if you[3] are truthful?' **30** Say: 'For you (there is) the appointment of a Day. You will not delay it by an hour, nor will you advance (it by an hour).'

31 Those who disbelieve say, 'We will not believe in this Qur'ān, nor in that which was before it.' If (only) you[4] could see when the evildoers are made to stand before their Lord, (how) some of them hurl the blame at others. Those who were weak will say to those who were arrogant, 'If not for you, we would have been believers.' **32** Those who were arrogant will say to those who were weak, 'Did we keep you from the guidance after it had come to you? No! You (yourselves) were sinners.' **33** Those who were weak will say to those who were arrogant, 'No! (It was your) scheming by night and day, when you commanded us to disbelieve in God and to set up rivals to Him.' They will be full of secret regret when they see the punishment. We shall put chains on the necks of those who disbelieved. Will they be repaid (for anything) except for what they have done?

34 We have not sent any warner to a town, except that its affluent ones said, 'Surely we are disbelievers in what you are sent with.' **35** And they (also) said, 'We (have) more wealth and children, and we shall not be punished.' **36** Say: 'Surely my Lord extends (His) provision to whomever He pleases, and restricts (it), but most of the people do not know (it).' **37** Neither your wealth nor your children are the things which bring you near to Us in intimacy, except for whoever believes and does righteousness. And those – for them (there is) a double payment for what they have done, and they will be secure in exalted rooms. **38** But those who strive against Our signs to obstruct (them) – those will be brought forward to the punishment. **39** Say: 'Surely my Lord extends (His) provision to whomever He pleases of His servants, and restricts (it) from him (whom He pleases). Whatever thing you contribute, He will replace it, (for) He is the best of providers.'

40 On the Day when He gathers them all together, He will say to the angels, '(Was it) you these were serving?' **41** They will say, 'Glory to You! You are our ally, not they. No! They used to serve the jinn – most of them believed in them.' **42** 'So today none of you has power to (cause) another benefit or harm.' And We shall say to those who did evil, 'Taste the punishment of the Fire, which you called a lie.'

43 When Our clear signs are recited to them, they say, 'This is only a man who wants to keep you from what your fathers have served.' And they say, 'This is nothing but a forged lie.' Those who disbelieve say to the truth, when it comes to them, 'This is nothing but clear magic' **44** – though We have not given them any Books to study, nor have We sent to them any warner before you. **45** Those who were before them (also) called (it) a lie, though they have not reached (even) a tenth of what We gave them. They (too) called My messengers liars, and how was My loathing (of them)!

---

3. *you*: plur.
4. *you*: sing.

Sheba

46 Say: 'I give you only one admonition, (namely) that you stand before God, in pairs or singly, (and) then reflect: (there are) not any jinn in your companion. He is only a warner for you in the face of a harsh punishment.' **47** Say: 'I have not asked you for any reward, but it was (only) for your own sake. My reward (depends) only on God. He is a witness over everything.' **48** Say: 'My Lord hurls the truth – Knower of the unseen.' **49** Say: 'The truth has come! Falsehood (can) neither bring (anything) about, nor restore (it).' **50** Say: 'If I go astray, I go astray only against myself, but if I am guided, it is by what my Lord inspires me (with). Surely He is hearing (and) near.'

51 If (only) you[5] could see when they are terrified and (there is) no escape, and they are seized from a place nearby, **52** and say, 'We believe in it (now).' Yet how will they reach (it) from a place far away, **53** when they disbelieved in it before? They conjecture about the unseen from a place far away. **54** But (a barrier) has been set between them and what they desire, as was done with their parties before. Surely they (too) were in grave doubt indeed (about it).

---

5. *you*: sing.

35 ✦ Creator

In the Name of God, the Merciful, the Compassionate

1 Praise (be) to God, Creator of the heavens and the earth, (who) makes the angels messengers having two, and three, and four wings. He adds to the creation whatever He pleases. Surely God is powerful over everything. 2 Whatever mercy God opens to the people, (there is) no withholder of it, and whatever (mercy) He withholds, (there is) no sender of it after that. He is the Mighty, the Wise.

3 People! Remember the blessing of God on you. (Is there) any creator other than God, (who) provides for you from the sky and the earth? (There is) no god but Him. How are you (so) deluded? 4 If they call you a liar, (know that) messengers have been called liars before you. To God all affairs are returned.

5 People! Surely the promise of God is true, so (do) not let this present life deceive you, and (do) not let the Deceiver deceive you about God. 6 Surely Satan is an enemy to you, so take him as an enemy. He only calls his faction so that they may be among the companions of the blazing (Fire). 7 Those who disbelieve – for them (there is) a harsh punishment, but those who believe and do righteous deeds – for them (there is) forgiveness and a great reward.

8 Is the one whose evil deed is made to appear enticing to him, and he perceives it as good, (like the one who is rightly guided)?[1] Surely God leads astray whomever He pleases and guides whomever He pleases. So do not exhaust yourself in regrets over them. Surely God is aware of what they do.

9 (It is) God who sends the winds, and it stirs up a cloud, and We drive it to some barren land, and by means of it give the earth life after its death. So (too) is the raising up. 10 Whoever desires honor – honor (belongs) to God altogether. To Him good words ascend, and the righteous deed – He raises it. But those who scheme evil deeds – for them (there is) a harsh punishment, and their scheming – it will be in vain.

11 God created you from dust, then from a drop, (and) then He made you pairs. No female conceives or delivers, except with His knowledge, and no one grows old who grows old, or is diminished in his life, except (it) is in a Book. Surely that is easy for God.

---

1. *(like the one who is rightly guided)*: something like this must be supplied to complete the sentence (cf. Q47.14).

12 The two seas are not alike: this one is sweet, fresh, good to drink, and this (other) one is salty (and) bitter. Yet from each you eat fresh fish, and bring out of it an ornament which you wear, and you see the ship cutting through it, so that you may seek some of His favor, and that you may be thankful. **13** He causes the night to pass into the day, and causes the day to pass into the night, and He has subjected the sun and the moon, each one running (its course) for an appointed time. That is God, your Lord – to Him (belongs) the kingdom, and those you call on, instead of Him, do not possess even the skin of a date seed. **14** If you call on them, they do not hear your calling, and (even) if they heard, they would not respond to you. On the Day of Resurrection they will deny your association. No one (can) inform you like One who is aware.

15 People! You are the ones in need of God, and God – He is the wealthy One, the Praiseworthy. **16** If He (so) pleases, He will do away with you and bring a new creation. **17** That is no great matter for God.

18 No one bearing a burden bears the burden of another. If one heavy-burdened calls for his load (to be carried), nothing of it will be carried, even though he be a family member. You warn only those who fear their Lord in the unseen, and (who) observe the prayer. Whoever purifies himself, only purifies (himself) for (the sake of) his own self. To God is the (final) destination. **19** The blind and the sighted are not equal, **20** nor are the darkness and the light, **21** nor the shade and the heat. **22** The living and the dead are not equal. Surely God causes whomever He pleases to hear. You will not cause those who are in the graves to hear **23** – you are only a warner. **24** Surely We have sent you with the truth, as a bringer of good news and a warner. (There has) not (been) any community except that a warner has passed away in it. **25** If they call you a liar, (know that) those who were before them called (their messengers) liars. Their messengers brought them the clear signs, and the scriptures, and the illuminating Book. **26** Then I seized those who disbelieved, and how was My loathing (of them)!

27 Do you not see that God sends down water from the sky, and by means of it We bring forth fruits of various colors? And in the mountains (there are) streaks (of) white and red – their colors are diverse – and (of) deep black. **28** And among people and (wild) animals and livestock – their colors are diverse as well. Only those of His servants who have knowledge fear God. Surely God is mighty, forgiving.

29 Surely those who recite the Book of God, and observe the prayer, and contribute from what We have provided them, in secret and in open, hope for a transaction – it will not be in vain – **30** so that He may pay them their rewards in full, and increase them from His favor. Surely He is forgiving, thankful.

31 What We have inspired you (with) of the Book – it is the truth, confirming what was before it. Surely God is indeed aware of His servants (and) sees (them). **32** Then We caused those of Our servants whom We chose to inherit the Book. Some of them do themselves evil, and some of them are moderate, and some of them are foremost in good deeds, by the permission of God. That is the great favor!

33 Gardens of Eden – they will enter them. There they will be adorned with bracelets of gold and (with) pearls, and there their clothes (will be of) silk. **34** And they will say, 'Praise (be) to God, who has taken away all sorrow from us! Surely our Lord is indeed forgiving, thankful, **35** who out of His favor has settled us in a lasting Home. No fatigue will touch us here, and no weariness will touch us here.'

36 But those who disbelieve – for them (there is) the fire of Gehenna. (Death) is not decreed for them, and so they do not die, nor will any of its punishment be lightened for them. In this way We repay every ungrateful one. **37** There they will cry out, 'Our Lord, bring us out! We will do righteousness instead of what we used to do.' 'Did We not give you a long life, enough of it for the one who would take heed to take heed? The warner came to you, so taste (the punishment)! The evildoers will have no helper.'

38 Surely God knows the unseen (things) of the heavens and the earth. Surely He knows what is in the hearts. **39** He (it is) who made you rulers on the earth. Whoever disbelieves, his disbelief (will be) on him. Their disbelief only increases the disbelievers in hatred in the sight of their Lord. Their disbelief only increases the disbelievers in loss. **40** Say: 'Have you seen your associates whom you call on instead of God? Show me what part of the earth they have created. Or do they have any partnership in (the creation of) the heavens?' Or have We given them a Book, so that they (stand) on a clear sign from it? No! The evildoers promise each other nothing but deception.

41 Surely God holds the heavens and the earth, or they would move. If indeed they moved, no one would hold them after Him. Surely He is forbearing, forgiving. **42** They have sworn by God the most solemn of their oaths: if a warner comes to them, they will be more (rightly) guided than one of the (other) communities. But when a warner came to them, it only increased them in aversion (to it), **43** (and) in arrogance on the earth, and in scheming evil. Yet evil scheming only overwhelms its own people. Do they expect anything but the customary way of those of old? You will find no change in the customary way of God. You will find no change in the customary way of God. **44** Have they not traveled on the earth and seen how the end was for those who were before them, though they were stronger than them in power? But God is not one that anything in the heavens or on the earth should escape Him. Surely He is knowing, powerful. **45** If God were to take the people to task for what they have earned, He would not leave on it any living creature. But He is sparing them until an appointed time. When their time comes – surely God sees His servants.

36 ❈ Yā' Sīn

In the Name of God, the Merciful, the Compassionate

1 Yā' Sīn.

2 By the wise Qur'ān! **3** Surely you are indeed one of the envoys, **4** on a straight path, **5** a sending down of the Mighty, the Compassionate, **6** so that you may warn a people. Their fathers have not been warned, and so they are oblivious.

7 Certainly the word has proved true against most of them: 'They will not believe.' **8** Surely We have placed chains on their necks, and it (reaches up) to the chin, and so they (are forced to) hold their heads up. **9** We have made a barrier before them and a barrier behind them, and We have covered them, and so they do not see. **10** (It is) the same for them whether you warn them or you do not warn them. They will not believe. **11** You warn only the one who follows the Reminder and fears the Merciful in the unseen. So give him the good news of forgiveness and a generous reward. **12** Surely We – We give the dead life and We write down what they have sent forward and their traces (left behind). And everything – We have counted it up in a clear record.

13 Strike a parable for them: the companions of the town, when the envoys came to it. **14** When We sent two men to them, and they called them liars, We reinforced (them) with a third. They said, 'Surely we are envoys to you.' **15** They said, 'You are nothing but human beings like us. The Merciful has not sent down anything. You are only lying.' **16** They said, 'Our Lord knows that we are indeed envoys to you. **17** Nothing (depends) on us except the clear delivery (of the message).' **18** They said, 'Surely we have an evil omen about you. If indeed you do not stop, we shall indeed stone you, and a painful punishment from us will indeed touch you.' **19** They said, 'Your evil omen refers to yourselves. If you had taken heed – No! You are a wanton people!' **20** (Just then) a man came running from the farthest part of the city. He said, 'My people! Follow the envoys! **21** Follow those who do not ask you for any reward, and (who) are (rightly) guided. **22** Why should I not serve Him who created me? You will (all) be returned to Him. **23** Shall I take (other) gods instead of Him? If the Merciful intends any harm for me, their intercession will be of no use to me at all, nor will they save me. **24** Surely then I would indeed be far astray. **25** Surely I believe in your Lord, so listen to me!' **26** It was said, 'Enter the Garden!' He said, 'Would that my people knew **27** that my Lord has forgiven me, and made me one of the honored.' **28** We did not send down on his people after him any force from the sky, nor are

Yā' Sīn

We (in the habit of) sending down (such a force). **29** It was only a single cry, and suddenly they were snuffed out. **30** Alas for the servants! Not one messenger comes to them whom they do not mock. **31** Do they not see how many generations We destroyed before them, (and) that they do not return to them? **32** But every one of them will be brought forward before Us.

33 A sign for them is the dead earth: We give it life, and bring forth grain from it, and from it they eat. **34** And We have placed in it gardens of date palms and grapes, and We have caused springs to gush forth in it, **35** so that they may eat from its fruit and what their hands have made. Will they not be thankful? **36** Glory to the One who created pairs of all that the earth grows, and of themselves, and of what they do not know.

37 A sign for them is the night: We strip the day from it, and suddenly they are in darkness. **38** And the sun: it runs to a dwelling place (appointed) for it. That is the decree of the Mighty, the Knowing. **39** And the moon: We have determined it by stations, until it returns like an old palm branch. **40** It is not fitting for the sun to overtake the moon, nor does the night outrun the day, but each floats in (its own) orbit.

41 A sign for them is that We carried their descendants in the loaded ship, **42** and We have created for them (ships) like it (in) which they sail. **43** If We (so) please, We drown them, and then (there is) no cry (for help) for them, nor are they saved, **44** except as a mercy from Us, and enjoyment (of life) for a time.

45 When it is said to them, 'Guard (yourselves) against what is before you and what is behind you, so that you may receive compassion' – **46** yet not a sign comes to them from the signs of their Lord without their turning away from it. **47** When it is said to them, 'Contribute from what God has provided you,' those who disbelieve say to those who believe, 'Shall we feed one whom, if God (so) pleased, He would have fed? You are only far astray!'

48 They say, 'When (will) this promise (come to pass), if you are truthful?' **49** They are only waiting for a single cry – it will seize them while they are (still) disputing, **50** and then they will not be able to make a bequest, nor will they return to their (own) families.

51 There will be a blast on the trumpet, and suddenly they will come swooping down from the graves to their Lord. **52** They will say, 'Alas for us! Who has raised us up from our sleeping place? This is what the Merciful promised, and the envoys were truthful.' **53** It was only a single cry, and suddenly they are all brought forward before Us. **54** 'Today no one will be done evil at all, nor will you be repaid (for anything) except what you have done.' **55** Surely the companions of the Garden today are busy rejoicing **56** – they and their spouses – reclining on couches in (places of) shade. **57** There they have fruit, and they have whatever they call for. **58** 'Peace!' – a word (of greeting) from a compassionate Lord. **59** 'But separate (yourselves) today, you sinners! **60** Did I not make a covenant with you, sons of Adam, that you should not serve Satan – surely he is a clear enemy to you

Yā' Sīn

– **61** and that you should serve Me? This is a straight path. **62** Certainly he has led astray many multitudes of you. Did you not understand? **63** This is Gehenna, which you were promised. **64** Burn in it today for what you have disbelieved!'

65 Today We will set a seal on their mouths, but their hands will speak to Us, and their feet will bear witness about what they have earned. **66** If We (so) pleased, We would indeed have obliterated their eyes, and they would race to the path, but how could they see? **67** And if We (so) pleased, We would indeed have transformed them where they were, and they could not go on, nor could they return. **68** (To) whomever We grant a long life, We reverse him in (his) constitution. Do they not understand?

69 We have not taught him the (art of) poetry, nor is it fitting for him. It is nothing but a Reminder and a clear Qur'ān, **70** so that he may warn whoever is living, and that the word may be proved true against the disbelievers.

71 Do they not see that We created for them – from what Our hands have made – livestock, and (that) they are their masters? **72** We have made them subservient to them, and some of them they ride, and some they eat. **73** And they have (other) benefits in them, and drinks. Will they not be thankful? **74** But they have taken (other) gods, instead of God, so that they might be helped. **75** (But) they cannot help them, (for) they will be brought forward before them as a group. **76** So do not let their saying cause you sorrow. Surely We know what they keep secret and what they speak aloud.

77 Does the human not see that We created him from a drop? Yet suddenly he is a clear adversary. **78** He has struck a parable for Us and forgotten (the fact of) his creation. He says, 'Who will give the bones life when they are decayed?' **79** Say: 'He will give them life who produced them the first time. He has knowledge of all creation, **80** who has made fire for you from the green tree – and so you (too) light a fire from it.' **81** Is not the One who created the heavens and the earth able to create their equivalent? Yes indeed! He is the Creator, the Knowing. **82** His only command, when He intends something, is to say to it, 'Be!' and it is. **83** Glory to the One in whose His hand is the kingdom of everything! To Him you will be returned.

37 ❖ The Ones Who Line Up

In the Name of God, the Merciful, the Compassionate

1 By the ones who line up in lines, **2** and the shouters of a shout, **3** and the reciters of a reminder! **4** Surely your God is one, **5** Lord of the heavens and the earth, and of whatever is between them, and Lord of the Easts.

6 Surely We have made the sky of this world appear enticing by means of the splendor of the stars, **7** and (We have made them) a (means of) protection from every rebelling satan. **8** They do not listen to the exalted Assembly, **9** but they are pelted from every side, driven off – for them (there is) punishment forever – **10** except for the one who snatches a word, and then a piercing flame pursues him. **11** So ask them for a pronouncement: 'Are they a stronger creation, or those (others) whom We have created?' Surely We created them from sticky clay.

12 But you are amazed when they ridicule, **13** and, when they are reminded, do not take heed, **14** and, when they see a sign, ridicule, **15** and say, 'This is nothing but clear magic. **16** When we are dead, and turned to dust and bones, shall we indeed be raised up? **17** And our fathers of old (too)?' **18** Say: 'Yes, and you will be humbled.' **19** (For) it will only be a single shout, and suddenly they will see, **20** and say, 'Woe to us! This is the Day of Judgment.' **21** 'This is the Day of Decision, which you called a lie. **22** Gather those who have done evil, and their wives, and what they used to serve, **23** instead of God, and guide them to the path of the Furnace. **24** And stop them (there), (for) they are to be questioned: **25** "What is (the matter) with you (that) you do you not help each other?" **26** No! Today they are resigned.' **27** Some of them will approach others asking each other questions. **28** They will say, 'Surely you used to come to us from the right (side).' **29** They will say, 'No! You were not believers. **30** We had no authority over you. No! You were a people who transgressed insolently. **31** So the word of our Lord has proved true against us. Surely we are indeed tasting (it). **32** We made you err (because) we were in error.' **33** Surely on that Day they will be partners in the punishment. **34** Surely in this way We deal with the sinners.

35 Surely they – when it was said to them, '(There is) no god but God,' they became arrogant, **36** and said, 'Are we to abandon our gods for a possessed poet?' **37** 'No! He has brought the truth and confirmed the envoys. **38** Surely you will indeed taste the painful punishment, **39** and you will not be repaid (for anything) except what you have done.'

The Ones Who Line Up

40 – Except for the devoted servants of God. **41** Those – for them (there will be) a known provision **42** (of) fruits, and they will be honored **43** in Gardens of Bliss, **44** on couches, facing each other, **45** (and) a cup from a flowing spring will be passed around among them – **46** white, delicious to the drinkers, **47** (there is) no ill effect in it, nor do they become drunk from it. **48** With them (there will be maidens) restraining (their) glances, wide-eyed, **49** as if they were hidden eggs.

50 Some of them will approach others asking each other questions. **51** One of them will say, 'Surely I had a comrade, **52** who used to say, "Are you indeed one of the confirmers? **53** When we are dead, and turned to dust and bones, shall we indeed be judged?"' **54** (Another) will say, 'Are you looking (down)?' **55** So he looks (down) and sees him in the midst of the Furnace. **56** He will say, 'By God! You nearly brought me to ruin. **57** Were it not for the blessing of my Lord, I (too) would have been one of those brought forward (to the punishment). **58** So do we not die, **59** except for our first death, and are we not punished? **60** Surely this – it indeed is the great triumph! **61** Let the workers work for something like this!'

62 Is that better as a reception, or the tree of al-Zaqqūm? **63** Surely We have made it a test for the evildoers. **64** It is a tree which comes forth from the root of the Furnace. **65** Its fruits are like the heads of the satans, **66** and they eat from it, and fill their bellies from it. **67** Then on (top of) it they have a drink of boiling (water). **68** Then their return is to the Furnace.

69 Surely they found their fathers astray, **70** and they run in their footsteps. **71** Certainly most of those of old went astray before them, **72** even though We sent warners among them. **73** See how the end was for those who were warned **74** – except for the devoted servants of God.

75 Certainly Noah called on Us, and excellent indeed were the responders! **76** We rescued him and his family from great distress, **77** and We made his descendants – they were the survivors. **78** We left (this blessing) upon him among the later (generations): **79** 'Peace (be) upon Noah among all peoples!' **80** In this way We repay the doers of good. **81** Surely he was one of Our believing servants. **82** Then We drowned the others.

83 Surely Abraham was indeed of his party: **84** When he came to his Lord with a sound heart, **85** when he said to his father and his people, 'What do you serve? **86** (Is it) a lie – gods other than God – you desire? **87** What do you think about the Lord of all peoples?' **88** And he took a look at the stars, **89** and said, 'Surely I am sick.' **90** So they turned away from him, withdrawing. **91** But he turned to their gods, and said, 'Do you not eat? **92** What is (the matter) with you (that) you do not speak?' **93** So he turned on them, striking (them) with the right (hand). **94** Then they came running to him. **95** He said, 'Do you serve what you carve, **96** when God created you and what you make?' **97** They said, 'Build a building for him, and cast him into the blazing (Fire)!' **98** They intended a plot against him, but We brought them down.

99 He said, 'Surely I am going to my Lord. He will guide me. **100** My Lord, grant me one of the righteous.' **101** So We gave him the good news of a forbearing boy. **102** When he had reached the (age of) running with him, he said, 'My son! Surely I saw in a dream that I am going to sacrifice you. So look, what do you think?' He said, 'My father! Do what you are commanded. You will find me, if God pleases, one of the patient.' **103** When they both had submitted, and he had laid him face down, **104** We called out to him, 'Abraham! **105** Now you have confirmed the vision. Surely in this way We repay the doers of good. **106** Surely this – it indeed was the clear test.' **107** And We ransomed him with a great sacrifice, **108** and left (this blessing) on him among the later (generations): **109** 'Peace (be) upon Abraham!' **110** In this way We repay the doers of good. **111** Surely he was one of Our believing servants.

112 And We gave him the good news of Isaac, a prophet, one of the righteous. **113** We blessed him and Isaac, and some of their descendants are doers of good, and some clearly do themselves evil.

114 Certainly We bestowed favor on Moses and Aaron, **115** and We rescued them and their people from the great distress. **116** We helped them, and they were the victors. **117** We gave them both the clarifying Book, **118** and guided them to the straight path, **119** and left (this blessing) on both of them among the later (generations): **120** 'Peace (be) upon Moses and Aaron!' **121** In this way We repay the doers of good. **122** Surely they were two of Our believing servants.

123 Surely Elijah was indeed one of the envoys: **124** When he said to his people, 'Will you not guard (yourselves)? **125** Do you call on Baal, and abandon the best of creators **126** – God – your Lord and the Lord of your fathers of old?' **127** Yet they called him a liar. Surely they will indeed be brought forward (to the punishment) **128** – except for the devoted servants of God. **129** And We left (this blessing) on him among the later (generations): **130** 'Peace (be) upon Elijah!' **131** In this way We repay the doers of good. **132** Surely he was one of Our believing servants.

133 Surely Lot was indeed one of the envoys: **134** When We rescued him and his family – all (of them) – **135** except for an old woman among those who stayed behind. **136** Then We destroyed the others. **137** Surely you indeed pass near them in the morning **138** and in the night. Will you not understand?

139 Surely Jonah was indeed one of the envoys: **140** When he ran away to the loaded ship, **141** and cast lots, but was one of the losers. **142** So the fish swallowed him, seeing that he was to blame. **143** Were it not that he was one of those who glorified (God), **144** he would indeed have remained in its belly until the Day when they are raised up. **145** But We tossed him on the desert (shore) while he was (still) sick, **146** and We caused a gourd tree to grow over him. **147** We sent him to a hundred thousand, or more, **148** and they believed. So We gave them enjoyment (of life) for a time.

149 Ask them for a pronouncement: 'Does your Lord have daughters while they have sons? **150** Or did We create the angels female while they were witnesses?'

The Ones Who Line Up

151 Is it not a fact that out of their own lie they indeed say, **152** 'God has begotten'? Surely they are liars indeed! **153** Has He chosen daughters over sons? **154** What is (the matter) with you? How do you judge? **155** Will you not take heed? **156** Or do you have any clear authority? **157** Bring your Book, if you are truthful.

158 They have fabricated an affiliation between Him and the jinn. Yet certainly the jinn know that they will indeed be brought forward (to the punishment) **159** – glory to God above what they allege! – **160** except for the devoted servants of God.

161 Surely you and what you serve – **162** you will not tempt (anyone to rebellion) against Him, **163** except for the one who is (destined) to burn in the Furnace. **164** (There is) not one of us who does not have an assigned position. **165** Surely we – we indeed are the ones who line up, **166** and surely we – we indeed are the ones who glorify (God).

167 If they were to say, **168** 'If (only) we had a reminder from those of old, **169** we would indeed have been the devoted servants of God.' **170** Yet they have disbelieved in it. Soon they will know! **171** Certainly Our word has (already) gone forth to Our servants, the envoys. **172** Surely they – they indeed are the ones who will be helped. **173** Surely Our army – they indeed are the victors. **174** So turn away from them for a time, **175** and observe them. Soon they will observe! **176** Do they seek to hurry Our punishment? **177** When it comes down in their (own) courtyard, (how) evil the morning will be for those who were warned! **178** So turn from away them for a time, **179** and observe (them). Soon they will observe!

180 Glory to your Lord, Lord of honor, above what they allege! **181** Peace (be) upon the envoys, **182** and praise (be) to God, Lord of all peoples!

38 ✣ ṢĀD

In the Name of God, the Merciful, the Compassionate

1 Ṣād.

By the Qur'ān, containing the Reminder! 2 – No! Those who disbelieve are in false pride and defiance. 3 How many a generation We have destroyed before them! They (all) called out, but there was no time for escape. 4 Yet they are amazed that a warner has come to them from among them. The disbelievers say, 'This (man) is a magician, a liar! 5 Has he made the gods (into) one god? Surely this is an amazing thing indeed.' 6 The assembly of them set out (saying): 'Walk (away), and remain steadfast to your gods. Surely this is a thing to be desired indeed. 7 We have not heard of this in the last creed. This is only a fabrication. 8 Has the Reminder been sent down on him (alone) among us?' No! They are in doubt about My Reminder! No! They have not yet tasted My punishment! 9 Or do they have the storehouses of the mercy of your Lord, the Mighty, the Giver? 10 Or do they have the kingdom of the heavens and the earth, and whatever is between them? Let them ascend on the ropes. 11 An army of the factions will be routed there. 12 Before them the people of Noah called (it) a lie, and 'Ād, and Pharaoh, he of the stakes,[1] 13 and Thamūd, and the people of Lot, and the people of the Grove – those were the factions. 14 Each of them called the messengers liars, and My retribution was justified. 15 What do these (people) expect but a single cry, for which (there will be) no delay.

16 They say, 'Our Lord, hurry our share to us before the Day of Reckoning!' 17 Bear with what they say, and remember Our servant David, (who was) endowed with strength. Surely he turned regularly (in repentance). 18 Surely We subjected the mountains (along) with him to glorify (Us) in the evening and at sunrise, 19 and the birds (too), gathered together, all regularly turning to Him (in praise). 20 We strengthened his kingdom, and gave him wisdom and a decisive word.

21 Has the story of the dispute come to you? When they climbed over the wall of the place of prayer, 22 when they entered upon David, and he was terrified of them, but they said, 'Do not fear! (We are) two disputants: one of us has acted oppressively toward the other. So judge between us in truth, and do not be unjust, and guide us to the right path. 23 Surely this (man) is my brother. He has ninety-nine ewes, and I have (only) one ewe. He said, "Give her into my charge,"

---

1. *he of the stakes*: meaning obscure.

Ṣād

and he overcame me in the argument.' **24** He said,[2] 'Certainly he has done you evil in asking for your ewe (in addition) to his ewes. Surely many (business) partners indeed act oppressively toward one another, except those who believe and do righteous deeds – but few they are.' And David guessed that We had (somehow) tested him, so he asked his Lord for forgiveness, and fell down, bowing, and turned (in repentance). **25** So We forgave him that. Surely he has intimacy indeed with Us, and a good (place of) return.

26 'David! Surely We have made you a ruler on the earth, so judge among the people in truth, and do not follow (vain) desire, or it will lead you astray from the way of God. Surely those who go astray from the way of God – for them (there is) a harsh punishment, because they have forgotten the Day of Reckoning.' **27** We did not create the sky and the earth, and whatever is between them, without purpose. That is the conjecture of those who disbelieve. So woe to those who disbelieve on account of the Fire! **28** Or shall We treat those who believe and do righteous deeds the same as the ones who foment corruption on the earth? Or shall We treat the ones who guard (themselves) the same as the depraved? **29** A blessed Book – We have sent it down to you, so that those with understanding may contemplate its verses and take heed.

30 To David We granted Solomon – an excellent servant he was! Surely he turned regularly (in repentance). **31** When the standing horses were presented before him in the evening, **32** he said, 'Surely I have loved the love of good (things) more than the remembrance of my Lord, until the sun has (now) been hidden by the veil. **33** Return them to me!'[3] Then he began to stroke their legs and necks. **34** Certainly We tested Solomon, and placed on his throne a (mere) image. Then he turned (in repentance). **35** He said, 'My Lord, forgive me, and grant me a kingdom (such as) will not be fitting for anyone after me (to have). Surely You – You are the Giver.' **36** So We subjected the wind to him, to blow gently at his command wherever he decided, **37** and (also) the satans, every builder and diver, **38** and others (as well) bound in chains: **39** 'This is Our gift, so bestow or withhold without reckoning.' **40** Surely he had intimacy indeed with Us, and a good (place of) return.

41 And remember Our servant Job: When he called out to his Lord, 'Surely I – Satan has touched me with weariness and punishment.' **42** 'Stamp with your foot! This (will become) a cool (place for) washing and a drink.' **43** And We granted him his household, and their equivalent with them, as a mercy from Us, and a reminder to those with understanding. **44** 'And take in your hand a bunch, and strike with it, and do not refuse.' Surely We found him patient – an excellent servant he was! Surely he turned regularly (in repentance).

45 And remember Our servants Abraham, Isaac, and Jacob: endowed with strength and vision. **46** Surely We purified them with a pure (thought): remembrance of the Home. **47** Surely with Us they are indeed among the chosen, the good.

---

2. *He said*: David now decides the dispute.
3. *Return them to me*: the meaning of this episode is obscure.

Ṣād

48 And remember Our servants Ishmael, Elisha, and Dhū-l-Kifl: each (of them) was one of the good.

49 This is a Reminder. Surely for the ones who guard (themselves there is) indeed a good (place of) return: **50** Gardens of Eden, (where) the gates are open for them, **51** where they recline, (and) where they call for abundant fruit and drink. **52** With them (are maidens) restraining (their) glances, (all) of the same age. **53** 'This is what you were promised for the Day of Reckoning. **54** Surely this is indeed Our provision – (there is) no end to it. **55** (All) this!'

But surely for the insolent transgressors (there is) indeed an evil (place of) return: **56** Gehenna, (where) they will burn – it is an evil bed! **57** (All) this! So make them taste it – boiling (water) and rotten (food), **58** and other (torments) of (this) kind in pairs. **59** 'This is a crowd rushing in with you – for them (there is) no welcoming. Surely they will burn in the Fire.' **60** They say, 'No! It is you for whom (there is) no welcoming. You sent it forward for us, and it is an evil resting place!' **61** They say, 'Our Lord, whoever sent this forward for us, give him a double punishment in the Fire!' **62** And they say, 'What is (the matter) with us (that) we do not see men (here) whom we used to count among the evil? **63** Did we take them in ridicule? Or has (our) sight turned aside from them?' **64** Surely that is true indeed – the disputing of the companions of the Fire.

65 Say: 'I am only a warner. (There is) no god but God, the One, the Supreme, **66** Lord of the heavens and the earth, and whatever is between them, the Mighty, the Forgiver.'

67 Say: 'It is a great story **68** from which you turn away. **69** I had no knowledge of the exalted Assembly when they disputed. **70** I am only inspired that I am a clear warner.' **71** (Remember) when your Lord said to the angels: 'Surely I am going to create a human being from clay. **72** When I have fashioned him, and breathed some of My spirit into him, fall down before him in prostration.' **73** So the angels prostrated themselves – all of them together **74** – except Iblīs. He became arrogant, and was one of the disbelievers. **75** He said, 'Iblīs! What prevented you from prostrating yourself before what I created with My two hands? Have you become arrogant, or are you one of the exalted?' **76** He said, 'I am better than him. You created me from fire, but You created him from clay.' **77** He said, 'Get out of here! Surely you are accursed! **78** Surely My curse (is going to remain) on you until the Day of Judgment.' **79** He said, 'My Lord, spare me until the Day when they are raised up.' **80** He said, 'Surely you are one of the spared **81** – until the Day of the known time.' **82** He said, 'Then, by Your honor, I shall indeed make them err – all (of them) **83** – except for Your devoted servants among them.' **84** He said, '(This is) the truth, and the truth I say: **85** I shall indeed fill Gehenna with you and those of them who follow you – all (of you)!'

86 Say: 'I do not ask you for any reward for it, nor am I one of the pretenders. **87** It is nothing but a reminder to all peoples. **88** You will indeed know its story after a time.'

39 ✵ The Companies

In the Name of God, the Merciful, the Compassionate

1 (The) sending down of the Book is from God, the Mighty, the Wise. **2** Surely We have sent down to you the Book with the truth. So serve God, devoting (your) religion to Him.

3 Is it not (a fact) that pure religion is for God (alone)? But those who take allies instead of Him – 'We only serve them so that they may bring us near to God in intimacy' – surely God will judge between them concerning their differences. Surely God does not guide anyone who is a liar (or) ungrateful. **4** If God wanted to take a son, He would indeed have chosen whatever He pleased from what He created. Glory to Him! He is God, the One, the Supreme.

5 He created the heavens and the earth in truth. He wraps the night around the day, and wraps the day around the night, and He has subjected the sun and the moon, each running (its course) for an appointed time. Is He not the Mighty, the Forgiver? **6** He created you from one person, (and) then made from him his wife, and He sent down to you four kinds of livestock. He creates you in the bellies of your mothers, creation after creation, in three darknesses. That is God, your Lord. To Him (belongs) the kingdom. (There is) no god but Him. How (is it that) you are turned away? **7** If you are ungrateful – surely God is wealthy (enough) without you. Yet He does not approve ingratitude in His servants. If you are thankful, He approves it in you. No one bearing a burden bears the burden of another. Then to your Lord is your return, and He will inform you about what you have done. Surely he knows what is in the hearts.

8 When hardship touches a person, he calls on his Lord, turning to Him (in repentance). Then, when He bestows blessing on him from Himself, he forgets what he was calling to Him for before, and sets up rivals to God to lead (people) astray from His way. Say: 'Enjoy (life) in your disbelief for a little. Surely you will be one of the companions of the Fire.' **9** Or is he who is obedient in the hours of the night, prostrating himself and standing, bewaring the Hereafter and hoping for the mercy of his Lord [. . .]?[1] Say: 'Are those who know and those who do not know equal?' Only those with understanding take heed.

10 Say: 'My servants who believe! Guard (yourselves) against your Lord. For those who do good in this present world, (there is) good, and God's earth is wide.

---

1. [. . .]?: the reader must supply 'like the one who does not do these things.'

The Companies

Surely the patient will be paid their reward in full without reckoning.' **11** Say: 'I have been commanded to serve God, devoting (my) religion to Him, **12** and I have been commanded to be the first of those who submit.' **13** Say: 'Surely I fear, if I disobey my Lord, the punishment of a great Day.' **14** Say: 'I serve God, devoting my religion to Him. **15** So serve whatever you please instead of Him.' Say: 'Surely the losers are those who lose their (own) selves and their families on the Day of Resurrection. Is that not – it is the clearest loss! **16** For them (there are) coverings of fire above them, and coverings (of fire) below them. That is what God frightens His servants with: "My servants! Guard (yourselves) against Me!"'

17 Those who avoid al-Ṭāghūt[2] – for fear that they serve it – and turn to God (in repentance) – for them (there is) good news. So give good news to My servants, **18** those who listen to the word and follow the best of it. Those are the ones whom God has guided, and those – they are those with understanding. **19** So is the one against whom the word of punishment is proved true – will you save the one who is (already) in the Fire? **20** But those who guard (themselves) against their Lord – for them (there will be) exalted rooms, above which exalted rooms are built, (and) below which rivers flow – the promise of God! God will not break the appointment.

21 Do you not see that God has sent down water from the sky, and put it into the earth as springs, (and) then by means of it He brings forth crops of various colors, (and) then they wither, and you see them turning yellow, (and) then He makes them broken debris? Surely in that is a reminder indeed to those with understanding.

22 Is the one whose heart God has expanded to Islam, and so he (depends) on a light from his Lord [. . .]?[3] Woe to those whose hearts are hardened against the remembrance of God! Those are clearly astray.

23 God has sent down the best proclamation – a Book, resembling (itself), oft-repeating. The skins of those who fear their Lord shiver from it. Then their skins and their hearts soften to the remembrance of God. That is the guidance of God. He guides by means of it whomever He pleases, but whoever God leads astray has no guide.

24 Is he who guards (himself) with his face against the evil of the punishment on the Day of Resurrection [. . .]?[4] But it will be said to the evildoers, 'Taste what you have earned!' **25** Those who were before them called (it) a lie, and the punishment came upon them from where they did not realize (it would). **26** So God made them taste disgrace in this present life, but the punishment of the Hereafter is indeed greater, if (only) they knew.

---

2. *al-Ṭāghūt*: meaning uncertain; perhaps 'other gods' or 'idols' (cf. Q2.256; 16.36), but elsewhere another name for Satan (Q4.60, 76).
3. [. . .]?: the reader must supply 'like the hard-hearted.'
4. [. . .]?: the reader must supply 'like the one who does not guard (himself).'

The Companies

27 Certainly We have struck in this Qur'ān every (kind of) parable for the people, so that they may take heed **28** – an Arabic Qur'ān, without any crookedness, so that they may guard (themselves). **29** God has struck a parable: a man concerning whom partners are quarreling, and a man belonging to one man. Are they both equal in comparison? Praise (be) to God! No! But most of them do not know (it).

30 Surely you are mortal, and surely they are mortal, **31** and surely on the Day of Resurrection you[5] will dispute in the presence of your Lord. **32** Who is more evil than the one who lies against God, and calls the truth a lie when it comes to him? Is there not a dwelling place in Gehenna for the disbelievers? **33** But the one who brings the truth and confirms it, those – they are the ones who guard (themselves). **34** They will have whatever they please with their Lord. That is the payment of the doers of good **35** – so that God may absolve them of the worst of what they have done, and pay them their reward for the best of what they have done. **36** Is God not sufficient for His servant, when they frighten you with (gods) other than Him? Whoever God leads astray has no guide, **37** but whoever God guides – no one (will) lead him astray. Is God not mighty, a taker of vengeance?

38 If indeed you ask them, 'Who created the heavens and the earth?,' they will indeed say, 'God.' Say: 'Do you see what you call on instead of God? If God intends any harm for me, will they be removers of His harm? Or if He intends any mercy for me, will they be withholders of His mercy?' Say: 'God is enough for me. In Him the trusting put their trust.' **39** Say: 'My people! Do as you are able. Surely I am going to do (what I can). Soon you will know **40** on whom punishment will come, disgracing him. On him a lasting punishment will descend.'

41 Surely We have sent down on you the Book for the people with the truth. Whoever is (rightly) guided, is guided only for himself, and whoever goes astray, goes astray only against himself. You are not a guardian over them.

42 God takes the self at the time of its death, and that which has not died in its sleep, and He retains the one for whom He has decreed death, but sends back the other until an appointed time. Surely in that are signs indeed for a people who reflect.

43 Or have they taken intercessors instead of God? Say: 'Even if they possess nothing and do not understand?' **44** Say: 'Intercession (belongs) to God altogether. To Him (belongs) the kingdom of the heavens and the earth. Then to Him you will be returned.'

45 When God is mentioned alone, the hearts of those who do not believe in the Hereafter shrink, but when those (gods) are mentioned instead of Him, suddenly they welcome the good news. **46** Say: 'God! Creator of the heavens and the earth, Knower of the unseen and the seen, You will judge between your servants concerning their differences.' **47** (Even) if those who have done evil had what is on the earth – all (of it) – and as much again, they would indeed (try to) ransom

---

5. *you*: plur.

(themselves) with it from the evil of the punishment on the Day of Resurrection. But what they were not counting on will become apparent to them from God, **48** and the evils of what they have earned will become apparent to them, and what they were mocking will overwhelm them.

49 When hardship touches a person, he calls on Us. Then, when We bestow blessing on him from Us, he says, 'I have only been given it because of knowledge.' No! It is a test, but most of them do not know (it). **50** Those who were before them said it (too), but what they earned was of no use to them, **51** and the evils of what they earned smote them. And those of these (people) who have done evil – the evils of what they have earned will smite them (too), and they will not be able to escape. **52** Do they not know that God extends (His) provision to whomever He pleases, and restricts (it)? Surely in that are signs indeed for a people who believe.

53 Say: 'My servants who have acted wantonly against themselves! Do not despair of the mercy of God. Surely God forgives sins – all (of them). Surely He – He is the Forgiving, the Compassionate. **54** Turn to your Lord (in repentance), and submit to Him, before the punishment comes upon you, (for) then you will not be helped. **55** Follow the best of what has been sent down to you from your Lord, before the punishment comes upon you unexpectedly, when you do not realize (it)' **56** – in case anyone (should) say, 'Alas for me, in regard to what I neglected concerning God, for I was indeed one of the scoffers!' **57** Or say, 'If only God had guided me, I would indeed have been one of those who guard (themselves)!' **58** Or say, when he sees the punishment, 'If only I had (another) turn, and (could) be one of the doers of good!' **59** 'Yes indeed! My signs did come to you, but you called them a lie, and were arrogant, and were one of the disbelievers.'

60 On the Day of Resurrection you will see those who lied against God, their faces blackened. Is there not a dwelling place in Gehenna for the arrogant? **61** But God will rescue those who guarded (themselves) in their (place of) safety. Evil will not touch them, nor will they sorrow. **62** God is the Creator of everything. He is guardian over everything. **63** To Him (belong) the keys of the heavens and the earth. Those who disbelieve in the signs of God, those – they are the losers.

64 Say: 'Do you command me to serve (anyone) other than God, you ignorant ones?' **65** You have been inspired, and those who were before you: 'If indeed you associate, your deed(s) will indeed come to nothing, and you will indeed be one of the losers.' **66** No! Serve God, and be one of the thankful.

67 They have not measured God (with) due measure, when the entire earth will be His handful on the Day of Resurrection, and the heavens will be rolled up in His right (hand). Glory to Him! He is exalted above what they associate. **68** There will be a blast on the trumpet, and whoever is in the heavens and whoever is on the earth will be thunderstruck, except for those whom God pleases. Then there will be another blast on it, and suddenly they will stand up, looking around. **69** And the earth will shine with the light of its Lord, and the Book will be laid down,

The Companies

and the prophets and witnesses will be brought, and it will be decided between them in truth – and they will not be done evil. **70** Each one will be paid in full for what he has done, (for) He knows what they do.

71 Those who disbelieved will be driven in companies into Gehenna, until, when they have come to it, its gates will be opened and its keepers will say to them: 'Did messengers not come to you from among you, reciting to you the signs of your Lord and warning you about the meeting of this Day of yours?' They will say, 'Yes indeed! But the word of punishment has proved true against the disbelievers.' **72** It will be said, 'Enter the gates of Gehenna, there to remain.' Evil is the dwelling place of the arrogant!

73 But those who guarded (themselves) against their Lord will be driven in companies into the Garden, until, when they have come to it, and its gates will be opened, and its keepers will say to them: 'Peace (be) upon you! You have been good, so enter it, to remain (there).' **74** They will say, 'Praise (be) to God, who has fulfilled His promise to us, and has caused us to inherit the earth! We (may) settle in the Garden wherever we please.' Excellent is the reward of the doers!

75 And you will see the angels completely surrounding the throne, glorifying their Lord with praise. It will be decided between them in truth, and it will be said, 'Praise (be) to God, Lord of all peoples!'

40 ✤ Forgiver

In the Name of God, the Merciful, the Compassionate

1 Hā' Mīm.

2 (The) sending down of the Book is from God, the Mighty, the Knowing, 3 Forgiver of sin and Accepter of repentance, harsh in retribution, full of forbearance. (There is) no god but Him. To Him is the (final) destination.

4 No one disputes about the signs of God, except those who disbelieve. Do not let their comings and goings in the lands deceive you. 5 The people of Noah before them (also) called (it) a lie, and the factions after them, and each community was determined to seize its messenger, and disputed by means of falsehood to refute the truth. So I seized them – and how was My retribution? 6 In this way the word of your Lord has proved true against those who disbelieve: 'They are the companions of the Fire.'

7 Those who bear the throne, and those around it, glorify their Lord with praise, and believe in Him, and they ask forgiveness for those who believe: 'Our Lord, You comprehend everything in mercy and knowledge, so forgive those who turn (in repentance) and follow Your way. Guard them against the punishment of the Furnace, 8 Our Lord, and cause them to enter the Gardens of Eden, which You have promised them – and anyone who was righteous among their fathers, and their wives, and their descendants. Surely You – You are the Mighty, the Wise. 9 And guard them against evil deeds. Whoever You guard against evil deeds on that Day, You have had compassion on him. That is the great triumph!'

10 Surely those who disbelieved will be called to: 'God's hatred is indeed greater than your hatred of one another, when you were called to belief and you disbelieved.' 11 They will say, 'Our Lord, You have caused us to die twice, and You have given us life twice. (Now) we confess our sins. (Is there) any way to get out?' 12 That is because, when God was called on alone, you disbelieved, but if (another) was associated with Him, you believed. Judgment (belongs) to God, the Most High, the Great.

13 He (it is) who shows you His signs, and sends down provision for you from the sky, but no one takes heed except the one who turns (in repentance). 14 So call on God, devoting (your) religion to Him, (even) though the disbelievers dislike (it).

15 Exalter of ranks, Holder of the throne, He casts the spirit of His command on whomever He pleases of His servants, to warn of the Day of Meeting. 16 On the

Day when they go forth, nothing of theirs will be hidden from God. 'To whom (belongs) the kingdom today?' 'To God, the One, the Supreme! **17** Today each person will be repaid for what he has earned. (There will be) no evil (done) today. Surely God is quick at the reckoning.'

18 Warn them of the Day of the Impending, when (their) hearts will be in (their) throats, choking (them). The evildoers will not have any loyal friend or intercessor (who) will be obeyed. **19** He knows the treachery of the eyes and what the hearts hide. **20** God will decide in truth, while those they call on instead of Him will not decide at all. Surely God – He is the Hearing, the Seeing.

21 Have they not traveled on the earth and seen how the end was for those who were before them? They were stronger than them in power, and in the traces (they left behind) on the earth. Yet God seized them in their sins, and they had no defender against God. **22** That was because they – (when) their messengers came to them with the clear signs – they disbelieved. So God seized them. Surely He is strong, harsh in retribution.

23 Certainly We sent Moses with Our signs and clear authority **24** to Pharaoh, and Haman, and Qārūn, but they said, 'A magician, a liar!' **25** When he brought them the truth from Us, they said, 'Kill the sons of those who believe with him, and keep their women alive.' Yet the plot of the disbelievers always goes astray. **26** Pharaoh said, 'Let me kill Moses, and let him call on his Lord. Surely I fear that he will change your religion, or that he will cause corruption to appear on the earth.' **27** Moses said, 'I take refuge with my Lord and your Lord from every arrogant one (who) does not believe in the Day of Reckoning.'

28 A (certain) man, a believer from the house of Pharaoh, (who) concealed his belief, said, 'Will you kill a man because he says, "My Lord is God," when he has brought you the clear signs from your Lord? If he is a liar, his lie is on him, but if he is truthful, some of what he promises you will smite you. Surely God does not guide anyone who is wanton (and) a liar. **29** My people! Today the kingdom (belongs) to you (who) prevail on the earth, but who will help us against the violence of God, if it comes upon us?'

Pharaoh said, 'I only show you what I see, and I only guide you to the right way.' **30** But the one who believed said, 'My people! Surely I fear for you something like the Day of the Factions, **31** like the case of the people of Noah, and 'Ād, and Thamūd, and those who (came) after them. Yet God does not intend any evil to (His) servants. **32** My people! Surely I fear for you the Day of Calling, **33** the Day when you will turn back, retreating, having no protector from God. Whoever God leads astray has no guide. **34** Certainly Joseph brought you the clear signs before, but you did not stop doubting about what he brought you, until, when he perished, you said, "God will never raise up a messenger after him." In this way God leads astray anyone who is wanton (and) a doubter.'

35 Those who dispute about the signs of God, without any authority having come to them – (that) is a very hateful thing in the sight of God and those who believe. In this way God sets a seal on the heart of every arrogant tyrant.

36 Pharaoh said, 'Haman! Build a tower for me, so that I may reach the ropes, 37 the ropes of the heavens, and look upon the god of Moses. Surely I think he is a liar indeed.' In this way the evil of his deed was made to appear enticing to Pharaoh, and he was kept from the way. But the plot of Pharaoh only (came) to ruin.

38 Certainly the one who believed said, 'My people! Follow me, and I shall guide you to the right way. 39 My people! Surely this present life is enjoyment, but surely the Hereafter – it is the permanent Home. 40 Whoever does an evil deed will only be repaid the equal of it, but whoever does a righteous deed, whether male or female – and is a believer – those will enter the Garden, where they will be provided for without reckoning. 41 My people! Why is it that I call you to salvation, but you call me to the Fire. 42 You call me to disbelieve in God, and to associate with Him what I have no knowledge of, but I call you to the Mighty, the Forgiving. 43 (There is) no doubt that what you call me to has no calling to in this world or in the Hereafter, and that our return is to God, and that the wanton – they will be the companions of the Fire. 44 You will remember what I say to you, and (now) I commit my affair to God. Surely God sees His servants.' 45 So God guarded him against the evils of what they devised, and the evil punishment overwhelmed the house of Pharaoh. 46 The Fire – they will be presented to it morning and evening. On the Day when the Hour strikes: 'Cause the house of Pharaoh to enter the harshest punishment!'

47 When they argue with each other in the Fire, and the weak say to those who were arrogant: 'Surely we were your followers, so are you going relieve us (now) of any portion of the Fire?' 48 Those who were arrogant will say, 'Surely we are all in it. Surely God has already rendered judgment among (His) servants.' 49 Those who are in the Fire will say to the keepers of Gehenna, 'Call on your Lord to lighten for us one day of the punishment!' 50 They will say, 'Did your messengers not bring you the clear signs?' They will say, 'Yes indeed!' They will say, 'Then call!' But the call of the disbelievers only goes astray.

51 Surely We do indeed help Our messengers and those who believe, (both) in this present life and on the Day when the witnesses arise 52 – the Day when their excuse will not benefit the evildoers. For them (there will be) the curse, and for them (there will be) the evil home. 53 Certainly We gave Moses the guidance, and caused the Sons of Israel to inherit the Book, 54 as a guidance and reminder to those with understanding. 55 So be patient![1] Surely the promise of God is true. Ask forgiveness for your sin, and glorify your Lord with praise in the evening and the morning.

---

1. *be patient*: sing. imperative (as are the two following).

Forgiver

56 Surely those who dispute about the signs of God, without any authority having come to them – they have their minds set only on greatness, but they will not reach it. So take refuge in God![2] Surely He – He is the Hearing, the Seeing. **57** Indeed the creation of the heavens and earth is greater than the creation of the people, but most of the people do not know (it).

58 The blind and the sighted are not equal, nor are those who believe and do deeds of righteousness and the evildoer. Little do you take heed! **59** Surely the Hour is coming indeed – (there is) no doubt about it – but most of the people do not believe. **60** Your Lord has said, 'Call on Me! I shall respond to you. Surely those who are too proud to serve Me will enter Gehenna humbled.'

61 (It is) God who made the night for you to rest in, and the day to see. Surely God is indeed full of favor to the people, but most of the people are not thankful (for it). **62** That is God, your Lord, Creator of everything. (There is) no god but Him. How are you (so) deluded? **63** In this way those who denied the signs of God were (also) deluded. **64** (It is) God who made the earth a dwelling place for you, and the sky a dome. He fashioned you, and made your forms well, and provided you with good things. That is God, your Lord. Blessed (be) God, Lord of all peoples! **65** He is the Living One. (There is) no god but Him. Call on Him, devoting (your) religion to Him. Praise (be) to God, Lord of all peoples!

66 Say: 'I am forbidden to serve those whom you call on, instead of God, when the clear signs have come to me from my Lord, and I am commanded to submit to the Lord of all peoples.' **67** He (it is) who created you from dust, then from a drop, then from a clot, then He brings you forth as children, then (He provides for you) so that you may reach your maturity, then that you may become old men – though among you (there is) one who is taken before (this) – and that you may reach an appointed time, and that you may understand. **68** He (it is) who gives life and causes death, and when He decrees something, He simply says to it, 'Be!' and it is.

69 Do you not see those who dispute about the signs of God? How they are turned away? **70** – Those who call the Book a lie and what We sent Our messengers with? Soon they will know! **71** – When (there are) chains on their necks, and they are dragged (by) chains **72** into the boiling (water), (and) then they are poured into the Fire. **73** Then it will be said to them, 'Where is what you used to associate, **74** instead of God?' They will say, 'They have abandoned us. No! We were not calling on anything before!' In this way God leads the disbelievers astray. **75** 'That is because you gloated on the earth without any right, and because you were jubilant. **76** Enter the gates of Gehenna, there to remain.' Evil is the dwelling place of the arrogant!

77 So be patient! Surely the promise of God is true. Whether We show you some of that which We promise them, or take you, to Us they will be returned. **78** Certainly We sent messengers before you: some of whom We have recounted to you,

---

2. *take refuge* ... : sing. imperative.

and some of whom We have not recounted to you. But it was not for any messenger to bring a sign, except by the permission of God. When the command of God comes, it will be decided in truth, and the perpetrators of falsehood will lose.

79 (It is) God who made the livestock for you, for you to ride some of them and some of them to eat 80 – and (there are other) benefits for you in them – and for you to reach any place you set your mind on, and on them, and on the ship (as well), you are carried. 81 He shows you His signs – so which of the signs of God do you reject?

82 Have they not traveled on the earth and seen how the end was for those who were before them? They were more numerous than them, and stronger in power, and in the traces (they left behind) on the earth. Yet what they earned was of no use to them. 83 When their messengers brought them the clear signs, they gloated over what knowledge they (already) had, and what they were mocking overwhelmed them. 84 Then, when they saw Our violence, they said, 'We believe in God alone, and we disbelieve in what we were associating (with Him).' 85 But their belief did not benefit them when they saw Our violence – the customary way of God, which has already occurred in the past concerning His servants – and then the disbelievers were lost.

41 ❖ Made Distinct

In the Name of God, the Merciful, the Compassionate

1 Ḥā Mīm.

2 A sending down from the Merciful, the Compassionate. **3** A Book – its verses made distinct – an Arabic Qur'ān for a people who know.

4 (He is) a bringer of good news and a warner. But most of them have turned away, and they do not hear. **5** They say, 'Our hearts are covered from what you call us to, and (there is) a heaviness in our ears, and between us and you (there is) a veil. So do (as you are able). Surely we are going to do (what we can).' **6** Say: 'I am only a human being like you. I am inspired that your God is one God. So go straight with Him, and ask forgiveness from Him. But woe to the idolaters, **7** who do not give the alms, and (who) are disbelievers in the Hereafter! **8** Surely those who believe and do righteous deeds – for them (there is) a reward without end.'

9 Say: 'Do you indeed disbelieve in the One who created the earth in two days, and do you set up rivals to Him? That is the Lord of all peoples. **10** He placed on it firm mountains (towering) above it, and blessed it, and decreed for it its (various) foods in four days, equal to the ones who ask. **11** Then He mounted (upward) to the sky, while it was (still) smoke, and said to it and to the earth, "Come, both of you, willingly or unwillingly!" They both said, "We come willingly." **12** He finished them (as) seven heavens in two days, and inspired each heaven (with) its affair. And We adorned the sky of this world with lamps, and (made them) a protection. That is the decree of the Mighty, the Knowing.'

13 If they turn away, say: 'I warn you of a thunderbolt like the thunderbolt of 'Ād and Thamūd.' **14** When the messengers came to them from before them and from behind them (saying): 'Do not serve (anyone) but God,' they said, 'If our Lord had (so) pleased, He would indeed have sent down angels. Surely we are disbelievers in what you are sent with.' **15** As for 'Ād, they became arrogant on the earth without any right, and said, 'Who is stronger than us in power?' Did they not see that God, who created them, was stronger than them in power? They denied Our signs. **16** So We sent a furious wind against them in the days of calamity, so that We might make them taste the punishment of disgrace in this present life. But the punishment of the Hereafter is indeed more disgraceful, and they will not be helped. **17** As for Thamūd, We guided them, but they preferred blindness over the guidance. So the thunderbolt of the punishment of humiliation took them for what they had earned. **18** But We rescued those who believed and guarded (themselves).

19 On the Day when the enemies of God are gathered to the Fire, and they are arranged (in rows) **20** – until, when they have come to it, their hearing and their sight and their skins will bear witness against them about what they have done, **21** and they will say to their skins, 'Why did you bear witness against us?' They will say, 'God, who gave speech to everything, has given us speech. He created you the first time, and to Him you are (now) returned. **22** You did not protect yourselves against your hearing and your sight and your skins bearing witness against you. You thought that God would not know much of what you had done. **23** And that – the thought you thought about your Lord – has brought you to ruin. (Now) you are among the losers.'

24 If they persist, the Fire will be a dwelling place for them, and if they ask to make amends, they will not be among the ones allowed to make amends. **25** We have allotted to them comrades, and they have made what is before them and behind them appear enticing to them. The word about the communities of jinn and humans (which) have passed away before them has proved true against them (as well). Surely they were losers.

26 Those who disbelieve say, 'Do not listen to this Qur'ān, but talk frivolously about it, so that you may overcome (them).' **27** We shall indeed make those who disbelieve taste a harsh punishment, and We shall indeed repay them for the worst of what they have done. **28** That is the payment of the enemies of God – the Fire – where they will have the Home of Eternity as payment for their having denied Our signs.

29 Those who disbelieve (will) say, 'Our Lord, show us those of the jinn and humans who led us astray. We shall place them beneath our feet, so that they may be among the lowest.' **30** Surely those who have said, 'Our Lord is God,' (and) then have gone straight – the angels will come down on them (saying): 'Do not fear, and do not sorrow, but welcome the good news of the Garden which you were promised. **31** We are your allies in this present life and in the Hereafter, where you will have whatever you desire, whatever you call for **32** – a reception from One forgiving, compassionate.'

33 Who is better in speech than the one who calls (people) to God, and does righteousness, and says, 'Surely I am one of those who submit'? **34** The good deed and the evil deed are not equal. Repel (evil) with that which is better, and suddenly the one with whom (there was) enmity between you and him (will behave) as if he were an ally. **35** Yet no one will receive it except those who are patient, and no one will receive it except one who possesses great good luck. **36** If any provocation from Satan provokes you, take refuge with God. Surely He – He is the Hearing, the Knowing.

37 Among His signs are the night and the day, and the sun and the moon. Do not prostrate yourselves before the sun or before the moon, but prostrate yourselves before God, who created them, if you serve Him. **38** If they are (too) proud, those who are in the presence of your Lord glorify Him by night and day, and do not become tired. **39** (Another) of His signs is that you see the earth barren, (and) then, when We send down water on it, it stirs and swells. Surely the One who gives it life is indeed the giver of life to the dead. Surely He is powerful over everything. **40** Surely those who pervert Our signs are not hidden from Us. Is the one who is cast into the Fire better, or the one who comes (out) secure on the Day of Resurrection? Do whatever you please. Surely He sees what you do.

41 Surely those who disbelieve in the Reminder when it comes to them – surely it is a mighty Book indeed! **42** Falsehood does not come to it, (either) from before it or from behind it. (It is) a sending down from One wise, praiseworthy. **43** Nothing is said to you except what has already been said to the messengers before you. Surely your Lord is indeed full of forgiveness, but (also) full of painful retribution. **44** If We had made it a foreign Qur'ān, they would indeed have said, 'Why are its signs not made distinct? Foreign and Arabic?' Say: 'It is a guidance and healing for those who believe, but those who do not believe – (there is) a heaviness in their ears, and for them it is a blindness. Those – (it is as if) they are being called from a place far away.'

45 Certainly We gave Moses the Book, and then differences arose about it. Were it not for a preceding word from your Lord, it would indeed have been decided between them. Surely they are in grave doubt indeed about it.

46 Whoever does righteousness, it is for himself, and whoever does evil, it is (likewise) against himself. Your Lord is not an evildoer to (His) servants.

47 Knowledge of the Hour is reserved for Him. No fruit comes forth from its sheath, and no female conceives or delivers, except with His knowledge. On the Day when He will call to them, 'Where are My associates?,' they will say, 'We proclaim to You: (there is) no witness among us.' **48** What they called on before will abandon them, and they will know (that there is) no place of escape for them.

49 The human does not tire of calling for good, but if evil touches him, he is in despair (and) downcast. **50** If indeed We give him a taste of mercy from Us, after hardship has touched him, he will indeed say, 'This is mine! I do not think the Hour is coming. If indeed I am returned to my Lord, surely I shall have the best (reward) indeed with Him.' We shall indeed inform those who disbelieve about what they have done, and indeed make them taste a stern punishment. **51** When We bless a person, he turns away and distances himself, but when evil touches them, he is full of long prayers.

52 Say: 'Do you see? If it is from God, and you disbelieve in it – who is farther astray than the one who is in extreme defiance?'

53 We shall show them Our signs in the skies and in themselves, until it becomes clear to them that it is the truth. Is it not sufficient in (regard to) your Lord that He is a witness over everything? **54** Is it not a fact that they are in doubt about the meeting with their Lord? Is it not a fact that He encompasses everything?

42 ❖ Consultation

In the Name of God, the Merciful, the Compassionate

1 Hā Mīm. 2 'Ayn Sīn Qāf.

3 In this way He inspires you, and those who were before you – God, the Mighty, the Wise. 4 To Him (belongs) whatever is in the heavens and whatever is on the earth. He is the Most High, the Almighty. 5 The heavens are nearly torn apart from above, when the angels glorify their Lord with praise, and ask forgiveness for those on the earth. Is it not a fact that God – He is the Forgiving, the Compassionate? 6 Those who have taken allies other than Him – God is watcher over them. You are not a guardian over them.

7 In this way We have inspired you (with) an Arabic Qur'ān, so that you may warn the Mother of Towns and those around it, and so that you may warn of the Day of Gathering – (there is) no doubt about it – (one) group in the Garden, and (another) group in the blazing (Fire). 8 If God had (so) pleased, He would indeed have made them one community. But He causes whomever He pleases to enter into His mercy. The evildoers will have no ally and no helper.

9 Or have they taken allies other than Him? God – He is the (true) Ally. He gives the dead life. He is powerful over everything. 10 Whatever you differ about, judgment of it (belongs) to God. That is God, my Lord. In Him I have put my trust, and to Him I turn (in repentance). 11 (He is) the Creator of the heavens and the earth. He has made pairs for you from yourselves, and pairs (also) from the livestock. He scatters you by this means. There is nothing like Him. He is the Hearing, the Seeing. 12 To Him (belong) the keys of the heavens and the earth. He extends (His) provision to whomever He pleases, and restricts (it). Surely He has knowledge of everything.

13 He has instituted for you from the religion what He charged Noah with, and that which We have inspired you (with), and what We charged Abraham, and Moses, and Jesus with: 'Observe the religion, and do not become divided in it.' What you call them to is hard on the idolaters. God chooses for Himself whomever He pleases, and He guides to Himself whoever turns (to Him in repentance). 14 They did not become divided until after the knowledge had come to them, (because of) envy among themselves. Were it not for a preceding word from your Lord, until an appointed time, it would indeed have been decided between them. Surely those who inherited the Book after them are in grave doubt indeed about it. 15 So call (them) to that, and go straight as you have been commanded, and do not follow

their (vain) desires, but say: 'I believe in whatever Book God has sent down, and I have been commanded to act fairly among you. God is our Lord and your Lord. To us our deeds and to you your deeds. (There is) no argument between us and you. God will gather us together. To Him is the (final) destination.'

16 Those who (still) argue about God, after whatever response has been made to Him – their argument is refuted in the sight of their Lord. Anger (will fall) on them, and for them (there will be) a harsh punishment. **17** (It is) God who has sent down the Book with the truth, and (also) the scale. What will make you know? Perhaps the Hour is near. **18** Those who do not believe in it seek to hurry it, but those who believe in it are apprehensive about it, and know that it is the truth. Is it not a fact that those who are in doubt about the Hour are far astray?

19 God is astute with His servants, providing for whomever He pleases. He is the Strong, the Mighty.

20 Whoever desires the harvest of the Hereafter – We shall give him increase in his harvest, and whoever desires the harvest of this world – We shall give him some of it, but he will not have any portion in the Hereafter. **21** Or do they have associates who have instituted for them from the religion what God has not given permission for? Were it not for a decisive word, it would indeed have been decided between them. Surely the evildoers – for them (there is) a painful punishment. **22** You will see the evildoers apprehensive about what they have earned, when it falls on them, while those who believe and do righteous deeds are in meadows of the Gardens. They will have whatever they please in the presence of their Lord. That is the great favor!

23 That is the good news which God gives to His servants who believe and do righteous deeds. Say: 'I do not ask you for any reward for it, except love for family.' Whoever acquires a good (deed), We shall increase the good for him in it. Surely God is forgiving, thankful.

24 Or do they say, 'He has forged a lie against God?' If God pleases, He will set a seal on your heart, and God will blot out falsehood and verify the truth by His words. Surely He knows what is in the hearts.

25 He (it is) who accepts repentance from His servants and pardons evil deeds. He knows what you do.

26 He responds to those who believe and do righteous deeds, and gives them increase from His favor. But the disbelievers – for them (there is) a harsh punishment.

27 If God were to extend (His) provision to His servants, they would indeed act oppressively on the earth, but He sends down in measure whatever He pleases. Surely He is aware of His servants (and) sees (them).

28 He (it is) who sends down the rain after they have despaired, and displays His mercy. He is the Ally, the Praiseworthy.

29 Among His signs are the creation of the heavens and the earth, and the creatures He has scattered in both of them. He has power over gathering them

Consultation

whenever He pleases. **30** Whatever smiting may smite you is because of what your (own) hands have earned – yet He pardons much. **31** You cannot escape (Him) on the earth, and you have no ally and no helper other than God.

32 Among His signs are the (ships) running on the sea, like landmarks. **33** If He pleases, He stills the wind and they remain motionless on its surface. Surely in that are signs indeed for every patient (and) thankful one. **34** Or He wrecks them for what they have earned – yet He pardons much – **35** and (it is so that)[1] He may know those who dispute about Our signs. For them (there is) no place of escape.

36 Whatever things you have been given are (only) the enjoyment of this present life, but what is with God is better and more lasting for those who believe and put their trust in their Lord **37** – and (also for) those who avoid great sins and immoral deeds, and when they are angry, they forgive, **38** and those who respond to their Lord and observe the prayer, and their affair (is a matter of) consultation among themselves, and they contribute from what We have provided them, **39** and those who, when envy smites them, defend themselves (against it). **40** (The) payment for an evil deed is an evil like it, but whoever pardons and sets (things) right – his reward (depends) on God. Surely He does not love the evildoers. **41** Whoever indeed defends himself after he has suffered evil, those – against them (there is) no way. **42** The way is only open against those who do the people evil, and act oppressively on the earth without any right. Those – for them (there is) a painful punishment. **43** But whoever indeed is patient and forgives – surely that indeed is one of the determining factors in (all) affairs.

44 Whoever God leads astray has no ally after Him, and you will see the evildoers, when they see the punishment, saying, '(Is there) any way to return?' **45** You will see them presented to it, humbled by the disgrace, looking with furtive glance(s). And those who believe will say, 'Surely the losers are those who have lost their (own) selves and their families on the Day of Resurrection.' Is it not a fact that the evildoers (will remain) in lasting punishment? **46** They will have no allies to help them, other than God, and whoever God leads astray has no way.

47 Respond to your Lord, before a Day comes from God which cannot be turned back. You will not have any shelter on that Day, nor any denial (of what you have done). **48** If they turn away – We have not sent you as a watcher over them. Nothing is (dependent) on you except the delivery (of the message). Surely We – when We give a person a taste of mercy from Us, he gloats about it, but if some evil smites them because of what their (own) hands have sent forward – surely the human is ungrateful.

49 To God (belongs) the kingdom of the heavens and the earth. He creates whatever He pleases. He grants females to whomever He pleases, and He grants males to whomever He pleases, **50** or He pairs them males and females. He makes barren whomever He pleases. Surely He is knowing, powerful.

---

1. *and (it is so that)* ... : the grammatical connection with what precedes is problematic.

Consultation

51 It is not (fitting) for any human being that God should speak to him, except (by) inspiration, or from behind a veil, or (that) He should send a messenger and he inspire by His permission whatever He pleases. Surely He is most high, wise. **52** In this way We have inspired you (with) a spirit of Our command. You did not know what the Book was, nor (what) belief (was), but We have made it a light by means of which We guide whomever We please of Our servants. Surely you will guide (people) to a straight path, **53** the path of God, the One to whom (belongs) whatever is in the heavens and whatever is on the earth. Is it not a fact that all affairs are returned to God?

43 ✺ Decoration

In the Name of God, the Merciful, the Compassionate

1 Ḥā Mīm.

2 By the clear Book! 3 Surely We have made it an Arabic Qur'ān, so that you[1] may understand. 4 And surely it is in the mother of the Book, with Us, most high indeed, wise.

5 Shall We strike the Reminder away from you, on the excuse that you have been a wanton people? 6 How many prophets have We sent among those of old! 7 Yet not one prophet came to them whom they did not ridicule. 8 So We destroyed (those peoples who were) stronger than them in power, and the example of those of old has passed away.

9 If indeed you ask them, 'Who created the heavens and the earth?,' they will indeed say, 'The Mighty, the Knowing created them.' 10 (It is He) who made the earth as a cradle for you, and made (path)ways in it for you, so that you might be guided, 11 and (it is He) who sends down water from the sky in measure – and by means of it We give some barren land life, and in this way you (too) will be brought forth – 12 and (it is He) who created the pairs, all of them, and made for you what you ride on from the ship(s) and the livestock, 13 so that you may mount their backs, (and) then remember the blessing of your Lord when you are mounted upon them, and say, 'Glory to the One who has subjected this to us, when we (ourselves) were not fit for it. 14 Surely we are indeed going to return to our Lord.' 15 Yet they assign to Him a part of His (own) servants. Surely the human is clearly ungrateful indeed.

16 Or has He taken (for Himself) daughters from what He creates, and singled you out with sons? 17 When one of them is given news of what he has struck as a parable for the Merciful, his face turns dark and he chokes back his disappointment. 18 'One who is brought up in luxury, and he is not clear in the (time of) dispute?'[2] 19 Yet they have made the angels – those who are themselves servants of the Merciful – females. Did they witness their creation? Their testimony will

---

1. *you*: plur.
2. *... in the (time of) dispute?*: meaning obscure; nor is it clear whether this question is posed by the man in exasperation after the announcement of the birth of his daughter, or whether it is spoken by God in reference to his alleged 'daughters.' In any case the general point seems to be that a daughter is simply not as good as a son, whether for a human or divine father.

Decoration

be written down, and they will be questioned. **20** They say, 'If the Merciful had (so) pleased, we would not have served them.' They have no knowledge about that; they are only guessing. **21** Or have We given them a Book before it, and do they hold fast to it? **22** No! They say, 'Surely we found our fathers (set) on a community, and surely we are guided in their footsteps.' **23** In this way We have not sent any warner before you to a town, except that its affluent ones said, 'Surely we found our fathers (set) on a community, and surely we are following in their footsteps.' **24** He said,[3] 'Even if I bring you better guidance than what you found your fathers (set) on?' They said, 'Surely we are disbelievers in what you are sent with.' **25** So We took vengeance on them. See how the end was for the ones who called (it) a lie!

26 (Remember) when Abraham said to his father and his people, 'Surely I am free of what you serve, **27** except for the One who created me. Surely He will guide me.' **28** And he made it a lasting word among his descendants, so that they might return.

29 No! I gave these (people) and their fathers enjoyment (of life), until the truth came to them, and (also) a clear messenger. **30** But when the truth came to them, they said, 'This is magic. Surely we are disbelievers in it.'

31 They said, 'If only this Qur'ān had been sent down on some great man of the two towns.' **32** Do they distribute the mercy of your Lord? We have distributed their livelihood among them in this present life, and raised some of them above others in rank, so that some of them may take others in slavery. But the mercy of your Lord is better than what they accumulate. **33** If it were not that humankind would be one community, We would indeed have made for those who disbelieve in the Merciful roofs of silver for their houses, and stairways on which to ascend, **34** and doors for their houses, and couches on which to recline, **35** and (all manner of) decoration. Yet all that is but the enjoyment of this present life – the Hereafter with your Lord is for the ones who guard (themselves).

36 Whoever turns away from the reminder of the Merciful – We allot to him a satan, and he becomes his comrade. **37** Surely they indeed keep them from the way, even though they think that they are (rightly) guided, **38** until, when he comes to Us, he says, 'Would that (there were) between me and you the distance of the two Easts!' And:[4] 'Evil is the comrade! **39** It will not benefit you today – since you have done evil – that you are partners in the punishment.'

40 Can you make the deaf to hear, or can you guide the blind and the one who is clearly astray? **41** Whether We take you away – surely We are going to take vengeance on them – **42** or show you what We have promised them – surely We are powerful over them. **43** So hold fast to what you are inspired (with). Surely you

---

3. *He said*: one of the former prophets (another reading has 'Say,' but that does not fit here).
4. *And*: what follows is spoken by God to all of them.

Decoration

are on a straight path. **44** Surely it is a reminder indeed to you and to your people. Soon you will (all) be questioned. **45** Ask those of Our messengers whom We sent before you: Did We appoint any other gods than the Merciful to be served?

46 Certainly We sent Moses with Our signs to Pharaoh and his assembly. He said, 'Surely I am a messenger of the Lord of all peoples.' **47** But when he brought them Our signs, suddenly they began to laugh at them, **48** even though every sign We showed them was greater than the one before it. We seized them with the punishment, so that they might return. **49** They said, 'Magician! Call on your Lord for us by whatever covenant He has made with you, (and) surely we shall indeed be (rightly) guided.' **50** But when We removed the punishment from them, suddenly they broke (their promise). **51** Pharaoh called out among his people: 'My people! Is the kingdom of Egypt not mine, and these rivers (which) flow beneath me? Do you not see? **52** Am I not better than this (man), who is despicable and scarcely makes (things) clear? **53** If only bracelets of gold were cast (down) on him or the accompanying angels came with him.' **54** So he unsettled his people, and they obeyed him. Surely they were a wicked people. **55** When they had angered Us, We took vengeance on them and drowned them – all (of them)! **56** We made them a thing of the past, and an example for the later (generations).

57 When the son of Mary is cited as an example, suddenly your people keep (others) from it, **58** and they say, 'Are our gods better, or is he?' They only cite him to you as a (matter of) dispute. Yes! They are a contentious people. **59** He was only a servant whom We blessed, and We made him an example for the Sons of Israel. **60** If We (so) pleased, We could indeed make angels out of you to be rulers on the earth.

61 Surely it is indeed knowledge for the Hour, so do not be in doubt about it, but follow me. This is a straight path. **62** Do not let Satan keep you from (it). Surely he is a clear enemy to you.

63 When Jesus brought the clear signs, he said, 'I have brought you the wisdom, and (I have done so) to make clear to you some of your differences. Guard (yourselves) against God and obey me. **64** Surely God – He is my Lord and your Lord, so serve Him! This is a straight path.' **65** But the factions differed among themselves. Woe to those who have done evil, because of the punishment of a painful Day!

66 Are they looking for anything but the Hour – that it should come upon them unexpectedly, when they do not realize (it)? **67** Friends on that Day – some of them will be enemies to others, except for the ones who guard (themselves). **68** 'My servants! (There is) no fear on you today, nor will you sorrow **69** – those (of you) who believed in Our signs and submitted. **70** Enter the Garden, you and your wives, you will be made happy!' **71** Plates and cups of gold will be passed around among them, and there (they will have) whatever they desire and their eyes delight in. And: 'There you will remain.' **72** And: 'That is the Garden which you have been given as an inheritance for what you have done. **73** There you have many fruits from which you will eat.'

Decoration

74 Surely the evildoers will remain in the punishment of Gehenna. **75** It will not subside for them, and there they will be in despair. **76** We did not do them evil, but they themselves were the evildoers. **77** They will call out, 'Master![5] Let your Lord finish us off!' He will say, 'Surely you will remain. **78** Certainly we brought you the truth, but most of you were averse to the truth.'

79 Or have they woven some plot? We (too) are weaving (a plot). **80** Or do they think that We do not hear their secret and their secret talk? Yes indeed! Our messengers are present with them writing (it) down.

81 Say: 'If the Merciful had a son, I (would be) the first of the ones who served (him). **82** Glory to the Lord of the heavens and the earth, Lord of the throne, above what they allege!' **83** So leave them! Let them banter and jest, until they meet their Day which they are promised. **84** He (it is) who is God in the sky and God on the earth. He is the Wise, the Knowing. **85** Blessed (be) the One who – to Him (belongs) the kingdom of the heavens and the earth, and whatever is between them. With Him is the knowledge of the Hour, and to Him you will be returned. **86** Those whom they call on instead of Him have no power of intercession, except for the one who has borne witness to the truth – and they know (this). **87** If indeed you ask them, 'Who created them?,' they will indeed say, 'God.' How are they (so) deluded? **88** And his saying:[6] 'My Lord! Surely these are a people who do not believe.' **89** So excuse them, and say: 'Peace!' Soon they will know!

---

5. *Master*: or 'Mālik,' the name of the chief angel-guard of Hell.
6. *his saying*: the Prophet's.

44 ✣ The Smoke

In the Name of God, the Merciful, the Compassionate

1 Ḥā Mīm.

2 By the clear Book! 3 Surely We sent it down on a blessed night – surely We were warning – 4 during which every wise command was divided out, 5 as a command from Us – surely We were sending – 6 as a mercy from your Lord. Surely He – He is the Hearing, the Knowing, 7 Lord of the heavens and the earth, and whatever is between them, if you (would) be certain. 8 (There is) no god but Him. He gives life and causes death – your Lord and the Lord of your fathers of old.

9 No! They are in doubt (while) they jest. 10 So watch for the Day when the sky will bring a visible smoke 11 covering the people: 'This is a painful punishment! 12 Our Lord, remove the punishment from us! Surely We are believers.' 13 How will the reminder be for them, when a clear messenger has already come to them? 14 Then they turned away from him, and said, '(He is) tutored, (he is) possessed!' 15 'Surely We are going to remove the punishment a little, (but) surely you are going to revert!' 16 On the Day when We attack with the great attack, surely We are going to take vengeance.

17 Certainly before them We tested the people of Pharaoh, when an honorable messenger came to them: 18 'Deliver to me the servants of God! Surely I am a trustworthy messenger for you.' 19 And: 'Do not exalt yourselves against God! Surely I bring you clear authority. 20 Surely I take refuge with my Lord and your Lord, for fear that you stone me. 21 If you do not believe me, withdraw from me!' 22 So he called on his Lord: 'These are a sinful people.' 23 And: 'Journey with My servants by night. Surely you will be followed. 24 And leave the sea parted, (for) surely they are a force (to be) drowned.' 25 How many gardens and springs they left (behind), 26 and (fields of) crops, and an honorable place, 27 and prosperity in which they used to rejoice. 28 So (it was), and We caused another people to inherit them. 29 Neither the sky nor the earth wept for them, nor were they spared. 30 Certainly We rescued the Sons of Israel from the humiliating punishment, 31 (and) from Pharaoh. Surely he was haughty, one of the wanton. 32 Certainly We chose them, on (the basis of) knowledge, over all peoples, 33 and gave them signs in which (there was) a clear test.

34 Surely these (people) indeed say, 35 'There is nothing but our first death. We are not going to be raised. 36 Bring (back) our fathers, if you[1] are truthful!'

---

1. *you*: plur.

The Smoke

37 Are they better, or the people of Tubbaʿ,[2] and those who were before them? We destroyed them. Surely they were sinners. **38** We did not create the heavens and earth, and whatever is between them, in jest. **39** We created them only in truth, but most of them do not know (it). **40** Surely the Day of Decision is their meeting – all (of them) – **41** a Day when a protector will be of no use at all as a protector, and they will not be helped **42** – except for the one on whom God has compassion. Surely He – He is the Mighty, the Compassionate.

43 Surely the tree of al-Zaqqūm **44** is the food of the sinner, **45** like molten metal boiling in the belly, **46** as hot (water) boils. **47** 'Seize him and drag him into the midst of the Furnace. **48** Then pour over his head from the punishment of hot (water)!' **49** 'Taste (it)! Surely you are the mighty, the honorable! **50** Surely this is what you doubted about.'

51 Surely the ones who guard (themselves) are in a secure place, **52** in (the midst of) gardens and springs, **53** wearing clothes of silk and brocade, facing each other. **54** So (it is), and We shall marry them to (maidens) with dark, wide eyes. **55** There they will call for every (kind of) fruit, secure. **56** There they will not taste death, except the first death, and He will guard them against the punishment of the Furnace. **57** Favor from your Lord! That is the great triumph!

58 Surely We have made it easy in your language, so that they may take heed. **59** So watch! Surely they (too) are watching.

---

2. *Tubbaʿ*: the title of the kings of the Ḥimyarites of South Arabia (mentioned only here and at Q50.14).

45 ❖ The Kneeling

In the Name of God, the Merciful, the Compassionate

1 Ḥā Mīm.
2 (The) sending down of the Book is from God, the Mighty, the Wise.
3 Surely in the heavens and the earth (there are) signs indeed for the believers.
4 And in your creation, and what He scatters of the creatures, (there are) signs for a people who are certain. 5 And (in the) alternation of the night and the day, and what God sends down from the sky of (His) provision, and by means of it gives the earth life after its death, and (in the) changing of the winds, (there are) signs for a people who understand. 6 Those are the signs of God. We recite them to you in truth. In what (kind of) proclamation – after God and His signs – will they believe?

7 Woe to every liar (and) sinner! 8 He hears the signs of God recited to him, (but) then persists in being arrogant, as if he had not heard them. Give him the news of a painful punishment. 9 When he comes to know any of Our signs, he takes them in mockery. Those – for them (there is) a humiliating punishment. 10 Behind them is Gehenna, and what they have earned will be of no use to them at all, nor those whom they have taken as allies instead of God. For them (there is) a great punishment. 11 This is guidance, but those who disbelieve in the signs of their Lord – for them (there is) a punishment of painful wrath.

12 (It is) God who has subjected the sea to you, so that the ship may run on it by His command, and so that you may seek some of His favor, and that you may be thankful. 13 And He has subjected to you whatever is in the heavens and whatever is on the earth – all (of it is) from Him. Surely in that are signs indeed for a people who reflect.

14 Say to those who believe to forgive those who do not expect the days of God, so that He may repay a people for what they have earned. 15 Whoever does righteousness, it is for himself, and whoever does evil, it is (likewise) against himself – then to your Lord you will be returned.

16 Certainly We gave the Sons of Israel the Book, and the judgment, and the prophetic office. We provided them with good things and favored them over all peoples. 17 And We gave them clear signs of the matter. They did not differ until after the knowledge had come to them, (because of) envy among themselves. Surely your Lord will decide between them on the Day of Resurrection concerning their differences. 18 Then We placed you on a pathway of the matter. So

The Kneeling

follow it, and do not follow the (vain) desires of those who do not know. **19** Surely they will be of no use to you at all against God. Surely the evildoers are allies of each other, but God is the Ally of the ones who guard (themselves).

20 This is evidence for the people, and a guidance and mercy for a people who are certain. **21** Or do those who commit evil deeds think that We shall treat them as those who believe and do righteous deeds – alike in their life and their death? Evil is what they judge! **22** God created the heavens and the earth in truth, and so that each person may be paid for what he has earned – and they will not be done evil. **23** Have you seen the one who has taken his (vain) desire as his god? God has led him astray on (the basis of) knowledge, and set a seal on his hearing and his heart, and made a covering on his sight? Who will guide him after God? Will you[1] not take heed? **24** But they say, 'There is nothing but our present life. We die, and we live, and nothing destroys us but time.' They have no knowledge about that. They only conjecture. **25** When Our signs are recited to them as clear signs, their only argument is that they say, 'Bring (back) our fathers, if you[2] are truthful!' **26** Say: 'God gives you life, then causes you to die, (and) then He gathers you to the Day of Resurrection – (there is) no doubt about it. But most of the people do not know (it).'

27 To God (belongs) the kingdom of the heavens and the earth. On the Day when the Hour strikes, on that Day the perpetrators of falsehood will lose. **28** You will see each community kneeling, each community called to its Book: 'Today you will be repaid for what you have done. **29** This is Our Book – it speaks about you in truth. Surely We have been copying down what you were doing.' **30** As for those who have believed and done righteous deeds, their Lord will cause them to enter into His mercy. That is the clear triumph! **31** But as for those who have disbelieved: 'Were My signs not recited to you? Yet you became arrogant and were a sinful people. **32** And when it was said, "Surely the promise of God is true, and the Hour – (there is) no doubt about it," you said, "We do not know what the Hour is. We think (it is) only conjecture, and we are not certain."' **33** The evils of what they have done will become apparent to them, and what they were mocking will overwhelm them. **34** And it will be said, 'Today We forget you, as you forgot the meeting of this Day of yours. Your refuge is the Fire, and you have no helpers. **35** That is because you took the signs of God in mockery, and this present life deluded you.' So today they will not be brought forth from it, nor will they be allowed to make amends.

36 Praise (be) to God, Lord of the heavens and Lord of the earth, Lord of all peoples! **37** To Him (belongs) the greatness in the heavens and the earth. He is the Mighty, the Wise.

---

1. *you*: plur.
2. *you*: plur.

46 ❖ The Sand Dunes

In the Name of God, the Merciful, the Compassionate

1 Hā Mīm.

2 (The) sending down of the Book is from God, the Mighty, the Wise.

3 We did not create the heavens and the earth, and whatever is between them, except in truth and (for) an appointed time, but those who disbelieve are turning away from what they are warned of. 4 Say: 'Do you see what you call on instead of God? Show me what (part) of the earth they have created. Or do they have any partnership in (the creation of) the heavens? Bring me any Book before this (one) or any trace of knowledge, if you are truthful.' 5 Who is farther astray than the one who, instead of God, calls on those who will not respond to him until the Day of Resurrection, while they are (otherwise) oblivious of their calling? 6 When the people are gathered, they will be enemies to them, and will deny their service.

7 When Our signs are recited to them as clear signs, those who disbelieve say to the truth, when it has come to them, 'This is clear magic.' 8 Or do they say, 'He has forged it'? Say: 'If I have forged it, you (would) have no power at all to (help) me against God. He knows what you are busy with. He is sufficient as a witness between me and you. He is the Forgiving, the Compassionate.'

9 Say: 'I am not the first of the messengers, and I do not know what will be done with me or with you. I only follow what I am inspired (with). I am only a clear warner.'

10 Say: 'Do you see? If it is from God, and you disbelieve in it, and a witness from the Sons of Israel has borne witness to (a Book) like it, and believed, and you become arrogant – surely God does not guide the people who are evildoers.' 11 Those who disbelieve say to those who believe, 'If it had been something good, they would not have gotten to it before us' – even when they are not guided by it. And they say, 'This is an old lie!' 12 Yet before it was the Book of Moses as a model and mercy; and this is a Book confirming (it) in the Arabic language, to warn those who do evil, and as good news for the doers of good. 13 Surely those who say, 'Our Lord is God,' (and) then go straight – (there will be) no fear on them, nor will they sorrow. 14 Those are the companions of the Garden, there to remain – a payment for what they have done.

15 We have charged each person (to do) good to his parents – his mother bore him with difficulty, and she delivered him with difficulty – his bearing and his

The Sand Dunes

weaning are thirty months – until, when he reaches his maturity, and reaches forty years, he says, 'My Lord, (so) dispose me that I may be thankful for your blessing with which You have blessed me and my parents, and that I may do righteousness pleasing to You, and do right by me concerning my descendants. Surely I turn to You (in repentance), and surely I am one of those who submit.' **16** Those are the ones from whom We shall accept the best of what they have done, and We shall pass over their evil deeds. (They will be) among the companions of the Garden – the promise of truth which they were promised. **17** But the one who says to his parents, 'Uff to both of you! Do you promise me that I shall be brought forth, when generations have already passed away before me?,' while both of them call on God for help: 'Woe to you! Believe! Surely the promise of God is true!,' and he says, 'This is nothing but old tales' – **18** those are the ones against whom the word has proved true about the communities of jinn and humans (which) have already passed away before them. Surely they were losers. **19** For each (there are) ranks, according to what they have done, and so that He may pay them in full for their deeds – and they will not be done evil. **20** On the Day when those who disbelieve are presented to the Fire: 'You squandered your good things in your present life, and enjoyed them. So today you will be paid the punishment of humiliation because you became arrogant on the earth without any right, and because you have acted wickedly.'

21 Remember the brother of 'Ād: When he warned his people at the sand dunes – and warners had already passed away before him and after him – (saying): 'Do not serve (anyone) but God! Surely I fear for you the punishment of a great Day.' **22** They said, 'Have you come to defraud us of our gods? Bring us what you promise us, if you are one of the truthful.' **23** He said, 'The knowledge (of it) is only with God. I deliver to you what I was sent with, but I see you are an ignorant people.' **24** When they saw it as a cloud approaching their wādīs, they said, 'This is a cloud (which) is going to give us rain.' 'No! It is what you were seeking to hurry – a wind in which (there is) a painful punishment, **25** destroying everything by the command of its Lord.' And morning found them not to be seen, except for their dwelling places. In this way We repay the people who are sinners. **26** Certainly We had established them with what We have not established you, and We gave them hearing and sight and hearts. Yet their hearing and their sight and their hearts were of no use to them at all, since they denied the signs of God, and what they were mocking overwhelmed them. **27** Certainly We destroyed the towns around you, and varied the signs so that they might return. **28** Why did they not help them – those gods whom they had taken, instead of God, as a (means of) drawing near (to Him)? No! They abandoned them. That was their lie and what they had forged.

29 (Remember) when We turned a band of jinn to you to listen to the Qur'ān: When they were in its presence, they said, 'Be silent!' And when it was finished, they turned back to their people as warners. **30** They said, 'Our people! Surely

The Sand Dunes

we have heard a Book (which) has been sent down after Moses, confirming what was before it, guiding to the truth and to a straight road. **31** Our people! Respond to the caller of God, and believe in Him. He will forgive you some of your sins, and protect you from a painful punishment. **32** Whoever does not respond to the caller of God – there is no escaping (Him) on the earth, and he has no allies other than Him. Those are clearly astray.'

33 Do they not see that God, who created the heavens and earth, and was not tired out by their creation, is able to give the dead life? Yes indeed! Surely He is powerful over everything. **34** On the Day when those who disbelieve are presented to the Fire: 'Is this not the truth?' They will say, 'Yes indeed! By our Lord!' He will say, 'Taste the punishment for what you have disbelieved.'

35 Be patient, as the messengers of firm resolve were (also) patient. Do not seek to hurry it for them. On the Day when they see what they are promised, (it will seem) as if they had remained (in the grave) for only an hour of the day. A delivery! Will any be destroyed but the people who are wicked?

47 ❂ Muḥammad

In the Name of God, the Merciful, the Compassionate

1 Those who disbelieve and keep (people) from the way of God – He will lead their deeds astray. **2** But those who believe and do righteous deeds, and believe in what has been sent down on Muḥammad – and it is the truth from their Lord – He will absolve them of their evil deeds, and set their case right. **3** That is because those who disbelieve follow falsehood, and because those who believe follow the truth from their Lord. In this way God strikes parables for the people.

4 When you[1] meet those who disbelieve, (let there be) a striking of the necks, until, when you have subdued them, bind (them) securely, and then either (set them free) as a favor or by ransom, until the war lays down its burdens. That (is the rule). If God had (so) pleased, He would indeed have defended Himself against them, but (He allows fighting) so that He may test some of you by means of others. Those who are killed in the way of God – He will not lead their deeds astray. **5** He will guide them and set their case right, **6** and He will cause them to enter the Garden – He has made it known to them.

7 You who believe! If you help God, He will help you, and make firm your feet. **8** But those who disbelieve – (there will be) downfall for them, and He will lead their deeds astray. **9** That is because they disliked what God sent down, and so He has made their deeds worthless. **10** Have they not traveled on the earth and seen how the end was for those who were before them? God destroyed them. The disbelievers have examples of it. **11** That is because God is the Protector of those who believe, and because the disbelievers have no protector.

12 Surely God will cause those who believe and do righteous deeds to enter Gardens through which rivers flow. But those who disbelieve – they take their enjoyment and eat as the cattle eat. The Fire will be their dwelling place.

13 How many a town We have destroyed that was stronger in power than your town which expelled you![2] And there was no helper for them. **14** Is the one who (stands) on a clear sign from his Lord like the one who – the evil of his deeds is made to appear enticing to him, and they follow their (vain) desires?

15 A parable of the Garden which is promised to the ones who guard (themselves): In it (there are) rivers of water without pollution, and rivers of milk – its

---

1. *you*: plur.
2. *you*: sing.

taste does not change – and rivers of wine – delicious to the drinkers – and rivers of purified honey. In it (there is) every (kind of) fruit for them, and forgiveness from their Lord. (Are they) like those who remain in the Fire? They are given boiling water to drink, and it cuts their insides (to pieces).

16 (There are) some of them who listen to you, until, when they go forth from your presence, they say to those who have been given knowledge, 'What did he say just now?' Those are the ones on whose hearts God has set a seal, and they follow their (vain) desires. **17** But those who are (rightly) guided – He increases them in guidance, and gives them their (sense of) guarding (themselves). **18** So are they looking for anything but the Hour – that it will come upon them unexpectedly? The conditions for it have already come, and when it comes upon them, how will they have their reminder? **19** Know that He – (there is) no god but God. Ask forgiveness for your sin, and for the believing men and the believing women. God knows your comings and goings, and your dwelling place.

20 Those who believe say, 'If only a sūra were sent down.' But when a clearly composed sūra is sent down, and fighting is mentioned in it, you see those in whose hearts is a sickness looking at you with the look of one who faints at the point of death. Woe to them! **21** Obedience and rightful words (are called for)! When the matter is determined, and if they are true to God, it will indeed be better for them. **22** Is it possible, if you turned away, that you would foment corruption on the earth, and sever your family ties? **23** Those are the ones whom God has cursed, and made them deaf, and blinded their sight. **24** Do they not contemplate the Qur'ān, or (are there) locks on their hearts? **25** Surely those who have turned their backs, after the guidance has become clear to them – (it was) Satan (who) contrived (it) for them, but He has spared them. **26** That is because they said to those who disliked what God had sent down, 'We will obey you in part of the matter' – but God knows their secrets. **27** How (will it be) when the angels take them, striking their faces and their backs? **28** That is because they have followed what angers God, and have disliked His approval, so He has made their deeds worthless.

29 Or do those in whose hearts is a sickness think that God will not bring to light their malice? **30** If We had (so) pleased, We would indeed have shown them to you, and you would indeed know them by their marks – indeed you do know them by their devious speech. God knows your deeds, **31** and We shall indeed test you, until We know those of you who struggle and those who are patient, and We shall test the reports about you. **32** Surely those who disbelieve, and keep (people) from the way of God, and break with the messenger, after the guidance has become clear to them – they will not harm God at all, and He will make their deeds worthless.

33 You who believe! Obey God, and obey the messenger, and do not invalidate your (own) deeds. **34** Surely those who disbelieve and keep (people) from the way of God, (and) then die while they are disbelievers – God will not forgive them.

Muḥammad

35 Do not grow weak and call for peace, when you are the prevailing (force), and God is with you, and will not deprive you of your deeds. **36** This present life is nothing but jest and diversion, but if you believe and guard (yourselves), He will give you your rewards and not ask you for your wealth. **37** If He asks you for it, and presses you, you are stingy, and He brings to light your malice. **38** There you are! These (people)! You are called on to contribute in the way of God, and (there are) some of you who are stingy. Whoever is stingy is stingy only to himself. God is the wealthy One, and you are the poor (ones). If you turn away, He will exchange a people other than you. Then they will not be like you.

48 ❈ The Victory

In the Name of God, the Merciful, the Compassionate

1 Surely We have given you[1] a clear victory, **2** so that God may forgive you what is past of your sin and what is (still) to come, and complete His blessing on you, and guide you to a straight path, **3** and that God may help you with a mighty help. **4** He (it is) who sent down the Sakīna into the hearts of the believers, so that they might add belief to their belief – to God (belong) the forces of the heavens and the earth, and God is knowing, wise – **5** and that He may cause the believing men and the believing women to enter Gardens through which rivers flow, there to remain, and absolve them of their evil deeds – that is the great triumph in the sight of God! – **6** and that He may punish the hypocrite men and the hypocrite women alike, and the idolatrous men and the idolatrous women alike, and the ones who think evil thoughts about God. The wheel of evil (will turn) against them. God is angry with them, and has cursed them, and has prepared Gehenna for them – and it is an evil destination! **7** To God (belong) the forces of the heavens and the earth. God is mighty, wise.

8 Surely We have sent you as a witness, and as a bringer of good news and a warner, **9** so that you[2] may believe in God and His messenger, and support him, and respect him, and that you may glorify Him morning and evening. **10** Surely those who swear allegiance to you[3] swear allegiance to God – the hand of God is over their hands. So whoever breaks (his oath), only breaks it against himself, but whoever fulfils what he has covenanted with God – He will give him a great reward.

11 Those of the Arabs who stayed behind will say to you, 'Our wealth and our families kept us busy, so ask forgiveness for us.' They say with their tongues what is not in their hearts. Say: 'Who has any power for you against God, whether He intends harm for you or intends benefit for you? No! God is aware of what you do. **12** No! You thought that the messenger and the believers would never return to their families, and that was made to appear enticing in your hearts, and you thought evil thoughts, and became a ruined people.' **13** Whoever does not believe in God and His messenger – surely We have prepared for the disbelievers

---

1. *you*: sing.
2. *you*: plur.
3. *you*: sing.

a blazing (Fire). **14** To God (belongs) the kingdom of the heavens and the earth. He forgives whomever he pleases and punishes whomever He pleases. God is forgiving, compassionate.

15 The ones who stayed behind will say, when you[4] set out to take spoils, 'Let us follow you.' They want to change the word of God. Say: 'You will not follow us. So God has said before.' They will say, 'No! You are jealous of us.' No! They have not understood, except for a little. **16** Say to those of the Arabs who stayed behind: 'You will be called to (fight) a people of harsh violence. You will fight them or they will surrender. If you obey, God will give you a good reward, but if you turn away, as you turned away before, He will punish you with a painful punishment.' **17** There is no blame on the blind, and no blame on the disabled, and no blame on the sick. Whoever obeys God and His messenger – He will cause him to enter Gardens through which rivers flow; but whoever turns away – He will punish him with a painful punishment.

18 Certainly God was pleased with the believers when they were swearing allegiance to you under the tree, and He knew what was in their hearts. So He sent down the Sakīna on them, and rewarded them with a near victory, **19** and many spoils to take. God is mighty, wise. **20** And God has promised you[5] many (more) spoils to take, and He has hurried this for you, and has restrained the hands of the people from you. (This happened) so that it might be a sign to the believers, and guide you to a straight path. **21** The other (spoils) which you were not able (to take), God has already encompassed them. God is powerful over everything.

22 If those who disbelieve fight you,[6] they will indeed turn their backs, (and) then they will not find any ally or any helper. **23** (That was) the customary way of God (concerning) those who have passed away before, and you will find no change in the customary way of God. **24** He (it is) who restrained their hands from you, and your hands from them, in the heart of Mecca, after He gave you victory over them – God sees what you do. **25** They are those who disbelieved, and kept you from the Sacred Mosque, and (also) the offering, (which was) prevented from reaching its lawful place. If not for (certain) believing men and believing women, whom you did not know, or you would have trampled them, and guilt smitten you without (your) realizing (it) because of them – so that God may cause to enter into His mercy whomever He pleases – if they had been separated out (clearly), We would indeed have punished those among them who disbelieved with a painful punishment. **26** When those who disbelieved fostered a fury in their hearts – the fury of the (time of) ignorance – God sent down His Sakīna on His messenger and on the believers, and fastened to them the word of guarding (themselves). They have more right to it and are worthy of it. God has knowledge of everything.

---

4. *you*: plur.
5. *you*: plur.
6. *you*: plur.

The Victory

27 Certainly God has spoken the truth in the vision to His messenger: 'You[7] will indeed enter the Sacred Mosque, if God pleases, in security, your heads shaved, your hair cut short, not fearing.' He knew what you did not know, and besides that produced a near victory. **28** He (it is) who has sent His messenger with the guidance and the religion of truth, so that He may cause it to prevail over religion – all of it. God is sufficient as a witness.

29 Muḥammad is the messenger of God. Those who are with him are harsh against the disbelievers, (but) compassionate among themselves. You see them bowing and prostrating themselves, seeking favor from God and approval. Their marks on their faces are the trace of prostration. That is their image in the Torah, and their image in the Gospel is like a seed (that) puts forth its shoot, and strengthens it, and it becomes stout and stands straight on its stalk, pleasing the sowers – so that He may enrage the disbelievers by means of them. God has promised those of them who believe and do righteous deeds forgiveness and a great reward.

---

7. *You*: plur.

49 ❖ The Private Rooms

In the Name of God, the Merciful, the Compassionate

1 You who believe! Do not be forward before God and His messenger, but guard (yourselves) against God. Surely God is hearing, knowing. 2 You who believe! Do not raise your voices above the voice of the prophet, and do not be loud in (your) speech to him, like the loudness of some of you to others, or your deeds will come to nothing without your realizing (it). 3 Surely those who lower their voices in the presence of the messenger of God, those are the ones whose hearts God has tested for the guarding (of themselves). For them (there is) forgiveness and a great reward. 4 Surely those who call out to you from behind the private rooms – most of them do not understand. 5 If they were patient, until you come out to them, it would indeed be better for them. Yet God is forgiving, compassionate.

6 You who believe! If a wicked person brings you some (piece of) news, be discerning, or you will smite a people in ignorance, and then become regretful over what you have done. 7 Know that the messenger of God is among you. If he obeyed you in much of the affair, you would indeed be in distress. But God has made belief dear to you, and made it appear enticing in your hearts, and made disbelief and wickedness and disobedience hateful to you. Those – they are the right-minded. 8 Favor from God and a blessing! God is knowing, wise.

9 If two contingents of the believers fight, set (things) right between them, and if one of them oppresses the other, fight the one which oppresses until it returns to the command of God. If it returns, set (things) right between them with justice, and act fairly. Surely God loves the ones who act fairly. 10 Only the believers are brothers, so set (things) right between your two brothers, and guard (yourselves) against God, so that you may receive mercy.

11 You who believe! Do not let one people ridicule (another) people who may be better than them, or women (ridicule other) women who may be better than them. Do not find fault with each other, or insult each other with nicknames. A bad name is wickedness after belief. Whoever does not turn (in repentance), those – they are the evildoers.

12 You who believe! Avoid too much conjecture, (for) surely some conjecture is a sin. Do not pry or go behind each other's back. Would any of you like to eat the flesh of his dead brother? You would hate it! Guard (yourselves) against God. Surely God turns (in forgiveness), compassionate.

13 People! Surely We have created you from a male and a female, and made you different peoples and tribes, so that you may recognize one another. Surely the most honorable among you in the sight of God is the one among you who guards (himself) most. Surely God is knowing, aware.

14 The Arabs say, 'We believe.' Say: 'You do not believe. Rather say, "We submit," (for) belief has not yet entered your hearts. But if you obey God and His messenger, He will not deprive you of your deeds at all. Surely God is forgiving, compassionate. **15** The believers are only those who believe in God and His messenger, (and) then have not doubted but struggled with their wealth and their lives in the way of God. Those – they are the truthful.'

16 Say: 'Will you teach God about your religion, when God knows whatever is in the heavens and whatever is on the earth? God has knowledge of everything.'

17 (They think) they bestow a favor on you in that they have submitted! Say: 'Do not bestow your submission on me as a favor! No! God bestows a favor on you, in that He has guided you to belief, if you are truthful. **18** Surely God knows the unseen (things) of the heavens and the earth. God sees what you do.'

50 ✺ QĀF

In the Name of God, the Merciful, the Compassionate

1 Qāf.

By the glorious Qur'ān! 2 – No! They are amazed that a warner has come to them from among them, and the disbelievers say, 'This is an amazing thing! 3 When we are dead, and turned to dust [. . .]?[1] That is a far return!' 4 We know what the earth takes away from them, and with Us is a Book (that is) keeping watch. 5 No! They called the truth a lie when it came to them, and they are in a confused state. 6 Do they not look at the sky above them, how We have built it, and adorned it, and it has no cracks? 7 And the earth – We stretched it out, and cast on it firm mountains, and caused every beautiful kind (of plant) to grow on it, 8 as evidence and a reminder to every servant who turns (in repentance). 9 And We sent down blessed water from the sky, and caused gardens to grow by means of it, and grain for harvest, 10 and tall date palms with bunches (of fruit), 11 as a provision for the servants, and We give a barren land life by means of it. In this way the coming forth (will take place).

12 Before them the people of Noah called (it) a lie, and the people of al-Rass,[2] and Thamūd, 13 and 'Ād, and Pharaoh, and the brothers of Lot, 14 and the people of the Grove, and the people of Tubba'[3] – each (of them) called the messengers liars, and My promise was proved true.

15 Were We tired out by the first creation? No! They are in doubt about a new creation. 16 Certainly We created the human, and We know what his own self whispers within him, (for) We are closer to him than (his) jugular vein. 17 When the two meeters meet together, (one) seated on the right, and (one) on the left, 18 he does not utter a word without (there being) a watcher ready beside him. 19 The daze of death comes in truth: 'That is what you were trying to avoid!'

20 There will be a blast on the trumpet: 'That is the Day of Promise.' 21 Each person will come, (and) with him a driver and a witness. 22 'Certainly you were oblivious of this, so We have removed your covering, and today your sight is

---

1. *[. . .]*: the reader must supply something like, 'shall we really be raised up?' (see e.g. Q37.12-17).
2. *people of al-Rass*: reference obscure (they are mentioned only here and at Q25.38).
3. *Tubba'*: the title of the kings of the Ḥimyarites of South Arabia (mentioned only here and at Q44.37).

Qāf

sharp.' **23** His comrade will say, 'This is what I have ready.' **24** '(You two), cast into Gehenna every stubborn disbeliever, **25** preventer of the good, transgressor, doubter, **26** who set up another god with God. Cast him into the harsh punishment.' **27** His (other) comrade will say, 'Our Lord, I did not make him transgress insolently, but he was far astray.' **28** He will say, 'Do not dispute in My presence, when I have already sent forth the promise to you. **29** The word is not going to change with Me. I am not an evildoer to (My) servants.' **30** On the Day when We say to Gehenna, 'Are you filled?,' and it says, 'Are there any more (to come)?,' **31** and the Garden is brought near for the ones who guard (themselves) – (it is) not far: **32** 'This is what you were promised. (It is) for everyone who turns (in repentance and) keeps watch **33** – whoever fears the Merciful in the unseen, and brings a heart turning (in repentance). **34** Enter it in peace!' That is the Day of Eternity. **35** There they will have whatever they please, and with Us (there is still) more.

36 How many a generation We have destroyed before them! They were stronger than them in power, and they searched about in the lands – was there any place of escape? **37** Surely in that is a reminder indeed to whoever has a heart or listens attentively, and he is a witness.

38 Certainly We created the heavens and the earth, and whatever is between them, in six days. No weariness touched Us in (doing) that. **39** Be patient with what they say, and glorify your Lord with praise before the rising of the sun, and before its setting. **40** And glorify Him during part of the night, and at the ends of the prostration. **41** And listen for the Day when the caller will call from a place nearby. **42** The Day when they hear the cry in truth – that is the Day of Coming Forth. **43** Surely We – We give life and cause death, and to Us is the (final) destination.

44 On the Day when the earth is split open from them, (and they come forth from the graves) rushing – that is an easy gathering for Us. **45** We know what they say. You are not a tyrant over them. So remind, by means of the Qur'ān, anyone who fears My promise.

51 ✦ The Scatterers

In the Name of God, the Merciful, the Compassionate

1 By the scatterers (with their) scattering, 2 and the bearers (with their) burden, 3 and the runners (with their) effortlessness, 4 and the distributors (with their) affair! 5 Surely what you[1] are promised is true indeed! 6 Surely the Judgment is indeed going to fall!

7 By the sky with all its tracks! 8 Surely you differ indeed in what you say! 9 Whoever is deluded about it is (really) deluded. 10 May the guessers perish, 11 those who are in a flood (of confusion), heedless. 12 They ask, 'When is the Day of Judgment?' 13 The Day when they will be tried over the Fire: 14 'Taste your trial! This is what you were seeking to hurry.'

15 Surely the ones who guard (themselves) will be in (the midst of) gardens and springs, 16 taking whatever their Lord has given them. Surely before (this) they were doers of good. 17 Little of the night would they sleep, 18 and in the mornings they would ask for forgiveness, 19 and in their wealth (there was) a due (portion) for the beggar and the outcast.

20 In the earth (there are) signs for the ones who are certain, 21 and (also) in yourselves. Do you not see? 22 And in the sky is your provision and what you are promised. 23 By the Lord of the sky and the earth! Surely it is true indeed – (even) as what you (are able to) speak.

24 Has the story come to you of the honored guests of Abraham? 25 When they entered upon him, and said, 'Peace!,' he said, 'Peace! (You are) a people unknown (to me).' 26 So he turned to his family and brought a fattened calf, 27 and he placed it near them. He said, 'Will you not eat?' 28 And he began to feel a fear of them. They said, 'Do not fear!' And they gave him good news of a knowing boy. 29 And then his wife came forward in a loud voice, and struck her face, and said, 'An old woman, barren!' 30 They said, 'So (it will be)! Your Lord has said. Surely He – He is the Wise, the Knowing.' 31 He said, 'What is your business, you envoys?' 32 They said, 'Surely we have been sent to a sinful people, 33 to send (down) on them stones of clay, 34 marked by your Lord for the wanton.' 35 We (would have) brought out any of the believers who were in it, 36 but We found in it only one house of those who had submitted. 37 And We left in it a sign for those who fear the painful punishment.

---

1. *you*: plur.

The Scatterers

38 And (there is also a sign) in Moses: when We sent him to Pharaoh with clear authority. **39** But he turned away with his supporter(s), and said, 'A magician or a man possessed!' **40** So We seized him and his forces, and tossed them into the sea, (for) he was to blame.

41 And (there is also a sign) in 'Ād: when We sent upon them the desolating wind. **42** It left nothing it came upon, but made it like decayed (ruins). **43** And (there is also a sign) in Thamūd: when it was said to them, 'Enjoy (yourselves) for a time!' **44** But they disdained the command of their Lord, and the thunderbolt took them while they were looking on, **45** and they were not able to stand, nor were they helped. **46** And the people of Noah before (them) – surely they were a wicked people.

47 The sky – We built it with (Our own) hands, and surely We were (its) extenders indeed. **48** And the earth – We spread it out. Excellent were the smoothers! **49** And We created pairs of everything, so that you might take heed. **50** So flee to God! Surely I am a clear warner for you from Him. **51** And do not set up another god with God. Surely I am a clear warner for you from Him.

52 (Even) so, not a messenger came to those who were before them, except they said, 'A magician or a man possessed!' **53** Have they bequeathed it to each other? No! They are a people who transgress insolently. **54** So turn away from them, (for) you are not to be blamed, **55** but remind (them). Surely the Reminder will benefit the believers.

56 I did not create jinn and humans except to serve Me. **57** I do not desire any provision from them, nor do I desire that they should feed Me. **58** Surely God – He is the Provider, One full of power, the Firm.

59 Surely for the ones who do evil (there will be) a portion like the portion of their companions. Let them not seek to hurry Me! **60** Woe to those who disbelieve on account of their Day which they are promised!

52 ❂ The Mountain

In the Name of God, the Merciful, the Compassionate

1 By the mountain **2** and a Book written **3** on parchment unrolled! **4** By the inhabited House! **5** By the roof raised up **6** and the sea surging! **7** Surely the punishment of your Lord is indeed going to fall! **8** (There is) no one to repel it.

9 On the Day when the sky will shake, **10** and the mountains fly away, **11** woe that Day to the ones who called (it) a lie, **12** who – they were jesting in (their) banter. **13** On the Day when they will be shoved forcefully into the fire of Gehenna: **14** 'This is the Fire that you called a lie! **15** Is this magic or do you not see? **16** Burn in it! Bear it patiently or do not bear it patiently – (it is) the same for you. You are only being repaid for what you have done.'

17 Surely the ones who guard (themselves) will be in Gardens and bliss, **18** rejoicing in what their Lord has given them, and (because) their Lord has guarded them against the punishment of the Furnace. **19** 'Eat and drink with satisfaction, (in return) for what you have done.' **20** (There they will be) reclining on couches lined up, and We shall marry them to (maidens) with dark, wide eyes. **21** (For) those who believe, and whose descendants followed them in belief, We shall join their descendants with them, and We shall not deprive them of any of their deeds. Each person (is held) in pledge for what he has earned. **22** We shall increase them with fruits and meat of whatever (kind) they desire. **23** There they will pass (around) a cup to each other in which there is no frivolous or sinful talk, **24** and among them will circulate boys of their own, as if they were hidden pearls. **25** Some of them will approach others asking each other questions. **26** They will say, 'Surely we were fearful among our family before, **27** but God has bestowed favor on us, and guarded us against the punishment of the scorching (Fire). **28** Surely we used to call on Him before. Surely He – He is the Beneficent, the Compassionate.'

29 So remind (them)! By the blessing of your Lord, you are neither an oracle-giver nor possessed. **30** Or do they say, 'A poet, for whom we await the uncertainty of Fate'? **31** Say: '(Just) wait! Surely I shall be one of those waiting with you.' **32** Or do their minds command them (to do) this, or are they a people who transgress insolently? **33** Or do they say, 'He has invented it?' No! They do not believe. **34** Let them bring a proclamation like it, if they are truthful. **35** Or were they created out of nothing? Or were they the creators? **36** Or did they create the heavens and the earth? No! They are not certain. **37** Or are the storehouses of

The Mountain

your Lord with them, or are they the record-keepers? **38** Or do they have a ladder on which they (can) listen? Then let their listener bring clear authority. **39** Or does He have daughters while you have sons? **40** Or do you ask them for a reward, so that they are burdened with debt? **41** Or is the unseen in their keeping, so that they are writing it down? **42** Or do they intend a plot? Then those who disbelieve will be the ones plotted against. **43** Or do they have a god other than God? Glory to God above what they associate! **44** Even if they see fragments of the sky falling, they will say, 'A heap of clouds!' **45** So leave them, until they meet their Day on which they will be thunderstruck **46** – the Day when their plot will be of no use to them at all, and they will not be helped. **47** Surely for those who do evil (there is) a punishment before that, but most of them do not know (it).

48 Be patient for the judgment of your Lord. Surely you are in Our sight. Glorify your Lord with praise when you arise, **49** and glorify Him during part of the night, and (at) the setting of the stars.

53 ❖ THE STAR

In the Name of God, the Merciful, the Compassionate

1 By the star when it falls! **2** Your companion has not gone astray, nor has he erred, **3** nor does he speak on a whim. **4** It is nothing but an inspiration inspired. **5** One harsh in power has taught him **6** – One full of strength! He stood poised, **7** while He was on the highest horizon, **8** then He drew near and came down. **9** He was two bow-lengths tall, or nearly. **10** And so He inspired His servant (with) what He inspired. **11** His heart did not lie about what it saw. **12** Will you dispute with him about what he sees?

13 Certainly he saw Him at a second descent, **14** by the Lote Tree of the Boundary, **15** near which is the Garden of the Refuge, **16** when (there) covered the Lote Tree what covered (it). **17** His sight did not turn aside, nor did it transgress. **18** Certainly he saw one of the greatest signs of his Lord.

19 Have you seen al-Lāt, and al-'Uzzā, **20** and Manāt, the third, the other?[1] **21** Do you have male (offspring) while He has female? **22** Then that (would be) an unfair division! **23** They are only names which you have named, you and your fathers. God has not sent down any authority for it. They only follow conjecture and whatever they themselves desire – when certainly the guidance has come to them from their Lord. **24** Or will a person have whatever he longs for? **25** To God (belongs) the last and the first.

26 How many an angel there is in the heavens whose intercession is of no use at all, until God gives permission to whomever He pleases and approves. **27** Surely those who do not believe in the Hereafter indeed name the angels with the names of females. **28** But they have no knowledge about it. They only follow conjecture, and surely conjecture is of no use at all against the truth. **29** So turn away from the one who turns away from Our reminder and desires nothing but this present life. **30** That is the extent of their knowledge. Surely your Lord – He knows who goes astray from His way, and He knows who is (rightly) guided. **31** To God (belongs) whatever is in the heavens and whatever is on the earth, so that He may repay those who do evil for what they have done, and repay those who do good with the best (reward).

---

1. *al-Lāt...al-'Uzzā...Manāt...*: said to be 'goddesses' connected with three shrines in the region of Mecca, but they are probably angels, as the section immediately following (Q53.26–31) makes clear.

The Star

32 Those who avoid great sins and immoral deeds, except for inadvertent ones – surely your Lord is embracing in forgiveness. He knows about you, when He produced you from the earth, and when you were (still) embryos in the bellies of your mothers. So do not claim purity for yourselves. He knows the one who guards (himself).

33 Do you see the one who turns away, **34** and gives little, and (then) grudgingly? **35** Is knowledge of the unseen in his keeping, and so he sees (it)? **36** Or has he not been informed about what is in the pages of Moses **37** and Abraham, who paid (his debt) in full? **38** – That no one bearing a burden bears the burden of another; **39** and that a person will receive only what he (himself) strives for; **40** and that his striving will be seen, **41** (and) then he will be paid for it with the fullest payment; **42** and that to your Lord is the (ultimate) goal; **43** and that He causes laughter and causes weeping; **44** and that He causes death and gives life; **45** and that He created pairs, the male and the female, **46** from a drop, when it is emitted; **47** and that the second growth (depends) on Him; **48** and that He enriches (people) and gives wealth; **49** and that He is the Lord of Sirius; **50** and that He destroyed 'Ād of old, **51** and Thamūd – He did not spare (them) **52** – or the people of Noah before (them) – surely they were – they (were) evil and insolent transgressor(s) – **53** and the overturned (cities) He overthrew, **54** when (there) covered them what covered (them). **55** So which of the blessings of your Lord will you[2] dispute?

56 This (man) is a warner, of the warners of old. **57** The impending (Hour) is impending! **58** There is no one to remove it, other than God. **59** Are you amazed at this proclamation? **60** And do you laugh and not weep, **61** while you amuse yourselves? **62** Prostrate yourselves before God and serve (Him)!

---

2. *your...you*: sing. (cf. the refrain of Q55).

54 ❊ The Moon

In the Name of God, the Merciful, the Compassionate

1 The Hour has drawn near, and the moon has been split open! **2** Yet if they see a sign, they turn away, and say, 'Non-stop magic!' **3** They call (it) a lie, and follow their (own vain) desires, yet everything is set. **4** Certainly enough of the story has come to them to act as a deterrent – **5** far-reaching wisdom (it is) – but warnings are of no use. **6** So turn away from them. On the Day when the Caller will call to a terrible thing: **7** with sight downcast, they will come forth from the graves as if they were locusts spreading, **8** rushing to the Caller. The disbelievers will say, 'This is a hard day!'

9 The people of Noah called (it) a lie before them, and they called Our servant a liar, and said, 'A man possessed!' He was deterred **10** and called on his Lord: 'I am overcome. Help (me)!' **11** So We opened the gates of the sky with water pouring (down), **12** and made the earth gush forth with springs, and the water met for a purpose already decreed. **13** We carried him on a vessel of planks and nails, **14** running before Our eyes – a payment for the one who was disbelieved. **15** Certainly We left it as a sign, yet (is there) anyone who takes heed? **16** How were My punishment and My warnings?

17 Certainly We have made the Qur'ān easy for remembrance, yet (is there) anyone who takes heed?

18 'Ād called (it) a lie. How were My punishment and My warnings? **19** Surely We sent a furious wind against them on a day of non-stop calamity. **20** It snatched the people away as if they were trunks of uprooted date palms. **21** How were My punishment and My warnings?

22 Certainly We have made the Qur'ān easy for remembrance, yet (is there) anyone who takes heed?

23 Thamūd called the warnings a lie, **24** and said, 'Shall we follow a single human being from among us? Surely then we would indeed be astray and raving mad. **25** Has the Reminder been cast (down) on him (alone) among us? No! He is an impudent liar.' **26** 'Tomorrow they will know who the impudent liar is! **27** We are sending the she-camel as a test for them, so watch them and be patient. **28** And inform them that the water is to be divided between them, each drink is to be brought (in turn).' **29** But they called their companion, and he took (a sword) and wounded (her). **30** How were My punishment and My warnings? **31** Surely We sent against them a single cry, and they were like the rubble (used by) the fence maker.

The Moon

32 Certainly We have made the Qur'ān easy for remembrance, yet (is there) anyone who takes heed?

33 The people of Lot called the warnings a lie. 34 Surely We sent a sandstorm against them, except for the house(hold) of Lot. We rescued them at dawn 35 – a blessing from Us. In this way We repay the one who is thankful. 36 Certainly he had warned them of Our attack, and they disputed the warnings. 37 Certainly they solicited him for his guest(s), but We obliterated their eyes: 'Taste My punishment and My warnings!' 38 Certainly in the morning a set punishment came upon them: 39 'Taste My punishment and My warnings!'

40 Certainly We have made the Qur'ān easy for remembrance, yet (is there) anyone who takes heed?

41 Certainly the warnings came to the house of Pharaoh. 42 They called Our signs a lie – all of it – so We seized them with the seizing of a mighty, powerful (One).

43 Are your disbelievers better than those? Or do you have an exemption in the scriptures?

44 Or do they say, 'We shall all be victorious'? 45 They will be routed and turn their back! 46 Yes! The Hour is their appointed time, and the Hour is grievous and bitter.

47 Surely the sinners are astray and raving mad! 48 On the Day when they are dragged on their faces into the Fire: 'Taste the effect of Saqar!'[1] 49 Surely We have created everything in measure, 50 and Our command is but a single (act), like a blink of the eye. 51 Certainly We have destroyed your parties (before), yet (is there) anyone who takes heed?

52 Everything they have done is in the scriptures, 53 and every small and great (deed) is inscribed. 54 Surely the ones who guard (themselves) will be in (the midst of) gardens and a river, 55 in a sure seat in the presence of a powerful King.

---

1. *Saqar*: another name for Hell (cf. Q74.26-27, 42).

55 ◈ The Merciful

In the Name of God, the Merciful, the Compassionate

1 The Merciful **2** has taught the Qur'ān. **3** He created the human. **4** He taught him the explanation. **5** The sun and the moon (move) in predictable paths, **6** and the star and the tree prostrate themselves. **7** The sky – He raised it, and He laid down the scale **8** – do not transgress insolently concerning the scale, **9** but establish the weight in justice, and do not cheat concerning the scale. **10** And the earth – He laid it down for all living creatures. **11** On it (there are) fruit, and date palms with sheaths, **12** and grain with its husk, and fragrant herbs. **13** Which of the blessings of your Lord will you two call a lie?

14 He created the human from clay like pottery, **15** and He created the jinn from a mixture of fire. **16** Which of the blessings of your Lord will you two call a lie?

17 Lord of the two Easts, Lord of the two Wests. **18** Which of the blessings of your Lord will you two call a lie?

19 He let loose the two seas (which) meet. **20** Between them (there is) a barrier (which) they do not seek (to cross). **21** Which of the blessings of your Lord will you two call a lie?

22 Pearl and coral come forth from both of them. **23** Which of the blessings of your Lord will you two call a lie?

24 His are the (ships) running, raised up on the sea like landmarks. **25** Which of the blessings of your Lord will you two call a lie?

26 All who are on it pass away, **27** but the face of your Lord remains, full of splendor and honor. **28** Which of the blessings of your Lord will you two call a lie?

29 (All) who are in the heavens and the earth make requests of Him. Every day He (is engaged) in some task. **30** Which of the blessings of your Lord will you two call a lie?

31 Soon We shall be free (to attend) to you, you two burdens! **32** Which of the blessings of your Lord will you two call a lie?

33 Assembly of jinn and humans! If you are able to pass beyond the confines of the heavens and the earth, pass! You will not pass beyond (them) except by authority. **34** Which of the blessings of your Lord will you two call a lie?

35 A flame of fire and a furious wind will be sent against you, and you will not (be able to) defend yourselves. **36** Which of the blessings of your Lord will you two call a lie?

The Merciful

37 When the sky is split open and turns red like oil – **38** Which of the blessings of your Lord will you two call a lie?

39 – on that Day neither human nor jinn will be questioned about his sin. **40** Which of the blessings of your Lord will you two call a lie?

41 The sinners will be known by their mark, and they will be seized by the hair and the feet. **42** Which of the blessings of your Lord will you two call a lie?

43 This is Gehenna which the sinners called a lie. **44** They will go around between it and hot, boiling (water). **45** Which of the blessings of your Lord will you two call a lie?

46 But for the one who fears the position of his Lord, (there are) two gardens – **47** Which of the blessings of your Lord will you two call a lie?

48 – with branches – **49** Which of the blessings of your Lord will you two call a lie?

50 – in both (there are) two flowing springs – **51** Which of the blessings of your Lord will you two call a lie?

52 – in both (there are) two of every (kind of) fruit – **53** Which of the blessings of your Lord will you two call a lie?

54 – (they are) reclining on couches lined with brocade, and fresh fruit of both gardens is near (at hand) – **55** Which of the blessings of your Lord will you two call a lie?

56 – in them (there are maidens) restraining (their) glances – no man or jinn has had sex with them before them – **57** Which of the blessings of your Lord will you two call a lie?

58 – as if they were rubies and coral – **59** Which of the blessings of your Lord will you two call a lie?

60 Is the payment for good anything but the good? **61** Which of the blessings of your Lord will you two call a lie?

62 And besides these two (there are another) two gardens – **63** Which of the blessings of your Lord will you two call a lie?

64 – deep green – **65** Which of the blessings of your Lord will you two call a lie?

66 – in both (there are) two springs gushing forth – **67** Which of the blessings of your Lord will you two call a lie?

68 – in both (there are) fruit, and date palms, and pomegranates – **69** Which of the blessings of your Lord will you two call a lie?

70 – in them (there are) good and beautiful (maidens) – **71** Which of the blessings of your Lord will you two call a lie?

72 – dark-eyed (maidens), confined in tents – **73** Which of the blessings of your Lord will you two call a lie?

The Merciful

74 – no man or jinn has had sex with them before them – **75** Which of the blessings of your Lord will you two call a lie?

76 – (they are) reclining on green cushions and beautiful carpets – **77** Which of the blessings of your Lord will you two call a lie?

78 Blessed (be) the name of your Lord, full of splendor and honor.

56 ❈ The Falling

In the Name of God, the Merciful, the Compassionate.
1 When the falling falls **2** – at its falling there will be no calling (it) a lie – **3** bringing low, raising high, **4** when the earth is violently shaken, **5** and the mountains utterly crumble, **6** and become scattered dust, **7** and you become three classes: **8** the companions on the right – what are the companions on the right? **9** And the companions on the left – what are the companions on the left? **10** And the foremost.

The foremost **11** – those are the ones brought near, **12** in Gardens of Bliss – **13** a host from the ones of old, **14** but few from the later (generations) – **15** on well-woven couches, **16** reclining on them, facing each other. **17** Boys of eternal youth will circulate among them, **18** with cups and pitchers, and a cup from a flowing spring **19** – they do not suffer any headache from it, nor do they become drunk – **20** and with fruit of their own choosing, **21** and the meat of birds of their own desiring, **22** and (maidens) with dark, wide eyes **23** like hidden pearls **24** – a reward for what they have done. **25** There they will not hear any frivolous or sinful talk, **26** only the saying, 'Peace! Peace!'

27 The companions on the right – what are the companions of the right? **28** (They will be) in (the midst of) thornless lote trees, **29** and acacia trees one after another, **30** and extensive shade, **31** and flowing water, **32** and many fruits **33** – unlimited, unforbidden – **34** and raised couches. **35** Surely We produced them specially, **36** and made them virgins, **37** amorous, (all) of the same age, **38** for the companions on the right. **39** A host from the ones of old, **40** and a host from the later (generations).

41 The companions on the left – what are the companions on the left? **42** (They will be) in (the midst of) scorching (fire) and boiling (water), **43** and a shadow of black smoke, **44** neither cool nor kind. **45** Surely before (this) they were affluent, **46** and persisted in the great refusal, **47** and used to say, 'When we are dead, and turned to dust and bones, shall we indeed be raised up? **48** And our fathers of old (too)?' **49** Say: 'Surely those of old and the later (generations) **50** will indeed be gathered to the meeting of a known Day. **51** Then surely you – you who have gone astray and called (it) a lie! – **52** will indeed eat from the tree of Zaqqūm,[1] **53** and fill your bellies from it, **54** and drink on (top of) it from boiling water, **55** drinking

---

1. *tree of Zaqqūm*: a tree in Hell (see Q37.62; 44.43; cf. Q17.60).

The Falling

like the thirsty (camel) drinks.' **56** This will be their reception on the Day of Judgment.

57 We created you. Why will you not affirm (it)? **58** Do you see what you emit? **59** Do you create it, or are We the Creators? **60** We have decreed death (to be) among you – We are not (to be) outrun – **61** so that We may exchange the likes of you, and (re)produce you in what you do not know. **62** Certainly you have known the first growth. Why will you not take heed? **63** Do you see what you cultivate? **64** Do you (yourselves) sow it, or are We the Sowers? **65** If We (so) pleased, We could indeed make it broken debris, and you would be left rejoicing, **66** 'Surely we have incurred debt indeed! **67** No! We have been robbed!' **68** Do you see the water which you drink? **69** Do you send it down from the clouds, or are We the Ones who send (it) down? **70** If We (so) pleased, We could make it bitter. Why are you not thankful? **71** Do you see the fire which you ignite? **72** Do you produce the timber for it, or are We the Ones who produce (it)? **73** We have made it a reminder and a provision for the desert dwellers. **74** So glorify the name of your Lord, the Almighty.

75 I swear by the fallings of the stars **76** – surely it is a great oath indeed, if (only) you[2] knew – **77** surely it is an honorable Qur'ān indeed, **78** in a hidden Book! **79** No one touches it but the purified. **80** (It is) a sending down from the Lord of all peoples.

81 Do you[3] hold this proclamation in disdain, **82** and do you make it your living to call (it) a lie? **83** Why not, when the life of the dying man leaps into his throat, **84** and you are looking on **85** – though We are nearer to him than you, only you do not see (Us) – **86** why, if you are not (to be) judged, **87** do you not return it, if you are truthful? **88** If he[4] is one of those brought near, **89** (there will be) comfort, and fragrance, and a Garden of Bliss. **90** And if he is one of the companions on the right: **91** 'Peace (be) to you, from the companions on the right!' **92** But if he is one of those who called (it) a lie (and) went astray, **93** (there will be) a reception of boiling (water) **94** and burning in a Furnace. **95** Surely this – it indeed is the certain truth. **96** So glorify the name of your Lord, the Almighty.[5]

---

2. *you*: plur.
3. *you*: plur.
4. *he*: the dying man.
5. *So glorify…*: sing. imperative.

57 ❖ Iron

In the Name of God, the Merciful, the Compassionate

1 Whatever is in the heavens and the earth glorifies God. He is the Mighty, the Wise. **2** To Him (belongs) the kingdom of the heavens and the earth. He gives life and causes death. He is powerful over everything. **3** He is the First and the Last, the Outer and the Inner. He has knowledge of everything. **4** He (it is) who created the heavens and the earth in six days. Then He mounted the throne. He knows what penetrates into the earth, and what comes forth from it, and what comes down from the sky, and what goes up into it. He is with you wherever you are. God sees what you do. **5** To Him (belongs) the kingdom of the heavens and the earth, and to God (all) matters are returned. **6** He causes the night to pass into the day, and causes the day to pass into the night. He knows what is in the hearts.

7 Believe in God and His messenger, and contribute from what He has made you inheritors in. Those of you who believe and contribute – for them (there will be) a great reward. **8** What is (the matter) with you that you do not believe in God, when the messenger calls you to believe in your Lord, and He has already taken a covenant with you, if you are believers? **9** He (it is) who sends down on His servant clear signs, so that He may bring you forth from the darkness to the light. Surely God is indeed kind (and) compassionate with you.

10 What is (the matter) with you that you do not contribute in the way of God, when the inheritance of the heavens and the earth (belongs) to God? The one among you who contributed and fought before the victory is not equal. They are higher in rank than those who contributed and fought after that. Yet to each God has promised the good (reward). God is aware of what you do. **11** Who is the one who will lend to God a good loan, and He will double it for him? For him (there will be) a generous reward.

12 On the Day when you see the believing men and the believing women: their light will run before them, and at their right (hands): 'Good news for you today! Gardens through which rivers flow, there to remain. That is the great triumph!'

13 On the Day when the hypocrite men and the hypocrite women will say to those who believed: 'Wait for us! Let us borrow your light!' It will be said, 'Turn back and search for a light!' And a wall with a door will be set up between them: on the inside of it (there is) mercy, and on the outside of it – facing (it) – (there is) the punishment. **14** They will call out to them: 'Were we not with you?' They will say, 'Yes indeed! But you tempted yourselves, and you waited and doubted, and wishful thinking deceived you, until the command of God came, and the Deceiver deceived you about God. **15** So today no ransom will be accepted from you, nor from those who have disbelieved. Your refuge is the Fire – it is your protector – and it is an evil destination!'

16 Is it not time for those who believe that their hearts become humble before the Reminder of God, and (before) what has come down of the truth, and (that) they not be like those to whom the Book was given before, and for whom the time lasted too long, so that their hearts became hard, and many of them were wicked? **17** Know that God gives the earth life after its death. We have made clear to you[1] the signs, so that you may understand.

18 Surely the charitable men and the charitable women, and (those who) have lent to God a good loan – it will be doubled for them, and for them (there will be) a generous reward. **19** Those who believe in God and His messengers, those – they are the truthful and the martyrs in the sight of their Lord – they have their reward and their light. But those who disbelieve and call Our signs a lie – those are the companions of the Furnace.

20 Know that this present life is nothing but jest and diversion, and a (passing) splendor, and a (cause for) boasting among you, and a rivalry in wealth and children. (It is) like rain: the vegetation it produces pleases the disbelievers, (but) then it withers and you see it turning yellow, (and) then it becomes broken debris. In the Hereafter (there is) a harsh punishment, **21** and forgiveness from God and approval. But this present life is nothing but the enjoyment of deception. Race toward forgiveness from your Lord, and a Garden – its width is like the width of the sky and the earth – prepared for those who believe in God and His messengers. That is the favor of God. He gives it to whomever He pleases. God is full of great favor. **22** No smiting smites in the earth or among yourselves, except that it was in a Book before We brought it about – surely that is easy for God – **23** so that you may not grieve over what eludes you, nor gloat about what has come to you. God does not love anyone who is arrogant (and) boastful, **24** (nor) those who are stingy and command the people to be stingy. Whoever turns away – surely God – He is the wealthy One, the Praiseworthy.

25 Certainly We sent Our messengers with the clear signs, and We sent down with them the Book and the scale, so that the people might uphold justice. And We sent down iron – in which (there is) harsh violence, but (also) benefits for the people – and (We did so) in order that God might know who would help Him and His messengers in the unseen. Surely God is strong, mighty.

26 Certainly We sent Noah and Abraham, and We placed among their descendants the prophetic office and the Book. Yet (there was only the occasional) one of them who was (rightly) guided, but many of them were wicked. **27** Then in their footsteps We followed up with Our messengers, and We followed up with Jesus,

---

1. *you*: plur.

son of Mary, and gave him the Gospel, and placed in the hearts of those who followed him kindness and mercy. But monasticism, they originated it. We did not prescribe it for them. (It) only (arose out of their) seeking the approval of God. Yet they did not observe it as it should have been observed. So We gave those of them who believed their reward, but many of them were wicked.

28 You who believe! Guard (yourselves) against God and believe in His messenger! He will give you a double portion of His mercy, and will make a light for you by means of which you will walk, and He will forgive you – God is forgiving, compassionate – **29** so that the People of the Book may know that they have no power over any of the favor of God, and that favor is in the hand of God. He gives it to whomever He pleases. God is full of great favor.

58 ✲ The Disputer

In the Name of God, the Merciful, the Compassionate

1 God has heard the words of the woman who disputes with you about her husband, and (who) complains to God, and God hears the discussion of the two of you. Surely God is hearing, seeing. **2** Those of you who declare their wives to be as their mothers' backs – they are not their mothers. Their mothers are only those who gave them birth. Surely they indeed say a wrong word and a falsehood. Yet surely God is indeed pardoning (and) forgiving. **3** Those who declare their wives to be as their mothers' backs, (and) then return to what they have said, (the penalty is) the setting free of a slave before the two of them touch each other. That is what you are admonished. God is aware of what you do. **4** Whoever does not find (the means to do that), (the penalty is) a fast for two months consecutively, before the two of them touch each other. And whoever is not able (to do that), (the penalty is) the feeding of sixty poor persons. That is so that you may believe in God and His messenger. Those are the limits (set by) God – and for the disbelievers (there will be) a painful punishment.

5 Surely those who oppose God and His messenger have been disgraced, as those before them were disgraced. We have already sent down clear signs – and for the disbelievers (there will be) a humiliating punishment, **6** on the Day when God will raise them up – all (of them) – and inform them about what they have done. God has counted it up, though they have forgotten it. God is a witness over everything.

7 Do you not see that God knows whatever is in the heavens and whatever is on the earth? There is no secret talk of three men but He is the fourth of them, nor of five men but He is the sixth of them, nor less than that, nor more, but He is with them wherever they may be. Then on the Day of Resurrection He will inform them about what they have done. Surely God has knowledge of everything.

8 Do you not see those who were forbidden from secret talk, (and) then return to what they were forbidden, and converse secretly in sin and enmity and disobedience to the messenger? And when they come to you, they greet you with what God does not greet you with, and they say within themselves, 'If only God would punish us for what we say.' Gehenna will be enough for them, where they will burn – and it is an evil destination!

9 You who believe! When you converse secretly, do not converse in sin and enmity and disobedience to the messenger, but converse in piety and the guarding (of yourselves). Guard (yourselves) against God, to whom you will be gathered.

The Disputer

10 Secret talk is only from Satan, so that he may cause those who believe to grieve. But he will not harm them at all, except by the permission of God. In God let the believers put their trust.

11 You who believe! When it is said to you 'Make room in the assemblies,' make room! God will make room for you. And when it is said, 'Rise up,' rise up! God will raise in rank those of you who have believed and those who have been given knowledge. God is aware of what you do.

12 You who believe! When you converse privately with the messenger, send forward a freewill offering before your private talk. That is better for you and purer. If you do not find (the means to do so) – God is forgiving, compassionate. **13** Are you afraid to send forward freewill offerings before your private talk? When you do not (do so), and God has turned to you (in forgiveness), observe the prayer and give the alms, and obey God and His messenger. God is aware of what you do.

14 Do you not see those who have taken as allies a people with whom God is angry? They are neither of you nor of them. They swear upon lies – and they know (it). **15** God has prepared a harsh punishment for them. Surely they – evil indeed is what they have done! **16** They have taken their oaths as a cover, and kept (people) from the way of God. For them (there will be) a humiliating punishment. **17** Neither their wealth nor their children will be of any use against God. Those are the companions of the Fire. There they will remain. **18** On the Day when God will raise them up – all (of them) – they will swear to Him as they swear to you, and think they (are standing) on something. Is it not a fact that they – they are the liars? **19** Satan has prevailed over them, and made them forget the Reminder of God. Those are the faction of Satan. Is it not a fact that the faction of Satan – they are the losers? **20** Surely those who oppose God and His messenger – they will be among the most humiliated. **21** God has written, 'I shall indeed conquer – I and My messengers!' Surely God is strong, mighty.

22 You will not find a people who believe in God and the Last Day loving anyone who opposes God and His messenger, even if they were their fathers, or their sons, or their brothers, or their clan. Those – He has written belief on their hearts, and supported them with a spirit from Him, and will cause them to enter Gardens through which rivers flow, there to remain. God is pleased with them, and they are pleased with Him. Those are the faction of God. Is it not a fact that the faction of God – they are the ones who prosper?

59 ❊ The Gathering

In the Name of God, the Merciful, the Compassionate

1 Whatever is in the heavens and whatever is on the earth glorifies God. He is the Mighty, the Wise. **2** He (it is) who expelled those of the People of the Book who disbelieved from their homes for the first gathering. You[1] did not think that they would go forth, and they thought that their strongholds would defend them against God. But God came upon them from where they were not expecting, and cast dread into their hearts. They destroyed their houses with their (own) hands and the hands of the believers. Learn a lesson, you who have sight! **3** If God had not prescribed exile for them, He would indeed have punished them in this world – and for them (there is) the punishment of the Fire in the Hereafter. **4** That is because they opposed God and His messenger. Whoever opposes God – surely God is harsh in retribution.

5 Whatever palm trees you cut down, or left standing on their roots – (it was) was by the permission of God, and (it was) so that He might disgrace the wicked. **6** What God has given to His messenger (as spoils) from them – you did not spur on any horse or camel for it, but God gives authority to His messengers over whomever He pleases. God is powerful over everything. **7** What God has given to His messenger (as spoils) from the people of the towns (belongs) to God and to the messenger, and to family, and the orphans, and the poor, and the traveler, so that it does not (just) circulate among the wealthy of you. Whatever (spoils) the messenger gives you, take it, and whatever he forbids you, stop (asking for it). Guard (yourselves) against God! Surely God is harsh in retribution.

8 (Spoils belong) to the poor emigrants, who were expelled from their homes and their wealth, seeking favor from God and approval, and helping God and His messenger. Those – they are the truthful. **9** And those who settled in 'the home'[2] and in belief before them, they love whoever emigrates to them, and do not find in their hearts any need for what they have been given, but prefer (emigrants) above themselves, even though there is poverty among them. Whoever is guarded against his own greed, those – they are the ones who prosper. **10** Those who came after them say, 'Our Lord, forgive us and our brothers, who preceded us in

---

1. *You*: plur., referring to the believers throughout this section.
2. *'the home'*: said to be a reference to Medina.

belief, and do not place any rancor in our hearts toward those who believe. Our Lord, surely You are kind (and) compassionate.'

11 Do you[3] not see those who have played the hypocrite? They say to their brothers who disbelieve among the People of the Book, 'If indeed you are expelled, we shall indeed go forth with you, and we shall never obey anyone concerning you. And if you are fought against, we shall indeed help you.' God bears witness: 'Surely they are liars indeed!' **12** If indeed they are expelled, they will not go forth with them, and if indeed they are fought against, they will not help them. And if indeed they do help them, they will indeed turn their backs. Then they will not be helped. **13** Indeed you[4] (strike) greater fear in their hearts than God. That is because they are a people who do not understand. **14** They will not fight against you all together, except in fortified towns or from behind walls. Their violence among themselves is (so) harsh, you (might) think them all (united) together, but their hearts are divided. That is because they are a people who have no sense. **15** (They are) like those who shortly before them tasted the consequence of their action – for them (there is) a painful punishment. **16** (They are) like Satan, when he said to the human, 'Disbelieve!,' and when he disbelieved, he said, 'Surely I am free of you. Surely I fear God, Lord of all peoples.' **17** So the end of both of them is: they will both be in the Fire, (and) there they both will remain. That is the payment of the evildoers.

18 You who believe! Guard (yourselves) against God, and let each person look to what he sends forward for tomorrow. Guard (yourselves) against God! Surely God is aware of what you do. **19** Do not be like those who forgot God, and He caused them to forget their own selves. Those – they are the wicked. **20** The companions of the Fire and the companions of the Garden are not equal. The companions of the Garden – they are the triumphant. **21** If We had sent down this Qur'ān on a mountain, you would indeed have seen it humbled (and) split apart out of the fear of God. These parables – We strike them for the people so that they will reflect.

22 He is God, the One who – (there is) no god but Him – is the Knower of the unseen and the seen. He is the Merciful, the Compassionate.

23 He is God, the One who – (there is) no god but Him – is the King, the Holy One, the Peace, the Faithful, the Preserver, the Mighty, the Sole Ruler, the Magnificent. Glory to God above what they associate!

24 He is God – the Creator, the Maker, the Fashioner. To Him (belong) the best names. Whatever is in the heavens and the earth glorifies Him. He is the Mighty, the Wise.

---

3. *you*: sing.
4. *you*: the believers.

60 ❖ The Examined Woman

In the Name of God, the Merciful, the Compassionate

1 You who believe! Do not take My enemy and your enemy as allies. Do you offer them friendship when they have disbelieved in the truth which has come to you, expelling the messenger and you because you believe in God your Lord? If you have gone forth to struggle in My way, and to seek My approval, do you keep secret (your) friendship for them? I know what you hide and what you speak aloud. Whoever of you does that has gone astray from the right way. **2** If they come upon you, they will be enemies to you, and will stretch out their hands and their tongues with evil against you, and want you to disbelieve. **3** Neither your family ties nor your children will benefit you on the Day of Resurrection. He will distinguish between you. God sees what you do.

4 There was a good example for you in Abraham, and those who were with him, when they said to their people, 'Surely we are free of you and what you serve instead of God. We repudiate you, and between us and you enmity has shown itself, and hatred forever, until you believe in God alone' – except for Abraham's saying to his father: 'I shall indeed ask forgiveness for you, but I have no power from God to (benefit) you at all' – 'Our Lord, in You we put our trust, to You we turn (in repentance), and to You is the (final) destination. **5** Our Lord, do not make us an (object of) persecution for those who disbelieve, but forgive us, Our Lord. Surely You – You are the Mighty, the Wise.' **6** Certainly there was a good example for you in them – for whoever hopes in God and the Last Day. But whoever turns away – surely God – He is the wealthy One, the Praiseworthy.

7 It may be that God will (yet) establish friendship between you and those of them with whom you are on hostile terms. God is powerful, and God is forgiving, compassionate. **8** God does not forbid you regarding those who have not fought you in the (matter of) religion, and have not expelled you from your homes, that you should do good and act fairly toward them. Surely God loves the ones who act fairly. **9** God only forbids you regarding those who have fought you in the (matter of) religion, and have expelled you from your homes, and have supported your expulsion, that you should take them as allies. Whoever takes them as allies, those – they are the evildoers.

10 You who believe! When believing women come to you as emigrants, examine them – God knows their belief – and if you know them to be believers, do not return them to the disbelievers. They are not permitted to them, nor are they are permitted to them. Give them what they have spent. (There is) no blame on you if you marry them, when you have given them their marriage gifts. Do not hold to ties with disbelieving women, but ask (back) what you have spent, and let them ask (back) what they have spent. That is the judgment of God. He judges between you, and God is knowing, wise. **11** If any of your wives escape from you to the disbelievers, and you take retribution, give those whose wives have gone off the equivalent of what they have spent. Guard (yourselves) against God, in whom you believe.

12 Prophet! When believing women come to you, swearing allegiance to you on (the condition) that they will not associate anything with God, and will not steal, and will not commit adultery, and will not kill their children, and will not bring a slander they have forged between their hands and their feet, and will not disobey you in anything right, accept their oath of allegiance, and ask forgiveness for them from God. Surely God is forgiving, compassionate.

13 You who believe! Do not take as allies a people with whom God is angry. They have despaired of the Hereafter, even as the disbelievers have despaired of the companions of the graves.

61 ✵ The Lines

In the Name of God, the Merciful, the Compassionate

1 Whatever is in the heavens and whatever is on the earth glorifies God. He is the Mighty, the Wise.

2 You who believe! Why do you say what you do not do? **3** It is very hateful in the sight of God that you say what you do not do. **4** God loves those who fight in His way, (drawn up) in lines (for battle) as if they were a solid building.

5 (Remember) when Moses said to his people, 'My people! Why do you hurt me, when you already know that I am the messenger of God to you?' Then, when they turned aside, God caused their hearts to turn aside, (for) God does not guide the people who are wicked. **6** And (remember) when Jesus, son of Mary, said, 'Sons of Israel! Surely I am the messenger of God to you, confirming what was before me of the Torah, and bringing good news of a messenger who will come after me, whose name will be Aḥmad.' Then, when he brought them the clear signs, they said, 'This is clear magic.' **7** Who is more evil than the one who forges lies against God, when he is called to Islam? God does not guide the people who are evildoers. **8** They want to extinguish the light of God with their mouths, but God will perfect His light, even though the disbelievers dislike (it). **9** He (it is) who has sent His messenger with the guidance and the religion of truth, so that He may cause it to prevail over religion – all of it – even though the idolaters dislike (it).

10 You who believe! Shall I direct you to a transaction that will rescue you from a painful punishment? **11** You (should) believe in God and His messenger, and struggle in the way of God with your wealth and your lives – that is better for you, if (only) you knew. **12** He will forgive you your sins, and cause you to enter Gardens through which rivers flow, and good dwelling places in Gardens of Eden – that is the great triumph! – **13** and another thing which you love: help from God and a victory near (at hand). Give good news to the believers!

14 You who believe! Be the helpers of God, as Jesus, son of Mary, said to the disciples, 'Who will be my helpers to God?' The disciples said, 'We will be the helpers of God.' One contingent of the Sons of Israel believed, and (another) contingent disbelieved. So We supported those who believed against their enemy, and they were the ones who prevailed.

62 ✤ The Assembly

In the Name of God, the Merciful, the Compassionate

1 Whatever is in the heavens and whatever is on the earth glorifies God, the King, the Holy One, the Mighty, the Wise.

2 He (it is) who has raised up among the common people a messenger from among them, to recite His signs to them, and to purify them, and to teach them the Book and the wisdom, though before (this) they were indeed clearly astray **3** – and others of them who have not (yet) joined them. He is the Mighty, the Wise. **4** That is the favor of God. He gives (it) to whomever He pleases. God is full of great favor.

5 Those who have been loaded down with the Torah, (and) then have not carried it, are like a donkey carrying books. Evil is the parable of the people who have called the signs of God a lie. God does not guide the people who are evildoers. **6** Say: 'You who are Jews! If you claim that you are the allies of God, to the exclusion of the people, wish for death, if you are truthful.' **7** But they will never wish for it because of what their (own) hands have sent forward. God knows the evildoers. **8** Say: 'Surely the death from which you flee – surely it will meet you. Then you will be returned to the Knower of the unseen and the seen, and He will inform you about what you have done.'

9 You who believe! When the call to prayer is made on the day of assembly, hurry to the remembrance of God, and leave business aside. That is better for you, if (only) you knew. **10** Then, when the prayer is finished, disperse in the land and seek some favor from God, and remember God often, so that you may prosper. **11** But when they see (the chance of) some (business) transaction or diversion, they rush off to it, and leave you standing. Say: 'What is with God is better than any diversion or transaction. God is the best of providers.'

Sūra 62

63 ✺ The Hypocrites

In the Name of God, the Merciful, the Compassionate

1 When the hypocrites come to you, they say, 'We bear witness that you are indeed the messenger of God.' God knows that you are indeed His messenger, and God bears witness: 'Surely the hypocrites are liars indeed!' 2 They have taken their oaths as a cover, and have kept (people) from the way of God. Surely they – evil is what they have done. 3 That is because they believed, (and) then they disbelieved. So a seal was set on their hearts, and they do not understand. 4 When you see them, their bodies please you, but when they speak, you hear their speech as if they were planks of wood propped up. They think every cry is against them. They are the enemy, so beware of them. God fight them! How deluded they are! 5 When it is said to them, 'Come, the messenger of God will ask forgiveness for you,' they shake their heads, and you see them turning aside, and they become arrogant. 6 (It is) the same for them whether you ask forgiveness for them or you do not ask forgiveness for them: God will not forgive them. Surely God does not guide the people who are wicked. 7 They are those who say, 'Do not contribute to those who are with the messenger of God until they disperse,' when the storehouses of the heavens and the earth (belong) to God. But the hypocrites do not understand (this). 8 They say, 'If indeed we return to the city, the mightier in it will indeed expel the lowlier,' when all honor (belongs) to God, and to His messenger, and to the believers. But the hypocrites do not know (this).

9 You who believe! Do not let your wealth or your children divert you from the remembrance of God. Whoever does that, those – they are the losers. 10 Contribute from what We have provided you, before death comes upon one of you, and he says, 'My Lord, if only You would spare me for a time near (at hand), so that I might make a freewill offering, and become one of the righteous.' 11 But God will not spare anyone when his time comes. God is aware of what you do.

64 ❖ Mutual Defrauding

In the Name of God, the Merciful, the Compassionate

1 Whatever is in the heavens and whatever is on the earth glorifies God. To Him (belongs) the kingdom, and to Him (belongs) the praise. He is powerful over everything. 2 He (it is) who created you. One of you is a disbeliever, and one of you a believer. God sees what you do. 3 He created the heavens and the earth in truth. He fashioned you, and made your forms well. To Him is the (final) destination. 4 He knows whatever is in the heavens and the earth. He knows what you keep secret and what you speak aloud. God knows what is in the hearts.

5 Has the story not come to you[1] of those who disbelieved before, and tasted the consequence of their action, and for whom (there was) a painful punishment? 6 That was because their messengers brought them the clear signs, and they said, 'Will a human being guide us?' So they disbelieved and turned away, but God had no need (of them). God is wealthy, praiseworthy.

7 Those who disbelieve claim that they will not be raised up. Say: 'Yes indeed! By my Lord! You will indeed be raised up, (and) then you will indeed be informed about what you have done. That is easy for God.' 8 So believe in God and His messenger, and the light which We have sent down. God is aware of what you do. 9 On the Day when He will gather you for the Day of Gathering – that will be the Day of Mutual Defrauding.[2] Whoever believes in God and does righteousness – He will absolve him of his evil deeds, and cause him to enter Gardens through which rivers flow, there to remain forever. That is the great triumph! 10 But those who disbelieved and called Our signs a lie – those are the companions of the Fire, there to remain – and it is an evil destination!

11 No smiting smites, except by the permission of God. Whoever believes in God – He will guide his heart. God has knowledge of everything. 12 Obey God, and obey the messenger! If you turn away – only (dependent) on Our messenger is the clear delivery (of the message). 13 God – (there is) no god but Him. In God let the believers put their trust.

---

1. *you*: plur.
2. *Day of Mutual Defrauding*: the idea may be that the tables have now been turned, and the believers will get the better of the disbelievers, but the exact meaning remains obscure.

Mutual Defrauding

14 You who believe! Surely among your wives and children (there is) an enemy to you. So beware of them. If you pardon and excuse and forgive – surely God is forgiving, compassionate. **15** Surely your wealth and your children are a trial, but God – with Him (there is) a great reward. **16** Guard (yourselves) against God as much as you are able, and hear and obey, and contribute! (That is) better for yourselves. Whoever is guarded against his own greed, those – they are the ones who prosper. **17** If you lend to God a good loan, He will double it for you, and will forgive you. God is thankful, forbearing, **18** Knower of the unseen and the seen, the Mighty, the Wise.

65 ❖ Divorce

In the Name of God, the Merciful, the Compassionate

1 Prophet! When you divorce women, divorce them when they have reached (the end of) their waiting period. Count the waiting period, and guard (yourselves) against God your Lord. Do not expel them from their houses, nor let them leave, unless they commit clear immorality. Those are the limits (set by) God. Whoever transgresses the limits (set by) God has done himself evil. You[1] do not know, perhaps after that God may bring about a new situation. **2** When they reach their term, either retain them rightfully, or part from them rightfully. Call in two of your just men as witnesses, and conduct the witnessing (as if) before God. That is what anyone who believes in God and the Last Day is admonished. Whoever guards (himself) against God – He will make a way out for him, **3** and will provide for him from where he was not expecting. Whoever puts his trust in God – He will be enough for him. Surely God attains his purpose. God has appointed a measure for everything.

4 (As for) those of your women who have no hope of (further) menstruation: if you[2] are in doubt, their waiting period is three months, and (also for) those who have not (yet) menstruated. (As for) those who are pregnant, their term (is) when they deliver what they bear. Whoever guards (himself) against God – He will bring about some relief for him from His command. **5** That is the command of God, which He has sent down to you. Whoever guards (himself) against God – He will absolve him of his evil deeds, and make his reward great.

6 Let them reside where you are residing, according to your means, and do not treat them harshly, so that you cause distress for them. If they are pregnant, support them until they deliver what they bear. If they nurse (the child) for you, give them their payment, and consult together rightfully. But if you encounter difficulties, another woman will nurse (the child) for him. **7** Let a man of means spend out of his means, and whoever is limited in provision, let him spend out of what God has given him. God does not burden anyone except (according to) what He has given him. God will bring about some ease after hardship.

8 How many a town disdained the command of its Lord and His messengers, and We made a harsh reckoning with it, and punished it with a terrible punishment.

---

1. *You:* sing.
2. *you:* plur.

Divorce

9 So it tasted the consequence of its action, and the result of its action was loss. **10** God prepared a harsh punishment for them. Guard (yourselves) against God, those (of you) with understanding!

(You) who believe! God has sent down to you a reminder **11** – a messenger reciting over you clear signs of God, so that He may bring those who believe and do righteous deeds out of the darkness to the light. Whoever believes in God and does righteousness – He will cause him to enter Gardens through which rivers flow, there to remain forever. God has made good provision for him.

12 (It is) God who created seven heavens, and of the earth a similar (number) to them. The command descends in the midst of them, so that you may know that God is powerful over everything, and that God encompasses everything in knowledge.

66 ❁ THE FORBIDDING

In the Name of God, the Merciful, the Compassionate

1 Prophet! Why do you forbid what God has permitted to you, seeking the approval of your wives? God is forgiving, compassionate. **2** God has already specified (what is) obligatory for you[1] in the absolution of your oaths. God is your Protector. He is the Knowing, the Wise.

3 When the prophet confided a (certain) story to one of his wives, and when she informed (another) about it and God disclosed it to him, he made known part of it, and avoided a part. And when he informed her about it, she said, 'Who informed you of this?' He said, 'The Knowing (and) the Aware informed me.' **4** If both of you[2] turn to God (in repentance), both your hearts are (well) inclined, but if both of you support each other against him, surely God – He is his Protector, and Gabriel (too), and the righteous among the believers, and beyond that the angels are (his) supporters. **5** It may be that, if he divorces you,[3] his Lord will give him in exchange better wives than you – women who have submitted, believing, obedient, repentant, worshipping, fasting – (both) previously married and virgins.

6 You who believe! Guard yourselves and your families against a Fire – its fuel is people and stones – over which are angels, stern (and) harsh. They do not disobey God in what He commands them, but they do what they are commanded. **7** 'You who disbelieve! Do not make excuses today, (for) you are only being repaid for what you have done.'

8 You who believe! Turn to God in sincere repentance. It may be that your Lord will absolve you of your evil deeds, and cause you to enter Gardens through which rivers flow. On the Day when God will not disgrace the prophet or those who believe with him: their light will run before them, and at their right (hands) [...],[4] and they will say, 'Our Lord, perfect our light for us, and forgive us. Surely You are powerful over everything.'

---

1. *you*: plur.
2. *both of you*: the dual is taken to refer to Ḥafṣa and 'Ā'isha.
3. *you*: plur.
4. *at their right (hands) [...]*: there is a lacuna here, but it can be restored on the basis of the parallel at Q57.12: 'Good news for you today!'

The Forbidding

9 Prophet! Struggle against the disbelievers and the hypocrites, and be stern with them. Their refuge is Gehenna – and it is an evil destination!

10 God has struck a parable for those who disbelieve: the wife of Noah and the wife of Lot. They were under two of Our righteous servants, but they both betrayed them. Neither of them was of any use at all to either of them against God, when it was said, 'Enter the Fire, both of you, with the ones who enter!'

11 And God has struck a parable for those who believe: the wife of Pharaoh, when she said, 'My Lord, build a house in the Garden for me in Your presence, and rescue me from Pharaoh and his deed(s), and rescue me from the people who are evildoers.' **12** And Mary, daughter of 'Imrān, who guarded her private part: We breathed into her some of Our spirit, and she affirmed the words of her Lord and His Books, and became one of the obedient.

67 ✻ The Kingdom

In the Name of God, the Merciful, the Compassionate

1 Blessed (be) He in whose hand is the kingdom – He is powerful over everything – **2** who created death and life to test which of you is best in deed – He is the Mighty, the Forgiving – **3** who created seven heavens in stories (one upon another). You[1] do not see any mistake in the creation of the Merciful. Cast your sight again! Do you see any fissure? **4** Then cast your sight again and again! Your sight will come crawling back to you, worn out.

5 Certainly We adorned the lower heaven with lamps, and made them missiles for the satans – and We have prepared for them the punishment of the blazing (Fire). **6** For those who disbelieve in their Lord (there is) the punishment of Gehenna – and it is an evil homecoming! **7** When they are cast into it, they will hear its panting, as it boils up **8** (and) nearly bursts apart from rage. Whenever a crowd is cast into it, its keepers will ask them, 'Did a warner not come to you?' **9** They will say, 'Yes indeed! A warner did come to us, but we called (him) a liar, and said, "God has not sent down anything. You are simply terribly astray."' **10** And they will say, 'If (only) we had heard or understood, we would not have been among the companions of the blazing (Fire).' **11** And so they confess their sin. Away with the companions of the blazing (Fire)! **12** Surely those who fear their Lord in the unseen – for them (there is) forgiveness and a great reward.

13 Keep your word secret or speak it publicly – surely He knows what is in (your) hearts. **14** Does the One who created not know, when He is the Astute, the Aware? **15** He (it is) who made the earth subservient to you. So walk about in its regions, and eat from His provision, but to Him is the raising up.

16 Do you feel secure that the One who is in the sky will not cause the earth to swallow you, and then suddenly it shakes? **17** Or do you feel secure that the One who is in the sky will not send a sandstorm against you, and then you will know how My warning is? **18** Certainly those who were before them called (it) a lie, and how was My loathing (of them)?

19 Do they not see the birds above them, spreading (their wings), and they fold (them)? No one holds them (up) but the Merciful. Surely He sees everything. **20** Or who is this who will be a (fighting) force for you to help you, other than the Merciful? The disbelievers are only in delusion. **21** Or who is this who will

---

1. You: sing.

The Kingdom

provide for you, if He withholds His provision? No! But they persist in (their) disdain and aversion. **22** Is the one who walks bent over on his face better guided, or the one who walks upright on a straight path?

23 Say: 'He (it is) who produced you, and made for you hearing and sight and hearts – little thanks you show!'

24 Say: 'He (it is) who scattered you on the earth, and to Him you will be gathered.'

25 They say, 'When (will) this promise (come to pass), if you[2] are truthful?' **26** Say: 'The knowledge (of it) is only with God. I am only a clear warner.'

27 When they see it near at hand, the faces of those who disbelieve will become sad, and it will be said, 'This is what you have been calling for.'

28 Say: 'Have you considered? If God destroys me and whoever is with me, or has compassion on us, who will protect the disbelievers from a painful punishment?'

29 Say: 'He is the Merciful. We believe in Him, and in Him we put our trust. Soon you will know who it is (who is) clearly astray.'

30 Say: 'Have you considered? If one morning your water should sink (into the ground), who would bring you flowing water?'

---

2. *you*: plur.

68 ❖ THE PEN

In the Name of God, the Merciful, the Compassionate

1 Nūn.

By the pen and what they write! 2 You are not, by the blessing of your Lord, possessed. 3 Surely for you (there is) indeed a reward without end, 4 (for) surely you (are) indeed on a great undertaking. 5 So you will see, and they will see, 6 which of you is the troubled one. 7 Surely your Lord – He knows who goes astray from His way, and He knows the ones who are (rightly) guided. 8 So do not obey the ones who call (it) a lie. 9 They wish that you would compromise, and then they would compromise.

10 And do not obey any despicable swearer, 11 a slanderer (who) trades in gossip, 12 a hinderer of the good, a transgressor (and) sinner, 13 crude, and besides all that, a bastard, 14 (just) because he has wealth and sons. 15 When Our signs are recited to him, he says, 'Old tales!' 16 We shall brand him on the snout!

17 Surely We have tested them as We tested the owners of the garden, when they swore they would indeed harvest it in the morning, 18 but did not make exception. 19 And so a circler from your Lord went around it while they were sleeping, 20 and in the morning it was as if it had been harvested. 21 They called to each other in the morning: 22 'Go out early to your field, if you are going to harvest (it).' 23 So they set out, murmuring among themselves: 24 'No poor person will enter it today in your presence.' 25 They went out early, able to (their) task. 26 But when they saw it, they said, 'Surely we have gone astray indeed! 27 No! We have been robbed!' 28 The most moderate one of them said, 'Did I not say to you, "Why do you not glorify (God)?"' 29 They said, 'Glory to our Lord! Surely we have been evildoers!' 30 So some of them approached others blaming each other. 31 They said, 'Woe to us! Surely we have been insolent transgressors! 32 It may be that our Lord will give us a better one in exchange for it. Surely we turn in hope to our Lord.' 33 Such was the punishment. Yet the punishment of the Hereafter is indeed greater, if (only) they knew.

34 Surely for the ones who guard (themselves) (there will be) Gardens of Bliss with their Lord. 35 Shall We treat those who submit like the sinners? 36 What is (the matter) with you? How do you judge? 37 Or do you have a Book which you study? 38 Surely you (would) have in it whatever indeed you choose! 39 Or do you have guarantees from Us, reaching to the Day of Resurrection? Surely you (would) have whatever indeed you judge! 40 Ask them which of them will

guarantee that. **41** Or do they have associates? Let them bring their associates, if they are truthful. **42** On the Day when the leg will be bared, and they will be called to (make) prostration, but are unable: **43** their sight will be downcast, and humiliation will cover them, because they had been called to (make) prostration when they were able.

44 So leave Me (to deal with) anyone who calls this proclamation a lie. We shall lead them on step by step without their realizing it. **45** And I shall spare them – surely My plan is strong.

46 Or do you ask them for a reward, so that they are burdened with debt? **47** Or is the unseen in their keeping, and so they are writing (it) down?

48 Be patient for the judgment of your Lord, and do not be like the companion of the fish,[1] when he called out, choked with distress. **49** If a blessing from his Lord had not reached him, he would indeed have been tossed on the desert (shore), condemned. **50** But his Lord chose him, and made him one of the righteous.

51 Surely those who disbelieve almost indeed make you stumble with their look, when they hear the Reminder. They say, 'Surely he is possessed indeed!' **52** Yet it is nothing but a reminder to all peoples.

---

1. *companion of the fish*: probably Jonah (see Q21.87–88; 37.139–148).

69 ✺ The Payment Due

In the Name of God, the Merciful, the Compassionate

1 The payment due! **2** What is the payment due? **3** And what will make you[1] know what the payment due is? **4** Thamūd and 'Ād called the striking a lie. **5** As for Thamūd, they were destroyed by the outbreak. **6** And as for 'Ād, they were destroyed by a furious, violent wind, **7** which He forced on them for seven nights and eight days consecutively, and during which you (could) see the people lying flat, as if they were the trunks of collapsed date palms. **8** Do you see any remnant of them (now)? **9** And Pharaoh (too) – and those who were before him, and the overturned (cities) – committed sin, **10** and they disobeyed the messenger of their Lord, so He seized them with a surpassing seizing. **11** Surely We – when the waters overflowed – We carried you in the running (ship), **12** so that We might make it a reminder to you, and (that) an attentive ear might attend to it.

13 When a single blast is blown on the trumpet, **14** and the earth and the mountains are lifted up and shattered with a single shattering, **15** on that Day the falling will fall, **16** and the sky will be split open, (for) on that Day it will be frail, **17** and the angels (will stand) on its borders, and they will bear the throne of your Lord above them on that Day – eight (of them). **18** On that Day you will (all) be presented – not a secret of yours will be hidden.

19 As for the one who is given his book in his right (hand), he will say, 'Take (and) read my book. **20** Surely I thought that I would meet my reckoning.' **21** And he will be in a pleasing life, **22** in a Garden on high, **23** its clusters (of fruit) near (at hand). **24** 'Eat and drink with satisfaction, (in return) for what you did in days past.' **25** But as for the one who is given his book in his left (hand), he will say, 'Would that I had not been given my book, **26** and not known what my reckoning is! **27** Would that it had been the end! **28** My wealth is of no use to me. **29** My authority has perished from me.' **30** 'Seize him and bind him! **31** Then burn him in the Furnace, **32** (and) then put him in a chain of seventy cubits. **33** Surely he never believed in God, the Almighty, **34** nor did he ever urge the feeding of the poor. **35** So today he has no friend here, **36** nor any food except refuse, **37** which only the sinners eat.'

38 I swear by what you[2] see **39** and what you do not see! **40** Surely it is indeed the word of an honorable messenger. **41** It is not the word of a poet – little do

---

1. *you*: sing.
2. *you*: plur.

you believe! **42** Nor (is it) the word of an oracle-giver – little do you take heed! **43** (It is) a sending down from the Lord of all peoples. **44** If he had forged any (false) words against Us, **45** We would indeed have seized him by the right (hand). **46** Then We would indeed have cut his (main) artery, **47** and not one of you could have defended him from it. **48** Surely it is a reminder indeed to the ones who guard (themselves). **49** Yet surely We indeed know that some of you are calling (it) a lie. **50** Surely it will be a (cause of) regret indeed to the disbelievers. **51** Yet surely it is the certain truth indeed. **52** So glorify the name of your Lord, the Almighty.

70 ❊ The Stairways

In the Name of God, the Merciful, the Compassionate

1 A questioner questioned about the punishment going to fall 2 – the disbelievers have no one to repel it! – 3 from God, controller of the stairways. 4 The angels and the spirit ascend to Him in a day, the measure of which is fifty thousand years. 5 So be patient with a patience that becomes (you). 6 Surely they see it as far off, 7 but We see it as near 8 – the Day when the sky will be like molten metal, 9 and the mountains will be like (tufts of) wool, 10 and friend will not question friend. 11 (As) they come into sight of each other, the sinner will wish that he (could) ransom (himself) from the punishment of that Day with his sons, 12 and his consort, and his brother, 13 and his family who gave him refuge, 14 and whoever is on the earth – all (of them) – (wishing that) then it might rescue him. 15 By no means! Surely (there is) a flame, 16 a scalp remover! 17 It will call the one who turned and went away, 18 and (who) accumulated and hoarded.

19 Surely the human was created anxious (for gain). 20 When misfortune touches him, (he is) complaining, 21 but when good touches him, refusing (to give), 22 except for the ones who pray 23 (and) who continue at their prayers, 24 and in whose wealth (there is) an acknowledged (portion) due 25 for the beggar and the outcast, 26 and who affirm the Day of Judgment, 27 and who are apprehensive of the punishment of their Lord 28 – surely no one feels secure (against) the punishment of their Lord – 29 and who guard their private parts, 30 except concerning their wives or what their right (hands) own[1] – surely then they are not (to be) blamed, 31 but whoever seeks beyond that, those – they are the transgressors – 32 and those who keep their pledges and their promise(s), 33 and who stand by their testimonies, 34 and who guard their prayers. 35 Those will be honored in Gardens.

36 What is (the matter) with those who disbelieve, rushing toward you, 37 from the right (hand) and from the left in groups? 38 Is every person among them eager to enter a Garden of Bliss? 39 By no means! Surely We have created them from what they know. 40 I swear by the Lord of the Easts and the Wests! Surely We are able indeed 41 to exchange (others who are) better than them – We are not (to be) outrun! 42 So leave them! Let them banter and jest, until they meet their Day which they are promised, 43 the Day when they will come forth from the graves rushing – as if they were running to some goal – 44 their sight downcast, humiliation covering them. That is the Day which they were promised.

---

1. *what their right (hands) own*: i.e. their female slaves (cf. Q4.3, 24).

71 ✸ Noah

In the Name of God, the Merciful, the Compassionate

1 Surely We sent Noah to his people: 'Warn your people before a painful punishment comes upon them.' **2** He said, 'My people! I am a clear warner for you. **3** Serve God, and guard (yourselves) against Him, and obey me! **4** He will forgive you your sins, and spare you until an appointed time. Surely the time of God, when it comes, cannot be postponed. If (only) you knew!'

5 He said, 'My Lord, surely I have called my people night and day, **6** but my calling has only increased them in flight. **7** Surely I – whenever I called them, so that You might forgive them, they put their fingers in their ears, and covered themselves with their clothes, and persisted (in disbelief), and became very arrogant. **8** Then surely I called them publicly, **9** then surely I spoke openly to them, and I confided to them in secret, **10** and I said, "Ask forgiveness from your Lord, surely He is forgiving, **11** and He will send the sky (down) on you in abundance, **12** and increase you with wealth and sons, and make gardens for you, and make rivers for you. **13** What is (the matter) with you that do not expect seriousness (of purpose) on the part of God, **14** when He created you in stages? **15** Do you not see how God created seven heavens in stories, **16** and placed the moon in them as a light, and placed the sun (in them) as a lamp? **17** And God caused you to grow from of the earth, **18** (and) then He will return you into it, and bring you forth again. **19** God has made the earth an expanse for you, **20** so that you may traverse its open (path)ways."'

21 Noah said, 'My Lord, surely they have disobeyed me, and followed one whose wealth and children increase him only in loss, **22** and they have schemed a great scheme, **23** and said, "Do not forsake your gods, and do not forsake Wadd, nor Suwā', nor Yaghūth, and Ya'ūq, and Nasr."[1] **24** And they have led many astray. Increase the evildoers only in going astray!'

25 They were drowned on account of their sins, and forced to enter a fire, and they found they had no helpers other than God. **26** Noah said, 'My Lord, do not leave any of the disbelievers as an inhabitant on the earth. **27** Surely You – if You leave them, they will lead Your servants astray, and will give birth only to depraved disbeliever(s). **28** My Lord, forgive me and my parents, and whoever enters my house believing, and the believing men and the believing women, and increase the evildoers only in destruction!'

---

1. *do not forsake Wadd, nor Suwā', nor Yaghūth, and Ya'ūq, and Nasr*: gods presumably worshipped in the time of Noah (mentioned only here).

72 ❖ The Jinn

In the Name of God, the Merciful, the Compassionate

1 Say: 'I am inspired that a band of the jinn listened, and they said, "Surely we have heard an amazing Qur'ān! **2** It guides to the right (course). We believe in it, and we shall not associate anyone with our Lord. **3** And (we believe) that He – exalted (be) the majesty of our Lord! – He has not taken a consort or son. **4** And that the foolish among us used to say an outrageous thing against God. **5** And that we had thought that humans and jinn would never say any lie against God. **6** And that some humans used to take refuge with some jinn, and they increased them in depravity. **7** And that they thought as you (also) thought, that God will not raise up anyone. **8** And that we touched the sky and found it filled with harsh guards and piercing flames. **9** And that we used to sit there on seats to listen (in), but whoever listens now finds a piercing flame lying in wait for him. **10** And that we do not know whether evil is intended for those who are on the earth, or whether their Lord intends right (guidance) for them. **11** And that some of us are righteous, and some of us are other than that – we are on different roads. **12** And that we (now) think that we shall not be able to escape God on the earth, and shall not escape Him by flight. **13** And that when we heard the guidance, we believed in it, and whoever believes in his Lord will not fear any deprivation or depravity. **14** And that some of us have submitted, and some of us are the ones who have deviated. Whoever submits, those have sought out right (guidance), **15** but as for the ones who have deviated, they have become firewood for Gehenna!"'

16 And (We say) that if they[1] had gone straight on the road, We would indeed have given them water to drink in abundance, **17** so that We might test them concerning it. Whoever turns away from the remembrance of his Lord – He will place him in hard punishment. **18** And that the mosques (belong) to God, so do not call on anyone (along) with God. **19** And that when the servant of God stood calling on Him, they were almost upon him in hordes.

20 Say: 'I call only on my Lord, and I do not associate anyone with Him.'

21 Say: 'Surely I possess no power over you, either for harm or for right (guidance).'

---

1. *And (We say) that if they ...*: while the same construction ('And that ...') continues, the speaker suddenly switches from the jinn to God (or the angels), and 'they' now refers to humans.

The Jinn

22 Say: 'No one will protect me from God, and I shall not find any refuge other than Him. **23** (I bring) only a delivery from God and His messages.' Whoever disobeys God and His messenger, surely for him (there is) the Fire of Gehenna, there to remain forever. **24** – Until, when they see what they are promised, they will know who is weaker in helper(s) and fewer in number.

25 Say: 'I do not know whether what you are promised is near, or whether my Lord will appoint a (distant) time for it. **26** (He is) the Knower of the unseen, and He does not disclose His unseen to anyone, **27** except to a messenger whom He has approved, and then He dispatches before him and behind him (watchers) lying in wait, **28** so that He may know that they have delivered the messages of their Lord. He encompasses all that is with them, and He counts everything by number.'

73 ❖ THE ENWRAPPED ONE

In the Name of God, the Merciful, the Compassionate

1 You, enwrapped one! **2** Stay up through the night, except a little **3** – half of it or a little less, **4** or a little more – and arrange the Qur'ān very carefully. **5** Surely We shall cast upon you a heavy word. **6** Surely the first part of the night – it is more efficacious and more suitable for speaking. **7** Surely during the day you have protracted business, **8** but remember the name of your Lord, and devote yourself to Him completely.

9 Lord of the East and the West – (there is) no god but Him, so take Him as a guardian, **10** and be patient with what they say, and forsake them gracefully. **11** Leave Me (to deal with) the ones who call (it) a lie – (those) possessors of prosperity – and let them be for a little (while). **12** Surely We have chains and a Furnace, **13** and food that chokes, and a painful punishment, **14** on the Day when the earth and the mountains will quake, and the mountains will become a heap of shifting sand.

15 Surely We have sent to you a messenger as a witness over you, as We sent to Pharaoh a messenger. **16** But Pharaoh disobeyed the messenger, and We seized him harshly. **17** If you disbelieve, how will you guard (yourselves) against a Day which will turn the children grey, **18** on which the sky will be split open and His promise comes to pass? **19** Surely this is a Reminder, and whoever pleases takes a way to his Lord.

20 Surely your Lord knows that you[1] stay up nearly two-thirds of the night – or a half of it or a third of it – and (so do) a contingent of those with you. God determines the night and the day. He knows that you[2] do not count it up, and He has turned to you (in forgiveness). So recite[3] what is easy (for you) of the Qur'ān. He knows that some of you are sick, and others are striking forth on the earth, seeking some of the favor of God, and (still) others are fighting in the way of God. So recite what is easy (for you) of it, and observe the prayer and give the alms, and lend to God a good loan. Whatever good you send forward for yourselves, you will find it with God – it will be better and greater as a reward. Ask forgiveness from God. Surely God is forgiving, compassionate.

---

1. *you*: sing.
2. *you*: plur. (here and throughout the rest of this section).
3. *recite*: plur. imperative.

74 ❈ THE CLOAKED ONE

In the Name of God, the Merciful, the Compassionate

1 You, cloaked one! **2** Arise and warn! **3** Magnify your Lord, **4** and purify your clothes, **5** and flee from the defilement! **6** Do not confer a favor to gain more, **7** and be patient before your Lord. **8** When there is a blast on the trumpet, **9** that Day will be a hard Day **10** – far from easy on the disbelievers.

11 Leave Me (to deal with) him whom I created alone, **12** and for whom I supplied extensive wealth, **13** and sons as witnesses, **14** and made everything smooth for him. **15** Then he is eager that I should do more. **16** By no means! He is stubborn to Our signs. **17** I shall burden him with a hard climb. **18** Surely he thought and decided – **19** so may he perish (for) how he decided! **20** Once again, may he perish (for) how he decided! **21** Then he looked, **22** then he frowned and scowled, **23** then he turned back and became arrogant, **24** and said, 'This is nothing but ordinary magic. **25** This is nothing but the word of a human being.' **26** I shall burn him in Saqar![1]

27 And what will make you[2] know what Saqar is? **28** It spares nothing, and leaves nothing, **29** scorching all flesh. **30** Over it are nineteen. **31** We have made only angels as keepers of the Fire, and We have made their number only as a test for the disbelievers, so that those who have been given the Book may be certain, and that those who believe may increase in belief, and that those who have been given the Book and those who believe may not be in doubt, and that those in whose hearts is a sickness and the disbelievers may say, 'What did God intend by this as a parable?' In this way God leads astray whomever He pleases and guides whomever He pleases. No one knows the (angelic) forces of your Lord but Him. It is nothing but a reminder to humankind.

32 By no means! By the moon, **33** and the night when it retreats, **34** and the morning when it brightens! **35** Surely it is indeed one of the greatest things **36** – a warning to humankind – **37** to whoever of you pleases to go forward or lag behind.

38 Each person (is held) in pledge for what he has earned, **39** except for the companions on the right. **40** In Gardens they will ask each other questions **41** about the sinners: **42** 'What put you into Saqar?' **43** They will say, 'We were not among the

---

1. *Saqar*: another name for Hell (cf. Q54.48).
2. *you*: sing.

The Cloaked One

ones who prayed, **44** and we did not feed the poor, **45** and we bantered with the banterers, **46** and we called the Day of Judgment a lie, **47** until the certainty came to us.' **48** The intercession of the intercessors will not benefit them.

49 What is (the matter) with them, turning away from the Reminder, **50** as if they were frightened donkeys **51** fleeing from a lion? **52** No! Each one of them wants to be given scrolls unrolled. **53** By no means! No! They do not fear the Hereafter. **54** By no means! Surely it is a reminder, **55** and whoever pleases takes heed of it. **56** But they will not take heed unless God pleases. He is worthy of guarding (oneself) against, and worthy of (dispensing) forgiveness.

75 ✺ The Resurrection

In the Name of God, the Merciful, the Compassionate

1 I swear by the Day of Resurrection! **2** And I swear by the accusing self! **3** Does the human think that We shall not gather his bones? **4** Yes indeed! We are (even) able to fashion his fingers (again). **5** Yet the human (still) wants to know what is in store for him. **6** He asks, 'When is the Day of Resurrection?' **7** When the sight is dazed, **8** and the moon is eclipsed, **9** and the sun and moon are brought together, **10** on that Day the human will say, 'Where is the escape?' **11** By no means! (There is) no refuge! **12** The (only) dwelling place on that Day will be to your Lord. **13** On that Day the human will be informed about what has he sent forward and kept back. **14** No! The human will be a clear proof against himself, **15** even though he offers his excuses.

16 Do not move your tongue with it to hurry it. **17** Surely on Us (depends) its collection and its recitation. **18** When We recite it, follow its recitation. **19** Then surely on Us (depends) its explanation.

20 By no means! No! You[1] love this fleeting (world), **21** and neglect the Hereafter. **22** (Some) faces that Day will be radiant, **23** looking to their Lord, **24** and (other) faces that Day will be scowling, **25** thinking that a calamity will be visited on them. **26** By no means! When it reaches the collarbones, **27** and it is said, 'Who will carry (him) off?,' **28** and he thinks that the parting has come, **29** when leg is tangled with leg, **30** the (only) drive on that Day will be to your Lord.

31 (For) he did not affirm (it), nor did he pray, **32** but he called (it) a lie and turned away. **33** Then he went to his household with an arrogant swagger. **34** Nearer to you and nearer! **35** Once again, nearer to you and nearer! **36** Does the human think that he will be left to go about at will? **37** Was he not a drop of semen emitted? **38** Then he was a clot, and He created and fashioned (him), **39** and made from it the two sexes, the male and the female. **40** Is that One not able to give the dead life?

---

1. *You*: plur.

76 ❋ THE HUMAN

In the Name of God, the Merciful, the Compassionate

1 Has (there) come upon the human a period of time when he was a thing not mentioned? 2 Surely We created the human from a drop, a mixture – We test him – and We made him hearing (and) seeing. 3 Surely We guided him to the way, (to see) whether (he would be) thankful or whether (he would be) ungrateful.

4 Surely We have prepared for the disbelievers chains and fetters and a blazing (Fire). 5 Surely the pious will drink from a cup containing a mixture of camphor, 6 (from) a spring at which the servants of God drink, making it gush forth abundantly. 7 They fulfill (their) vows, and fear a Day – its evil is (already) in the air – 8 and they give food, despite their love for it, to the poor, and the orphan, and the captive: 9 'We feed you only for the face of God. We do not desire any payment or thanks from you. 10 Surely we fear a grim (and) ominous Day from our Lord.' 11 So God has guarded them against the evil of that Day, and made them encounter radiance and happiness, 12 and repaid them for their patience with a Garden and silk. 13 Reclining there on couches, 14 they do not see there any (hot) sun or bitter cold, and its shades are close upon them, and its clusters (of fruit) near (at hand). 15 Vessels of silver and cups made of crystal are passed around among them 16 – crystal of silver which they have measured very exactly. 17 There they are given a cup to drink, containing a mixture of ginger, 18 (from) a spring there named Salsabīl. 19 And boys of eternal youth circulate among them. When you[1] see them, you (would) think them scattered pearls. 20 When you see (it all), then you will see bliss and a great kingdom. 21 On them are green clothes of silk and brocade, and they are adorned with bracelets of silver, and their Lord gives them a pure drink to drink. 22 'Surely this is a payment for you, and your striving is thanked.'

23 Surely We – We have sent down on you the Qur'ān once and for all. 24 So be patient for the Judgment of your Lord, and do not obey any sinner (or) ungrateful one among them. 25 But remember the name of your Lord morning and evening, 26 and part of the night, and prostrate yourself before Him, and glorify Him all night long.

27 Surely these (people) love the fleeting (world), and leave behind them a heavy Day. 28 We created them and strengthened their constitution, and when We

---

1. *you*: sing.

The Human

please, We shall exchange the likes of them. **29** Surely this is a Reminder, and whoever pleases takes a way to his Lord. **30** But you will not (so) please unless God pleases. Surely God is knowing, wise. **31** He causes whomever He pleases to enter into His mercy, but the evildoers – He has prepared a painful punishment for them.

77 ❊ The Ones Sent Forth

In the Name of God, the Merciful, the Compassionate

1 By the ones sent forth in succession, and the ones blasting (with their) blast! 2 By the scatterers 3 (with their) scattering, 4 and the ones splitting asunder, 5 and the ones casting a reminder, 6 as an excuse or warning! 7 Surely what you are promised is indeed going to fall!

8 When the stars are obliterated, 9 and when the sky is split open, 10 and when the mountains are scattered (as dust), 11 and when the messengers' time is given – 12 for what Day are these things appointed? 13 For the Day of Decision!

14 And what will make you know what the Day of Decision is? 15 Woe that Day to the ones who call (it) a lie!

16 Did We not destroy those of old? 17 Then We caused later (generations) to follow them. 18 In this way We deal with the sinners. 19 Woe that Day to the ones who call (it) a lie!

20 Did We not create you from despicable water, 21 and put it in a secure dwelling place 22 for a known term? 23 We determined (it) – excellent were the Ones able (to do that)! 24 Woe that Day to the ones who call (it) a lie!

25 Did We not make the earth as a container 26 of the living and dead? 27 And did We not place on it lofty mountains, and give you fresh water to drink? 28 Woe that Day to the ones who call (it) a lie!

29 Depart to what you called a lie! 30 Depart to a three-branched shadow 31 – (it affords) no sheltering (shade) and (it is of) no use against the flame. 32 Surely it shoots out sparks, (each one) the size of a castle, 33 as if it were (the color) of yellow camels. 34 Woe that Day to the ones who call (it) a lie!

35 This is a Day when they will not speak, 36 nor will it be permitted to them to make excuses. 37 Woe that Day to the ones who call (it) a lie!

38 'This is the Day of Decision. We have gathered you and those of old together. 39 If you have a plot, plot against Me!' 40 Woe that Day to the ones who call (it) a lie!

41 Surely the ones who guard (themselves) will be in (the midst of) shades and springs, 42 and fruits of whatever (kind) they desire: 43 'Eat and drink with satisfaction (in return) for what you have done.' 44 Surely in this way We repay the doers of good. 45 Woe that Day to the ones who call (it) a lie!

46 'Eat and enjoy (life) a little. Surely you are sinners!' **47** Woe that Day to the ones who call (it) a lie!

48 When it is said to them, 'Bow down,' they do not bow down. **49** Woe that Day to the ones who call (it) a lie!

50 In what proclamation will they believe after this?

78 ✺ The News

In the Name of God, the Merciful, the Compassionate

1 What are they asking each other questions about? 2 About the awesome news, 3 concerning which they differ. 4 By no means! Soon they will know! 5 Once again, by no means! Soon they will know!

6 Have We not made the earth as a bed, 7 and the mountains as stakes? 8 We created you in pairs, 9 and made your sleep as a rest, 10 and made the night as a covering, 11 and made the day for (your) livelihood. 12 We have built above you seven firm (heavens), 13 and made a blazing lamp. 14 We have sent down water from the rainclouds, pouring forth, 15 so that by means of it We may bring forth grain and vegetation, 16 and luxuriant gardens.

17 Surely the Day of Decision is an appointed time: 18 the Day when there will be a blast on the trumpet, and you will come in crowds, 19 and the sky will be opened and become gates, 20 and the mountains will be moved and become a mirage. 21 Surely Gehenna lies in wait 22 as a (place of) return for the insolent transgressors, 23 there to remain for ages. 24 They will not taste there any coolness or drink, 25 except for boiling (water) and rotten (food) 26 – a fitting payment! 27 Surely they were not expecting a reckoning 28 when they called Our signs an utter lie. 29 But We have counted up everything in a Book. 30 So: 'Taste (it)! We shall only increase you in punishment.'

31 Surely for the ones who guard (themselves) (there is) a (place of) safety: 32 orchards and grapes, 33 and full-breasted (maidens), (all) of the same age, 34 and a cup full (of wine) 35 – in which they will not hear any frivolous talk, nor any lying 36 – a payment from your Lord, a gift, a reckoning!

37 Lord of the heavens and the earth, and whatever is between them, the Merciful, of whom they have no power to speak. 38 On the Day when the spirit and the angels stand in lines, they will not speak, except the one to whom the Merciful has given permission, and he will say what is correct. 39 That is the true Day. Whoever pleases takes a (way of) return to his Lord. 40 Surely We have warned you of a punishment near (at hand), on the Day when a person will see what his hands have sent forward, and the disbeliever will say, 'Would that I were dust!'

79 ❁ The Snatchers

In the Name of God, the Merciful, the Compassionate

1 By the ones who snatch violently! **2** By the ones who draw out completely! **3** By the ones who glide smoothly, **4** and race swiftly, **5** and direct the affair! **6** On the Day when the (earth)quake quakes, **7** and that which ensues follows it, **8** hearts on that Day will pound, **9** their sight downcast. **10** They will say, 'Are we indeed being turned back into (our) former state? **11** When we were rotten bones?' **12** They will say, 'That would then be a losing turn!' **13** Yet it will only be a single shout, **14** and suddenly they will be awakened.

15 Has the story of Moses come to you? **16** When his Lord called to him in the holy wādī of Ṭuwā: **17** 'Go to Pharaoh! Surely he has transgressed insolently. **18** And say: "Do you have (any desire) to purify yourself? **19** And: "I would guide you to your Lord, and then perhaps you will fear (Him)."' **20** So he showed him the great sign, **21** but he called (it) a lie and disobeyed. **22** Then he turned away in haste, **23** and he gathered (his people) and called out, **24** and said, 'I am your Lord, the Most High!' **25** So God seized him with the punishment of the last and the first. **26** Surely in that is a lesson indeed for whoever fears.

27 Are you a stronger creation or the sky? He built it. **28** He raised its roof and fashioned it. **29** He darkened its night and brought forth its morning light. **30** And the earth, after that, He spread it out. **31** He brought forth from it its water and its pasture **32** – and the mountains, He anchored it (to them) – **33** a provision for you and for your livestock.

34 When the great overwhelming comes, **35** on the Day when a person will remember what he strove for, **36** and the Furnace will come forth for all to see: **37** as for the one who transgressed insolently, **38** and preferred this present life, **39** surely the Furnace – it will be the refuge. **40** But as for the one who feared the position of his Lord, and restrained himself from (vain) desire, **41** surely the Garden – it will be the refuge.

42 They ask you about the Hour: 'When is its arrival?' **43** What do you have to do with the mention of it? **44** To your Lord is its (ultimate) goal. **45** You are only a warner for whoever fears it. **46** On the Day when they see it, (it will seem) as if they had remained (in the grave) for only an evening or its morning light.

80 ❂ He Frowned

In the Name of God, the Merciful, the Compassionate

1 He frowned and turned away, **2** because the blind man came to him. **3** What will make you[1] know? Perhaps he will (yet) purify himself, **4** or take heed, and the Reminder will benefit him. **5** As for the one who considers himself independent, **6** you give your attention to him. **7** Yet it is not (dependent) on you if he does not purify himself. **8** But as for the one who comes running to you, **9** and (who) fears (God), **10** from him you are distracted.

11 By no means! Surely it is a Reminder **12** – and whoever pleases (may) take heed of it – **13** (written) in honored pages, **14** exalted (and) purified, **15** by the hands of scribes, **16** (who are) honorable (and) dutiful.

17 May the human perish! How ungrateful he is! **18** From what did He create him? **19** From a drop! He created him, and determined him, **20** then He made the way easy for him, **21** then He caused him to die and buried him, **22** then, when He pleases, He will raise him (again). **23** By no means! He[2] has not accomplished what He commanded him.

24 Let the human consider his food: **25** We pour out water in abundance, **26** then We split open the earth in cracks, **27** and We cause grain to grow in it, **28** and grapes and green plants, **29** and olives and date palms, **30** and lush orchards, **31** and fruits and herbs **32** – a provision for you and your livestock.

33 When the blast comes, **34** on the Day when a person will flee from his brother, **35** and his mother and his father, **36** and his consort and his sons, **37** each of them that Day will have some matter to keep him busy. **38** (Some) faces that Day will be shining, **39** laughing, rejoicing at the good news. **40** But (other) faces that Day – dust will be upon them, **41** (and) darkness will cover them. **42** Those – they are the disbelievers, the depraved.

---

1. *you*: sing.
2. *He*: the human.

81 ❊ THE SHROUDING

In the Name of God, the Merciful, the Compassionate

1 When the sun is shrouded, 2 and when the stars become dim, 3 and when the mountains are moved, 4 and when the pregnant camels are abandoned, 5 and when the wild beasts are herded together, 6 and when the seas are made to surge, 7 and when selves are paired, 8 and when the buried baby girl is asked 9 for what sin she was killed, 10 and when the pages are spread open, 11 and when the sky is stripped off, 12 and when the Furnace is set ablaze, 13 and when the Garden is brought near, 14 (then each) person will know what he has presented.

15 I swear by the slinking (stars), 16 the runners, the hiders, 17 by the night when it departs, 18 by the dawn when it breathes! 19 Surely it is indeed the word of an honorable messenger 20 – one full of power, secure with the Holder of the throne, 21 one (to be) obeyed, (and) furthermore trustworthy. 22 Your companion is not possessed. 23 Certainly he did see Him on the clear horizon. 24 He is not grudging of the unseen. 25 It is not the word of an accursed satan. 26 So where will you go? 27 It is nothing but a reminder to all peoples 28 – to whoever of you pleases to go straight. 29 But you will not (so) please unless God pleases, the Lord of all peoples.

82 ❊ The Rending

In the Name of God, the Merciful, the Compassionate

1 When the sky is rent, 2 and when the stars are scattered, 3 and when the seas are made to gush forth, 4 and when the graves are ransacked, 5 (then each) person will know what he has sent forward and kept back.

6 Human! What has deceived you about your generous Lord, 7 who created you and fashioned you and balanced you? 8 He constructed you in whatever form He pleased. 9 By no means! No! You (still) call the Judgment a lie. 10 Surely (there are) indeed watchers over you, 11 honorable, writing. 12 They know whatever you do. 13 Surely the pious will indeed be in (a place of) bliss, 14 and surely the depraved will indeed be in a Furnace. 15 They will burn in it on the Day of Judgment, 16 and from it they will not be absent.

17 What will make you[1] know what the Day of Judgment is? 18 Once again, what will make you know what the Day of Judgment is? 19 The Day when no one will have any power to (help) another. The command on that Day (will belong) to God.

---

1. *you*: sing.

83 ❊ The Defrauders

In the Name of God, the Merciful, the Compassionate

1 Woe to the defrauders, 2 who take full measure when they measure against the people, 3 but give less when they measure for themselves or weigh for themselves. 4 Do those (people) not think that they will be raised up 5 for a great Day, 6 a Day when the people will stand before the Lord of all peoples? 7 By no means! Surely the book of the depraved is indeed in Sijjīn. 8 And what will make you[1] know what Sijjīn is? 9 A written book. 10 Woe that Day to the ones who call (it) a lie, 11 who call the Day of Judgment a lie! 12 No one calls it a lie except every transgressor (and) sinner. 13 When Our signs are recited to him, he says, 'Old tales!' 14 By no means! No! What they have earned has rusted on their hearts. 15 By no means! Surely on that Day they will indeed be veiled from their Lord. 16 Then surely they will indeed burn in the Furnace. 17 Then it will be said to them, 'This is what you called a lie.'

18 By no means! Surely the book of the pious is indeed in 'Illiyyīn. 19 And what will make you know what 'Illiyyīn is? 20 A written book. 21 The ones brought near bear witness to it. 22 Surely the pious will indeed be in (a place of) bliss, 23 (lying) on couches gazing about. 24 You will recognize in their faces the radiance of bliss. 25 They are given a pure, sealed wine to drink, 26 its seal is musk – for that let the seekers seek! – 27 and its mixture contains Tasnīm, 28 (from) a spring at which the ones brought near drink.

29 Surely those who sinned used to laugh on account of those who believed, 30 and when they passed them by used to wink at each other. 31 And when they turned back to their people, they turned back amused, 32 and when they saw them, they said, 'Surely these (people) have gone astray indeed!' 33 Yet they had not been sent as watchers over them. 34 So today those who believed are laughing on account of the disbelievers, 35 (as) they gaze about (lying) on couches. 36 Have the disbelievers been rewarded for what they have done?

---

1. *you*: sing.

84 ❀ The Splitting

In the Name of God, the Merciful, the Compassionate

1 When the sky is split open, 2 and listens to its Lord and is made fit, 3 and when earth is stretched out, 4 and casts forth what is in it and becomes empty, 5 and listens to its Lord and is made fit, 6 you human – surely you are laboring to your Lord laboriously and are about to meet Him.

7 As for the one who is given his book in his right (hand), 8 he will receive an easy reckoning, 9 and turn back to his family, rejoicing. 10 But as for the one who is given his book behind his back, 11 he will call out for destruction, 12 and burn in a blazing (Fire). 13 Surely he used to be among his family, rejoicing. 14 Surely he thought that he would not return. 15 Yes indeed! Surely his Lord was watching him.

16 I swear by the twilight, 17 by the night and what it envelops, 18 by the moon when it becomes full! 19 You will indeed ride story upon story.

20 What is (the matter) with them that they do not believe, 21 and when the Qur'ān is recited to them, do not prostrate themselves? 22 No! Those who disbelieve call (it) a lie. 23 Yet God knows what they hide away. 24 So give them news of a painful punishment 25 – except for those who believe and do righteous deeds. For them (there is) a reward without end.

85 ❖ The Constellations

In the Name of God, the Merciful, the Compassionate

1 By the sky full of constellations, **2** by the promised Day, **3** by a witness and what is witnessed! **4** May the companions of the Pit perish **5** – the Fire full of fuel – **6** when they are sitting over it, **7** and they (themselves) are witnesses of what they have done to the believers. **8** They took vengeance on them only because they believed in God, the Mighty, the Praiseworthy, **9** the One who – to Him (belongs) the kingdom of the heavens and the earth. God is a witness over everything.

10 Surely those who persecute the believing men and the believing women, (and) then have not turned (in repentance) – for them (there is) the punishment of Gehenna, and for them (there is) the punishment of the burning (Fire). **11** Surely those who believe and do righteous deeds – for them (there are) Gardens through which rivers flow. That is the great triumph!

12 Surely your Lord's attack is harsh indeed. **13** Surely He – He brings about (the creation) and restores (it). **14** He is the Forgiving, the Loving, **15** Holder of the throne, the Glorious, **16** Doer of what He intends.

17 Has the story of the forces come to you,[1] **18** of Pharaoh and Thamūd? **19** No! But those who disbelieve persist in calling (it) a lie. **20** Yet God surrounds them from behind.

21 Yes! It is a glorious Qur'ān, **22** in a guarded Tablet.

---

1. *you*: sing.

86 ❖ The Night Visitor

In the Name of God, the Merciful, the Compassionate

1 By the sky and the night visitor! **2** And what will make you[1] know what the night visitor is? **3** The piercing star! **4** Over every person (there is) a watcher. **5** So let the human consider: what was he created from? **6** He was created from spurting water. **7** It comes forth from (a place) between the spine and the ribs. **8** Surely He is able indeed to bring him back, **9** on the Day when (all) secrets will be examined, **10** and he will have no power (and) no helper.

11 By the sky full of returning (rain), **12** by the earth full of cracks! **13** Surely it is a decisive word indeed! **14** It is no joke.

15 Surely they are hatching a plot, **16** but I (too) am hatching a plot. **17** So let the disbelievers be, let them be for a little (while).

---

1. *you*: sing.

87 ✻ The Most High

In the Name of God, the Merciful, the Compassionate

1 Glorify the name of your Lord, the Most High, 2 who creates and fashions, 3 who determines and guides, 4 who brings forth the pasture, 5 and then turns it into darkened ruins. 6 We shall make you recite, and you will not forget – except whatever God pleases. 7 Surely He knows what is spoken publicly and what is hidden. 8 We shall make it very easy for you. 9 So remind (them), if the reminder benefits. 10 He who fears will take heed, 11 but the most miserable will turn away from it 12 – who will burn in the great Fire. 13 Then he will neither die there nor live.

14 Prosperous is he who purifies himself, 15 and remembers the name of his Lord, and prays. 16 No! But you prefer this present life, 17 when the Hereafter is better and more lasting. 18 Surely this is indeed in the former pages, 19 the pages of Abraham and Moses.

88 ❈ The Covering

In the Name of God, the Merciful, the Compassionate

1 Has the story of the Covering come to you?[1] 2 (Some) faces that Day will be downcast, 3 laboring, weary. 4 They will burn in a scorching Fire. 5 They will be made to drink from a boiling spring. 6 They will have no food except dry thorns, 7 (which) neither nourishes nor satisfies hunger. 8 (Other) faces that Day will be blessed, 9 content with their striving, 10 in a Garden on high 11 – where they will hear no frivolous talk, 12 where (there is) a flowing spring, 13 where (there are) raised couches, 14 and cups laid down, 15 and cushions lined up, 16 and carpets spread out.

17 Will they not look at the camels, how they were created, 18 and at the sky, how it was raised up, 19 and at the mountains, how they were constructed, 20 and at the earth, how it was spread flat?

21 So remind (them)! You are only a reminder. 22 You are not a record-keeper over them 23 – except for the one who turns away and disbelieves. 24 God will punish him with the greatest punishment. 25 Surely to Us is their return. 26 Then surely on Us (depends) their reckoning.

---

1. *you*: sing.

89 ☸ The Dawn

In the Name of God, the Merciful, the Compassionate

1 By the dawn **2** and ten nights! **3** By the even and the odd! **4** By the night when it journeys on! **5** (Is there) in that an oath for a person of understanding?

6 Do you[1] not see how your Lord dealt with 'Ād, **7** Iram of the pillars, **8** the like of which was never created in (all) the lands, **9** and Thamūd, who carved out the rock in the wādī, **10** and Pharaoh, he of the stakes, **11** who (all) transgressed insolently in (their) lands, **12** and spread (too) much corruption there? **13** So your Lord poured on them a scourge of punishment. **14** Surely your Lord indeed lies in wait.

15 As for the human, whenever his Lord tests him, and honors him and blesses him, he says, 'My Lord has honored me.' **16** But whenever he tests him, and restricts his provision for him, he says, 'My Lord has humiliated me.' **17** By no means! No! You do not honor the orphan, **18** nor do you urge the feeding of the poor, **19** yet you devour the inheritance greedily, **20** and love wealth passionately.

21 By no means! When the earth is shattered with a double shattering, **22** and your Lord comes, and the angels, line after line, **23** and Gehenna is brought (forth) on that Day – on that Day the human will (finally) take heed, but how will the reminder be for him? **24** He will say, 'Would that I had sent forward (righteous deeds) for my life!' **25** On that Day no one will punish as He punishes, **26** and no one will bind as He binds. **27** 'You, secure one! **28** Return to your Lord, approving (and) approved! **29** Enter among My servants! **30** Enter My Garden!'

---

1. *you*: sing.

90 ❖ The Land

In the Name of God, the Merciful, the Compassionate

1 I swear by this land **2** – and you are a lawful (resident) in this land – **3** by a begetter and what he begot! **4** Certainly We created the human in trouble. **5** Does he think that no one has power over him? **6** He says, 'I have squandered vast wealth!' **7** Does he think that no one has seen him? **8** Have We not made two eyes for him, **9** and a tongue, and two lips? **10** And have We not guided him to the two ways? **11** Yet he has not attempted the (steep) ascent.

12 And what will make you know what the (steep) ascent is? **13** The setting free of a slave, **14** or feeding on a day of hunger **15** an orphan who is related, **16** or a poor person (lying) in the dust. **17** Then he has become one of those who believe, and (who) exhort (each other) to patience, and (who) exhort (each other) to mercy.

18 Those are the companions on the right. **19** But those who disbelieve in Our signs, they are the companions on the left. **20** A fire (will be) closed over them.

91 ❋ The Sun

In the Name of God, the Merciful, the Compassionate

1 By the sun and her morning light! 2 By the moon when he follows her! 3 By the day when it reveals her! 4 By the night when it covers her! 5 By the sky and what built it! 6 By the earth and what spread it! 7 By the self and what fashioned it, 8 and instilled it with its (tendency to) depravity and its (sense of) guarding (itself)! 9 He has prospered who purifies it, 10 and he has failed who corrupts it.

11 Thamūd called (it) a lie by their insolent transgression, 12 when the most miserable (one) of them was raised up, 13 and the messenger of God said to them, 'The she-camel of God and her drink!' 14 But they called (him) a liar and wounded her. So their Lord covered them over for their sin and leveled it. 15 He was not afraid of its outcome.

92 ✦ The Night

In the Name of God, the Merciful, the Compassionate

1 By the night when it covers! **2** By the day when it reveals its splendor! **3** By what created the male and the female! **4** Surely your striving is indeed (to) divided (ends). **5** As for the one who gives and guards (himself), **6** and affirms the best (reward), **7** We shall ease him to ease. **8** But as for the one who is stingy, and considers himself independent, **9** and calls the best (reward) a lie, **10** We shall ease him to hardship. **11** His wealth will be of no use to him when he perishes. **12** Surely on Us indeed (depends) the guidance. **13** Surely to Us indeed (belong) the last and the first.

14 I have warned you of a flaming Fire. **15** Only the most miserable will burn in it: **16** the one who called (it) a lie and turned away. **17** But the one who guards (himself) will avoid it: **18** the one who gives his wealth to purify himself, **19** and (confers) no blessing on anyone (expecting) to be repaid, **20** but only seeks the face of his Lord, the Most High. **21** Soon indeed he will be pleased.

93 ❈ The Morning Light

In the Name of God, the Merciful, the Compassionate

1 By the morning light! 2 By the night when it darkens! 3 Your Lord has not forsaken you, nor does He despise you. 4 The last will indeed be better for you than the first. 5 Soon indeed your Lord will give to you, and you will be pleased.

6 Did He not find you an orphan and give (you) refuge? 7 Did He not find you astray and guide (you)? 8 Did He not find you poor and enrich (you)?

9 As for the orphan, do not oppress (him), 10 and as for the beggar, do not repulse (him), 11 and as for the blessing of your Lord, proclaim (it).

94 ❖ The Expanding

In the Name of God, the Merciful, the Compassionate

1 Did We not expand your heart for you, **2** and deliver you of your burden, **3** which had broken your back? **4** Did We not raise your reputation for you? **5** Surely with hardship (there is) ease. **6** Surely with hardship (there is) ease. **7** So when you are free, work on. **8** And to your Lord set (your) desire.

95 ✹ The Fig

In the Name of God, the Merciful, the Compassionate

1 By the fig and the olive! 2 By Mount Sinai! 3 By this secure land! 4 Certainly We created the human in the finest state. 5 Then We reduce him to the lowest of the low 6 – except for those who believe and do righteous deeds. For them (there is) a reward without end. 7 What will call you a liar after (that) in (regard to) the Judgment? 8 Is God not the most just of judges?

96 ❋ The Clot

In the Name of God, the Merciful, the Compassionate

1 Recite in the name of your Lord who creates, **2** creates the human from a clot. **3** Recite, for your Lord is the Most Generous, **4** who teaches by the pen, **5** teaches the human what he does not know.

6 By no means! Surely the human transgresses insolently indeed, **7** for he considers himself independent. **8** Surely to your Lord is the return.

9 Have you seen the one who forbids **10** a servant when he prays? **11** Have you seen whether he (relies) on the guidance, **12** or commands the guarding (of oneself)? **13** Have you seen whether he calls (it) a lie, and turns away? **14** Does he not know that God sees? **15** By no means! If indeed he does not stop, We shall indeed seize (him) by the hair – **16** (his) lying, sinful hair. **17** So let him call his cohorts! **18** We shall call the guards of Hell. **19** By no means! Do not obey him, but prostrate yourself and draw near.

97 ✤ The Decree

In the Name of God, the Merciful, the Compassionate

1 Surely We sent it down on the Night of the Decree. 2 And what will make you[1] know what the Night of the Decree is? 3 The Night of the Decree is better than a thousand months. 4 The angels and the spirit come down during it, by the permission of their Lord, on account of every command. 5 It is (a night of) peace, until the rising of the dawn.

---

1. *you*: sing.

98 ❖ The Clear Sign

In the Name of God, the Merciful, the Compassionate

1 Those who disbelieve among the People of the Book, and the idolaters, were not (to be) set free until the clear sign had come to them **2** – a messenger from God, reciting purified pages, **3** in which (there are) true books. **4** Those who were given the Book did not become divided until after the clear sign had come to them. **5** They were commanded only to serve God, devoting (their) religion to Him, (being) Ḥanīfs, and to observe the prayer and give the alms. That is the right religion.

6 Surely those who disbelieve among the People of the Book, and the idolaters, will be in the Fire of Gehenna, there to remain. Those – they are the worst of creation. **7** Surely those who believe and do righteous deeds, those – they are the best of creation. **8** Their payment is with their Lord – Gardens of Eden through which rivers flow, there to remain forever. God is pleased with them, and they are pleased with Him. That is for whoever fears his Lord.

99 ✵ The Earthquake

In the Name of God, the Merciful, the Compassionate

1 When the earth is shaken with her shaking, 2 and the earth brings forth her burdens, 3 and a person says, 'What is (the matter) with her?' 4 On that Day she will proclaim her news, 5 because your Lord has inspired her (with it). 6 On that Day the people will come forth separately to be shown their deeds. 7 Whoever has done a speck's weight of good will see it, 8 and whoever has done a speck's weight of evil will see it.

100 ❈ The Runners

In the Name of God, the Merciful, the Compassionate

1 By the runners panting, **2** and the strikers of fire, **3** and the chargers at dawn, **4** when they kick up a (cloud of) dust, **5** and pierce through the midst of it all together! **6** Surely the human is indeed an ingrate to his Lord, **7** and surely he is indeed a witness to that, **8** and surely he is indeed harsh in (his) love for (worldly) goods. **9** Does he not know? When what is in the graves is ransacked, **10** and what is in the hearts is extracted **11** – surely on that Day their Lord will indeed be aware of them.

101 ✺ The Striking

In the Name of God, the Merciful, the Compassionate

1 The striking! 2 What is the striking? 3 And what will make you[1] know what the striking is? 4 The Day when the people will be like scattered moths, 5 and the mountains will be like (tufts of) wool. 6 As for the one whose scales are heavy, 7 he will be in a pleasing life, 8 but as for the one whose scales are light, 9 his mother will be Hāwiya.[2] 10 And what will make you know what she is? 11 A scorching Fire!

---

1. *you*: sing.
2. *Hāwiya*: meaning uncertain, but the final verse implies it is another name for Hell.

102 ✸ Rivalry

In the Name of God, the Merciful, the Compassionate

1 Rivalry diverts you, 2 until you visit the graves. 3 By no means! Soon you will know! 4 Once again, by no means! Soon you will know! 5 By no means! If (only) you knew (now) with the knowledge of certainty: 6 you will indeed see the Furnace. 7 Once again, you will indeed see it with the eye of certainty. 8 Then, on that Day, you will indeed be asked about (what) bliss (is).

103 ✹ The Afternoon

In the Name of God, the Merciful, the Compassionate

1 By the afternoon! 2 Surely the human is indeed in (a state of) loss 3 – except for those who believe and do righteous deeds, and exhort (each other) in truth, and exhort (each other) in patience.

104 ❈ The Slanderer

In the Name of God, the Merciful, the Compassionate

1 Woe to every slanderer, fault finder, **2** who accumulates wealth and counts it over and over! **3** He thinks that his wealth will make him last. **4** By no means! Indeed He will be tossed into al-Ḥuṭama.¹ **5** And what will make you² know what al-Ḥuṭama is? **6** The Fire of God ignited, **7** which rises up to the hearts. **8** Surely it (will be) closed over them **9** in extended columns (of flame).

---

1. *al-Ḥuṭama*: meaning uncertain; probably another name for Hell.
2. *you*: sing.

105 ❖ THE ELEPHANT

In the Name of God, the Merciful, the Compassionate

1 Have you[1] not considered how your Lord did with the companions of the elephant? **2** Did He not make their plot go astray? **3** He sent against them birds in flocks **4** – (which) were pelting them with stones of baked clay – **5** and He made them like chewed-up husks (of straw).

---

1. *you*: sing.

106 ❖ Quraysh

In the Name of God, the Merciful, the Compassionate

1 For the uniting of Quraysh, 2 for their uniting for the caravan of the winter and the summer: 3 Let them serve the Lord of this House, 4 who has fed them on account of (their) hunger, 5 and secured them on account of (their) fear.

107 ☸ Assistance

In the Name of God, the Merciful, the Compassionate

1 Have you[1] seen the one who calls the Judgment a lie? **2** That is the one who shoves away the orphan, **3** and does not urge (people) to the feeding of the poor.

4 Woe to the ones who pray, **5** who – they are heedless of their prayers, **6** who – they (only) make a show, **7** and withhold assistance!

---

1. *you*: sing.

108 ❋ Abundance

In the Name of God, the Merciful, the Compassionate

1 Surely We have given you[1] the abundance. 2 So pray to your Lord and sacrifice. 3 Surely your hater – he is the one cut off!

---

1. *you*: sing.

109 ❖ The Disbelievers

In the Name of God, the Merciful, the Compassionate

1 Say: 'You disbelievers! **2** I do not serve what you serve, **3** and you are not serving what I serve. **4** I am not serving what you have served, **5** and you are not serving what I serve. **6** To you your religion and to me my religion.'

110 ❖ Help

In the Name of God, the Merciful, the Compassionate

1 When the help of God comes, and the victory, **2** and you[1] see the people entering into the religion of God in crowds, **3** glorify your Lord with praise, and ask forgiveness from Him. Surely He turns (in forgiveness).

---

1. *you*: sing.

111 ✵ The Fiber

In the Name of God, the Merciful, the Compassionate

1 The hands of Abū Lahab[1] have perished, and he has perished. **2** His wealth and what he has earned were of no use to him. **3** He will burn in a flaming Fire, **4** and his wife (will be) the carrier of the firewood, **5** with a rope of fiber around her neck.

---

1. *Abū Lahab*: or 'Father of Flame' (said to refer to the Prophet's uncle, 'Abd al-'Uzzā).

112 ❈ Devotion

In the Name of God, the Merciful, the Compassionate

1 Say: 'He is God. One! **2** God the Eternal! **3** He has not begotten and was not begotten, **4** and He has no equal. None!'

113 ❈ The Daybreak

In the Name of God, the Merciful, the Compassionate

1 Say: 'I take refuge with the Lord of the daybreak, **2** from the evil of what He has created, **3** and from the evil of darkness when it looms, **4** and from the evil of the women who blow on knots, **5** and from the evil of an envier when he envies.'

114 ✺ Humans

In the Name of God, the Merciful, the Compassionate

1 Say: 'I take refuge with the Lord of (all) humans, **2** King of (all) humans, **3** God of (all) humans, **4** from the evil of the whispering one, the slinking one, **5** who whispers in the hearts of humans, **6** of jinn and humans.'

INDEX TO THE QUR'ĀN

Aaron (*Hārūn*)
brother and assistant of Moses, 7.142; 10.75, 87; 20.29-34, 90-94; 21.48; 23.45; 25.35; 26.13; 28.34-35; 37.114-120; a prophet, 4.163; 6.84; 19.53; family of, 2.248; sister of, 19.28; Lord of, 7.122; 20.70; 26.48

Abel *see* Adam, two sons of

ablutions *see* washing

Abraham (*Ibrāhīm*)
abandons idolatry, 6.74-84; 21.51-71; 26.69-102; 29.16-25; 37.83-101; 43.26-28; 60.4; abandons his father, 9.114; 19.41-49; visited by angels, 11.69-76; 15.51-60; 29.31-32; 51.24-34; sacrifice of son, 37.102-113; religion of, a Ḥanīf and Muslim, 2.130-135; 3.67, 95; 4.125; 6.161; 16.120-123; 22.78; builds/purifies God's House, with Ishmael, 2.125-129; 3.96-97; 22.26-31; not a Jew or Christian, 2.140; 3.65-68; God took him as a friend, 4.125; community of, 2.134, 139-141; pages of, 53.36-37; 87.19; prayer of, 14.35-41 (and title); also 2.124 (an *imām*), 136, 258; 3.33, 84; 4.54, 163; 9.70; 12.6, 38; 19.58; 22.43; 33.7; 38.45; 42.13; 57.26

abrogation *see* cancelation

Abū Lahab
111.1

acacia trees
in Paradise, 56.29

'Ād
people to whom Hūd was sent, 7.65-72; 11.50-60; 26.123-40; 46.21-26; 54.18-21; 69.4-8; also 7.74; 9.70; 14.9; 22.42; 29.38; 38.12; 40.31; 41.13, 15; 50.13; 51.41-42; 53.50; 89.6-7

Adam (*Ādam*)
God made him 'ruler on earth' and taught him 'all the names,' 2.30-33; worshipped by angels, except Iblīs, 2.34; 7.11; 15.28-31 (not named); 17.61; 18.50; 20.116; 38.71-74 (not named); eats from forbidden tree and expelled from Garden, 2.35-39; 7.19-25; 20.120-124; two sons of (not named), 5.27-31; descendants of Adam ('sons of Adam'), 7.26, 27, 31, 35; 17.70; 36.60-61; God's covenant with the 'sons of Adam,' 7.172-174; creation of first human, 6.98; 7.189-193; 15.28; 39.6; also 3.33, 59; 19.58

adultery *see* sexual immorality

Aḥmad
Jesus predicts his coming, 61.6

Alexander the Great *see* Dhū-l-Qarnayn

alliances
between believers and emigrants, 8.72; between hypocrites and disbelievers, 4.138-139; renunciation of with disbelievers; 9.1-12; forbidden with disbelievers, 4.144; 9.23 (among family); Jews and Christians, 5.51; hypocrites, 4.88-89

alms
by itself, 7.156; 23.4; 41.7; alms and prayer together, 2.43, 83 (Israelites), 110, 177; 4.77, 162; 5.12 (Israelites), 55; 9.5, 11, 18, 71; 19.31 (Jesus), 55 (Ishmael); 21.73; 22.41, 78; 24.37, 56;31.4; 33.33; 58.13; 73.20; 98.5; contrasted with usury, 2.276; 30.39; *see also* contributions

alteration of scripture
2.59, 75; 3.78; 4.46; 5.13, 41; 7.162; concealing of scripture, 2.42, 76–77, 140, 146, 159, 174; 3.71; 5.15; forging of scripture, 2.79

Alyasaʻ *see* Elisha

angels
winged messengers of God, 35.1; agents of revelation, 16.2; 37.3; 77.5; 97.4; glorify God, 7.206; 21.20; 37.166; 39.75; 40.7; bear his throne, 40.7; 69.17; intercede for believers, 40.7–9; not gods, but servants, 21.26–29; 37.149–150; 43.19; wrongly given fem. names, 53.27; recording angels, 6.61; 50.18; 82.10–12; 86.4; seize people at death, 7.37; 32.11; 50.17; present at Judgment, 37.165; 89.22; descend at God's command, 19.64; on the 'Night of Power,' 97.3–4; ascend to God, 70.4; worshipped Adam, 2.34; 7.11; 15.30; 17.61; 18.50; 20.116; 38.73; disbelievers want revelation from angels, 15.6–9; help believers in battle, 3.124; 8.9; guardians of Hell, 74.31; 96.18; *see also* Gabriel; Hārūt; Mārūt; spirit

animals
2.164; 5.4; 6.38 (form communities); 15.20; 22.18, 36; 25.49; 29.60; 31.10; 34.14; 35.28; 42.29; 45.4; 55.10; *see also* ants; apes; bees; birds; camels; elephant; fish; horses; hudhud; livestock; quails

anṣār *see* helpers

ants
27.18 (and title)

apes
sabbath-breakers turned into, 2.64; 5.60; 7.166

apostasy
warning against, 5.54; will not be pardoned, 4.137; punishable, 3.86–90; 9.74; 88.23–24; except under compulsion, 16.106

Arabic
'an Arabic Qur'ān,' 12.2; 20.113; 39.28; 41.3, 44; 42.7; 43.3; Qur'ān in 'clear Arabic,' 16.103; 26.195; also 13.37; 46.12

Arabs
unsatisfactory attitude of, 9.90, 97–100, 101–106; relations with the Prophet, 48.11–17; not true believers, 49.14–17; also 33.20

ʻArafāt
2.198

arbitration
of disputes between husband and wife, 4.35

ark
cult object of the Israelites, 2.248; Moses cast into, 20.39; *see also* ship (Noah's)

armor
given by God, 16.81

atonement
in forgoing retaliation, 5.45; for breaking an oath, 5.89; for hunting in state of sanctity, 5.95; *see also* compensation; ransom

Index to the Qur'ān

augury
7.131; 17.13; 27.47; 36.18

Ayyūb *see* Job

Āzar
Abraham's father, 6.74; *see also* Abraham

Baal (*Ba'l*)
false god, 37.125; *see also* Elijah

Babylon (*Bābil*)
2.102

Badr
God's help at the battle of, 3.123; also 3.13; 8.7–17, 42–44

Be!
God's creative word, 2.117; 3.47, 59; 6.73; 16.40; 19.35; 36.82; 40.68

Becca (*Bakka*)
'first House' founded at, 3.96

bees
inspired by God, 16.68 (and title)

behavior *see* social etiquette

belief (selected references)
2.3, 285; 4.136; 7.158; 9.2; 10.9; 30.56; 33.22; 42.52; 48.4; 49.7, 14; 52.21; 58.22; 59.9–10; 74.31; *see also* believers

believers (selected references)
duties and character of, 4.135; 5.8, 35; 9.71, 123; 22.77–78; 23.1–9, 57–61 (and title); 27.2–3; 32.15–16; 33.41–42; 48.29; 59.18–19; rewards of, 2.25; 5.9; 6.48; 8.1–4; 9.72, 111; 13.28–29; 22.23; 32.17; 37.40–49; 38.49–55; 44.51–57; 52.17–28; 55.46–78; 56.10–40; 57.12, 19–21; 65.11; 78.31–36; 98.8; warnings about disbelief, 3.100, 102–106; 5.57–61; 57.16; 63.9–11; 64.14–17; 66.6, 8; believers to be tested, 29.2–6; belief only by God's permission, 10.100

birds
form communities, 6.38; their ability to fly a sign, 16.79; 67.19; their praise a sign, 21.79; 24.41; 34.10; 38.19; Abraham's sacrifice of, 2.260; their language known to Solomon, part of his army, 27.16, 20; clay birds brought to life by Jesus, 3.49; 5.110; sent by God against the 'companions of the elephant,' 105.3; *see also* augury; hudhud

blood
forbidden as food, 2.173; 5.3; 6.145; 16.115; plague on Egypt, 7.133; bloodshed prohibited, 2.84; angels predict that humans will shed blood, 2.30; fake blood on Joseph's shirt, 12.18; blood relations, 8.75; 25.54; 33.6; also 16.66; 22.37

Book (selected references)
referring to the Qur'ān, 2.2; 3.3, 7; 5.48; 6.92, 155; 11.1; 12.1; 13.1; 14.1; 15.1; 18.1; 19.16, 41, 51, 54, 56; 31.1; 32.1; 40.2; 41.3; 43.2; 44.2; 45.2; 46.2; referring to the Torah, 3.48 (Jesus); 3.187 (Jews); 5.110 (Jesus); 6.154 (Moses); 13.36; 19.12 (John), 30 (Jesus); 23.49 (Moses); 29.27 (Abraham's descendants); 37.117 (Moses and Aaron); 52.2–3(?); referring to the Torah and Gospel, 3.48 (Jesus); 5.110; 19.30(?); referring to the heavenly archetype, 13.39; 43.4; 56.78(?); referring to the heavenly record of deeds, 18.49; 23.62; 69.19, 25; 84.7, 10; referring to the heavenly book of destiny, 6.38, 59; 9.36 ('Book of God'); 10.61; 11.6; 13.38; 22.70; 57.22; *see also* Gospel; pages; Psalms; Qur'ān; Tablet(s); Torah

Book, People of the
appealed to, 3.64–68; 4.171; 5.67–69, 77; warning to, 3.98–99; warning about, 2.104–110; 5.57–66; diatribe against, 3.69–85, 98–99; 4.44–57, 153–162, 171–173; 5.12–19, 59; believers among, 3.113–117, 199; 28.52–55; disbelievers among, 98.1; fighting against, 9.29–35; 33.26–27; expulsion of, 59.2–4; are 'brothers' of the hypocrites, 59.11–17; to pay tribute, 9.31; also 4.123; 5.65–66; 29.46; 57.29; 98.1, 6; *see also* Gospel, People of the; Reminder, People of the

brass
barrier built by Dhū-l-Qarnayn, 18.96; spring of molten brass created for Solomon, 34.12

bribery
of judges prohibited, 2.188

Byzantines *see* Romans

Cain *see* Adam, two sons of

calendar *see* months

calf, the
worshipped by Israelites, 2.51, 92; 4.153; 7.148; story of, 20.83–98

camels
their creation one of God's signs, 88.17; she-camel of Ṣāliḥ a sign, 7.73–78; 11.64; 17.59; 26.154–159; 54.27–31; 91.13–14; passing through the eye of the needle, 7.40; may be eaten, 6.144

camphor
a drink in Paradise, 76.5

cancelation
God cancels and replaces verses, 2.106; 13.39; 16.101; God cancels satanic verses, 22.52

captives
taking of, 8.57, 60; ransoming of, 2.85; 47.4

cattle *see* livestock

cave, companions of the
their story, 18.9–26 (and title)

children
nursing of, 2.233 (regulations); 31.14; 46.15; rules for inheritance, 4.11; a trial, 8.28; 64.14–15; not to be killed, 6.137, 140; 16.59; 17.31; 60.12; 81.8–9; God has none, 6.101; 21.26; 23.91; 25.2; *see also* daughters; sons

Christians (Naṣārā)
believe in God and Last Day, 2.62; 5.69; are friends of believers, 5.82–85; their monasteries and churches, 22.40; their errors, 2.111, 116, 135, 140; 3.67; 4.171; 5.14–18, 51 (not to be taken as friends), 72–75; 9.30–32; 23.50–56; 98.4; invented monasticism, 57.27; challenge to, 3.61–68; among the religions God will judge, 22.17; *see also* Book, People of the; Gospel; Jesus; Messiah

churches
22.40

city, the (al-madīna)
9.101, 120; 33.60; 63.8; also 7.111 (plur.), 123; 12.30; 15.67; 18.19, 82; 26.36, 53 (plur.); 27.48; 28.15, 18; 36.20; *see also* Yathrib

clot
humans created from, 22.5; 23.14; 40.67; 75.38; 96.2 (and title)

clothing
made by Adam and his wife, 7.22; sent down by God, 7.26 (to cover nakedness); 16.81 (as protection from the elements); to be worn in mosques, 7.31; of women, 24.31;

Index to the Qur'ān

53.39; 'clothes of fire' as punishment for disbelievers, 22.19

clouds
one of God's signs, 2.164; 7.57; 13.12; 24.43; 30.48; 35.9; 56.69; 78.14; overshadowed Israel, 2.57; 7.160; God will come in the shadow of, 2.210; will be split on Last Day, 25.25; mountains will appear like on Last Day, 27.88; disbelievers will mistake the falling sky for on Last Day, 52.44

commerce
by ship, 16.14; 17.66; permissible during pilgrimage, 2.198; measures to be just, 17.35; *see also* trading

Compassionate, the (*al-Raḥīm*)
attribute of God, 1.1 (and *basmala*), 3; 2.37, 54, 128, 160, 163; 7.151; 9.104, 118; 10.107; 12.64, 92, 98; 15.49; 21.83; 23.109, 118; 26.9, 68, 104, 121, 140, 159, 175, 191, 217; 27.30; 28.17; 30.5; 32.6; 34.2; 36.5; 39.53; 41.2; 42.5; 44.42; 46.8; 52.28; 59.22

compensation
for unintentional homicide, 4.92; none accepted at Judgment, 2.48, 123; 6.70; 31.33; *see also* atonement; ransom

constellations *see* stars

contributions
to God's cause, 2.195, 254, 261–262, 267, 270, 272, 274; 3.92, 180; 4.37–39; 34.39; to family, orphans, the poor etc., 2.215, 273; voluntary contributions (*ṣadaqāt*), 2.196 (in place of pilgrimage), 263, 271, 276; 4.114; 9.58–59, 60 (for the poor, slaves, debtors etc.), 79, 103–104 (as purification); 58.12 (before an audience with the Prophet); as marriage gifts to women, 4.4; *see also* alms

coral
55.22, 58

couch
earth created as a, 2.22; believers recline on in Paradise, 15.47; 18.31; 36.56; 37.44; 52.20; 55.54; 56.15, 34; 76.13; 83.23, 35; 88.13; also 43.34

covenant
with Adam, 20.115; with 'sons of Adam,' 7.172; with the prophets, 3.81; 33.7; with Israel, 2.83–85, 93; 3.187; 5.12; with Christians, 5.14

creation (selected references)
of the heavens and earth, 10.5–6; 13.2–3; 31.10–11; 41.9–12; in six days, 7.54; 10.3; 11.7; 25.59; 32.4; 41.9–12; 50.38; 57.4; of human(s), 4.1; 6.2; 7.11; 16.4; 22.5; 32.7–9; 35.11; 40.67; 76.2; 86.6–7; of humans and jinn, 15.26–27; 51.56; of animals, 16.5–8; 24.45; creation purposeful, 21.16; 30.8; *see also* God

crystal
Solomon's palace of, 27.44; cups of in Paradise, 76.15

customary way (*sunna*)
of God, 17.77; 33.38, 62; 35.43; 40.84; 48.23; of previous generations, 4.26; 8.38; 15.13; 18.55; 35.43

darkness
created by God, 6.1; God leads out of, 2.257; 5.16; 33.43; 57.9; 65.11; leaves disbelievers in, 2.17; 6.39, 122; 10.27; al-Ṭāghūt leads into, 2.257; Moses leads out of, 14.5; the Prophet leads out of, 14.1; Dhū-l-Nūn calls out in, 21.87; of Last Day, 80.41; evil of, 113.3; also 6.63, 97; 13.16; 24.40; 27.63; 35.20; 36.37; 39.6 ('three darknessess')

date palms
  2.266; 6.99, 141; 13.4; 16.11, 67; 17.91; 18.32; 19.23, 25; 20.71; 23.19; 26.148; 36.34; 50.10; 54.20; 55.11, 68; 69.7; 80.29

daughters
  prejudice against, 16.58–59; 43.17; ascribed to God, 16.57; 17.40; 53.21; God has none, 37.149, 153; 43.16; 52.39; *see also* children; sons

David (*Dāwūd*)
  killed Goliath, 2.251; a prophet, given Psalms, 4.163; 17.55; given judgment and knowledge, 21.78; 27.15; mountains and birds join him praising God, 34.10; 38.17–20; story of the lamb and his repentance, 38.21–25; made a ruler, 38.26; cursed disbelieving Israelites, 5.78; given Solomon, 38.30; also 6.84; 34.13

day *see* night and day

death
  occurs at a fixed time (*ajal*) by God's will, 3.145; 16.61; 39.42; angels summon at death, 4.97; 6.61, 93; 7.37; 8.50; 16.28, 32; 32.11 (angel of death); 47.27; 50.17–19; disbelievers' experience of death, 75.26–30; it will seem only a short time between death and resurrection, 20.103; 23.112–114; 46.35; also called 'the certainty' (*al-yaqīn*), 15.99; 74.46–47; reference to possible death of Muḥammad, 3.144

debts
  rules for recording of, 2.282–283; relief for debtors, 9.60; also 4.11, 12; 52.40; 56.66; 68.46

Deliverance, the (*al-furqān*)
  2.53, 185; 3.4; 8.29, 41 ('Day of Deliverance'); 21.48; 25.1 (and title)

demons *see* satans

Devil *see* Iblīs, Satan

Dhū-l-Kifl
  a prophet, 21.85; 38.48

Dhū-l-Qarnayn
  Alexander the Great(?), story of, 18.83–98

Dhū-l-Nūn
  a prophet (Jonah) 21.87; 68.48

diatribe
  against Jews and Christians, 2.111–121; against the Israelites, 5.70–71; against the Jews, 3.21–27, 181–189; 62.5–8; against the People of the Book, 3.69–85; 4.44–57, 153–162, 171–173; 5.12–19; against the Christian doctrine of the trinity, 5.72–77; against the disbelievers, 5.103–105; 6.25–32; 52.29–47; against the hypocrites, 4.138–149; 9.50–57, 61–70, 73–80; against the Arabs, 49.14–18

disbelievers (selected references)
  a seal on their hearts, a covering over their sight, 2.7; 4.155; 6.25; 9.93; 10.74; 16.108; 17.46; 45.23; 47.16; associate other gods with God, 3.151; 6.1, 64, 94, 100, 136–137; 7.190; 13.16, 33; 14.30; 16.54; 29.65; 30.33, 35; 34.27; 40.12, 73–74; disrespect the Prophet, 6.25; 8.30; 15.6; 21.36; 25.5; 27.68; 37.35; 41.26; 44.14; 50.2–3; 52.30, 33; 68.51; stubborn, 2.6; 7.193; 26.5; 36.10; 50.24; 74.16; arrogant, 2.87; 4.172–173; 6.93; 7.36, 40, 75; 10.75; 14.21; 16.22; 23.66–67; 25.21; 29.39; 31.7; 34.32; 37.35; 38.2; 39.59–60; 40.26; 41.15; 45.8, 31; 46.20; 63.5; 71.7; 74.21–26; the Prophet's break with, 109.1–6 (and title); believers to fight them, 47.4; among the People of the Book, 98.1; punishment of, 3.10; 7.40–41; 14.29–30;

22.19–22, 72; 25.11–14; 27.5; 33.64; 36.64; 40.71–72, 76; 64.5–6; 67.6–11; see also idolaters

disciples
Jesus' followers and God's helpers, 3.52; 61.14; are 'Muslims,' 5.111; ask for a table from heaven, 5.112–115

divination arrows
forbidden, 5.3, 90

divorce
various regulations concerning, 2.228–32, 236, 241; 33.49; 65.1–7 (and title); use of a certain formula of forbidden, 58.1–4; the Prophet's wives threatened with, 66.5

dogs see hunting

donkeys
created by God for transport, 16.8; voice of hateful, 31.19; also 2.259; 62.5; 74.50

dreams
of Abraham to sacrifice his son, 37.102; of the Prophet about the enemy, 8.43; of Joseph, 12.4–5; of Joseph's fellow prisoners, 12.36; of the king of Egypt, 12.43; Joseph a dream interpreter, 12.6, 37–41, 101; disbelievers call the revelation a 'jumble of dreams,' 21.4

earth
created by God, 2.164; 3.190–191; 65.12; in two days, 41.9; in six days, 7.54; 10.3; 11.7; 25.59; 50.38; 57.4; spread out by God, 13.3; 15.19; 50.7; 79.30; 91.6; stands fast by God's command, 30.25; creation of purposeful, 21.16; 38.27; nothing hidden from God in, 3.3; 14.38; 22.70; 27.75; 34.2; 57.4; will give up its dead on Last Day, 84.3–5; will be changed into something else, 14.48; kingdom of the heavens and earth belongs to God, 3.189; 5.17, 18, 40, 120; 7.158; 9.116; 24.42; 25.2; 39.44; 42.49; 43.85; 45.27; 48.14; 57.2, 5; 85.9

earthquake
destroys the people of Thamūd, 7.78; of Midian, 7.91; 29.36; of Moses, 7.155; sign of the Last Day, 22.1; 99.1 (and title)

Eden (*'Adn*)
Gardens of, 9.72; 13.23; 16.31; 18.31; 19.61; 20.76; 35.33; 38.50; 40.8; 61.12; 98.8; see also Paradise

Egypt (*Miṣr*)
2.61; 10.87; 12.21, 99; 43.51; plagues against, 7.130, 133–135; see also Moses; Pharaoh

elephant, the
companions of, 105.1 (and title)

Elijah (*Ilyās*)
one of the envoys, opposed worship of Baal, 37.123–132; of the descendants of Abraham, 6.85

Elisha (*Alyasa'* or *al-Yasa'*)
6.86; 38.48

emigrants (*muhājirūn*)
encouragement to emigrate, 4.100; mentioned with 'helpers,' 9.100, 117; will be rewarded, 16.41, 110; 22.58–59; wealthy to support them, 24.22; receive part of the spoils, 59.8; treatment of emigrant women, 60.10

Enoch see Idrīs

envoy see messengers

Eve
Adam's wife, but not mentioned by name, 2.35; 7.19–23; 20.117–121; 39.6

evil
2.169; 4.79, 85; 6.160; 10.27; 12.53; 16.90; 24.21; 29.4; 41.46; 45.15; 91.7–10; 99.8; 113.2

Index to the Qur'ān

Ezra (*'Uzayr*)
regarded by Jews as the son of God, 9.30; *see also* Idrīs

factions
referring to the people of Thamūd, Lot, and the Grove, 38.13; after Noah, 40.5; the Day of, 40.31–32 (people of Noah, 'Ād, and Thamūd); of Jews and Christians, 11.17; 13.36; 19.37; 23.53; 43.65; of the men of the cave, 18.12; of hostile disbelievers, 33.20, 22 (and title)

fasting
prescribed for believers in Ramaḍān, 2.183–185, 187; vowed by Mary, 19.26; as compensation, 4.92 (for unintended homicide); 5.89 (for breaking an oath), 95 (for hunting in state of sanctity); 58.4 (for using a forbidden formula of divorce)

fathers
disbelievers follow the errors of their fathers, 2.170; 5.104; 7.28, 173; 11.109; 21.52–53; 26.74–76; 31.21; 34.43; 37.69–70; 43.23–24; disbelievers demand that their fathers be made alive, 45.25; disbelieving fathers to be treated as enemies, 9.23; 58.22; *see also* parents

fig
95.1 (and title)

fighting
for the cause of God, 2.190, 216–218, 244; 3.142; 4.71, 95; 5.35, 54; 8.39, 65, 72, 74; 9.12–14, 19–20, 24, 29–31, 36, 123; 22.39–40; 47.4; 49.15; 61.11; fighting in the sacred months, 2.217; 9.36; reluctance to fight, 2.246; 4.77; 9.38, 42–49, 86; 47.20; dying for the cause of God, 2.154; 3.157, 169, 195; 47.4–6; also 9.41, 73; 22.78; 66.9

fire
created by God, 36.80; humans ignite it, 56.71–72

Fire, the *see* Hell

fish
permissible to eat, 5.96; 16.14; 35.12; of Jonah, 37.142; 68.48; also 7.163; 18.61–63

flood
of Noah, 11.40–44; 23.27–29; 54.11–15; 69.11–12; plague against Egypt, 7.133; of 'Arim, 34.16

food, regulations concerning
forbidden: carrion, blood, pig, what is dedicated to another god, 2.173; 5.3 (with additions); 6.121, 145; 16.115; most foods permissible, 2.168–172; 3.93 (except what Israel/Jacob forbade); 5.1, 4 (including game caught by hunting dogs), 5 (also the food of the People of the Book), 87; 6.118–119, 142; 16.114; special food laws for the Jews, 3.93; 4.160; 6.146; 16.118; other lawful foods, 5.96 (fish); violation of food laws pardonable, 5.93; 6.119; also 6.143; 10.59; 16.116; *see also* camels, livestock, wine

forgiveness
of believers, 24.22; 42.37; of disbelievers, 45.14; better than retaliation, 42.37–43; *see also* repentance

Friday
'day of assembly' for prayer, business temporally suspended, 62.9–10

Furqān *see* Deliverance

Gabriel (*Jibrīl*)
mentioned by name, 2.97, 98 (with Michael); 66.4 (supports the Prophet)

gambling
forbidden, 2.219; 5.90

garden
parables about earthly gardens, 18.32–44; 68.17–33; *see also* Paradise

Garden(s) *see* Paradise

Garden of the Refuge
theophany near, 53.15

Gehenna (*Jahannam*) *see* Hell

God (selected references)
God's power and providence, 6.95–99; 7.54–58; 10.3–6; 13.2–4, 8–17; 14.32–34; 15.16–25; 16.3–18, 65–74, 78–83; 17.12; 21.30–33; 22.5–7, 61–66; 23.12–22, 78–83; 24.41–46; 25.45–62; 28.68–73; 29.19; 30.20–27, 46–54; 31.10–11, 29–32; 32.4–9; 35.1–17, 44; 36.33–44, 71–76; 37.6–11; 39.5–7, 21; 40.56–68, 79–81; 41.9–12, 37–40; 42.9–12, 27–35, 49; 45.3–13; 51.20–23, 47–50; 56.57–74; 78.6–16; 79.27–33; 88.17–20; knowledge, 6.59–60; 10.61; 11.5–6; 13.8–10; 22.70; 27.65; 58.7; benevolence, 2.268; 10.58–60; 35.3; 55.1–28; 80.24–32; the only deity, 16.51; 23.116–117; 27.59–64; 37.4–5; 38.65–66; 39.2–3, 64–66; 112.1–4; has the best names, 7.180; 17.110; 20.8; 59.24; has no son or daughter, 2.116; 6.101; 10.68; 17.111; 19.88–95; 37.149–157; 43.16, 81; 72.3; 112.3; determines a person's fate, 3.145; 45.26; 57.22; *see also* creation

gods *see* idols, false gods

Gog (*Yājūj*)
and Magog (*Mājūj*), barbarous peoples confined behind a wall by Dhū-l-Qarnayn, 18.93–97; released before the Day of Judgment, 21.96

gold
3.14, 91; 9.34; 43.53; bracelets of in Paradise, 18.31; 22.23; 35.33; plates and cups of in Paradise, 43.71

Goliath (*Jālūt*)
killed by David, 2.249–251

Gospel (*Injīl*)
book given to Jesus, 3.3, 48, 65; 5.46, 47, 66, 68, 110; 9.111; 48.29; 57.27; predicts coming of the Prophet, 7.157

Gospel, People of the
5.47; *see also* Book, People of the; Reminder, People of the

grapes
2.266; 6.99; 13.4; 16.11, 67; 17.91; 18.32; 23.19; 36.34; 78.32; 80.28

greed
3.180–181; 4.37; 9.34–35; 47.38; 70.21

greetings *see* social etiquette

Grove, people of the
story of, 26.176–189 (Shu'ayb sent to them); also 15.78; 38.13; 50.14

guidance
Qur'ān as guidance, 2.2, 97, 159, 185; 3.138; 6.157; 7.52, 203; 9.33; 10.57; 12.111; 16.64, 89, 102; 17.94; 27.2, 76; 31.3; 39.23; 41.44; 45.20; 47.25, 32; 48.28; 53.23; 61.9; 72.13; 96.11; Torah and Gospel as guidance, 3.3–4; 5.44, 46; 6.91, 154; 7.154; 17.2; 28.43; 32.23; 40.53–54; God's House as guidance, 3.96; revelation in general as guidance, 2.16, 38, 120, 175, 185; 3.73; 4.115; 6.71, 84–90; 7.193; 16.37; 18.13, 55; 19.76; 20.47, 123; 22.8; 28.37, 50; 32.13; 34.24; 41.17; 43.24; 47.17; 92.12

Ḥajj *see* pilgrimage

Hāmān
associate of Pharaoh, 28.6, 8, 38; 29.39–40; 40.24, 36

Ḥanīf
Abraham, 2.135; 3.67, 95; 4.125; 6.79, 161; 16.120, 123; the Prophet, 10.105; 30.30; also (in plur.) 22.31; 98.5

Index to the Qur'ān

Hārūn *see* Aaron

Hārūt
angel in Babylon, 2.102

Heaven *see* Paradise

heavens
seven heavens created by God, 2.29; 17.44; 23.17, 86; 41.12; 65.12; 67.3–5; 71.15; 78.12; kingdom of the heavens and earth belongs to God, 3.189; 5.17, 18, 40, 120; 7.158; 9.116; 24.42; 25.2; 39.44; 42.49; 43.85; 45.27; 48.14; 57.2, 5; 85.9; *see also* sky

heights
men on the, 7.46–49 (and title)

Hell (selected references)
descriptions of, 38.55–58; 70.15–18; 73.12–13; 74.26–31; 104.4–9; punishment in it eternal, 2.81; 20.74; 43.74–78; has seven gates, 15.44; guarded by angels, 40.49–50; 74.30–31; its lust to possess sinners, 11.106; 21.98–100; 25.11–12; 67.6–8; will be filled with jinn and humans, 7.179; 11.119; 32.13; 38.85; 50.30

helpers (*anṣār*)
Jesus' disciples, 3.52; 61.14; and 'emigrants,' 9.100, 117; all believers to be 'helpers of God,' 61.14

al-Ḥijr
its people disobeyed and were punished, 15.80–84 (and title)

holy spirit *see* spirit

homosexuality
transgression of Lot's people, 26.165–166; 27.55; 29.28–29; also 4.16(?)

honey
produced from bees, 16.69; rivers of in Paradise, 47.15

horses
created by God as transport, 16.8; enjoyment of, 3.14; cavalry of believers, 8.60; 59.6; of Iblīs, 17.64; of Solomon, 38.31–35

Hour, the *see* Judgment, Day of

House, the (*al-bayt*)
founded by Abraham and Ishmael, 2.125–127; 22.26; 'this House,' 106.3; *see also* Ka'ba; Mosque, the Sacred

houses
created by God for rest, 16.80

Hūd
messenger sent to 'Ād, 7.65–72; 11.50–60, 89 (and title); 26.123–140; 46.21–26

hudhud
a messenger-bird for Solomon, 27.20–28

human, humans, humankind (selected references)
creation of, 6.98; 7.189; 15.26, 28; 39.6; prenatal development, birth, growth, 22.5; 23.12–14; 40.67; 75.37–39; 76.2; 86.5–7; 96.1–2; originally one community, 2.213; 10.19; God's covenant with, 7.172; subject to death, 21.34–35; created weak, 4.28; taken by God at night, 6.60; 39.42; prone to satanic influence, 114.4–6 (and title); *see also* Adam

Ḥunayn
battle of, 9.25

hunting
use of dogs in, 5.4; forbidden in a state of sanctity, 5.1, 2, 94

al-Ḥuṭama
name of Hell(?), 104.4

hypocrites (*munāfiqūn*)
false believers, 4.61, 88, 138–145; 8.49; 9.64–68, 73; 29.11; 33.1, 12–13,

24, 48, 60, 73; 48.6; 57.13; 63.1–8 (and title); 66.9; 'those in whose hearts is a sickness,' 2.10; 5.52; 8.49; 9.125; 22.53; 33.12, 32, 60; 47.20, 29; 74.31; among the Arabs, 9.101

Iblīs
an angel who refused to worship Adam, 2.34; 7.11–18; 15.28–42; 17.61–65; 20.116–117; 38.71–85; 'one of the jinn', 18.50; also 26.95 (his forces); 34.20; *see also* Satan

Ibrāhīm *see* Abraham

idolaters (*mushrikūn*)
believe in God but 'associate' other gods with him, 6.22, 68, 136; 23.84–89; 29.61, 63, 65; 43.9–15; are in a state of ritual defilement and banned from the 'mosques of God,' 9.17; and 'Sacred Mosque,' 9.28; are like a spider, 29.41; not to be prayed for, 9.113; renunciation of treaty with, 9.1–17; command to fight against, 9.36; also 2.105, 135; 5.82; 10.28, 66; 22.17; 48.6; *see also* disbelievers

idolatry (selected references)
'association' of other gods with God unforgivable, 4.48, 116; also 3.64, 151; 4.36; 5.72; 6.151; 7.33, 190; 12.38; 13.36; 18.38, 110; 22.26, 31; 29.8; 31.13; 35.14; 39.64; 60.12; 72.2, 20

idols, false gods
are powerless, 7.191–198; 16.20–22; 25.3; 35.40; unable to intercede, 6.94; 10.18; 30.13; 39.3, 38; turn against their worshippers at Judgment, 10.28–29; 16.86; 18.52; 19.82; 29.25; 30.13; 35.14; 46.5–6; various gods named, 53.19–20; 71.23; some regarded as females, 16.57; 17.40; 37.149–155; are jinn or angels, 6.100;

34.40–41; are merely names, 7.71; 12.40; 53.23; *see also* daughters; al-Ṭāghūt

Idrīs
a prophet (probably Ezra, sometimes identified with Enoch), 19.56; 21.85

'ifrīt
a type of jinnī, 27.39

'Illiyyīn
a book(?), 83.18–19

Ilyās *see* Elijah

imām
'leader' or 'model,' 2.124 (Abraham); 9.12 (of disbelief); 21.73 (Isaac and Jacob); 25.74 (believers); 28.5 (people of Israel), 41 (Pharaoh and his forces); 32.24 (people of Israel); also 11.17; 46.12 (Book of Moses); 15.79; 17.71; 36.12 (record of a person's deeds)

'Imrān
father of Mary, 3.33–35 (and title); 66.12

Injīl *see* Gospel

incest
rules against, 4.22–23; 33.4

infanticide *see* children

inheritance
rules concerning, 4.7–9, 11–12, 19 (of women), 176; wills, 2.180–182, 240–241; 5.106–108; also 89.19; *see also* orphans

inspiration (selected references)
3.44; 4.163–164; 5.111; 6.19, 50, 93, 106, 121 (by satans); 7.117; 10.2, 15; 11.36–37; 12.3, 109; 16.43, 123; 18.27, 110; 20.13, 77, 114; 21.7, 21, 45, 73; 23.27; 29.45; 33.2; 35.31; 41.12; 42.3, 7, 13, 51–52; 53.4, 10; 72.1; 99.5

intercession
none permitted at Judgment, 2.48, 123, 254; 26.100; 40.18; 74.48; except by God's permission, 2.255; 6.51, 70; 10.3; 19.87; 20.109; 21.28; 32.4; 34.23; 39.43-44; intercession of other gods useless, 10.18; 30.13; 43.86; 53.26 (of angels); *see also* prayer

Iram
a place, 89.7

iron
sent down by God, 57.25 (and title); made malleable for David's armor, 34.10; barrier of built by Dhū-l-Qarnayn, 18.96; hooked rods of in Hell, 22.21

'Īsā *see* Jesus

Isaac (*Isḥāq*)
son of Abraham, a prophet, 4.163; 6.84; 11.71; 14.39; 19.49; 21.72; 29.27; 37.112-113; also 2.133, 136, 140; 3.84; 12.6, 38; 38.45

Ishmael (*Ismā'īl*)
son of Abraham, a prophet, 2.133, 136, 140; 3.84; 4.163; 6.86; 14.39; 19.54-55; 21.85; 38.48; covenant with Abraham and Ishmael, they purify/build God's House, 2.125-127; as sacrifice, 37.102-111

Islam (*Islām*)
as name of the religion, 3.19, 85; 5.3; 6.125; 39.22; 61.7; as 'submission' (to God), 9.74; 49.17

Israel (*Isrā'īl*)
3.93; 19.58; *see also* Jacob

Israel, Sons of (*Banū Isrā'īl*)
2.40, 47, 83, 122, 211, 246; 3.49, 93; 5.12, 32, 70, 72, 78, 110; 7.105, 134, 137, 138; 10.90, 93; 17.2, 4, 101, 104; 20.47, 80, 94; 26.17, 22, 59, 197; 27.76; 32.23; 40.53; 43.59; 44.30; 45.16; 46.10; 61.6, 14; disobedience of, 2.54-66, 83-87; 4.153-162; 5.20-26, 70; 23.49-56 (and Christians); *see also* Jews

Jacob (*Ya'qūb*)
given to Abraham, 6.84; 11.71; 19.49-50; 21.72; 29.27; a prophet, 3.84; 4.163; 11.49; 19.6; one of the chosen, 38.45-47; father of Joseph, 12.6, 38, 68; charge to his sons, 2.132-134

Jālūt *see* Goliath

Jesus (*'Īsā*)
a prophet, messenger, 2.87, 253; 3.48-51; 5.46, 110; 43.63-65; 57.27; 61.6; his announcement and birth, 3.45-47; 19.16-34; supported by his disciples, 3.52; 5.111; 61.14; God's word, a spirit from him, 4.171; not crucified, 4.157-159; God raised him, 3.55; 4.158; a created being, like Adam, 3.59; 'only a messenger,' not a god or son of God, 4.171; 9.30; 19.34-35; 43.59; miracles of, 5.110; sending down of heavenly table, 5.112-115; predicts the coming of Aḥmad, 61.6; cursed disbelievers, 5.78; also 2.136; 3.84; 4.163; 6.85; 33.7; 42.13; *see also* Gospel; Mary, son of; Messiah

Jews (*Yahūd, Hūd, alladhīna hādū*)
2.62, 111, 113, 120, 135, 140; 3.67; 4.160; 5.18, 44, 51, 64, 69, 82; 6.146; 9.30; 16.118; 22.17; 62.6; appeal to, 2.40-44, 47-53, 122-123; 3.64; 5.15; criticism of, 2.88-96, 111-115; 3.72-85; 4.44-57, 150-161; 5.64, 78-82; 62.6-8; their alteration and forging of scripture, 2.75-82; 4.46; 5.13, 41; religion of Abraham superior, 2.130-141; 3.65-71; 5.44-50; expulsion of, 59.2-5; some believe in the Prophet and the Qur'ān, 3.199; *see also* diatribe; Israel, Sons of

Jibrīl *see* Gabriel

al-Jibt
other gods, idols(?), 4.51

jinn
created from fire, 15.27; 55.15; created to serve God, 51.56; lead people astray, 41.29; Hell filled with jinn and humans, 6.128; 11.119; 32.13; 41.24; part of Solomon's forces, worked for him, 27.17, 39–40; 34.12–14; Iblīs one of them, 18.50; *'ifrīt* a type of, 27.39; listened to the Qur'ān and believed, 46.29–32; 72.1–19; messengers sent to them, 6.130; worshipped by humans, 6.100; also 55.33; *see also* possession; satans

Job (*Ayyūb*)
a prophet, 4.163; 6.84; his sufferings, 21.83–84; 38.41–44

John the Baptist (*Yaḥyā*)
his birth, 3.38–41; 19.2–15; 21.90; also 6.85

Jonah (*Yūnus*)
a prophet, 4.163; 6.86; his story, 37.139–148; 68.48–50; his people alone believed, 10.98 (and title); *see also* Dhū-l-Nūn

Joseph (*Yūsuf*)
his story, 12.3–108 (and title); also 6.84; 40.34

Judaism *see* Jews; Israel, Sons of; rabbis; synagogues

al-Jūdī
resting place of Noah's ark, 11.44

Judgment, Day of (also 'the Day,' 'the Last Day,' 'the Day of Resurrection,' 'the Hour' etc.)
comes suddenly, 6.31; 7.187; 12.107; 22.55; 43.66; 47.18; signs of, 20.105–108; 22.1–2; 36.53; 39.68; 50.20; 54.1; 56.1–7; 69.13–17; 73.14, 17–18; 74.8; 75.7–10; 77.8–13; 78.18–20; 79.6–7; 80.33–36; 81.1–14; 82.1–5; 84.1–6; descriptions of, 7.6–9; 11.103–108; 21.47; 75.12–15; 77.28–50; 78.38–40; 79.6–14; 80.33–42; 84.7–15; each will face it alone, 31.33; 82.19; date known only to God, 7.187; 79.42–44; God is judge, 1.4; 22.56; 40.20; *see also* intercession; scale

Judgment scenes
6.93–94, 128–135; 7.38–51; 14.21–23; 16.24–32, 84–89; 18.47–49, 52–53; 19.85–87; 25.17–19, 22–29; 27.82–90; 28.62–67, 74–75; 30.55–57; 34.31–33, 51–54; 37.12–34; 39.67–75; 40.10–12, 69–76; 41.19–23, 29–32, 47–48; 43.66–78; 45.27–35; 50.20–35; 57.12–15; 69.19–37; 89.21–30

Ka'ba
5.95, 97 ('Sacred House'); *see also* House, the; Mosque, the Sacred

Khalīfa *see* ruler, rulers

killing
4.29, 89, 92–93; 5.32; 6.137, 140; 9.5; 17.33; 60.12

king
God, 20.114; 23.116; 25.2; 59.23; 62.1; 114.1–2; Saul, 2.246–248; David, 2.251; of Egypt, 12.43, 50, 54, 72, 76; also 27.34

kingdom
of the heavens and earth, 2.107; 3.189; 5.17, 18, 40, 120; 6.74; 7.158, 185; 9.116; 24.42; 25.2; 38.10; 39.44; 42.49; 43.85; 45.27; 48.14; 57.2, 5; 64.1; 85.9; of God, 3.26; 6.73; 17.111; 22.56; 23.88; 25.26; 35.13; 36.83; 39.6; 40.16; 67.1 (and title); God gives it, 2.247; 3.26; of Abraham (and Israel), 2.258; 4.54; of Solomon, 2.102; 38.35; of David, 2.251; 38.20; of Egypt, 12.101; 43.51

Korah *see* Qārūn

languages
diversity of one of God's signs, 30.22

Last Day *see* Judgment, Day of

al-Lāt
a goddess (or angel?), 53.19

leader *see* imām

light
created by God, 6.1; God is, 24.35 (and title); God leads out of darkness to, 2.257; 5.16; 24.35; 28.71; 33.43; 57.9, 28; 65.11; sends down clear, 4.174; 5.15; perfects his, 9.32; 61.8; 66.8; Torah and Gospel contain, 5.44, 46; 6.91; 21.48; Qur'ān as, 7.157; 42.52; 64.8; Moses leads out of darkness to, 14.5; the Prophet leads out of darkness to, 14.1; of believers, 57.12, 13, 19; 66.8; disbelievers want to extinguish, 9.32; 61.8; on Last Day, 39.69; also 6.122; 13.16; 24.40; 39.22

lightning
one of God's signs, 13.12; 24.43; 30.24; parable of thunder and, 2.19

livestock
includes sheep, goats, camels, cattle, 6.143–144; 39.6; created by God, 6.136; 16.5; 36.71; 39.6 ('sent down'); 40.79; 42.11; 43.12; for transport and food, 6.142; 23.21–22; 36.72–73; 40.79–80; 43.12–13; God's provision for, 10.24; 32.27; 79.33; 80.32; 'pagan' rituals concerning, 5.103; 6.136, 138; also 3.14

Lot (*Lūṭ*)
sent to his people, 7.80–84; 21.74–75; his people punished, 11.77–83; 15.57–74; 26.160–173; 27.54–58; 29.26, 28–35; 37.133–138; 54.33–40; also 6.86; 11.70, 74, 89; 21.71; 22.43; 38.13; 50.13; 66.10 (his wife a warning)

Lote Tree of the Boundary
theophany near, 53.14, 16

lote trees
34.16; 56.28 (in Paradise)

Luqmān
a sage who imparted wisdom to his son, 31.12–19 (and title)

Magians (*Majūs*)
22.17

magic, magician
taught by satans in the time of Solomon, and by angels Hārūt and Mārūt in Babylon, 2.102; Pharaoh's magicians, 7.111–122; 10.79–81; 26.36–51; Moses accused of magic, 7.109; 10.76–77; 20.57; 26.34–35, 49; 27.13; 40.24; 51.39; Jesus accused of magic, 5.110; 61.6; the Prophet accused of magic, 10.2; 34.43; 37.15; 38.4; 43.30; 46.7; 74.24; also 51.52

Magog (*Mājūj*)
and Gog (*Yājūj*), barbarous peoples confined behind a wall by Dhū-l-Qarnayn, 18.94–97; released before the Day of Judgment, 21.96

Majūs *see* Magians

Manāt
a goddess (or angel?), 53.20

manna
and quails 'sent down,' 2.57; 7.160; 20.80

marriage
forbidden with idolaters, 2.221; permitted with believers, and Jewish and Christian women, 5.5; marriage of widows, 2.234–235; marriage with female slaves, 4.3, 25; 23.6; 70.30; up to four wives, 4.3; sex in marriage, 2.223; rules against incest, 4.22–23; 33.4; various rules, 4.4 (dowries), 24–28, 127–129; 24.26, 32–33; 60.10–11

Index to the Qur'ān

(of fugitives); the Prophet's wives, 33.6 ('mothers of believers'), 28–34, 50–52 (slaves as concubines), 53–55, 59; 66.3–5; *see also* divorce; women

martyrs
2.154; 3.140, 143, 169; 4.69, 72; 57.19

Mārūt
angel in Babylon, 2.102

al-Marwa
2.158

Mary (*Maryam*)
birth and upbringing, 3.35–44; announcement and birth of Jesus, 3.45–47; 19.16–33 (and title); slandered, 4.156; a messenger, 23.50–51; example of, 66.12; also 4.171; 21.91

Mary, son of
'son of Mary' (alone), 23.50; 43.57; 'Jesus, son of Mary', 2.87, 253; 3.45; 4.157, 171; 5.46, 78, 110, 112, 114; 19.34; 33.7; 57.27; 61.6, 14; 'the Messiah, son of Mary', 5.17, 72, 75; 9.31; *see also* Jesus

al-Masīḥ *see* Messiah, the

maysir *see* gambling

Mecca (*Makka*)
48.24

Medina *see* city, the

men
rank above women, 2.228; are responsible for them, 4.34; modest behavior for, 24.30; not to marry idolaters, 2.221; permitted with believers, and Jewish and Christian women, 5.5; marriage with widows, 2.234–235; marriage with female slaves, 4.3, 25; 23.6; 70.30; up to four wives permitted, 4.3; sex in marriage, 2.223; rules against incest, 4.22–23; 33.4; as witnesses, 2.283; 65.2; *see also* divorce; inheritance;

marriage; menstruation; sexual immorality; women

menstruation
men not to have sex with women during, 2.222

Merciful, the (*al-Raḥmān*)
attribute of God, 1.1(and *basmala*), 3; 2.163; 27.30; 41.2; 59.22; as a proper name of God, 13.30; 17.110; 19.18, 26, 44, 45, 58, 61, 69, 75, 78, 85, 87, 88, 91, 92, 93, 96; 20.5, 90, 108, 109; 21.26, 36, 42, 112; 25.26, 59, 60, 63; 26.5; 36.11, 15, 23, 52; 43.17, 19, 20, 33, 36, 45, 81; 50.33; 55.1 (and title); 67.3, 19, 20, 29; 78.37, 38

messengers
are human, 7.35, 63, 69; 10.2; 11.27; 12.109; 14.10–11; 16.43; 18.110; 21.3, 7; 23.24, 33–34; 26.154, 186; 36.15; or angels, 22.75; 35.1; no distinction among messengers, 2.136; 3.84; 4.150, 152; some preferred over others, 2.253; 27.15; Muḥammad is the messenger of God, 33.40; self-designation of the Prophet, 7.158; the Prophet similar to previous messengers, 4.163–165; 40.78; messengers speak the language of their people, 14.4; 19.97; 46.12; always face opposition, 15.10–11; 23.44; 46.35; 51.52; Satan tampers with their revelation, 22.52; as bringers of good news and warners, 4.165; 6.48; 18.56; their message, 16.36; 21.25; 23.23, 32; 71.1–3; perform miracles only by God's permission, 13.38; 40.78; *see also* prophets

Messiah, the (*al-Masīḥ*)
announcement of his birth, 3.45; not crucified, 4.157; 'only a messenger,' not divine, 4.171; 5.17, 72, 75; 9.30; *see also* Jesus; Mary, son of

373

Michael (*Mīkāl*)
2.98 (with Gabriel)

Midian (*Madyan*)
people to whom Shuʿayb was sent, 7.85–93; 11.84–95; 29.36–37; Moses among them, 20.40; 28.22–28; also 9.70; 22.44; 28.45

milk
created by God, 16.66; rivers of in Paradise, 47.15

model *see* imām

monasteries
22.40; *see also* monks

money
qinṭār, 3.14, 75; 4.20; dīnār, 3.75; dirham, 12.20

monks
found among Christians, friendly to believers, 5.82; worshipped by Christians, 9.31; consume people's wealth, 9.34; monasticism invented by Christians, not prescribed by God, 57.27; *see also* Christians; monasteries

month
twelve months prescribed in the 'Book of God,' 9.36; four are sacred, 9.5, 36; intercalary month forbidden, 9.37; the sacred month, 2.194, 217 (and fighting); 5.2, 97 (appointed by God); *see also* Ramaḍān

moon
subject to God's command, 7.54; 13.2; 14.33; 16.12; 29.61; 31.29; 35.13; 39.5; prostrates itself before God, 22.18; created for reckoning time, 6.96; 10.5; 36.39; 55.5; provides light, 10.5; 25.61; 71.16; Abraham turned from worshipping, 6.77; worship of forbidden, 41.37; in Joseph's dream, 12.4; new moons, 2.189; split on Last Day, 54.1 (and title); 75.8, 9; in oaths, 74.32; 84.18; 91.2; also 21.33; 22.18; 36.40

Moses (*Mūsā*)
childhood, 20.37–40; 28.3–21; in Midian, 28.22–28; called to be a prophet and deliver Israelites, 14.5–14; 19.51–53; 20.9–23; 26.10–17; 27.7–14; 28.30–35; sent to Pharaoh, 7.103–136; 10.75–89; 17.101; 20.24–73; 23.45–48; 26.18–51; 28.36–42; 40.23–50; 43.46–56; 51.38–40; 79.15–26; the exodus, 7.137–141; 10.90; 20.77–82; 26.52–67; on Sinai, 7.142–147, 154–157; God spoke to Moses directly, 4.164; given the Book (Torah), 2.53 (and Furqān), 87; 6.91, 154; 11.110; 17.2; 23.49; 25.35; 28.43; 32.23; 40.53; 41.45; 46.12; pages of, 53.36; 87.19; story of the calf, 2.51–56; 7.148–153; 20.83–98; miracles of, 2.60; 7.160 (strikes the rock); 20.17–24, 47, 56; 27.10–14 ('nine signs'); calls Israelites to enter the land, 5.20–26; sacrifice of a cow, 2.67–73; story of Moses and 'the servant,' 18.60–82; also 2.92, 108, 136, 246; 3.84; 4.153; 6.84; 7.159; 11.17, 96; 21.48; 22.44; 28.48, 76; 29.39; 33.7, 69; 46.30; 61.5

Mosque, the Distant (*al-masjid al-aqṣā*)
17.1

Mosque, the Sacred (*al-masjid al-ḥarām*)
direction of prayer toward, 2.144, 149; pilgrimage to, 2.196; 9.19, 28 (idolaters to be banned from); treaty made at, 9.7; disbelievers kept believers from, 2.217; 5.2; 8.34; 22.25; 48.25; believers will enter it, 48.27; *see also* House, the; Kaʿba

mosques
2.114 (of God), 187; 9.17–18 (only believers permitted in, idolaters banned); 22.40; 72.18

mother of the Book (*umm al-kitāb*) heavenly archetype of scripture, 3.7(?); 13.39; 43.4; *see also* Book

Mother of Towns (*umm al-qurā*) 6.92; 42.7

mothers
to be treated well for bearing and raising children, 31.14; 46.15; *see also* parents

mountain *see* Sinai

mountains
created by God, hold the earth in place, 13.3; 15.19; 16.15; 21.31; 31.10; 50.7

muhājirūn *see* emigrants

Muḥammad
3.144 ('only a messenger'); 33.40; 47.2 (and title); 48.29; *see also* Aḥmad; messengers; Prophet, the

mules
created by God for transport, 16.8

munāfiqūn *see* hypocrites

Muslim, Muslims (*Muslim, Muslimūn*) meaning 'submitted' (to God), 2.128, 133, 136; 3.52, 102; 6.163; 7.126; 10.72, 84, 90; 11.14; 12.101; 15.2; 16.89, 102; 21.108; 27.31, 38, 42, 81, 91; 29.46; 30.43; 33.35; 39.12; 41.33; 43.69; 46.15; 48.16; 51.36; 66.5; 68.35; 72.14; meaning 'Muslim,' 3.64; 22.78; 28.53; *see also* believers; Islam

Naṣārā *see* Christians

Nasr
a god, 71.23

New Testament *see* Gospel

nicknames
forbidden, 49.11

night, blessed (*laylat mubārak*) Qur'ān 'sent down' on it, 44.3

night and day
created by God for rest and sight, 10.67; 17.12 ('two signs'); 25.47; 27.86; 28.73; 30.23; 40.61; 78.10–11; also 6.13, 96; 28.71–72

Night of the Decree (*laylat al-qadr*) Qur'ān 'sent down' on it, 97.1–3

Noah (*Nūḥ*)
a prophet, his story, 7.59–64; 10.71–73; 11.25–34; 23.23–30; 26.105–121; 37.75–82; 71.1–28 (and title); his people destroyed by a flood, 11.36–49; 25.37; 29.14–15; 54.9–15; his wife a disbeliever, 66.10; also 3.33–34; 4.163; 6.84; 7.69; 9.70; 11.89; 14.9; 17.3, 17; 19.58; 21.76–77; 22.42; 33.7; 40.5, 31; 42.13; 50.12; 51.46; 53.52; 57.26; 69.11–12

nudity
Adam and his wife realize they are naked, 7.20–22; 20.120–121; Satan stripped them of their clothing, 7.27; clothing 'sent down' to cover, 7.26

oaths
to be kept, 16.91–92; warning about, 2.224–225; absolution of 66.2; atonement for broken oaths, 5.89; penalty for breaking oaths of alliance with the community, 3.77; oaths sworn in the Qur'ān, 36.2; 37.1–3; 51.1–4; 52.1–6; 77.1–6; 79.1–5; 89.1–5; 91.1–8; 93.1–3; 95.1–5; 100.1–5

offerings
for the pilgrimage, 2.196; 48.25; not to be profaned, 5.2; at the Ka'ba, 5.95, 97; *see also* sacrifice

old age
  worst stage of life, 16.70; 22.5; 30.54; also 17.23

Old Testament *see* Torah; Psalms

olives
  6.99, 141; 16.11; 80.29; 95.1

olive tree
  23.20; 24.35

oracle-giver
  Prophet not one, 52.29; 69.42

orphans
  to be supported, 2.83, 177, 215; 4.36; 76.8; 90.14–15; to be treated fairly, 2.220; 4.8; 89.17; 93.9; 107.2; property to be respected, 4.2, 6, 8, 10; 6.152; to receive their share of spoils, 8.41; 17.34; 59.7; marriage of female orphans, 4.3, 127

pages (*ṣuḥuf*)
  'scriptures' of previous prophets, 20.133; 53.36–37 (of Moses and Abraham); 80.13 (the Qur'ān); 87.18–19 (of Abraham and Moses); record of a person's deeds, 74.52; 81.10; heavenly archetype(?), 98.2–3; *see also* Book

parables
  of the fire at night, 2.17–18; the cloudburst, 2.19–20; the crier, 2.171; grain of corn, 2.261; smooth rock, 2.264; garden on a hill, 2.265; freezing wind, 3.117; the dog, 7.176; rain, 10.24; blind and deaf, 11.24; disbelievers, 14.18; good and bad trees, 14.24–27; two slaves, 16.75; two men, 16.76; a city, 16.112–113; two men with two gardens, 18.32–44; rain, 18.45; God's light, 24.35; the spider, 29.41; master and slaves, 30.28; the disbelieving city, 36.13–29; slave with several masters, 39.29; parable of the wives of Noah, Lot, and Pharaoh, 66.10–11; the ruined garden, 68.17–33

Paradise (heavenly 'Garden,' 'Gardens')
  promise and description of, 2.25; 3.15, 133, 195; 4.57, 124; 9.72, 111; 10.9–10; 11.108; 13.23–24; 18.31; 37.40–49; 43.68–73; 44.51–57; 47.4–6, 15; 50.31–35; 52.17–28; 55.46–76; 56.11–40; 57.21; 68.34; 76.12–22; 78.31–36; 79.40–41; 85.11; 88.8–16; also 7.44, 47–51; 37.50–61; 75.23

parents
  to be treated well, 2.83; 4.36; 6.151; 17.23; 19.14, 32; 29.8; 31.14; 46.15; not to be obeyed if idolaters, 29.8; 31.15

path, straight
  1.6–7; 2.142, 213; 3.51, 101; 4.68, 175; 5.16; 6.39, 87, 126, 153, 161; 7.16; 10.25; 11.56; 15.41; 16.76, 121; 19.36; 22.54; 23.73–74; 24.46; 36.4, 61; 37.118; 42.52–53; 43.43, 61, 64; 48.2, 20; 67.22; also 14.1; 19.43; 20.135; 22.24; 34.6; 36.66; 37.23; 38.22; *see also* roads; way

pearls
  22.23; 35.33; 52.24; 55.22; 56.23; 76.19

pen
  3.44; 31.27; 68.1 (and title); 96.4

People of the Book *see* Book, People of the

persecution
  2.191, 217; 8.39; 10.83, 85–86; 16.110; 29.10; 60.5; 85.10

Pharaoh (*Fir'awn*)
  Moses (and Aaron) sent to, 7.103–137; 10.75–92; 11.96–97; 17.101–103; 20.24–36, 42–79; 26.10–67; 28.30–42; 40.23–46; 43.46–56; 44.17–31; 51.38–40;

79.15–25; 'nine signs' to, 17.101; 27.12; plagues against, 7.130, 133–135; Israel rescued from 'house of Pharaoh,' 2.49–50; 7.141; 14.6; 44.30–31; orders Haman to build a tower, 28.38; 40.36–37; also 3.11; 8.52, 54; 28.3–6; 29.39; 38.12; 50.13; 54.41–42; 66.11 (wife of); 69.9; 73.15–16; 85.17–18; 89.10

pilgrimage (*ḥajj*)
regulations concerning, 2.196–203; 22.27–33 (and title); at time of new moon, 2.189; al-Ṣafā and al-Marwa included, 2.158; a duty to God, 3.97; hunting forbidden during, 5.1–2, 94–96; fishing permitted, 5.96; sacrifices, 22.33–36; *see also* 'umra

Pit, companions of the
85.4–8

poet
the Prophet accused of being one, 21.5; 37.36; 52.30; Prophet not one, 36.69; 37.37; 69.41; poets condemned, 26.224–226 (and title)

polygamy *see* marriage

polytheism *see* idolatry; idolaters; idols

pomegranates
6.99, 141; 55.68

poor, the
to be supported and fed, 2.83, 177, 215, 271, 273; 4.8, 36; 9.60; 17.26; 22.28; 24.22; 30.38; 69.34; 74.44; 76.8; 89.18; 90.12–16; 107.3; to receive their share of spoils, 8.41; 59.7, 8; also 2.184; 4.135; 5.89, 95; 24.32; 47.38; 58.4; 68.24; 93.8

possession
by jinn, an accusation leveled against every messenger, 51.52; against Noah, 23.25; 54.9;
against Moses, 26.27; 51.39, against the Prophet, 15.6; 23.70; 37.36; 44.14; 68.51; denial of, 7.184; 34.8; 37.37; 52.29; 68.2; 81.22

prayer
only to God, 13.14; 40.60; who answers prayer, 2.186; 3.38; 6.41; 14.39; 19.4; 27.62; 40.60; other gods do not, 7.194; 13.14; 35.14; 46.5; toward Sacred Mosque, 2.144; times of, 2.238; 3.41; 6.52; 11.114; 13.15; 17.78; 18.28; 20.130; 24.36; 30.17; 32.15–16; 33.42; 48.9; 50.39–40; 76.25; Friday prayer, temporary cessation of business, 62.9–10; regulations concerning, 4.43; 5.6; 6.52; 17.110; 107.4–7; shortening of in dangerous situations, 2.239; 4.101–103; Israel commanded to pray, 2.43, 45, 83; 5.12; prophets commanded to pray, 14.40 (Abraham); 21.73 (Isaac and Jacob); 10.87; 20.14 (Moses); 19.31 (Jesus); 11.114; 17.78; 29.45; 73.20 (the Prophet); true believers observe prayer, 2.3, 110, 177, 277; 4.162; 5.55;6.72, 92; 7.170; 8.3; 9.71; 13.22; 14.31; 22.35, 41, 78; 24.37, 56; 27.3; 30.31; 35.18, 29; 42.38; 98.5; marks of prostration on believers, 48.29; no prayer for idolaters, even if relatives, 9.113; prayer for hypocrites useless, 9.80; 63.5–6; deceptive prayer of hypocrites, 4.142; no funeral prayer for disbelievers, 9.84; People of the Book ridicule, 5.58; Satan hinders from, 5.91; also 31.17; 33.33; 58.13; *see also* intercession; prostration

priests
found among Christians, friendly to believers, 5.82; *see also* Christians; monks

Index to the Qur'ān

Prophet, the
addressed as, 7.158 (*ummī*); 8.64–65; 9.61, 73, 113, 117; 66.1, 3, 9; 'seal of the prophets,' 33.40; a warner, 19.97; 33.45; 34.28; 46.9; 48.8; 74.2; 92.14; a bringer of good news, 19.97; 33.45; 34.28; 45.8; 48.8; 84.24; a messenger of God, 7.158; 46.9; a reminder, 88.21; a mercy to all peoples, 21.107; a witness, 33.45; 48.8; close to believers, 33.6; not a guardian or watcher, 17.54; 42.48; 88.22; universality of his mission, 25.1; 34.28; plots against him, 8.30; his visions, 53.4–18; 81.22–25; does not know future, 6.50; 11.31; his 'night journey,' 17.1; accusations of magic and possession, 7.184; 15.6; 51.52; 74.24 (*see also* magic, magician; oracle-giver; poet; possession); accusation of forgery, 10.38; 11.13, 35; 21.5; 25.4; 32.3; 34.8, 43; 42.24; 46.8; 52.33; an example to believers, 33.21; to be saluted and respected, 33.56; 49.2; to pray for forgiveness, 4.106; 47.19; given advice, 7.199–206; 41.33–36; 47.16–19; 50.38–45; given encouragement, 2.196–198; 4.79–84; 6.33–36; 11.12–16, 112–123; 13.30–32, 36–43; 15.88–99; 18.27–31; 22.77–78; 28.85–88; 35.18–26; 40.77–78; 41.53–54; 42.16–18; 43.40–45; 93.1–5(?); preserved from error, 4.113; 22.52; his wives, 33.6 ('mothers of believers'), 28–34, 53–55, 59; 66.3–5

prophetic office
3.79; 6.89; 29.27; 45.16; 57.26

prophets
sent by God, 2.213; 5.20; 43.6; 45.16; God's covenant with, 3.81; each has an enemy, 6.112; 25.31; Israel opposed and killed its prophets, 2.61, 87, 91; 3.21, 112, 181; 4.155; 5.70; lists of prophets, 3.84; 4.163; 6.83–89; 19.58; 29.27; 33.7; 57.26; some preferred over others, 17.55; 27.15; Muḥammad the 'seal of the prophets,' 33.40; also 2.177; 3.80; 4.69; 5.44; 21 (title); 39.69; *see also* messengers

prostitution
female slaves not to be forced into, 24.33

prostration
of the angels before Adam, 2.34; 7.11; 15.29–31; 17.61; 18.50; 20.116; 38.72–73; of the angels before God, 7.206; of the heavens and earth before God, 13.15; 16.48–49; 22.18; 55.6; Israelites to enter town in, 2.58; 4.154; 7.161; of Egyptian magicians, 7.120; 20.70; 26.46; of stars, sun, and moon before Joseph in his dream, 12.4; of Joseph's family before him, 12.100; of Sheba before the sun, 27.24–25; of Mary, 3.43; of the People of the Book, 3.113; of the Prophet, 15.98; of believers, 9.112; 22.77; 25.65; 26.219; 48.29; believers fall down in when Qur'ān recited, 17.107–109; 19.58; 32.15 (and title); believers' marks of, 48.29; command to before the Merciful, 22.60; before God, 41.37; 53.62; not before sun or moon, 41.37; on the Last Day, 68.42–43; also 2.125; 4.102; 22.6; 39.9; 50.40; *see also* prayer

Psalms (*zabūr*)
a book given to David, 4.163; 17.55; 21.105; as a plur. (*zubur*) 'scriptures'(?), 3.184; 16.44; 23.53; 26.196; 35.25; 54.43, 52 (record books?)

purification
of pollution, 4.43; 5.6

Index to the Qur'ān

Qārūn
associate of Pharaoh, 29.39–40; 40.23–25; swallowed by the earth, 28.76–82

qibla (direction of prayer)
change from Jerusalem(?) as *qibla*, 2.142, 143; believers now to face Sacred Mosque, 2.144–150; houses in Egypt a *qibla* for Moses and the Sons of Israel, 10.87

quails
and manna 'sent down,' 2.57; 7.160; 20.80

Qur'ān
10.15, 61; 13.31; 15.1 ('clear'); 17.106; 36.69 ('clear'); 41.44 ('foreign'); 56.77; 72.1; 85.21; 'an Arabic Qur'ān,' 12.2; 20.113; 39.28; 41.3; 42.7; 43.3; 'the Qur'ān,' 2.185; 4.82; 5.101; 7.204; 9.111; 15.87, 91; 16.98; 17.45, 46, 60, 78, 82; 20.2; 25.32; 27.1, 6, 92; 36.1; 38.1; 46.29; 47.24; 50.1, 45; 54.17, 22, 32, 40; 55.2; 73.4, 20; 76.23; 84.21; 'this Qur'ān,' 6.19; 10.37; 12.3; 17.9, 41, 88, 89; 18.54; 25.30; 27.76; 30.58; 34.31; 39.27; 41.26; 43.31; 59.21; also 75.17–18; *see also* Book; Reminder

Quraysh
106.1 (and title)

rabbis
5.44, 63; *see also* teachers; Israel, Sons of

al-Raḥmān *see* Merciful, the

rain *see* water

Ramaḍān
month in which the Qur'ān was 'sent down,' fasting in it, 2.185; *see also* month

ransom
of Abraham's son, 37.107; of captives, 2.85; 47.4; of slaves, 2.177; 9.60; for not fasting, 2.184; for not shaving head at pilgrimage, 2.196; for dissolving a marriage, 2.229; none accepted at Judgment, 3.91; 5.36; 10.54; 13.18; 39.47; 57.15; 70.11; *see also* atonement, compensation

al-Raqīm
mentioned with 'companions of the cave,' 18.9

al-Rass
its people disbelievers, 25.38; 50.12

rasūl *see* messengers

record book
of human deeds, 15.79; 17.71; 18.49; 23.62; 36.12; 45.28–29; 50.4; 69.19, 25; 74.52; 84.7, 10

redemption *see* atonement; compensation; ransom

religion (*dīn*)
God sole object of, 7.29; 39.2, 11, 14; 40.14, 65; 98.5; religion with God is Islam, 3.19; 5.3; believers to fight until the religion is God's, 2.193; 8.39; no compulsion in religion, 2.256; 10.99; believers are brothers in religion, 9.11; 33.5; religion of believers that of Abraham, 2.132–135; 22.78; 42.13 (and of Noah, Moses, Jesus); idolaters have their religion, the Prophet his, 109.6; also 42.21; *see also* Abraham

Reminder
referring to the Qur'ān, 3.58; 6.68; 15.6, 9; 16.44; 21.24, 50; 23.71; 25.18; 25.29; 36.11; 38.8, 49; 41.41; 43.5; 51.54; 57.16; 58.19; 68.52; 73.19; 74.49; 76.29; 80.11; referring to the Torah, 21.105; referring to the Prophet, 65.10–11; 88.21; also 38.1; 54.25

Index to the Qur'ān

Reminder, People of the
16.43; 21.7; *see also* Book, People of the; Gospel, People of the

repentance (selected references)
4.16–18; 5.39; 9.5 (and title); 16.119; 19.60; 25.70; 39.54; 42.47; 85.10; *see also* forgiveness

resurrection
certainty of, 4.87; 16.38–40; 19.66–68; 22.5–7; 45.24–26; 46.33–35; 50.15–22; disbelievers doubt, 13.5–6; 17.49–52; 19.66; 27.67–72; 32.10–14; 34.7–8; 36.78–79; 37.15–19; 44.34–38; 45.24–25; 50.2–5; 75.3–11; 79.10–14; revival of the earth a sign of, 7.57–58; 22.5; 30.19, 50; 35.9; 50.9–11; parallel to creation, 29.19; 36.79, 81; 46.33; 50.15; parallel to human birth, 75.36–40 (and title); 80.18–22; period between death and, 2.259; 20.102–104; 23.112–115; 30.55–56; emptying of graves, 82.4; 84.3–4; 100.9

retaliation
regulations concerning, 2.178–179, 194; prescribed in the Torah, 5.45; not to exceed injury, 16.126; 42.40; also 22.39, 60

ritual, rituals
Abraham's request for, 2.128, performed at the pilgrimage, 200; assigned to each community, 22.34, 67; *see also* offerings; sacrifice

roads
placed in the earth by God, 16.15; 20.53; 21.31; 43.10; 71.19–20; road to Hell, 4.168–169; 37.23; separate roads of Jews, Christians, and Muslims, 5.48; jinn called to a straight road, 46.30; different roads of righteous and wicked, 72.11 (jinn), 16 (humans); 90.10; *see also* path, straight; way

Romans (*Rūm*)
30.2 (and title)

rubies
55.58

ruler, rulers
God appoints Adam as, 2.30; Aaron, 7.142; David, 38.26; different peoples as, 6.165; 7.129; 10.14; 24.55; 27.62; 35.39; angels as, 43.60

Sabā' *see* Sheba

Sabians (*Ṣābi'ūn*)
community of believers, along with Jews and Christians, 2.62; 5.69; 22.17 (also with Magians)

sabbath
Jewish day of rest, 4.154; 16.124; punishments for those who transgressed, 2.65; 4.47; 7.163

sacrifice
offered by Adam's sons, 5.27; Abraham's sacrifice of birds, 2.260; Abraham's sacrifice of his son, 37.102–107; sacrifice of cow by Moses, 2.67–71; sacrifice commanded, along with prayer, 108.2; name of God to be invoked over, 22.34, 36; God not fed by, 22.37; at the pilgrimage, 2.196; 48.25; also 3.183; *see also* offerings

al-Ṣafā
2.158

Sakīna
2.248; 9.26, 40; 48.4, 18, 26

ṣalāt *see* prayer

Ṣāliḥ
messenger sent to Thamūd, 7.73–79; 11.61–68; 26.141–158; 27.45–53; people of, 11.89

Salsabīl
a spring in Paradise, 76.18

al-Sāmirī
created golden calf, 20.85–96
Saqar
name of Hell(?), 54.48; 74.26, 42
Satan (*al-Shayṭān*)
provokes humans to evil, their enemy, 2.36, 168, 208, 268; 3.155; 4.38, 60, 117–120; 6.43, 142; 7.22, 27, 200; 8.48; 12.5; 16.63; 17.53, 64; 27.24; 28.15; 29.38; 35.6; 36.60; 41.36; 43.62; whispers in their hearts, 7.20; 20.120; 114.4–6; tampers with revelation to prophets, 22.52; false god, 4.117; also 2.275; 3.36, 175; 4.76, 83; 5.90; 6.68; 7.175; 8.11; 12.42, 100; 14.22; 16.98; 17.53; 18.63; 19.44; 24.21; 25.29; 31.21; 38.41; 47.25; 58.10, 19; 59.16; *see also* Iblīs; satans

satans (*shayāṭīn*)
lead humans astray, 6.71, 121; 7.27; 19.83; 22.3; 26.221–222; individually assigned to incite a person to evil, 19.83; 23.97; 41.25; 43.36; taught humans magic, 2.102; associated with Solomon, 2.102; 21.82; 38.37; eavesdrop on heavenly secrets, 15.17–18; 37.7–8; 67.5; believers take refuge with God from, 23.97–98; 'satans of the humans and jinn,' 6.112; false gods, 2.14; 7.27; Qur'ān not brought down by them, 26.210–211; 81.25; also 17.27; 19.68; *see also* Iblīs; jinn; Satan

Saul (*Ṭālūt*)
king of Israel, 2.247–249

scale
to be used justly, 6.152; 7.85 (Midian); 11.84; 55.9; established by God, 55.7–8; 57.25 ('sent down'); set up on Day of Judgment, 21.47; 55.7; 101.6, 8

scribes
2.282–283; 80.15

scriptures *see* Book

sea
ships on the sea a sign of God's providence, 2.164; 14.32; 16.14; 17.66; 22.65; 31.31; 42.32; 45.12; 55.24; God guides in darkness of land and sea, 6.63, 97 (by stars); 27.63; God brings safely to land from, 10.22; 17.67; Israelites passed through, 2.50; 7.138; 10.90; 20.77; 26.63; 44.24; seas will boil on Last Day, 81.6; 82.3; the two seas (fresh and salt), 18.60; 25.53; 27.61; 35.12; 55.19–20; if the sea were ink, there would not be enough to record God's words, 18.109; 31.27

seal of the prophets (*khātam al-nabiyyīn*)
title applied to Muḥammad, 33.40

semen
humans created from, 16.4; 18.37; 22.5; 23.13; 32.8; 35.11; 36.77; 40.63; 53.46; 75.37; 76.2; 77.20; 86.6

Seven Sleepers *see* cave, companions of the

sexual immorality (*zinā*)
forbidden, 17.32; 25.68; to be punished by confinement, 4.15–16; by flogging, 24.2; restrictions on marriage, 24.3, 26; four witnesses needed against women, 4.15; punishment for false accusations of, 24.4–10, 23

Sheba (*Sabā'*)
a land ruled by a queen, who eventually 'submits' to God, 27.22–44; a people punished for their ingratitude, 34.15–19 (and title)

ship
Noah's 'ark,' 7.64; 10.73; 11.37–44; 23.27; 26.119; 29.15; 36.41; 37.140; *see also* sea

Shu'ayb.
messenger sent to Midian, 7.85–93; 11.84–95; 29.36–37; and to the people of the Grove, 26.176–189

signs (selected references)
as natural phenomena, 2.164; 3.190; 6.95–99; 7.57–58; 10.5–6, 101; 13.2–4; 16.65–67; 29.19–23; 30.46; 36.33–44; 41.37–40; 42.29, 32–35; 45.3–6; 50.20–21; as miracles, 3.13 (in battle), 49 (Jesus); 5.110, 114 (Jesus); 6.109–111; 7.73 (Ṣāliḥ), 130–137 (Moses); 15.73–77; 17.59, 101 (Moses); 20.17–24, 47, 56 (Moses); 27.10–13 (Moses); 29.24; 30.58; 40.78; 43.46–48 (Moses); 54.13–15; demand for, 6.37; 13.7; 21.5; as recited verses (or revelation), 2.106; 6.57; 8.2, 31; 11.17; 16.101; 24.1; 31.2, 7; 39.71; 41.3; 45.6, 25; 46.7; 47.14; 62.2; 65.11; 68.15; 83.13

Sijjīn
a book(?), 83.7–8

silk
18.31; 22.23; 35.33; 44.53; 76.12, 21

silver
3.14; 9.34; 43.33; vessels of in Paradise, 76.15; bracelets of in Paradise, 76.21

Sinai
'Mount Sinai,' 23.20; 95.2; 'the Mountain,' 2.63, 93; 4.154; 7.171; 19.52; 20.80; 28.29, 46; 52.1 (and title)

Sirius (al-Shi'rā)
the star, 53.49

sky
lowest of the seven heavens, 37.6; 41.12; erected by God as a 'dome,' 2.22; 40.64; as 'a guarded roof,' 21.32; 50.6; 51.47 ('built by hand'); 55.7; 79.27–28; 88.18; 91.5; held up by God, 22.65; stands fast by God's command, 30.25; nothing hidden from God in, 14.38; 21.4; 22.70; 27.75; 34.2; 57.4; God directs affairs from, 32.5; creation of purposeful, 21.16; 38.27; sends down water from, 2.22, 164; 6.6, 99; 8.11; 13.17; 14.32; 15.22; 16.10, 65; 20.53; 23.18; 25.48; 27.60; 29.63; 30.24; 31.10; 35.27; 39.21; 43.11; 78.14; a sign from, 26.4; punishment from, 2.59; 7.162; 8.32 (demand for); 29.34; 34.9; 52.44; 67.17; demand for the Prophet to make the sky fall, 17.92; 26.187; demand for the Prophet to ascend into, 17.93; demand for a Book from, 4.153; a table from, 5.112–115; promise of blessings from, 7.96; a ladder to, 6.35; told to stop for Noah, 11.44; did not weep for Pharaoh, 44.29; constellations in, 15.16; 25.61; 85.1; touched by jinn, 72.8; will be rolled up on Last Day, 21.104; will be split on Last Day, 25.25; 55.37; 69.16; 73.18; 77.9; 78.19; 82.1; 84.1; will fill with smoke on the Last Day, 44.10; will shake on Last Day, 52.9; will be like molten metal on Last Day, 70.8; will be stripped off on Last Day, 81.11; also 6.125; 15.14; 17.95; 18.40; 21.16; 22.15, 31; 29.22; 30.48; 36.28; 41.11; 43.84; 51.7; 86.1, 11; *see also* heavens

slander
4.112; 24.4, 23; 33.58

slaves
treatment of, 4.36; manumission of, 2.177; 4.92; 5.89; 9.60; 24.33(?); 58.3; marrying them off, 24.32–33; young female slaves not to be forced into prostitution, 24.33 (God will forgive them if they are)

sleep
created by God for rest, 25.47; 30.23; 78.9; a person's 'self' returns to God

in sleep, 39.42; God does not sleep, 2.255; *see also* night and day

social etiquette
modesty for men and women, 24.30–31, 60; 33.59 (the Prophet's wives); walking in humility, 17.37; 25.63; proper greetings, 4.86; 6.54; 24.61; 25.63; domestic privacy respected, 24.27–28; household etiquette, 24.58–60; proper eating in other houses, 24.61; respect for the Prophet's houses, 33.53; 49.4–5; voices not raised in the Prophet's presence, 49.2–3; avoidance of private meetings, 58.8–10

Solomon (*Sulaymān*)
satans in his reign, 2.102; controls wind and satans/jinn, 21.78–82; 34.12–13; 38.36–40; understands language of birds, 27.15–21; horses of, 38.31–35; and Queen of Sheba, 27.22–44; his death, 34.14; also 4.163; 6.84

sons
desirable, 3.14; 9.24; 17.40; 18.46; 43.16; 68.14; preferable to daughters, 37.149, 153; 43.16; 52.39; adopted, 33.4, 37; God provides wealth and, 16.72; 17.6, 40; 26.133; 71.12; 74.13; wrongly ascribed to God, 6.100; God has none, 6.101; 21.26; 23.91; 25.2; *see also* Adam (sons of); children; daughters; Israel, Sons of

spider
parable of, 29.41 (and title)

spirit
God's spirit breathed into the first human, 15.29; 32.9; 38.72; into Mary, 21.91; 66.12; spirit sent to Mary, 19.17; the holy spirit supported Jesus, 2.87, 253; 5.110; Jesus is a spirit from God, 4.171; spirit sent down (from God), 16.2 (with angels); holy spirit brought down the Qur'ān, 16.102; trustworthy spirit brought down revelation, 26.192–195; 40.15; descended on the Night of the Decree, 97.4 (with angels); inspired the Prophet, 42.52; comes from God's command, 17.85; 40.15; 42.52; ascends to God, 70.4 (with angels); stands in line with angels on Last Day, 78.38; God's spirit supports believers, 58.22; *see also* angels; Gabriel

spoils
belong to God and the Prophet, 8.1 (and title); 59.6–10; a 'fifth' to be given to God, 8.41; future spoils promised, 48.15, 19–21

stars
created by God, to guide humans on land and sea, 6.97; 7.54; 16.12, 16; prostrate themselves before God, 22.18; 55.6; Abraham turned from worshipping, 6.76; 37.88–89; blotted out on Last Day, 77.8; 81.2; shooting stars chase satans away from heaven, 15.16–18; 37.6–10; 67.5; 72.8–9; constellations, 15.16; 25.61; 85.1 (and title); *see also* Sirius

submission *see* Islam

successors
different peoples succeed others, 7.69, 74, 169; 10.73; 19.59

ṣuḥuf *see* pages

Sulaymān *see* Solomon

sun
subject to God's command, 7.54; 14.33; 16.12; 29.61; 31.29; prostrates itself before God, 22.18; provides light, 10.5; 71.16; worship forbidden, 41.37; Abraham turned from worshipping, 6.78; worshipped by Queen of Sheba, 27.24; sun and its brilliance in oath, 91.1 (and title); brought together with the moon, shrouded on Last Day, 75.9; 81.1

Index to the Qur'ān

sunna *see* customary way

sūra
opponents challenged to bring one, 2.23; 10.38; 11.13 ('ten'); also 9.64, 86, 124, 127; 24.1; 47.20

Suwā'
a god, 71.23

swearing *see* oaths

swearing allegiance
of the women, 60.12; under the tree, 48.18; *see also* covenant

synagogues
10.87(?); 22.40

table
Jesus' miracle of the, 5.112–115 (and title)

Tablet(s)
of Moses, 7.145, 150, 154; referring to the heavenly archetype (or Qur'ān written on one), 85.21–22

al-Ṭāghūt
2.256, 257; 4.51, 60, 76; 5.60; 16.36; 39.17

Ṭālūt *see* Saul

Tasnīm
a spring in Paradise, 83.27

Tawrāt *see* Torah

teachers
5.44, 63; 9.31, 34; *see also* rabbis

Thamūd
people to whom Ṣāliḥ was sent, 7.73–79; 11.61–68; 26.141–158; 27.45–53; 51.43–45; 54.23–31; 91.11–15; also 9.70; 11.95; 14.9; 17.59; 22.42; 25.38; 29.38; 38.13; 40.31; 41.13, 17; 50.12; 53.51; 69.4; 85.18; 89.9

theft
punishment for, 5.38

throne
of God, 2.255; 7.54; 9.129; 10.3; 11.5; 13.2; 17.42; 20.5; 21.22; 23.86, 116; 25.59; 27.26; 32.4; 39.75; 40.7, 15; 43.82; 57.4; 69.17; 81.20; 85.15; of Egypt, 12.100; of Solomon, 38.34; of Queen of Sheba, 27.23, 38, 41–42

thunder
2.19; praises God, 13.13 (and title)

Torah (*Tawrāt*)
book given to Moses 3.3, 48, 50, 65, 93; 5.43–46, 66, 68, 110; 9.111; 48.29; 61.6; 62.5; predicts coming of the Prophet, 7.157

trading
2.275, 282; 4.29; *see also* commerce

treasure
11.12; 18.82; 25.8; 26.58; 28.76

treaties
9.1, 7–13; violation of treaties with the Prophet, 8.55–58

Tree of Immortality
in the Garden, 20.120–121; also 2.35; 7.19–22

trees
God causes their growth, 27.60; 56.72; prostrate themselves before God, 22.18; 55.6; God created fire from, 36.80; theophany to Moses at one, 28.30; oath of allegiance to the Prophet at one, 48.18; parable of good and bad trees, 14.24–27; if all were pens, they could not record God's words, 31.27; in the Garden ('this tree'), 2.35; 7.19–22; also 20.120–121; *see also* acacia trees; Lote Tree of the Boundary; lote trees; olive tree; al-Zaqqūm

tribes
descendants of Jacob/Israel, 2.136, 140; 3.84; 4.163; 7.160 (twelve)

tribute
  to be paid by People of the Book who do not practice Islam, 9.29
trinity
  Christian doctrine rejected, 4.171; 5.73
trumpet
  announcing Last Day, 6.73; 18.99; 20.102; 23.101; 27.87; 36.51; 39.68; 50.20; 69.13; 74.8; 78.18
Tubba'
  people of, 44.37; 50.14
Ṭuwā, wādī of
  place of Moses' call, 20.12; 79.16; also 28.30
'umra
  mentioned with the pilgrimage, 2.158, 196
usury
  forbidden to Muslims, 2.275–281; 3.130; 30.39; practiced by Jews, though forbidden to, 4.161
'Uzayr see Ezra
al-'Uzzā
  a goddess (or angel?), 53.19
victory
  2.89; 3.147; 5.52; 8.19; 14.15; 32.28–29; 48.1 (and title), 18, 24, 27; 57.10; 61.13; 110.1
visions
  of the Prophet, 17.60; 53.4–18; 81.22–25
Wadd
  a god, 71.23
waiting period
  before remarriage, 2.226, 228, 231, 234–235; 65.1, 4
washing
  as preparation for prayer, 4.43; 5.6

water
  all life created from, 21.30; 24.45; 25.54; God's throne upon, 11.7; sent down by God as rain, 2.22, 164; 6.6, 99; 8.11; 13.17; 14.32; 15.22; 16.10, 65; 20.53; 23.18; 25.48; 27.60; 29.63; 30.24; 31.10; 35.27; 39.21; 43.11; 78.14; giving of to pilgrims, 9.19; those in Hell will beg for, 7.50; *see also* flood; semen; washing
way (selected references)
  of God, 2.190, 195, 218, 246, 261–262, 273; 3.169, 195; 4.74–76, 100; 6.153; 8.72, 74; 9.19–20; 22.58; 24.22; 47.4, 38; 49.15; 57.10; 61.11; 73.20; God guides to the, 4.137; leads astray from, 4.88, 143; 42.46; right way, 2.108; 5.12, 60, 77; 7.146; wrong way, 4.115; no middle way, 4.150; of al-Ṭāghūt, 4.76; of the workers of corruption, 7.142; disbelievers keep people from, 2.217; 5.77; 6.116; 7.45, 86; 8.36, 47; 9.9; 11.19; 14.3; 16.88; 22.8, 25; 31.6; 47.1, 32, 34; 58.16; People of the Book keep people from, 3.99; 4.44, 160; 9.34; hypocrites keep people from, 63.2; no way against the righteous, 9.91; ways of peace, 5.16; *see also* path, straight; roads
wills see inheritance
wind
  controlled by God, one of his signs, 2.164; 7.57; 15.22; 25.48; 27.63; 30.46, 48; 35.9; 42.32; 45.5; sent by God against an enemy, 33.9; against 'Ād, 41.16; 46.24; 51.41; 54.19; 69.5; parables of 3.117; 14.18; 18.45; 22.31; Solomon's control of, 21.81; 34.12; 38.36

Index to the Qur'ān

wine
there is sin in it (*khamr*), but also benefit, 2.219; an abomination, 5.90–91; wine (*sakar*) from dates and grapes permissible, 16.67; rivers of wine (*khamr*) in Paradise, 47.15

wisdom
2.129, 151, 231, 251, 269; 3.48, 81, 164; 5.110; 16.125; 17.39; 31.12; 33.34; 38.20; 43.63; 54.5; 62.2

witnesses
2.282–283; 4.6, 15, 41; 5.106; 24.4–6; 65.2

women
regulations concerning, 4.127–130 (and title); men rank above them, 2.228; are responsible for them, 4.34; modest behavior for, 24.31; 33.59; not to marry idolaters, 2.221; nursing of children, 2.233; rules for widows, 2.234; provision for widows, 2.240; treatment of rebellious women, 4.34; treatment of women refugees and runaway wives, 60.10–12; as witnesses, 2.283; *see also* divorce; inheritance; marriage; men; menstruation; sexual immorality

Yaghūth
a god, 71.23

Yaḥyā *see* John the Baptist

Yājūj *see* Gog

Ya'qūb *see* Jacob

al-Yasa' *see* Elisha

Yathrib
siege of, 33.9–27; *see also* city, the

Ya'ūq
a god, 71.23

Yūnus *see* Jonah

Yūsuf *see* Joseph

Zabūr *see* Psalms

Zachariah (*Zakariyyā*)
father of John (the Baptist), 3.38–41; 19.2–11; 21.89–90; guardian of Mary, 3.37; one of the righteous, 6.85

zakat *see* alms

al-Zaqqūm
a tree in Hell, 37.62; 44.43; 56.52; also 17.60(?)

Zayd
former husband of one of the Prophet's wives, 33.37

www.ingramcontent.com/pod-product-compliance
Lightning Source LLC
Chambersburg PA
CBHW070732170426
43200CB00007B/508